CW01465469

Dictionary of Organs

AND

Organists

EDITED BY

Frederick W. Thornsby

Price: SIX SHILLINGS, NETT

1912

BOURNEMOUTH   H LOGAN & COMPANY

Dictionary of Organs & Organists

PUBLISHERS' INTRODUCTION:

INTEREST in the Organ has developed enormously during the last few years, and some of the largest instruments in the world are being built at the present time. Hitherto, there has been no publication in existence attempting to keep a record, in concrete form, of the various changes that are constantly taking place in Organ construction. This, therefore, is the function of this publication, and although, at present, far from complete, is at least an effort to give, in a collective form, brief particulars of the principal Organs in the British Isles.

Included also, are many special articles, written by trustworthy writers, and, as an addendum is the " Organists' Who's Who," giving brief biographies of the leading Organists throughout the country.

It can be claimed with sincerity, that such a collection has never before been issued, and is only done now with the help which we have received from the Organists and Organ builders, whose instruments are represented in the work.

We have been at pains to make the lists, both of Organs and Organists thoroughly representative, and every endeavour has been made to secure full and accurate details for the publication. For the specifications and biographies, consent has been duly obtained, proofs submitted, and correction made.

The issue of a book, ranging over so wide a field, necessarily absorbs a considerable amount of time, and we have to express some regret that, even before the pages leave the printers' hands, some few records, mainly of a personal character, are out of date. This was inevitable, but we think it well to mention the fact, believing our readers will judge of our efforts as a whole, and not condemn us because of unavoidable errors and omissions.

We hope that the work will prove that the public appreciates the comprehensiveness and reliability of the publication, and take this opportunity of rendering our thanks to all who have in any way assisted in its compilation.

H. LOGAN & Co.,

December, 1912.   *Publishers.*

Dictionary of Organs & Organists

A Brief History of the Organ.

By The Editor.

IN the following outline sketch of the organ and its history, it is quite unnecessary to enter into details and technicalities of a more or less elaborate nature, as these can easily be met with by organists, students, and others by consulting the well-known works of leading experts on this subject ; also there are various technical, etc., matters of a special kind, which are dealt with elsewhere in this volume.

The early history of the organ is both remote and obscure. The earliest records we have are of a somewhat classical nature.

Vitruvius alludes to an instrument blown by wind — hydraulicon or hydraulic organ ; also Athenæus mentions a kind of water organ instrument. In a treatise on Pneumatics by Hero of Alexandria, there are both fairly clear descriptions and drawings of pneumatic and hydraulic organs. This early record is, if authentic, somewhat remarkable, as in the said drawings the pipes appear arranged much in the same way as seen to-day. At Constantinople, on the Obelisk of Theodosius (fourth century), there is a piece of carving representing an instrument with pipes. There are also shown the figures of two men standing on bellows, thus appearing to furnish the instrument with the necessary wind pressure.

Organs of the above primitive kind began to be first used for public worship, it is supposed, some time during the latter part of the first thousand years after Christ, but the notes could only have been sounded one at a time, and must have been a very slow and laborious task for the organist or operator, as the keyboard does not seem to have been invented until some time afterwards. The notes only numbered about ten, but as time elapsed each note had several pipes attached to it. No keyboard appears to be mentioned in what is supposed to be about the earliest treatise on organ construction, a work by the monk Theophilus, in the early part of the eleventh century, though much of the text is unintelligible.

In the early organs with keyboards, the keys appear to have been of great length, and about three inches broad, and required, it is said, pummelling with the fist to make the keys go down. It is thus probable that the chief use they were put to would be merely to sound the notes for the Plainsong. About the first mention of a keyboard was one consisting of 16 keys, in Madgeburg Cathedral, about the end of the eleventh century. It is believed that narrow keys, and the shorter semitone ones, were first introduced during the fourteenth century, though there is no certainty upon this point.

In many cases the naturals were of a black colour, with white short keys—the reverse as in use now—though there are numerous examples of the above still extant in Great Britain and on the Continent ; as also there are harpsichords having black keyboards· The church at Heiligenblut, in the Tyrol, owns, or did own, a very curious organ. It consists of two manuals, one manual having black naturals and white semitones, and the other manual vice versa ; also iron levers, moving right and left, operate the stops.

The method of blowing about the time of the introduction of keyboards was similar to so many magnified kitchen bellows with a valve. A man had charge of a couple, which he had to work with his feet and weight, holding on to a bar above with his hands the while.

The mode now in general use in Germany is but a development of the above with certain modifications, etc., the bellows having diagonal hinges, etc., whereas the British system of horizontal reservoirs and feeders has far superior advantages. There was nothing at the above early time of the nature of stops. All the pipes in connection with any one note sounded whenever that note was used, the apparent object of this being to give a powerful and dominating character to these single notes, and thus making them acting and important factors in leading the church song. Whilst the notes of these early organs were few, and each note had a multiplicity of pipes, the system of forming a chord on each note originated, and we have a kind of survival of this in our modern mixture stop.

It was not until about the fifteenth century that the invention of the pedal came about, and soon after this the Continental, and especially the German organs, began to assume generally a form similar in many respects to that in vogue up to recent times. England was some hundreds of years behind the Continent in adopting pedals, and before the nineteenth century, at which time they became more generally used, a lighter voicing and absence of heavy bass were noticeable features with the organs of this country. Many of these ancient organs possessed handsome cases of most ornate pattern, and there are some fine examples of these old cases still extant, especially on the Continent.

During the Revolution in the seventeenth century most of the organs in England fell a prey to the zealous fury of the Puritans and were destroyed, but at the Restoration of the Stuarts came a busy time for organ builders in replacing these, and as a natural consequence of the reaction following the rigid Cromwellian rule, organs were being required all over the country. Bernard (or Father) Smith, a German, and Thomas and René Harris, Frenchmen, were in most repute at this time, and their work has borne the test of time to a wonderful degree.

The invention of the swell, with the peculiar quality of the English swell reeds as a natural accompaniment to its development, was the work of the two Jordans, father and son, and marks the first important step in English organ construction. It was first used in an organ for St. Magnus' Church, near London Bridge, about the year 1712.

Most of the old "Echoes" of the German and Continental builders were gradually transformed into "Swells" during the eighteenth century, and the rule soon became almost universal as regards England.

There is a man named Hancock who is mentioned about this time as a good "reed voicer," and who worked with one Crang in changing the old "Echoes" into "Swells."

It was not until about the middle of the nineteenth century that the compass arrangement in vogue in England (F, or G, to tenor c or d) was superceded by the German one of two and a half octaves (C—f). The great advantage of this was that it enabled the practical study of such classical organ works as belonging to Bach and Mendelssohn, etc., which before the change had been impossible.

About this period we have that most useful mechanical invention by Bishop, an English organ builder, for conveniently dealing with groups of stops—the Composition Pedal.

As to the general mechanical action of the organ, this was improved about the year 1850 by the introduction of the pneumatic lever into many of the larger instruments, and the further later improvements of Willis practically revolutionised the whole mechanism of the organ.

Now, in our modern march of progress, we have the tubular-pneumatic and electro-pneumatic, etc., actions, various mechanical blowing apparatus in place of manual labour, the somewhat bewildering array of couplers, composition pedals, pistons, and other valuable—and otherwise—adjuncts, that it seems as though the day may not be far off when we may see the " mechanical " organist push his " flesh and blood " brother off the stool.

In conclusion, it would appear that the English organ builders, with their national slowness and conservatism, preferred (or were perhaps otherwise incapable) to learn thoroughly the fundamental points from their Continental brothers to being pioneers, but they have not neglected opportunities to improve upon those points, and are to a degree in many respects ahead of their original instructors, and the English organ of to-day is probably all round superior—or at any rate equal—to that of any other country.

F. T.

PNEUMATIC TRANSMISSION.

By Professor Dr. Bedart, University of Lille.

TUBULAR-PNEUMATIC TRANSMISSION BY EXHAUST.

THE prototype of this interesting system was realised in France by Moitessier, organ builder of Montpelier, for the 46 stops organ of Notre Dame de la Dalbade, Toulouse, in 1847. His patent dated from 1840 ; it was the exhaust system, now commonly used by all organ-builders !

Moitessier called it " abregé pneumatique " (abregé in French is the name of set of rollers transmitting key motion to pallets), and thus describes it : " All backfalls and rollers are replaced by tubes —each key having its particular tube. This tube opens under a piston running into a small cylinder cut out of a solid piece of wood ; the piston is affixed by a sticker to the pallet of the wind chest, and the spring of the pallet combined with the wind pressure keeps the piston in upward position corresponding to the closed pallets."

The tube was, at its other end, in communication with the air by an open valve ; but as soon as the key was depressed, this valve was closed and the tube put in communication with an exhaust chamber ; therefore, the under face of the piston being by the tube in communication with attenuated air, the piston by the atmospheric pressure, acting against its upper face, went down and opened the pallet.

This organ of la Dalbade, Toulouse, was a large three manual with 46 speaking stops. It was inspected by the committee on the 18th February, 1850, and lasted for 38 years, being in 1889 overhauled and refitted by Puget with the Barker lever to each manual and electro-pneumatic action to the pedal.

The workmanship of this organ was a masterpiece of joinery, but with time the wood cylinders did not remain quite true with the pistons ; there was a great loss of power, the pistons not being airtight. As Dr. Hinton tells us (in his lectures delivered for the Royal College of Organists, 1901), if " Moitessier had only covered the upper end of the cylinders with a bit of leather tied fast, like paper on a jam-pot, he could have got more power from the motor thus formed." Notwithstanding, this prototype of tubular pneumatic organs, conceived in 1840, and built in 1850 by Moitessier, worked in good order for 30 years at least, before being overhauled 38 years after its erection, and is *quite an historical* organ.

TUBULAR-PNEUMATIC TRANSMISSION BY COMPRESSED
AIR.

In the year 1854 Galy Cazelat in France, and L. Clarke in
England, made applications for a patent concerning a device for
moving (by compressed or attenuated air through long tubes,) tin
boxes containing letters or small parcels.   In 1859 Doctor Upham,
of Boston, succeeded in transmitting for a distance the heart
beat for physiological demonstrations by tubes containing air ;
but in the same year Tœpffer and Shœdel in Berlin were building
house bells in which, instead of pulling down the ordinary bellrope,
the bells were put in action by a tube containing compressed air.
In 1858 Professor Ch. Buisson, in Paris, transmitted movements of heart to a distance with the aid of a lead tube filled with
water, but after 1860, he used air instead of water with greater
success, with the collaboration of Marey, the future inventor of
chromo-photography and the cinematograph.

It is not until 1864 that we find the application of this mode of
transmission to organs ; the first trial was performed by Peschard,
during his researches upon electricity applied to organs.   Peschard
(a rich amateur organist of Caen, LL.D.) began about the year
1860, to lift the introduction valve of the Barker lever, by the action
of an electro magnet ; in 1862 he tried the action of electro
magnets not directly upon the introduction valve of Barker lever,
but upon the smaller valve of an auxiliary (very small) Barker lever,
which . governed the introduction valve of the great Barker
lever acting the pallets of channels.   He used for this purpose, not
only an electro magnet, but also a " membrane at the end of a
tube for pneumatic transmission," as Professeur Marey used for his
then far-famed physiological experiments.   But Peschard left air
transmission for electro-pneumatics, and from his collaboration
with Barker were built the electric organ of Salon Bouches du
Rhone in 1866, St. Augustin, Paris, 1868, and Montrouge 1869,
this latter being destroyed by the bombardment of 1870.

In 1867 Fermis, a schoolmaster in Hauterive (near Toulouse,
France), erected in the Church of Foix, Departement de l'Ariege, a
large 28 stops organ with a complete system of tubular action.
Fermis knew very well the Moitessier exhaust tubular system in
la Dalbade's organ, and took rather the counterpart by using
compressed air.   The keys opened valves introducing wind
into tubes, by which the bellows of an ordinary pneumatic Barker
machine were inflated ; it is the system by inflation, with the
outside pneumatic motors.

Now the pneumatic motors are put inside the wind chest, and
are flattened by deflating, when the tubular action lifts the valve
giving communication with the air.

Fermis had exhibited the swell of Foix organ in the 1867 Exhibition, and Dr. Hinton in his " Organ Construction " reports

(page 114) that " Mr. Henry Willis was much struck by a system of tubular pneumatics which was introduced in an organ shewn at the Paris Exhibition of 1867, and, thus stimulated, turned his energies to developing an improved form of tubular work, and turned into a new and definite school of organ building."

This *historical* organ of Foix is still in good order, and has not been repaired since its erection. It is under survey of Th. Puget, the well-known French organ builder of Toulouse, who writes that this tubular action, although not possessing the quickness in answering of our modern tubular, is a tolerable one after 40 years, being only a great wind " eater." In 1869 Fermis built a similar organ for the Black Friars, Oudinot Street, Paris, which was still in good order in 1904. Associated with Percy, Fermis built in 1878 the large 66 speaking stop in St. François Xavier, Paris, which stands as a fine organ, artistically played by Marty, the blind organist. Cavaillé Coll interposed a pneumatic lever between the keyboards and the chest supplying wind to tubes inflating the outside primitive motors, so the original tubular part built by Fermis remained unaltered. This organ is also a great wind " eater," wanting five blowers with foot-treadles !

Consequently in tubular pneumatic transmission, the names of Moitessier, (La Dalbade's Toulouse organ, 1850 exhaust system), of Fermis' (organ in Foix Church, 1867 inflation system), ought to be retained.

ELECTRO-PNEUMATIC TRANSMISSION.

After the early experiments of H."J. Gauntlet (1852), who inserted in his patent these words including the germ of all that has since been realized in electro-pneumatics : " *The apparatus known as pneumatic lever may be worked with magnet and armature,*" the definite results were attained by Dr. Albert Peschard, of Caen, who began his experiments in electro-pneumatics in 1860, and early in 1861 communicated his discoveries to Barker. Born in 1836, Peschard died in 1903.

It is surprising that the name of Peschard is not mentioned in Robertson's Practical Treatise of Organ-Building ; Hopkins also never speaks of Peschard's important discoveries.

Peschard's name, as remarks Dr. Hinton in his " Story of the Electric Organ " (1909), was first brought before the English public in a leader upon " Electric Organs " which appeared in the *Musical Standard* (May 23rd, 1891) : " The honours of combined electricity and pneumatics must remain divided between the Frenchman Albert Peschard and the Englishman Charles Barker."

In 1892 Peschard published a pamphlet entitled : *The Electric Organ is not an American Invention* (Paris Larousse, Editor). It was an answer to the dicta of Schmœle and Mols returning from

Philadelphia and claiming to be the inventors of electro-pneumatic system.

M. Peschard was entitled to do so, for, with the collaboration of Barker, he had built in 1866 the organ of St. Laurent Parish Church in Salon, near Marseilles, quite a remarkable electric organ, for actually forty-six years after its opening (1912) it is in good order, working upon the primitive electro-pneumatic apparatus, only cleaned in partial repairs of 1893 and 1904.   Many lovers of organ music have heard in St. Augustin the famous organist Gigout ; from 1868 to 1898 he played the organ, built by Peschard and Barker with electro-pneumatic system—that is, an electro magnet controlling the escape valve of a pneumatic motor put inside the chest.

Since 1862 Peschard and Barker had conceived this combination of pneumatic lever and of electricity, and in 1864 Peschard obtained a patent for the action of an electric magnet upon a valve covering a *multi-perforated surface* and allowing a very small raising for the valve ;   consequently the Hope-Jones improvement was not a new one.

In 1869 they introduced in the organ of St. Pierre de Montrouge, Paris (destroyed by shells during the Commune, 1870), the combination of a very small pneumatic lever (governing the valve of the great pneumatic bellow acting the pallet), the electro magnet had only to move the tiny valve commanding the auxiliary small pneumatic lever ;   and in 1862 Peschard had tried a sequel of four pneumatic levers, of decreasing size, from the chest-pallet to the electro magnet. Consequently the trial of a series of pneumatic levers " in cascade," as well as their application in the organ of Montrouge in 1869, is not an American one ;   Peschard and Barker found and applied with success the disposition on which all the electro-pneumatic systems have been built, with slight variations.

English Organ-Cases.

By Andrew Freeman.

I T is quite impossible in a short article to deal at all adequately with this subject, for in spite of the regrettable fact that only about one in every fifty organs in England possesses a case of any merit, the majority of the others being little better than eye-sores, yet England is such a land of organs that the number of good organ-cases, some of them really beautiful, is by no means inconsiderable. Happy to relate this number is added to each year, thanks to the interest now taken by many of our ablest architects in this so long neglected branch of ecclesiology.

No one will contend that our English cases can compare in majestic grandeur with such Continental specimens as Bois-le-Duc, Chartres, Tarragona or Lubeck (Marien-Kirche), and, sad to say, none can lay claim to the antiquity of Salamanca (Old Cathedral, *c*. 1380), Sion (*c*. 1390), and at least a score of other well-known organs dating from the Fifteenth Century. But in respect of perfect proportions, variety in design, exquisite carving and skilled workmanship—that is, in all except size and age, many English cases will hold their own. Where shall we find more beautiful cases than those at King's College, Cambridge, [58 and 59] St. Paul's Cathedral, Little Bardfield [69], or All Hallows, Barking [66], to mention four only of the older ones ; or the Sheldonian Theatre [75], and Brasenose College [74] (both at Oxford) ; St. Bartholomew's, Armley ; St. Paul's, Burton-on-Trent ; St. Mary's, Nottingham [56] ; or the Parish Church, Stratford-on-Avon, amongst those constructed during the last fifty years ? It would be quite easy to extend this list to some three or four dozen without including in it any but really fine cases.

The inferiority in size of the older English cases was due to a combination of circumstances, chief amongst which were the smallness of the instruments themselves, the comparative lowness of the roof of the majority of English churches, and the place in which the organ was situated.

The first of these no longer holds, but for centuries English organ-builders were much behind those on the Continent in developing their art. No English organ contained more than two manuals until after the Restoration of 1660 ; few of them had pedals till

NOTE.—The numbers enclosed in square brackets refer to the illustrations.

about the year 1790,[1] while the earliest to have a 32ft. stop was that at York Minster (1829), and the first with a 32ft. front that at Birmingham Town Hall (1834). On the Continent we find a complete instrument erected in the Church of St. Martin at Danzig, in 1585, consisting of three manual and two pedal departments, with a total of 55 sounding stops (including one of 32ft.). Pedals certainly date back to 1468 (St. Sebald, Nuremberg), and probably to 1418 (Beeskow, near Frankfort-on-Oder), whilst 32ft. pipes formed the front of the Halberstadt instrument as long ago as 1361. A hundred years ago it was a rare thing to find an English organ with more than 30 stops. Both at St. Paul's Cathedral and at York Minster, the organ contained only 27 stops, with no separate pipes to the pedal " pull-downs " ; that at Westminster Abbey had an octave of Pedal Pipes, but only 21 manual stops.

Nowadays large organs with a plentiful supply of 16ft. and 32ft. pipes are fairly common, and the newer cases show an increase in size which is often considerable. None, however, are to be found, even in Concert Halls, which will compare in size with the large foreign cases before mentioned. The reason for this can, perhaps, be made clear by an example :—

The Church of St. Margaret, Westminster, standing in the shadow of the Abbey, looks small by comparison with its mother-church. It seats about nine hundred and fifty, and is therefore a fair specimen of the average parish church. But this church, tower and all (the latter 85ft. high) could easily stand under the Abbey roof, which reaches to a height of 101 feet above the pavement—being, in fact, the highest vault in England. Yet the Bois-le-Duc organ, which is 40 feet wide and (with its gallery) 100 feet high, would not stand at the west end of the Abbey, unless taken out of its gallery, and even then it would be two feet too wide for the Abbey nave.[2] The Bois-le-Duc case is certainly the largest in the world, and, curiously enough, the largest of its front pipes is only 24ft. speaking length ; but other large cases, containing 32ft.

[1] There is one isolated and remarkable instance—the organ built by Robert Dallam for Jesus College Chapel, Cambridge, in 1634, at a cost of £200, and to which, according to the Dictionary of National Biography, " in 1635 he added pedals . . . for 12*l*." These, however, may possibly have been pedals to work shifting movements. Another instance, much later in point of time, was St. Paul's, for Burney, writing in 1785, tells us that Handel, upon his first arrival in England, frequently went " to play on that organ for the exercise it afforded him in the use of the pedals." This shows that there were *pedals* at St. Paul's as early as *c.* 1710, or very little later, but there were no separate *pedal pipes* there till 1826. At Westminster Abbey, Avery added pedal pipes in 1780—apparently the first in England.

[2] The height of the vault of several of our Cathedrals is given for the sake of comparison with some typical foreign churches—York, 99ft. ; St. Paul's, 89ft. ; Ripon, 88ft. ; Peterborough, 78ft. ; Chester, 75ft. ; Ely, 72ft. ; Rochester, 55ft. ; Amiens, 140ft. ; Palma (Majorca), 140ft. ; Chartres, 122ft. ; St. Jan, Bois-le-Duc, 120ft.

fronts, are frequently to be found on the Continent, some of them approaching very near to it in point of size. Most of them are very shallow, this one being only about 10 feet from back to front.[3] If one can picture it standing outside St. Margaret's, reaching to some 15 feet above the highest pinnacle of the tower, one is better able to imagine how much smaller its case would have to be made, in order that the same sized organ should be placed inside at the west end, over the entrance. Much more compression would be needed if it were to be placed at the other end of the church, in the north aisle, where the St. Margaret's organ is situated. And yet, previous to its being rebuilt in 1901, the Bois-le-Duc instrument had actually seven stops less than has that at St. Margaret's, the numbers being 41 and 48 respectively. The St. Margaret's organ displays a 16ft. speaking front towards the aisle —not a very common feature of church organs in this country.

This has brought us to the third of the reasons mentioned above—the situation of the organ in English Churches and Cathedrals, and its effect upon the size of the case.

I believe that previous to the Reformation only two organs are known to have been placed at the west end of an English Church. One was so placed at Croyland Abbey (where there was a second organ in the quire) and the other in a small subsidiary building, namely the Beauchamp Chapel attached to St. Mary's Parish Church, Warwick. I believe, also, that there are very few instances of Cathedral organs being placed on the screen until after that same landmark in our history had been passed[4]—the most usual position being on one side of the quire—though organs in Parish Churches were usually placed in the rood loft, which was generally roomy enough to contain the small instruments then in vogue. At the Reformation the screens in Parish Churches were destroyed, and thereafter, until the Gothic revival of the Nineteenth Century the majority of parochial organs were set up at the west end, and of cathedral organs on the quire screen. During the latter half of the last century many Cathedral organs were removed from their commanding position on the screen and re-erected, generally on one or both sides of the quire, but occasionally in one of the transepts, whilst the ordinary church organ made a similar migration eastwards, usually to be buried in some wretched hole called an organ-chamber, on one side or other of the chancel. It is not my intention to make lamentation over the destruction of many splendid old cases during this period of transition ; in the first place because

---

[3] The large organ at the west end of the Marien-Kirche at Lübeck contains 82 sounding stops. The case itself is nearly 80ft. high and 40ft. wide, though only 7ft. in depth. In the Cathedral Church at Perpignan is an ancient organ (c. 1490) with a 32ft. front. Its dimensions are 45ft. high by 23ft. wide by 3ft. 6in. deep !

[4] At Ripon, York and Durham, organs were placed on the screen, but these were not generally the chief instruments in use.

it is no use, and in the second because it led directly to the designing and construction of such fine cases as those at Chester, Ely and Bangor Cathedrals, St. John's College, Cambridge, Nottingham Parish Church [56] and others.   My purpose is to point out that the only position suited for a case of large proportions—the west end of a cathedral church—was never adopted here in England, and that if the quire screen or west gallery could not accomodate a large case the circumstances are even less favourable in the positions now chosen—an exception being made where the transept position has been selected, and also where a new church has been specially designed to take and make the most of an adequate instrument.

In fairness to our early organ-builders it should be said that the size of the organ was, to some extent at least, influenced by the position chosen.   Wherever it was, east or west, on the screen or over the stalls, it was always near to the body of singers whom its chief purpose was to accompany.   Consequently a large organ was not felt to be a necessity.

Since the organ found its way into our churches in very early times—certainly not later than A.D. 700—it may not be un-profitable if we attempt to show, in as brief a manner as possible, how the simple superstructure of early organs, hardly to be called a "case," developed into the magnificent "fronts" which are sometimes to be met with at home and abroad.

It is not possible to illustrate this evolution by means of re-productions of contemporary English organ-cases because, as has been said before, so few of our existing organs are really old, and none of them can be called ancient.   Many modern cases, however, are founded on ancient models and can be used to illustrate certain typical features and periods of development.

It should be stated here that the following attempt to trace the development of the organ case is founded almost entirely upon a careful examination of the seventy or eighty plates and a collation of the dates in the accompanying letterpress in Mr. Arthur G. Hill's two splendid volumes dealing with "Organ Cases and Organs of the Middle Ages and Renaissance."   *So far as dates are con-cerned it should be noted that they are merely those of the organs in which certain features are earliest found.   The features them-selves may have been, and probably were in many instances, found at earlier dates than those given.   I have only given the earliest I have been able to ascertain.*   It is hardly necessary to say that the various features illustrated would scarcely have made their appear-ance in different countries at the same time.   Due allowance must be made for the comparative isolation of certain provinces, or even countries, for local influences, and, especially in detail and ornamentation, for national characteristics which often led to complete transformation and much overlapping of styles. Moreover, one of the chief methods of determining the date of a case depends upon an examination of the style and execution of its carved detail—a phase of architectural history much beyond the scope of the present article, and therefore only here and there hinted at. The difficulty of determining the date of a case is often increased by the substitution of later ornamentation in place of older work— for instance of carved wings for folding shutters, of late Renaissance pipe shades for earlier Gothic tracery, or of storied campaniles above the towers for the former steeple-like roofs.

Early organs possessed no case-work above the impost, if we except the simple band of wood which held the front pipes in position, taking the place of the rack-board so far as these pipes were concerned. In these primitive instruments the pipes were generally arranged semitonally and almost directly over the broad-keyed clavier. A faithful representation of such an organ has been preserved to us in the beautiful Cecilia panel, painted by the Van Eycks for the church of St. Bavon, Ghent, but now at Berlin. It was painted in the early part of the fifteenth century.

As the compass increased and larger pipes were added, the pipes could no longer stand over their own keys—especially when the latter were reduced in size. The natural consequence was that the upper portion was made to overhang the lower on either side.[5] Many examples of this most characteristic feature of Gothic organ cases will be seen in the accompanying illustrations. Most of Father Smith's cases once possessed it, and some of them still retain it in spite of subsequent alterations and enlargements. An example of its use as late as 1717 is found in Schreider's instrument still, happily, to be seen at St. Mary's Church, Finedon, Northants [70].

By providing such an organ with sides, back, a canopy above and hinged doors to the front to protect the pipes from damp and dust, we arrive at the first real organ-case. Though the upper portion would be similar in outline to a wardrobe, yet such a case, properly proportioned, with richly carved tracery above the pipes and an open-work parapet along the top of the cornice, and with the whole of the wood-work enriched with painting and gilding, could be made to look very beautiful.

The custom of gilding the pipes and cases of organs is a very old one. Adhelm, who died A.D. 709, tells us that the Anglo-Saxons frequently embellished their organs in this manner.

The next step was to divide the pipes into compartments by means of buttresses or pilasters, and afterwards to break the line of

---

[5] An increase in the number of stops was the probable reason of a similar overhanging of the front, but this form of " hang-over " would obviously be later than the other.

the cornice by making one or more of the compartments higher than the rest, forming flat towers.

The Theddingworth organ [48] has an unbroken cornice, whilst those at Weybridge [50] and Stockcross [49] are examples of that type of case in which the cornice is irregular—all of them, of course, quite modern in construction though early in style. The Theddingworth instrument is one of the few in England provided with doors, these appendages being here adorned with pictures of angels playing on musical instruments. The ogee-form of the tracery here employed was a characteristic feature of fourteenth century design in England, but in the earliest organs the tops of the pipes would not have been hidden by the tracery. The front pipes are gilt, with slight decorations about their mouths, and a diagonal band painted in red, blue, white and black. The central compartment contains five pipes, the other two, four each. The lower portion of the case is painted dark green and reddish brown, with stencilled patterns in black and white, with the text " Sing praises unto the Lord " written along the front under the impost. Above the impost the case is decorated in white, red, light blue and gold. It was designed by the late Rev. F. H. Sutton (Author of " Church Organs, their Position and Construction "), who was vicar of the parish from 1864 to 1873, and about whom I shall have more to say later.

The case at Stockcross is closely modelled on that in the Conventual Church at Sion, Switzerland (*c.* 1390), though it overhangs in front instead of at the sides, and, being of plain oak, lacks the picturesque doors and elaborate colour scheme of its prototype. The treatment of the outside of the gable over the central flat and of the crestings of the two side towers, and the arrangement of its front pipes are almost identical, but there is a considerable variation in the carved tracery beneath the cornices, that at Sion being much the lighter and richer of the two, while the under edge of the gable differs from that at Stockcross in being quite plain.

The front of the Weybridge organ seems to have been modelled on two ancient cases—the one in the Chapel of San Bartholomé in the Old Cathedral at Salamanca (c. 1380) and the other in the church of San Petronio at Bologna (1470-5). In outline it resembles the former, but in the arrangement of the pipes in its three towers and in the treatment of its traceried pipe-shades (particularly in the engrailing of the lower edge of these to fit over the top of the individual pipes) it closely follows the design of the latter. (The ancient custom of leaving the pipes their natural length is to be seen in the Salamanca and Bologna examples but not at Weybridge, where the tops are cut so as to present a symmetrical appearance). The case is of oak and the pipes are of plain metal, with gilt decorations about their mouths and tops. It was designed by the late Mr. J. L. Pearson.

Still another early variety of case is the Ecchinswell one [51] which is distinctive of its designer, the late Mr. G. F. Bodley. Its front pipes, divided into three compartments, are of plain type-metal. Its wood-work is painted red and decorated in gold, with texts in red and black lettering on white scrolls. The pipe shades are of the simplest description, the carving being limited to the single line of cresting above the cornices of the canopies.

Another of Mr. Bodley's cases is at the church of St. John the Evangelist, Cowley Road, Oxford (the Church of the Cowley Fathers) [54]. This is a "hanging organ," placed high up on the north wall of the church above the screen, and is rather more elaborate than the Ecchinswell one, having more carved work about it. The pipes are divided into four compartments, the two central ones being separated by a well-carved image of an angel. Being silvered, the pipes show up well against the wood-work of the case—the latter painted green with stencilled patterns at the side in a darker shade of green, and with the pendant portion painted blue, the whole being relieved by a good deal of gilding. A graceful effect is produced by slightly curving the upper edges of the central portion of the cornice, instead of making them form a straight-edged V. It is not unlike the beautiful little hanging organ in the nave of the cathedral at Freiburg-in-Bresgau, built in 1515.

The next step was the vertical sub-division of one or more compartments into two or more tiers, stories, or stages, of which an example occurs as early as *c.* 1420, in the organ at San Pablo, Zaragoza. Occasionally, the whole composition was thus divided into two well-marked portions, as at the Cathedral at Zaragoza (1413). Here the lower story consists of eight compartments—six of them containing small pipes and the other two pierced tracery—while the upper story is made up of five flats, three of which, standing higher than the others and forming towers, are surmounted by concave roofs, or steeples,[6] with crocketed ribs and finials.

Another form of ornament—triangular and semicircular pediments above the cornices of the towers—made its appearance in the case at St. George's, Nordlingen (1466). In cases of later date these pediments were frequently "broken," as at Trinity College, Cambridge [see Frontispiece] and at Finedon Church [70].

A few words may here be said about the pipe-shades. When describing the Theddingworth organ-case, it was mentioned that in the earliest organs these shades, which were merely horizontal fringes or bands of tracery, were kept clear of the pipe-tops. Very soon, however, we find instances where they were made to follow,

[6] This is the earliest known appearance of these steeples—the precursors of the campaniles of the Renaissance period. Palma Cathedral, Majorca (*c.* 1420), has five such steeples—one above each of its three towers and two intermediate compartments.

more or less exactly, the rake of the latter,[7] while at least as early as 1413 (Zaragoza Cathedral) we find the tops of the pipes hidden by their means. The design of the carved work on these shades was, of course, determined by the prevailing architectural style of the period and country.

The lower extremities of the pipes were, in all early examples, placed so that they stood along the impost itself, and (a little later) along other portions of the frame-work parallel with it.[8]

The lines, curved or straight, formed by the mouths of a group of pipes were of necessity a feature in the design of every case. At first these lines were horizontal because the pipe-feet of each group (at the Old Cathedral, Salamanca) or of all the groups (at Sion) were of equal length. Very soon, however, they were made to form various angles with the impost, by making the foot either proportional to the length of the pipe (Amiens, 1429) or inversely so (Zaragoza Cathedral). The latter method was by far the most usual, and since the lines, or curves, so formed generally proceeded in a direction contrary to those of the lower edges of the pipe shades, the effect was greatly enhanced. Two of these methods can be seen in the case of the Stanford instrument [62] and the third in that at Ecchinswell [51], whilst all three are combined in the fine and elaborate case at Exeter Cathedral.

Both the usual forms of pipe-mouth—those in which the upper lip was pointed, or leaf-shaped, and those in which it was rounded (generally termed the " French " shape)—were in use from the earliest times. The more ornamental types do not appear to have been used until the early part of the sixteenth century.

With no other means than those that have been mentioned, namely, the horizontal and vertical sub-division of the front into compartments and stories respectively, the hang-over at the sides, the hinged-door, or shutter, and the infinite variety obtained by different methods of pipe arrangement and by the more purely ornamental additions in the form of elaborately-wrought carving and painted decoration, magnificent cases can be, and were, designed, of which those at the Marien-Kirche, Lubeck (1504), Barcelona Cathedral (1546), Tarragona Cathedral (1563) and the Church at Argentan (c. 1550) are probably the most splendid.

But long before the possibilities of this kind of case had been exhausted, the resources at the disposal of the designer were infinitely increased by the adoption of an irregular plan of impost.

[7] San Petronio, Bologna (1470), and its English understudy at Weybridge have already been mentioned. The custom of leaving pipes their natural length, and clear of the pipe-shades, lasted quite as late as 1657, the date of the elaborate and beautifully contrived case at Sta. Maria di Carignano, Genoa ; in fact, it may never have quite died out in Italy.

[8] The earliest known instance of making the line of their feet form an angle with the impost seems to have been St. John's, Luneburg (c. 1550).

Thus we find V-shaped towers at Chartres Cathedral (1475)[9], large semi-circular towers at the Marien-Kirche, Dortmund (*c.* 1480), and a large three-sided breast at the Church at Wisel, near Cleve (c. 1490).

A few examples may now be taken, from the large number in this country, to show how diverse are the forms which may be given to a case, of quite moderate dimensions but with an impost of irregular plan, without departing from the strict Gothic style.

A small but complete Gothic case of considerable charm, is to be found above the stalls on the north side of the chancel of the Chapel of Jesus College, Cambridge [52]. It was built in 1849, and was the gift of Sir John Sutton, fellow commoner of the college and elder brother of the Rev. F. H. Sutton before mentioned. In all probability it was designed by the donor. It consists of two flats, of seven pipes each, separated by a V-tower containing five larger pipes, and has overhanging sides and hinged doors— the inner sides of the latter covered with paintings of angels playing upon musical instruments. The pipe shades and the panels of the lower portion of the case are carved, and the whole is painted in shades of red and decorated with gilt.

At the west end of the same building is a newer and larger organ [53] erected in 1885. Its elaborate case, added a few years later, is decorated to match the chancel organ. It has two angels at the top and carved wings at the sides.

It may be worth mentioning that both these ornamental appendages had made their appearance on organ cases towards the end of the fifteenth century, the Hombleux organ (*c.* 1500) being one of the first known to display carved angels, whilst that at Strasbourg (1489) seems to have been the earliest to have side-wings. The last named adjuncts gradually superseded the picturesque folding doors, becoming in late Renaissance times much exaggerated in size.[10]

A still more ornate case is to be found in the Parish Church at St. Ives (Hunts) [55]. This organ is very curiously and exceptionally placed above the screen, where it entirely blocks out the view of the upper part of the chancel.[11] The ingenious way in which the organ-front is made to embody the Holy Rood with the

9 The case was much enlarged in 1513 in the Renaissance style. It is excelled by one case only—that at Bois-le-Duc.

10 *e.g* Aire-sur-la-Lys and Bruges (S. Sauveur). It is a curious fact that the original design for the Strasbourg case (which is still preserved) shows a painted, hinged door, outstretched, on one side, and one of the present pierced and carved wings on the other side—evidently for the sake of comparison. (See the *Musical Times* for September, 1910.)

11 At Stratford-on-Avon, where the organ is similarly situated—only in a loft instead of on the screen—there is much more room above the arch, so that the view of the chancel is not obstructed in the slightest degree.

attendant images of the Virgin and St. John is worthy of notice. The wood-work of organ and screen is elaborately decorated in gold, white, and red on a green ground, and the general effect is rich, though with a tendency to gaudiness. The keys are not contained in the tribune which overhangs the screen door, but are placed in a detached console on the chancel floor.

Sir Gilbert Scott's fine case at St. Mary's Parish Church, Nottingham [56], is another elaborate case with richly carved pipe-shades and wings, and brattished cresting above. It occupies a comparatively small space on the north side of a chancel that is none too wide, the upper portion of the case considerably over-hanging the lower in front and at the sides. Owing to its position the excellencies of its design are not at once apparent, and for the same reason, and because of its loftiness, a good photograph is an impossibility, if taken from below, as the accompanying one had to be.

At St. Alban's Cathedral [57] a well-designed divided case stands against the wall, on either side, above the only complete ancient Rood screen still remaining in England. The two cases (which bear some resemblance to that at Strasbourg) are identical except that the mouths of the pipes in the north case are leaf-shaped, while those of the south are rounded—a difference so minute that one is inclined to wonder why it was made. The cathedral is very light, so that the case with its new oak and plain metal front pipes scarcely shows to advantage—a matter which the flow of Time will set right.

In the spacious and lofty church of St. Michael and All Angels, Croydon [60], designed by Mr. Pearson,[12] there is another fine double-fronted case of Mr. Bodley's. The organ is splendidly placed in a chamber over the north aisle of the chancel, with a 16ft. front (divided into five flats) to the transept, and an 8ft. front to the chancel. The latter front contains two large semi-circular towers with several compartments of smaller pipes arranged in two tiers. The organist's seat is immediately under the front pipes, in a tribune that projects over the choir below him in the chancel. Here, at least, is to be found that ideal combination—a splendid organ with a beautiful case, situated in the best possible position in a church with fine acoustic properties and no inconsiderable claims to architectural distinction.

Many other fine and interesting organ-cases could be dealt with, did space permit, but at this point we must take up the tale of development with the oldest cases now left in England—those which belong to the pre-Restoration period.

All too few are these, but when one remembers how sweeping

12 In many respects it served as a sort of study for Mr. Pearson's master-piece at Truro. The vault is over 50 feet high.

was the destruction meted out to this form of church furniture during the Great Rebellion, and how many cases (beautiful and otherwise) suffered later on at the hands of the early Gothic revivalists, the wonder is that a single one of these treasures should have been spared to us. Those that are undoubtedly of this period are at least ten in number, some of which (marked *) now stand in buildings other than those for which they were originally constructed. They are :—

  1. St. Stephen's, Old Radnor, *c.* 1500.
 *2. St. Lawrence's, Appleby, before 1571.
  3. Gloucester Cathedral—*Choir case only,* 1579. (The remainder dates from 1663-5).
  4. King's College Chapel, Cambridge, 1606.
  5. Hatfield House, *c.* 1609.
 *6. St. Nicholas, Stanford-on-Avon (Northants), *c.* 1625 (possibly *c.* 1580).
  7. Dean Bargrave's organ at Canterbury Cathedral, 1629.
 *8. St. Mark's, Old Bilton (near Rugby), 1635-6.
 *9. Tewkesbury Abbey Church, 1637 (possibly *c.* 1580).

To complete the list a small chamber instrument should be added :—

*10. A " Positive " organ known as " Queen Elizabeth's organ," 1592, whilst one other organ-case has strong claims to be considered as belonging to this period :—
*11. Framlingham Parish Church (Suffolk), 1674, the case dating in all probability from *c.* 1550.

All of these deserve more than passing mention, but our notice of each must be brief.

The case of the organ at St. Stephen's, Old Radnor, [61] is undoubtedly the oldest now remaining in these islands. It has been exhaustively dealt with, and well illustrated, in the Rev. F. H. Sutton's " Church Organs." In dimensions it is comparatively small, being only 18ft. high, 9ft. 4in. wide, and 2ft. 6in. deep. Formerly a complete wreck, bereft of mechanism and pipes, it was, in 1872, most carefully restored under the direction of Mr. Sutton and fitted with a new instrument. The front has three V-towers, containing the larger pipes, and two flats—each of the latter consisting of two tiers of small pipes. The lower part of the front and the whole of the sides are almost entirely covered with intricate and well-carved napkin-pattern panels. In the upper portion of the front there is a good deal of rich carving, particularly in the cresting. The latter, which extends along the whole of the top, is debased in style but exceedingly effective, consisting of a series of pinnacles, semi-circles, and grotesque animals. In addition to the usual Gothic features of overhanging front and sides, this organ had, and still has, an extension of the lower part of the case at the back to give more bellows' room. Mr. Hill says that it appears to belong to the days of Henry VIII.

There is good reason for believing that the case and front pipes of the organ now in use in the Church of St. Lawrence, Appleby, once belonged to the " one pair of organnes " which is mentioned in an inventory of Carlisle Cathedral, taken in 1571. The Dean and Chapter of the Cathedral, on the completion of their new organ in 1684, presented the old one to Appleby Church, where it has been ever since. It was first erected in the west gallery, when it was enlarged in 1746, but in 1863 it was removed to a chapel on the north side of the chancel. In 1891 it was again enlarged.[13] The case itself is painted and is decorated with floral designs. Across the front, in gilt letters, is inscribed the text " Glory to God in the Highest." The three semi-circular towers are supported by large cherubs, while the cornices at the top of the case are gilded, and there is a cherub's head at each corner.

Mr. Hill states that the choir-organ case at Gloucester dates from 1579. It is certainly much older in style than the main case above it, which was completed in 1666. The treatment of the tower cornices of the two cases is very different, those of the choir being surmounted by cresting of an essentially English type. The carving on the pipe shades of the smaller case evidently served as a model for the corresponding portions of the larger one. The two cases blend exceedingly well, and together form a front which is as excellent as it is typically English.

The Chapel of King's College, Cambridge is divided into two portions, chapel and ante-chapel, by what is generally acknowledged to be the finest Renaissance screen in this country, above which stands a beautiful double-fronted organ [58 and 59]. Both fronts are kept low in the centre in order not to obstruct the *vista* more than necessary, the consequence being that the outlines are peculiarly graceful. There is a choir organ case above the screen door in the east, or chapel, front, which consists of a central V-tower, two semi-circular towers, and two connecting flats, with a crown above each of the semi-circular towers. The main case above it is similar in design, only the flats are much wider in proportion and the two end towers are larger than semi-circles. The latter are placed corner-wise, have crowns on their summits and are supported by curious bird-like men. The west front comprises two V-towers and seven intermediate compartments, of which latter the central one slightly projects. The two angels, with uplifted trumpets, which stand upon the two large western towers are modern restorations of an old feature in the design, the original angels having been

---

[13] These particulars are taken from Mr. Nicholson's Account of the Organs and Organists of Carlisle Cathedral, published in 1907. The description of the case is from information kindly supplied by Miss Mary Ridge, organist of Appleby Church.

supplanted early in the eighteenth century by two ghastly and cumbrous pinnacles. The small central flat is surmounted by a figure of King David with his harp. The pipes of all the towers (in both fronts) have inverted shades at their feet as well as the ordinary pipe shades above, those above being in some instances cut so as to fit each pipe—a noticeable feature in later Renaissance work. The carving of these shades is thrown into relief by a background painted green. The front pipes, now gilt, were formerly embossed and coloured. The case is of oak, dark, but by no means black, with age.

The organ was originally built by Thomas Dallam, of London, in 1606, at a cost of £214. The case, by Chapman and Hartop, cost another £156. The instrument itself has been enlarged and improved from time to time by Lancelot Pease (a Cambridge man who added the choir *organ*, and, possibly, the choir *case*, in 1661) ; Thomas Thamer (of Peterborough) in 1675-6 ; Renatus Harris, in 1686-7-8 and again in 1710 ; Avery, in 1804 ; and subsequently by Messrs. Hill and Son.

One of the chief treasures of the unrestored (and therefore unspoilt) fourteenth Century Church of St. Nicholas, Stanford-on-Avon (Northants), is the unique organ-case which stands in a loft at the west end of the nave [62]. Unfortunately the whole mechanism is a complete and grievous wreck, the only internal pipe remaining being a large reed-pipe belonging to the " Bass Trumpet." It has been in this unplayable condition for years. Though it consists of but a single manual it has two cases, the smaller one, however, merely serving as a screen to the player. This pseudo-choir-case consists of a single row of dummy wooden pipes, arranged in three compartments, and painted to match the beautiful embossed and decorated pipes in the main case above it, while the flat pipe shades are covered with stencilled patterns in cream, in lieu of the usual carving. This smaller case blends well with the larger one, though it is much less elaborate both in design and finish, and is most certainly a subsequent addition.

The three-sided central tower of the larger case is surmounted by a crown placed over a mitre which rests on a cushion with hanging ribbons—these several emblems being effectively decorated in gold, red and blue. Above each of the semi-circular side towers stands a quaint little angel blowing a trumpet, while underneath is a cherub. The central tower is likewise supported by *two* cherubs.

The case, which is of deal, was formerly painted. In the full glory of its original colouring, its appearance must have been really gorgeous.

There are legends that connect this organ with the old Palace of Whitehall. One states that it was removed from Whitehall to Stanford during the Commonwealth, while another (and more likely) story is to the effect that it was presented by Charles II. to Sir Thomas Cave, of Stanford, who set it up in the church.   The legends differ as to its original home, one mentioning the Banqueting House and the other the Chapel Royal.   Though direct documentary evidence is at present lacking, I have some grounds for believing that the organ was originally in the Chapel Royal, that a choir organ was added shortly before 1638, that it was " embezled " during the Commonwealth, but recovered and set up in its original position in the Chapel in 1660, and that, finally, about the year 1663 it was removed, *together with its loft*, to Stanford, in order to make room for a new organ built by Father Smith.

Mr. Hill dates this case *c.* 1625, but it is possibly much older than that, and *c.* 1580 would, in all probability, be not very wide of the mark.[14]

During the cleaning of a room over the Cathedral Treasury at Canterbury in 1910, the workmen came across the remains of a small organ which is undoubtedly the one which the Dean and Chapter bought for the use of the Dean (Dr. Isaac Bargrave) in 1629, at a cost of £22.   It probably stood in the Dean's Chapel (destroyed in 1651), and was apparently lost sight of for some two hundred and fifty years.   Pipes, key-board, and bellows have entirely disappeared, but the oak case, with its folding doors, still remains, as well as the sound-board and some of the action.   There appear to have been eight stops, four on either side of the key-board, but only four of these remain.   These are all on the left side, and consist of iron levers, which work by being moved from left to right.

In the centre of the panel of each of the case-doors is a coat of arms, on the right that of Christ Church, Canterbury, and on the left that of Dean Bargrave.

This interesting relic, having been carefully cleaned, has now found a home in the Cathedral Library.   Its dimensions are— *height*, 2ft. 2½in. ; *width*, 3ft. ; and *depth*, 2ft. 1½in. ; but the carved oak stand upon which the instrument is mounted brings the total height to 4ft. 7in., to which another two or three inches should be added for the feet of the stand, which have rotted off.[15]

In the years 1635-6 a new one-manual instrument with its case was built by Robert Dallam (a son of the Thomas Dallam who had built the King's College organ) for St. John's College Chapel, Cambridge.   It contained six stops and cost £185.   Thamar, who

[14] See *Musical Times* for November, 1911, for a fuller account of this organ and its case.

[15] For the above information I am indebted to a short account of this organ by the Rev. C. E. Woodruff, in the *Canterbury Diocesan Gazette* for January, 1911.   Can there be more of these old instruments stored away in forgotten lumber rooms of our greater churches ?

had charge of the instrument after the Restoration, probably added the choir organ case.[16] The organ underwent repairs from time to time, and was rebuilt and considerably enlarged in 1838 by Hill. In 1868 the organ was still further enlarged, preparatory to its being removed into the new Chapel, and at this period both the cases were discarded. The old Dallam case was purchased by the late Rev. H. O. Assheton, Rector of St. Mark's, Old Bilton, near Rugby, [63] where it was fitted with a new organ by Messrs. Nicholson and Company, of Worcester. Here, the case projects from the north wall of the chancel above the keyboards, the organ being placed in the vestry behind. Mr. Sutton, who supervised the fitting of the case to its new position was responsible for the " hang-over " of the front and for the three " spirettes " which adorn the cornices of the towers. Otherwise it was not interfered with—except to restore it to its original shape which had been slightly altered in 1838. The Tudor Rose and Portcullis embodied in the pipe shades are emblamatic of the Lady Margaret, foundress of St. John's College. The case is of oak, picked out with gilt, and the front pipes (which have rounded and gilded mouths), are of plain metal, and the general effect is one of simple dignity.[17]

Tewkesbury Abbey possesses two organs, one of which is enclosed in a beautiful case of great historical interest. The organ itself was built by Harris (grandfather of Renatus Harris) for Magdalen College Chapel, Oxford, in 1637, but seeing that the instrument consisted of two manuals with thirteen stops, and that the amount paid seems to have been only £40, there is some[18] justification for thinking that the case of a former organ was used. This theory is quite consistent with the style of the case, the details being very early Renaissance in character, not at all inconsistent with a date as early as *c.* 1580. The carving on the pipe-shades is very similar in design to that at Stanford. It also resembles the instrument in that place in the possession of beautifully embossed pipes, but is more fortunate in that it is in good playing order and in constant use in the services.

It was removed from Magdalen College to Hampton Court Palace, by Oliver Cromwell, and restored to the College in 1660. Here, after repairs at the hands of Renatus Harris, chiefly in 1686,

[16] The curved plan of the two curtains of pipes which connect the three towers of this choir case seems to point to a somewhat later date, but extracts from the College account books prove that in the year 1669 there were either two cases (great and choir) or two distinct and separate organs.

[17] The Choir case, similarly fitted with a new organ, found a home in Brownsover Church, a mile or two the other side of Rugby, where its otherwise charming appearance is somewhat spoilt by some modern carving which was added to its lower portion. The original organ (much enlarged) at St. John's College was provided with new cases in 1888. These are Gothic, and were designed by Mr. J. O. Scott. Their effect is excellent.

[18] Compare this price with the £370 paid for that at King's College.

it was superseded by a new organ, and found a fresh resting-place on the screen at Tewkesbury Abbey, in 1737. Since it has been at Tewkesbury it has been rebuilt by Holland, in 1796, and, in 1848, by Father Willis. It now stands on the south side of the quire.

A curious Positive of beautiful design and finished workmanship deserves a few words, though it is a chamber instrument, pure and simple. It is of Flemish origin and was constructed by E. Hoffheimer in 1592—apparently for the Earl of Montrose, whose arms and monogram are worked into the exquisite carving. All the pipes are of wood and are elaborately carved so as to resemble a Scotch thistle. There is nothing to show that this organ ever belonged to Queen Elizabeth, though it may have been the property of *Princess* Elizabeth, daughter of Charles I., seeing that it was in the Isle of Wight—where the Princess died—for so many years. It is now in the possession of Mr. W. H. Head, who exhibited it at the Music Loan Exhibition, held at Fishmongers' Hall in July, 1904.

The organ at Framlingham Parish Church, Suffolk, had, and, it is to be hoped still has, a double case. The main case came from the Chapel of Pembroke College, Cambridge, in 1707, for which it had been built by Thamar, in 1674. Here again there is some reason to believe that an old case was used up to contain Thamar's new instrument, for its style led both Mr. Sutton and Mr. Hill to ascribe it to the reign of Henry VIII., though it is only fair to add that Mr. Hill withdrew from this position upon learning the dates given above. In the second volume of his " Organ Cases," he has this to say, when dealing with this particular instrument :—" It will be observed that old English organs generally appear to be of a considerably earlier date than is really the case, showing the continuance of older architectural traditions in organ building, after the styles had been more fully altered in regard to other branches of artistic woodwork."

The chief features of this (main) case are the unusual form of the cornices of the three towers (two of them V-shaped, with a three-sided central one) which with two intermediate flats constitute the front, the quaint way in which the said towers are supported (a small full length figure under each of the end towers and five scroll-like brackets under the middle one), the two panels carved in imitation of a groined interior, the overhanging sides, the carving of the pipe shades, and the flowing diaper-pattern on the front pipes.

The small case which serves as a screen to the player was originally part of the front of a former organ in the church, but whether of earlier or later date than 1660, I am unable to say. It is almost oblong in form, is filled with a large number of quite small pipes and some florid and well-executed carving.

The number of organs which survived the period of the Commonwealth was considerably larger than was at one time supposed, but all, except those above named, seem to have met with an evil fate at one time or another. That which stood on the north side of the choir in Old St. Paul's fell a victim to the flames which destroyed the Cathedral during the Great Fire of 1666. It had a Gothic case with a crocketed gable and hinged doors, and, if we except small organs like Dean Bargrave's, seems to have been one of the last two surviving examples of an Old English case so provided of which we have any record. The other was the organ built by Robert Dallam, for Jesus College Chapel, Cambridge, in 1634, and either rebuilt by Renatus Harris in 1688, or superseded by a new organ by the latter maker.[19] In 1790 it was given to *Old* All Saints' Church, Cambridge, where it remained until the destruction of the church about the year 1864, when it seems to have been broken up. Another organ, built by Robert Dallam, in 1632, for York Minster, lasted till 1829, in which year it was destroyed by a fire which did considerable damage to the interior of the Minster. Three others by various builders were supreseded at various dates, namely, that at Christ's College, Cambridge, about the year 1706 ; that at St. John's College, Oxford, in 1766 ; and that at Lincoln Cathedral, in 1826. Many others underwent similar experiences, but lack of space forbids even mention of them here.

The numerous cases of organs which have been erected in England since the Restoration may, for our purpose, be divided into two groups, corresponding, roughly, with the periods from 1660 to *c.* 1830, and from *c.* 1830 to the present time. The first of these periods, which commenced with many extremely fine Renaissance cases, ended most ingloriously, after a long period of decline in workmanship as well as in design, with a large number of wretched specimens in the debased Gothic style, whose appearance is suggestive of smugness cultivated to the point of sanctity. The second period began with the Gothic Revival, which was a crusade against the debased and crudely complacent erections which had long usurped the name of Gothic. Its originators founded their methods upon a careful study of ancient examples, and the training of skilled workmen in the lost art of carving. Like all other revolutionary movements, its early achievements were unfortunately marred by the irreparable damage wrought by its all-too-eager disciples, but whatever their mistakes—and they were not few— it is to the Gothic Revival that we owe not only our more intimate knowledge of the purer Gothic forms, but a proper recognition and appreciation of the best architecture of all styles and all periods. With English organ-cases of this latter period we have already partly dealt, and we shall have more to say after consideration of those which were constructed between 1660 and 1830, or thereabouts.

[19] See Note 1. The organ was taken down in 1642-3 and set up again at the Restoration.

Considering that the building, repairing and tuning of church organs had been suspended for nearly twenty years, it is surprising to find how many organ-builders were plying their trade immediately after the return of the Merry Monarch. Amongst them were the three sons of old Thomas Dallam—Robert, Ralph and George—James White (partner of, and successor to the last-named), Preston of York, Thamar of Peterborough, Lancelot Pease of Cambridge, Robert Hayward of Bath, Robert Taunton of Bristol, and John Loosemore of Exeter.

Through the kindness of my friend Mr. S. W. Harvey, I am able to reproduce a photograph of a beautiful and remarkable design for an organ-case belonging to the early years of the Restoration Period. This is none other than that built by Lancelot Pease, of Cambridge, for Canterbury Cathedral, in 1662-4 [64]. The original is a sepia drawing, the work of one George Woodroffe, whose name appears in the right-hand bottom corner of the drawing in the writing of the period. Full particulars of this instrument will be found in the *Organist and Choirmaster* for August, 1908, from the pen of Mr. H. H. Battley, so that, space being limited, only a brief reference to it will be made here.

Pease's agreement shows that the organ consisted of two manuals, Great and Choir, with thirteen and six stops respectively. The dimensions of the cases (for there was a separate one for the Choir organ although it is not shown in the drawing) were—Great case, 16ft. wide by 23ft. high " to the upper part of the Cornish " ; Choir case, 7ft. wide by 9ft. high by 3ft. deep. The cost was £650 and the old Pre-Restoration organ which had been badly damaged but not destroyed in 1642 by soldiers under the command of Colonel Sandys, and which had been made playable, in some manner, shortly after the Restoration of Charles II.

Pease's organ was placed on the north side of the quire, over the stalls, and, though the interior was replaced, or at least renewed, by subsequent builders, here it remained till it was superseded by Green's unsightly organ of 1784—the last-named being placed on the screen.

This unique design may be cited in further support of Mr. Hill's remarks on the survival of the older architectural styles in English organ-case designs. (See above, under Framlingham.)

The case of the famous organ which Loosemore built for Exeter Cathedral in 1665, still remains in its original position on the screen, though the two great towers of pipes which stood against the piers at either end of the screen were, unfortunately, taken away some years ago. These contained the largest pipes ever made in England until the introduction of pedal pipes, the largest one being 20ft. 6in. speaking length. These pipes were of tin, and the towers which they formed were finished off with cornices similar to those on the main case between them. When these large towers were destroyed, all the other front pipes, which were also of tin, and many of which were beautifully embossed, were melted down. Notwithstanding these vandalisms, the case presents several points of interest, amongst which may be mentioned the treatment of the central flat tower of the east front, in which the middle pipe of the five which compose it is made to project beyond the others, the V-shaped additions to both bracket and cornice thus rendered necessary, adding considerably to the effect. The end towers of this front are larger than semi-circles, while all three towers of the west front are semi-circular. In both fronts the intermediate spaces are divided into tiers, but whereas the lower tiers are very similar, and both fronts have small circular compartments in the second stage, the east front has additional features in the form of two small towers placed high up between the circular compartments and the outer towers. The choir organ case which was at one time placed towards the nave has now been restored to its proper position, facing east. The instrument, which has overhanging sides, has a commanding appearance. The pipe-shades are cut so as to fit each pipe separately. The only point that can be urged against this splendidly executed, and in all other respects, finely designed case, is that the caps of the two circular towers of its east front are rather too heavy.

Within a year or two of the Restoration of Charles II, the English builders above enumerated were joined by Thomas Harris, and his son Renatus (son and grandson, respectively, of the Harris who had built the organ now at Tewkesbury, already described), both of whom had been living and working in France for some years, and by the most celebrated of all these old craftsmen, Bernard, or Father Smith, a German (or according to others, a Dutchman). Smith, who brought over with him his two nephews, Gerard and Christian, seems always to have had plenty of work, but the Harrises were not so fortunate until the death of Robert Dallam, in 1665, and of his brother Ralph, in 1672, whereafter Renatus Harris became Smith's most serious rival.

The cases of these two celebrated builders form a class by themselves, and will be so considered.

Sir John Sutton, writing in 1847,[20] says :—" The cases which were built by Schmidt, in the latter part of the seventeenth Century, are far better than anything that has been built since, for although the detail is not ecclesiastical, still the old form is kept up, and the general appearance is the same as those erected in Germany and Flanders, from the latter end of the sixteenth century, and the carved work is bold, and consists only of open work panelling in imitation of foliage and flowers, with large angels' heads, and at the

[20] In " A Short Account of Organs Built in England " (published anonymously)—pp. 96-7.

present time, with the assistance of a hundred and sixty years, they really look very venerable, especially when they have diapered pipes, which is the case in the Durham Cathedral organ, and some others. . . ."

" The cases of Harris are much more elaborate than those of Schmidt, and many of the details are those which were in common use in fitting up the apartments of the court and nobility of France, during the reign of Louis the Fourteenth ; wreaths of flowers and indelicate fat cupids, by way of angels, with drapery used for every purpose but to cover their nakedness. It is needless to comment further on such ornaments, as it must be evident to everyone that, to say the least of them, they are very much out of place in a church, and offensive to the feelings of right-minded persons."

This criticism, though not altogether unmerited, is rather less than just to Renatus Harris and his father. Several of their instruments have (or had) overhanging sides, amongst which those at St. Lawrence Jewry, and at St. Andrew Undershaft [65] may be named, whilst if the figures reclining above the cornices of the flats of the noble case at All Hallows, Barking [66], would be more accurately described as " Graces," that distinction ought also to be conferred upon the two denizens of the upper regions who were similarly situated on the old case of Father Smith's at the Temple Church (removed in 1842, when the present Gothic case was substituted for it). Moreover, a large number of Harris's cases never possessed these angels, graces, or cupids (call them what one will), and though it is true that many of the carved emblems are not of an ecclesiastical character, yet, in common with those of Smith, the modest and dignified proportions of the cases, with their massive cornices, gilded pipes and excellent carving, go a long way to make up for any indiscretion in the choice of ornamental detail.

The Temple Church organ-case, above referred to, does not seem to have come up to the same standard of high excellence usually maintained by its famous builder, but it presented the rather unusual feature of rounded towers, larger than semi-circles, placed at the angles. The treatment of the carving on the caps of the three towers was similar to that on the smaller organ, by the same builder, still to be found in Manchester Cathedral.

In some respects the cases of Smith and Harris were similar. Their towers were never divided into tiers, though the intermediate flats, which were always straight in plan, were frequently made in two stories. The most usual form of tower was the semi-circular. Flat towers and V-shaped towers were less used. At Gloucester Cathedral, the central tower of both east and west fronts (which differ only in slight particulars) is almost identical in treatment with the central tower of the east front of Exeter Cathedral, already described. The main case was added by T. and R. Harris in 1665-6, and is one of the most beautiful to be found in any of our Cathedrals. (The small choir case was described earlier in the course of this article).

Instances of the use of two, three and four towers by each of these craftsmen remain. Their cases seem always to have terminated with a tower at either end, and never with a flat. Except when there were only two towers, the central portion was nearly always the highest, caused either by placing the largest pipes in the middle tower (or towers), or exceptionally, as at All Hallows, Lombard Street and St. Clement's, East Cheap, by putting a small central tower above a flat—in these instances a large circular flat, which by no means improves the appearance of the case. These were exceptions to this rule, but they were few and far between, one that may be mentioned being that at St. Sepulchre's, Holborn Viaduct.

So great was the variety obtainable by adopting various combinations of the three forms of towers above mentioned, with different treatment of the cornices of the intermediate flats, that it is safe to say that where a repetition of a design is to be met with, it was at the wish of the client and not because the designer had come to an end of his resources.

Amongst cases so duplicated (none quite exactly) are those at Christ Church Cathedral, Oxford (1680), St. Mary's University Church, Cambridge (1697), the Banqueting House Chapel (Royal), Whitehall (1699), [67], and Eton College Chapel (c. 1700). Of these, the first named, alone, has a choir case which has recently been restored to its proper place behind the organist, whilst the last is now at Hawkesyard Park, Rugeley, Staffs. Most famous of all is that which was removed from the Chapel Royal to the church of St. Peter ad Vincula, Tower of London, in 1890, where it still is. Nearly all writers on English organs have united in describing it as the first instrument built by Father Smith in this country, namely in 1660, whereas it was not built till the old Chapel Royal had been destroyed by fire, namely, in 1699.[21]

Harris's instrument at St. Nicholas (now the Cathedral), Newcastle-on-Tyne, was a curious instance of a double duplication, its front bearing a close resemblance to that at St. Sepulchre's, Holborn Viaduct, and its back being similar to that at St. Andrew's, Holborn—two churches within a few hundred yards of each other, whose organs were also by Harris.

The towers of both builders were supported either by a cherub's head (sometimes two or three were used) or by a bracket covered with foliated carving, and were finished off with a heavily moulded cornice. Occasionally, as in two of the four towers of the old

[21] See *Musical Times* for September, 1911.

portion of the case at Trinity College, Cambridge [see Frontispiece], the upper orders of the cornice moulding above a flat tower were left out, and a semi-circular pediment substituted.   (The Trinity case was judiciously enlarged some years ago by the addition of an extra flat and a large tower to each end).

Frequently some kind of ornament was added above the towers,—the crown and mitre (as at Christ Church, Newgate Street), vases with gilded flames (as at St. Clement Danes, Strand), and cupolas (as at St. Bride's, Fleet Street and at St. Sepulchre's).

The last named instrument, built by Harris in 1670 or 1677 (the date is variously given) was removed from the West End of the church to the North Chapel in 1891-2, when it was shorn of its cupolas and choir organ case, being at the same time considerably extended in width.   It still retains the coat of arms over its central tower and the two winged "supporters," while the two angels ("indelicate fat cupids"!) continue to recline on the two halves of the broken, rounded pediment, which are placed above the two inner flats.

The St. Bride's organ is more fortunate in retaining its west gallery position and all its adornments.   In this case the pipes in the lower story on each side of the central tower are arranged in upright oval compartments, while the cupola on each of the side towers terminates with a mitre, and that on the central tower with a crown.

The organ which Harris built in 1696 for St. Andrew Undershaft, [65], had, before its removal to the east end of the south aisle, in 1875, in addition to the two angels above the cornices of the side flats, a singular erection above its central tower.   For sheer exuberance of this species of cornice adornment, however, the same builder's design for the organ which he built in 1710 for Salisbury Cathedral [68] probably stands unrivalled.[22]   Though little, if at all, larger than the generality of the most important cases of the period, being 20ft. in width, it sprouted to such effect that the crown on the top reached to a height of 40ft.   Of all Harris's cases that I have met with this is the one that most merits the condemnation of Sir John Sutton, but apart from its excessive ornamentation and the unsightly excrescences above the towers, it is a very good example of its period, immeasurably superior to Green's miserable specimen of "correct" Gothic which succeeded it in 1792.   Above the three towers of the choir case were three small figures, or statues.   At least two other organs by the same builder still have similar figures above their towers.   These are those built for St.

[22] An excellent reproduction of this design appeared in the *Musical Times* for February, 1903.   Part of the organ, including the choir organ case, was used up in the organ erected by Green and Blyth in Helston Church in 1799. Thence it was removed to Shaugh Church (Devon), and later to Braunton Church, but the case has now entirely disappeared.

Peter Mancroft, Norwich (now placed in the south aisle of the chancel at Yarmouth Parish Church, where it forms the back of one portion of the divided organ[23]), and King James' "New Popish Chapell," at Whitehall, built in 1637 (now at St. James' Piccadilly, to which church it was given by Queen Mary, in 1691). The central tower of the former is still surmounted by a finely carved statue of St. Peter, while the latter has no less than six figures—an angel blowing a trumpet on each side of the towers, a larger one reclining above each of the two flats, and two more figures above the large central tower. These two cases are both noble specimens of the craftman's art, the Whitehall one having been carved by Grinling Gibbons.

Large figures are also to be found on the truly magnificent divided case at St. Paul's Cathedral Those above the main towers were added by Sir Christopher Wren (who himself designed the case) in order to hide the tops of the long pipes which Father Smith had used, and over which architect and builder had quarrelled. These figures are placed in pairs, with an altar between them. The case is in the Italian Renaissance style, and adorned with some of the finest carving in the world, mostly by the master hand of Grinling Gibbons. It remained on the screen from its erection in 1697 till 1860, when it was removed to the second arch on the north side of the quire, and temporarily robbed of its choir case. In 1872 it was divided, the original front, together with the choir case, being placed over the stalls on the north side of the quire, whilst the "back" case, for which a replica of the choir case was made, was set up on the opposite side. At the same time the sides of each of the main cases were fitted with pipes, so that there are now six speaking fronts. The choir cases are very similar to the large cases above them—merely two flat towers with a flat compartment between—and the front pipes are gilded. The present situation is ideal, and it is difficult to imagine the state of mind of anyone who would wish it altered in any way, or differently situated—but who knows ? Vandals are a hardy species, and will probably outlive the poor !

Before leaving the cases of Smith and Harris, it may be mentioned that the ornamentation of the cornices *between* the towers was not limited to the reclining angels instanced above. The upper edge was sometimes finished off with carved foliage (as at St. Mary at Hill and St. Clement Danes, Strand), but more frequently

---

[23] The case of the old Yarmouth instrument (by Jordan, 1733) does similar duty to the other half of the organ in the north aisle. This, too, has a large figure above its central tower. Curiously enough, the side towers of this case are surmounted by crowns, and of the St. Peter's case by mitres. Both cases are very much alike, only the Jordan case has its intermediate compartments slightly curved. Jordan's case at Bath Abbey (1703) had large figures of King David, St. Peter and St. Paul It was ruthlessly destroyed in 1838.

the ornamentation took the form of the more or less heavy scroll-work, of which examples still remain at St. Peter ad Vincula [67], Trinity College, Cambridge [see Frontispiece], and several other places.   Of course, in many cases, the cornices both of towers and of flats, consisted of plain mouldings alone, without any form of super-structure.   A perfect example of a small organ of this type and period is to be seen at St. Katherine's, Little Bardfield, Essex [69]—surely one of the most charming cases that was ever devised.   It was built by Harris, and is said to have come to Little Bardfield from Jesus College, Cambridge.   It still retains nearly, if not quite, all its original pipes, including a mounted cornet.

For some time after the death of Father Smith, in 1708, good cases were made by his son-in-law, Schreider, his two nephews, Gerard and Christian, and their contemporaries, but few of these were up to the standard of the earlier master, and many cases of poor design crept in amongst them, and in increasing numbers.

That made by Schreider, in 1717, for St. Mary's Church, Finedon, Northants [70], is an exceptionally good one, and is still, happily, in its original position in the west gallery.   Its two side towers, which are flat, terminate in broken, curved pediments, whilst the spaces above the lower compartments and between the three towers, are entirely filled in with two well-carved screens of scroll-work.   The brackets which support the overhanging sides are also in the form of scrolls.   In spite of successive alterations, much of the old pipe work, including the front pipes with their original decorations, remains.   This organ has been ascribed to Gerard Smith by various writers, but Mr. A. C. Edwards, in his "Organs and Organ Building," is quite positive that it was built by Schreider.

At St. Helen's Church, Abingdon, is another old case so like the main case of the Salisbury instrument, above described, that several writers have concluded that they are one and the same. This is not so, however, for the Abingdon instrument was built by Abraham Jordan in 1725, and in the contract for the rebuilding, which was entrusted to Byfield, England and Russell, *c.* 1780, it was expressly stated that the old case was to be retained.   The Harris instrument remained at Salisbury till 1792.   The gilded representation of King David and his harp once adorned the west gallery (where the organ stood till its removal to its present position in the south chancel aisle).   It scarcely merits its prominent place on this fine old organ-case.

Many other excellent cases could be described, but lack of space compels us to mention two only, the first a late, but exceedingly graceful one built by Richard Bridge for St. Andrew's Parish Church, Enfield,[24] in 1753 [71].   The ogee-curve was a favourite

[24] The same design—more or less exact, and sometimes with additional

one in work of this period, and used with discretion, as at Enfield, was a means of beauty. (Its use in the *plan* as well as in the elevation of the curtains between the towers should be noticed). A close examination of the carving enables me to testify to its excellence. Most of the internal pipes and mechanism of this instrument now form part of an enlarged organ nearer the chancel. Would that other equally beautiful specimens of well-designed and well-executed wood-work had been preserved in the same way ! Here, at Enfield, the back has been cut away and front of the case set back to within two or three feet of the wall, so that little room has been lost by the retention of this interesting link with past generations of worshippers.

A still later case, which though far inferior to the Enfield one, is still above the average for its period, is to be seen in the west gallery at St. Botolph's, Aldersgate Street, E.C. [72] It was built by Samuel Green, in 1778. Its worst points are the meanness of the cornices of the two flats, the inferior character of the carving, and the lack of skill shown in the management of the brackets which support the towers. A few alterations in the lines of the case, more particularly in those of the two ugly flats, combined with a richer form of carving, properly distributed, would make this quite a fine case. Its most noticeable features are the central group of three towers and the festoons which take the place of the pipe-shades of earlier cases.

Similar groups of three towers were to be found in the organs in St. Alfege, Greenwich and in St. Mary Redcliffe, Bristol—the latter long since destroyed.

At this point Sir John Sutton may again be quoted. He says :[25] " Early in the reign of George the Third, attempts were made to restore the Gothic style, at least in the restorations made in old churches ; with what success may be seen by examining the stalls at Westminster Abbey, the Altar and organ screens at St. George's Chapel, at Windsor, and other works executed about the same period. Green, who was at that time at the height of his popularity, and was very much patronised by King George the Third, was obliged to conform to the prevailing taste, and began to engraft innumerable pinnacles and incorrect Gothic details upon his tasteless boxes. And their effect was, if possible, worse than the plain ones which preceded them. Many of our Cathedrals, College Chapels and Parish Churches, are disfigured by these unsightly organ-cases, which became every day larger and more heavy looking, and the ornamental parts resemble the barley sugar ornaments we see about Christmas time in pastrycooks' windows, displayed in all their glory on a twelfth cake. From time to time slight improve-

ornament above the cornices—was used for several other organ-cases of the period,—for instance, at St. Margaret Pattens, E.C.

[25] ".A Short Account of Organs," pp. 98-100.

ments were made in the details, though they were injudiciously applied. Every part of a church has been copied for the organ-case, and attempts have been made at one time to make the organ look like a tomb, at another like a screen, at another the canopies of the stalls have been placed on the top of the organ, and latterly, as if in despair of producing any thing decent, the organ has been put out of sight altogether."

Amongst the cases which more or less merit the above condemnation, may be cited those at St. Katherine's, Regent's Park (1778), Greenwich Hospital (1789—fine workmanship thrown away on a poor design), New College Chapel, Oxford (1776—a barbarous erection, now destroyed, with a hole through the middle of it to allow a " peep " at the Reynolds window)—all by Green ; York Minster (Elliott and Hill, 1829) and Leeds Parish Church (a weird mass of " carvery " in the form of a shrine, without a single pipe showing). Many others are to be met with in smaller churches which are even more horrible, but it does not seem quite fair to put the latter into the same pillory of architectural depravity as the more important churches just mentioned, where the foremost architects of the day found congenial occupation, presumably to the mutual satisfaction of all concerned.

When Gothic architecture began to be properly studied, and its principles mastered, a great change rapidly came about. One of the earliest fruits of the Revival, so far as organ-cases are concerned, is to be found at the University Church of St. Mary the Virgin, at Oxford. Here, in 1827, the Revivalist architect, one Thomas Plowman, found an interesting Father Smith case on the screen dividing the chancel from the nave, and set about altering the nave front to make it fit in with his notions of what an organ-case in a Gothic church should look like. Without altering the disposition of the pipes, but merely by the substitution of perpendicular caps, shades, tracery and panels for the old Renaissance work (leaving only the foliated pipe shades of two of the compartments and the cherubs that form the brackets to the three towers), he completely transformed it. Though not at all happy, the result is much better than most of this kind and period.[73][26] The chancel front, (which is really only a more or less ornamental back, consisting of three flat towers and two-storied intermediate flats, each filled with flattened wooden dummy pipes, painted a dull red-brown) he left, though in a somewhat mutilated condition, so that we are able to compare it with the " restored " case, and form an estimate of its original appearance.

The Oxford Architectural Society and the Cambridge Camden Society, both founded about 1839, did much to foster and direct

[26] At Norwich Cathedral a Harris organ-case was similarly treated in 1833, and again in 1899, only much less successfully ; in fact, this twice-tinkered case is not now worthy of its position in so splendid a building.

the new movement, and the organ-case was not overlooked. The two Suttons exerted no little influence, the elder one in his " Short Account of Organs " (for which Pugin supplied a set of five suggestive designs), and the younger in his " Church Organs," first published in 1866 under the title " Some Account of the Mediæval Organ-case still existing at Old Radnor," and illustrated with etchings of existing old organs and some extremely interesting designs for new ones in the earlier Gothic styles. In this connection the most remarkable and unique design prepared by William Burges, for the Cathedral of Lille (but never constructed) must be noticed. Mr. Audsley describes it as a " Castle of Sound and Music . . . designed for the reception of a complete polychromatic embellishment, which, had it been carried out under Mr. Burges' careful supervision, would unquestionably have made the work the most expressive and artistic of its class ever designed."[27]

Amongst the earliest of the really fine Gothic cases were those designed by Sir Gilbert Scott for Ely (1851), St. Mary's, Nottingham [56] (1871), Manchester (1872), Chester (1876), and Ripon (1878), and Mr. R. C. Carpenter's case for Sherborne Abbey. Possibly the noblest of them all is that at St. Bartholomew's, Armley, which seems to have been erected about the year 1880, but I am unable to give the architect's name. Mention should be made of the cases at St. Barnabas, Pimlico, and St. John the Divine, Kennington (G. F. Bodley) ; Halifax and Croydon Parish Churches (J. O. Scott, 1899 and 1893 respectively) ; Northington Church, Hants (T. G. Jackson) ; Chichester and Peterborough Cathedrals (A. G. Hill, 1888 and 1904 respectively) ; St. Mary's, Portsea (Sir A. Blomfield) ; St. Alban's, Teddington (A. H. Skipworth) ; St. Martin of Tours, Epsom (Sir C. Nicholson) ; Chiswick Parish Church and Westminster Abbey (J. L. Pearson) ; Stratford-on-Avon and St. Augustine's, Pendlebury (Bodley and Garner) ; St. Paul's, Morton, near Gainsborough (J. T. Micklethwaite and Somers Clarke, 1893) , St. John's, Stanstead Mountfitchet and Winchester College Chapel (W. D. Caröe, 1891 and 1911 respectively) ; the Lady Chapel of the new Cathedral at Liverpool (Gilbert Scott) ;—also Holy Trinity, Rugby ; Marlborough College Chapel ; Selby Abbey ; Lichfield Cathedral ; Rawtenstall Parish Church , St. Paul's, Burton-on-Trent ; Holy Trinity, Bracknell , Great Bardfield ; Great Saling and Littlebury—the three last-named quite small organs in village churches in Essex. Some of these are splendid : all are good.

The revival of Gothic led to a similar revival in Renaissance, and the concluding section of this article will be devoted mainly to organ cases designed in this style, most of which were built during the past thirty years.

Mr. T. G. Jackson has some exceptionally fine organ-cases to his credit, amongst which may be quoted those at Hampstead

[27] " The Art of Organ Building," Vol. I., p. 149.

Parish Church (with campaniles above its tower-cornices), Hertford College Chapel, Oxford (a well proportioned case in light oak, with a campanile above its central V-tower, and angels worked into the carving of the pierced screens above the two compartments which connect this central tower with the rounded ones at either end), and Brasenose College Chapel, Oxford [74]. The latter, which was constructed in 1892, encloses quite a small two-manual instrument. It is placed on the screen dividing the chapel from the ante-chapel, to each of which it presents a differently planned front of gilded pipes. The east, or chapel front, has three rounded towers. Above the central one, which is the smallest, is seated an angel, playing on a viol. Two peacocks are to be seen in the pipe-shades of each of the three towers. The west front has two V-shaped towers (whose supporting brackets terminate in small heads of angels), and a rounded one between. Above the latter, which is placed at a lower level than the others, is an angel blowing a trumpet, and included in the carving of its pipe shade is a peacock. Four angels take the place of peacocks in the remaining towers of this front. The case is of light oak, embellished with gold, and the overhanging sides add to its graceful and dignified appearance.

Finer still, however, is the same architect's case in the Sheldonian Theatre, in the same city, constructed in 1877 [75]. Beautiful alike in outline, detail, and colour, it harmonizes splendidly with the architecture, internal fittings, and decorative scheme of Wren's famous building. The treatment of the wings of large metal pipes at the back, and the way in which the central breast and its flanking towers are connected with the gallery front, are especially worthy of notice. The small carved wings on either side of the front are just what such appendages ought to be, and add not a little to a case of many charms—a case to which I, for one, always turn with feelings of admiration and pleasure, and one which seems little short of perfection.

Mr. A. G. Hill's grandest case is at Sydney Town Hall, New South Wales,[28] but a good example of a plainer and painted case, designed by him in the Renaissance style, is to be seen at the Guildhall, Cambridge [76]. The projecting tubas are a somewhat unnecessary feature, and there is but little in the way of ornamentation, but there are many points about this excellently proportioned

[28] It is certainly the finest 32ft. front that ever emanated from England, where few of our architects seem to know how to deal with such large pipes. Only two such cases are even tolerably successful—those at Leeds Town Hall and St. George's Hall, Liverpool,—the others (such as those at the Albert Hall and Alexandra Palace) being only more or less (and generally less) successful attempts at grouping 32ft. pipes with little in the way of case. Two attempts at 32ft. fronts in churches (at Carlisle Cathedral and at Eton College Chapel) are miserable failures, the impression given being that of enormous stove-pipes whose manipulation was beyond the power of the architect. The effect at Eton is not greatly (if at all) improved by the elaborate scheme of decoration.

16ft. case, which might well serve as a model where the space allowed is wide in proportion to its height, and where an expensive case is out of the question.

At the Queen's Hall, Langham Place, W., there is another case, on similar lines, but more elaborately carved and decorated, designed by Mr. T. E. Knightley, the architect of the hall. It is painted in delicate tints and enriched with gold.

Reading Town Hall [77] possesses a fine and imposing oak case, with a 16ft. speaking-front of plain metal pipes. It is so planned that a considerable number of the larger pipes are displayed on its three sides without any of its compartments being broken up into stories. It was designed by Mr. Lainson.

Clapham Parish Church (dedicated to the Holy Trinity, not to St. Mary, as stated in Hopkins and Rimbault) possesses at the present time two organs. The older one [—], though still playable, has not been used since the erection of the new instrument in the chancel in 1909. It still occupies its original position in the west gallery, where it was erected by the late Mr. J. C. Bishop, in 1845. Many Renaissance churches—this one is of the watered-down-Renaissance species—which were either built or re-fitted in the first half of the last century, had the good taste to refuse the cases designed in the debased and nasty forms then in vogue, and so, here and there, we find reversions to older and better types. This one is an instance of a case out of its period by some seventy or eighty years. What little ornamentation there is is in good taste, and it is a pleasure to find it still retaining its west gallery position.[29]

At the other end of the church, in a specially constructed loft on the north side of the chancel is a fine new organ by Messrs. Hunter and Son.[78] The oak case, made by the builders, is in accordance with the designs of Mr. Beresford Pite. Personally, I do not like to see the tops of the pipes showing above the wood-work of the case, and I cannot say that I admire either the fret-carving which is so much in evidence, or the curve given to the cornices which connect the towers with the wings ; but these blemishes—if blemishes they are—are not sufficient to detract from the air of strength conveyed by what is really a fine and original case. I have nothing but admiration to express for the fine quality of workmanship both of case and instrument.

The practice, above referred to, of leaving the tops of the pipes exposed above the highest part of the case-work, became the rule rather than the exception with organs made in England during the greater part of the nineteenth century. This is altogether contrary to the usage observed in all the finest of the older organ-

[29] Perhaps the best of all these " old-fashioned " cases is that built by J. Booth, in 1827, for Brunswick Chapel, Leeds. It has seven towers and the usual flats in the great case, and a choir organ in front of the gallery.

cases, both English and Continental. In this connection it is worth while recalling Wren's disgust and indignation when he found Father Smith's pipes protruding above the cornice of his case at St. Paul's, and the pains he took to conceal them by designing additional carving for the top of the case. I venture to say that even so gifted an architect as Sir Gilbert Scott was unable to produce a faultless case when he departed—as he often did—from this important principle of mediæval organ-design. Fine cases can be, and have been made, but perfect ones—never!

There was a certain type of case which was constructed about the middle of the last Century, when architects gave over copying old English cases and tried to evolve something new, and, to their minds, more in keeping with the Renaissance and Classic buildings which they were called upon to build or restore. This was before the older Continental cases had been studied, hence their achievements in this direction, though not lacking in originality, were generally rather heavy in appearance. Some of them, however, were not without a certain air of distinction. Amongst them may be noted those at St. Martin-in-the-Fields (T. Allom, 1854—a double case) ; St. Peter's, Manchester[30] (E. Salomons, 1856) ; Providence Congregational Church, Cleckheaton ; and Halifax Place Wesleyan Church, Nottingham.

The above types have been succeeded by others in which the Renaissance forms are used with greater freedom and boldness. Some of these have already been described more or less briefly ; others are to be found at Wadham and Corpus Christi Colleges, Oxford ; and Radley College, near Abingdon (T. G. Jackson—the effect of the Radley organ is somewhat marred by its carved wings, which are somewhat obtrusive) ; Douglas Castle, Isle of Man (H. Wilson, 1896—a pleasing and original composition with its pipe shades for the most part solid, evidently on account of the smallness of the chapel) ; St. Catherine's College, Cambridge (T. Garner, 1895—with a choir case in front) ; the Victoria Hall, Halifax (A. G. Hill, 1901—a case in three divisions, at the back and sides of the stage, connected by perforated screens), and Haileybury College Chapel (Reginald Blomfield, 1901—a fine, bold and original example).

It is curious that the debased taste prevalent during the eighteenth Century should have had such different results here and abroad, but so it was. Here in England, after the ineffectual attempt at more florid forms (as exemplified in some of Renatus Harris's later instruments), the downward movement ended in flat cases meanly ornamented with poor, stiff carving. On the Continent (though to a lesser degree in France than in Spain, Germany and the Netherlands) the tendency was from the first

---

[30] The organ, but not the case, is now at St. Bride's Church, Old Trafford, where it was removed on the destruction of St. Peter's Church in 1907.

towards organ-cases with wildly exaggerated excrescences at the sides and above, enormous carved figures and rococo ornament. It is, perhaps, only natural that the revulsion of feeling against these debased forms of art should have first set in the country where the worst cases were to be found—namely, in England. In Germany, on the other hand, however much one finds to criticise in the matter of design, it has to be admitted that organ-cases of the period were frequently examples of splendid workmanship, and often of no little magnificence. In fact, in most of them it is only the ornamental detail that is at fault, the lines being good and the proportions excellent. As a result, we find that many quite modern German cases in the Renaissance style exhibit the same regrettable tendencies in the way of fantastic cornices and florid ornamentation that characterized the majority of cases constructed in the 18th Century.

The revival of Gothic architecture in France, Germany and the Netherlands, accompanied as usual by a destruction of much ancient and beautiful ecclesiastical furniture, has scarcely advanced beyond that stage, which, in England, earned Sir John Sutton's severe condemnation. Few of the modern cases " in the Gothic style " to be seen in these countries are better than Blore's erections at Winchester and Peterborough—the last named, fortunately, now no more.

I do not hesitate to say that in organ-cases produced within the last fifty or sixty years, both Gothic and Renaissance, England stands unrivalled.

In conclusion, I venture to suggest that one or two ancient devices, which seem to have been almost wholly neglected by architects of our modern organ-fronts, might be more frequently used with the happiest results. For instance, if, instead of trimming the pipes with a view to symmetry, or of covering their upper extremities with pipe-shades, the shades are kept clear above the pipes, and the latter are allowed to display the whole of their natural speaking lengths, a certain quaint beauty, otherwise unobtainable, is achieved.

The shades themselves can be either quite symmetrical, or the lowest edges can be so treated that they follow, more or less exactly, the rake of the pipes, hovering, so to speak, above the top of each individual pipe. Excellent examples of organs with pipes and pipe-shades so treated, are those at Barcelona Cathedral (1546), Tarragona Cathedral (1563) and St. Filiu, Gerona (c. 1575). At San Petronio, Bologna (1470), some of the shades are symmetrical, while others are cut so as to follow the pipe levels more exactly. I cannot recall any English case where this treatment is to be observed, for at Weybridge both pipes and shades are symmetrical.

Then, for church organs, especially those placed in a loft

over the chancel aisle, or at the West end, I would advocate the revival of folding-doors or shutters. Such an organ as that at St. Michael and All Angels, Croydon [60], would gain much by such appendages, especially if enriched with appropriate paintings, while the shutters would be of no little utility at church cleaning times. In addition to those at Theddingworth [48] and Jesus College, Cambridge [52 and 53], already described, two other organ-cases which are so provided deserve a word of praise, one at St. Andrew the Less, Barnwell, Cambridge, and the other at St. Hugh's Chapel, Bishop's Hostel, Lincoln. The first of these seems to have been designed by Sir John Sutton. The other is a very beautiful example by Mr. Temple Moore, than whom no one seems happier or more successful in the treatment of Gothic organ-cases, judging from his designs for the organ-fronts at All Saints', Tooting Graveney, and at Skirbeck Church, near Boston.

The separate choir-organ case seems also to have gone out of fashion of late years, though a few organs recently built have part of their cases advanced somewhat after the manner of a choir-case—one instance being that at Clapham Parish Church.[78]. Yet a hanging choir-organ case can be made one of the most charming features in a design, and many organ fronts would be greatly improved by such an addition.

I am quite sure that our architects would have something fresh and beautiful to show us if they included these special features just named amongst the other forms and devices which we now know they can use with such skill and originality.

English Organ Cases.

Index to Illustrations. · · ·--   ·

All reproduced from Copyright Photographs by Andrew Freeman.

ORGAN IN ALL SAINTS' CHURCH, THEDDINGWORTH,
LEICESTERSHIRE.

ORGAN IN ST. JOHN'S CHURCH, STOCKCROSS,
Near NEWBURY.

ORGAN IN ST. JAMES' CHURCH WEYBRIDGE.

ORGAN IN ST. LAWRENCE'S CHURCH, ECCHINSWELL,
Near NEWBURY.

CHANCEL ORGAN, JESUS COLLEGE CHAPEL, CAMBRIDGE.

WEST END ORGAN, JESUS COLLEGE CHAPEL,
CAMBRIDGE.

ORGAN IN THE CHURCH OF ST. JOHN THE
EVANGELIST, COWLEY ROAD, OXFORD
(THE CHURCH OF THE COWLEY FATHERS).

ORGAN IN ALL SAINTS' PARISH CHURCH,
ST. IVES (Hunts).

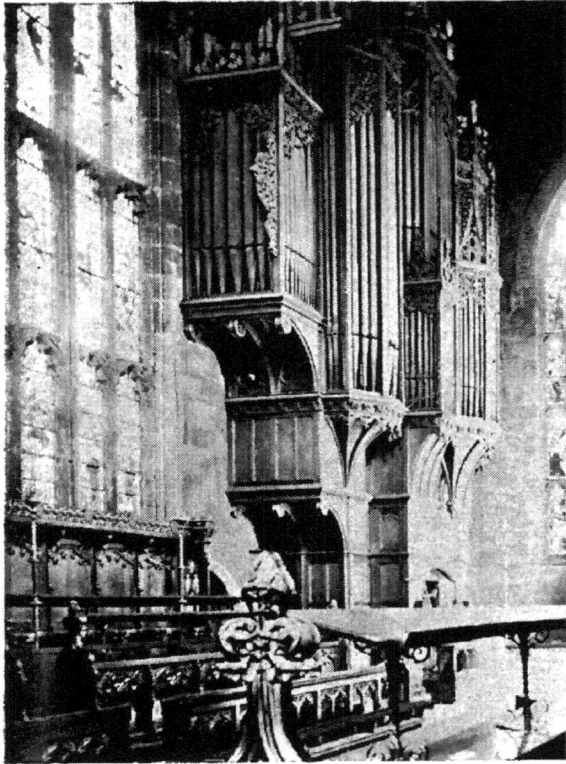

ORGAN IN ST. MARY'S PARISH CHURCH, NOTTINGHAM.

ORGAN IN ST. ALBAN'S CATHEDRAL.

ORGAN IN KING'S COLLEGE CHAPEL, CAMBRIDGE
(EAST FRONT).

ORGAN IN KING'S COLLEGE CHAPEL, CAMBRIDGE
(WEST FRONT),

ORGAN IN ST. MICHAEL AND ALL ANGELS
CHURCH, CROYDON.

ORGAN IN ST. STEPHEN'S CHURCH, OLD RADNOR.
FROM THE REV. F. H. SUTTON'S MONOGRAPH ON]THE
OLD RADNOR ORGAN (1866).

ORGAN IN ST. NICHOLAS' CHURCH.
STANFORD ON-AVON, NORTHANTS.

ORGAN IN ST. MARK'S CHURCH, OLD BILTON,
Near RUGBY.

DESIGN OF CASE FOR OLD ORGAN (1662) IN
CANTERBURY CATHEDRAL.
FROM A CONTEMPORARY SEPIA DRAWING.

THE ORGAN, ST. ANDREW UNDERSHAFT, LONDON.
FROM GOODWIN'S "LONDON CHURCHES" (1838).

THE ORGAN, ALL HALLOW'S, BARKING.

THE ORGAN, ST. PETER AD VINCULA, TOWER OF LONDON.

THE OLD ORGAN (1754) SALISBURY CATHEDRAL.
FROM THE REV. PETER HALL'S " PICTURESQUE
MEMORIALS OF SALISBURY." 1834.

ORGAN IN ST. KATHERINE'S CHURCH,
LITTLE BARDFIELD, ESSEX.

ORGAN IN ST. MARY'S CHURCH, FINEDON,
NORTHANTS.

ORGAN IN ST. ANDREW'S PARISH CHURCH, ENFIELD.

ORGAN IN ST. BOTOLPH CHURCH,
ALDERSGATE STREET, LONDON.

ORGAN IN THE UNIVERSITY CHURCH OF ST. MARY
THE VIRGIN, OXFORD (WEST FRONT).

ORGAN IN BRASENOSE COLLEGE CHAPEL, OXFORD.

ORGAN IN SHELDONIAN THEATRE, OXFORD.

ORGAN IN THE GUILDHALL, CAMBRIDGE.

ORGAN IN READING TOWN HALL.

CHANCEL ORGAN IN HOLY TRINITY PARISH
CHURCH, CLAPHAM.

[COPYRIGHT.]

THE RELATION OF ORGANIST AND CLERGY.

A Commentary, on the Model Agreement for the . Clergy and Organists of the Church of England.

As prepared by
Herbert Westerby, Mus. Bac. Lond., F.R.C.O., L.Mus.T.C.L.

THE position of Organist and Choirmaster in connection with the Parish Churches of England and Wales as it exists to-day in the eyes of the Law is one of distinct peculiarity ; as one that is unrecognized in Ecclesiastical Law, and yet that is in the present universality of highly ornate musical services, responsible for a considerable and highly important portion of these services, it is exceedingly necessary that the conditions governing the successful maintenance of such a delicately balanced situation should be stated in full detail.

The peculiarity of the position lies in the fact that it is not so much in what is made legally binding on both Church Authorities and Organist (though that necessarily has its place), but in the knowledge of, on both sides, the various customs and usages which obtain with regard to the same. These latter, along with various suggestions towards realizing that perfect harmony and co-operation which should exist between the Clergy and the profession are stated in detail in the following *Disquisition*.

It will be seen, therefore, that this " Commentary " is really of more importance than the Agreement itself.* It is hoped that the following Commentary will be found to anticipate, as far as possible, any sources of misunderstanding appertaining to the relationship of Incumbent with Organist and Choirmaster :—

> " Successful co-operation can only come from mutual confidence and loyalty in promoting the same aims. At the same time, it is quite right that there should be a *clear agreement* as to the time and services for which the Organist is to be responsible."
>
> REV. T. E. LINDSAY,
> *Rural Dean* of Scarborough
> (now Archdeacon).

* It is suggested that the Agreement should be (1) used only as a *guide* to find out what may be expected ; (2) to be produced when an agreement form is necessary.

" Nearly all the misunderstandings between Parson
and Organist are owing to want of *definiteness* as to what
is and what is not expected of the Organist."

REV. T. P. BROCKLEHURST,
Formerly Vicar of Brocklehurst.

To the Organist.

(1). The position of Organist and Choirmaster in the Parish
Churches of England is *not* known to Ecclesiastical Law, and therefore the professional Organist, in common with other professional
classes who give their services in part only to various persons or
institutions, is subject to, and governed by, the ordinary laws of
the realm, *i.e.*, the *Common Law*. Briefly put, it follows that
whatever is agreed upon between the contracting parties should
be put into the usual form of a Contract, and duly signed and
witnessed, if possible, under the supervision of the legal agents of
both parties.

(2). The *specification of duties* in such Contract should be
precise and clear in every detail, and, as a matter of business,
avoiding generalities of any kind which would place the office-
holder in a similar position to one who gives up his whole time
to the Church. The list of services, choral and non-choral, ordinary
and special, therefore, at which the Organist or his deputy is expected to be present, and the duties he is supposed to undertake
in connection with the Choir, should be fully and completely
detailed. To this end such clauses should be deleted or added
as is thought necessary to govern the circumstances of the case,
and the form of Agreement as amended should be submitted to
the legal agents of both parties for their approval. Care should
be taken that all that is verbally agreed upon should be added to
the Contract, as " it is a well-known rule of Common Law that
oral evidence shall not be given to add to, subtract from, or alter
or vary the terms of a written Agreement." [1] A very *simple form
of Contract* consists of a written *List of Duties, Privileges* and
Liabilities signed by both parties. This form may suffice in many
cases. [2]

(3). As the time given by the Professional Parish Organist
and Choirmaster to his duties as such (as contrasted with the
Cathedral Organist) is but small in comparison with that given
to his ordinary professional avocations, it is only right and a
matter of business that he should be protected from " undue
demands on his time." [3] And as the remuneration usually bestowed
in his case does not follow on the higher scale, it is advisable that
he should be allowed *Deputies* (duly approved) " for the comparatively unimportant portions of his duty." [3]

[1] " The Law of Organs and Organists," by *W. C. A. Blew*, of the Inner
Temple, Esq., Barrister-at-Law.
[2] See " The Organist's Simple Contract Form," page 98.
[3] *Dr Chas. W Pearce*, Mus. Doc. Cantab , F.R.C O., Member of the Council
of the R C.O.

(4). An Organist " cannot be compelled to perform any duties foreign to " (*a*) such as are duly specified in the Contract. If the necessity arises for new or *additional work* or assistance in the musical services of the Church (such as additional daily or evening services), or preparation for the same, the new demands on his professional labour and time should, as a matter of business, be made the subject of an amicable business arrangement.

(5). An Incumbent cannot rightly and legally interfere with an Organist's obtaining or performing *other professional duties* in whatsoever sphere (church or secular) so long as these duties do not interfere with the particular Contract spoken of, nor are derogatory in any way to the nature of the same.

(6). The Churchwardens *or members of the Vestry* who are primarily responsible, are usually associated with the Incumbent in the written guarantee of *payment of the stipend* accruing to the office of Organist and Choirmaster.

> " Like many other old churches, my church is governed by the Vestry, and the Clergy have no control over the musical engagements."
>
> *(The late)* DR. E. H. TURPIN,
> Hon. Sec., Royal College of Organists.

The Incumbent is not responsible for the Organist's stipend unless he sign an agreement to that effect, either by himself or in conjunction with the Churchwardens, or unless he has given a written guarantee " to some third party that he would pay the stipend if the amount could not be collected in any other way."(*b*)

> " The Churchwardens, who are the purse-bearers of the congregation, should have a voice in the appointment."
>
> REV. T. P. BROCKLEHURST.

(7). *The Incumbent* can elect an Organist, but " cannot compel the Parish to pay his appointee."(*c*)

The Churchwardens (members of " Vestry " or of " Select Vestry ") can elect an Organist " if authorized by the Parish and allowed by the Incumbent."(*d*) Their choice, however, should be duly approved by the Incumbent as the person legally responsible for the whole of the services of the Church.

The Churchwardens " if authorized by the Parish " may undertake to pay the Organist's stipend.(*e*)

" *If the Parish* find the Organist's stipend and are allowed to elect him, it is doubtful whether the minister can dismiss him."(*f*)

The Incumbent may, subject to the terms of the express or implied Contract, " dispense with the *services* of the duly appointed Organist," but if " appointed and paid by some third party he may not have the power " to deprive him of his stipend.(*g*)

a *(Blew.)*
b *(Blew).* All References a to l.

(7a). The arrangement made with the Churchwardens binds them only for the year of their office.

" If the Churchwardens make an arrangement with an Organist for a period exceeding the duration of their office, they may render themselves personally liable on the Contract."(*h*)

> " I have always claimed and used the power, as Incumbent, of appointing and dismissing an Organist, but have, as a matter of courtesy, acted with the knowledge and consent of the Wardens. These are a ' Corporation ' with charge of the offertories, and are morally if not legally bound to continue the engagement of their predecessors, should any change in their number occur.'
>
> THE VEN. ARCHDEACON LINDSAY.

Whatever arrangement is come to it should be clearly stated in the agreement *who is responsible for* the payment of the *stipend* attached to the office in question. It is also advisable when the Churchwardens, members of the Vestry, or third parties assume responsibility for the stipend, that such responsibility is transferred on their resignation to their successors, space being left for the purpose in the Agreement, the alterations to be initialled by both parties. The form of Contract should be signed by both parties and duly witnessed, preferably through the legal agents of both, and a copy provided for the Incumbent and the Organist.

(8). The length of notice required for termination of the Contract should be duly stated.*

(8a). *Termination on the part of the INCUMBENT without notice* is possible on the ground of wilful breach of the terms, unlawful absence from or neglect of duties, moral, pecuniary, or other misconduct reflecting on or derogatory to the nature of his office. The accused can, however, always enter a petition-at-law for damages for wrongful dismissal or for any action calculated to injure him in his profession.

(8b). On the other hand, *termination on the part of the ORGANIST without notice* is possible on the ground of wilful breach of the terms of the Contract, such as failure to pay stipend when due on the part of those responsible, any attempt, without due notice, to relieve him of any portion of the responsibilities delegated to him by the Contract, etc.†

(9). An Organist is entitled to a true and correct appreciation of the professional duties performed by him in connection with any church.

* On the determination of the agreement the Organist will " deliver up to the Vicar and Churchwardens all books and music and other documents, instruments, things or property belonging to the Vicar and Churchwardens then in his custody or power." (From an agreement.)

† A Parish Organist's stipend is due at the close of the Sunday Service.

(10). An organ *legally*[A] placed in a parish church becomes, *in the absence of a proviso* to the contrary,[B] the property of the parish. As the property of the parish, the organ comes under the care of the Churchwardens except during the time of divine service when it comes under the legal control of the Incumbent.

" The Churchwardens' care of, and the Minister's control over, the organ, when there is no service in the church, may very briefly be described as negative. Neither of the parties can authorize its use, yet neither can nullify the sanction of the other."

(10a). It will be necessary, therefore, that for the usual privilege of the Organist's own practice, for lessons to pupils, and pupils' practice, the written consent of both Churchwardens and Incumbent be obtained. Any limitation, also, of practice restriction as to hours, as well as the provision of the means for practice, should be duly stated in the Agreement.

(10b). It is customary and reasonable to leave the *sole charge of* so complex an instrument as *the organ* entirely in the Organist's hands, making him responsible for its safe keeping, and as the only means of attaining its efficient control, allowing him opportunities for daily practice.

(10c). As a matter of courtesy, the Incumbent and Churchwardens will respect this charge by not giving access to the organ to others, and the Organist will observe similar restrictions (pupils and deputies always excepted) where due permission for the same has not already been obtained.*

(10d). The Organist is *not responsible* in any way for the upkeep, *repair*, or tuning *of the organ*—this falling to the Builders or Tuners, according to the usual Contract ; and though he may volunteer to put any minor disorder right that may make no particular demand on his professional time, it is no part of his duties, and he cannot be compelled to execute the same. Nevertheless, it would be his duty to notify the Incumbent of any failing in the instrument.

(11). As Choirmaster the Organist is not only responsible for the training of the voices, but is at least responsible for order or the *discipline of the choir* generally at practices.

A ' No organ can be legally set up in, or removed from, a consecrated church without a faculty from the Ordinary " (" the Bishop of the Diocese and his Chancellor "). (*Blew.*)

B ' In which case the property in the organ may remain in, or revert to, the person placing it in the church." (*Blew.*)

* " I quite endorse what you say in reference to repairs and use of organ." (*Rev. T. E. Lindsay*).

> " It is *infra dig* on the part of the choirmaster to expect the clergy to keep order at the practices—the clergy destroy the morale of the choir if they interfere with discipline."
>
> REV. E. P. BROCKLEHURST.[†]

(11a). Mention might be made of the conditions regarding the Choirmaster's *power to elect* or dispense with members of the *Choir*, together with any assistance in the organization of the Choir that he may look for from the Incumbent or his deputies :—

> " As in the choice of an Organist, so in that of Choristers, the ultimate object is not music but worship ; therefore the incumbent must, if he be true to his responsibilities, choose men of good life and character, and dispense with them if they fail to justify their position in the church. Their fitness as musicians would, of course, be decided by the Organist and Choirmaster."
>
> REV. T. E LINDSAY,
> Rural Dean of Scarborough.

Before proposed members are admitted to any form of choir work it is advisable that the name should be submitted to the clergy for enquiry.

With regard to the *dismissal of choir* members :—

> " The Incumbent ought to get rid of them on the representation of the Organist."
>
> SIR FREDERICK BRIDGE,
> (Westminster Abbey).

> " As the Choristers are formally admitted to office by the Incumbent, so their dismissal should come from him, even though it be the act of the Organist."
>
> REV. T. E. LINDSAY,
> Rural Dean of Scarborough.

The difficulty of Dual Control (moral and musical) of the Choir is simplified if the Vicar and Organist observe their respective practical spheres of interest. And, as the position of Choir Members is primarily a musical one, it follows that in the :—

1. *Admission* of Choristers.—Ascertainment of musical fitness by the Organist should come first
2a. *Dismission* —Moral grounds on the part of the Vicar, or
2b. Musical or disciplinary reasons on the part of the Organist should suffice.

In 1 *permission* is necessary, in 2b *confirmation* on the part of the Vicar

(12). Details as to the fixing or alteration of choir-practice night should be arranged with the Incumbent.

(12a). Mention might be made of the *facilities*—room and instrument—usually provided *for* choir *practice*.

[†] An Organist may amicably consent to occasionally help the Incumbent, his deputy, the curate or choir chaplain, to a more correct and artistic rendering of his part—(usually arranged as a matter for private tuition).

(13). The medium and responsibility for *payment of the choir* members and choristers should be fixed.

(13a). The Organist should also consult with the Vicar and Churchwardens before incurring any outlay, such as for new music on behalf of the Choir.*

(14). It is necessary that the Organist should appoint his own minor officials (secretary and others) to fulfil minor duties in connection with the Choir for which he may be responsible—notification of choir practices and of absentees, provision of choir lists, lists of services, occasional MS. copies of music (secretary), supervision and care of music (librarians), cassocks, surplices, etc (monitors).

(15). Particulars as to recitals, occasional musical festival or oratorio performances, with the portion to be received from the offertories of same, etc.

(15a). Fees at Weddings, Funerals, and Baptisms, etc., should be mentioned likewise. With regard to fees for Weddings, the procedure obtains in some places of referring such applications to the Clerk to the Vestry. In such case there is generally " an inclusive fee, covering the use of the organ, the blowing, the services of the Organist, and, for a further fee, the attendance of the Choir boys," such fee being paid to the Clerk.

(15b) Provision should also be made for the offerings on Organist's Sunday where the custom obtains.

(16). The *provision of Deputies* for holidays, absence or illness should also be made and responsibility of payment of same should be stated.

(17). It is desirable that the Choirmaster and Organist should as far as possible have the *choice of the music*—" A most important question to the highly-trained and capable organist " (Pearce). The latter would, of course, bear in mind the character of the services agreed upon, its suitability to the occasion or for the particular season of the Church's year. The clergyman frequently reserves the choice of the hymns, and sometimes suggests some particular anthem. Much, however, depends on the Choir Practice, the attendance at the Services, the " form " in which the Choirmaster finds his Choristers (especially with a Voluntary Choir), that it is advisable to give him as free a hand as possible. General conditions can be best arranged as in 18 (Sir Frederick Bridge).

* When the Organist's privilege of discount rates is borrowed it is only businesslike that he should be promptly reimbursed for the amount, plus inclusive postages.

By The Bishop of Richmond—
> "With the Organist and Choir-trainer rests the choice of music. If the composer gives his best the Organist must choose the best. The Organist's first duty is to separate the wheat from the chaff, to discern the true ring of spiritual worship in anthem, service, chant, and hymn tune.
> "He should consider 'how much shall be sung,' and 'the voices at his disposal.'"

(18). The Organist will find it useful to have an occasional conference with the Incumbent in order to talk over arrangements for the musical services and "on any matter affecting the general welfare of the choir."

Legally speaking, the Incumbent has entire control over, and is responsible for, the services of the church in every detail, whether musical or otherwise.

> "The choice of music to be sung belongs to the Vicar as much as the prayers and the sermon. He may delegate it to his Organist, but has no right to make an Agreement to tie his hands from discharging his duty."
> REV. T E LINDSAY.

It is, perhaps, an anomaly that one who is neither a professional nor an expert in the realm of music "should have the power to control and nullify the judgment and experience of one" who is both. The "result is to be attributed to modern requirements rather than to a defect in the law," "the organist has his *moral* right, and the principle upon which incumbent and organist must proceed must be essentially one of *co-operation*.[A] In their relations with each other, incumbent and organist should carefully discriminate between suggestions on the one hand, and commands or interference on the other."[k] " The additional importance now claimed, and rightly so, for the office of organist and the technical knowledge and skill an average organist now possesses" should "make an incumbent cautious how he interferes with him."[1]

Sir Hubert Parry (the then President of the Royal College of Organists) in a public address has said in effect, that having appointed the best man possible (under the circumstances) the incumbent should give him a *free hand ;* or, in the words of a model agreement drawn up by a Yorkshire clergyman, [B] "the organist and choirmaster should have a free hand within the reasonable limits mentioned in this (agreement), so that he may feel every interest in increasing and developing the musical character of the services." This being so, the following quotation seems also reasonable :—

(19). "The Organist and Director of the Choir will regard

A " Blew "—(Barrister-at-Law), 1878.
B Rev. T. P. Brocklehurst.

himself as being one of the ministers of the church, and will be so regarded by his *colleagues*, the Vicar and other ministers of the church."

Etiquette, therefore, on the part of the *Clergyman*, would forbid (after the general style of the musical service has been decided upon) interference as to his colleague's accompaniments to the service or as to the pieces played on the organ (except a request be preferred for certain music on special occasions) or in the detailed choice of music made by the Choirmaster, who naturally is the best judge of what is musically appropriate and what is suited to the capabilities of his choir.

(19a). What has been said already as to the impolicy, not to speak of etiquette, of interference on the part of the incumbent naturally applies more strongly to the same on the part of his deputies, the curate, choir chaplain, or precentor.[*]

(19b). "It is no part of the *Churchwardens'* duty to interfere with the way the service is performed—they cannot order the Organist to play, nor can they forbid him to do so." The office of Churchwarden is one of "observation and complaint, but not control with regard to divine worship" (*Lord Stowell*). Such "complaint" would be referred to the Ordinary ("The Bishop of the Diocese and his Chancellor").

In the further interests of friendly co-operation of both incumbent and organist it will be seen that the following warning uttered by *Dr. Pearce*, of the Council of the Royal College of Organists, should be mutual, applying equally to both parties. "The wise organist will suffer no man, *nor woman*, to occupy an intermediate and interfering position between himself and his clergyman or minister."

To further emphasize the need of co-operation we quote from an address given by *Dr. Madely Richardson* at the annual conference of the Incorporated Society of Professional Musicians held in Dublin in January, 1903.

The Clergy and Organist and Choirmaster "should act side by side, shoulder to shoulder, representing respectively the theological and musical side of Church life."

"The musical welfare of the Choir should be very near the heart of the clergy, but the initiative in matters concerning it should come from the Organist."

(20). *FINALLY*, to quote again from the Agreement mentioned in Article 18, " the incumbent and churchwardens should

---

[*] The Precentor is "unknown to ecclesiastical law," and neither choir, Chaplain, Precentor, Curate, or other presiding cleric can, " unless requested by the Vicar, have the right to say anything about the service." (*Blew*.)

(in consideration that the time an Organist and Choirmaster gives to the Church is not remunerated at the usual rate of professional work) in every legitimate way do their best to further the professional welfare of the organist and choirmaster " (Brocklehurst), on the ground that he " makes it a point of honour to do his utmost for the church with that limited portion of time which he has at his disposal " (*Pearce*).

> " It is the bounden duty of the Vicar to help his
> Organist to get teaching, and thus supplement the paltry
> stipend which he probably receives."
> REV. H. T. SPINNEY.

If the Organist consents, in addition, to occasionally assist the choir when they offer (by means of concerts, etc.) to relieve the Churchwardens of a portion of their financial responsibility in the provision of new music, etc., he will have a further claim on their gratitude.

ADDENDUM.

(21). " A great deal can be said in favour of a better secured fixity of tenure for the members of our profession."—(*Dr. Pearce*). " What is more desirable is that the organist should become a recognized church officer, holding his position on conditions similar to those of a curate, with, perhaps, reference to the Bishop in cases of real hardship."—(*Musical News*). A Bishop's license has been frequently advocated as a remedy for the state of affairs, but as the relationship of organist and choirmaster in parish churches is purely a business one, it is perhaps best for him on the whole to remain entirely free of ecclesiastical law. Moreover, it is understood that Bishops and Convocation have no legal power in the matter. Nevertheless, it is hoped that a petition to Convocation may result in a moral recommendation :—*

(1). That the Incumbent, when making a change of parish or receiving a new appointment, would earnestly consider the advisability of continuing the existing agreement with the organist and choirmaster of the new church ;

(2). That consideration be given to the advisability of recognizing, in common with decayed clergy, the moral claim of organists who have grown old in the service of the church to pecuniary assistance in their old age.

---

* "A memorial to Convocation would, of course, point out that an Organist is utterly unprotected in Church Law. Under the Canons of the Scottish Episcopal Church an appeal to the Bishop is allowed in the case of a dispute as to the use of the organ at services, practices, ' or other times.' " (*Clement A. Harris.*)

N.B.—Special care should be taken in the case of appointments in the Colonies, or United States, enquiries being directed to the London offices of the Agents-General for the respective Colonies, or to the United States, for information as to the validity of documents signed in this country, and other matters concerning the appointment.

CLERGYMEN also are warned against the policy of negotiating with holders of American degrees, or of bogus diplomas issued in this country.

ENQUIRIES may be directed to the Secretary of the Union of the University Graduates in Music (University of London, South Kensington), or to the Secretary of the Royal College of Organists, Kensington Gore, S.W.)

PARTICULARS of the career of University Graduates in music may, as a rule, be obtained in the Calendar issued by that Society.

NOTES OF INTEREST FROM VARIOUS SOURCES.

The Organist in Relation to CONGREGATION, CHOIR, *and* CLERGY.

" The Organist also needs to be a tactful individual ; he has to please congregation, choir, and clergy. From the purely musical point of view each of them may make demands which grate upon the feelings of the trained musician, but the latter is by no means free to indulge his own tastes without restriction. To him, *congregational singing* may be an abomination, yet it is his duty to encourage it, because his work involves higher considerations than mere musical perfection.

" So also with his *choir*. Careful on the one hand to preserve the rights of the people he will also be zealous in the championship of his singers. With a voluntary choir he will not be rash enough to expect the finished renderings possible to professional singers ; he will, with certain reservations, consult their tastes and desires, recognizing that his forces, if not paid in money, may not unreasonably look for the recompense of their services in music and in the enhancement of the reputation of the choir for character and performance.

" His relations with the *clergy* also depend for their amicableness upon this invaluable quality of tact, which, it may be said, should be thoroughly mutual. Here again it is satisfactory to note a growing improvement. The clergy as a rule are not and cannot be as technically conversant with music as organists, but by virtue of their position they govern the situation, and it is fatuous to ignore this cardinal fact. An organist who desires to occupy a post in peace and quietness, and at the same time to preserve his ideals of church music, must be prepared to give and take, and to regard his parson as a superior colleague in church work."—*Musical News*, June 16th, 1906.

———

" Very often *the clergyman* overlooks the fact that in his organist he has a special officer, whose department of work is special in character, demanding many of the same qualities of tact and patience that are necessary in his own incumbency, besides particular acquirements which, like preparation for the clerical calling, have involved much study and expense."—Leader, *Musical News*, March 31st, 1906.

———

" *Some remarks* made recently by an Anglican minister in acknowledging the great and often unrecognized services which are rendered to the church by its organists,—now a very large body of men and women :—
" ' The organist needs all the help that we can give him. Remember that, of the income that he must make to live in decent comfort (especially if he is a family man), his stipend as organist forms only a very small part. We expect a good deal from him, and we do not as a rule (in fact, we cannot) pay him on a scale which errs on the side of undue liberality. He has many difficulties and many critics. Much of his best work is done quietly and unostentatiously, and is not noticed. His mistakes are spotted at once, and are criticised with a keenness which is not inspired by good nature or by musical knowledge. A congregation wakes up to the fact that the church choir has improved enormously during the last two or three years. It does not strike them that the improvement is due mainly to the patient, unwearying grind and practice, week by week and month by month, of the organist with his choir.' "—*Musical Opinion.*

———

From the Report of the Committee appointed in October, 1903, by the Worcester Diocesan Conference " to investigate the principles which should govern the use of music in churches."
" That systematic facilities for leave of absence (apart from usual vacations) from work on Sundays at least once in every three months should be afforded to all organists and choirmasters with a view of
Providing them with regular relief from very arduous duties.
Enabling them to worship at times amongst the people.
Enabling them to hear other services than their own.
Preventing them from getting into a groove in their organ
    playing and methods generally."

ORGANISTS AND CLERGY.

From a Paper read at the I.S.M., May 11th, 1901, by Percy Ramsey :—

" III.   In the third place, we want to cultivate more those two important qualifications of a successful organist and choirmaster,—sympathy and tact.   One great cause of unpleasantness with the clergy can be traced directly to the want *of sympathy* on an organist's part *with his vicar's religious opinions.*   An organist of pronounced Protestant or Low Church views is bound to feel out of place at a church where there is a high mass or missa cantata every Sunday.   Similarly, a Catholic or High Church organist would scarcely feel at home appointed to a church where a preacher in a black gown continually insisted on his eternal damnation. And I think an organist of ' no church ' views has scarcely a right to be a church organist at all.   We ought to consider more, when we apply for a post, whether we should be really happy on our appointment to that post.

" Lastly, and this is by no means the least important point, have a *definite agreement* in black and white, signed by your vicar and yourself, so that you may know how far you are responsible for the behaviour of the choir boys in church, what holidays you may rightly claim, at what services besides the usual Sunday services your attendance is required, and how much of your work may be occasionally performed by deputy.   Above all, *accept no dual responsibility.*   No choir can serve two masters.   Personally, I think it highly desirable that the vicar or one of his curates should be placed in charge of the spiritual and social welfare of the choir, preparing the boys for confirmation, explaining to them all acts of reverence, etc., also arranging excursions for them in the summer and entertainments or suppers in the winter ; but in such a case there must be a distinct understanding with the choirmaster so that there can be no interference with his legitimate duties."

AUTHORITIES.

CLERGY.

	Section in Commentary.
Bishop of Richmond, Quotation	11a
Rev. T. E. Lindsay, Archdeacon of Scarborough	1, 7b, 10c, 11a, 18
Rev. T. P. Brocklehurst	1, 6, 11, 20

MUSICAL.

Sir Frederick Bridge, Mus. Doc., M.V.O. of Westminster Abbey, Ex-President of R.C.O.	11a, 17
Sir Hubert Parry, Mus. Doc., Ex-President of R.C.O.	18
Dr. Chas. W. Pearce, Mus. Doc., F.R.C.O., Member of Council of R.C.O.	3, 17, 19c, 20, 21
Dr. Madely Richardson, Mus. Doc., F.R.C.O., late of Southwark Cathedral	19c
Clement A. Harris	Addendum, 21

LEGAL.

W. C. A. Blew, Esq., Barrister-at-Law of the Inner Temple. " The Law of Organs and Organists "	... 2, also references a to 1
Lord Stowell	19b

[COPYRIGHT.]

Model Agreement for the Clergy and Organists of the Anglican Church.

Prepared by
Herbert Westerby, Mus. Bac., Lond., F.R.C.O., L.Mus.T.C.L.

N.B.—It is suggested that the following Agreement Form may, in the first place, be treated by the Organist as a Guide to what may be expected of him.

[For detailed Guide to the above, with opinions of both Clergy and Organists, see " The Relation of Organist and Clergy, a Commentary on the Model Agreement."

[The Form may be amended to suit varying circumstances.]

MEMORANDUM OF AGREEMENT made the ....
day of ...., 190..., *BETWEEN* ....
................, of, &c. (hereinafter called " the Vicar "), of the first part, ..., of, &c., and ....,
of, &c. (hereinafter called " the Churchwardens ") [1] of the second part, and ...., of, &c., of the third part, as follows :—

(1)   The said Vicar and Churchwardens on the one hand and the said .... on the other hand DO HEREBY bind themselves to observe the following contract as set forth in the following *terms and conditions.*

(2)   The said Vicar and Churchwardens DO HEREBY agree to pay to the said .... as *stipend* the sum of £...... (........................ pounds) per annum, payable by equal .... payments on the........ ...., the first of such payments to be made on the .... day of .... next, and in consideration of such payments as aforesaid the said .... HEREBY undertakes to perform such professional duties as Organist and Choirmaster at the .... Church of .... aforesaid as are hereinafter mentioned.

[1] Substitute " Members of the Vestry " or " Members of the Select Vestry " where necessary.

(3) The *principal duties* of the said ....
shall be to officiate at the following musical services
held on Sundays, namely Morning and Evening Service,[1a] (" Commentary," Sec. 2) ....
likewise at the[2] ....

(4) THE said .... shall officiate also at
the following [3]..

(5) THE said .... shall preside at the
following Special Services, of which reasonable notice
will be given [4] ....

(6) THE said .... shall receive the following *additional fees* for Weddings—choral....................
guineas, non-choral .... guineas, in both cases
payable by ....
  Baptisms .... guineas
  Funerals .... guineas
also offerings on Organist's Sunday.

  In case the party wishes to have the services of another
  Organist at Weddings, Baptisms, or Funerals, the usual
  fee shall be paid to the said ....
  (" Commentary," Sec. 15a).

(7) THE Vicar and Churchwardens agree to accept *approved
deputies* for the following services [5]...........................
and also in the event of the absence of the said ....
.... from duty owing to sickness or any
other reasonable cause (" Commentary," Sec. 3).

(8) THE Vicar and Churchwardens will also allow the said
.... weeks' *vacation* in
the month of .... in every year, and also
the following *relaxation from duty* ....
after the greater Festivals of [6]...............................

[1a] Sunday *afternoon* service held every .... Sunday of, etc., and at
the following seasons of the year :—Easter, Whitsuntide, Christmas Day.

[2] Sunday afternoon services held in connection with the following Festivals
(Harvest, Children's Dedication, etc.), as well as on the following special
occasions on Sunday (Early Choral Celebrations, etc.).

[3] Week-day services, namely, the evening week-night service held on
........, the special services held on Christmas Day, Christmas Eve, Ascension Day, All Saints' Day, Ash Wednesday, Holy Innocents' Day, services
in Holy Week (Good Friday, morning and afternoon, three hours' service,
Maundy Thursday, Easter Eve).

[4] Funeral services (choral) (non-choral), services held on occasions of
national rejoicing or mourning, Midnight Service on New Year's Eve, Confirmation Service, etc.

[5] Week-night, Ascension Day, etc.
[6] Easter, Whitsuntide, Christmas.

.... the deputies in each case to
be duly approved   The said........................... shall
provide all deputies at .... expense, and
on the other hand shall receive all *fees earned* by such
deputies both at ordinary and extraordinary services,
including Weddings, Baptisms, &c.) ("Commentary,"
Sec. 16).

(9) THE principal *duties of* the said ....
as *Choirmaster* shall be to train the choir of the said
church "with all diligence and to the best of his
ability," and to that end will hold at least ....
.... practice in each week, giving such
time as he thinks necessary for the preparation of the
services ("Commentary," Sec. 2).

(10) THE said .... shall consult with the
Vicar as to the fixing, *alteration*, omission, or absence
from the principal *practice* night ("Commentary," Sec.
12).

(11) THE said .... shall after reference to
the Vicar as to general suitability have *power to elect*
after due trial of voice any new *members for the choir*
("Commentary," Sec. 11a).

(12) IN the *provision* of *new members* (junior and senior) he
will have the assistance of the Vicar or his deputy, and
will also have powers of *dismissal of members*, but will
previously refer in both cases to the Vicar for permission
or confirmation respectively ("Commentary," Sec. 11a).

(13) THE Choirmaster *as deputed by the Vicar* shall be responsible for order and *discipline* at the *choir-practices*
("Commentary," Sec. 11).

(14) THE Choirmaster shall if he think fit appoint his own
Secretary, Librarian, and other *minor officials* (see
"Commentary," Sec. 14), and be responsible for (if
requested) the distribution of the various money pay-
ments to the choir ·provided by the Churchwardens
("Commentary," Sec. 13).

(15) IN the event of the said .... being
called upon to perform new and *additional musical
labours* in connection with the said Church, he shall
receive an additional fee or stipend (according to
arrangement) in consideration of such labours being
carried out by him or his deputy ("Commentary,"
Sec. 4.)

(16) THE said .... will consult with the Churchwardens before incurring any expense or making any *outlay*, such as for *new music*, choir lists, etc., on behalf of the choir ("Commentary," Sec. 13a).

(17) THE said .... after due conference with the Vicar shall have the *choice of* the *music* with the exception of the hymns, bearing in mind the character of the services agreed upon and its suitability for the particular season of the Church's year or the nature of the occasion ("Commentary," Sec. 17).

(18) THE said .... generally speaking "will have a *free hand* within the reasonable limits mentioned in this agreement " ("Commentary," Sec. 18).

(19) THE Vicar and Churchwardens in whose hands lies the custody of the *organ* will allow the said .... to have *sole charge* of the same in the said Church, and the said .... will be made responsible for its safe keeping " (Commentary," Sec. 10b), and, in order that he may have the means of attaining and maintaining efficient control of the same he shall be allowed the privilege of daily practice ("Commentary," Sec. 10a) [7] ....

(19a) The Vicar and Churchwardens will also provide the usual instrument and Room for Practice with the Choir ("Commentary," Sec. 12).

(20) THE said .... shall not be held responsible in any way for the upkeep, *repair*, or tuning *of the organ* in the said Church (this falling to the Builders or Tuners according to the usual contract), but he shall report any failing in the instrument to the Vicar or Churchwardens in order that the matter may be put right ("Commentary," Sec. 10d).

The Vicar and Churchwardens will allow the said .... to give *lessons to pupils* on the organ in the said Church without charge (except for the cost of .... power utilized at the rate of .... per hour ("Commentary," Sec. 10a).

(21) THE Vicar and Churchwardens will also allow the said .... to give .... (limit, if any) *Organ or Oratorio Recitals* (after due consultation with the Vicar as to proposed date and other

[7] Here insert limitations (if any), or any limit in the use of gas or motor power, and charge for same beyond the limit, also any restrictions as to the hours of practice.*

preliminaries) in the aforesaid Church, and to receive the proceeds or .... of same [8].....................
(" Commentary," Sec. 15).

(23) THE Vicar and Churchwardens will " In every legitimate way do their best to further the professional welfare of their Organist and Choirmaster,* on the understanding that he " makes it a point of honour to do his utmost for the Church with that limited portion at his disposal."**

(24) THE Contract hereby made shall be determinable at any time on either the Vicar and Churchwardens giving to the said .... or the said .... giving to the said Vicar and Churchwardens .... months' *notice of termination* in writing of their or his intention so to determine it.

AS WITNESS the hands of the parties hereto.

SIGNED by the said ....⎫
.... and ....⎬
in the presence of   ⎭

SIGNED by the said ....⎫
.... in the presence of ⎬

SIGNED by............................⎫
in the presence of   ⎬

SIGNED by............................⎫
in the presence of   ⎭

†*WE* the undersigned ....
being the successors to ....
the Churchwardens mentioned in the within-written agreement do hereby undertake all responsibility financial and otherwise incurred by the said ....
in respect of the within-written Agreement.

Dated this .... day of ...., 191...

* From an agreement drawn up by Rev. Brocklehurst.
** Address by Dr. Pearce referred to. (" Commentary," Sec. 20.)
[8] The said .... shall also have the benefit of one Sunday's offertories in the course of the year on what is known as " Organist Sunday."
† Optional Form for Renewal by New Churchwardens. (See " Commentary," Sec. 7a.)

The Organist's Simple Contract Form (Copyright).

Prepared by Mr. Herbert Westerby, Mus. Bac. London, F.R.C.O., L. Mus. T.C.L.

Organist and Choirmastership _____ Church of

_____

Stipend _____ Per Annum, Payable in _____ Instalments.

By _____

Duties
AS
ORGANIST
	{ Sunday Services:—
	  Weekly Services:—
	  Festivals (Weekly):—
	  Special Occasions:—

DEPUTIES allowed for :—

VACATIONS :—   and

ADDITIONAL FEES	{ Weddings.
	  Funerals.
	  Baptisms.

PROCEEDS OF	{ Recitals:—
	  Oratorios:—
	  Collections :—Organist's Sunday.

AS CHOIRMASTER, DUTIES	{ (Boys) Practices Weekly Full ,, ,,

POWERS	{ Election of Choir Members by Confirmed by
	  Dismissal ,, ,, ,, ,, ,,
	  Discipline ,, ,, ,,
	  Election of Minor Offices (Choir Secretary, &c.) by

OUTLAYS	{ Payment of Members by Purchase of Music, &c., by Sum allowed

ORGAN	{ Choice of Music by
	  Charge of Organ deputed to
	  Organ Pupils (facilities)
	  Facilities for Practice, Organist Charge, if any
	                        Pupils ,, ,,

Termination of Contract   Notice by Organist
                                        Notice by

Signed _____ Organist.

_____ Vicar or Clergy.

_____ (Churchwarden.)

_____ Vestry, Session, or
                                    Deacon's Clerk.

Date _____ 19____

INDEX TO COMMENTARY AND AGREEMENT.

Advice to Young Choirmasters.

By Herbert Westerby, Mus. Bac., F.R.C.O.

(Quoted from " Musical News," December 28th, 1907, with additions by H. W.)

" The primary necessity for a young choirmaster is to be able to impress his vicar and his choir with his musical ability, with his modesty of demeanour, and with his high sense of the duties of his position."—" With regard to BOYS, a good many young choirmasters, with excellent intentions, make a great mistake in being too familiar with them." " Under favourable circumstances a good deal may be done to make their position as church servants a desirable one "—" but the choirmaster must never let them forget that he is their master." Where there are LADIES in the choir and " with MEN who give their services voluntarily, it is necessary to pursue a course of conciliation," tempered, of course, with firmness. " Grown men will not submit to open correction, as if they were boys, and if the choirmaster desires to retain their goodwill, he will not single out individuals, whatever their mistakes." Separate part practice, or as a last resort, " a gentle hint in private " that the weak member " should look at his part at home," will probably suffice. Impress the choirmen " with your sincerity and singleness of purpose," give them " some music which will interest them without being beyond their capability " and " let them feel that you and they are fellow labourers in a high and holy calling," and you " will have little or no trouble with choir-men." This will naturally apply also to the whole of the choir.

As to relations with the CLERGY, it should be recognised that in the Church of England final authority rests with the vicar, and the wise man will consult his wishes " as to what degree the service is to be a musical one."

In Nonconformist and other churches, the circumstances are not the same, the " vestry," " session " or " deacons' court " having some say in the matter ; but, if the Organist and Clergy are united in purpose, the former can count on things going smoothly. The young Organist and Choirmaster should also " make friends of the members of the congregation as far as he can,"—" that through their personal esteem they may come to hold his office in higher regard " and lead them " to a better appreciation of the music of the church." He will be wise also to " display interest," " in the undertakings of the church " and thereby " earn the affection of his fellow-workers." He will also " be cautious and slow in his innovations at any time, and particularly so while he is new to his choir." He will thus tactfully introduce " his own method " by degrees, and remember that everything comes " to him who knows how to wait."

Position and Prospects of the Organist in Scotland.

By Mr. Herbert Westerby, Mus. Bac. London, F.R.C.O., &c.

PUT briefly, these are, on the whole, certainly more favourable than in England. The Church of Scotland is more popular in its constitution than the Church of England, and the position of the organist, so long as he is competent and does his duty, is more secure, since in case of disagreement with the Kirk Session, he can always appeal to the Presbytery. His Choir work is lighter, since he has the invaluable foundation of women's voices, and he can get more *artistic* and *expressive* results with half the work necessitated by the training of young boys.

There is a keener demand for musical (and general) education in Scotland, and the "bogus" musical examining institutions which run riot without legal "let or hindrance" in the working-class towns of England can scarcely find a footing in Scotland. The properly qualified teacher's position, therefore, is more secure and he is more "looked up to."

At my request the Rev. Dr. George Bell, and the Rev. John M. Hunter have very kindly contributed the following valuable papers on the position of the organist in the Church of Scotland.

(Contribution by the Rev. George Bell, M.A., Mus. D., Minister of St. Kenneth's, Holmfauldhead, Govan (Glasgow), Member of the Psalmody and Hymns Committee of the General Assembly of the Church of Scotland, and Hon. President of the Glasgow Society of Organists.)

I. *As regards the Clergy.* (1) The appointment and dismissal are somewhat differently regulated from what exists in England, *i.e.*, these are not exclusively vested in the incumbent of the parish, but in its Kirk Session. This is the lowest ecclesiastical court in Scotland, and consists of the minister as Moderator, with his elders, sitting as assessors. The latter correspond in function to churchwardens in England, and they vary in number according to the size and circumstances of the parish. In a very small rural charge there may only be two elders, while in a large urban one as many as forty-five are to be found : the average number, however, is from six to eight (2) A well-educated and competent organist in the Church of Scotland occupies a social position which is in no respect inferior, but, if anything, superior, to that of his brother organist in the South.   The remuneration of the organist in Scotland is higher, on the whole, than in the average parish in England.   (3) The ordering of the services rests entirely with the minister of the parish, who is answerable, not to the Kirk Session, but to its superior judicatory, the Presbytery.   While the selection of psalms and hymns is retained in the hands of the parish minister, the choice of tunes, chants, anthems, etc., is assigned, by practically universal custom, to the Organist.   No objection is raised by the Kirk Session to his giving lessons in organ playing, or to the practising of his pupils on the instrument.

II. *As regards the Congregation.* This is scarcely a question of much practical importance, but it may be said that if the organist employs a generous allowance of familiar tunes, preferably for the old Scottish Psalms, in which the people can readily join, he may depend on having the happiest relations with all concerned.

III. *As regards the Choir.* The organist sometimes acts as choirmaster ; where singers receive remuneration, their appointment and dismissal are generally made either directly by himself or by the Kirk Session at his recommendation.   Choir practices are mostly held once a week.

IV. *The Services of the Church of Scotland* differ from those of the sister Establishment in England in two marked ways— (1) by the use of a traditional form of service with unprescribed prayers and many formulæ of considerable antiquity. and (2) by the employment of a much greater proportion, during the service, of metrical psalms and hymns over what is to be found in an English parish In some places, however, responses are coming into use. A series of excellent volumes, drawn up by and published with the authority of the Church, affords ample material for a church service of much musical interest.   These include the *Scottish Hymnal,* the *Church Hymnary,* the *Scottish Mission Hymnal,* the *Scottish Metrical Psalter, with Tunes,* the *Scottish Prose Psalter,* pointed for chanting, and the *Scottish Anthem Book.* There is, indeed, little to be desired in the musical rendering of Divine service in places like the ancient Cathedrals of St. Mungo, at Glasgow, and St. Giles, at Edinburgh, to mention but two out of many instances which might be given of highly efficient choirs.   During the last half-century an organ has been erected in nearly every important parish church, abbey, or cathedral in Scotland ; and throughout the land many notable examples are to be found of the most modern achievements in organ-building.

*Contribution by the Rev. John M. Hunter, B.D.,
Minister of Abbotshall Parish Church, Kirkcaldy.*

It seems quite unnecessary for me to add anything to the admirable and succinct article contributed by Dr. Bell, unless it be in regard to the courts of the Church to which appeals, in cases of dispute, may be made ; for it is really wonderful how ignorant the average English Churchman is of our position and Church government in Scotland. Presbyterians, moreover, are not even supposed to have any order of service, but sing, pray, and preach as the spirit may move them !

The governing ecclesiastical body of each parish is the *Kirk Session* (Kirk is Scots for Church), and we owe it to John Knox that the powers similar to those of the Anglican vicar are vested with the Kirk Session This body is composed of the Moderator (or chairman), who is the minister of the parish, and certain communicants who are called elders or presbyters From this fact our church is Presbyterian *in its government.* (The word Presbyterian is wrongly used when it refers to certain forms of worship.) These elders must be parishioners or townsmen, of age and of proved religious bearing. They are elected by the Session, although in practice the congregation is sometimes asked to nominate suitable persons.

This body is the lowest judicatory in the Church, and its meetings are frequent. The court above it is the *Presbytery*, which meets about six times yearly. To it every parish sends its minister and 'an elder. If there be a University in the Presbyterial district it is entitled to send its Professor of Divinity if also a minister. About twelve parishes form a Presbytery. Glasgow, however, has about one hundred. The shifting of the population, of course, accounts for the variation in the numbers constituting the various Presbyteries

The next court is the *Synod*, the membership of which is exactly the same as the Presbytery. This court meets twice in the year. Three or more Presbyteries compose a Synod.

The highest court is the *General Assembly*, which meets once a year and sits for ten lawful days. Each Presbytery sends one minister for every four ministers and one elder for every six. The Royal Burghs are entitled to send an elder Edinburgh has the privilege of sending two, while the Universities may each send either an elder or a minister, as also the Church in India. The King is represented at this court in the person of the Lord High Commissioner.

So far as I can discover, the *position of an organist in Scottish Ecclesiastical Law* is undefined, which is, of course, a matter for congratulation. The law is for the unlawful ! When the law was in the process of being made, there were no such beings as organists dreamt of. Of course there was the precentor or *Master of Song*, and I presume that our modern organists are legally entitled to whatever legal position these precentors occupied. I only know of one organist who calls himself the Master of Song—Mr Whalley, late of Peebles Parish Church, and now of St. George's, Edinburgh. It seems to be the legal title.

Now the Kirk Session has full power over the precentor, as to his appointment and dismissal, and naturally they have similar powers over the organist. It may cheer some organists who are superstitiously inclined, that although the Session may appoint an organist, they may not appoint a doorkeeper nor a gravedigger— which momentous decisions were given in the Court of Session in a case raised by St. Andrew's Session against the Town Council of Edinburgh ! No Committee—Psalmody or otherwise—can do any more than recommend, etc., to the Session. *In practice*, congrega- tions are sometimes asked to vote ; sometimes a body of experts advise ; sometimes a well-known organist judges from a short leet—but *the Kirk Session appoints*. They are also responsible for the organist's salary and for the proper upkeep of the organ.

Most *choirs* are voluntary, and the organist has to depend upon his own persuasive powers to keep the numbers sufficient. There is no law on the subject. There may, of course, be usages which, though not prescribed by enactment, have the force of law.

I am glad that Dr. Bell emphasises the fact that the *Order of Service* rests with the minister alone, and he is responsible not to the Kirk Session but to the Presbytery. No minister, however, who has the welfare of his church at heart would think of intro- ducing drastic changes without consulting his elders in a friendly way. Most congregations prefer the " old " tunes, *i.e.*, the tunes they heard in their childhood. I have known a congregation, *e g.*, convinced that Orlington (1860) was a far grander tune (because " older ") than Wiltshire ! It had been sung in the days of their childhood.

It is a sore point between some ministers and organists as to who should *choose the tunes* for the psalms or hymns. Custom is usually followed, and in practice there is never really any difficulty *where neither the minister nor the organist happens to be stupid* ! If either or both, there is always some unpleasantness. Quite recently a minister reproved his organist from the pulpit for playing the " wrong " tune to a certain hymn. The organist went on playing the " wrong " tune—and as a result was dismissed by the Kirk Session at their first meeting, without a testimonial. I leave my readers to judge as to who was to blame. The organist did not appeal to the Presbytery.

Organ Building and Organ Builders of New York City.

By Chas. A. Radzinsky.

THE following facts have never, I believe, appeared in print before. Certainly not in a collected form. Fragmentary as the information is, it may prove of interest, and the above statement will, I trust, be considered a sufficient apology for the appearance of this little contribution to the history of organ building in America.

The first builder of whom we have any definite information, was John Geif, who came from Philadelphia Pa. to New York City, and in 1802, built an organ for St. George's Church in Beekman Street, New York, and in 1810 he built an organ for Grace Church, then in Lower Broadway, New York. The Grace Church organ, which possessed the handsomest case in America, was destroyed by fire three years later.

Geif also built pianos, and the writer has tuned several of these instruments bearing his name, but further than this, no more seems to be known of him.

Thomas Hall, who began business in Philadelphia, came to New York in 1820, and having formed a partnership with his brother-in-law, Henry Erben, under the name of Hall and Erben, built organs for several years. No record of their work seems to have been kept, and if any organs were built for New York churches, they have completely disappeared.

In 1824 this firm dissolved partnership, and Henry Erben began business on his own account. Erben was borne in 1800, and from 1824 till his death in 1884, practically commanded the best trade of New York City. He was without doubt the most eminent builder of his time, and was admittedly a fine mechanic and a master organ builder, his organs being considered the best, as to workmanship, mechanically and tonally.

During his long and honourable career, he built 146 organs for New York City alone, beside several hundred organs which were scattered all over the United States His masterpiece was undoubtedly the great organ in Trinity Church, Wall Street, New York. This organ was built in 1846, under the direction of Dr. Edward Hodges, formerly of Bristol, England, and was unique in many ways. The ordinary 8ft. stops were carried down to 16ft., the 4ft. to 8ft. and so on, in the Great Organ. The organ has 3

manuals, 31 stops, and only 1 pedal stop, but that one stop was a
32ft. open diap.—of wood. A solo organ of 7 stops has since been
added, by Erben in 1869, and the organ till the beginning of 1907
was as Erben left it, save for some new reeds and some alteration
of the action. This, after daily use for over 60 years, speaks volumes
for Erben's work. In 1907 the organ was mechanically reconstructed by Hook and Hastings, of Boston, Mass. The pipes were retained, and not altered in any way. This organ is noted for its
grand tone, and is not surpassed by any in New York City. Erben
was distinguished by his unswerving fidelity to his work, and also for
his plain speech. He met many reverses latterly, and died a poor
man. The business was taken over by L. C. Harrison, a former
employé, and he having removed from New York, little is left to
remind one of the greatest builder of his time but his organs.

Thomas Hall, in the meantime, had entered into a partnership
with a party named La Bagh, and they built many organs under
the name of Hall and La Bagh, but the quality of work was not
like the former standard when Hall and Erben were together.
Later on, about 1865, Mr. James Kemp was admitted to the firm,
and on Mr. Hall's death, in 1877, the firm was known as La Bagh
and Kemp. Among organs built by this firm were those in Baltimore
Cathedral, St. Thomas P. E. Church, Church of the Strangers,
and Trinity Chapel, the last three in New York. About 1885 the
firm gave up business.

Richard M. Ferris was another old time builder, and during
his life time built many good, plain, and substantial instruments.
Among them being organs for Calvary Baptist Church, New York ;
Broadway Tabernacle, New York ; Brick Presbyterian Church,
New York ; and All Souls' Unitarian Church, New York. Later on
Ferris was in partnership with L. U. Stuart, a relative by marriage.
Mr. Ferris died 40 years ago, and his business was discontinued
as he left no one capable of carrying it on.

Another old and fine builder was Thomas Robjohn, who
with his brother William, had been in the employ of Gray and
Davison, in London, England. Robjohn built several organs, all
of them of artistic construction, but he was hampered for lack of
funds, and was accustomed to do organ work in churches where
he could, putting up a work bench or benches as he needed. He
was probably the most accomplished mechanic the writer ever
knew, either in wood or metal, and a most finished voicer. Among
organs built by him are those in the South Reformed Church, New
York ; St. John's Chapel, New York ; and the Wesleyan Church,
Troy, New York. The organ in the South Reformed Church was
noted for having the first independent pedal of 7 stops ever built
in New York City.

During the Civil War, Mr. U. C. Burnap, then organist of the Church, imported a Vox Humana, and had it placed in this organ. This also was an innovation, as it was the first stop of the kind to be used here. This organ also had a pneumatic action, but of what type I have never heard. On Robjohn giving up business as a builder, both he and his brother William were in the employ of Odell and Company, until the death of both of them. Thomas died in 1875 and William in 1879.

In 1834, George Jardine, who was a relative of the Jardines of Manchester, England, began his career as an organ builder in New York. Later he associated his four sons with him, and on his death, about 1880, two grandsons were admitted to the firm. For over 60 years this firm built organs, and their work is to be found all over the United States. Of a cheaper grade, there was a great demand for their work, and many large organs came from their factory. They were particularly famous for fine case work. In 1900, on the death of three members of the firm, it went out of existence, the remaining member being now with a firm in the West.

In 1840, or thereabouts, Messrs. L. U. Stuart and Brother, began business, and built many organs of medium size and fair workmanship One of the larger being for Broadway Tabernacle, New York ; and one for Holy Trinity P.E. Church, New York. Richard M. Ferris, above mentioned, was associated with the Stuarts for a short time. The Stuarts are, I believe, still in business in a small way in Albany, New York.

In 1859, John H. and Cales S. Odell, who had been employed for some years by Stuart Brothers, above mentioned, began business in a small way, at 163, Seventh Avenue, New York. In a short time they had attained a commanding position in the trade, due to the artistic excellence of their work—mechanically and tonally—and to the maintenance of the high standard they had set. This firm continued until 1892, when on the death of Mr. C. S. Odell, his son, William H., and nephew, George W. were admitted to the firm, and in 1900, on the death of John H. Odell, the two survivors formed the new firm, which still continues. During a long and honourable business career, from 1859 to 1907, this firm here built over 200 organs for New York City alone, besides 500 for other parts of the country, all of the highest type of excellence. Their most important organs are those in the Temple Emmanuel, St. Nicholas Dutch Reformed Church, Second Christian Science Temple—all of New York, and the First Baptist Church of Newark, N J. All of 4 manuals each At the present time this is the only firm of organ builders in New York proper.

In 1872, Mr. H. L. Roosevelt began organ building in West 18th Street, New York, and until his death in 1886, he built many important instruments. His work was marked by great excellence and artistic finish, and he undoubtedly exercised a great and beneficial influence on the trade, for he was an organ enthusiast of the first magnitude, and his death was certainly a loss to all. Among his larger organs were those in Garden City Cathedral, 4 manuals and 115 stops ; Grace P.E. Church, New York, 4 manuals and 71 stops ; and Calvary P.E. Church, New York. On the death of Mr. Roosevelt, his brother Frank took over the business, and continued it until 1893 on a larger scale. During his control of it, he built the organ for the Auditorium, Chicago, S.A., 4 manuals and 107 stops ; M.E. Church, Denver, Colorado, 4 manuals and 68 stops, and many others. In 1893 Mr. Frank Roosevelt retired from business, and his patents, stock, etc., were purchased by the Farrand and Votey Company, of Detroit, Mich.

About 1850 Mr. Alexander Mills began the building of small organs in New York, and so continued for many years, and while still living is not actually engaged in building organs. None of his organs were large, but all bore a good reputation.

Probably the oldest family of organ builders in New York, is that of Davis and Son. In 1798, Morgan Davis, of London, who had been in the employ of Broadwood, of London, piano-makers, came to New York and made pianos until 1835. On his death, his son, William H. Davis, took control of the work, and in 1840, he built his first organ, which is still doing duty in St Lucip Church, Jersey City, N.J. The first large organ he built, was for Calvary P.E. Church, New York, and contained Barker's pneumatic lever, the first in America. A curious feature of this organ was a conceit of the rector's, who had the draw stops arranged in the form of a cross. Mr. William H. Davis died in 1888, and was succeeded by his older son, Albert E. On the death of the latter, a younger son, Mr. Henry L. Davis, became the head of the firm, and now has admitted his son to membership, thus making four generations engaged in musical instrument making without a break. During the career of this firm, they have built many organs of medium size, and are still doing a safe and conservative business.

Another old timer in the organ business in New York was Francis X. Engelfreid, who came to New York in 1853, and until 1875, when he died, built a number of organs, which were of fine tone, but not satisfactory mechanically. They were constructed on the German system, viz., individual pallet chests, with tracker and roller action, box bellows, with stirrup and strap blowing apparatus, and were generally 50 years behind the times. His sons, Charles and George, were employed by Roosevelt as voicers, and were considered among the best in the trade. Engelfreid's largest work was the organ in St. Vincent de Paul R C. Church, New York, and in the R.C. Church of the Redeemer, New York.

The last of the New York organ builders to be mentioned is Reuben Midmer, who came from England when about 16 years of age, and served an apprenticeship with Hall and La Bagh, of New

York. In 1860 he began for himself in High Street, Brooklyn, New York. Mr. Midmer continued building organs until 1888, when he retired from active work, and his son, Reed Midmer, took control. Mr. Midmer, Senr., died in 1895, and the firm is composed of his son as above mentioned. The firm have built many organs for all parts of the country, and for Brooklyn alone have built 113. Among the more prominent are those in St. Francis Xavier's R.C. Church, St. Luke's P.E. Church, Thompkins Aru Congregational Church, St. Anthony's R.C. Church—all of Brooklyn, and First Congregational Church, Paughkeepsie, New York. The firm have lately built a large new factory in Merrick, L.I., New York, and are doing a large and important business.

This closes the first consecutive, though incomplete history of organ-building in New York City. The industry seems in late years to have drifted away from New York, and have gone to the Eastern and Western States. In the recollection of the writer, seven firms have gone out of existence in New York alone, leaving but one in the City proper at the present time, viz., Odell and Company. In Boston, Mass., are several large firms, also in Hartford, Conn, and in Chicago, Ill., are three at least, some of these being the largest in America. This article, however, has to do only with organ-builders of New York, and the history of others must wait for a future time.

PART II.

Brief Specifications of the Principal Organs in the British Isles.

London Organs.

CITY.—ALL HALLOWS BARKING-BY-THE-TOWER CHURCH, Great Tower Street. Built 1908 by Harrison. Opened by Dr. Madeley Richardson, of Southwark Cathedral. 3 manuals and pedal, 32 speaking stops, 9 couplers, 4 combination pedals, 8 combination pistons, 2 balanced crescendo pedals, reversible piston to Great to Pedal. Tubular pneumatic action. Blown by electric motor. Organist: Arthur Poyser.

CITY.—AUSTEN FRIARS DUTCH CHURCH. Built 1864 by Hill. 2 manuals, 29 speaking stops, 3 couplers, etc. Vox humana an exact copy of the celebrated one at Haarlem Cathedral, Holland. Bell on top of each pipe. Is of singular beauty. Organist: Rudolph J. Loman.

CITY.—BISHOPSGATE CHAPEL, (CONGREGATIONAL). Built 1855 and rebuilt 1898 by Bevington & Son, London. Re-opened by the late Mr. Fountain Meen. 2 manuals, 18 speaking stops, 6 couplers, 6 composition pedals, about 1,000 pipes. Blown by hydraulic engine. Detached and reversed console. Tubular pneumatic throughout. Organist and Choirmaster: Walter Lawrence Eggleton.

CITY.—GUILDHALL SCHOOL OF MUSIC. Built 1907 by Norman & Beard. 3 manuals CC to C 61 notes, 26 speaking stops, 8 other stops, 1,560 pipes. Tubular pneumatic action. Pedal CCC to G 32 notes; concave and radiating. Blown by patent Kinetic blower and electric motor. Detached console. Choir organ enclosed in swell box.

CITY.—MERCERS' HALL, CHAPEL. Built 1884 by Bevington. 2 manuals, 17 speaking stops, 9 other stops. Hydraulic blowing. Organist: Percy Younge.

CITY.—ST. ALBAN'S CHURCH, WOOD STREET, E.C. Built 1728 by Harris & Byfield. Restored 1850 and 1872. 3 manuals, 21 speaking stops, 9 other stops. Organist: Richard D. Metcalfe, MUS. BAC. (DUNELM), A.R.A M.

CITY.—ST. ANDREW UNDERSHAFT. Built 1696 by Renatus Harris. 3 manuals, 29 speaking stops, 10 other stops, 1,716 pipes. Organist: Herbert George Preston, 18, Ailsa Road, Westcliff-on-Sea.

CITY.—ST. AUGUSTINE AND ST. FAITH CHURCH, WATLING STREET. Built by Willis. 3 manuals, 26 speaking stops, 6 other stops, 6 composition pedals. Great to pedal "on and off." Double-acting pedal controlling pedal open Diap. Organist: Sydney H. Lovett, F.R.C.O.

CITY.—ST. BARTHOLOMEW HOSPITAL. Built by Gray & Davison. 2 manuals. Organist: Bruce Steane.

CITY.—St. Botolph Without, Bishopsgate. Built 1753 by John Byfield, jun. Removed from West gallery to East end, 1868, by Willis; rebuilt and enlarged 1887 by Willis; put back in West Gallery 1893, by Lewis, and divided into two portions, with electro pneumatic action for Northern half. New electro pneumatic action supplied to Northern half in 1902 by Walker. Completely rebuilt, much enlarged, and electro pneumatic console provided at East end of South gallery by Norman & Beard, 1912. 3 manuals, 45 stops. Organist: John Ernest Borland, MUS. DOC. OXON., F.R.C.O.

CITY.—St. Bride's Church, Fleet Street. Built by Renatus Harris. Rebuilt 1886 by Gray & Davison. 3 manuals, 33 speaking stops, 8 couplers, 5 composition pedals. Organist: Herbert Townsend.

CITY.—St Dunstan's in the West Church, Fleet Street. Rebuilt and enlarged 1897 by Eustace Ingram. 3 manuals, 27 speaking stops, 7 other stops.

CITY.—St. Giles' Church, Cripplegate. Built 1899 by Walker. 3 manuals, 27 speaking stops, 8 couplers, 6 composition pedals, 1 double-acting pedal controlling Great to Pedal coupler. Tubular pneumatic action to manuals, pedals, and draw-stops. Blown by hydraulic engines.

CITY.—St. Magnus the Martyr. Built 1712 by Abraham Jordan. Opened by J. Robinson. Restored 1760 by Sedgewick, 1782 by Parker, 1804 by Parsons, 1855 by Gray & Davison, 1861 by Hill, 1879 by Brindley & Foster. 3 manuals, 31 speaking stops, 7 other stops. Organist: George Fredk. Smith.

CITY.—St. Mary-le-Bow Church, Cheapside. Built 1877 by Walker. 3 manuals, 34 speaking stops. 12ft. quint on Pedal. Pedal compass CC to G 32 notes. Pedals concave and radiating. Horn diapasons on Great unusually good. 5 reeds; one wind pressure for whole organ. Tracker action. Blowing by Kinetic Swanton Company, 1904.

CITY.—St. Michael's Church, Cornhill. Built 1684 by Renatus Harris. Rebuilt 1790 by Green; 1849 by Robson; 1868 electric action applied by Bryceson and subsequently removed by Hill & Son; 1885 and 1901 by Hill. Detached Console. Opened by G. F. Vincent. 3 manuals, 38 speaking stops, 8 couplers and 13 pneumatic pistons. Diapasons and delicate stops remarkably good. Blown by two Kinetic electric blowers. Organist: George F. Vincent.

CITY.—St. Mildred's Church, Bread Street. Built 1744 by Thomas Griffin Alterations and additions since 1806 by Gray & Davison. 3 manuals, 24 speaking stops, 5 other stops. Organist: Henry Tolhurst, Clevedon, 166, High Road, Lee, S.E.

CITY.—St. Nicholas Cole Abbey, Queen Victoria Street. Built 1881. and reconstructed 1890 by Henry Speechly. Opened by Sir G. Martin 3 manuals, 28 speaking stops, 7 couplers, 1,404 pipes. Organist: Herbert Hodge, A.R.C M., F.R.C.O.

CITY.—St. Paul's Cathedral. Built by Bernard Schmidt. Rebuilt by Willis. 5 manuals, 76 speaking stops, 26 other stops, 4,822 pipes. Organist and Director of the Music: Sir George Clement Martin, M.V.O., MUS. DOC. OXON ET CANTUAR, F R C.O., HON. R.A.M.

CITY.—St. Stephen's Church, Coleman Street. Built 1775 by Avery. Rebuilt and revoiced by T S. Jones 3 manuals, 31 speaking stops, 7 couplers, 1,811 pipes, 6 composition pedals ("on and off"), pedal for Great to Pedals. Tubular pneumatic action to Pedal organ. Blown by electric motor.

CITY.—St. Stephen's Church, Walbrook. Built 1888 and modernised 1907 by Hill. 3 manuals, 35 speaking stops, 12 other stops, 2,008 pipes. Tubular pneumatic action throughout. Blown by high pressure hydraulic engine. Exceptionally fine instrument; very handsome case. Organist : H J. White. Appointed 1873.

CITY.—South Place Chapel. Built 1876 by Hill. 2 manuals, 14 speaking stops, 3 other stops, 813 pipes. Blown by hand. Organist : Henry Smith Webster, A R C O.

BATTERSEA.—Church of The Ascension, Lavender Hill. Rebuilt 1894 by Beall & Thynne. 2 manuals, 15 speaking stops, 5 other stops, 770 pipes, 3 composition pedals. Tracker action. Organist : William John White Honey.

BATTERSEA.—Northcote Road Baptist Church. Built 1887 and enlarged 1912 by Bevington. 2 manuals, 17 speaking stops, 7 other stops. Blown by rotary fan and Sterling motor. Tubular action. Organist : William Reuben Hitchcock, A.T S.C

BATTERSEA.—St John's College. Built 1850 by Bishop Restored 1897. 3 manuals, 14 speaking stops, 6 other stops, 563 pipes Pneumatic action to pedal. Organist : Edward Mills, MUS. B. OXON.

BATTERSEA.—St. Mary's Parish Church; Rebuilt 1896 by Bishop. 2 manuals, 22 stops Good tone. Organist : Arthur F. Adcock.

BELSIZE PARK.—See Hampstead.

BETHNAL GREEN.—Parish Church. Built 1861 and restored and improved 1901 and 1912 by Jones. 2 manuals, 28 speaking stops, 1,492 pipes. Organist : Charles Henry Ockelford.

BLACKHEATH.—See Lewisham.

BRIXTON.—See Lambeth.

CAMBERWELL.—All Saints' Church, West Dulwich. Built by Norman & Beard. Fine instrument of 3 manuals. Organist : Frederick William Holloway, F.R.C O.

CAMBERWELL.—Camden Parish Church. Memorial organ to Sir Gilbert Scott and John Ruskin. Built by Hill. Opened by Dr. Madeley Richardson 1907. Partly destroyed by fire. Restored by Gray & Davison 1908. 3 manuals, 37 stops, 8 pneumatic pistons, 5 composition pedals. Blown by electricity. Choir organ in separate chamber in chancel. Great and Swell organs in transept. Organist : C. Hastings Kirby, A R.C.O.

CAMBERWELL.—Dulwich College. Built 1885 by Martin. Enlarged 1907 by Martin & Coate. 4 manuals, 38 speaking stops, 11 other stops, 2,054 pipes. Opened by John Ivimey. Organist : H. V. Doulton, M A.

CAMBERWELL.—DULWICH COLLEGE CHAPEL. Built 1759 by England. Restored 1888 by Norman & Beard. 3 manuals, 19 speaking stops, 6 other stops. Organist : M. Gordon Burgess.

CAMBERWELL.—EMMANUEL CHURCH. Built by Robson. 2 manuals, 20 stops (more prepared for), 7 compositions, swing Swell pedal. Richly toned diapasons. Situated in West gallery. Organist : Cecil A. J. Peirce.

CAMBERWELL.—EMMANUEL CHURCH, WEST DULWICH, Restored 1900 by Hill. 3 manuals. Excellent tone. Organist and Choirmaster ; Walter W. Stark.

CAMBERWELL.—LICENCED VICTUALLERS' ASYLUM CHAPEL, PECKHAM. Built 1905 by Kearsley-Brown Opened by W. J. Kipps, A.R A.M., F.R.C.O. 2 manuals, 16 speaking stops, 3 other stops 848 pipes Organ in West gallery. Pine case. Tracker action except pedals, which are pneumatic. Organist : Arthur Kipps.

CAMBERWELL.—RYE LANE BAPTIST CHURCH, PECKHAM. Built 1903 by Brindley & Foster. Opened by present organist. 2 manuals, 20 speaking stops, 6 other stops, 1,034 pipes. Blown by electric motor. Detached console. Pneumatic action throughout. Organist : Joseph Ernest Green, MUS. B., L. MUS. T C.L.

CAMBERWELL.—ST. ANDREW'S CHURCH, PECKHAM. Built by Bevington, 1865. 2 manuals, 17 speaking stops, 8 couplers.

CAMBERWELL.—ST. GILES' CHURCH. Built 1844 by Bishop 3 manuals, 43 speaking stops. Built from a specification by late Dr. S. S. Wesley, at one time organist. Organist : John Carter Jenner, A.R.C.M.

CAMBERWELL.—ST. JAMES' CHURCH. Built 1881 by Walker. Opened by W. S. Hoyte, F.R.C.O. 3 manuals, 28 speaking stops, 6 other stops, 1,684 pipes. Organist : H. Harvey Pinches, MUS. B. OXON.

CAMBERWELL.—ST. MARK'S CHURCH, PECKHAM. Built 1868 for St. John's, Hammersmith. Enlarged 1894 by Bevington. 3 manuals, 23 speaking stops, 11 couplers. Part tubular pneumatic. Organist : Miss K Pearman.

CAMBERWELL.—ST. MARY MAGDALENE CHURCH (PARISH CHURCH OF PECKHAM). Built 1893 by Bevington. Removed to gallery in chancel 1910 by Norman & Beard. 3 manuals, 25 speaking stops, 14 other stops. Blown by Kinetic electric fan blower. Tubular pneumatic action. Organist : Harold W. W. James.

CAMDEN.—See CAMBERWELL.

CANONBURY.—See ISLINGTON.

CATFORD.—See LEWISHAM.

CHARLTON.—See GREENWICH.

CHELSEA.—CONGREGATIONAL CHURCH, MARKHAM SQUARE. Built and restored (1894) by Bishop. 3 manuals, 25 speaking stops, 8 other stops, about 1,300 pipes. Fine diapasons. Organist and Choirmaster : Alfred R. Stock, A.R.C.O.

CHELSEA —HOLY TRINITY CHURCH, SLOANE STREET. Built 1891 by Walker 4 manuals, 50 speaking stops, 13 other stops Blown by six water engines. Stops controlled by pistons and composition pedals Great contains four fine diapasons. One of the finest and largest church organs in London. Organist· Henry Lucas Balfour, MUS. BAC., F.R.C.O

CHELSEA.—ST. LUKE'S PARISH CHURCH Built 1823 by Gray Restored 1895 by Jones 3 manuals, 37 speaking stops, 7 couplers. Old flue work. Situated in West gallery. Organist : John Nicholson Ireland, MUS. BAC., F.R.C.O., A.R.C.M.

CLAPHAM.—See WANDSWORTH.

CLERKENWELL.—See FINSBURY.

CROUCH HILL —See ISLINGTON.

CROFTON PARK.—See LEWISHAM.

DALSTON.—See HACKNEY.

DENMARK HILL —See LAMBETH.

DEPTFORD —GOLDSMITHS' COLLEGE, NEW CROSS. Built 1891 by Abbott & Smith Opened by Dr. J. Churchill Sibley· 4 manuals, 52 speaking stops, 10 couplers, 25 combination pistons and pedals. Electric blown. Tubular pneumatic and pneumatic lever action.

DEPTFORD.—ST. CATHERINE'S CHURCH, HATCHAM. Rebuilt 1904 by Norman & Beard· Opened by W. M. Wait. 3 manuals, 29 speaking stops, 6 other stops, 1,512 pipes, 7 composition pedals· Gt. to pedal by D.A. pedal. Balanced Swell. Tremulant by pedal Tracker action to manuals ; tubular pneumatic to pedals. Organist : F. W E· Charrosin, 189, Waller Road, New Cross, London, E.C.

DULWICH.—See CAMBERWELL.

EAST FINCHLEY.—See HAMPSTEAD.

EAST GREENWICH.—See GREENWICH.

FINSBURY.—CHURCH OF THE HOLY REDEEMER, CLERKENWELL.ˈ Built by Willis. Organist : Frederick James Karn, MUS BAC. CANTAB., MUS. DOC. TRIN UNIVERSITY TORONTO·

FINSBURY.—ST JAMES' CHURCH, CLERKENWELL. Built 1792 by England. Reconstructed 1877 by Gray & Davison. 3 manuals, 33 stops ; 10 on Swell, Great 9, Choir 5, Pedals 3, 6 couplers and tremulant ; 5 composition pedals, Great 3, Swell 2 ; Swell Pedal, and Swell Pedal to Choir organ (Cremona). Organist : David Beardwell, A R A M , M I S.M

FINSBURY.—WESLEY'S CHAPEL, CITY ROAD. Built 1891 by Brindley & Foster. Restored 1906 by Norman & Beard, who added electro pneumatic action 3 manuals, 27 speaking stops, 9 other stops, 1,500 pipes Organ divided Console 80 feet distant and on ground floor facing choir and pulpit. Excellent tone of stops. Organist : Charles F. Warner, A.R.C.O.

FROGNAL —See HAMPSTEAD.

GREENWICH.—CHRIST CHURCH, EAST GREENWICH Built by Noble. 3 manuals, 30 speaking stops, 7 couplers, 8 pneumatic composition pistons. Tubular pneumatic action throughout. Blown by hydraulic engine. 1,862 pipes.

GREENWICH.—HOLY TRINITY CHURCH, CHARLTON Built 1894 by Bevington. 2 manuals, 19 speaking stops, 8 couplers. Part tubular. Part of Great separated and fixed on face of chancel wall. Organist : George Davies.

GROSVENOR PARK.—See SOUTHWARK.

HACKNEY.—CHRIST CHURCH, SOUTH HACKNEY. Built 1876 by Bevington. 2 manuals and pedal, 18 speaking stops, 3 couplers. Organist : W. Meacham Haley.

HACKNEY.—ST BARTHOLOMEW'S CHURCH, DALSTON. Built 1885 by Eustace Ingram. 2 manuals, 21 speaking stops, 4 couplers. Tracker action. Thoroughly cleaned and overhauled and pneumatic action added to pedals, 1909. Organist : Clement Meek, A.R.C.O.

HACKNEY.—ST MATTHEW'S CHURCH, UPPER CLAPTON. Built 1870 by Gray & Davison. Rebuilt and enlarged 1912 by Spurden Rutt. 3 manuals, 37 speaking stops (12 on Great, 12 Swell, 7 Choir, 6 Pedal), 10 other stops, 1,944 pipes Tremulant to Swell, also acts on Choir. 13 composition pistons, 8 composition pedals. Balanced crescendo pedals to Swell and Choir Blown by 4 h.p. electric motor and " Discus Blower." Pneumatic action throughout. Key tablets grouped above the Swell manual take the place of stop knobs. Organist : W. G. Low.

HAMMERSMITH.—OAKLANDS CONGREGATIONAL CHURCH, UXBRIDGE ROAD. Built by Norman & Beard 3 manuals, 40 stops, 8 pistons, 2 Swell pedals, 9 composition pedals, 1,600 pipes Blown by Sterling Blower and 3½ h p. motor. Organist : Alfred George Woodham, F R.C O

HAMMERSMITH.—RIVERCOURT WESLEYAN CHURCH. Built 1875 by Bevington. 3 manuals, 28 speaking stops, 11 couplers. Organist : Mrs. Braithwaite.

HAMPSTEAD.—ALL SAINTS' CHURCH, EAST FINCHLEY. Built 1897 by Hill. Opened by W. Neal. 2 manuals, 14 speaking stops (Great 7, Swell 6 to tenor C only). 2 couplers Swell to Great, Great to Pedal. Temporary organ put together from various organs Organist : George R. Ceiley, L R A M , A.R.C O

HAMPSTEAD.—ROSSLYN HILL UNITARIAN CHURCH. Built by Hill 1896, 3 manuals, 40 speaking stops and accessories. Choir organ in separate Swell box. Blown by Kinetic Blower. Organist . Charles J. Pemberton.

HAMPSTEAD.—ST. ANDREW'S PRESBYTERIAN CHURCH, FROGNAL. Built 1904 by Brindley & Foster 3 manuals, 36 speaking stops, 9 other stops, 2,379 pipes, 7 pistons to Great, 7 to Swell. Contrivance allowing Swell reeds to speak on Choir, thus giving all other stops for use as accompaniment Organist : Arthur E. Godfrey, A R.A.M.

HAMPSTEAD.—St. Luke's Church. Built 1901 by Willis. Opened by
E Milne. Added to in 1910 by Hele 3 manuals, 32 speaking stops,
8 other stops Blown by 2 hydraulic engines. Finely carved oak
case. Console under oak pannelled canopy. Fine diapasons.

HAMPSTEAD.—St Paul's Church, Avenue Road. Built 1898 by Lewis.
3 manuals, 27 speaking stops, 8 other stops, 6 pistons, 6 composition
pedals. Tubular pneumatic action throughout. Organist : Edward
George Croager, A R.A.M.

HAMPSTEAD.—St. Peter's, Belsize Park. Built 1843 and restored 1901
by Bevington. 3 manuals, 30 speaking stops, 8 other stops, 1,980
pipes. Tubular action. Choir organ on face of Chancel wall ; Pedal
organ in South Transept gallery. Blown by gas engine. Organist :
Louis D. Marsden, A.R.C.O.

HAMPSTEAD —St. Saviour's Church, South Hampstead. Built 1856
by Bevington Restored 1887 by Hill and 1907 by Norman & Beard.
3 manuals, 30 speaking stops, 6 other stops.

HAMPSTEAD.—2, Kidderpore Avenue, the residence of Mr W. M Peters.
Built by Noterman. 2 manuals, and pedal organ, 18 speaking stops,
5 couplers, 916 pipes. 3 combination pedals to Great organ and 3 to
Swell organ. Balanced swell pedal and balanced crescendo pedal on
stops without affecting knobs or tablets Fitted with an automatic
playing device. Arranged on each side of the entrance hall. Dark oak
case. Tubular pneumatic action. Blown by self-regulating hydraulic
engine.

HATCHAM.—See Deptford

HERNE HILL.—See Lambeth.

HIGHBURY —See Islington.

HOLBORN.—Freemasons' Hall Built by Gray & Davison Restored
1912 and electric blower added by H Dyer & Son 2 manuals, 14
speaking stops, 4 couplers, 750 pipes. Opened (1912) by John W.
Ivimey, B. MUS OXON., F R.C.O., A.R C.M.

HOLBORN.—John's Street Baptist Church, Bedford Row. Built 1897
by Bevington. 2 manuals, 13 speaking stops, 10 couplers. Tubular
pneumatic action throughout.

HOLBORN —St. Andrew's Church. Built 1904 by Hill 3 manuals,
45 speaking stops, 8 couplers. Tubular pneumatic action. Hydraulic
blowing Organist : F. G M. Ogbourne.

ISLINGTON.—Christ Church, Highbury Built 1903 by Norman &
Beard. Opened by Dr H W. Richards. 3 manuals, 25 speaking
stops, 9 other stops, 1,482 pipes. Balance Swell pedal, clarionet Choir
prepared for. 6 composition pedals. Tubular pneumatic action.
Hydraulic engines. Organist : Miss Ellen Mary Cooper.

ISLINGTON —Crouch Hill Presbyterian Church. Built by Monk.
3 manuals, 32 stops. Built half each side of Church. Partly tubular
pneumatic action. Organist : Louis F. Goodwin·

ISLINGTON.—HOLLY PARK WESLEYAN CHURCH, CROUCH HILL. Built 1887 by Kirkland. 3 manuals, 27 speaking stops, 7 couplers, tremulant, etc., 1,554 pipes, 8 composition pedals. Placed in South Chancel arch. Chancel and Nave fronts. Organist and Choirmaster. Arthur William Robinson.

ISLINGTON —PARK CHURCH (U.P.), HIGHBURY. Built by Young. 3 manuals and pedal, 33 speaking stops, 7 couplers, 8 composition pedals 1,940 pipes.

ISLINGTON.—ST. MARY'S PARISH CHURCH. Built by Byfield & Green 1772 Enlarged by Holdich, 1872 ; restored by Hill, 1904. 3 manuals, 27 speaking stops, 6 couplers Finely carved polished Spanish mahogany case with gilt pipes Organist : Alfred Markham Colchester, A R C O.

ISLINGTON.—ST. PAUL'S CHURCH, CANONBURY Built 1828 by Timothy Russell. Rebuilt 1875 by Robson and 1901 by Eustace Ingram. Re-opened by D Wetton, MUS. DOC. 3 manuals, 31 speaking stops, 6 other stops, 1,704 pipes. Blown by hydraulic engine Organist . George Norman Meachen, M.D., B.S., LONDON, M.R C.P., A. MUS. T.C L.

ISLINGTON —UNION CONGREGATIONAL CHAPEL Built 1878 by Willis. Opened by Mr W S Hoyte 3 manuals, 37 speaking stops, 5 other stops, 2,214 pipes Hydraulic blowing Pneumatic lever to Great, Swell and Pedal. Organist : Julius Alan Greenway Harrison.

KENNINGTON.—See LAMBETH.

KENSINGTON.—BOLTONS ST. MARY'S CHURCH, BROMPTON. Built 1882 by Hill Rebuilt and enlarged 1908 by Hill. 52 speaking stops, 12 couplers. Organist : R. Meyrick Roberts.

KENSINGTON —DENBIGH ROAD WESLEYAN CHURCH. Built 1865 by Bevington. Restored 1888 2 manuals, 20 speaking stops, 5 other stops, 1,236 pipes, 5 composition pedals Blown by hand Part tubular. Organist W C Crouch, L L C M.

KENSINGTON —HOLY TRINITY CHURCH. Built 1889 by Abbott & Smith. 2 manuals, 19 speaking stops, 4 couplers, 5 combination pedals, 1 double-acting pedal to Great. Powerful Swell. Handsome carved case. Organist : Henry Beck.

KENSINGTON —ROYAL ALBERT HALL. Built 1869 by Willis 4 manuals, and Pedal organ, Choir 20 stops, Great 25, Swell 25, Solo 20, Pedal 21 , total, 111. 14 couplers. Eight patent pneumatic combination pistons govern the whole of the stops of each Manual organ. These 32 pistons appear immediately below and in front of each clavier, concentrated so as to be at all times within reach by the hands of the performer. Six pedals govern the stops of the Pedal organ by means of ventils Six pedals govern and combine in various ways all the other accessories. and thus, by one instantaneous operation of the performer, vary the effect of the whole instrument at once. Two tremulants, governed by pedals (one to the Swell and one to the Solo organ) are applied. These tremulants act only upon suitable stops The general construction of the instrument is of the most elaborate and beautiful kind, of the best material and workmanship. The internal metal pipes consist of 5-9ths lamb-stamp commercial tin and 4-9ths soft lead, and the scales of these, as well as those of the front, are suitable to the proportions of the building. All the front pipes are made of tin 90 and lead 10 in 100 parts, and are burnished and polished in the same manner as those of the best Continental organs. The key fittings are elegant in design, the combination pistons being plated with gold and engine turned. The claviers are made of very thick ivory The main reservoirs in which the compressed air is forced are placed in a chamber prepared in a clean and dry locality. The feeders supplying the air by steam power are of the most ample size, and constructed to receive their wind from the room above, and not from the locality in which they are placed. To carry out this arrangement (of the highest importance) passages are provided for the wind shafts to and from the organ to the chamber in which the main reservoirs are placed. The main reservoirs deliver their wind to numerous reservoirs in immediate connection with the pipes. Organist and Assistant Conductor to the Albert Hall Royal Choral Society Henry Lucas Balfour, MUS. BAC., F R C.O.

KENSINGTON.—ST. COLUMBS' CHURCH, LANCASTER ROAD. Built by Bishop 23 speaking stops, 7 other stops Organist : Francis Burgess, F S A. (Scot).

KENSINGTON—ST. CUTHBERT'S CHURCH. Built 1900 by Hunter. 4 manuals, 53 speaking stops, 15 other stops Swanton high pressure water engines. Tubular pneumatic action throughout Case of handsome decorated iron and copper screens Organist : Rev. Cyril W. Miller, MUS. BAC. DUNELM, F.R.C.O.

KENSINGTON —ST JOHN BAPTIST CHURCH, HOLLAND ROAD. Built by Gern Restored 1912 by Noterman, Shepherds Bush 4 manuals, 33 speaking stops, 13 couplers and accessories, 1,792 pipes. Blown by hydraulic power. Beauty of tone in string toned stops. Organist ; Healey Willan, F.R C.O.

KENSINGTON.—ST JOHN'S PRESBYTERIAN CHURCH. Built 1882 by Bevington 20 speaking stops, 10 couplers Part tubular. Choir organ and extra stops on Pedal organ by Bishop, 1904.

KENSINGTON —ST. JUDE'S CHURCH Built by Wedlake. Entirely rebuilt and enlarged 1896 by Walker. 3 manuals, 43 speaking stops, 8 couplers, 8 composition pistons, 4 composition pedals, 1 double-acting pedal, 5 complete new ranks of pipes added since 1901. Tubular pneumatic action to key and pedal action Tubular pneumatic draw-stop action. Blown by two hydraulic engines (Watkins high pressure). Organist : Reginald Yarrow.

KENSINGTON.—ST. LUKE'S CHURCH, REDCLIFFE SQUARE. Built by Jones. 3 manuals, 26 speaking stops, 5 other stops. Organist : Charles Hoby, A R.C.M , L.R A.M.

KENSINGTON —ST. MARY ABBOT'S CHURCH Built 1872 by Hill Opened by James Turle, Organist Westminster Abbey. Restored 1892 by Hill. 4 manuals, 46 speaking stops, 9 other stops, 2,674 pipes Blown by two hydraulic engines Fine diapasons in Great, magnificent Swell and Tuba on 9in. wind Organist Henry Richard Bird, F.R C O., F T.C.L.

KENSINGTON.—ST. MARY'S CHURCH. Built 1903 by Jones. 3 manuals, 29 speaking stops, 6 other stops, 6 composition pedals. Tremulant pedal. Organist: Albert H. Edwards, MUS. D , F.R.C.O.

KENSINGTON.—St. Paul's Church, Onslow Square. Built 1886 by Lewis. Rebuilt 1900 by Walker. Opened by Guilmant in 1886 and Lemare in 1900. 4 manuals, 42 speaking stops, 10 couplers, etc. Console 12ft. away from organ. Fine oak case. Organist : Geoffrey O'Connor-Morris.

KENSINGTON —St. Paul's Church, Vicarage Gate. Built 1888 by Hill. 3 manuals, 33 speaking stops, 7 other stops. Organist : Walter B. C. Wiltshire, F.R.C.O., A.R.C.M.

KENSINGTON—St. Peter's Church, Cranley Gardens. Built 1893 by Willis. Rebuilt 1908 by Walker. 4 manuals, 54 speaking stops, 18 couplers, 16 combination pistons, 8 combination pedals, 2 balanced swell pedals. One double-acting pedal-piston, and one double-acting thumb piston. Organist : Ernest Read, A.R.A.M., L.R.A.M., F.R.C.O., 7, Neville Terrace, South Kensington, S.W.

KENSINGTON.—Trinity Presbyterian Church, Kensington Park Road. Built 1884 by Bevington. 2 manuals, 20 speaking stops, 5 couplers, etc., 1,220 pipes, 7 composition pedals, centre balanced swell-pedal. Placed in South transept. Organist and Choirmaster : Ernest Victor Page.

KENTISH TOWN.—See St. Pancras.

KNIGHTSBRIDGE.—See Westminster.

LAMBETH—Brixton Independent Church. Built 1870 by Willis. Enlarged 1901 by Lewis ; reconstructed and enlarged 1905 and 1911 by Norman & Beard. 4 manuals, 52 speaking stops, 12 couplers, 22 composition pedals and pistons. Divided organ ; electro pneumatic action. Blown by Kinetic blower driven by electric motor. Organist Sidney Hann, A.R.A.M.

LAMBETH.—Holy Trinity Church. Built 1894 by Gern. Opened by Dr. Alcock. 2 manuals, 13 speaking stops, 4 other stops. Organist · S. R. Philpot, 23, Gresham Road, Brixton, London, S.W.

LAMBETH.—Methodist Church, Herne Hill. Built 1888 by Adams. 2 manuals, 12 speaking stops, 3 other stops, 646 pipes. Opened by Dr. Turpin. Console detached 40ft. Organist : H Williams Mills

LAMBETH —Mostyn Road Wesleyan Church, Brixton. Built 1882 by Bevington. 2 manuals, 18 speaking stops, 10 couplers. Part tubular.

LAMBETH —Presbyterian Church, Kennington Road. Built about 1820 by H. Tarncason. 1 manual, 6 speaking stops, 220 pipes. Organist · N. Edward Sanger.

LAMBETH.—St. Agnes' Church, Kennington. Built by Brindley & Foster. 3 manuals, 33 speaking stops, 7 couplers and tremulant, 10 pneumatic pistons, Swell to Great. Reversing pedal. Tubular pneumatic action throughout. Blown by electric motors. Divided organ.

LAMBETH.—St. Ann's Church. Built by Bevington, 1876. 3 manuals, 25 speaking stops, 13 couplers. Extended tracker action.

LAMBETH.—St. John Evangelist Church, Norwood   Built 1882 by Lewis. Action renewed and console moved to North Side, under Organ, January, 1913. 3 manuals, 35 speaking stops, 5 couplers. Organ planned by Mr. Eyre in consultation with Mr. Lewis. 2 pedal stops prepared for pneumatic action.   Organ in lofty chamber on North side above chancel Very fine tone. Organist: Alfred J Eyre, M R.A.M , F.R C.O.

LAMBETH —St Luke's Church, Norwood. Built 1872 and rebuilt 1903 by Bevington 3 manuals, 29 speaking stops, 11 other stops. Blown by hand. Part tubular. Organist: Percy Sibthorpe Bright, MUS. BAC. (London), A.R C.O.

LAMBETH.—St. Matthew's Church, Denmark Hill. Built by Hill, added to by Walker & Bishop Rebuilt by Hunter 3 manuals, 42 speaking stops and couplers, 2,118 pipes Pedal trombone in Swell box   Organist. John Warriner, MUS. DOC. TRIN. COLL. DUBLIN, F T.C.L.

LAMBETH.—St. Paul's Church, Herne Hill Built by Holdich. Restored 1902 by Kirkland. 31 stops. Organist: W. Vivian W. Vine, F.R C.O , L.R.A M.

LAMBETH.—St. Saviour's Church, Brixton Hill Built 1875 by Brindley & Foster Restored and added to 1885 and 1895 by Jones. 3 manuals, 25 speaking stops, 7 other stops, 1,560 pipes

LEE.—See Lewisham.

LEWISHAM —Catford Wesleyan Church, Rushey Green. Built 1910 by Arundell Opened by Sir Frederick Bridge. 3 manuals, 23 speaking stops, 7 couplers, 1 tremulant, 6 pneumatic pistons, and 1,226 pipes. Balanced Swell. Tubular pneumatic action throughout. Blown by a Watkins & Watson's " Discus Blower." Driven by electric motor. Organist: Alfred J Blake, 238, Verdant Lane, Hither Green, S E.

LEWISHAM.—Christ Church, Lee Park   Rebuilt 1893. 4 manuals, 46 speaking stops, 12 other stops.   Two hydraulic engines   Opened by present organist. Organist: J. T Field, L.T C L

LEWISHAM.—Church of the Ascension, Blackheath   Repaired 191[1] by Bevington. Opened by Dr Warriner. 2 manuals, 19 speaking stops, 6 couplers. Organist: F W. Brinkworth, A R.C.O.

LEWISHAM —Crystal Palace Concert Organ. Built 1854 by Gray & Davison. 4 manuals, 68 speaking stops, 12 couplers, 2 tremulants Blown by high pressure hydraulic engine by Watkins and Watson. Organist. Walter W. Hedgcock.

LEWISHAM.—Holy Trinity Church, Lee. Built by Robson. Enlarged under the direction of Frederick Archer when he was organist. 2 manuals, 21 speaking stops, 4 couplers. Organist: Ernest G. White.

LEWISHAM.—Private residence of S. Prestige, Blackheath   Built 1909 by Bevington 3 manuals, 30 speaking stops, 6 couplers, 11 pistons, 2 pedals Tubular pneumatic. Blown by compound hydraulic engines.

LEWISHAM.—St. Augustine's Church, Lee   Built 1889 by Forster & Andrews. Opened by Sir Frederick Bridge. 3 manuals, 19 speaking stops, 7 other stops, 1,002 pipes Detached console. Tracker action except pedals which are tubular pneumatic Blown by hand Pedals straight concave—CCC to F.

LEWISHAM.—St. Bartholomew's Church, Sydenham.   Restored 1900 by Hill.   3 manuals, 28 speaking stops, 5 other stops.   Organist : Frederick G. Shinn, mus. doc. (Dunelm), a.r.c.m., f.r.c.o.

LEWISHAM —St. Hilda's Church, Crofton Park, S.E.   Built by Conacher. 3 manuals and pedal, 32 speaking stops, 11 couplers, 11 combination pistons, 8 combination pedals.   Tubular pneumatic action throughout. Oak case.   Organist : Herbert N. G. Newlyn.

LEWISHAM.—St. Laurence Church, Catford.   Built 1887 by Eustace Ingram.   3 manuals, CC to G, 22 speaking stops (11 more prepared for), 6 other stops, 1,254 pipes   Tracker action throughout.   Blown by hand.   Choir organ in Swell box.   Pedals straight and concave, CCC to F.   Organist and Director of the Choir : Burman Herrick Edwards.

LEWISHAM —St. Margaret's Parish Church, Lee.   Built 1850 by Bishop. Rebuilt 1875 by Walker and 1899 by Bishop, who substituted tubular pneumatic action for Tracker action.   3 manuals, 31 speaking stops, 9 other stops, 1,950 pipes.   Two stops in Great prepared for.   16ft. on Swell divided at middle C.   Blown by hydraulic engine in chamber under church.   Organist : Frederic Leeds, mus bac cantab., f.r.c.o.

LEWISHAM.—St. Mary's Parish Church   Built 1882 by Brindley & Foster.   3 manuals, 42 stops and couplers, 6 composition pedals. Tracker action.   Blowing apparatus by Watkins & Watson.   A new hydraulic engine installed in 1905.   Organist : William Whitehead.

LEWISHAM —St Peter's Church, Brockley.   Built by Hill   Rebuilt 1910 by Lewis   3 manuals, 38 speaking stops, 14 couplers, 2,182 pipes, 2 tremulants, 12 pistons, 9 composition pedals   Tubular pneumatic throughout.   Organist : Charles Joseph Frost, mus doc. cantab , f.r c.o.

LIMEHOUSE.—See Stepney.

MAIDA HILL.—See Paddington.

MARYLEBONE.—All Saints' Church, Margaret Street   Built 1910 by Harrison & Harrison, to the specification of present organist.   4 manuals, 69 speaking stops, 29 couplers, 5 combination pedals, 25 combination pistons, 3 reversible pistons, 2 reversible pedals, 3 balanced crescendo pedals.   Tubular pneumatic action throughout.   Blown by hydraulic engines.   Organist : Walter S. Vale, 84, Margaret Street, London, W.

MARYLEBONE.—Christ Church.   3 manuals, 25 speaking stops, 5 other stops.   Organist : Sidney H. Sheppard, a.r.c.o., l.t.c.l.

MARYLEBONE.—Hinde Street Wesleyan Methodist Church.   Built 1807 by Bishop.   2 manuals, 16 speaking stops, 2 other stops.   Situated in back gallery behind congregation.   Organist : Frederick J. Gill.

MARYLEBONE.—Holy Trinity Church.   Built 1828 by Bishop.   Restored and enlarged 1902 by Vincent.   Rebuilt 1911 by Norman & Beard.   Opened by present Organist.   4 manuals, 42 speaking stops, 10 other stops.   Balance Swell crescendo pedal and balance.   Swell to Solo organ, 3 composition pedals and pedal for Swell tremulant. Detached console.   Electro pneumatic action throughout.   Organist : Hugh Blair, m.a., mus. doc ch. coll. cambridge.

MARYLEBONE.—MIDDLESEX HOSPITAL CHURCH (Private Chapel). Built 1870 by Lewis. Opened by present Organist. Restored 1910. 2 manuals, 13 speaking stops. Blown by electric motor. Organist: J. C. Spanswick.

MARYLEBONE.—Private residence of Montague Ballard, Esq., Regent's Park. Built 1911 by Bevington. 3 manuals, 29 speaking stops, 8 couplers, 9 pistons, 4 pedals, 2 tremulants, 3 crescendo pedals Tubular pneumatic action throughout. Electric blowing. Private Organist: H. Robinson.

MARYLEBONE.—ST. CYPRIAN'S CHURCH. Built by Bishop & Starr. 2 manuals. Organist: Charles George Thomas, L.T.S.C., DIPLOMA LEIPZIG ROYAL CONS.

MARYLEBONE.—ST. MARY'S CHURCH, BRYANSTON SQUARE. Built 1912 by Harrison. 3 manuals, 41 speaking stops, 16 couplers, 5 combination pedals, 14 combination pistons, 2 reversible pistons, 1 reversible pedal, 2 reversible toe pistons for tremulants, 2 balanced crescendo pedals. Tubular-pneumatic and electro-pneumatic. Blowing by electricity. Organist: Reginald J. Foort, F.R.C.O.

MARYLEBONE.—ST. PETER'S CHURCH, VERE STREET. Built 1855 by Hill. Restored and enlarged on four occasions since. 3 manuals, 29 speaking stops, 7 couplers. Tracker action; pneumatic action to Pedal organ. Blown by hand. Originally in West gallery, but removed to East end about 1885. Heavy touch, but good organ for size. Organist: Augustus Toop, F.R.C.O.

MARYLEBONE —SELFRIDGE'S, OXFORD STREET. Built 1912 by Norman & Beard Opened by Edwin H. Lemare. 3 manuals and pedal, 27 speaking stops, 17 couplers.

MARYLEBONE.—TRINITY COLLEGE OF MUSIC. Built 1908 by Vincent. 4 manuals, 28 stops. Pneumatic action. Electric blower. Opened by Sir Frederick Bridge, M.V.O., MUS. DOC., M.A.

MARYLEBONE.—WEST LONDON SYNAGOGUE, UPPER BERKELEY STREET. Built 1908 by Harrison and Harrison. 4 manuals, 55 speaking stops, 15 couplers, 6 combination pedals, 17 combination pistons, 6 solo pistons, 3 reversible pedals, 2 balanced crescendo pedals to Swell and Solo organs. Tubular pneumatic action throughout, except manual to pedal coupling action, which is mechanical Blown by hydraulic engines. Organist: Dr. Percy R. Rideout, A.R.C.M.

MAYFAIR —See WESTMINSTER.

MILE END.—See STEPNEY.

NEW CROSS.—See DEPTFORD.

NEWINGTON.—See SOUTHWARK.

NORWOOD.—See LAMBETH.

PADDINGTON.—ALL SAINTS' CHURCH, NORFOLK SQUARE. Built 1896 by Hill 3 manuals. Organist: William Wolstenholme, MUS. BAC. OXON.

PADDINGTON.—CATHOLIC APOSTOLIC CHURCH, MAIDA HILL. Built by Brindley & Foster. 3 manuals, 38 speaking stops, 6 couplers and tremulant, 7 composition pedals Tubular throughout. Blown by hydraulic engine. Organist: J. Stedman.

PADDINGTON.—CHRIST CHURCH, LANCASTER GATE. Built 1880 by Walker Rebuilt 1903 by Norman and Beard. Opened by H. W Richards. 4 manuals, 40 speaking stops, 10 other stops. Electric connection. Blown by three engines. Organist: Henry W Richards, MUS. DOC., F.R.C O , HON. R.A.M

PADDINGTON.—ST. SAVIOUR'S CHURCH. Built by Gray & Davison. Rebuilt by Monk. 3 manuals, 43 stops. Organist: Leonard Hart. F.R.C.O., A.R.A.M.

PECKHAM.—See CAMBERWELL.

PIMLICO.—See WESTMINSTER.

PUTNEY.—See WANDSWORTH.

RUSHEY GREEN.—See LEWISHAM.

ST. PANCRAS.—CHRIST CHURCH, ALBANY STREET. Built by Jones. 3 manuals, 35 speaking stops.

ST. PANCRAS —CHURCH OF THE HOLY CROSS, CROMER STREET. Built by Monk. 20 stops. Detached console. Tubular pneumatic action.

ST. PANCRAS —FOUNDLING HOSPITAL CHAPEL. Built 1855 by Bevington. Enlarged 1884 by Willis and later by Hill 3 manuals, 50 speaking stops, 16 couplers Organist: Dr. H. Davon Wetton, F R C.O., 19, Sheldon Road, Cricklewood, London, N.W.

ST. PANCRAS.—NORTH LONDON COLLEGIATE SCHOOL FOR GIRLS. Built 1879 by Bevington. 3 manuals, 16 speaking stops. 4 couplers. Organist: Miss Ada H. Green, F.R.C O , A.R.C.M.

ST. PANCRAS.—REGENT'S PARK BAPTIST CHAPEL. Built by Hill. Rebuilt 1897 by Ingram. Re-opened by present organist. 19 speaking stops, tremulant and couplers. Organist: Charles Edwin Smith.

ST. PANCRAS.—ST. BARNABAS' CHURCH, KENTISH TOWN. Built 1880 by Monk. 3 manuals, 35 stops. Choir organ in Swell box.

ST. PANCRAS —ST. BARTHOLOMEW'S CHURCH, GRAY'S INN ROAD. Built about 1810. Restored 1907 by Hele. 3 manuals, 30 stops and couplers. Situated in East gallery over Communion table. Organist: George Shinn, MUS BAC , CANTAB

ST. PANCRAS —ST. MARY'S CHURCH, SEYMOUR STREET. Built 1875 by Bevington. 2 manuals (third prepared for), 26 speaking stops, 10 couplers.

SHOREDITCH.—SHOREDITCH BOROUGH PARISH CHURCH. Built by Bridge in 1757 3 manuals, 25 speaking stops, 4 couplers. Organ much in its original state. Black naturals, white sharps with a thin streak of black. No composition pedals Compass great GG to E 3in. alt, Choir GG to E 3in alt, while the Swell, from Fiddle G to E 3 in alt. Has beautiful case and stands in West Gallery Organist: William Alfred Warren, F.I.S.C

SOUTH HACKNEY.—See HACKNEY.

SOUTH HAMPSTEAD.—See HAMPSTEAD.

SOUTHWARK.—ALL SAINTS' CHURCH, SURREY SQUARE. Built by Hill. 2 manuals, 15 stops.

SOUTHWARK.—ALL SOULS' CHURCH (NEWINGTON), GROSVENOR PARK. Built 1871 by Bevington. 2 manuals, 17 speaking stops, 3 other stops, 1,138 pipes. Organ prepared for five extra stops and a third manual.

SOUTHWARK.—CATHEDRAL, THE. Built 1897 by Lewis. 4 manuals, 13 pedal stops, including three of 32ft. Fine solo organ, 40 combination key touches. Electric action throughout. Organist: Edgar S. Cook, F.R.C.O , L.R.A.M.

SOUTHWARK.—ST. MARK'S CHURCH, EAST STREET, WALWORTH. Built 1724 by Renatus Harris. Restored 1868 by Gray & Davison; 1879, by Waley, Young & Oldknow; and 1885 by Ingram. 3 manuals. 36 speaking stops, 9 other stops. The Great to Pedal coupler can be worked by a wedge situated on the left hand side of the pedal board, which is slightly radiating and concave. The last organ built by Renatus Harris. Fine old case and some of the original pipes still in use. Organist: C. Norman Mills.

SOUTHWARK.—ST. MARY'S PARISH CHURCH, NEWINGTON. Built 1877 by Lewis. Opened by the late Dr. E. J. Hopkins. 3 manuals, 36 speaking stops, 7 composition pedals, 5 couplers. Pneumatic action to Great organ. Carved oak case. Gift of W. Tarn, Esq., in memory of his father. Organist and Choirmaster: William Rayment Kirby, MUS. BAC. DUNELM, F.R.C.O.

SOUTHWARK.—ST. STEPHEN'S CHURCH, WALWORTH. Built 1871 by Bevington. 2 manuals, 15 speaking stops, 7 couplers.

STEPNEY.—GREAT ASSEMBLY HALL, MILE END. Built 1886 by Bevington. 3 manuals, 37 speaking stops, 14 couplers. Blown by gas engine. Director of Music: G. Day Winter, 30, Tredegar Square, Bow.

STEPNEY.—ST. ANNE'S PARISH CHURCH, LIMEHOUSE. Built 1851 by Gray & Davison. 3 manuals, 34 speaking stops, 6 other stops. In West end Gallery. Blown by hand. Oak case, front gilded pipes.

STEPNEY.—ST. DUNSTAN'S CHURCH. Built 1903 by Norman & Beard. Opened by A. Madeley Richardson. 3 manuals, 27 speaking stops, 10 other stops, 7 composition pedals. Pneumatic pistons Balanced swell pedal Blown by Swanton-Kinetic electric blower. Organist: Percy Walter Downes.

STEPNEY.—ST. JOHN'S CHURCH, WAPPING. Restored 1879 by Eustace Ingram. 2 manuals, 18 speaking stops, 16ft. pedal, 3 couplers. Well balanced tone. Supposed to be built in eighteenth century. Organist: W. H. Maisey.

STEPNEY.—SPITALFIELD PARISH CHURCH. Built 1735 by R. Bridge. Repaired and enlarged 1832 by Bishop; 1837 by Lincoln; 1852 by Gray & Davison; 1870 by Lewis; and 1898 by Northcott. 3 manuals, 42 speaking stops, 8 couplers. Situated in West Gallery and has fine appearance.

STOKE NEWINGTON.—St. Mary's Church. Built by Gray & Davison. Rebuilt 1906 by Hill. 4 manuals, 44 speaking stops, 12 other stops. Balanced Swell pedal, crescendo and dim pedal for all stops in sequence. Blown by electric motor. Tubular pneumatic, Choir organ in chancel, Console in chancel, rest of organ in South Transept. Organist : Henry T. Pringuer, MUS. DOC. (OXON), F.R.C O.

STOKE NEWINGTON.—St. Michael's Church. Built 1897 by Hill. 29 speaking stops, 7 couplers. Electric action, electric blowing. Organist : B J Pirie.

STREATHAM.—See Wandsworth.

SYDENHAM —See Lewisham.

TOOTING.—See Wandsworth.

UPPER CLAPTON —See Hackney.

UPPER TOOTING.—See Wandsworth.

WALWORTH —See Southwark.

WANDSWORTH.—All Saints' Church, Tooting Graveney. Built 1907 by Harrison. 3 manuals, 41 speaking stops, 11 couplers, 4 combination pedals, 11 combination pistons, 1 reversible piston, 2 balanced crescendo pedals Tubular pneumatic. Blown by Kinetic blower and 4 h p. electric motor. Hon. Organist : H Walter Wheeler. Assistant Organist : E. Carrick.

WANDSWORTH.—Congregational Church, Grafton Square. Built 1902 by Hunter. 3 manuals, 39 speaking stops, 9 other stops, 2,260 pipes, 21 pistons, 7 composition pedals Tubular pneumatic action throughout Opened by the late J. P. Attwater, MUS. BAC , F.R.C.O., L R.A.M. Organist : Francis W. Sutton, A.R.C O.

WANDSWORTH —Holy Trinity Parish Church, Clapham. Built 1909 by Hunter 3 manuals, 42 speaking stops, 10 couplers, 21 pistons, 12 composition pedals, concave and radiating pedal board. The manual, pedal, drawstop and composition actions are tubular pneumatic. Blown by electric motor Organist : Herbert Edward Thorne.

WANDSWORTH.—Immanuel Church, Streatham Common. Built 1865 by Hill 3 manuals, 28 speaking stops, 7 couplers, etc., 1,646 pipes. Tubular pneumatic action to Pedal only Organist : Andrew Freeman, B.A , MUS. B. (CANTAB), F.R.C O

WANDSWORTH.—Magdalene Hospital, Streatham. Built 1868 by Hill. 2 manuals, 15 speaking stops, 3 other stops, 844 pipes, 4 composition pedals. Detached Console Organist : Miss Grace Ivorsen, A.R A.M , A.T.C M , A G.S.M.

WANDSWORTH—Mitcham Road Baptist Church, Streatham. Built 1910 by Bevington. 2 manuals, 13 speaking stops, 13 couplers, 8 pistons. Tubular action Blown by hydraulic engine.

WANDSWORTH —St Alban's Church, Streatham. Built 1889 by Walker. 3 manuals, 22 speaking stops, 5 other stops. Organ incomplete Prepared for 30 speaking stops

WANDSWORTH.—St. Barnabas Church, Clapham Common. Built 1899 by Vowles. Cost £1,000. Opened by Dr. Longhurst. 3 manuals, 30 speaking stops, 6 couplers, 1 tremulant. Blown by electric motor. Fine oak case. Organist: Norman Alfred Lilwall. Appointed 1905.

WANDSWORTH.—St. John's Church, Clapham Rise. Built 1912 by Brindley & Foster. 3 manuals, 28 speaking stops, 7 other stops, 24 pneumatic combination accessories, 8 composition pedals. Blown by electric motor.

WANDSWORTH.—St. John the Baptist Church, Putney. Built by Walker. 2 manuals. Organist: Matthew Dunn, A.R.C.M., F.I.S.C.

WANDSWORTH.—St. John the Evangelist Parish Church, Clapham. Built 1883 by Bishop. Restored 1912 by Brindley & Foster. 3 manuals, 28 speaking stops, 16 other stops, 1,632 pipes. Transformers and bringradus pedal. Organist: Thomas Curry.

WANDSWORTH.—St. Leonard's Parish Church, Streatham. Built 1905 by Walker. 3 manuals, 31 speaking stops, 8 other stops. Blown by hydraulic engine. Organist: Cuthbert Harris, MUS. DOC. DUNELM, F.R.C.O.

WANDSWORTH.—St. Margaret's Church, Streatham Hill. Built 1907 by Harrison. 3 manuals, 36 speaking stops, 11 couplers, 4 combination pedals, 8 combination pistons, 1 reversible piston, 2 balanced crescendo pedals. Tubular pneumatic. Blown by Kinetic blower and 5½ h.p. National gas engine. Organist Sydney V. Sherwood, F.R.C.O.

WANDSWORTH.—St. Mary Magdalene Church, Wandsworth Common. Built 1908 by Nicholson. 31 speaking stops, 13 other stops. Pneumatic action, detached console, stop-keys, 28 pneumatic pistons. Tromba on Choir. Special combination action

WANDSWORTH.—St Mary the Virgin Parish Church, Putney. Built 1879 and enlarged 1901 by Walker. 3 manuals, 36 speaking stops, 6 couplers, 7 combination pedals. Tubular pneumatic action added to Pedal organ in 1901. Organist: H. Wharton Wells, F.R.C.O., L.R.A.M., L. MUS. T.C.L.

WANDSWORTH.—St. Peter's Church, Streatham Built 1912 by Hill. 4 manuals, 46 speaking stops, 9 couplers, and tubular pneumatic action. Electric blowing. Organist: B. Greek-Stoneman.

WANDSWORTH.—Trinity Presbyterian Church, Clapham. Built 1882 by Bevington. 3 manuals, 36 speaking stops, 14 couplers Part tubular pneumatic. Hand blown. Organist: Colin MacAlpin.

WANDSWORTH.—Trinity Road Baptist Church, Upper Tooting. Built 1906 by Bevington. 2 manuals, 15 speaking stops, 5 other stops. Tubular action. Blown by hand. Organist: Arthur G. Webb.

WANDSWORTH.—Wesleyan Church, High Street, Clapham. Built by Hunter. Opened by Alfred Hollins. 3 manuals, 34 speaking stops, 8 other stops. Blown by two hand blowers. Organist: Wesley Hammet, A.R.C.O.

WANDSWORTH.—Wesleyan Church, Putney. Restored and enlarged 1906 by Binns. Opened by present organist. 3 manuals, 30 speaking stops, 11 other stops, 2,000 pipes. Pneumatic action throughout.

Pedals concave radiating : each manual on different wind pressure. Feeders and large reservoir in chamber beneath organ Organist : John Curran, F.R.C.O.

WEST DULWICH —See CAMBERWELL.

WESTMINSTER —ABBEY, THE. Built 1895 by Hill 5 manuals and pedal, 78 speaking stops, 22 couplers, 10 pneumatic combination pedals, 10 combination pistons, 3 crescendo pedals, 3 tremulants. Organist : Sir Frederick Bridge, C.V O , M A., MUS. DOC. OXON.

WESTMINSTER.—ALL SAINTS' CHURCH, GROSVENOR ROAD Built 1876 by Bevington. 2 manuals, 15 speaking stops, 7 couplers.

WESTMINSTER —CHRIST CHURCH, MAYFAIR. Built by Bevington. Restored 1906 and (after fire) enlarged 1911 by Bevington 2 manuals, 15 speaking stops, 5 other stops, 820 pipes. Part tubular Blown by electric motor. Organist : J. Herbert Olding, A.R.C.O., F. GLD. O.

WESTMINSTER.—CHURCH HOUSE. Built 1899 by Lewis Gift of The Hon Richard Strutt. 3 manuals and pedal, 30 speaking stops, 8 couplers, 1,764 pipes, 6 combination pedals Tremulant, balanced Swell pedal, balanced Crescendo. Electro pneumatic action

WESTMINSTER —CLAVERTON STREET WESLEYAN CHURCH Built 1888-93 by Bevington Opened by Ralph Dunstan, MUS DOC 2 manuals, 18 speaking stops, 5 other stops, 1,096 pipes. Blown by hand Tubular pneumatic action to pedals Organist : A. White Comben.

WESTMINSTER —FARM STREET R.C CHURCH. Built by A Grammont, Belgium. 3 manuals, 50 speaking stops. Organist : John Francis Brewer.

WESTMINSTER.—FRENCH PROTESTANT EPISCOPAL CHURCH OF THE SAVOY, SHAFTESBURY AVENUE. Built 1870 by Bryceson. Opened by A. L. Tamplin Improved by builders 1886, when a new pedal clavier and another stop in the Swell organ were inserted. Enlarged 1892, when 5 stops to Great organ and wind reservoir were added under the superintendence of present organist 2 manuals (3 prepared for), 15 speaking stops, 3 couplers. Organist : W. H. Treffry.

WESTMINSTER.—HOLY TRINITY CHURCH, KINGSWAY. Rebuilt 1894 by Walker. Opened by Dr. E H. Turpin Rebuilt (upon rebuilding of Church) 1911 by Hill. 2 manuals, 18 speaking stops, 3 couplers. Choir organ prepared for. 6 composition pedals Organist : Miss Maria J Cope

WESTMINSTER —KING's COLLEGE. Built 1854 by Willis, London 3 manuals 40 stops. Organist : John Edward Vernham.

WESTMINSTER.—KING's COLLEGE HOSPITAL CHAPEL. Built 1889 by H. Jones 2 manuals, 10 speaking stops, 2 composition pedals. Blown by hydraulic power. Organist . Miss Maria J. Cope

WESTMINSTER.—LINCOLN's INN CHAPEL. Built by Hill Rebuilt and enlarged 1905 by Norman & Beard. 3 manuals, 36 speaking stops, 8 couplers, 10 composition pedals, 11 pistons, tremulant by pedal. Spring Swell pedal Organist and Director of Choir : Reginald Steggall, F.R.A.M., Professor R A M.

WESTMINSTER.—LONDON COLLEGE OF MUSIC. Built 1906 by Rieger Bros. 3 manuals, 21 speaking stops, 15 other stops, 1,244 pipes. Balanced swell and choir pedal. Tubular pneumatic action. Blown by electric motor. Oak case and silvered front pipes. Organist. George Augustus Holmes, Director of Examinations, L.C.M.

WESTMINSTER.—MARLBOROUGH HOUSE CHAPEL. Built by Snetzler. Enlarged 1863 by Hill. 2 manuals, 16 speaking stops, 2 other stops.

WESTMINSTER.—NATIONAL SCOTTISH CHURCH. Built 1910 by Bevington. 3 manuals, 24 speaking stops, and 9 other stops. Tubular action. Blown by electricity. Organist: G. H. Rees.

WESTMINSTER.—ST. BARNABAS CHURCH. Built 1852 by Flight. 3 manuals, 40 speaking stops, 37 other stops. Tubular pneumatic action. Controlled pneumatic switches. Organist: William J. Phillips, MUS. DOC OXON, F.R.C.O., A.R.C.M.

WESTMINSTER.—ST. JOHN THE EVANGELIST CHURCH. Built 1910 by Hill. 3 manuals, 31 speaking stops, 8 couplers. Placed in West gallery. Tubular pneumatic action throughout. Blown by electric motor operating a " Discus " blower. Organist: E. F. Horner, MUS D., F R C O, 19, Beverley Road, Anerley, S E.

WESTMINSTER.—ST MARGARET'S CHURCH. Built 1897 by Walker. Opened by E. H. Lemare. 3 manuals, 48 speaking stops, 14 couplers. Blown by two electric motors. Organist and Choirmaster: Reginald Goss Custard.

WESTMINSTER.—ST. MARTIN'S-IN-THE-FIELDS CHURCH. Built 1854 by Bevington. Rebuilt and enlarged 1912 by Hill. 3 manuals, 39 speaking stops, 12 couplers. Tubular pneumatic action throughout. Handsome case. Choir organ in separate case behind player. Organist William John Kipps, A.R.A.M., F.R.C.O.

WESTMINSTER.—ST. MICHAEL'S CHURCH, CHESTER SQUARE, S.W. Built 1899 by Hope Jones. 4 manuals, 35 speaking stops, 26 other stops. Echo organ at West end, 36 miles of wire. Organist: Thomas J. Crawford, MUS. BAC. (DUNELM), F.R C O., M I.S.M.

WESTMINSTER.—ST. PAUL'S CHURCH, COVENT GARDEN. Built 1862 by Bevington. 3 manuals, 27 speaking stops, 5 couplers. Compass of manuals, CC to A, 58 notes. Pedals CCC to F, 30 notes. Swell organ only going to Tenor C. Organist: Harry E Wall.

WESTMINSTER.—ST. PAUL'S CHURCH, KNIGHTSBRIDGE. Built 1888 by Willis. 4 manuals, 54 stops. Organist: John Edward Vernham.

WESTMINSTER.—ST. PETER'S CHURCH, EATON SQUARE, S.W. Built 1902 by Lewis. 4 manuals and pedal, 67 speaking stops, 14 couplers, 2 tremulants, 33 pistons, 8 combination pedals.

WESTMINSTER.—ST. SAVIOUR'S CHURCH, PIMLICO. 3 manuals, 26 speaking stops, 7 other stops. Organist: Philip Herrmann Coxall, F.R.C.O.

WESTMINSTER.—WESLEYAN CHURCH HOUSE—CENTRAL HALL. Built 1912 by Hill. 4 manuals, 42 speaking stops, 12 couplers, 24 pistons, electric blowing. Tuba and carillon placed in a Swell box with the rest of the Solo organ. Fine case, with two front towers of 32ft. metal open pipes. Organist: J. A. Meale, F.R.C.O.

Provincial Organs.

ABERDARE.—St. Elvan's Church. Built 1888 and rebuilt 1911 by Vowles. 3 manuals, 30 speaking stops, 8 couplers. Console on N. and organ on S. side of chancel. Pneumatic action throughout. Electric blower.

ABERDARE.—Trinity Chapel. Built 1910 by Vowles. 3 manuals. College of Organists' scale of pedals. Pneumatic action throughout. Organist: J. Arkite Phillips.

ABERDEEN.—Beechgrove United Free Church. Built by Abbott & Smith. . 2 manuals and pedal, 26 speaking stops, 5 couplers, Tremulant to Swell, 7 composition pedals. Blown by hydraulic engine and separate feeders. Erected on both sides of Chancel. Detached Console. Tubular pneumatic action throughout. Organist : A. Rebacca, 24, Osborne Road, Aberdeen.

ABERDEEN.—East United Free Church. Built 1901 by Lewis. Destroyed by fire, 1902. Rebuilt by Lewis 1903, to specification by Dr. Peace. 3 manuals, 27 speaking stops, 13 couplers, 1,676 pipes, 7 combination pedals, detached console. Tubular pneumatic action throughout. Concave and radiating pedal board. Organist: T. Ayrton.

ABERDEEN.—Holburn Parish Church. Built 1885 by Harrison. Opened by G. F. Dawson, a.r.c.o. 2 manuals, 22 speaking stops. Organist : William A. Herd.

ABERDEEN.—St. Machar's Cathedral. Built 1892 by Willis. 3 manuals, 33 speaking stops, 9 other stops, about 2,000 pipes. Opened by Dr Peace. Organist : George Cummings Dawson, f.r.c.o.

ABERGAVENNY.—Llanthewy Skirrid Parish Church. Built 1879, and enlarged 1883 by Vowles. Opened 1883 by present organist 2 manuals, 15 speaking stops, 4 couplers, 1,084 pipes, and 4 composition pedals; spotted metal throughout, every stop runs through. Organist : Charles Claggett Caird.

ABERGAVENNY.—St. Mary's Parish Church. Rebuilt by Conacher. 3 manuals, 30 stops. Blown by hydraulic engine. Organist : W. R. Carr, a.r.c.o.

ABERTILLERY.—Parish Church. Built by Vowles. 3 manuals and pedal, 38 speaking stops, 7 couplers, 2 tremulants, 9 pistons, 6 combination pedals, 2 double-acting pedals, 2,084 pipes. Detached console. Pneumatic action throughout. Electric blowing Organist . A. Harding.

ABERYSTWYTH.—English Congregational Church. Built 1876 by Stringer, Hanley. Opened by Prof. J. Parry. Renovated 1903 by Nicholson, Worcester. 2 manuals, 20 speaking stops, 5 other stops. Blown by hand. Organist : G. Stephen Evans, a.r.c.o.

ABERYSTWYTH.—HOLY TRINITY CHURCH. Built by Conacher. 3 manuals (choir prepared), 18 speaking stops, 6 other stops, 964 pipes. Choir organ : 6 stops (2 Gt., 1 Sw , 1 Ped. stop), and 2 couplers (prepared for). Excellent tone, pneumatic action. Organist : Arthur Charles Edwards, MUS. BAC. OXON., F.R.C.O.

ABERYSTWYTH.—WELSH C.M. TABERNACLE CHAPEL. Built 1905 by Harrison Opened by E T. Davies, F.R.C.O. 3 manuals, 27 speaking stops, 7 other stops, 1,490 pipes. Detached console, Swell and Choir crescendo on balanced principle, radiating and concave pedal board. Blown by 2 hydraulic engines. Tubular-pneumatic system throughout. Organist : J. Charles McLean.

ACCRINGTON.—PARISH CHURCH. Built 1835 Restored and enlarged 1880 by Gray and Davison. Memorial to Benjamin Hargreaves, of Arden Hall 2 manuals, 19 stops, etc. Organist : Eli Smith

ACCRINGTON.—ST. PETER'S CHURCH. Built 1907 by Abbott & Smith. Opened by Dr. Pyne. 3 manuals, 38 speaking stops, 9 other stops and 2,174 pipes. Organist : S. H. Fielding.

ACCRINGTON.—UNION STREET WESLEYAN CHAPEL. Restored 1904 by Jardine Re-opened by present organist. 3 manuals, 28 speaking stops, 7 other stops, 5 composition and 1 reversible pedals. Organist : William Spencer Walker.

ACTON —ALL SAINTS' CHURCH, SOUTH ACTON. Built 1874 by Walker. Enlarged 1887 by Bishop. 3 manuals, 36 speaking stops, 8 other stops, 2,086 pipes. Tubular pneumatic action. A complete set of composition pedals to Great, Swell, and Pedal. Organist : T. King Holtham.

ACTON —CONGREGATIONAL CHURCH. Built by Gray & Davison. Restored 1903 by Noble. 2 manuals, 20 speaking stops, 4 couplers. Organist : Charles Edgcome Richards, F.R C.O.

ACTON.—ST. DUNSTAN'S CHURCH. Built 1912 by Hill Tubular pneumatic action. 23 speaking stops, 7 couplers.

ADDLESTON.—ST. PAUL'S CHURCH. Rebuilt 1911 by Vincent. Opened by E. W. Gayton 3 manuals, 34 stops. Tubular pneumatic action. Electric blower.

ALDERSHOT —ST. GEORGE'S CHURCH (Military). Built 1908 by Hele. Opened by Dr. Prendergast 2 manuals, 29 speaking stops, 4 couplers, 1,494 pipes, 8 composition pedals Great to pedal off and on by pedal. Console detached Blown by electric motor. Organist : Arthur C. Goodyear.

ALDERSHOT.—ST. PETER'S PARISH CHURCH, ASH. Built 1902 by Martin and Coate, to specification by present organist. 2 manuals, 15 speaking stops, 4 other stops. Admired for its exceptional beauty of tone. Organist : William Henry Bates, F G O.

ALFRETON —PRIMITIVE METHODIST ZION CHURCH, SOUTH NORMANTON. Built by Steele and Keay, Burslem. 2 manuals, 14 speaking stops, 4 couplers, 748 pipes. Case of selected pitch pine.

ALNWICK.—ST. PAUL'S CHURCH. Built 1887 by Nicholson, Newcastle-on-Tyne. Opened by T. H Collison, MUS. BAC. 3 manuals, 26 speaking stops, 6 other stops. Blown by electric motor

ALSAGER, CHESHIRE —St. Mary Magdalene Church. Built 1905 by Steele & Keay, Burslem. Opened by C. W. Perkins. 3 manuals, 37 speaking stops, 8 other stops. Organist: Gilbert H. Greenwood, MUS. BAC.

ALTON.—All Saints' Church. Built 1884 by Hill. Opened by Humphrey Stark, MUS. BAC. OXON. 2 manuals, 15 speaking stops, 4 other stops and 750 pipes. Pedals, straight and concave. Organist: Henry Piggott, MUS. BAC., L. MUS. T.C.L.

ALTON.—St. Lawrence's Parish Church. Built 1866 and restored 1898 by Henry Speechly. Opened by Dr. W. G. Alcock. 3 manuals, 34 speaking stops, 6 couplers, tremulant, and 1,944 pipes. Blown by 2 h.p. gas engine. Tubular pneumatic action. Decorated pipes. Organist: James Everitt, MUS. BAC. D_URHAM.

ALTRINCHAM.—Christ Church, Timperley (Parish Church). Built 1899 by Wadsworth. Opened by Dr. Pyne. 3 manuals, 24 speaking stops, 4 other stops. Very fine diapasons. Good reeds. Organist: H. Mozart Sheaves, MUS. BAC. (VICT.), F.R.C.O., A.R.C.M., A.R.M.C.M.

ALTRINCHAM.—St. George's Church. Built 1903 by Brindley & Foster. 3 manuals, 29 speaking stops, 8 couplers, and 6 composition pedals. Blown by Crossley gas engine. Organist: W. H. Holloway.

ALTRINCHAM —St. John the Evangelist Church. Built 1886 by Jardine. Restored 1901 by Wadsworth. Re-opened by W. Henry Maxfield. 3 manuals, 30 speaking stops and 7 other stops. Action, Tracker—tubular pneumatic. Organist: W. Henry Maxfield, MUS. BAC., F.R.C.O.

AMESBURY —Parish Church. Built 1888 by Monk. Rebuilt and renovated 1910. 2 manuals, 19 speaking stops, 3 couplers. Built on screen with console under organ. Tubular pneumatic action. Organist and Choirmaster: Edmund J. Brown.

ARDROSSAN.—New Parish Church. Built 1889 by Wadsworth. Restored 1902 by Ingram. Organist: James Broom Lawson.

ARMAGH —Ancient Cathedral of St. Patrick. Built 1839 by Walker. 3 manuals (Compass, *fff* to F in Alt), 21 speaking stops, 3 couplers. Originally placed on gallery, South Transept; removed to North Transept and enlarged, 1854; rebuilt, 1870, and compass altered to CC to F 54 notes, etc. Has a remarkably sweet tone, diapasons being particularly good. Organist: T. Osborne Marks, MUS. BAC. OXON., MUS. DOC. T.C.D.

ARUNDEL.—Parish Church. Built about 1814 by two amateur musicians. Restored by Walker and Corps. Tuned and regulated since 1876 by Hill. New case, new pedals, and tubular pneumatic action, to pedal organ have also been added. 3 manuals, 28 stops, and 1 prepared for (intended for Clarion). Organist: Edward Bartlett, F.R C.O.

ASCOT.—All Saints' Church. Built 1866 by Hill. 2 manuals, 17 speaking stops and 3 couplers. Organist: William Millard.

ASHBOURNE.—Wesleyan Church. Built by Steele & Keay. 2 manuals and pedal, 18 speaking stops, 4 couplers, 6 double-acting composition pedals, self-balancing crescendo pedal. Tubular pneumatic action to Pedal. Pitch pine case. Organist: A. H. Osborne, The Ivies, Ashbourne, Derbyshire.

ASHTON-IN-MAKERFIELD.—CONGREGATIONAL CHURCH Built 1875 by Conacher. Renovated and enlarged 1901 by Whiteley. Opened by H. Cooke Re-opened by Jas. Dawber 2 manuals, 21 speaking stops, 4 other stops, and 1,240 pipes. Blown by hydraulic engine. Organist: William Aspinall; Deputy: Samuel Hart.

ASHTON-UNDER-LYNE —ALBION CONGREGATIONAL CHURCH Built 1894 by Lewis Opened by Dr Peace 4 manuals, 43 speaking stops, 7 other stops, tubular pneumatic throughout. Blown by gas engine Organist: Charles Stanley Grundy, MUS. B. DUNELM, L R.A.M.

ASHTON-UNDER-LYNE.—CHRIST CHURCH. Built 1901 by Wadsworth. Opened by Dr. Pyne. 3 manuals, 28 speaking stops, 6 other stops, 1,666 pipes. Organist: Albert Edward Knott, A.R.C.O., M I.S M.

ASHTON-UNDER-LYNE —ST. MICHAEL'S PARISH CHURCH. Built 1845 by Hill. Restored 1889 by Wordsworth, and in 1904 by Norman and Beard 3 manuals, 47 stops. Tubular pneumatic action. Blown by electric motor, working by crank shaft upon 3 vertical feeders. Organist: George Frederick Wrigley.

ASHTON-UNDER-LYNE.—WESLEYAN CHURCH, STAMFORD STREET Built 1875, and rebuilt 1904 by Young, Manchester. Opened by Charles Wrigley and Irvine Dearnaley. 3 manuals, 30 speaking stops, 6 couplers, 1,639 pipes Tracker action throughout. Blown by two hand levers. Organist and Choirmaster: James Buckley Thompson.

ASHTON - UPON - MERSEY.—ST. MARY MAGDALENE PARISH CHURCH. Built 1875 by Jardine 3 manuals, 28 speaking stops, 7 other stops. Organist: J. A Ingham.

AXMINSTER.—PARISH CHURCH. Built 1905 by Norman and Beard. 3 manuals, 28 speaking stops, pedal board concave and radiating. Balanced Swell pedal. Organist: Chas. F. Seymour, A.L C.M.

AYR.—DARLINGTON PLACE U.F. CHURCH. Built 1898 by Brindley and Foster 2 manuals, 27 stops. 4 " Brinovus " pistons to each keyboard. Pneumatic action. Blown by hydraulic engine. Organist: Ernest E. Mills.

AYR.—NEW PARISH CHURCH. Built 1901 by Norman & Beard. Gift of J. L. Holdsworth, Esq 3 manuals, 9 stops Great, 11 stops Swell, 7 stops Choir, 4 stops Pedal; 8 couplers; Tremulant to Swell, Tremulant to Choir, 7 composition pedals; 7 pistons; Choir in Swell box; Swell do Tubular pneumatic action. Hydraulic engines Organist and Choirmaster D. H. Markham-Lee, M I.S M., A.R.C O

AYR.—NEWTOWN PARISH CHURCH. Built 1910 by Vincent. 3 manuals, 35 stops. Pneumatic action. Detached console. Electric blower. Organist: W. Kennedy.

AYR.—ST. LEONARD'S PARISH CHURCH. Built 1890 by Harrison Rebuilt and enlarged 1910 by Vincent. 3 manuals, 36 stops, 4 pistons and 4 composition pedals to Swell, 3 pistons and 3 pedals to Great, 3 pistons to Pedal. Pneumatic action Blown by electric motor, 2½ B.H.P. Organist John Mactaggart, A.R.C.M., L.R.A.M., F.T.S.C., etc.

BALLATER —CRATHIE PARISH CHURCH, BALMORAL. Built 1895 by Willis, Rebuilt and enlarged 1911 by Vincent. Opened by Mr John Kirby. 3 manuals, 16 speaking stops, 5 other stops, and 616 pipes. Organist: Samuel S. Page.

BANBURY.—PARISH CHURCH. Built by Snetzler. Restored 1874 by Walker. Altered and added to 1882 by Martin, Oxford. 3 manuals, 29 stops (few of Snetzler's). Organist : W. C. Luttman.

BANGOR.—CATHEDRAL, THE. Built 1873 by Hill, rebuilt 1897 4 manuals, 64 speaking stops, 23 other stops, 3,742 pipes. Blown by hydraulic engine. French pitch. Tubular pneumatic action throughout. Detached console 3 balanced crescendo pedals. Organist. Roland Rogers, MUS. DOC. OXON.

BANGOR.—TWRGWYN CHAPEL. Built 1900 by Conacher. 2 manuals. Tubular Pneumatic action. Blown by electric motor, Organist : Miss Olwen Rowlands.

BARNET —SOUTH MIMS CHURCH. Built 1894 by Bevington. 2 manuals, 15 speaking stops, 3 couplers, 4 composition pedals, and swell pedal. Blown by hand Organist : H. N Clarke

BARNSLEY.—PARISH CHURCH. Old portion built 1785 ; restored 1820-45-64-85-1903 New portion built by Brindley & Foster. 3 manuals, 31 speaking stops, couplers, etc Pneumatic action. Blown by electric motor. Organist : H. N. Horton, F.R.C.O., A R.C.M.

BARNSLEY.—ST. GEORGE'S CHURCH. Built 1824 by Greenwood, Leeds. Restored 1893 by Binns. Re-opened by Dr. Peace. 3 manuals, 33 speaking stops, 12 other stops, and 1,998 pipes. Binn's tubular pneumatic action throughout. Compass CC to C, 61 notes Hydraulic blowing apparatus with Ch. and Sw. organs enclosed in Sw boxes. Balanced pedals. Organist Bernard Langdale, L I S M., A R.C.O

BARROWFORD.—PARISH CHURCH Built 1871 by Bevington. 2 manuals, 18 speaking stops, 9 couplers, etc.

BATH.—CHRIST CHURCH. Built 1800 by Avery. Rebuilt 1887 by Vowles. Re-voiced and added to 1892 by Sweetland, and Griffen & Stroud. 3 manuals, CC to G, 31 speaking stops, and 6 other stops Tracker action ; T pedal on and off Gr. to pedals ; 6 composition pedals. Blown by Ross hydraulic valve engine, with automatic starter. Organist : Henry James Davis, L R A M.

BATH —ST. ANDREW'S CHURCH, WALCOT. Restored by Griffen & Stroud. 3 manuals, 37 speaking stops, and 8 other stops. Hydraulic blowing. Organist : Frederick E Hollingshead, F R C O , A.R.C.M.

BATH —ST. JAMES' CHURCH. Built 1781 by Richard Seed, Bristol. Restored and enlarged 1902, and electric motor for blowing installed 1906 by Griffen & Stroud. Opened 1903 by Sir Frederick Bridge, C.V O 3 manuals, 34 speaking stops, and 6 couplers Was originally a GG organ of 2 manuals, 13 stops, without pedals. Choir organ added 1800, small Pedal organ, 1811. Organist : Herbert Charles Toms Gill, A.R.C O

BATH —ST. MARK'S CHURCH Restored by Vowles, 1900 2 manuals (Choir organ prepared for), 20 speaking stops, 6 couplers Blown by hand. Organist : S. M. Popplestone, F.R.C O

BATH.—ST. MATTHEW'S CHURCH. Built 1896 by Norman & Beard. Opened by Percy Buck 2 manuals, 24 speaking stops, 3 couplers and tremulant to swell, 1,412 pipes. Organist : L. C. Cooper.

BATH.—St. Michael's Church. Built 1846 and restored 1900 by Sweetland. 2 manuals, 21 speaking stops, 6 other stops, 1,148 pipes. Organist : Henry Keel, appointed 1907.

BATH.—St. Paul's Church. Built 1896-7 by Griffen & Stroud. Opened
by T. W. Dodds, MUS. DOC. 3 manuals, 35 speaking stops, 7 other
stops, and 2,042 pipes; 7 composition pedals. Builders' Pneumatic
action applied to manual and pedal organs. Blown by two hydraulic
engines. Organist : Herbert Jeffrey Harding, F.I.G.C.M.

BATTLE.—St. Mary's Church. Built 1869 by Bevington. 3 manuals,
24 speaking stops, 10 couplers. Organist : Bertram Weller, Speedwell,
Clepbourne Road, Bexhill

BECKENHAM.—Congregational Church. Built 1907 by Hunter.[?] 3
manuals, 43 speaking stops, 9 couplers, 21 pistons. Tubular pneumatic
throughout. 2 water engines. Reeds spotted metal throughout.
Organist : E. W. Lewis.

BEDALE.—Parish Church (St. Gregory's). Rebuilt 1890 by Abbott &
Smith. 2 manuals, 21 speaking stops, 3 couplers, and 6 composition
pedals. Choir organ prepared for. Organist : Charles Frank Rowden.

BEDFORD.—Bunyan Meeting House. Built 1867 by Forster & Andrews.
Opened by R. Rose. 2 manuals, 23 speaking stops, 3 other stops,
1,424 pipes. Organist : Thomas James Ford.

BEDFORD.—Grammar School Chapel. Built 1907. 2 manuals and 14
speaking stops. Organist : H. A. Harding.

BEDFORD.—Holy Trinity Church. Built 1891 by Walker. 3 manuals,
33 stops. Organist : Henry T. Tiltman, F.R.C.O., L.R.A.M.

BEDFORD.—Modern School, (Boys). Built 1881 by Trustam, Bedford.
3 manuals, 21 speaking stops, 7 couplers, 5 composition pedals. Organist : Henry William Stewardson, F.T.C.L.

BEDFORD.—Moravian Church, St. Peter's. Built 1715 by Gerhard
Schmidt. Restored 1888 by Brindley & Foster. 3 manuals, 27 speaking
stops, 7 other stops. Blown by electric rotasphere, tubular pneumatic
throughout. Diapason tone and reeds good. Organist : E. Bandey.

BEDFORD.—St. Cuthbert's Church. Built 1880 by Trustam ; enlarged
1912 by Speechley. 2 manuals, 26 speaking stops, 3 couplers, 6 composition pedals. Blown by hydraulic engine. Oak case. Organist :
John Henry Adams, A.R.C O., L.R.A.M.

BEDFORD.—St. Paul's Church. Built 1898 by Norman & Beard. 3
manuals, 45 stops. Organist : H. A. Harding, MUS. DOC. OXON,
F.R C.O., L.R.A.M., also Corporation Organist and Hon. Sec. Royal
College of Organists.

BEDFORD.—St. Paul's Wesleyan Church Built 1869 by Wadsworth ;
restored 1900 by Norman & Beard. Opened by Henry Rose ; re-
opened by P. H. Diemer, R.A.M. Presented by Sir Frederick Howard,
J.P. 3 manuals, 32 speaking stops, 9 other stops, 1,848 pipes. R.C.O.
pedals. Tracker action. Very fine diapasons ; excellent wood flute
stops. Blown by hydraulic engine. Organist : W. H. Nutting.

BEDFORD.—St. Peter de Merton, Parish Church. Built 1903 by Binns. Opened by present organist. 3 manuals, 25 speaking stops, 11 other stops and 1,365 pipes. Choir organ over choir stalls, remainder in recess on North side. Detached console. Organist. Samuel William Churchill, A R C M., L.R.A.M., A.R C.O.

BELFAST.—Fisherwick Presbyterian Church. Built 1901 by Walker. 2 manuals, 25 speaking stops, 6 couplers, 8 composition pedals, double-acting pedal-controlling Great to Pedal coupler, balanced Sw. Ped., tremulant by pedal, pedal board radiating and concave. Tubular pneumatic action to manuals, pedals and drawstops Blown by electricity ; hand-blowing apparatus in case of emergency. Organist : Thomas H. Crowe.

BELFAST.—St. Anne's Cathedral. Built 1906 by Harrison. 3 manuals, 48 speaking stops, 15 couplers, 6 combination pedals, 11 combination pistons, 3 patent adjustable pistons, 2 balanced crescendo pedals. Tubular pneumatic action Blown by 3 hydraulic engines. Organist : Charles John Brennan, mus. bac. (dunelm), f.r.c o , l.r.a.m.

BELFAST —SS. Philip and James' Church, Holywood. Built and restored 1897 by Forster & Andrews. 3 manuals. Organist : E. Godfrey Brown.

BELFAST.—St. James' Church Rebuilt by Hill. 3 manuals, 31 speaking stops, 6 couplers. Tubular pneumatic action. Hydraulic blowing. Organist : Laurence Walker, mus. doc., a.r.c.o.

BELFAST —St. Thomas's Church. Rebuilt 1906 by Hill. Opened by Dr. J. O. Marks. 3 manuals, 33 speaking stops, 9 other stops. Originally a 2-manual tracker, but rebuilt in tubular pneumatic throughout. One of the finest church organs in Belfast Organist : W. H. Derrick-Large.

BELFAST.—Ulster Hall. Built 1863 and restored 1903 by Hill. 4 manuals, 62 speaking stops, couplers, etc. Tubular action. Organist : Charles John Brennan, mus. bac. (dunelm), f r c o., l.r a m.

BELPER —Wesleyan ° Church. Built 1873 by Faulkner, Manchester. Rebuilt 1896 by Cousans, Lincoln. Re-opened by W. H. Richardson, a.r c o 2 manuals, 19 speaking stops, 5 other stops, and 1,200 pipes, 6 composition pedals. Tubular pneumatic action. Organist : John B. Gough.

BERWICK-ON-TWEED —Parish Church Built 1905 by Harrison 3 manuals, 12 stops on Great, 12 on Swell, 10 on Choir, 7 on Pedal, and 7 couplers Organist : Charles Trevor Gauntlett.

BEVERLEY.—Minster, the. Built 1767 by Snetzler Rebuilt 1885 by Hill. Re-opened by Dr. Naylor. 4 manuals, 58 speaking stops, 10 other stops and 3,576 pipes. Originally GGG organ, Pedal 24ft pipes added 1846, continued in present organ to CCCC, 32ft. reed, 16ft and 8ft tubas on Solo, 2 gemshorns, 8ft. and 4ft on Swell, old tierces retained in the mixtures. Organist : John Camidge.

BEVERLEY.—St. Mary's Church. Built 1908 by Lewis to specification by present organist. 3 manuals, 53 speaking stops, 12 couplers, tubular pneumatic action throughout. Blown by hydraulic engine (Watkins

& Watson). 3 tremulants, 7 combination pedals, 31 pistons, 3 balanced pedals, balanced crescendo pedal over entire organ. Organist: C. Carte Doorly.

BEXHILL-ON-SEA.—ST. BARNABAS' CHURCH. Built by Norman and Beard. Opened by Dr. W. S. Hoyte. 3 manuals, 25 speaking stops, 8 couplers and 1,388 pipes. Pneumatic action. Pedals radiating and concave, R.C.O. pattern. Balanced Swell pedal, D to Swell and Choir. Very fine organ, especially diapasons. Blown by Watkins' & Watson's "Discus" Blower. Organist: Albert Percy Howe, Mus. Bac., F.R.C.O., L. MUS. T.C.L.

BEXHILL-ON-SEA.—ST PETER'S OLD PARISH CHURCH. Built 1891 by Hunter. 3 manuals, 32 speaking stops, 8 other stops, 6 pneumatic pistons. Fine oak case on North side of Chancel. Rebuilt by Norman & Beard 1908. Organist: T. S. Guyer, F.R C.O.

BEXLEY.—CHRIST CHURCH. Built 1892 by Hunter. Opened by Percy Starnes. 2 manuals, 22 speaking stops, and 6 couplers. Sound boards carried an octave beyond manuals, thus making the supers effective throughout Organist: Edmund Whomes.

BICESTER.—ST EDBURG'S CHURCH. Built by Gray and Davison. 2 manuals, 11 speaking stops, 2 other stops and 559 pipes.

BICKLEY —ST. GEORGE'S CHURCH. Built 1909 by Hill. 37 speaking stops, 9 couplers. Tubular pneumatic action. Detached console. Electric blowing Organist: W. G. Clarke.

BIRKENHEAD.—ALL SAINTS' CHURCH, OXTON —Built 1880 by Hall, Birkenhead. Restored 1911 by Rushworth & Dreaper 2 manuals, 13 speaking stops, 3 other stops. Blown by hand.

BIRKENHEAD.—PRENTON PARISH CHURCH. Built 1899 by Conacher Opened by F. H. Burstall. Restored 1909 by Gray & Davison. Re-opened by present Organist. 3 manuals, 30 speaking stops and 10 other stops Tubular pneumatic throughout. Blown by electric motor. Organist: C. Whitaker-Wilson

BIRKENHEAD.—ST. ANNE'S CHURCH. Built by Willis. Removed from North Transept to Chancel, 1893, by Hardy, Stockport. Opened by present organist. 2 manuals, 24 speaking stops, 4 other stops and 1,308 pipes. Tubular pneumatic action to pedal organ only. Organist: Millward Hughes.

BIRKENHEAD —ST. JAMES' CHURCH. Built 1906 by Rushworth & Dreaper. 3 manuals, 30 speaking stops, 9 couplers, 9 composition pedals. Tubular pneumatic action throughout. Blown by electric motor. Organist: H. Hall-Jones.

BIRKENHEAD.—ST. MARK'S CHURCH. Built 1892 by Willis. 3 manuals, 34 speaking stops, 6 other stops, 1,860 pipes. Pneumatic action throughout Reeds and diapasons particularly fine. Organist: Benjamin Sandberg Lee.

BIRKENHEAD.—ST MARY'S PARISH CHURCH. Built 1911 by Rushworth & Dreaper. 3 manuals, 32 speaking stops, 10 couplers, 8 composition pedals, 4 pistons. Tubular pneumatic action throughout. Blown by electric motor. Organist: G. Hutchence.

BIRKENHEAD.—St. Paul's Presbyterian Church. Built 1886 by Young, Manchester. Rebuilt 1900. 2 manuals, 22 speaking stops, 5 other stops, 1,281 pipes, centre balanced swell pedal, 8 composition pedals. Console extended out so as to be nearer choir. Organist: Henry Glynn Wylie.

BIRKENHEAD.—St. Peter's Parish Church, Rock Ferry. Built by Willis. 3 manuals, 30 speaking stops, 5 other stops. Blown by hydraulic engine. Great organ stops on left of player. Organist: Robert Wordsworth Davies.

BIRKENHEAD.—St. Saviour's Church, Oxton. Built 1897 by Hope Jones. Rebuilt and converted to tubular pneumatic action 1908 by Norman & Beard. 3 manuals, 42 stops. Wind pressure from 6 to 15 inches. Wind supplied by two Kinetic Blowers, driven by 7½ h.p. electric motor. Organist: R. E. Parker, F.R.C.O.

BIRMINGHAM.—Aston Parish Church. Built 1901 by Banfield. 3 manuals, 30 speaking stops, 8 couplers. Tubular pneumatic action throughout. Organist: Thos. F. Thomason, MUS. BAC.

BIRMINGHAM.—Birchfields Wesleyan Church, Mansfield Road, Aston. Built by Young. 2 manuals and pedal, 9 speaking stops, 4 couplers, 2 double-acting compositions. Balanced Swell. Organist: Frank Lowe.

BIRMINGHAM.—Bristol Road Wesleyan Church. Built 1910 by Steele & Keay. 2 manuals and pedal, 26 speaking stops, 5 couplers, 8 combination pistons, 1 reversible pedal, self-balancing crescendo pedal. Tubular pneumatic action throughout. Pitch pine case. Organist: D. Jameson.

BIRMINGHAM.—Christ Church, Summerfield. Built 1889 by Nicholson (Worcester). Opened by present organist. 3 manuals, 24 speaking stops, 6 other stops, 1,478 pipes, 6 composition pedals, crescendo pedal to Swell, Gt. to pedals on and off, and tremulant pedal. Organist: T. Johnson, MUS. BAC. CANTAB.

BIRMINGHAM.—Edgbaston Parish Church. Built 1891 by Hill. 3 manuals, 31 speaking stops, 8 other stops and 6 composition pedals. Balanced Swell pedal. Kinetic electric blower. Tubular pneumatic action throughout. Organist: Henry Taylor, MUS. BAC. CANTAB., F.R.C.O.

BIRMINGHAM.—Hagley Road Baptist Church. Rebuilt 1882 by Bevington. 2 manuals, 24 speaking stops, 10 other stops. Organist: Herbert Grice.

BIRMINGHAM.—Handsworth Parish Church. Built 1895 by Gray & Davison; rebuilt 1906 by Norman & Beard. 3 manuals, 45 stops. Tubular pneumatic action. Blown by electric power, Kinetic blower. Organist: Alfred J. Silver, MUS. DOC. DUNELM, F.R.C.O.

BIRMINGHAM.—Harborne Parish Church. Built 1884 by Conacher. 3 manuals, 37 stops. Blown by hand. Erected on North side of Chancel. Organist: Franklyn Mountford, A.R.C.M., L.R.A.M.

BIRMINGHAM.—King's Heath Parish Church. Built 1892 by Flight & Robson. 2 manuals, 25 speaking stops, 5 other stops, and 6 composition pedals. Opened by J. H. Maunder. Organist: J. Thomas.

BIRMINGHAM.—Moseley Parish Church. Built 1887 by Jones. 3 manuals, 31 speaking stops, 6 other stops and 2 composition levers to Sw., and 2 to Gt. and tremulant. Organist: George Howard Mann.

BIRMINGHAM.—St. Anne's Church, Moseley. Built 1907 by Brindley & Foster. 2 manuals, 25 speaking stops, 5 couplers, 1,402 pipes, 5 double acting composition pedals to Great, 5 to Swell, 7 transformers to Swell, pneumatic transference of Swell reeds to Great manual, and 3 " Cut outs," controlled by draw stops. Organist: W. Berridge-Hicks.

BIRMINGHAM.—St. Barnabas Church, Ryland Place. Rebuilt 1889 by Bevington. 3 manuals, 27 speaking stops, 13 couplers, etc. Organist: John W. Brittain.

BIRMINGHAM.—St. Clement's Church, Nechells. Built for St. James', West Derby, Liverpool, 1846 by Bewsher & Fleetwood. Removed to this Church and added to, 1869. Restored 1906 by Halmshaw & King 2 manuals and pedals, 20 speaking stops, 5 couplers, 1,036 pipes. Manual blowing. Open diapasion and harmonic flute (4ft) in Great organ are particularly good stops. Organist and Choirmaster. H. A. Needham.

BIRMINGHAM.—St. George's Church, Edgbaston. Built 1890 by Brindley and Foster. Opened by present organist. 3 manuals, 30 speaking stops, 10 other stops. Blown by hand. Organist: C. J. B Meacham, MUS. BAC. CANTAB.

BIRMINGHAM.—St. James' Church, Handsworth Built 1909 by Norman & Beard. Opened by C. W. Perkins. 3 manuals, 38 speaking stops, 9 other stops, 2,300 pipes, 11 pistons, 8 composition pedals, 1 reversible pedal. Tubular pneumatic action throughout. Kinetic blower, worked by electric motor. Radiating and concave pedal board Magnificent tone. Organist: Alfred G. Smith, F.R.C O, L R A M.

BIRMINGHAM.—St. John's Church, Ladywood. Built 1858-1881 by Bevington. 3 manuals, 31 speaking stops, 10 other stops. Blown by hand. Organist: W. E Robinson, F R C.O, L.R.A.M.

BIRMINGHAM.—St. Martin's Parish Church. Built by Harrison, 1906. 3 manuals, 61 speaking stops, 15 couplers, 3,600 pipes, 5 combination pedals, 15 combination pistons, 3 patent adjustable pistons, 2 reversible pistons, 1 reversible pedal, 2 balanced crescendo pedals Blown by a 7½ h p. electric motor. Tubular pneumatic action throughout. Organist: Dr. W. John Reynolds.

BIRMINGHAM.—St. Paul's Church. Rebuilt 1871 by Bevington. 3 manuals, 25 speaking stops, 11 couplers, etc.

BIRMINGHAM.—St. Paul's Church, Balsall Heath Built by Willis. Restored 1902 by Positive Co. Opened by C. W. Perkins. 3 manuals, (Solo and Choir on one), 36 speaking stops, 19 other stops, and 2,152 pipes. Casson's pedal helps, divided pedal and melody attachment. Organist: John Heywood, M.I.S.M.

BIRMINGHAM.—St. Philip's Cathedral. Built 1715 by Schwarbrick. Re-constructed 1804 by England; 1892 by Nicholson (Worcester). 34 speaking stops, 10 other stops. Removed 1883 from West to East end Fine front. Modern set of pedals up to G have been added, with 32ft. Acoustic Bass from Pedal open, and reeds re-tongued. Organist: Edwin Stephenson.

BIRMINGHAM.—THE OLD MEETING CHURCH. Built 1909 by Harrison. Gift of Mrs. Charles Harding. 3 manuals, 45 speaking stops, 16 couplers, 10 composition pedals, 16 combination pistons, 2 reversible pistons, 3 reversible pedals, 2 balanced crescendo pedals to Solo and swell organs. Tubular pneumatic action throughout, except to pedal coupling action which is mechanical. Wind pressures vary from 4 to 12 inches; 7 reservoirs in the organ. Low " French " pitch (c 517 vibrations). Blown by 6 h.p. electric motor. Stands in lofty chamber on North side of Chancel. Organist: A. J. Cotton, 10, Grove Avenue, Moseley, Birmingham.

BIRMINGHAM.—THE ORATORY CHURCH. Built 1909 by Nicholson. 3 manuals, 42 speaking stops, 16 other stops, 14 to be added later. 45 pneumatic pistons, 13 stops on Pedal, including double open, 32ft. 9 miles of pneumatic tubing. Stop keys and special combination knobs. Blown by fan and 6 h.p. electric motor. 2 balanced swell pedals. Heavy claribella on Great organ.

BIRMINGHAM.—TOWN HALL. Built 1834. Restored 1890 by Hill. 4 manuals, 68 speaking stops, 9 other stops, 4,350 pipes. Blown by hydraulic engine. Organist: C. W. Perkins.

BIRMINGHAM.—WARWICK ROAD WESLEYAN CHURCH, SPARKHILL. Built 1909 by Steele & Keay. 2 manuals and pedal, 25 speaking stops, 4 couplers, 6 double-acting composition pedals, self-balancing crescendo pedal. Tubular pneumatic action to pedal and front pipes. Pitch pine case. Organist: Henry H. Mason.

BISHOPS CASTLE.—PRIMITIVE METHODIST CHURCH. Built 1905 by Steele & Keay. 2 manuals and pedal, 13 speaking stops, 4 couplers, 4 double-acting composition pedals. Blown by hydraulic engine. Pitch pine case. Organist: A. M. Pugh.

BISHOPS STORTFORD.—ST. MICHAEL'S PARISH CHURCH. Built 1888 by Kirkland. Opened by W. T. Best. 3 manuals, 32 speaking stops, 5 couplers, 1,900 pipes, 7 composition pedals, and 1 double acting, Gt. to pedals. Pneumatic action to Great organ and couplers.

BLACKBURN.—CHURCH OF ST. JOHN THE EVANGELIST. Restored 1900 by Binns. Opened by Alfred Hollins. 3 manuals, 31 speaking stops, 12 other stops. Blown by electric motor. Tubular pneumatic action. Organist: Frederick Herbert Wood, MUS. BAC. (DUNELM), A.R.C.M. (singing).

BLACKBURN.—PARISH CHURCH. Built on the Ventil system 1875, by Cavaillé-Coll. Paris. 3 manuals. Every stop of full compass. Hydraulic engines, feeders and main reservoir placed in crypt, 60ft. from organ. As is usual with French organs in general, reed work is very fine. Harmonic flute (8ft.) and Double Trumpet (16ft.) being chief features. Contains a mixture of 7 ranks, a peculiar feature which worries the tuners a great deal. Organist: Henry P. Coleman, F.R.C.O.

BLACKBURN.—ST. ANN'S CATHOLIC CHURCH.—Built 1854 by Parvin, Bolton. Restored 1889 by Ainscough. 3 manuals, 23 speaking stops, 6 other stops. Blown by hand. Organist: John Hayhurst.

BLACKBURN.—ST. JAMES' CHURCH. Built 1906 by Binns. 3 manuals, 31 speaking stops, 10 other stops, 1,871 pipes, 8 compound combination pedals, 1 reversible pedal controlling Great to Pedal, and 1 balanced crescendo Pedal to Swell. Wind supplied by electric blower. Organist: Arthur Abbot, A.R C.O.

BLACKBURN.—ST. PETER'S CHURCH. Built 1872 by Willis. Opened by W. T. Best. 4 manuals, 42 speaking stops, 9 other stops, 12 combination pistons, and 4 combination pedals to Pedal organ. Fine tone, well balanced. Organist: D. Albert Slater, F.R.C.O.

BLACKPOOL.—ADELAIDE STREET FREE CHURCH. Built 1903 by Conacher. 3 manuals, 33 speaking stops, 10 couplers, 6 double acting composition pedals and balanced crescendo pedals to Swell and Choir. Tubular pneumatic action throughout. Blown by electric power. Organist: J. S. Warburton, A. MUS. T.C.L.

BLACKPOOL.—CHRIST CHURCH. Built 1867 and rebuilt 1904 (to specification by Dr. Kirtland) by Wadsworth. Opened 1904 by Dr. J. Varley Roberts. 3 manuals, 40 speaking stops, etc. Wind supplied by a Crossley gas engine. Organist: Herbert William Cliffe.

BLACKPOOL.—HOLY TRINITY CHURCH, SOUTHSHORE. Built 1903 by Hill. 3 manuals, 32 speaking stops, 6 couplers. Tubular pneumatic action. Electric blowing. Organist: C. W. Fisher, MUS. BAC. CANTAB., F.R.C.O.

BODMIN.—ST. PETROC'S CHURCH. Built by old German maker; rebuilt and enlarged 1883 by Hele. 3 manuals, 28 speaking stops, 7 other stops, 1,644 pipes. Pneumatic action to Great controlled by Barker's pneumatic lever. Organist: R. R. Glendinning, MUS. BAC. OXON., Sunnyside, Beacon R$_o$ad, Bodmin.

BOLTON.—BANK STREET UNITARIAN CHURCH. Built 1877 by Holt, Leeds, and Gray & Davison. Opened by Dr Pyne. Rebuilt and enlarged 1907 by Norman & Beard. 3 manuals, 29 speaking stops, 10 couplers, and 1,612 pipes. Organist: John Thomas Flitcroft, MUS. BAC., T.U.T., F.R.C O, L.R.A.M , F.T.C.L.

BOLTON.—DEANE PARISH CHURCH (ST. MARY'S). Built about 1827 by Wren & Boston, Manchester. Rebuilt 1901 by Young, Manchester. Opened by present organist. 3 manuals, 28 speaking stops, 8 other stops, and 2 tremulants. Choir organ in swell box. All stops through entire manuals. Pedal board radiatory and concave. CCC to F. Organist: John Miles.

BOLTON.—HOLY TRINITY CHURCH. Built 1861 for Manchester Cathedral, by Nicholson (Worcester). Restored 1905 by Jardine. 3 manuals, 41 speaking stops, 6 other stops, 2,346 pipes, 2 solo stops on Choir manual, 4ft. flute, 8ft. grand ophideide, 8 composition pedals, double action couplers Great to Pedal, and Swell to Pedal. Blown by hydraulic engine. Organist: Frederick William Pacey, MUS. BAC. OXON.

BOLTON.—ST. ANNE'S CHURCH, TURTON. Built 1872, and restored 1911, by Willis. 2 manuals (CC to G), and pedal (CCC to F). 18 speaking stops, 5 composition pedals, and usual couplers. Organist and Choirmaster: Alfred Edward Bostock.

BOLTON.—ST. GEORGE'S CHURCH. Built 1836; enlarged 1842; repaired 1865. Rebuilt 1876 by Brindley & Foster. 3 manuals, 25 speaking stops, 5 couplers, tremulant and 2 composition pedals to Great only. Organist: Thomas Booth, MUS. BAC. (DUNELM), A.R.C.O.

BOLTON.—St. Matthew's Church, Little Lever. Built 1885, and restored 1911, by Brindley & Foster. 3 manuals, 28 speaking stops, 10 other stops. Blown by hand. Organist: Walker Crossley, Mus. Bac. (Dunelm), F.R.C.O.

BOLTON.—Town Hall. Built 1874 and rebuilt 1907 by Gray & Davison. 4 manuals and pedal, 51 speaking stops, peal of 37 bells. 2 tremulants, 12 couplers, 3 swell boxes, 30 pneumatic pistons and pedal touches. 3,473 pipes. Tubular pneumatic action throughout. Blown by " Kinetic " fans driven by a 10 h.p electric motor at 850 revolutions per minute. Organist: Arthur E Jones, F R C O , L T C L

BOLTON.—West Houghton Parish Church. Built 1874 by Hill. Opened by Sir Frederick Bridge. 3 manuals, 24 speaking stops, 6 other stops, 1,366 pipes. Organist: Ralph Worthington Brown, F GLD.O., A.T.C.L.

BOSTON —Parish Church. Built by 1717 Christian Schmidt. Restored 1908 by Norman & Beard. Contains work by Nicholls (1820), Hill (1853), Bishop (1868) and Brindley (1871) 3 manuals, 41 speaking stops, 9 couplers, 11 thumb pistons, 12 composition pedals. Organist: George Herbert Gregory, Mus. Bac. Oxon., F.R.C.O.

BOSTON.—Wesleyan Church, Red Lion Street Built 1913 by Cousans, to replace organ destroyed by fire in 1909 3 manuals, 31 speaking stops, 8 couplers, heavy wind for the reeds Pneumatic throughout. Blown by gas engine and Cousans "Turbine " Organist · George Dennis Haller, F.R.C.O.

BOULTON.—Parish Church Built 1892 by Porrit Opened by A. F. Smith, F R C O , Mus Bac. 2 manuals, 14 speaking stops, and 3 other stops Tracker action, and very easy. Organist : Robert S. Walker.

BOURNEMOUTH —Catholic Church Built 1847 by Hill. 2 manuals 10 speaking stops, 2 other stops. Organist: Felix D. Blackbee (Junr.).

BOURNEMOUTH.—Charminster Road Congregational Church. Built 1885 by Brindley & Foster. Opened by Enos J. Watkins, F R.C.O., A.R C M. 2 manuals, 27 speaking stops, 4 couplers, 7 composition pedals Pedal board radiating and concave. Tracker action replaced by tubular pneumatic to Great, Swell and Pedal organs. Organist Hugh Vernon Sloper.

BOURNEMOUTH.—Congregational Church, Boscombe. Built 1906 by Brindley & Foster. Opened by Enos J. Watkins, F.R.C.O., A.R C M. 2 manuals, 13 speaking stops, 5 other stops. Independent Pedal organ, with pneumatic action throughout. Blown by electric motor. Organist: P. D. Mundy, Southbourne Grove.

BOURNEMOUTH.—Corpus Christi R.C. Church, Boscombe. Restored 1908 by Griffen & Stroud. 2 manuals. Organist : E. Clinton Hoste, B.A Oxon , " St. Mary's," St. James' Square, Boscombe Park.

BOURNEMOUTH.—Lansdowne Baptist Church. Built by Burton, Winchester , added to 1903. 2 manuals, 12 speaking stops, 4 couplers, and 2 composition pedals. Organist : T. Hadley Watkins.

BOURNEMOUTH.—Richmond Hill Congregational Church. Built 1907 by Lewis. 3 manuals, 34 speaking stops, 11 other stops, and 1,932 pipes. 2 tremulants by pedal. Tubular pneumatic action throughout. Compass, 5 octaves. Spotted metal throughout (50% tin). Reeds on heavy wind pressure. Organist : Enos James Watkins, F.R.C.O., A.R.C.M. (Singing).

BOURNEMOUTH.—ROYAL ARCADE, BOSCOMBE. Built by Beale. Restored by Burton. 3 manuals, 28 speaking stops and 8 other stops. Organist : Allan Biggs, L.R.A.M., F.R.C.O.

BOURNEMOUTH.—ST. ANDREW'S CHURCH, BOSCOMBE. Built 1898 by Hill. Opened by Dr. Prendergast. 3 manuals and pedals, 23 speaking stops, tremulant and 8 couplers. Blown by " Kinetic " Blower driven by electric motor. Enclosed in handsome oak case. Organist : Arthur Marston, A.R.C.O.

BOURNEMOUTH.—ST. ANDREW'S PRESBYTERIAN CHURCH. Built 1893 by Monk. 3 manuals, 26 speaking stops, 5 couplers. Opened by Dr. Turpin.

BOURNEMOUTH.—ST. AUGUSTIN'S CHURCH. Built by Bevington. 2 manuals, 9 speaking stops and 3 other stops. Organist : Frederick John Phillips.

BOURNEMOUTH.—ST. KATHARINE'S CHURCH, SOUTHBOURNE-ON-SEA. Built by Jones. 3 manuals, 24 speaking stops and 4 other stops. Organist : Allan Biggs, L.R.A.M., F.R.C.O.

BOURNEMOUTH.—ST. MARK'S PRESBYTERIAN CHURCH. Built by Burton. 2 manuals and pedal, 20 speaking stops, 7 couplers, 1,006 pipes, 6 composition pedals. Blown by " Kinetic " blower. Organist . Fred P. Brazier.

BOURNEMOUTH.—ST. PETER'S CHURCH. Built by Willis. 22 speaking stops, 5 other stops, and 1,292 pipes. Instrument though small, has some fine work in it, and is about to be enlarged. Organist : James D. Chandler, F.R.C.O.

BOURNEMOUTH.—WESLEY CHURCH, HOLDENHURST ROAD. Built 1910 by Compton. 2 manuals, 38 speaking stops. Electro-pneumatic action. All pipes enclosed in two swell chambers. Blown by electric motor. Organist : Dr. F. Muller.

BOVEY TRACEY.—ST. THOMAS-A-BECKET PARISH CHURCH. Probably built by Webster Bros. Orginally the property of Professor Russel Lockner, and built in a hall attached to his residence in Lancaster Road, W. Brought to Bovey Tracey 1890 ; re-constructed and enlarged by Hele. 4 manuals (arranged into 3), 42 speaking stops, 10 couplers and 2,709 pipes. Swell of 68 notes, and Pedal of 42 extra notes for octave couplers. Lever-pneumatic action. Blown by 3 men ; electric blowing contemplated. Organist : Melbourne Holman.

BRADFORD.—BAPTIST CHAPEL, GIRLINGTON. Built 1878 by Conacher. 3 manuals, 26 speaking stops, 6 other stops. Tracker action to all parts except pedals which are pneumatic. Organist . Arthur Whitaker.

BRADFORD.—EASTBROOK HALL. Built 1846. Restored 1875 and rebuilt 1903 by Hill. Opened 1846 by Thomas Adams. 3 manuals, 41 speaking stops, 8 couplers. Tubular pneumatic action. Electric blowing. Organist : Oliver Knapton.

BRADFORD.—PARISH CHURCH. Built 1903 by Hill. 3 manuals, 39 speaking stops, 6 couplers. Tubular pneumatic action. Electric blowing. Organist : Henry Coates.

BRADFORD.—St. Mary Magdalene's Church. Built 1877 by Hill.
3 manuals, 32 speaking stops, and 5 other stops. Organist and Choir
Master : George Smith.

BRADFORD.—Wesley Church, Lowmoor. Restored 1895 by Driver
& Haigh, Bradford. Opened 1895 by W. T. Crossley, A.R.C.O. 2
manuals, 19 speaking stops, 5 other stops. Diapasons (Conacher)
very good. Fine Salcional in Swell organ. Organist : William T.
Crossley, A R.C.O.

BRADFORD.—Westgate Baptist Church, Manningham. Built 1902 by
Binns. 3rd manual (Choir) added by Andrews, Bradford. Opened
by Alfred Hollins, after restoration by H. A. Fricker. 3 manuals,
38 speaking stops, 12 other stops Console in front of choir stalls.
Electric blowing. Organist : Arthur Pearson.

BRADFORD-ON-AVON.—Holy Trinity Parish Church. Built 1875,
and restored 1900, by Sweetland. 2 manuals, 20 speaking stops,
5 other stops. Blown by hand. Organist : E. P. Bartlett.

BRECHIN.—Cathedral, The. Built by Conacher. Restored by Miller,
Dundee, 1902. 3 manuals, 30 speaking stops, couplers, etc., 8 composition pedals, and 2 pneumatic pistons. Tubular pneumatic action
throughout. Blown by hydraulic engine

BRECON.—St. John's Priory Church. Built 1886 by Hill. Opened
Dr. Langdon Colborn. 3 manuals, 30 speaking stops, 6 other stops
Blown by hand. Organist : Rees Thomas Heins, High Street, Brecon
Appointed 1879.

BRECON.—St Mary's Church. Built 1877 by Walker. 2 manuals,
19 speaking stops, 4 other stops, 1,297 pipes Organist : W. H. Webb,
R.A.M., M·I.S.M., HON. F.G.O., M.G·C·M·, L·V.C·M·

BRIDGNORTH.—St. Leonard's Church. Built 1869 by Walker. Rebuilt
and enlarged 1911 by Johnson 3 manuals, 39 speaking stops, 13
other stops, 2 tremulants. Blown by fan driven by gas engine.
Organist : J Turton Smith, F R C O., L R.A.M.

BRIDGNORTH.—St. Mary Magdalene Built 1870 by Jones 2 manuals,
20 speaking stops, and 5 other stops. Pneumatic action to Swell.
Tracker to Great and Pedal. Ross valve blowing engine. Organist :
James Simpson

BRIDLINGTON.—Priory Church Built 1889 by Anncesseens, Grammont,
Belgium ; rebuilt by Abbott & Smith 3 manuals, 45 speaking stops,
10 couplers, 2,325 pipes, 9 combination pistons, 10 composition pedals.
Tubular pneumatic action throughout Organist : A. P. Stephenson,
F R.C.O

BRIGHOUSE.—Congregational Church. Restored 1896 by Conacher.
3 manuals, 34 speaking stops, 6 couplers and 6 composition pedals
Tremulant in choir. Organist : Arthur Nettleton, A R.C o

BRIGHTON.—Chapel Royal. Built 1883 by Willis Opened by Frank
Butler, F R.C o 2 manuals, 19 speaking stops, 3 other stops and
tremulant, 1,092 pipes. Original specification was for a 3 manual
organ, and space is provided for Choir organ, together with 2 Pedal
stops and other additions to Great, 7 composition pedals Organist ·
Horace W. Gates A.R C.O.

BRIGHTON.—CHURCH OF THE SACRED HEART (R.C.). Built 1887 by Bevington. 3 manuals, 32 speaking stops, 13 couplers.

BRIGHTON.—ST. AUGUSTINE'S CHURCH. Built 1896 by Morgan & Smith. Opened by Dr. Herbert Botting. 2 manuals, 22 speaking stops, 6 other stops, 1,268 pipes. Tracker action to manuals, pneumatic pedals. Blown by 1 h.p. electric motor with Coote's patent controller. Organist : Alfred William Abdey, MUS. BAC. OXON., F.R.C.O.

BRIGHTON.—ST. BARTHOLOMEW'S CHURCH. Built by Walker. Rebuilt, divided and fitted with detached Console and enlarged by Morgan & Smith, 1906. 3 manuals, 26 speaking stops, 8 couplers. Blown by two hydraulic motors. Pneumatic action throughout. Organist : Henry Madle.

BRIGHTON.—ST. JAMES'S CHURCH. Built by Corps. 3 manuals, 40 speaking stops, 8 couplers. Rich tone. Organist : Norman Richards.

BRIGHTON.—ST. LUKE'S CHURCH. Built 1885 by Bevington. 2 manuals, 23 speaking stops, 10 couplers.

BRIGHTON.—ST. MARGARET'S CHURCH. Built 1875 by Gray and Davison : restored 1904 by Morgan and Smith. Opened by Dr. Botting. 3 manuals, 40 speaking stops, 10 other stops and 2,000 pipes. Tubular pneumatic action. Blown by 2 electric motors. Organist : W. Wilson Macpherson, M.I.S.M.

BRIGHTON.—ST. MARY'S CHURCH. Built 1859 and enlarged 1879 and 1904 by Bevington. 3 manuals, 30 speaking stops, 12 other stops. Blown by hand. Part tubular. Organist : W. Norman Roe.

BRIGHTON.—ST. SAVIOUR'S CHURCH. Built 1899 by Morgan & Smith. 3 manuals, 29 speaking stops, 6 couplers. Pneumatic action throughout. Blown by electric motor.

BRIGHTON.—THE DOME, ROYAL PAVILION. Built 1870 by Willis. Opened by W. Best. 4 manuals, 44 speaking stops and couplers. Varying pressures of wind for orchestral and other stops. Organist : Alfred King, MUS. DOC. OXON., F.R.C.O., L.T.C.L.

BRIGHTON.—THE COLLEGE. Built 1912 by Morgan & Smith. Some of the stops used from the original organ by Bishop. 3 manuals, 27 speaking stops, 8 couplers. Pneumatic action throughout. Blown by electric motor. Case designed by Mr Morgan, the builder, and executed by T. B. Colman, of Brighton. Organist : Percy C. Taylor, A.R.C.O.

BRIGHTON.—UNION CONGREGATIONAL CHURCH. Built 1910 by Morgan & Smith. 2 manuals, 27 speaking stops, 5 couplers. Pneumatic action throughout. Blown by electric motor. Organist : Miss Celia Burleigh, MUS. BAC., F.R.C.O., 78, Ditchling Road, Brighton.

BRISTOL.—ALL SAINTS' CHURCH. Built 1910 by Binns. 3 manuals, 34 speaking stops, 13 couplers, 6 interchangeable combination pistons, 8 combination pedals, balanced crescendo pedal to Swell organ. Tubular pneumatic action throughout. Blown by electric motor. Organist : William Ernest Fowler, L.R.A.M., A.R.C.M.

BRISTOL.—CATHEDRAL, THE. Built 1907 by Walker. Opened by Sir Walter Parratt. 4 manuals, 61 speaking stops, 15 other stops, 3,388 pipes, 18 pneumatic combination pistons, 13 pedals to combinations, couplers, etc. Blown by 3 electric motors. Organist : Hubert W. Hunt.

BRISTOL.—CHURCH OF THE HOLY NATIVITY, KNOWLE. Built 1887, enlarged 1890, by Vowles. 3 manuals, 28 speaking stops, 8 other stops and 7 composition pedals. Blown by hand. Organist and Choirmaster: A. J. Baker.

BRISTOL.—CLIFTON COLLEGE CHAPEL. Built 1910 by Harrison. 4 manuals, 42 speaking stops, 19 couplers, 4 combination pedals, 14 combination pistons, 3 reversible pedals, 2 crescendo pedals. Tubular pneumatic action throughout. Blown by 6 h p. electric motor. Organist: A. H. Peppin, B.A.

BRISTOL.—COLSTON HALL. Built 1900 by H. Willis. Re-arranged and enlarged 1905 by Norman & Beard. Opened by George Riseley. 5 manuals, 109 speaking stops, 21 other stops, 6,112 pipes. Blown by electricity. Organist: Geo. Risley

BRISTOL.—GRAMMAR SCHOOL, THE.—Built 1879 by Vowles. 3 manuals, 31 speaking stops, 10 other stops, 2,000 pipes, 8 composition pedals, 1 ventil to Pedal organ. Blown by " Otto " gas engine, which operates on 2 double acting pumps and feeders. Organist: Chas. W. Stear.

BRISTOL.—ST. BARNABAS PARISH CHURCH, WARMLEY. Built 1886 by Jones. 2 manuals, 16 speaking stops, 4 other stops Full scale instrument and is prepared for further additions. Fine tone of diapasons. Organist: Gilbert Burchill, M.I.S.M., R.C.O.

BRISTOL.—ST. JOHN'S PARISH CHURCH, BEDMINSTER. Built 1860, and restored 1901, by Vowles. 3 manuals, 36 speaking stops and 5 other stops. Tubular pneumatic action. Organist: Frederick William Hek, A R.C.O.

BRISTOL.—ST. MARY REDCLIFFE CHURCH. Original organ built 1726 by Harris and Byfield; rebuilt and considerably enlarged by Vowles 1867, when removed from the West end of the Church. New organ built 1911 by Harrison. 4 manuals, 64 speaking stops, 23 couplers, etc., 26 combination pistons, 4 reversible pistons, 7 combination pedals, 3 reversible pedals, 3 balanced crescendo pedals to Swell and Echo organs Electro-pneumatic action throughout. Blown by two electric motors of 10½ h p. An unusual feature is the insertion in the swell box of two heavy-pressure Pedal reed stops of 32ft. and 16ft. pitch. Organist: R. T. Morgan.

BRISTOL.—ST. MARY'S CHURCH, TYNDALL'S PARK, CLIFTON. Built 1885 by Vowles. 3 manuals, 36 speaking stops, 7 couplers, 7 composition pedals. Organist and Choirmaster: Chas. W. Stear.

BRISTOL.—ST. NICHOLAS' CHURCH. Built by Smith, Bristol, and Vowles. Rebuilt by Hele. Opened by H. W. Hunt. 3 manuals, 35 speaking stops, 8 other stops, 1,788 pipes, 5 composition pedals to Great and Pedal tremulant, 3 composition pedals to Swell, 1 pedal acting on Great to Pedal coupler Pedal organ on North side of Chancel, Swell, Great and Choir on South side. Organist: Arthur Sydney Warrell, F.R.C O.

BRISTOL.—STAPLETON UNION CHAPEL. Built 1911 by Bevington. Opened by R. T. Morgan, of St. Mary Redcliffe. 2 manuals, 16 speaking stops, 3 other stops, 780 pipes. Blown by hand. Organist: Francis George Willson.

BRISTOL.—VICTORIA ROOMS, CLIFTON. Built 1900 by Norman and Beard (Hope-Jones electric action). Originally a large 4 manual Hill organ, built for the Panoptican, Leicester Square, and also stood for some time in the South transept of St. Paul's Cathedral, erected in the above Rooms about 30 years ago. 4 manuals, 50 stop keys, 17 double-acting combination pistons, placed under each manual, 6 double-touch composition pedals, and a stop-switch (by key and pedal). Blown by electric motor and fan. Organist : Chas. W. Stear.

BROADSTAIRS.—HOLY TRINITY PARISH CHURCH. Built 1883 by Gern. Opened by Dr. Prior. 3 manuals, 24 speaking stops and 6 other stops. Tubular pneumatic action throughout. Hydraulic blowing.

BROADSTAIRS.—ST. PETER THE APOSTLE IN THANET. Built 1885, enlarged 1894, by Walker; further enlarged and improved 1908. 3 manuals, 24 speaking stops, 6 couplers and 1,436 pipes. Blown by hand, very good diapason work and excellent reeds. Organist : Harold Bartrum Osmond, F.R.C.O.

BROMBOROUGH.—ST. BARNABAS' PARISH CHURCH. Built 1911 by Rushworth & Dreaper. 3 manuals, 30 speaking stops, 9 couplers, 9 composition pedals. Tubular pneumatic action throughout. Organist : James P. King.

BROMLEY.—PARISH CHURCH. Built 1874 by Walker. Rebuilt 1894 by Young. 3 manuals, 35 speaking stops, 8 couplers, 7 composition pedals, and 10 composition pistons. Organist : Frederic Fertel, "Holmcroft," Holwood Road, Bromley, Kent. Appointed 1896; also Conductor, Bromley Choral Society.

BROMLEY.—ST. MARY'S CHURCH. Built 1882 by Hill. Opened by present organist. 3 manuals, 39 speaking stops, 7 other stops. Blown by hydraulic engine. Organist : F. Lewis Thomas.

BROMSGROVE.—ST. PETER'S CHURCH. Built 1912 by Brindley & Foster. 2 manuals, 17 speaking stops, 7 acoustic stops, 954 pipes, 18 pneumatic combination accessories, 9 composition pedals, tremulant, balanced swell pedal. Blown by hydraulic engine. Organist : Mr. Walter Daniel.

BROUGHTON ASTLEY.—BAPTIST CHURCH, SUTTON-IN-THE-ELMS. Built 1906 by Hewitt, Leicester. 2 manuals, 13 speaking stops, 4 other stops and 708 pipes. Opened by Arthur Pickett. Organist : Frank Hall, " Haydn House," L.C.V., I.U.M.

BURNLEY.—BRUNSWICK CHAPEL. Built 1909 by Brindley & Foster. Opened by H. A. Fricker, MUS. BAC. 3 manuals, 38 speaking stops, 32 other stops (including transformers) and 2,333 pipes. Accessories, transformers and stops total 85. Blown by electric motor. Organist : Matthew Watson.

BURNT-ISLAND.—PARISH CHURCH. Built 1909 by Cousans. Opened by Mr. David Stephen. 2 manuals, 19 speaking stops, 5 couplers. Pneumatic throughout. Hydraulic blowing. Organist : Hutton Rogers Laidlaw, A.I.C.M., 23, E. Hermitage Place, Leith.

BURSLEM.—HILL TOP METHODIST FREE CHURCH. Built 1905 by Steele & Keay. 3 manuals and pedal, 29 speaking stops, 7 couplers, 6 double-acting composition pedals, 2 pneumatic pistons, 1 reversible pedal, 1 self-balancing crescendo pedal. Tubular pneumatic to Pedal. Blown by " Kinetic " blower driven by 2 h.p. electric motor.

BURSLEM.—St. Paul's Church. Built 1902 by Steele & Keay. 3 manuals, 34 speaking stops, 7 couplers, 6 double-acting composition pedals, self-balancing crescendo pedal to Swell. Tubular pneumatic action to Pedal and front pipes.

BURTON-ON-TRENT.—Parish Church. Built 1899 by Norman & Beard. 4 manuals, and 55 stops. Electric action. Organist : Harry William Tupper, mus. bac. oxon., f.r.c.o., l. mus. t.c.l.

BURTON-ON-TRENT.—St. Chad's Church. Built by Conacher. Gift of the late Lord Burton. 3 manuals and pedal, 28 speaking stops, 1 tremblant, 10 couplers, 8 composition pedals, 11 combination pistons. Tubular pneumatic action throughout. Blown by electric motor and rotary fan. Handsome oak case. Organist : J. E. Collins (appointed 1884).

BURTON-ON-TRENT St John's Parish Church, Horninglow. Built 1895 by Nicholson & Lord (Walsall). Opened by Sir J. Frederick Bridge. 3 manuals, 27 speaking stops, 7 other stops, and 1,510 pipes Re-constructed, provided with proper organ chamber and an electric blower, 1912. Organist : Arthur William Read, f.r.c.o., a.r.c.m.

BURTON-ON-TRENT.—St. Paul's Church. Built 1896 by Hope Jones. Opened by A. B. Plant. 4 manuals, 31 speaking stops and 20 other stops. Choir, Great and Swell organ in chancel, Pedal and Solo in transept. Organist : Arthur Blurton Plant, mus. doc. oxon., f.r.c.o.

BURY.—Parish Church. Built by Jardine. 3 manuals, 46 stops. Organist : Walter Williams, mus. bac. oxon., f.r.c o., a.r.c.m.

BURY ST. EDMUNDS.—St. James' Church. Restored 1864 by Walker. 3 manuals, 36 speaking stops, and 6 couplers. Vox Humana in separate box, played from Choir organ, and on pneumatics. Organist : C. J. H. Shann.

BURY ST. EDMUNDS.—St. Mary's Parish Church. Restored 1898 by Walker. Opened by G. W. M. Boutell. 3 manuals, 41 speaking stops, 6 couplers, 1 tremulant. Tracker action on all except bottom $1\frac{1}{4}$ octaves, on Great and Pedals which are pneumatic. $3\frac{1}{2}$in. pressure to manuals, and $6\frac{1}{2}$in. to pedal, tuba, and pneumatics. Organist : E. Percy Hallam.

BUXTON.—Wesley Chapel, Higher Buxton. Built by Young. 3 manuals and pedal, 24 speaking stops, 6 couplers, 1,372 pipes, 6 composition pedals.

CALLANDER.—Parish Church. Built 1903 by Willis. Rebuilt and enlarged 1911 by Vincent. 3 manuals, 28 stops. Pneumatic action. Hydraulic blower. Organist : T. Hainsworth, a.r.c.o.

CALNE.—Bowood Chapel. (Private Chapel of the Marquis of Lansdowne). Built by Blennerhassett. 3 manuals. Blown by electric motor. Organist : W. R. Pullein.

CALNE.—Castle House. Private residence of Henry G Harris, j.p. Built 1896 by Conacher. 5 manuals, 40 speaking stops, 13 accessories, 2,348 pipes, 4 combination pistons. Handsome case of dark oak, richly carved. Tubular pneumatic action throughout. Blown by 2 h.p. Crossley gas engine. Choir and Echo organs enclosed in seperate boxes. Organist : W. R. Pullein.

CALNE.—St. Mary's Parish Church. Built 1907-8 by Conacher. Gift of Henry G. Harris, J.P., of Castle House. Opened by W. Wolstenholme. 5 manuals, 54 speaking stops, 14 other stops, 4,500 pipes. Tubular pneumatic action throughout. Blown by Kinetic blower, ..ctuated by 8 h.p. Crossley gas engine. Organist : W. R. Pullein.

CAMBERLEY.—Royal Military College Chapel. Built 1879 by Bevington. 2 manuals, 21 speaking stops, 9 other stops. Blown by hydraulic ¬ngine. Organist : J. Spyer, F.R.C.C.

CAMBERLEY.—St. Anne's Parish Church, Bagshot. Built 1899 by Walker. Opened by Sir Walter Parratt. Excellent Vox Angelica, and two very soft gamba stops. Organist : Edwin J. Hickox, A.R.C.M., F.R.C.O.

CAMBORNE.—St. Martin's Church. Built by Nicholson (Worcester). 3 manuals (Choir prepared for), 21 speaking stops, 5 other stops, 1,288 pipes. Blown by electricity. Organist : Arthur Henry Baker, F.R.C.O., F.T.C.L., L.R.A.M., A.R.C.M.

CAMBRIDGE.—Church of our Lady and English Martyrs. Opened 1890. Built by Abbott & Smith. 3 manuals, 41 speaking stops. Blown by hydraulic engine.

CAMBRIDGE.—Clare College Chapel. Built 1911 by Harrison. 3 manuals, 26 speaking stops, 10 couplers, 8 combination pedals, 12 combination pistons, 1 reversible pedal, 1 reversible piston, 2 balanced crescendo pedals Tubular pneumatic. Blown by 3½-h.p. electric motor and discus fans. Organist : Noel T. Hopkins.

CAMBRIDGE.—Elsworth Parish Church. Built 1911 by Noterman. Opened by A. Halton. 2 manuals, 14 speaking stops, 6 other stops, 714 pipes. Blown by hand. Detached console. Contains the builder's long distance pneumatic action. Organist : Mrs. Tibbits, Elsworth Rectory, Cambridge.

CAMBRIDGE.—Emmanuel Congregational Church. Built 1880 by Father Willis. Restored and enlarged 1911 by Norman & Beard. Opened by Dr. A. H. Mann. 3 manuals, 30 speaking stops, 11 other stops. Blown by 4 h.p. electric motor. Fine diapasons and reeds. Great and Pedal reeds on heavy wind pressure, and Great reeds and horn in the Swell have harmonic trebles. Harmonic trumpet on the Great is also playable through the Choir keys. Tremulant to Choir and Swell. Organist : John Herbert Warmington, M.A.

CAMBRIDGE.—King's College. Rebuilt 1888 by Hill. 4 manuals, 55 speaking stops, 9 couplers Tubular pneumatic action Hydraulic blowing. Organist : Dr. A. H. Mann, M A , F R.C.O., F.R.A.M.

CAMBRIDGE.—Pembroke College Chapel. Built 1707-8 by Quarles, the pipes probably being by " Father Smith." Restored 1863 and 1873. by Hill, and 1903 by Norman & Beard. 3 manuals, 30 speaking stops, 5 other stops, 6 combination pedals, 1,800 pipes. Blown by hydraulic engine. Organ noted for its fine tone and voicing. Organist : Felix W. Morley, M.A., MUS. BAC.

CAMBRIDGE.—St. Andrew the Great Church. Built 1904 by Hill. 3 manuals, 27 speaking stops, 6 couplers. Tubular pneumatic action. Electric blowing

CAMBRIDGE.—St. John's College Chapel. Built 1635 by Robert
Dallam. Rebuilt 1839 and altered and added to 1868 and 1889, by Hill.
Rebuilt 1902 by Norman & Beard. 3 manuals, 53 speaking stops,
8 other stops, 11 composition pedals, and 10 pneumatic pistons.
Tubular pneumatic action, except Manual to Pedal. Blown by
hydraulic engines. Organist: Cyril Bradley Rootham, M.A., MUS. DOC.
CANTAB.

CAMBRIDGE.—Trinity College Chapel. Built 1706 by Smith; overhauled and improved 1767 by Parker; further work 1801 by Avery;
1808 by Lincoln; and 1819 by Flight & Robson. Extensive improvements 1836 by Gray; and 1853, 1870 and 1890 by Hill. Completely
rebuilt, restored and enlarged 1912 by Harrison. 4 manuals, 74
speaking stops, 17 couplers, 6 combination pedals, 22 combination
pistons, 2 reversible pedals, 2 reversible pistons, pedal for tremulant,
2 crescendo pedals Tubular pneumatic. Blown by 12 h.p. electric
motor and discus fan. Organist: Alan Gray, MUS. DOC. CANTAB., LL. M.

CANNOCK—St Chads. Built 1901 by Steele & Keay. Opened by T. Cox,
F R.C.O. 2 manuals, 18 speaking stops, 4 other stops, 1,022 pipes.
Blown by hand. Organist: Mr. E. W. Bird, F.I.G.C.M, F.V.C.M.

CANTERBURY.—Cathedral, The. Built 1885 by Willis. 4 manuals,
6 Stops on Solo, 13 on Swell, 8 on Choir, 15 on Great, 4 on Pedal; 10
couplers, 4 composition pedals, 4 composition pistons on each manual.
5 pedal stops and Kinetic blower, operated by 10 h.p. Bull electric motor,
added by Norman & Beard, 1905. Organist: C. Charlton Palmer,
MUS DOC. OXON., F R.C.O.

CANTERBURY.—St. Edmund's School. Restored 1893 by Browne.
2 manuals, 15 speaking stops, 5 other stops, 778 pipes, and 5 composition
pedals. Pneumatic action on Swell and Pedal. Organist; Pullen
Baker.

CARDIFF.—Clare Gardens Wesleyan Church. Built by Blackett &
Howden. 3 manuals and pedal, 24 speaking stops, 10 couplers, 1,015
pipes, 6 composition pedals Tubular pneumatic action throughout.
Detached console. Blown by hydraulic motor.

CARDIFF.—Ebenezer (Congregational) Church Built about 1893 by
Conacher. 2 manuals, 15 speaking stops, 3 other stops Blown by
hand. Organist: E. P. Mills, L.R.A.M,

CARDIFF.—Richmond Road Congregational Church. Built 1898 by
Harrison. Opened by Arthur Harrison. 3 manuals, 25 speaking
stops, 6 couplers, 1,442 pipes, 8 combination pedals. Blown by Ross
valve engine. Balanced swell pedal. Organist: George Bull, A R C.O.

CARDIFF.—St. Alban's Church. Built by Blackett & Howden. 2 manuals,
12 speaking stops, 3 couplers, 4 composition pedals, balanced swell
pedal. Tubular pneumatic action throughout. Detached console.

CARDIFF.—St. Margaret's Church, Roath. Built 1871 and restored 1888
by Bevington. 3 manuals, 19 speaking stops, 9 other stops. Organist:
G. Herbert Wyman, F R C.O

CARDIFF.—St. Mary The Virgin Church Restored 1896 by Coates.
Choir added 1906 by Phipps. 28 speaking and 5 other stops. Organist
T. Davies, A R.C.O., A. MUS. T.C.L., MUS. BAC. (DUNELM).

CARLISLE.—CATHEDRAL CHURCH OF THE HOLY AND UNDIVIDED TRINITY. Built 1856 by Willis. Rebuilt and enlarged 1907 by Harrison. 4 manuals, 58 speaking stops, 17 couplers, 3,322 pipes. Tubular pneumatic action throughout, 5 combination pedals, 10 combination pistons, 4 patent adjustable combination pistons, 2 reversible pistons, 1 reversible pedal, 2 balanced crescendo pedals, 2 tremulant pedals. Blown by 5 h.p. electric motor. Organist: Fred Wadely, M.A., MUS. B. CANTAB, F.R.C.O., 4, Victoria Place. Educated at Selyn College, Cambridge, and R.C.M.

CARLISLE.—OUR LADY AND ST. JOSEPH'S CHURCH. Built by Blackett & Howden. 3 manuals, 28 speaking stops, 10 couplers, 6 composition pistons, Great to Pedal, " on and off." Tubular pneumatic action throughout. Detached console. Blown by electric motor. Organist and Choirmaster: Felix Burns, " Arcade," Scotch Street, Carlisle.

CARLOW.—CATHEDRAL OF THE ASSUMPTION. Built by Bevington. 3 manuals, 28 speaking stops, and 4 other stops. Organist: Gust F. S. Haan, I.S M.

CARLOW.—ST. MARY'S CHURCH. Built 1845 by Walker. 2 manuals, 22 speaking stops, 3 couplers and 4 composition pedals. Organist Robert Malone, MUS. DOC. T.C.D.

CARMARTHEN.—CHRIST CHURCH. Built 1907 by Hunter. 3 manuals, 37 speaking stops, 10 couplers, 16 pistons. Tubular pneumatic action throughout. Blown by water engine. Reeds spotted metal throughout.

CARNARVON.—SILOH CALVINISTIC METHODIST CHURCH. Built by Blackett & Howden. 3 manuals, 25 speaking stops, 7 couplers, 6 composition pistons, balanced swell pedal. Tubular pneumatic action throughout. Blown by hydraulic motor.

CASTLEACRE.—ST. JAMES'S PARISH CHURCH. Built 1854 by Holdich. Restored 1890-4 by Norman & Beard. 3 manuals, 17 speaking stops, 948 pipes. An unusually long keyboard—66 notes. Formerly player sat with back to instrument. Organist: Francis Gardner Highe, F.I.G C.M., CERT. TRIN. COLL. LOND.

CATERHAM.—ST. MARY'S PARISH CHURCH. Built 1907 by Norman & Beard. 3 manuals, 26 speaking stops, 9 other stops, 6 composition pedals, 1 reversible pedal for Great to Pedal, 2 balanced Swell pedals, 9 combination pistons. Choir in a Swell box. Erected as memorial to late Vicar—Rev. Bright. Organist: W. C. S. Clark.

CHAGFORD.—ST. MICHAEL'S CHURCH. Built 1854 by Dicker. Restored and enlarged 1890 and 1901 by Hele. 3 manuals, 23 speaking stops, 6 other stops. Blown by hand, but electric prepared for. First comprised one manual and Swell pedal, and could also be played by means of handle with barrels. The second manual was added in 1890 and the third in 1901. Organist: R. Percy Collings, A.R.C O.

CHATHAM.—EBENEZER CONGREGATIONAL CHURCH. Built 1892 by Bevington. Opened by Ernest Dale, F.R.C.O., A.R.C M. 2 manuals, 21 speaking stops, 12 other stops. Blown by hydraulic engine. Choir organ prepared for. Extended tracker action. Organist: Edward J Bishop.

CHATHAM.—ST. ANDREW'S PRESBYTERIAN CHURCH. Built 1910 by Morgan & Smith. 2 manuals, 21 speaking stops, 5 couplers. Pneumatic action throughout. Organist: Lewis Harrison.

CHATHAM —St. John's Church. Built 1877 and enlarged 1905, by Bevington 3 manuals, 25 speaking stops, 11 other stops. Organist: A. V.
Dale, f.r.c.o.

CHELTENHAM.—Christ Church. Built by Hunter. Overhauled, new
reeds, many stops revoiced, by Price 3 manuals, 37 speaking stops.
Organist: Ralph Hamon Bellairs, m a., mus. doc. oxon., f.r.c.o.,
a r.c.m.

CHELTENHAM.—Church of the Holy Trinity Built 1896 by Price.
Opened by Dr. S. Bath. 3 manuals, 32 speaking stops, 5 other stops,
tremulant by piston, 1,940 pipes. Blown by hydraulic engine. Organist: Arthur W. H. Hulbert

CHELTENHAM.—Parish Church. Built 1883 by Nicholson. In three
sections so that stained glass should not be hidden Swell organ
in roof, Great organ between two windows. Pedal pipes lie on floor.
Organist: Leonard Vaughan Wheeler.

CHELTENHAM.—St. Matthew's Church. Built 1865. Restored 1876
by Willis 3 manuals, 41 stops, several of which are memorial presented by the late organist, the choir and various persons. Organist:
H. Marshall Sowry, f r.c.o., l.r.a.m.

CHELTENHAM —St Stephen's Church Built 1884 by Monk. Rebuilt
1912 by Norman & Beard 3 manuals and pedal, 32 speaking stops,
6 couplers, tremulant. Organist: H. E. C Townley.

CHESHUNT.—St. Mary's Parish Church Built 1891 by Hill. Opened
by present organist. 2 manuals, 20 speaking stops, 4 other stops.
Blown by hydraulic engine Organist: W. J. D. Butt, l. mus. t c l.

CHESTER —All Saints' Church, Hoole. Built 1901 by Whitely. 3
manuals, 26 speaking stops, 8 other stops, 1,412 pipes. Organist:
Richard B. Hamilton.

CHESTER.—Cathedral, the Built 1874 by Chas. Whiteley; improved
1895 by Gray & Davison, rebuilt 1910 by Hill. 4 manuals, 63 speaking stops, 14 couplers, 10 composition pedals, 20 pistons, 1 double-
acting pedal Blown by electric Kinetic fan. Pneumatic action.
Electric action also to Choir organ and Pedal. Organist: Joseph C.
Bridge, m a., mus. doc. oxon and dunelm, f.s a., hon. r.a.m, f.r.c.o.

CHESTER —Christ Church Built 1909 by Brindley & Foster. 2 manuals,
26 speaking stops, 5 other stops, 1,602 pipes, 25 pneumatic combination
accessories, 9 composition pedals, tremulant, balanced swell pedal.
Blown by electric motor. Organist: T Brooke Edwards, Canadian
Avenue, Hoole, Chester.

CHESTER.—Queen Street Congregational Church Built 1872 and
rebuilt 1912 by Charles Whiteley 2 manuals and pedal, 22 speaking
stops, 4 couplers, 1,127 pipes, 5 combination pedals Tracker action
to manuals Pneumatic action to pedals. Organist: James Skeldon.

CHESTER —St. John the Baptist Church, Alford. Built 1866 by Hill.
Opened by Mr. Gunton. Restored 1895 by Wenman 3 manuals, 15
speaking stops, 4 other stops, 798 pipes. Organist: John U. Scorah.

CHESTER —St. Mary's Parish Church. Built 1887 by Chas Whiteley;
repaired, and electric blower added, 1910, by Young. 3 manuals, 31
speaking stops, and 7 couplers Organist: Thomas Davidson Huxley,
f.r.c.o.

CHESTERFIELD.—ALL SAINTS' CHURCH, ASHOVER. Built 1886 by Abbott & Smith. 2 manuals, 14 speaking stops, 3 couplers. Tracker action to manuals and pedals; mechanical blowing and draw-stop actions. Cleaned and two stops added 1902. Organist : Bertram Hopkinson.

CHESTERFIELD.—CONGREGATIONAL CHURCH. Restored by Brindley & Foster. 2 manuals, 20 speaking stops and 4 other stops. Beautiful quality, soft stops. Organist : John H. Gaunt.

CHESTERFIELD.—PARISH CHURCH. Built 1756 by Snetzler. Rebuilt 1891 by Abbot & Smith. 3 manuals, 44 stops. Several original stops and autograph of original builder left. Organist and Choirmaster : J. Frederick Staton, MUS. BAC., F.R.C.O., L.R.A.M.

CHESTERFIELD.—ST. THOMAS' CHURCH. Built 1906 by Lloyd. 3 manuals, 29 speaking stops, 10 couplers, tremulant and six pistons. Organist : J. Lancaster.

CHICHESTER.—CATHEDRAL, THE. Built 1685 by Renatus Harris. Last restored 1904, by Hele. Contains work by Byfield, Knight, England, Gray & Davison, and Hill 3 manuals, 34 speaking stops, 7 other stops, and 2,080 pipes Tubular pneumatic action ; $2\frac{3}{4}$in pressure on all fine flue work, oboe, and clarionet ; 6in. on reeds and action. 4th manual and 32ft. pedal prepared for. Beautiful and mellow tone, considered one of the finest in England. Opened 1904 by present organist, assisted by the choirs and organists of Salisbury and Winchester Cathedrals. Organist : Frederick Joseph William Crowe, F.R.A.S., F.R. HIST SOC.

CHIGWELL.—ST. MARY'S PARISH CHURCH. Built 1889 by Hill. Opened by present organist 2 manuals, 19 speaking stops, 3 other stops and 1,068 pipes. Oak case. All stops carried through Organist : Henry Riding, F R.C.O.

CHIPPENHAM —PARISH CHURCH. Built 1879 by Gray & Davison. 3 manuals, 34 speaking stops, 6 other stops, and 2,000 pipes. Organist : W. T. Bradshaw, L R.A M., A R C.O.

CHISWICK.—PARISH CHURCH Built by Walker Added to 1884 by Bryceson. Renovated and enlarged 1907 by Lewis 3 manuals, 29 speaking stops, 7 other stops, 1,714 pipes. Tracker action. Organist and Choirmaster : William Adams, F R.C O., A.T C L.

CLEVEDON —CHRIST CHURCH. Built by Allen. 2 manuals, 18 speaking stops, 3 couplers, and 5 composition pedals. Organist : Miss Fanny Ellen Marchant, L.R A M.

CLEVEDON.—ST. ANDREW'S PARISH CHURCH. Built 1905 by Sweetland. 2 manuals, 15 speaking stops, 5 other stops. Blown by gas engine and electricity. Fine quality stops and powerful tone. Organist . Victor E. Cox.

CLEVEDON —ST JOHN THE EVANGELIST CHURCH. Built 1878 by Willis. Opened by E. Cook. 2 manuals, 13 speaking stops, 3 couplers, and 670 pipes. Blown by hydraulic engine. Organist : Walter Somerton.

CLITHEROE.—MOOR LANE CHAPEL. Built 1888 by Laycock. Opened by Dr. Spark. 2 manuals, 25 speaking stops, 5 other stops, 1,586 pipes. Organist : John W. Hayhurst.

CLONMEL.—PARISH CHURCH. Built 1861 by Telford. Restored 1907 by Chestnut. Re-opened by present organist. 3 manuals, 32 speaking stops and 6 other stops. Tracker action, pneumatic to pedals. Organist: Charles S. Craddock.

COLCHESTER.—ST. JAMES' CATHOLIC CHURCH. Built 1910 by Bevington. 2 manuals, 16 speaking stops, 6 couplers. Tubular action throughout. Electric blowing.

COLCHESTER.—ST. MARY AT WALLS CHURCH. Built 1886 by Hunter. Opened by Mr. Charles Osmond. 3 manuals, 30 speaking stops, 10 other stops. Blown by hand (two handles). Organist: W. F. Kingdon, MUS. BAC. OXON, F.R.C.O.

COLLIERLY.—ST. THOMAS' CHURCH. Built 1884 by Harrison. 2 manuals, 14 speaking stops, 4 couplers, 2 composition pedals to Great organ. Noted for its particular brilliancy and sweetness of tone. Organist: William Thomas Daglish.

COLNE.—PARISH CHURCH. Built 1909 by Brindley & Foster. 3 manuals, 33 speaking stops, 9 other stops, 1,937 pipes, 23 pneumatic combination accessories, 10 composition pedals, tremulant piston (on and off), balanced Swell pedal; Brindgradus (or crescendo pedal). Blown by electric motor controlled from console. Organist: Nelson Victor Edwards, F.R.C.O., L. MUS. T.C.L., L.I.S.M.

COLWYN BAY.—ST. JOHN'S ENGLISH WESLEYAN CHURCH. Built 1890 by Binns. Opened by S. W. Pilling. 3 manuals, 29 speaking stops, 9 couplers and tremulant to Swell, 1,548 pipes. Centre Swell pedal, balanced. All stops run through except voix celestes. Hydraulic blowing. Pneumatic action throughout (Binns) except to pedal couplers. Organist: Thomas Joseph Linekar.

CONGLETON.—ST. PETER'S PARISH CHURCH. Built 1824 by Renn & Boston. Opened by Mr. Wilkinson. Restored 1911 by Steele & Keay. 3 manuals, 31 speaking stops, 12 other stops, 1,914 pipes. Blown by gas engine and rotary fans. Tubular pneumatic throughout, extended console, magnificent oak case, 25ft. high and 21ft. wide. Organist: Frederick Green, A.R.C.M. (LOND.), L.R.A.M.

CONISBOROUGH.—PARISH CHURCH. Restored 1901 by Keates, when old organ was incoporated with the new one. 2 manuals, 17 speaking stops, 4 couplers, 4 combination pedals, balanced Swell pedal, reversible pedal. Organist: Albert Fletcher.

CONSETT.—WESLEYAN METHODIST CHURCH. Built by Abbott & Smith. 3 manuals and pedal, 24 speaking stops, 9 couplers, tremulant to Swell, 8 composition pedals. Blown by hydraulic engine. Tubular pneumatic action. Pitch pine case. Organist: Jas. E. Palliser.

CORFE CASTLE.—WESLEYAN CHURCH. Built 1907 by Burton. Opened by W. H Hardick. 2 manuals, 14 speaking stops, 3 other stops, pedals, concave and radiating. Tremulant by piston. Splendid tone. Organist: S. Charles Ford, Bucknowle House, Corfe Castle, Dorset. Appointed 1907.

CORK.—CATHEDRAL, THE. Built 1870 by Hill. Restored 1889 by Magaby, and 1907 by Hele. Opened 1907 by present organist. 4 manuals, 53 speaking stops, 13 other stops, and 3,040 pipes. Tubular pneumatic

throughout. Blown by 3 hydraulic engines. Built in chamber about
20ft. below level of floor. Organist: William George Eveleigh, MUS.
DOC. OXON., F.R.C.O., A.R.C.M.

CORK.—GLANMIRE PARISH CHURCH. Restored 1889 by Maghay. 2 manuals
20 speaking stops. Organist: Henry Brentnall, M.I.S M., F.G.O.

CORK.—ST. LUKE'S CHURCH. Built by Conacher. 3 manuals, 30 speaking
stops, 7 other stops. Tubular pneumatic action. Hydraulic blower.
Organist: Louis J. Garrett.

CORK —ST. MICHAEL'S CHURCH, BLACKROCK. Built 1887 by Magahy.
Opened by J. C. Marks, MUS. DOC. 2 manuals, 12 speaking stops, 4
other stops and 602 pipes. Organist: James Hurst.

CORSHAM.—ST. BARTHOLOMEW PARISH CHURCH. Built 1881 by Sweetland.
Opened by Henry Goold Spackman. Pneumatic action added to
Pedal organ 1906 by Griffen and Stroud. 2 manuals, 24 speaking stops,
5 other stops and 1,206 pipes. Sweet tone, flue work very good. Organist: Lewin Spackman.

COVENTRY.—BAPTIST CHURCH, QUEEN'S ROAD. Built 1896 by Norman &
Beard. 3 manuals, 21 speaking stops, 6 other stops. Opened by
Josiah Booth. Organist: Sidney Louis Coveney, F.R.C.O.

COVENTRY.—HOLY TRINITY CHURCH. Built 1855 by Foster & Andrews.
Restored 1900 by Hill. 4 manuals, 47 speaking stops, 11 other stops,
about 4,000 pipes. Opened by T Tertius Noble. Organist : Christie
Green, MUS. BAC. OXON., F.R C.O.

COVENTRY.—ST. MICHAEL'S CHURCH. Built 1887 by Willis. 4 manuals,
44 speaking stops, 10 other stops. Electric Kinetic blower. Organist.
Walter Hoyle, F.R.C.O. Assistant: Fred J. Harker.

COWES.—ST. MILDRED'S CHURCH, WHIPPINGHAM. Built by Willis. Opened
by Sir G. Elvey. 2 manuals, 22 speaking stops, 4 other stops. Trumpet
on Great put in for the wedding of H R.H. Princess Henry of Batten-
berg. Organ in West gallery. Oak case, plain metal front. Organist:
Miss Caroline Isabel May Scadding, L.L.C.M.

CREWKERNE.—PARISH CHURCH. Built 1906 by Rothwell 3 manuals,
30 speaking stops, 6 other stops. Patent Swell pedal. Pneumatic
action. Hydraulic blowing.

CRIEFF. — PARISH CHURCH. Restored and enlarged 1906 by Smith,
Glasgow. 2 manuals, 26 speaking stops, 5 other stops, and 1,266
pipes. Hydraulic motor in separate chamber outside chancel. Organist : Mark Dobinson, F.M.I C.

CRIEFF.—ST. COLUMBA'S EPISCOPAL CHURCH. Built 1878 and enlarged
1902 by Bishop. 2 manuals, 17 speaking stops, and 5 other stops.
Hand blown. Organist: Clement Antrobus Harris, A.R C O , A. MUS.
T C.L.

CROMER —ST. PETER AND ST. PAUL PARISH CHURCH. Built 1897 and
enlarged and brought up to date 1912 by Norman & Beard. 4 manuals,
54 speaking stops. Case from Bath Abbey. Organist: Alfred Heath.

CROYDON.—EMMANUEL CHURCH, S. CROYDON. Built by Walker. 3 manuals, 23 speaking stops, 7 other stops. Tubular pneumatic action throughout. Electric blowing. Organist: George Denham, L.R.A.M., A.R.C.O.

CROYDON.—MUSIC ROOM, ST. ERIC'S, UPPER NORWOOD (private residence of Mr. I. Clark Griffith). Built 1903 by Norman and Beard. Specification and opened by A. J Eyre, F.C.O. 3 manuals, 17 speaking stops, 8 other stops, 900 pipes. Detached console. Tubular pneumatic action. Blown by electric motor and Kinetic blower. Sweetness and delicacy of tone. Orchestral in quality.

CROYDON.—PARISH CHURCH (ST. JOHN BAPTIST). Built 1869 and rebuilt 1904 by Hill. Opened 1869 by F. Cambridge, MUS. BAC. 4 manuals, 67 stops, 3,290 pipes. Tubular pneumatic action throughout. Blown by Kinetic electric blower. Placed on N. side of choir. Organist and choirmaster: Frederick Rowland Tims, F.R.C.O.

CROYDON.—ROYAL NORMAL COLLEGE FOR THE BLIND, UPPER NORWOOD. Rebuilt 1902 by Hill. 26 speaking stops, 6 couplers. Tubular pneumatic action. Electric blowing. Principal: Sir Francis Campbell.

CROYDON.—ST. MARY'S CHURCH. Built 1899 by Hope Jones. Opened by Hugh Blair. 2 manuals, 14 speaking stops, 7 other stops, and 700 pipes Electric action, wind pressure, 10in. and 5in , supplied by Kinetic fan, and 2 h p. motor. Organist: Herbert Sayers.

CROYDON.—ST. MARY'S PARISH CHURCH, BEDDINGTON. Built 1869. Restored 1905 by Lewis. 3 manuals, 26 speaking stops, 7 other stops, 1,456 pipes, and 6 composition pedals. Blown by Crossley gas engine, in separate building. Beautifully voiced gambas. Very handsome case. Organist: Hugh Ware, F.R.C.O., L.T.C.L.

CROYDON.—ST. SAVIOUR'S CHURCH. Built 1905 by Lewis Opened by R. L. Balfour, MUS. BAC. 3 manuals, (4 pistons to each), 40 speaking stops, 13 other stops, and over 2,000 pipes. Part of Choir organ in Swell box. Balance swell pedals to Choir and Swell. Vox Humanica in separate box within Swell box. Pedal organ of 9 stops. Blown by Crossley gas engine. Organist: Edward William Groocock, F.R.C.O., A.R.C.M , L.R.A.M., A.G.S M.

DARLINGTON.—HOLY TRINITY CHURCH. Rebuilt by Nicholson & Lord. 3 manuals, 34 speaking stops, and 7 couplers. Very fine Cremona stop. Organist: G Holland Fox.

DARTFORD.—CITY OF LONDON MENTAL HOSPITAL CHAPEL. Built by Henry Speechly. Opened by present organist. Rebuilt 1912 by Norman & Beard. 3 manuals, 24 speaking stops, 6 other stops, 1,279 pipes. 3 composition pedals to Great and Swell organ, 1 reversible pedal for Great to Pedal Coupler. Choir organ in separate swell box. Tubular pneumatic action throughout. Blown by electric motor. Carved oak case. Organist: Henry Septimus Pratt.

DARTFORD.—HOLY TRINITY PARISH CHURCH. Built 1910 by Harrison. 3 manuals, 27 speaking stops, 13 couplers, 3 combination pedals, 10 combination pistons, 1 reversible piston, 2 balanced crescendo pedals. Tubular pneumatic. Blown by 3 h.p. electric motor and discus fans. Organist: W. Hall Graham.

DARWEN.—HOLY TRINITY PARISH CHURCH Built 1887 by Jardine. 3 manuals and pedals, Great 10 stops, Swell 12, Choir 6, 3 pedals, and 8 couplers, etc. Organist : Thomas Lane.

DARWEN.—PRIMITIVE METHODIST CHURCH, REDEARTH ROAD. Built by Abbott & Smith. 3 manuals and pedal, 23 speaking stops, 7 couplers, 5 composition pedals, balanced crescendo pedal to Swell. Blown by electric motor. Tubular pneumatic action throughout.

DEAL.—ST. GEORGE THE MARTYR CHURCH. Built 1880 by Browne. Opened by Dr Longhurst. 3 manuals, 27 speaking stops, 7 other stops. Fine oak case. Organist : J. Dixon Smith, F.R C.O.

DERBY.—COLLEGIATE CHURCH OF ALL SAINTS. Built by " Father Smith." Rebuilt 1879 by Stringer. Renovated and added to by Hill. 3 manuals, 38 speaking stops, and 6 other stops. Organist : Thomas Herbert Bennett, F.R.C.O , L.R.A.M., M.I.S.M.

DERBY.—LEY'S MALLEABLE CASTINGS CO , LTD , MESS ROOM. Built 1904 by Brindley & Foster. Opened by T. H. Bennett, at a banquet given by Sir Francis Ley, Bart , to his workpeople. 2 manuals, 15 speaking stops, 3 other stops, and 762 pipes. Tracker action to keyboards, and pneumatic to pedals. Very powerful for its size. Organist : Robert S. Walker

DERBY —MELBOURNE PARISH CHURCH Built 1860 by Bevington. 2 manuals, 21 speaking stops, 7 couplers, etc.

DERBY —MILFORD PARISH CHURCH. Built 1905 by Bevington. 2 manuals, 17 speaking stops, 9 couplers, etc. Part tubular.

DERBY —ST ALKMUND'S CHURCH 3 manuals, 31 speaking stops, 5 couplers, 7 double acting combination pedals, 2 balanced crescendo pedals. Tubular pneumatic action to pedal organ. Organist : Benard Fowles, L.R A M.

DERBY —ST. WERBURGH'S CHURCH. Rebuilt 1907 by Willis. Opened by Dr. Peace. 4 manuals, 49 speaking stops, and 10 other stops.

DERBY.—THE DRILL HALL. Built 1855-1870 by Bevington. 3 manuals, 35 speaking stops, 14 couplers, etc. Built for Paris Exhibition, 1855, and gained 1st class medal.

DEWSBURY.—ST. JOHN'S PARISH CHURCH, DEWSBURY MOOR. Re-built 1906 by Binns Opened by present organist. 2 manuals, improved tracker action, tubular pneumatic to pedals Organist : E. Inman Dawson, A.L.C M.

DISS.—CORN HALL. Restored 1893 by Samuel. 2 manuals. Organist : A Hemstock.

DISS.—ST MARY'S PARISH CHURCH. Built 1877 by Rayson. Opened by present organist. 3 manuals, 23 speaking stops, 5 couplers, and 1,400 pipes. Plan of organ very effective, having Swell organ behind front pipes, with Great and Choir organ divided on either side, connected underneath with slides. Organist · A. Hemstock.

DONCASTER.—CHRIST CHURCH Built 1863 by Schultze. 3 manuals, 24 speaking stops. Tracker action. Hand blown. Organist ; Alf. Taylor, Regent Square, Doncaster.

DONCASTER.—PRIORY PLACE WESLEYAN CHURCH. Built 1881 by Conacher. Opened by Dr. Turpin. 3 manuals, 31 speaking stops, 8 other stops. Organist: Asa Litchfield.

DONCASTER.—ST. GEORGE'S PARISH CHURCH. Built 1862. Restored 1894 by Schulze, Paulinzelle; and 1910 by Norman & Beard. Opened 1862 by H. Smart and 1910 by Sir Walter Parratt, M V.O. 5 manuals, 92 speaking stops, 15 other stops, 5,805 pipes, 15 composition pistons, 9 composition pedals, thunder pedal. Blown by 10 h p. electric motor. Beautiful flue work. Large sound boards and magnificent Pedal organ containing 25 stops. Organist: Wilfrid Ernest Sanderson, MUS. BAC. DUNELM , F.R.C O , L R A M.

DONCASTER.—ST. JAMES' CHURCH. Built 1858 and restored 1908 by Brindley & Foster. Opened by Mr. Hopkins. 3 manuals, 24 speaking stops, 4 other stops Blown by hand The pipes are old and were removed from the Parish Church, Doncaster. Organist: George Havelock, MUS. DOC.

DONCASTER —ST. OSWALD's CHURCH, CROWLE. Built 1906 by Wordsworth. 3 manuals, 26 speaking stops, and 7 other stops. Fine diapasons, rich reeds, orchestral stops exact prototype of instruments they represent. Organist : Mrs. Armstrong

DORCHESTER —HOLY TRINITY CHURCH 2 manuals. Enlarged 1902 by Hill. Situated in the Chancel, with additional front facing North Aisle. Organist and Choirmaster : Edgar Alfred Lane

DORCHESTER.—ST. NICHOLAS' CHURCH, ABBOTSBURY. Built 1886 by Walker. 1 manual, 6 speaking stops, 1 other stop Opened by Mr Thorne, Organist, Trinity Church, Weymouth Organist: Miss Claudia Augusta White, appointed 1906.

DOUGLAS.—See ISLE OF MAN.

DOVER.—COLLEGE CHAPEL. Built 1884 by Gern. Gift of the late Dr. Astley, of Dover. Enlarged 1907 by Browne, to the specification of present organist. Opened 1907 by present organist. 4 manuals, 37 speaking stops, 10 couplers, 15 combination pistons. Blown by Kinetic blower and electro-motor. Tubular pneumatic action throughout. Detached console. Organist: J Edis Tidnam, MUS. BAC. OXON., F R C.O.

DOVER.—COLLEGE REFECTORY Built by Gern. 3 manuals, 30 stops. Organist and Music Master : J. Edis Tidnam, MUS. BAC. OXON , F R C.O.

DOVER.—TOWN HALL. Built 1902 by Norman & Beard The gift of the late Dr Astley. Opened by present organist 4 manuals, 49 speaking stops, 15 other stops. Electro-pneumatic action Blown by electric motor. Console in North aisle, Great organ bracketed from East wall, in centre of platform ; Choir and Orchestral organ and the Solo organ, together with part of Pedal organ, in South gallery near platform ; the Swell organ and remainder of Pedal organ on opposite side. Noted for beautiful tone, orchestral effects, and peal of bells. Organist: Harry James T2ylor, F R C.O.

DOWNPATRICK.—DOWN CATHEDRAL. Erected at restoration of Cathedral 1817, by Wolfenden, Dublin. Presented by Arthur, Marquis of Downshire Experts believe it to be the work of Snetzler or Greene. Traditionally obtained through the kindness of George III 2 manuals,

28 speaking stops, and 3 other stops GG to F. 58 keys, pedals CCC to F. 1,652 pipes, 7 composition pedals. Hand blown, Tracker action. Imposingly erected on screen to West of nave Fine old oak case. Rich tone, mellow and sweet. Rebuilding under consideration. Organist : Albert John Humphrey Coulter.

DUBLIN.—ALL HALLOWS' COLLEGE. Built 1898 by Telford & Telford. 2 manuals and pedal, 20 speaking stops, 4 couplers, etc , 10 pneumatic combination pistons. Balanced swell pedal. Tubular pneumatic action throughout. Organist : V. O'Brien, 37, Rutland Square, Dublin.

DUBLIN.—CHRISTCHURCH CATHEDRAL. Built 1856 and restored 1878 by Telford 4 manuals, Great 12 stops, Swell 15, Choir 8, Solo 7, Pedal 5. Couplers Swell to Great, Swell to Choir, Solo to Great, Swell to Pedal, Great to Pedal, Sub and super octave to Swell, 7 composition pedals, tubular pneumatic action pedals Pneumatic levers Great, Swell. Organist : James F. FitzGerald, B.A., CANTAB.

DUBLIN —PARISH CHURCH, MONKSTOWN. Built 1898 by Gray & Davison. Opened by present organist. 3 manuals, 34 speaking stops, 6 other stops, 1,052 pipes, 10 composition pedals, 6 pneumatic pistons. Organist : Bartholomew Warburton Rooke, MUS. BAC.

DUBLIN.—ST GEORGE'S PARISH CHURCH. Built 1910 by Benson to specification of present organist. 3 manuals, 33 speaking stops, 8 couplers, 8 double acting pedals, 1,922 pipes Detached console Tubular pneumatic action throughout Blown by " Discus " blower. Driven by a 5 h p electric motor Pedal board radiating and concave. Organist and Choirmaster George Harrison.

DUBLIN —ST MARY'S ROMAN CATHOLIC CATHEDRAL. Built 1900 by Hill to specification of the present organist, by whom it was opened. 4 manuals, 50 speaking stops, 10 other stops, 3,000 pipes Detached console Tubular pneumatic action throughout 9 reservoirs and different pressures, 2 powerful hydraulic engines Fine variety of tone Solo organ possesses great variety of orchestral stops Fine tuba and vox humanica. Organist . Brenden J. Rogers.

DUBLIN.—ST. PHILIP'S CHURCH, UPPER RATHMINES. Built 1896 by Telford. Opened by W. H. Telford, MUS. BAC , T.C.D. and present organist. 2 manuals, 15 speaking stops and 4 other stops. Organist : E. H. Telford, 109, St Stephen's Green, Dublin.

DUBLIN.—ST SAVIOUR'S DOMINICAN CHURCH, DOMINICK STREET. Built 1897 by Telford & Telford. 4 manuals and pedal, 40 speaking stops, 8 couplers, etc , 7 composition pedals, 2,396 pipes.

DUBLIN —ST. STEPHEN'S CHURCH. Built 1889 by Conacher. Opened by present organist 4 manuals, 35 speaking stops, 12 other stops and 1,912 pipes. Organist : William H. Gater, B A , MUS. DOC., T C.D., L. MUS. T.C L.

DUDLEY.—ST. JOHN'S CHURCH Built 1886 by Conacher. 3 manuals, 22 speaking stops and 8 other stops. Organist : Alexander Clifford Duesbury, 15, Blackacre Road, Dixon's Green, Dudley. Appointed 1888.

DUDLEY —ST LUKE'S CHURCH. Restored 1911 by Nicholson & Lord. 3 manuals, 33 speaking stops, 8 other stops, 1,986 pipes. Organist : James Randall Cooke.

DUDLEY.—St. Thomas' Parish Church. Restored 1901 by Ingram & Co. Opened by H. C. Tonking. 3 manuals, 37 speaking stops, 8 other stops, 2,200 pipes. Set of *ad. lib.* stops for arranging previous combination, 6 pistons acting on whole of organ. Organist : Thomas William North.

DUMFRIES.—Pro Cathedral. Built 1899 by Cousens as a temporary organ for Lincoln Cathedral while old organ was being rebuilt and enlarged. Opened by Dr Bennett. 2 manuals, 21 speaking stops, 7 other stops, and about 1,400 pipes. Blown by hydraulic power. Organist : Frank Tipping.

DUMFRIES.—St. Michael's Church. Built 1890 by Willis. 2 manuals, 16 speaking stops, 4 other stops. Blown by Melvin hydraulic engine. Organist . J. W. Cheadle.

DUNDEE.—Gilfillan Memorial Church. Rebuilt 1906 by Norman & Beard. Opened by the late Dr. Peace. 4 manuals, 71 stops. Entirely electric. Organist : Fredk Gibson, L.R A M , L T C L.

DUNKELD.—Cathedral, The. Built 1909 by Bevington. 2 manuals, 13 speaking stops, 9 couplers, etc. Part tubular. Hydraulic blowing.

DUNS.—Boston U F. Church. Built by Conacher. 2 manuals and pedal, 10 speaking stops, 5 couplers, 4 composition pedals, 4 thumb pistons. Tubular pneumatic action. Detached console.

DUNS (SCOTLAND).—Parish Church. Built 1879 by Conacher to replace one destroyed by fire. First organ in Scotland sanctioned by the General Assembly. Organist : Johannes Albe, The Hawthorne, Duns.

DURHAM.—Cathedral, The. Built 1876 by Willis ; restored 1905 by Harrison. 4 manuals, 73 speaking stops, 17 couplers, 22 combination pistons, 6 combination pedals, 1 reversible piston, 4 stop-control switches, 3 balanced crescendo pedals. Blown by 3 electric motors. Organist : Rev. Arnold Duncan Culley, M A., Mus. Bac., F.R C.O., A R.C.M.

DURHAM.—St. Nicholas' Church. Built 1865 ; restored 1880 and 1909. 2 manuals, 24 speaking stops, 3 other stops. Radiating pedal board added in 1909. Organist . — Abbey, Old Elvet, Durham.

DURHAM.—Ushaw College. Built 1850 by Bishop. Restored by Bevington. 3 manuals, 29 speaking stops, 12 other stops, 1,717 pipes. Hydraulic engine. Organist. Rev. Edwin Bonney.

EALING.—All Saints' (Spencer Perceval Memorial) Church. Built 1905 by Norman & Beard. 3 manuals, 38 speaking stops, 6 other stops, nearly 2,000 pipes. Tubular pneumatic action throughout. Kinetic electric blowing. Separate console, giving player full view of choir. Same pattern as new R.C.O. organ. Opened by Dr W. G. Alcock (Organist Chapel Royal, St. James') Organist : — Horsey.

EALING.—Christ Church. Built by A. C. Lewis, Clapham. Opened by A. Thompson, F R.C.O. 3 manuals, 40 speaking stops, 12 other stops. Blown by two hydraulic engines. Electro pneumatic action. Console 80ft. from large organ and 25ft. from small organ, both organs being playable from same console. Organist : Albert Thompson, F R.C O.

EALING.—Parish Church. Built by Walker. 3 manuals, 40 stops. Organist . Herbert J. Dawson, MUS BAC. (CANTAB), L R.A M , F.R C.O.

EALING.—PERIVALE PARISH CHURCH. Built by Bishop. 2 manuals, 15 speaking stops, 6 other stops, 872 pipes. Pneumatic action, 5 composition pedals. Organist : Henry Armstone Ducket.

EALING.—ST. JAMES' CHURCH. Built 1909 by Bishop. Opened by present organist. 2 manuals, 16 speaking stops (Choir organ prepared for), also 12 other stops Blown by hand. 3 composition pedals. Organist : Frederick Lane, L.N.C.M.

EALING.—ST JOHN'S CHURCH. Built 1876. Restored 1907 by Forster & Andrews. 3 manuals, 37 stops. Blown by electric motor and Rotary blower. Fine tone and very large scale diapason (metal) pipes. Organist : Ernest Hartley Ford.

EALING.—ST. SAVIOUR'S CHURCH. Built 1903 by Willis. 3 manuals, 40 speaking stops, 13 other stops, 2,400 pipes. 6 pistons to each manual and 6 pedals to Pedal organ. All adjustable. Magnificent reeds. Organist. Henry Goss Custard, MUS BAC. OXON.

EALING.—TOWN HALL. Built 1862 by Bevington Opened by Verrinder. 4 manuals, 40 speaking stops, 20 other stops. Tubular action. Blown by electricity. Organist : Henry Goss Custard, MUS. BAC. OXON.

EALING.—WESLEYAN METHODIST CHURCH. Rebuilt 1903 and enlarged by Bishop. Opened by R. G. Custard. 3 manuals, 28 speaking stops, 9 other stops, 1,608 pipes. Tubular pneumatic action to manuals and couplers. Organist : Herbert W. Pierce, A.R.C.O.

EASTBOURNE —ALL SAINTS' CHURCH. Built 1885 by Hill. 3 manuals, 33 speaking stops, 11 other stops. Lever pneumatic action. Blown by hydraulic engine. Organist : M. P. Conway.

EASTBOURNE.—CENTRAL, WESLEYAN CHURCH. Built by Speechly. 3 manuals and pedal, 32 speaking stops, 9 couplers, 1,720 pipes, 8 composition pedals, 2 pneumatic pistons, swell crescendo' pedal. Pedal board radiating and concave. Tubular pneumatic action. Blown by hydraulic motors. Organist : George T. Cruse.

EASTBOURNE —CHURCH OF OUR LADY OF RANSON. Built 1903 by Morgan & Smith. 3 manuals, 40 speaking stops, 7 couplers. Divided organ. Pneumatic action throughout. Blown by two hydraulic engines and primary bellows placed in crypt.

EASTBOURNE.—ST. MARY'S PARISH CHURCH. Built 1854 by Walker. Rebuilt 1862-1868 and enlarged 1872. Reconstructed and enlarged 1908 by Nicholson. 3 manuals, 37 couplers, 9 couplers, 1,626 pipes. Tubular pneumatic action. Organist : Alfred Herbert Kerr.

EASTBOURNE.—ST. SAVIOUR'S CHURCH. Built 1882 by Walker Opened by the Reverend Sir Frederick A. Gore Ouseley. 4 manuals, 43 speaking stops, 11 other stops. Blown by electric " Discus " installation. Organist : James R Dear, MUS. BAC., F.R.C.O.

EAST HAM —CENTRAL HALL. Built 1907 by Brindley & Foster. 3 manuals, 36 speaking stops, 8 couplers, 10 combination pedals, reversing pedal, " Brindgradus " pedal and balanced crescendo pedal. Tubular pneumatic action. Blown by electric motor.

EAST MOLESEY.—ST PAUL'S PARISH CHURCH. Built 1872 by Bryson. Restored by Bishop. 3 manuals, 24 speaking stops, 5 other stops,

1,100 pipes. Blown by hand. Tubular pneumatic action to pedals, tracker action to manuals, tremulant to Swell. Several soft stops of beautiful tone. Organist : Phil. Macdonald.

ECCHINSWELL.—ST LAWRENCE'S CHURCH Built 1887 by Bevington Opened by the late J. Rost. 2 manuals, 9 speaking stops, 3 other stops Fine case (see page 51) designed by G. F. Bodley, A.R.A. Organist . Miss Hill.

EDINBURGH—BRAID CHURCH. Built 1898 by Blackett & Howden. 2 manuals, 24 speaking stops, 7 other stops, 1,511 pipes, 3 combination pedals to Great and Pedal, 3 to Swell, 1 to Tremulant, and 1 reversible Great to Pedal. Spotted metal pipes throughout. Electric motor Organist : Alfred Wm Tomlyn, MUS. BAC DUNELM, L. MUS , T C L.

EDINBURGH.—BROUGHTON PLACE CHURCH Built 1889 by Willis. Restored 1907 by Norman & Beard. Opened by T H. Collinson Reopened by present organist. 3 manuals, 34 speaking stops, 12 other stops, 1,920 pipes. Detached console Both hydraulic and electric blowing fitted, either of which can be used separately for practice ; for services both are used. Very fine diapasons and reeds. Organist : William Baird Ross, MUS. DOC. OXON., F.R C O.

EDINBURGH —FETTES COLLEGE. Built 1900 by Vincent. 2 manuals, 17 speaking stops, 7 other stops, 1,034 pipes and 6 thumb pistons Balanced Swell pedal Sforzando pedal Tubular pneumatic action throughout. Hydraulic blowing Organist : R. Sterndale Bennett.

EDINBURGH.—FREEMASONS' HALL. Built 1912 by Brindley & Foster 3 manuals, 34 speaking stops, 12 couplers, 1,791 pipes, 16 pneumatic combination accessories, 8 combination pedals, 2 tremulants, 2 balanced swell pedals. " Brindgradus " general crescendo pedal Blown by electric motor W. Grand Organist Arthur J Curle, 12, Seaview Terrace, Joppa, Edinburgh.

EDINBURGH —MUSIC CLASS ROOM. Rebuilt 1907 by Hill. 4 manuals, 54 speaking stops, 10 couplers, tubular pneumatic action. Hydraulic blowing.

EDINBURGH —NORTH LEITH U.F. CHURCH. Built 1875 and reconstructed 1899 by Hamilton. Opened 1899 by Mr. Alfred Hollins. 2 manuals, 24 speaking stops, 6 other stops and 1,316 pipes. Tubular pneumatic action Detached console. Electric blowing. Organist : Harold F. Morris, A. MUS., T.C L.

EDINBURGH.—PALMERSTON PLACE UNITED FREE CHURCH. Built 1901 by Norman & Beard. 2 manuals, 22 speaking stops, 5 couplers, 1,270 pipes, 7 combination and 1 tremulant pedals. Case designed by Washington Browne, R.S A. Organist : Samuel Warren, A.R.C.M.

EDINBURGH.—PILRIG U.F CHURCH. Built 1903 by Forster and Andrews Opened by Alfred Hollins, F.R.C.O. 2 manuals, 18 speaking stops and 7 other stops. Action noiseless. Tubular pneumatic action. Detached console. Organist : James C. Lumsden.

EDINBURGH.—PARISH CHURCH, BORTHWICK. Built 1893 by Forster & Andrews. 2 manuals and pedal, 14 speaking stops, 4 couplers, 2 composition pedals and 722 pipes. Organist : Andrew S Lumsden, A. MUS. T.C.L., L.C.M.

EDINBURGH.—St. Andrew's Parish Church. Built 1880 by Conacher Restored 1905 by Norman & Beard. Opened 1880 by Dr. Peace 3 manuals, 32 speaking stops, 5 couplers, 1 tremulant, 6 composition pedals, 1,890 pipes. Organist. James Smith Anderson, F R.C.O , MUS. BAC. OXON.

EDINBURGH.—St. Mary's Cathedral. Built 1879 by Willis. Electric action added 1897 by Hope Jones. 4 manuals, 49 speaking stops, 18 couplers, and 4 double-touch couplers Preparation for Sanctuary organ on Choir manual, and for various other stops. 20 compound composition keps, 2 Swell pedals, tremulant and stop switch. Electric motor and Willis patent cylinders. 3,160 pipes. Organist : T. H. Collinson, MUS. BAC. OXON., F.R C.O.

EDINBURGH.—St. Michael's Parish Church. Built 1895 by Brindley & Foster 2 manuals, 22 speaking stops, 5 other stops Blown by hydraulic engine. 3 stops added in 1911. Organist : Gavin Godfrey, L.R.A M., A R C O.

EDINBURGH.—St. Stephen's Parish Church. Organ built 1880 by Willis. 3 manuals, 32 speaking stops, 7 couplers, 6 composition pedals, tremolo. Blown by hydraulic engine. Organist and Choirmaster : Arthur J. Curle, 12, Seaview Terrace, Joppa, Edinburgh.

EDINBURGH.—St. Thomas' Church, Princes Street (West End). Built 1843 by Willis. Rebuilt 1883 by Brindley & Foster and 1906 by Scovell & Lewis Opened 1906 by F. l. Plummer, A R.C.M 3 manuals, 25 speaking stops, 8 other stops, 1,230 pipes, 6 pistons, 2 composition pedals, poppet pedal to Great to pedal coupler (reversible). Tubular pneumatic action throughout, blown by Melvin hydraulic engine, with patent starter at console. Wesley-Willis pedal board with all R C O recommendations. Separate console of oak Ivory draw-stops, keys, etc 7 couplers grouped over Swell manual Organist : Walter S. Abbott.

EDINBURGH.—South Leith Parish Church Built 1887 by Brindley & Foster. 3 manuals. Stops : Great 9, Swell 11, Choir 6, Pedal 5, 8 couplers, 6 composition pedals, 2 reversing pedals and 1,796 pipes. Organist : Charles Bradley.

EDINBURGH.—United Free Church, Portobello. Built by Burton. 2 manuals and pedal, 27 speaking stops, 7 couplers, 1,494 pipes Pneumatic action throughout. Detached console. Blown by hydraulic motor.

EDINBURGH.—West St. Giles' Parish Church. Built 1889 by Eustace Ingram. Opened by J. S Anderson, MUS BAC., F.R.C O. 2 manuals, 18 speaking stops, 4 couplers, 6 composition pedals and 1,068 pipes. Tubular pneumatic action throughout. Detached console 25 feet from organ. Blown by Barr hydraulic engine. Organist · Andrew J. Bell.

EGREMONT (CHESHIRE).—Presbyterian Church of England. Built 1908 by Rushworth & Dreaper to specification of present organist. 3 manuals, 36 speaking stops, 7 couplers, 8 composition pedals, 8 pistons Divided on both sides of Chancel Tromba (Great) on heavy wind pressure Choir organ stops in separate box, with independent tremulant. Tubular pneumatic action throughout, actuated by electric motors Blown by " Kinetic " fan. Organist and Choirmaster : S. Claude Ridley.

ELGIN.—PARISH CHURCH. Built 1844 by Willis. Opened by Dr. C. Peace. 2 manuals, 18 speaking stops, 4 other stops. Tracker action to manuals, pneumatic action to pedals. Blown by Swanton hydraulic engine. Organist : J. Chalmers

ELLESMERE.—ST. MATTHEW'S CHURCH, CRIFTINS. Built 1907 by Blackett and Howden. Opened by Mr. A. E. Floyd, Oswestry. 2 manuals, 9 speaking stops, 3 other stops, and 474 pipes Tubular pneumatic action to Pedal organ Swell pedal. Organist : Miss Jessie Gleaves. Appointed 1895.

ELSTREE.—ELSTREE SCHOOL. Built 1877. Rebuilt 1906 by Hill. Opened by David Beardwell and the late Mr. J. Farmer. 2 manuals, 10 speaking stops, 3 couplers, 510 pipes.

ELTHAM (KENT).—HOLY TRINITY CHURCH Built 1880 by Hill. Restored 1910 by Bishop. 3 manuals, 29 speaking stops, 5 other stops Organist: B. J. Hancock, MUS. B. OXON., F R.C.O.

ELTHAM (KENT).—WESLEYAN CHURCH Built by Burton. 2 manuals and pedal, 24 speaking stops, 7 couplers, 1,348 pipes. Tubular pneumatic action throughout.

ELY.—CATHEDRAL, THE. Built 1908 by Harrison 4 manuals, 69 speaking stops, 19 couplers, 7 combination pedals, 26 combination pistons, 1 reversible pedal, 2 reversible pistons, 2 balanced crescendo pedals. Choir, Solo and part of Great and Pedal electro-pneumatic ; Swell and remainder of Great and Pedal tubular pneumatic. Blown by 14 h.p. National gas engine and feeders. Organist : A. W. Wilson, MUS. D. OXON , F.R.C.O., The College, Ely.

ENFIELD.—ALL SAINTS' CHURCH, EDMONTON. Built 1772 by England. Restored 1869 by Walker. Rebuilt 1905 by Kirkland Opened by Dr E. H Turpin. 3 manuals, 30 speaking stops, 6 other stops. Organist : Edwin Arthur Crusha, F R.C.O., L. MUS. T.C.L.

ENFIELD.—BAPTIST CHURCH. Built 1890 and restored 1911 by Monk. 2 manuals, 13 speaking stops, 4 other stops. Mechanical blower Situated in Choir gallery at rear of church. Organist Herbert W. Davey.

ENFIELD.—BAPTIST CHURCH, ENFIELD WASH. Built 1896 by Bevington for Baptist College. Removed to Baptist Church 1909. 3 manuals, 20 speaking stops, 11 couplers. Part tubular action.

ENFIELD.—CHRIST CHURCH. Built 1898 by Monk. 3 manuals, 35 speaking stops, 5 couplers. Spotted metal pipes. Oak case.

ENFIELD.—ST. ANDREW'S CHURCH Built 1908 by Hill. 31 speaking stops, 7 couplers. Tubular pneumatic action. Organist : W. Lec-Jones

ENFIELD.—ST. PAUL'S PRESBYTERIAN CHURCH. Built 1912 by Vincent. 43 stops. Detached console. Electric blower. Organist. Paul E. Swainstead, B.A.

EPPING.—ST JOHN BAPTIST, PARISH CHURCH. Built 1895 by Wordsworth. Opened by Dr. W. J. Reynolds. Restored 1909 by Walker 4 manuals, 40 speaking stops, 10 couplers, 1 tremulant, 9 compositon pedals. Pedal board concave and radiating. Blown by two Discus blowers driven by two electric motors. Solo organ and Choir clarinet enclosed in separate Swell boxes. Organist : Donald William Henry Penrose.

EPSOM.—COLLEGE CHAPEL. Built 1896 by Gray & Davison 2 manuals, 21 speaking stops and 3 other stops Pedal board, straight and concave Tubular pneumatic action throughout Organist: Thomas Isaac Watts, M.A., MUS. BAC. CANTAB , F.R.C.O.

EXETER.—CATHEDRAL, THE. Built 1666 by Loosemore Rebuilt by Henry Speechly 4 manuals, 55 speaking stops, 9 couplers. Front pipes of pure tin, the only ones in existence in Great Britain. Organist: and Choirmaster : Dr. D. J. Wood, MUS. B. OXON., F R C O , L.T C L.

EXETER.—BEDFORD CHURCH. Built 1896 by Hele. Opened by Dr. D. J. Wood. 2 manuals, 15 speaking stops and 3 other stops. Well balanced Good tone. Organist : Henry W. Hawker.

EXETER.—MOUNT PLEASANT METHODIST CHURCH. Built 1912 by Burton. 2 manuals, 22 speaking stops, 6 combination pistons, tremulant. Blown by " Discus " blower. Organist : W. T. Slader.

EXETER.—ST. MATTHEW'S PARISH CHURCH. Built 1903 by Hele. Opened by Rev. Arnold Culley, MUS. BAC., F.R C.O. 2 manuals, 18 speaking stops, 4 other stops. Tubular pneumatic action and detached console. Choir organ prepared for. Blown by hand. Organist : F. G. Bradford, A.R C.O.

EXETER.—ST. MICHAEL'S CHURCH, HEAVITREE. Built 1896 Rebuilt 1909 by Hele Opened by present organist. 3 manuals, 37 speaking stops, and 8 other stops. Tubular pneumatic throughout. Fine diapason tone. Organist : Ferris Tozer, MUS. DOC. OXON.

FALKIRK —GRAHAMSTON PARISH CHURCH Built 1903 by Ingram. Opened by present organist. 2 manuals, 16 speaking stops, 8 other stops, 871 pipes. Blown by hydraulic engine. Built on the Ventil system, the draw-knobs all in front and contains : 8 double-acting ventils, 4 on Swell, 4 on Great. Organist : William Hamilton Wilson.

FALKIRK.—WEST U.F. CHURCH. Built 1896 by Bishop. Opened by T. H. Collinson. 2 manuals, 22 speaking stops, tremulant, 6 couplers, 6 combination pedals, 1,112 pipes. Tubular pneumatic action throughout Blown by Bamford hydraulic engine. Organist : T. W Blakey, M I S M.

FALMOUTH —PARISH CHURCH (KING CHARLES THE MARTYR). Restored 1898 by Hele. 3 manuals, 38 draw stops Pneumatic action. Organist: Robert E. Clark, MUS. BAC. OXON., A R.C M.

FARNBOROUGH —FARNBOROUGH SCHOOL. Built by Monk. Placed in chapel 1907 by Norman & Beard. 2 manuals. Organist : Archie Fairbairn Barnes, B A., MUS. BAC. OXON., F.R.C O.

FARNBOROUGH.—PARISH CHURCH. Built 1893 by Bevington. 2 manuals, 10 speaking stops, 3 other stops, 566 pipes. Front pipes decorated. Organist : R. F C. Holloway.

FARNHAM —ST. ANDREW'S PARISH CHURCH Restored 1847-67-84 by Walker. Opened 1884 by Sir George Martin. 3 manuals, 24 speaking stops, 5 other stops, and 1,536 pipes. Original builder unknown Organist : Percy R. Rowe, A.R.C M., " Esselmont," Ridgway Road, Farnham.

FAVERSHAM.—PARISH CHURCH. Built 1753 by Bridge. Repaired and improved 1825 by Elliott ; 1840 and 1852 by Hill ; 1863 Hill added Choir organ and improved Pedal ; 1867 instrument was tuned on equal temperament system ; 1892 removed from West Gallery and reconstructed in Chancel by Gern. 3 manuals, 10 stops on Great, 14 on Swell, 7 on Choir, 6 on Pedal, 9 couplers, 8 composition pedals and 8 pistons. Organist : William John Keech, MUS. BAC. DUNELM, F.R.C.O.

FELLING-ON-TYNE.—ST. PATRICK'S R.C. CHURCH. 2 manuals, 16 speaking stops, 3 other stops. Organist : Edmund Quigley.

FLEETWOOD.—ROSSALL SCHOOL. Built by Willis. 3 manuals, 22 speaking stops, 5 couplers, 6 composition pedals. Tracker action. Very old organ. Organist : Percy R. Tomlinson, M.A., MUS. BAC. CANTAB.

FOLKESTONE —CHRIST CHURCH. Restored 1905 by Norman & Beard. Opened by Mr. F. E. Fletcher 3 manuals, 40 speaking stops, 10 other stops. Blown by Kinetic-Swanton duplex blower. Organist Frank Edward Fletcher, MUS. BAC. (T.C.T.), F.R.C.O.

FOLKESTONE.—PARISH CHURCH. Built 1894 by Hill. 3 manuals, 35 speaking stops, 6 couplers. Pneumatic lever action to Great ; tracker to Swell and Choir ; 4 pistons Great ; 4 pistons Swell ; 4 pedals to Great, duplicating the pistons. Double acting pedal for Great to pedal coupler. Blown by electric motor. Organist : Cyril Gerard Church.

FOLKESTONE.—ST. MARY'S AND ST. EADBURG'S PARISH CHURCH, LYMINGE. Built 1896 by Beale & Thyne. Opened by Rev. C. J. Ridsdale. 2 manuals, 7 speaking stops, 4 other stops and 371 pipes. Two additional stops provided for. Built as a memorial to the late Canon Jenkins, Rector of Lyminge. Organist : William Edward Pitman.

FOREST GATE.—ST. ANTHONY'S R.C. CHURCH. Built by Vincent 1909. Opened by Mr. E. W. Taylor. 3 manuals, 38 stops (divided). Pneumatic action. Electric blower. Organist : Rev. Brother Joseph.

FORFAR.—PARISH CHURCH. Built 1900 by Forster & Andrews. 4 manuals, 12 stops on Great, Swell 14, Choir 6, Solo 5, Pedal 8, couplers, etc., 8. Organist : Charles Hopkins Old.

FORRES.—ST JOHN'S EPISCOPAL CHURCH. Built 1889 by Bevington. Restored 1906 by Wadsworth. 2 manuals, 13 speaking stops, 4 other stops, 696 pipes. Blown by hand. Gift of Lady Thurlow in memory of her daughter. Organist : Claude Alan Forster.

FORT WILLIAM.—ST. ANDREW'S CHURCH. Built 1882 by Bryceson Ellis. Restored 1911 by Forster & Andrews. 2 manuals, 18 speaking stops, 3 other stops. Blown by hydraulic engine. Organist : Chas. W. Todd.

GALASHIELS.—ST. JOHN'S CHURCH. Enlarged 1901 by Kirkland. 2 manuals, 12 speaking stops, 6 other stops, 596 pipes. Pneumatic action to pedals. Blown by hydraulic engine. Organist : William Taylor, A.R.C.O.

GAINSBOROUGH.—PARISH CHURCH. Built 1906 by Walker. Opened by Edgar Robinson, F.R.C.O. 3 manuals, 32 speaking stops, 9 other stops and 1,726 pipes. 7 composition pedals. Tubular pneumatic action to manuals, pedals, and couplers Balance Swell pedals to Swell and Choir. Organist : William Augustus Montgomery, MUS. BAC. (DURHAM), F.R.C.O., L.R.A.M., L. MUS. T.C.L.

GAINSBOROUGH.—WESLEYAN CHAPEL. Built by Young. 2 manuals and pedal, 25 speaking stops, 4 couplers, 7 composition pedals. Blown by hydraulic engine. Organist: G. H. Smithson, Lily Bank, Morton, Gainsborough.

GLASGOW.—ANDERSTON PARISH CHURCH. Built 1865 by Hill. Restored 1903 by Merrilees. Opened by Dr. Ives, Australia. 2 manuals. Organist: Thomas Freer.

GLASGOW.—BARONY PARISH CHURCH, THE. Built 1889 by Brindley & Foster. 3 manuals and pedal. Situated in large chamber on North side of the Chancel. Organist: Alfred Dinsdale, F.R.C.O.

GLASGOW.—BURNBANK UNITED FREE CHURCH. Built by Brindley & Foster. Restored 1909 by Mirrlees. 2 manuals, 18 speaking stops, 4 other stops. Blown by hydraulic engine. Organist: Albert J. Gray, L.T.S.C.

GLASGOW.—CATHEDRAL, THE. Built 1876 by Willis. Rebuilt and enlarged 1903. Opened 1876 by Dr A L Peace; 1903 by present organist. 4 manuals, 57 speaking stops, 22 other stops, 4,000 pipes. Interchangeable combinations. Tubular pneumatic action. Magnificent diapason tone. Blown by 3 12-h p electric motors. Organist: Herbert F. R. Walton, A.R.C.M.

GLASGOW.—CITY HALL. Built by Lewis. 4 manuals and pedal, 53 speaking stops, 21 couplers, 2 tremulants, 6 accessories, 4 adjustable combinations, 29 key touches, 9 composition pedals, 4 balanced crescendo pedals.

GLASGOW.—FINE ART GALLERIES. Built 1902 by Lewis. 3 manuals and pedal, 48 speaking stops, 14 couplers, 8 combination pedals, 3 balanced swell pedals, 2 tremulants, 30 combination pistons. Tubular pneumatic action throughout.

GLASGOW.—GOVAN PARISH CHURCH.—Built by Brindley & Foster. 3 manuals, 31 speaking stops, 6 other stops. Organist: Robert Fox Frew.

GLASGOW.—GOVAN TOWN HALL. Built 1900 by Norman & Beard. Opened by J. E. R. Senior, F.R.C.O. 4 manuals, Great, Swell, Choir and Solo. Blown by electric motor. Organist: J. E. R. Senior.

GLASGOW.—HYNDLAND CHURCH. Built 1886 by Willis. 3 manuals, 32 speaking stops, 5 other stops, 7 composition pedals, and 2,130 pipes. Organist: W. Forbes Forsyth, L.R.A.M., A.R.C.O.

GLASGOW.—PARK CHURCH. Built 1889 by Willis. 3 manuals, 39 speaking stops, 8 couplers, over 2,000 pipes, 7 composition pedals. Choir organ in Swell box. One reversible pedal for Great to Pedal. Compressed air movement to Pedal and Choir organs. Two Swell pedals, placed in centre of pedal-board. Key fittings and draw stop jambs of oak. Draw stop knobs of solid ivory. Organist: Purcell James Mansfield, F.R.C.O., A.R.C.M, L. MUS. T.C.L., L.L.C.M.

GLASGOW.—ST ANDREW'S HALL. Built 1877 and rebuilt 1905 by Lewis. 4 manuals and pedals, 75 speaking stops, 22 couplers, 5,093 pipes, 8 adjustable combinations, 50 pistons, 9 composition pedals, 3 balanced crescendo pedals, 3 tremulants. Tubular pneumatic action throughout. Blown by hydraulic engines.

GLASGOW.—St. Kenneth's Parish Church. Built 1906 by Vincent. 3 manuals, 40 stops   Tubular pneumatic action.

GLASGOW.—St. Mary's Church, Abercromby Street. Built 1906 by Wilkinson. 3 manuals, 28 speaking stops, 8 couplers, 8 combination pedals. Organist : Mr. Byatt.

GLASGOW.—St. Mary's Cathedral. Built 1909 by Harrison. 3 manuals, 54 speaking stops, and 15 couplers ; total, 69 stops. Action partly tubular-pneumatic and partly electro-pneumatic. Blown by discuss fans operated by an electric motor. Organist: G. T. Pattman, F.R.C.O.

GLASGOW.—Springburn Hall. Built 1902 by Binns. Opened by H. Walton. 3 manuals, 47 speaking stops, 14 couplers, 11 pistons, 8 combination pedals, 2,796 pipes   Binns' patent tubular pneumatic action throughout.   Two hydraulic engines

GLASGOW.—Tollcross U.F. Church, Main Street. Built 1904 by Brindley & Foster. Opened by Thomas Berry, MUS. BAC. (CANTAB). 2 manuals, 20 speaking stops, 6 other stops, 1,052 pipes and 6 composition pedals. Ball and Swell pedal. Tubular pneumatic action Organist : Daniel Patterson, A R.C O , A.M., T.C L.

GLASGOW.—University, The. Built 1904 by Lewis. Opened by Dr. A. L. Peace   4 manuals and pedal, 50 speaking stops, 24 couplers and accessories, 18 key-touches, 9 composition pedals, 3 balanced crescendo pedals. Blown by electric motors   Organist : A. M. Henderson, L.R.A.M.

GLASGOW.—Victoria Park United Free Church, Partick. Built 1911 by Abbott & Smith. Opened by Herbert Walton, organist Glasgow Cathedral. 3 manuals, 34 speaking stops, 18 couplers, 16 combination pistons and pedals. Probably the only church organ containing a large bass gong drum, also contains thunder pedal, dulcitone, etc. Blown by electric motor   Tubular pneumatic action throughout. Fine carved oak case.

GLASTONBURY.—St. John Baptist Church. Built 1817 by Flight. Restored 1859 by Willis and 1887 by Sweetland   3 manuals, 23 speaking stops, 4 couplers, 1,375 pipes. Incomplete Swell to Gamut G only. Choir to Swell coupler instead of Swell to Choir   Blown by hand. Organ not in use at present ; funds urgently needed for restoration. Organist : David Scott, A.R.C.

GLOSSOP —All Saints' Parish Church. Built by Brindley & Foster. Rebuilt 1899 by Young.   Opened by present organist.   3 manuals, 21 speaking stops, 6 other stops.   13 additional stops prepared for. Organist : Wilfred E. Cottrill.

GLOSSOP.—Wesleyan Church. Built by Conacher.   3 manuals and pedal, 32 speaking stops, 12 couplers, 8 composition pedals, 8 pneumatic pistons, reversible pedal for Great to Pedal " on and off," 2 balanced crescendo pedals, 1,658 pipes. Tubular pneumatic action throughout. Oak case.   Blown by electric motor.   Organist : Henry Fielding.

GLOUCESTER.—Churcham Church. Built by Vowles.   3 manuals and pedal, 12 speaking stops, 8 couplers, tremulant, 4 composition pedals. Detached console.   Pneumatic action throughout.

GLOUCESTER.—St. Mark's Church. Built 1907 by Hill. 3 manuals, 23 speaking stops, 6 couplers. Combination pistons to Great and Swell, combination pedals to Great. Tubular pneumatic action. Electric blowing (Kinetic-Swanton Co). Ordinary hand blowers, in case of necessity. Organist: Herbert Charles Deavin, A R C.O.

GLOUCESTER.—Southgate Congregational Church. Built 1878 by Henry Speechly. Opened by Mr. J. Stimpson. 2 manuals, 23 speaking stops, 5 couplers, 6 composition pedals, about 1,220 pipes. Organist: Franklin Higgs.

GODALMING.—Parish Church. Built by Hill. Restored by Brindley & Foster. 3 manuals, 36 speaking stops, 8 other stops, 6 pistons, tubular pneumatic action throughout. Blown by hydraulic motor. 4th manual prepared for. Organist: Alfred Alexander Mackintosh, F.R.C.O.

GORLESTON.—St. Andrew's Parish Church. Built by Bishop. 2 manuals, 22 speaking stops, 3 couplers, 3 composition pedals to Great and 3 to Swell. Tracker action throughout. Organist: W. Percy Jones.

GOSPORT.—St. Mary's Church, Alverstoke. Built 1869 by Hunter. 2 manuals, 22 speaking stops. Organist: Ernest Douglas, A.R.C.O.

GRAYS.—St. Peter & Paul, Parish Church. Built by Lewis. Rebuilt by Tirrell. 2 manuals, 11 speaking stops and 3 other stops. Fine open diapason on Great. Opened by Dr. Lewis after enlargement. Organist: William Henry Fraser, F.I G.C.M., L.I.C.M.

GREAT YARMOUTH.—Parish Church (St. Nicholas). Built 1733 by Jordan. Enlarged 1812 by England; 1844 by Gray & Davison; 1870 by Hill. Divided, enlarged and placed in Chancel aisle 1875 by Bishop. Entirely rebuilt and brought up-to-date 1902 by Binns. 4 manuals 66 speaking stops. Opened by Dr. Keeton. Organist: Haydon Hare F.R.C.O. A.R.C.M.

GREAT YARMOUTH.—St Mary's Parish Church, Southtown. Built 1867 by Mack. 2 manuals, 18 speaking stops, and 6 other stops. Fine flue work. Open diapason on Great. Organist: William Richard Hunn, F.R.C.O., A R.C.M., L.R.A.M.

GREAT YARMOUTH.—St. Peter's Church. Built by Bishop. 3 manuals 24 speaking stops, 5 other stops. Removed from gallery to Chancel, 1906. Organist: Charles Walter Moss, F.R.C.O., M.I.S.M.

GREENOCK.—Mid Parish Church. Built 1865 by Forster & Andrews. Restored 1912 by Mirlees. 3 manuals, 32 speaking stops, 10 other stops. Blown by hydraulic engine. Tubular pneumatic action to keyboard, pedal board and draw stop actions. Detached console. Organist: Latimer Tertius Sharp, A.R.C.O.

GREENOCK.—St. John's Episcopal Church. Built 1870 by Mirrlees. 3 manuals, 30 speaking stops. Organist: Thomas Bates.

GREENOCK.—St. Paul's Church. Built 1892 by Willis. 3 manuals, 28 speaking stops, 6 other stops, 6 composition pedals. Blown by two Ross valve engines.

GRIMSBY.—ALL SAINTS' CHURCH. Built 1912 by Brindley & Foster. 2 manuals, 21 speaking stops, 6 other stops, 1,237 pipes, 29 pneumatic combination accessories, 9 composition pedals, tremulant, balanced swell pedal. Blown by electric motor. Organist: Ernest Harrison, Thorsgarth, Park Avenue, Grimsby.

GRIMSBY.—ST. ANDREW'S CHURCH. Built 1866 by Forster & Andrews. Enlarged 1908 by Cousan. Opened by Dr. G J Bennett. 3 manuals, 23 speaking stops, 7 couplers Pneumatic throughout.

GRIMSBY.—WELHOLME ROAD CONGREGATIONAL CHURCH. Built 1908 by Cousans, incorporating a smaller instrument by Forster & Andrews. Opened by Mr. Goss Custard 3 manuals, 8 couplers, 37 speaking stops Detached console Pneumatic throughout. Electric blowing. Organist: J. Wintringham Smathurst.

GUERNSEY.—ST. STEPHEN'S CHURCH, ST. PETER'S PORT. Built 1866 by Robson Enlarged and improved successively by Dr. Hinton, Wedlake, Oldknow, Hicks, Beale & Thynne, Hope Jones, Ingram, Norman & Beard, and present organist 3 manuals, 33 speaking stops and 7 couplers. Organist. J. Matthews, R.C.M. DRESDEN.

GUILDFORD.—CATHOLIC APOSTOLIC CHURCH, ALBURY. Built 1860 by Holdich & Ingram; renovated 1912 by Gray & Davison. 2 manuals, 14 speaking stops and 4 other stops. Blown by hydraulic engine. . Organist: Gilbert H. Coe.

GUILDFORD —ST NICHOLAS' CHURCH, CRANLEIGH. Built 1875 by Hill. 2 manuals, 17 speaking stops, 3 other stops. Organist: Charles Henry Vince, A.T.C.L.

GUISBOROUGH.—ST NICHOLAS' CHURCH. Restored 1906 by Hopkins. Opened by present organist 3 manuals, 32 speaking stops, 8 other stops, and 1,763 pipes Originally a 2 manual Pedal board Wesley-Willis measurements, drawstop jambs at an angle, solid ivory drawstop knobs; pitch, R.S.A.; 3in wind pressure; blown by hydraulic engine and two independent feeders Organist: Charles Henry Fordham, F.G.C.M, L. MUS. V.C M.

HALIFAX.—ALL SAINTS' CHURCH 2 manuals, 20 speaking stops and 3 other stops (couplers). Organist: Geo. Horsfield.

HALIFAX —KING'S CROSS WESLEYAN CHURCH. Built 1898 by Norman & Beard 3 manuals, 34 speaking stops, 10 couplers. Blown by double feeders, electric motor. Organist: Robert Halliday Bruce.

HALIFAX.—PARISH CHURCH. Built 1766 by Snetzler, still contains some original pipe work. Opened by Joah Bates. Rebuilt 1878 and 1897 by Abbott & Smith 4 manuals, 49 speaking stops, 11 couplers, over 20 combination pistons and pedals Electric blown. Fine oak case. Organist: Joseph Soar, MUS. BAC DUNELM., A.R.C.M., F.R C.O

HALIFAX.—ST. JAMES' CHURCH. Built 1881 by Halnshaw Opened by Dr. Roberts. 3 manuals, 30 speaking stops, 6 other stops, 1,628 pipes. Placed in West gallery. Organist: William Horsfield, A.R.C O

HALIFAX.—ST MARY'S CHURCH Restored 1900 by Abbott & Smith. Original organ by Hill. Opened 1900 by H A. Fricker. 3 manuals, 26 speaking stops, 7 other stops, and 1,556 pipes. Organist: Edmund Mountain.

HALIFAX.—St. Paul's Church, King Cross. Built 1912 by Abbott & Smith. Opened by Sydney H. Nicholson, M A , MUS. BAC , Organist Manchester Cathedral. 3 manuals, 37 speaking stops, 10 couplers, 21 pistons and pedals. Electric blown. Tubular pneumatic action throughout. Organist : A. Ryder.

HALIFAX.—West Vale Baptist Church. Built 1909 by Rushworth & Dreaper. 3 manuals, 28 speaking stops, 8 couplers, 6 composition pedals. Tubular pneumatic action. Blown by hydraulic motor. Organist : E. Fielding.

HALSALL.—Parish Church. Built 1874 by Rushworth & Dreaper. 2 manuals, 24 speaking stops, 6 couplers, 6 composition pedals Renovated and improved by builders 1887. Tubular pneumatic action to Swell and pedal Organist : F. Jones.

HAMPTON —St. James' Church, Hampton Hill. Built about 100 years ago for St. Peter's, Eaton Square, S.W., by Bishop. Sold to Hampton Hill Church when the present organ by Lewis was built for St. Peter's Restored about 1881 by Bishop. Thoroughly rebuilt and modernised, with pneumatic action and patent stop keys by Hele, 1912. 26 speaking stops, 8 other stops, 1,417 pipes, including tremulant. Blown by " Sterling " fan driven by electric motor. Organist : Henry T; Gilberthorpe, F.R.C O , L. MUS. T.C.L.

HAMPTON —St. Mary the Virgin Church Built 1832 and restored 1898 by Bishop. 3 manuals, 32 speaking stops, 9 other stops, 1,842 pipes. Blown by water power Tubular pneumatic action Original organ gift of William IV. One of the earliest " Clarabellas," by J C. Bishop, inserted 1832. Organist : Cecil Ridgway, F R.C O , A.R.C M

HANWELL.—London County Asylum Chapel. Built 1901 by Bishop & Sons, Ipswich. Cost £300. 2 manuals, 13 speaking stops, 4 other stops, 683 pipes. Organist : Leonard Holmes Walker.

HARROGATE —Bilton Parish Church. Built 1905 by Hill 3 manuals, 31 speaking stops, 8 other stops Blown by hydraulic power The organ is placed on the North side of the choir stalls and the console at the South East side , the action is tubular pneumatic and is carried under the Chancel. Organist : S. W. Swainson, F.R C.O.

HARROGATE.—St Mary's Church Built 1894 by Binns. 3 manuals, 39 speaking stops, 8 other stops. Blown by hand Choir organ is contained in separate Swell box. Organist : J. C Stephenson, A.R.C.O.

HARROGATE.—St. Paul's Presbyterian Church Built 1896 by Abbott & Smith Opened by Sir Walter Parratt. 3 manuals, Choir organ prepared for, 30 speaking stops, 7 other stops, 1,879 pipes, 6 composition pedals, 1 double acting Great to Pedal coupler, pneumatic action to pedals Organist : John Adelberg Lawson, F.R.C.O , F.T.C L.

HARROGATE —St. Peter's Church. Built by Schultze. Restored 1903 by Binns Opened by W T. Best 3 manuals, 36 speaking stops, 12 other stops. Organist : John Pullein, F.R.C.O.

HARROGATE —Trinity Wesleyan Church. Built 1880 by Forster & Andrews. 3 manuals, 30 speaking stops, 6 other stops, 1,720 pipes. Organist and Choirmaster : J. W. Fitton, MUS. BAC., F.R.C.O.

HARROW.—TRINITY PRESBYTERIAN CHURCH. Built 1909 by Morgan & Smith. 2 manuals, 20 speaking stops, 5 couplers. Blown by electric motor. Organist : A. E. Burley.

HARTLEPOOL.—ST. HILDA'S CHURCH. Built by Conacher. 3 manuals, 26 speaking stops, 6 couplers and tremulant. Organist : J. H. Robson.

HASTINGS.—WELLINGTON SQUARE BAPTIST CHURCH. Rebuilt 1906 by S. F. Dalladay, A.R.C O. Opened by builder. 3 manuals, 61 notes, 26 speaking stops, 6 other stops, 1,647 pipes, 5 composition pedals. Organist : Hiram Alfred Hollands.

HAVERFORDWEST.—ST. MARY'S CHURCH. Built by England. Restored 1860 by Banfield ; further restored, enlarged and removed from West gallery to Chancel 1889 by Hill. Opened 1889 by Dr J A. Greenish. 3 manuals, 30 speaking stops, 8 other stops, 1,825 pipes. Possesses grand Swell organ, including a beautiful Vox Humana, the gift of Mrs. F. R. Greenish. Organist : Sidney Herbert Anstey, A.R.C.O.

HAWICH.—PARISH CHURCH. Built 1897 by Forster & Andrews. 3 manuals, 29 speaking stops, and 7 couplers ; 3 composition pedals to Great, 3 to Swell. Pneumatic action throughout. Organist : A. N. McLeod Colledge, L.L.C.M.

HECKMONDWIKE.—GEORGE STREET CONGREGATIONAL CHURCH. Built 1905 by Wordsworth. 3 manuals, 33 speaking stops, 10 other stops, 8,217 pipes. Blown by 4 feeders worked by 2 hydraulic motors. 6 interchangeable pistons and composition pedals. Opened by E. H. Lemare. Organist : John Bowling.

HECKMONDWIKE.—ST. JAMES PARISH CHURCH. Built 1878 by Brindley & Foster. Restored 1906 by Binns. 3 manuals, 23 speaking stops, 7 other stops, 1,384 pipes. Organist : Joel Allott.

HELENSBURGH.—ROW PARISH CHURCH. Restored 1903 by Hill. 3 manuals, 34 speaking stops, 6 other stops Very fine diapasons and trumpet on Great. Organist : Vernon Oswald Wright, A.R.C.M.

HELENSBURGH.—ST. COLUMBA'S CHURCH. Restored 1902 by Eustace Ingram Opened by Dr A. L. Peace. 2 manuals, 26 speaking stops, 5 couplers. Tubular pneumatic action. Organist : S. Townshend, L R.A.M.

HELENSBURGH —ST MICHAEL AND ALL ANGELS' EPISCOPAL CHURCH Built 1887 by Gern. Restored 1906 by Ingram. 3 manuals, 31 speaking stops, 13 other stops, and 1,975 pipes. 9 composition pedals, 14 pistons with indicators. Tubular pneumatic action throughout. Erected on each side of Chancel with detached console. Designed by present organist : T. W. Stanton.

HELENSBURGH.—WEST U.F. CHURCH. Built by Hill. 3 manuals. Organist : W. R. Wright, MUS. BAC. OXON.

HEMEL HEMPSTED.—PARISH CHURCH OF ST. MARY. Built 1910 by Walker Opened by Sir Frederick Bridge, C.V.O. 3 manuals, 21 speaking stops, 6 other stops. Splendid quality throughout. Organist : W. E Kirby, F.R.C.O.

HENDON.—St. Mary's Parish Church. Built 1894 by Hope-Jones. 4 manuals, 42 stops. Great and Swell organs in West gallery and Choir organ in North transept in chancel, all being connected by cable, 170ft. long. Organist : Thomas Rimmer.

HENFIELD.—St. Peter's Parish Church. Built 1882 and completed 1904 by Forster & Andrews. 2 manuals, 19 speaking stops, 5 other stops, 1,056 pipes. Tracker action. Blown by hand. Has excellent reeds and a good tone generally. Organist : John Crapps, F.R.C.O.

HEREFORD.—Cathedral, The. Restored 1892 and added to 1909 by Willis. Original organ built 1686 by Renatus Harris was presented by Charles II. Has been added to and altered by various builders. 4 manuals, 16 stops on Great ; Swell, 14 ; Choir, 10 ; Solo, 3 ; Echo, 7 ; Pedal, 10 ; couplers, 16 ; 3,455 speaking pipes ; 9 composition pedals ; 3 swell pedals ; 18 pneumatic combination pistons ; nearly 300 interchangeable pneumatic combination knobs. Tubular pneumatic action throughout. Blown by 5 hydraulic engines. Organist : George Robertson Sinclair, MUS. DOC., F.R.C.O., HON. R.A.M., L.R.A.M. Assistant Organist : Percy Clarke Hull, L.R.A.M., A.R.C.O.

HEREFORD.—Church of St. Francis Xavier. Built 1845 by Bevington. Rebuilt 1899 by Ingram. 2 manuals, 25 speaking stops, 4 couplers, and 1,426 pipes. Choir organ of 6 stops prepared for. Situated in West gallery. Blown by hydraulic power.

HERNE BAY.—Christ Church. Built 1880 by Forster & Andrews. 2 manuals, 21 speaking stops, 5 other stops. Organist : W. E. Hinchliffe.

HERTFORD —All Saints' Parish Church. Built 1900 by Willis. Opened by M. Heywood, A.R.A.M. 3 manuals, 30 speaking stops, 5 other stops, 1,658 pipes. Pneumatic action. 6 composition pedals and T pedal to Great to Pedal coupler on and off. Organist : James Lively Gregory, MUS. BAC. DURHAM, F.R.C.O.

HERTFORD.—Holy Trinity Church, Bengeo. Built 1878 by Walker. Opened by A. Shaw. 2 manuals, 13 speaking stops, 3 other stops, 750 pipes. Dulciana running through in metal. Organist : T. Merry.

HIGHGATE.—St. Joseph's Retreat. Rebuilt 1890 by Monk. 3 manuals, 40 stops. Detached console. Tubular pneumatic action Organist : Vernor Grant.

HIGH WYCOMBE.—All Saints' Parish Church. Built 1875 by Jones. Restored by Hill. 3 manuals, 31 stops, including 32ft. open diapason. Pedal organ. Organist : George F. Andrews, A.R.C.O.

HINCKLEY.—St. Mary the Virgin Parish Church. Built 1907 by Norman & Beard. 3 manuals, 40 speaking stops, 12 other stops, 2,120 pipes. Tubular pneumatic action throughout. 4 pistons to Great and Swell ; 3 to Choir ; 9 composition pedals and balanced Swells ; detached console. Blown by electric motor and rotary fan. Organist : Paul Rochard, A.R.C.M.

HONITON.—St. Paul's Parish Church. Built 1873 by Bishop & Starr. Opened by Dr. S. S. Wesley. 2 manuals ; 22 speaking stops: Great, 9 ; Swell, 10 ; Pedal, 3 ; couplers, 3 ; composition pedals : 3 to Great and 3 to Swell. Organist : Owen S. Jarratt.

HONLEY.—PARISH CHURCH. Built by Conacher. 3 manuals and pedal, 31 speaking stops, 10 couplers, 6 composition pedals, 6 composition pistons. Piston for Great to Pedal " on and off." Tubular pneumatic action throughout. Pedal board radiating and concave. Blown by hydraulic engine. Oak case.

HORNSEA.—PRIMITIVE METHODIST CHURCH Built 1905 by Wadsworth. Opened by C. F. Carter, MUS. BAC. 2 manuals, 16 speaking stops, tremulant, 4 couplers, and 842 pipes. 4 combination pedals: 2 to Swell, 2 to Great. Organist; R. T. C. Morrison.

HORNSEY.—ALEXANDRA PALACE, MUSWELL HILL. Built 1875 by Willis. 4 manuals, 89 speaking stops, 15 other stops, 5,849 pipes, 8 combination pedals To pedal organ, 32 combination pistons. Old organ burnt 1873. Organist ; G. D Cunningham.

HORNSEY.—HOLY INNOCENTS' CHURCH. Built 1872 by Walker. Opened by J. B. Ring 2 manuals, 20 speaking stops, 3 other stops. Blown by hand. Tracker action. Fine diapason tone. Removed into South Transept September, 1912. Organist and Choir Director : Arthur M. Flack.

HORNSEY —NEW PARISH CHURCH OF ST. MARY. Built 1889 by H. Willis. Opened by present organist. 3 manuals, 39 speaking stops, 7 couplers, 10 composition pedals and pistons. Pneumatic action to Swell, Great and Pedal organ. Blown by three hydraulic engines placed in basement. Organist: Henry John Baker, F.I.S SC., LONDON, Associate Philharmonic Society.

HORNSEY.—PARK CHAPEL, CROUCH END Built 1893 by Willis. Opened by Fountain Meen. 3 manuals, 36 speaking stops, 9 couplers, 2,080 pipes. Built upon compressed air system Wind supplied by hydraulic engines. Organist : Josiah Booth, A.R.A M.

HORNSEY.—ST. JAMES' CHURCH, MUSWELL HILL. Built 1912 by Harrison. 3 manuals, 47 speaking stops, 16 couplers, 6 combination pedals, 18 combination pistons, 2 reversible pistons, 1 reversible pedal, 2 balanced crescendo pedals Tubular pneumatic. Blown by electric motor and " Discus " fans Organist : G. D. Cunningham.

HORNSEY —ST. PETER IN CHAINS, STROUD GREEN. 3 manuals, 17 stops. Box organ with pipes in centre of choir gallery. Organist ; Francis S. Hales, CERT. S A.

HORSFORTH.—ST. MARGARET'S CHURCH. Built by Abbott & Smith. 3 manuals and pedal, 35 speaking stops, 13 couplers, 11 composition pedals. Blown by hand. Tubular pneumatic action.

HORSHAM.—ALL SAINTS' CHURCH, ROFFEY. Built 1879 by Walker. 2 manuals, 13 speaking stops, 3 couplers. Stands in gallery in tower. Played from back of choir stalls. Organist : Goodhart Godfrey.

HORSHAM —CHRIST'S HOSPITAL CHAPEL. Built 1902 by Kirkland. 4 manuals, 36 speaking stops, 10 other stops, 2,038 pipes. Divided in two—Great, Swell and Solo organs on one side of chapel ; Choir and Pedal organs on the other. Pneumatic action. Blown by electric motors. Organist : Robert Wilkinson.

HORSHAM.—CHRIST'S HOSPITAL, THE BIG SCHOOL. Built 1800 and rebuilt 1902 by Hill 3 manuals, 37 speaking stops, 6 other stops Pneumatic action. Blown by electric motors. Organist : Robert Wilkinson·

HORSHAM.—St. Mary's Parish Church. Built 1865 by Willis. Renovated 1909 by Norman & Beard. 3 manuals, 31 speaking stops, 8 couplers and tremulant, 1,856 pipes, 4 pedal stops, including ophicleide 16ft. Kinetic electric blower. Slow speed motor Beautiful mellow tone, especially diapasons. Placed on North side of Chancel. Organist : William Stanley Sutton, F.R.C.O., L.R.A.M

HORSHAM.—St. Peter's Church, Cowfold Built 1888 and rebuilt 1911 by Forster & Andrews. The gift of Colonel C. B. Godman. 2 manuals, 10 speaking stops and 3 other stops ; 535 pipes. Exceptionally good waldflute on Great. Organist : Frederick Charles Peacock.

HOVE —All Saints' Parish Church Built 1904 by Hill 3 manuals, Great organ 14 stops, Swell 13, Choir 12, Pedal 9, couplers 9, tremulants 2, 12 pistons and balanced swells to Swell and part of Choir. Tubular pneumatic action. Blown by 5 h p. electric motor, coupled direct to Kinetic blowing machine. Organist : Frank Butler.

HOVE.—St. Barnabas Church. Originally at Ker Gray Chapel, Albemarle Street, London. Rebuilt 1903 by Morgan & Smith. 3 manuals, 26 speaking stops, 7 other stops Pneumatic action throughout. Blown by electric motor. Organist : Miss Margaret Verrall.

HOVE —St Patrick's Church Built 1864 by Willis. Restored 1906 by Morgan & Smith. Opened 1906 by Dr. W Alcock 3 manuals, 39 speaking stops, 14 other stops, 16 pistons, 9 pedals, 2 Swell pedals, 2,338 pipes. Electro-pneumatic action. Detached console. Electric blower. Organist · Seymour Pile, M.A. CANTAB , L.R.A.M., F R.C O.

HOYLAKE —Congregational Church Built by Hope Jones Rebuilt 1906 by Norman & Beard. 3 manuals, 18 speaking stops, 13 other stops Electric organ

HUDDERSFIELD.—Buxton Road Sunday School, Built by Conacher 2 manuals and pedal, 10 speaking stops, 4 couplers, 4 composition pedals. Blown by hydraulic engine.

HUDDERSFIELD —Lindley Parish Church. Built by Conacher. 3 manuals, 31 speaking stops, 12 couplers (2 tremulants), 12 composition pedals, 7 pneumatic pistons, 2 double acting pistons. Tubular pneumatic action throughout. Blown by electric motor. Organist : Haydn H Sandwell, F R C.O.

HUDDERSFIELD.—Parish Church Built 1910 by Conacher. 4 manuals. Blown by hydraulic pressure. Organist : A Eaglefield Hull, MUS. DOC. OXON , F.R.C.O.

HUDDERSFIELD.—Queen Street Wesleyan Chapel. Built by Young 3 manuals and pedal, 40 speaking stops, 6 couplers, 10 thumb pistons, 10 composition pedals, 2,346 pipes Pedal board radiating and concave. Renovated 1911 by Messrs Peter Conacher & Co., of Huddersfield, who introduced their pneumatic action, stop-tabs over upper manual, thumb pistons and the new keyboard and pedal board, also new large open diapason on Great organ. Balanced crescendo pedals to Swell and Choir organs. Tremulants to Swell and Choir. Organist : Herbert Stather.

HUDDERSFIELD.—St. Paul's Church Built 1900 by Abbott & Smith. 3 manuals, 34 speaking stops, 8 other stops, 1,979 pipes Tubular pneumatic action throughout, except manual stop action. Handsome oak case Blown by hydraulic engine. Fine flue work, especially diapasons. Organist : Arthur Pearson.

HUDDERSFIELD.—TOWN HALL. Built 1878. Restored 1902 by Willis.
Opened by Sir Walter Parratt. Re-opened by E. H. Lemare. 4
manuals, 51 speaking stops, 16 other stops, over 3,000 pipes Tubular
pneumatic action throughout. Adjustable pistons, fine reeds;
perfect action. Organist: Arthur Pearson.

HUDDERSFIELD.—WESLEYAN CHURCH, GLEDHOLT. Built by Conacher.
3 manuals and pedal, 36 speaking stops, 8 couplers, 6 composition
pedals, double-acting pneumatic pistons to work the Swell to Great
and Great to Pedal. Couplers. Pitch pine case. Organist: John
Fletcher Sykes, F.R.C.O., 41a, Trinity Street, Huddersfield.

HUDDERSFIELD.—ZION METHODIST CHURCH, LINDLEY. Built 1871.
Restored 1890 by Brindley & Foster. 3 manuals, 32 speaking stops,
9 other stops, 1,874 pipes. Tubular pneumatic action throughout.
Blown by 2 hydraulic engines. Elaborate and splendidly decorated.
Unique tone, fine, mellow and powerful reeds. 32ft stop on pedals,
2 tremulants, 2 Swell pedals. Organist: Samuel E. Worton.

HULL.—ALBANY NEW WESLEYAN CHURCH. Built 1900 by Nicholson.
3 manuals, 28 speaking stops, 16 other stops, 1,524 pipes, 8 composition
pedals. Tubular pneumatic action to manuals. Blown by electric
motor.

HULL.—ALL SAINTS' CHURCH, HESSLE. Built 1891 by Forster & Andrews.
3 manuals. Organist: Philip Chignell, F.R.C.O.

HULL.—CITY HALL. Built 1911 by Forster & Andrews. Opened by Edwin
H. Lemare. 4 manuals, 125 stops, 5,505 pipes, 30 couplers, 19 other
movements, 35 combination pistons and pedals, balanced crescendo
pedal to Swell, Great, Pedal and couplers. Tubular bells, steel bars,
drums. First organ to have a Mustel Celesta and first concert organ
of this magnitude to have the advantages of a detached console.
Tubular pneumatic action throughout. Fine oak case. Electric
blowing by two patent " Discus " blowers and one " Booster." Two
six horse-power motors. One of the most up-to-date orchestral concert
organs in Great Britain.

HULL.—HOLY TRINITY PARISH CHURCH. Built 1876. Restored and
enlarged 1899 and 1908 by Forster & Andrews. 4 manuals, 12 stops
Great organ, 8 Solo, 15 Swell, 9 Choir, 9 Pedal; 15 couplers. Organist:
Fred K. Bentley, MUS. BAC. OXON., Pearson Park, Hull. Appointed
1881.

HULL.—PORTOBELLO P.M. CHURCH. Built by Conacher. 2 manuals and
pedal, 17 speaking stops, 4 couplers, 6 composition pedals. Tubular
pneumatic action to Pedal organ. Pedal board radiating and concave.
Blown by electric motor. Organist: John Richard Lawson, F.R.C.O.,
L.R.A.M.

HULL.—QUEEN's HALL. Built 1907 by Forster & Andrews. Opened by
J. A. Meale, F.R.C.O. 3 manuals, 47 speaking stops, 29 other stops,
2,597 pipes, 25 tubular bells, side drum, gong drum, thunder pedal,
2 Sforzando pedals, 15 composition pedals, 16 combination pistons,
6 adjustable and 3 balanced crescendo pedals. Solo and Choir organs
combined on top manual. Organist: Berkeley Mason, F.R.C.O., L R.A.M.

HULL.—ST JOHN's CHURCH. Built 1865 by Forster & Andrews. Opened
by Dr. Spark, Leeds. 3 manuals, 26 speaking stops, 4 other stops,
1,648 pipes. Tracker action. Flutes and diapasons very fine. All
solid work, no fancy stops. Organist: John Ellis.

180 *DICTIONARY OF ORGANS AND ORGANISTS*

HULL.—St. Stephen's Parish Church. Built by Hill. 3 manuals, 28 speaking stops, 4 other stops. Organist: Hubert Hogg, A.R.C.O.

HULL.—Sculcoates (All Saints') Parish Church. Built 1887 by Forster & Andrews. Enlarged 1908. Opened by present organist. 3 manuals, 37 speaking and 7 other stops. Organist: George Henry Smith, MUS. DOC. OXON.

HURSLEY.—Parish Church (of Keble fame). Built 1886 by Vowles. Rebuilt 1909 by Cusans Opened by Dr. Prendergast, A.R.C.O. 2 manuals, 24 speaking stops, 5 couplers. Pneumatic throughout. Organist: Mr. S. Argyle, A.R.C.O., Conductor of the Hursley and Ampfield Choral Society.

HYDE.—Wesleyan Church. Built 1896 by Wadsworth. Opened by Dr. J. Kendrick Pyne. 3 manuals, 27 speaking stops, 6 couplers, 1,454 pipes, 6 composition pedals, 1 tremulant, 2 balanced pedals.

ILFORD.—Holy Trinity Church, Barking Side. Built by Bryceson. 1 manual, 6 speaking stops. Organist: Josephine Frances Lach Szyrma, Barking Side Vicarage, Essex.

ILFORD.—St. Michael and All Angels' Church, Little Ilford. Built 1901 by Eustace Ingram. Rebuilt and enlarged by Gray & Davison, 1909. Opened (1901) by Mr W. H. Wilson (Organist St. Matthews' Parish Church, West Ham). 3 manuals, 26 speaking stops, 10 other stops (3 more prepared for), 1,433 pipes. Blown by " Discus " blower (Watkins & Watson). Organist: Frederick Ernest Wilson, F R.C.O , L R A.M. Assistant Organist: Albert Ernest Halls.

ILFORD.—St. James' Church, Little Heath. Built 1887 by White. 3 manuals, 15 speaking stops, 5 other stops, 736 pipes. Great and Choir on one sound-board. Organist: Arthur Emsley Dyster, A.R.C.O., 59, Cambridge Road, Seven Kings, Essex.

ILFRACOMBE —St. Peter's Church Built by Vowles. 3 manuals and pedal, 25 speaking stops, 7 couplers, 1,342 pipes. Tremulant, 5 combination pedals, double acting pedal for Great to pedals. Detached console. Pneumatic action throughout. Organist and Choirmaster: H. Watt-Smyrk, Kyrtonia, Croft's Lea Park, Ilfracombe.

ILKLEY —St. Margaret's Church. Built 1901 by Hill Opened by present organist, Dr. H. Walford Davies and Chas W Perkins. 3 manuals, 36 speaking stops, 7 other stops, 6 combination pistons. Tubular pneumatic action throughout. Hydraulic blowing, separate engines for light and heavy pressure. Organist: Arthur T. Akeroyd, A.R.C.M.

ILMINSTER.—St. Mary's Parish Church. Built 1906 by Minns. 3 manuals, 27 speaking stops, 5 other stops, 6 composition pedals. Organist: G. H. Fowler Sharpe.

INVERNESS.—Parish Church. Built 1892 by Willis. Opened by F. W. Whitehead. 2 manuals, 19 speaking stops, 3 other stops. Blown by Melvin hydraulic engine. Very fine tone.

IPSWICH.—All Saints' Parish Church. Built 1907 by Binns. Opened by Dr. W. J. Reynolds. 3 manuals, 26 speaking stops, 12 other stops, and 1,444 pipes Pedals CCC to F radiating and concave, 4 combination pedals to Great acting symmetrically on Pedal organ, 4 combination pedals to Swell—all double acting and fitted with Binns patent percussions. Organist : William Charles Frederick Brundell, A.R.C.O.

IPSWICH.—PUBLIC HALL. Built by Walker. 4 manuals, 47 speaking stops, 12 couplers, 12 pneumatic combination pistons, 8 pneumatic combination pedals, 1 double-acting pedal. Pedal-board radiating and concave Improved tubular pneumatic action to manuals, pedals, draw-stops and all manual couplers Blown by 3 hydraulic engines and a "Discus" blower, electrically driven. Organist James Price.

IPSWICH —ST. HELEN'S CHURCH. Built 1864 by Bryceson. 2 manuals, 15 speaking stops, 3 other stops, 630 pipes Pedals to R.C.O. scale, added in 1897, two composition pedals to Great lever Swell pedal in the centre. Organist : William George James Griggs, A.R.C.O.

IPSWICH —ST MARGARET'S PARISH CHURCH Built 1870 by Hill. Reconstructed 1907 by Binns. 3 manuals, 34 speaking stops, 10 couplers, tubular pneumatic action. Electric blowing. Fine tone of diapasons. Organist : Jonathan Job, F.R.C.O.

ISLE OF MAN.—KING WILLIAM'S COLLEGE CHAPEL, CASTLETOWN. Built 1897 by Wadsworth. Opened by present organist. 3 manuals, 27 speaking stops, 7 other stops, 1,302 pipes Blown by an hydraulic engine. Organist : Miss Edith L. McKnight

ISLE OF MAN.—PARISH CHURCH, BRADDAN. Built by Brindley & Foster. 2 manuals, 18 speaking stops and 5 couplers. Tubular pneumatic. Organist : Miss M. L. Wood, A R C.O.

ISLE OF MAN.—ST. THOMAS' CHURCH, DOUGLAS. Built 1912 by Hill. Tubular pneumatic action. 31 speaking stops, 7 couplers. Organist : F. C Poulter.

JERSEY.—ST MARK'S CHURCH. Built 1883 by Gray & Davison. 3 manuals, 26 speaking stops, 4 other stops and 1,622 pipes Choir organ and five stops prepared for. Organist : Charles Edward Russell Stevens.

JERSEY.—UNITED METHODIST CHURCH. Built 1889 by Eustace Ingram. Restored 1906 by Alfred Oldknow. 2 manuals, 21 speaking stops. Organist and Leader : Eliza Pallot.

KEIGHLEY.—ST. MICHAEL'S PARISH CHURCH, HAWORTH. Built 1883 by Binns, Leeds. Opened by W. T. Best. 3 manuals, 33 speaking stops, 7 other stops, and 2,064 pipes. Tone full and powerful. Organist : Robert Henry Moore.

KEIGHLEY —ST PETER'S CHURCH Built 1882 by Driver & Lupton. Opened by Dr Varley Roberts 3 manuals, 37 speaking stops, 6 other stops. Good diapason tone of Great organ Organist : Allen Fortune.

KENDAL.—PARISH CHURCH. Built 1877 and rebuilt 1905 by Willis. 4 manuals, 61 speaking stops and 20 couplers. Tubular pneumatic action throughout, interchangeable pistons. Detached console and key fittings in handsome oak. Solid ivory draw-stops Blown by 5-h.p. electric motor. 3 handles also provided in case of need Organist : William Granger.

KENDAL.—ST. GEORGE'S. Built 1883 by Wilkinson. 3 manuals, 32 speaking stops, 9 other stops, 6 combination pedals. Organist : John Whiteside, MUS. BAC. OXON., F.R.C O

KENDAL.—St. Thomas' Church. Built by Harrison. Enlarged 1909. 3 manuals, 30 speaking stops, 5 couplers. Organist: John Smallwood Winder.

KENILWORTH.—Parish Church. Built 1903 by Lee. Opened by H. C. Morris. 3 manuals, 28 speaking stops, 10 other stops, 1,522 pipes. Pneumatic action. Hydraulic blower by the Standard Engineering Company, Leeds.

KESWICK.—St. John's Parish Church. Built 1890 by Gern 3 manuals, 23 speaking stops, 9 other stops, 1,310 pipes. Kinetic blowing apparatus. Pedal board strait and concave. 7 composition pedals. Tubular pneumatic action. Organist: Percy W. de Courcy Smale.

KIDDERMINSTER.—St. George's Parish Church. Built 1869 by Hill. 3 manuals, 29 speaking stops, 6 couplers. Organist: R. A. Taylor, F.R.C.O.

KILBURN.—Church of the Sacred Heart. Built 1911 by Brindley & Foster. 2 manuals, 28 speaking stops, 6 other stops, 1,571 pipes, 29 pneumatic combination accessories, 9 composition pedals, tremulant, balanced swell pedal. Blown by electric motor.

KILBURN.—St. John's Church. Built 1880 by Bevington. 3 manuals, 23 speaking stops, 7 other stops, 1,348 pipes. Blown by hand. Organist: H. G. Mead.

KILBURN.—St. Luke's Church. Built 1884 by Bevington 2 manuals (third prepared for), 21 speaking stops, 9 couplers. Organist: Fred Manders.

KILBURN.—St. Mary's Church. Built by Bishop. 3 manuals. Tubular pneumatic action. Blown by hydraulic engine. Organist: Richard James Pitcher, MUS. BAC. DUNELM, F.R.C.O., A.R.C.M.

KILBURN.—Wesley Church, Quex Road. Built 1889 by Bevington. 2 manuals, 22 speaking stops, 12 couplers. Part tubular.

KILKENNY.—St. Canice's Cathedral. Built 1854 and 1906 by Bevington. 3 manuals, 32 speaking stops, 14 couplers, etc. Tubular throughout. Hydraulic blowing. Built for Dublin Exhibition, 1854. Organist: W. H. McClelland, MUS. BAC., DUBLIN, 17, Patrick Street, Kilkenny.

KILKENNY.—St. Canice Catholic Church. Built 1871 by Bevington. 3 manuals, 24 speaking stops, 10 couplers, etc

KILKENNY.—St. Mary's Catholic Cathedral. Built 1870 and 1906 by Bevington. 3 manuals, 32 speaking stops, 13 couplers, etc. Hydraulic blowing.

KILMARNOCK.—Coodham. Private Residence of Sir W. Houldsworth, Bart. Chapel organ built 1873 by Hill. Pneumatic action added, 1909. 3 manuals, 32 speaking stops, 8 other stops, 1,760 pipes. Hydraulic blowing.

KILMARNOCK.—Coodham. Organ in Billiard Room. Built 1868 by Hill. Removed from the Norbury Booths residence to Coodham, 1898. 3 manuals, 21 speaking stops, 7 other stops, 1,220 pipes. Oak Case Decorated Pipes. Hydraulic blowing.

KILMARNOCK.—KING STREET U.F. CHURCH Built 1895 by Walker & Co., Ludwigsburg. 3 manuals, 30 speaking stops, 13 pistons. Pneumatic action, detached console. Blown by hydraulic power. Balanced Swell and Choir pedals, also crescendo pedal Diapasons round and full, distinct tone Flutes and soft reeds particularly fine. Organist : H C. Jeffrey, A R.C.O.

KINGSTON-ON-THAMES.—H.M CHAPEL ROYAL, HAMPTON COURT PALACE. Built 1690 by Father Schmitt. Rebuilt 1856 and 1899 by Hill. 3 manuals, 30 speaking stops, 7 other stops, 1,542 pipes. Beauty of tone ; in rebuilding great care exercised to preserve original pipes and keep wind pressure at 2½in Blown by hydraulic engine. Good trombone on Pedal organ. Fine case, carving by Grinling Gibbons. Organist : Basil H. Philpott.

KINGSTON-ON-THAMES —ST. RAPHAEL'S CHURCH. Built 1848 by Bishop & Starr. Restored 1907 by Bishop. 2 manuals, 22 speaking stops, 3 couplers, 5 composition pedals, 1,296 pipes. Tremulant by pedal Organist : Clarence Lott.

KINGSTOWN.—MARINERS' CHURCH. Built 1900 by Abbott & Smith. 3 manuals, 35 speaking stops, 9 couplers, 16 combination pistons and pedals. Blown by two hydraulic engines. Oak case. Tubular pneumatic action throughout.

KINGS LYNN.—ALL SAINTS' CHURCH. Built 1850 by Holdich. Rebuilt 1900 by Street. Opened by present organist. 2 manuals, 10 speaking stops, 6 other stops. Organist : Walter Owen Jones.

KNARESBOROUGH.—PARISH CHURCH OF ST. JOHN. Rebuilt 1894 by Binns. 3 manuals, 41 speaking stops, 5 on pedal, 132ft. (4 pedal stops provided for), 6 couplers, 2,586 pipes, pneumatic action, balanced Swell pedal, 7 composition pedals, fine diapasons, 3 reeds on Choir in a separate Swell box Fine organ-case in oak, cost £320. Organist : George Edward Arnold, F.I.S C.

KILBRACHAN.—PARISH CHURCH Built 1904 by Hill. Opened by Dr. E. E. Harper, L. R A.M 3 manuals, 38 speaking stops, 10 pistons, 4 composition pedals, hanging swell pedals to Swell and reed stops on the Choir organ. Pneumatic action. Diapasons very fine and noble ; clarinet, orchestral oboe and gamba on the Choir organ, especially good. 7 stops on the Pedal organ Specification drawn up by Sir Frederick Bridge. Organist : William Griffith, MUS. BAC. DUNELM, F.R C.O , L. MUS. T.C.L.

LANCASTER.—ST. ANN'S CHURCH. Built by Bevington 3 manuals, 30 speaking stops, 13 couplers, etc.

LAUNCESTON.—ST. MARY MAGDALENE CHURCH. Restored 1903 by Hele. Opened by Dr M. J. Monk. 3 manuals, 32 speaking stops, 6 other stops, 1,688 pipes, 6 composition pedals Tubular pneumatic action to Pedal organ and 2 lowest octaves of Great and Swell. Hydraulic blowing. Organist : David John Coldwell, F.R.C.O.

LAUNCESTON.—WESLEYAN CHURCH. Built 1909 by Compton. 3 manuals, 31 speaking stops, 13 other stops. Blown by Kinetic Swanton hydraulic engine. 32ft. double open. Pedal controllers. " Extension " system. Organist : C. Stanley Parsonson, MUS. BAC. LONDON, L. MUS. T.C L.

LEAMINGTON SPA.—LILLINGTON PARISH CHURCH. Built 1902 by Bevington. 3 manuals, 22 speaking stops, 11 couplers, etc. Part tubular. Hand blown. Organist : A. E. Gibbs, MUS. BAC., " Lyndencote," 10, Lillington Road, Leamington Spa.

LEAMINGTON SPA.—ST. MARK'S PARISH CHURCH Built 1879 by Hill. Opened by Dr. Chipp. 4 manuals, 36 speaking stops, 5 other stops, 2,110 pipes 16ft. reed on Swell and Pedal. Pneumatic levers to Great. Manual blowing. Organist : George Kennett.

LEAMINGTON SPA.—ST. PETER'S ROMAN CATHOLIC CHURCH Built 1885 by Bevington. 3 manuals, 32 speaking stops, 11 other stops. Blown by hydraulic engine Organist : Walter Warren.

LEAMINGTON SPA.—WESLEYAN CHURCH, DALE STREET. Built 1905 by Nicholson. Opened by W. Perkins 3 manuals, 25 speaking stops, 15 other stops. Tremulant by rocking tablet, balanced swell pedals to Choir and Swell. Pedal for drawing Great to Pedal pistons on each manual. Stop keys instead of draw-knobs. Pneumatic action throughout. Blown by electric motor. Organist : Bennett Opie, A.R.C.O.

LEEDS.—ALL HALLOWS' CHURCH. Built 1900 by Abbott & Smith Opened by present organist. 3 manuals. Blown by hand. Organist : James Milnes.

LEEDS.—ALL SOULS' (HOOK MEMORIAL) CHURCH. Built 1877 and restored 1906 by Abbott & Smith. Opened 1881 by the late John Bowling. Electric blowing installation added in 1904. 3 manuals and pedal, 43 speaking stops, 9 couplers, 7 combination pedals, 8 pneumatic pistons, 2 balanced crescendo pedals Pistons for Great to Pedal and Swell to Great " on and off " Pedal board radiating and concave. Tubular pneumatic action throughout. Electric blowing. Carved oak case by A. Crawford Hick. Organist : C. L. Naylor, MUS. B

LEEDS.—BRUNSWICK CHAPEL. Built 1827 by Joseph Booth of Wakefield. Opened by Samuel Wesley, father of the late Dr. Sebastian Wesley. Rebuilt and enlarged 1903 by Abbott & Smith. 3 manuals, 41 speaking stops, 8 couplers, 8 composition pedals. Blown by three hydraulic engines Handsome carved mahogany case. Organist : Jer. Stones.

LEEDS.—BURLEY WESLEY CHURCH. Built 1911 by Keates 3 manuals, 35 speaking stops, 9 couplers, etc. Blown by hydraulic engine. Handsome figured pitch pine case. Pneumatic action.

LEEDS —CHRIST CHURCH, UPPER ARMLEY. Built 1900 by Binns. Opened by Dr. A. L. Peace. 3 manuals and pedals, 43 stops. Blown by hydraulic engine. Gothic case of fine pitch pine. Organist and Choirmaster : Dr. W. Bradley, F.R.C O.

LEEDS.—HEADINGLEY HILL CONGREGATIONAL CHURCH Built by Abbott & Smith. 3 manuals and pedal, 37 speaking stops, 14 couplers (2 tremulants), 8 composition pedals, 12 combination pistons, 2 balanced crescendo pedals. Blown by two hydraulic engines. Tubular pneumatic action.

LEEDS.—MASONIC HALL. Built by Abbott & Smith 2 manuals and pedal, 7 speaking stops, 4 couplers, 4 combination pistons. Tubular pneumatic action. Blown by hydraulic engine.

LEEDS.—MOOR ALLERTON CHURCH. Built by Abbott & Smith. 2 manuals, 14 speaking stops, 5 couplers, 4 composition pedals (2 on Great pedal, 2 on Swell). Blown by electric motor. Tubular pneumatic action.

LEEDS.—OXFORD PALACE WESLEYAN CHAPEL. Built 1912 by Binns. Opened by H. A. Fricker. 3 manuals, 40 speaking stops, 15 couplers, 3,371 pipes. Binn's patent tubular pneumatic action. Worked by electric motor and feeders.

LEEDS.—PARISH CHURCH. Built 1814. Rebuilt 1841 by Greenwood. Hydraulic blowing added 1859 by Holt and pipes added by Schulze. Entirely reconstructed 1883 by Abbott & Smith and modernised 1899. 5 manuals and pedal, 77 speaking stops, 14 couplers, 9 composition pedals, 16 combination pistons. Blown by electric motor. This organ is to be entirely re-planned, reconstructed and modernised in 1913. The Echo organ is to be placed in the bay between the side-chapel and the sanctuary nearest the East end. Organist: Edward C. Bairstow, MUS. DOC. DUNELM., F.R.C.O., 10, De Grey Road, Leeds.

LEEDS.—ST. AUGUSTINE'S CHURCH. Built 1875 by Bevington. 3 manuals, 28 speaking stops, 14 couplers, etc.

LEEDS.—ST. CHAD'S CHURCH, FAR HEADINGLEY. Built 1910 by Harrison. Gift of Mrs. W. Howard Stables. 3 manuals, 37 speaking stops, 8 couplers, 2 combination couplers, 4 combination pedals, 11 combination pistons, 2 reversible pistons, 2 balanced crescendo pedals. Blown by 7 h.p. electric motor. Oak case. Organist: H. Percy Richardson, F.R.C.O., A.R.C.M., 6, Monkbridge Road, Headingley, Leeds.

LEEDS.—ST. GEORGE'S CHURCH. Built 1871 by Gray & Davison. Opened by Dr. William Spark and Henry Smart. Restored 1903 by Wordsworth. 3 manuals, 46 speaking stops, 6 other stops, 3,000 pipes. Blown by hydraulic engine. Organist and Choirmaster: Horace Montague Dalton, A.R.C.O.

LEEDS.—ST. MICHAEL'S CHURCH, HEADINGLEY. Built by Abbott & Smith. 3 manuals and pedal, 46 speaking stops, 8 couplers, 10 composition pedals, 7 combination pistons. Tubular pneumatic action. Blown by two hydraulic engines. Organist: A. Hague, F.R.C.O.

LEEDS.—ST. OSWALD'S CHURCH, COLLINGHAM Built 1897 by Abbott & Smith. 2 manuals, 10 speaking stops, 3 other stops, 600 pipes. Tubular pneumatic action. Organist: Charles Hamer.

LEEDS.—SALEM CENTRAL HALL (CONGREGATIONAL), HUNSLET LANE. Revoiced and renovated 1907 by Wordsworth. 3 manuals, 32 speaking stops, 7 other stops, 1,658 pipes. Blowing apparatus removed to basement and screw starter for hydraulic engine fixed at console. Organ built many years ago. Organist: George Harry Farnell.

LEEDS.—TOWN HALL. Built by Gray & Davison; restored 1898 by Abbott & Smith. 5 manuals, 92 speaking stops, 16 other stops, 6,404 pipes, 10 composition pedals, 18 pneumatic pistons (some interchangeable), balanced Swell pedals, etc. Organist: Herbert Austin Fricker, F.R.C.O.

LEICESTER.—NEW TOWN HALL. Built 1912 by Taylor. The gift of Alfred Corah, Esq., of Scraptoft Hall 3 manuals, 41 speaking stops, 8 couplers, 2 tremulants, 12 thumb pistons, 4 combination pedals to Pedal organ. Tubular pneumatic action throughout. Wind pressures 3½ to 15 inches, the Pedal organ of 9 stops including an open of 32ft.

LEICESTER.—ST. GEORGE'S CHURCH. Built 1880 by Brystone & Ellis. Opened by W. T. Best. 3 manuals. Considerably damaged by water at a fire which partially burnt down the church, October 6th, 1911. Organist: W. H. Barrow, MUS. DOC.

LEICESTER.—ST. JAMES CHURCH. Built 1896 by Mills. Opened by W. H. Barrow. 3 manuals, 23 speaking stops, 4 other stops, 1,286 pipes. Organist : Sydney Weston.

LEICESTER.—ST. JOHN THE BAPTIST CHURCH, KNIGHTON. Built 1896 by Taylor. 4 manuals, 35 speaking stops, 12 other stops. Tubular pneumatic action. Organist : C. H. Kitson, MUS. DOC., OXON.

LEICESTER.—ST. JOHN THE DIVINE. Built 1904 by Taylor. Opened by present organist. 4 manuals, 40 speaking stops, 11 other stops, 2,010 pipes. Tubular pneumatic throughout. Builders' special interchangeable combination pistons. Organist and Choirmaster : John Henry Taylor.

LEICESTER.—ST. LEONARD'S CHURCH. Built 1877 by Taylor. 3 manuals, 16 speaking stops, 5 couplers Organist : R. T. Tuck.

LEICESTER.—ST. MARGARET'S CHURCH. Built by Father Smith. Rebuilt 1893 by Taylor. 3 manuals, 22 speaking stops, 5 couplers. Organist : W. Beaumont.

LEICESTER.—ST. MARTIN'S CHURCH. Built 1774 by Snetzler. Rebuilt 1873 by Walker. Opened by Best. 4 manuals, 49 speaking stops, 10 other stops, 3,021 pipes Fifth manual provided for. Electric motor for blowing. Snetzler diapasons very fine. Organist : Charles Hancock.

LEICESTER.—ST. MARY'S CHURCH. Built 1880 by Porritt. 3 manuals. Opened by H. B. Ellis, F R C O Organist : Benjamin Burrows.

LEICESTER.—ST. MATTHEW'S CHURCH. Built 1872 by Bishop Rebuilt 1901 by Taylor. 3 manuals, 28 speaking stops, 7 couplers. Tubular pneumatic. Organist : J. W. Wilson, F.R.C.O.

LEICESTER.—ST. MICHAEL AND ALL ANGELS' CHURCH. Built 1902 by Taylor. 2 manuals, 20 speaking stops (7 on Great, 9 on Swell, 4 on Pedal), 3 couplers. Organist : Jas. Maddocks.

LEICESTER.—ST. NICHOLAS CHURCH. Built 1890 by Porritt. Opened by Chas Hancock, MUS. BAC. 2 manuals, 18 speaking stops, 2 couplers, 1,156 pipes. Organist : Arthur Thomas Pole.

LEICESTER.—ST. PAUL'S CHURCH. Rebuilt by Taylor. 3 manuals, 23 speaking stops, 6 other stops. Organist : Cardinal Taylor, MUS. B., F.R.C.O.

LEICESTER. ST. PETER'S CHURCH. Built 1880 by Porritt. Rebuilt 1911 by Taylor. 3 manuals, 38 speaking stops, 14 other stops, 2,350 pipes. Blown by electric motor, and J. H. Taylor's patent blower. Great reeds and pedal reeds on 10 inch wind pressure ; Swell reeds on 6 inches ; flue work on 3½ inches Provision made for solo organ of 8 stops. Organist : Walter Joseph Bunney, F.R.C.O., L.R.A.M , A.R.C M.

LEICESTER.—ST. SAVIOUR'S CHURCH. Built 1880 by Taylor. 3 manuals, 18 speaking stops, 8 other stops, 7 others prepared for Fine spotted metal dia on Great organ (large scale). Organist : William Henry Scott.

LEICESTER.—VICTORIA ROAD CHURCH. Built 1869 by Nicholsons. Restored by Taylor and by Porritt. 3 manuals, 38 speaking stops, 9 other stops. Blown by electricity. Organist : Harold Parsons.

LEOMINSTER.—PRIORY CHURCH Repaired by Avery. Restored 1842 by Walker. 3 manuals, 24 speaking stops, 3 couplers. Put up in the west gallery (since taken down), 1737. A good Cremona, and 3 stopped diapasons (one on each manual), of very mellow quality. Organist: Herbert E. Crimp.

LETTERKENNY.—CATHEDRAL, THE. Built 1900 by Telford & Telford. 3 manuals and pedal, 54 speaking stops and couplers, 6 combination pistons.

LEVEN.—SCOOMB PARISH KIRK. Restored 1904 by Gern. Opened by James A. Crapper. 2 manuals, 17 speaking stops, 5 couplers, 790 pipes Fine specimen of Gern's work, the tone of soft stops being especially excellent. Organist: Andrew L. Baird.

LEYLAND.—ST. ANDREW'S PARISH CHURCH. Built 1876 by Jardine. Restored 1907 by Ainscough Re-opened by present organist. 3 manuals, 24 speaking stops, 6 other stops, and 1,268 pipes Blown by Ross engine (water). Special features: Good diapasons, a fine orchestral Gamba, and a really good Cornopean on the Swell on 3½in. wind. Organist: Henry Gerald Lockett, A.R.C M.

LEYTONSTONE.—HOLY TRINITY CHURCH. Built 1879 by Bevington. 2 manuals, 21 speaking stops, 10 couplers. Organist: H. J. Ellingford.

LICHFIELD.—CATHEDRAL THE. Rebuilt 1884 and 1908 by Hill. 4 manuals, 18 stops on Great, 16 on Swell, 9 on Choir, 9 on solo, 13 on Pedal, and 17 couplers, 7 composition pedals, 2 double acting pedals, 24 pneumatic pistons Organist. John B. Lott.

LICHFIELD.—ST. MICHAEL'S PARISH CHURCH. Built 1893 by Holdich. Rebuilt 1909, Nicholson & Lord Opened by J. B. Lott, MUS. BAC. 2 manuals, 20 speaking stops, 4 other stops. Tubular pneumatic action to pedals and drawstops. Organist: Harry Oram Burton, F.G.O., A.R.C.O.

LIMERICK.—ST. ALPHONSUS. Built 1910 by Hill. 32 speaking stops, 7 couplers. Tubular pneumatic action throughout. Electric blowing.

LIMPSFIELD.—CHURCH MISSIONARIES CHILDREN'S HOME CHAPEL. Built by Willis. Removed from Highbury Grove, London. Enlarged by Vincent. 2 manuals, 16 speaking stops, 3 couplers, 4 combination pedals, balanced Swell pedal Organist. Senior organ pupil.

LINCOLN.—ALL SAINTS' CHURCH. Built 1906 by Willis. Opened by Dr. G. J Bennett. 2 manuals, 19 speaking stops, 5 couplers. Blown by electricity (" Kinetic "). Organist: R. A. Cousans.

LINCOLN.—CATHEDRAL, THE. Built 1898 by Willis Opened by Sir Walter Parritt. 4 manuals, 58 speaking stops, 18 other stops, 3,228 pipes. Greater part of organ is on choir screen and keyboard on north side, but Swell organ and part of Pedal organ in Triforium, on north side. Blown by electricity, the bellows and two electric motors being in the Triforium. Organist: George John Bennett, MUS. DOC. CANTAB, F.R.A.M , F.R.C.O.

LINCOLN.—ST. MARTIN'S CHURCH. Built 1902 by Abbott & Smith. Opened by Dr. G. J. Bennett. 3 manuals, 32 speaking stops, 9 couplers, 15 combination pistons and pedals. Electric blown. " Kinetic " motor. Handsome oak case. Organist: Ernest Pullain.

LINCOLN.—St. Matthew's Church, Sutton Bridge. Built 1910 by Vincent. Opened by G. W. Pearce. 19 stops. Pneumatic action (divided). Blown by gas engine. Organist: Miss J. M. Hooton.

LINCOLN.—St. Paul's Church. Built 1910 by Cousans. Opened by G. J. Bennett, mus. d. 3 manuals, 23 speaking stops, 5 couplers. Pneumatic throughout. Electric blowing. Organist: A. E. Worland.

LINCOLN.—Wesley Chapel. Built 1860 by Sweetland. Restored by Nicholson, and Forster & Andrews. 3 manuals, 33 speaking stops, 4 other stops. Blown by Kinetic electric blower. Organist: Charles William Page.

LISBURN.—Cathedral, The. Built 1836 by Telford & Telford. 2 manuals, 25 speaking stops. Rebuilt and enlarged 1900. Organist: J. Henry McBratney.

LITTLE HULTON.—St. John The Baptist Parish Church. Built by George Benson. 2 manuals, 17 speaking stops, 4 other stops. 4 composition pedals and balanced Swell pedal. Hand blown. Organist: William Crompton, A.R.C.O.

LIVERPOOL.—All Hallow's Parish Church, Allerton. Flue work by Hill. Reeds by Cavaille-Coll. Rebuilt 1909 by Rushworth & Dreaper. 3 manuals, 31 speaking stops, 9 other stops, 1,800 pipes. Greatly admired for sweetness and mellowness of tone. Organ case of oak, beautifully carved. Organist: Joseph H. Hewitt.

LIVERPOOL.—Baptist Church, Myrtle Street. Built 1871 by Willis. Opened by W. T. Best. 2 manuals, 24 speaking stops, 6 other stops, 7 composition pedals, clarion and cornopean (heavy wind). Tremulant to Swell. Splendid reeds and fine tones diapasons. Organist and Choirmaster: Wilfrid Shaw.

LIVERPOOL.—Christ Church, Breeze Hill, Bootle. Built by Walker. 2 manuals, 17 speaking stops, 3 couplers, 1,082 pipes, 7 composition pedals. Beautiful quality of tone, especially diapasons. Organist: Frank Dibb, F.R.C.O.

LIVERPOOL.—Conservatoire of Music, 44, Princes Road. Restored 1903 by Nicholson. 2 manuals, 22 speaking stops Pedal open, diapason stops of good tone. Organist: Alexander Phipps, mus. bac.

LIVERPOOL.—Emmanuel Church, Everton. Built by Gray & Davison. Rebuilt 1912 by Rushworth & Dreaper. 3 manuals, 31 speaking stops, 9 couplers, 9 composition pedals. Blown by electric motor. Pneumatic action throughout. Organist: A. Thompson Parry.

LIVERPOOL.—Emmanuel Church, Fazakerley. Built 1912 by Rushworth & Dreaper. 2 manuals, 23 speaking stops, 9 couplers, 9 composition pedals. Tubular pneumatic action. Blown by electric motor. Organist: W. S. Wright.

LIVERPOOL.—Emmanuel Congregational Church. Built by Brindley & Foster. Restored 1901 by Norman & Beard, Norwich. Opened by W. J. Best, 1876, F. Burnstall, 1901. 3 manuals, 23 speaking 7 draw stops, stops, 1,292 pipes. Tubular pneumatic action throughout. Blown by Ross valve hydraulic engine. Organist: Albert E. Workman.

LIVERPOOL.—GREAT GEORGE STREET CONGREGATIONAL CHURCH. Rebuilt 1905 by Rushworth & Dreaper. 3 manuals, 49 speaking stops, 8 couplers, 8 composition pedals, 14 pistons. Tubular pneumatic action. Blown by " Duncan " water motor. Organist : R. H. Brewerton.

LIVERPOOL.—OUR LADY OF COMPASSION CHURCH, FORMBY. Built 1902 by Ainscough. Opened by J. Tomlinson. 3 manuals, 23 speaking stops, 7 other stops. Pneumatic action throughout, detached console with 6 controlling pistons. Stop keys in place of ordinary draw-stops. Organist : Wilfred John Chenoweth, A.R.C.O., M.I.S.M.

LIVERPOOL.—PRESBYTERIAN CHURCH, CHATHAM STREET. Built 1896 by Hill. 3 manuals. Pneumatic throughout. Organist : John Henry Roberts.

LIVERPOOL.—R.C. PRO. CATHEDRAL. Built 1870 by Willis. 2 manuals, 14 speaking stops, 5 other stops. Full ranges of pipes. Blown by hydraulic engine. Organist and Choirmaster : T. Bordonel Brown.

LIVERPOOL.—ST. AGNES' CHURCH, SEFTON PARK. Rebuilt 1908 by Rushworth & Dreaper and fitted with pneumatic action throughout. 3 manuals, 34 speaking stops, 7 couplers, 10 composition pedals, 8 pistons. Erected on columns, and occupying the entire North Transept. Blown by electric motor. Organist : I. H. Stammers, 4, Cumberland Avenue, Sefton Park, Liverpool.

LIVERPOOL.—ST. ANDREW'S CHURCH, AIGBURTH. Built 1871 by Bevington. Rebuilt 1909 by Gray & Davison. 2 manuals, 29 speaking stops, 4 couplers, etc. Organist . W H Windus, A.R.C.O.

LIVERPOOL.—ST. ANDREW'S CHURCH, LINACRE. Built 1907 by Rushworth & Dreaper. 2 manuals, 24 speaking stops, 6 couplers, 6 composition pedals. Tubular pneumatic action. Blown by electric motor. Organist : G. M Harvey.

LIVERPOOL.—ST. BEDE'S CHURCH. Built 1892 by Gray & Davison. 3 manuals, 34 speaking stops, 9 other stops, 1,964 pipes, 10 pneumatic pistons. Tubular pneumatic action. Front pipes of finest spotted metal. Organist : Ernest H. Smith, F.R.C.O.

LIVERPOOL.—ST. BRIDE'S CHURCH. Built by Gray & Davison. Rebuilt 1906 by Rushworth & Dreaper. 3 manuals, 29 speaking stops, 7 composition pedals, 5 couplers, 3 pistons, tubular pneumatic throughout. 2 h.p. electric motor.

LIVERPOOL.—ST. CLARE'S CHURCH. Built 1892 by Steele & Keay. Opened by Mr. Hague Kinsey. Removed to new organ loft 1900. 2 manuals, 20 speaking stops, 5 other stops, 6 composition pedals. Blown by hand. Balanced Swell pedal. Organist : H. D. Bowden.

LIVERPOOL.—ST. COLUMBA'S CHURCH. Built 1907 by Norman & Beard. Opened by J. H. England, MUS. BAC. DUNELM, F.R.C.O 2 manuals, 14 speaking stops, 5 other stops, 738 pipes, 4 composition pedals, balanced Swell pedal, tremulant by pedal, 1 keytouch to horn, 1 keytouch Great to Pedal. Revised R.C.O. pattern radiating and concave pedal. Tubular pneumatic action throughout. Organist : Claud S. Kershaw.

LIVERPOOL.—ST. EDWARDS COLLEGE. Built 1870 by Gray and Davison. 2 manuals, 14 speaking stops, 5 other stops. Full ranges of pipes. Blown by hand. Organist and Choirmaster : T. Bordonel Brown.

LIVERPOOL.—St. Francis Xavier's Church. Built 1907 by Hill. 4 manuals, 32 speaking stops, 9 couplers. Tubular pneumatic action. Electric blowing.

LIVERPOOL.—St. George's Hall. Built 1855 by Willis. Rebuilt and modernised 1898. Opened by Dr. A. L. Peace. 4 manuals, 100 speaking stops, 14 couplers, 36 pneumatic pistons, 6 composition pedals. Blown by two steam engines.

LIVERPOOL.—St. Luke's Church. Built 1906 by Rushworth & Dreaper. Opened by F. H. Burstall, F.R.C.O. 3 manuals, 36 speaking stops, 8 other stops, 4 composition pedals to Great, 4 to Swell, 1 to Choir. Blown by electric motor. Tubular pneumatic action except couplers. Placed on both sides of Chancel. Organist : Walter G. Withers, F.R.C.O.

LIVERPOOL.—St. Mary's Church for the Blind. Built 1892 by Jardine. Restored 1906 by Norman & Beard. Opened by Dr. A. L. Peace and present organist. 4 manuals, 39 speaking stops, 17 other stops. Organist : A. W. Pollitt, MUS. DOC. DURHAM, F.R.C.O., A.R.C.M., L.R.A.M., A.R.M.C.M.

LIVERPOOL.—St. Matthew's Church, Bootle. Built 1891 by Binns. 2 manuals, 16 speaking stops, 9 other stops. Blown by hand. Tubular pneumatic action. Organist and Choirmaster : Ernest A. Blackman, L.L.C.M.

LIVERPOOL.—St. Matthias' Church. Built 1911 by Rushworth & Dreaper. 2 manuals, 21 speaking stops, 7 couplers, 6 composition pedals. Tubular pneumatic action throughout. Organist : W. G. Mann.

LIVERPOOL.—St. Mary's Parish Church, Walton-on-the-Hill (the "Mother Church" of Liverpool). Built 1910 by Willis. 3 manuals, CC to C, 61 notes, Pedals CCC to F, 37 speaking stops, 11 couplers, 48 drawstops, 9 combination pedals, 12 combination pistons (adjustable) Tubular pneumatic action all through. Blown by electric motor. Organist and Choirmaster : Albert Orton, L.R.A.M., F.R.C.O.

LIVERPOOL.—St. Margaret's Church. Built 1870 by Hill. 3 manuals, 41 speaking stops, 9 other stops. Blown by 2 hydraulic engines. Very fine Swell and double open diapasons, 32ft. on pedal. Organist : William Faulkes.

LIVERPOOL.—St. Michael's-in-the-Hamlet. Built 1903 by Rushworth & Dreaper. 3 manuals, 25 speaking stops, 8 couplers, 9 composition pedals. Tubular pneumatic action. Blown by "Duncan" water motor. Organist : T. Ford.

LIVERPOOL.—St. Nicholas' ("Old" Church). Built 1868 by Willis, and rebuilt 1904 by Lewis. 3 manuals, 35 speaking stops, 11 other stops. Original specifications by W. T. Best and W. C. Ashlin. 4 reeds are on heavy pressure. Organist : C. W. Bridson, F.R.C.O.

LIVERPOOL.—St. Patrick's Roman Catholic Church. Built 1823 by Bishop. Restored by Lewis. Rebuilt and enlarged 1910 by Rushworth & Dreaper. 3 manuals, 27 speaking stops. Remarkably effective tone for size. Organist and Choirmaster : W. J. Bowden.

LIVERPOOL.—St. Peter's Parish Church, Woolton. Built 1895 by Forster & Andrews 3 manuals, 44 speaking stops, 9 couplers, 2,500 pipes. Blown by electric motor. Tubular pneumatic action throughout. Organist : Charles Kenneth James.

LIVERPOOL,—St. Peter's Pro. Cathedral. Built by Father Smith. Rebuilt and modernised 1899 by Rushworth & Dreaper. Old case and some of original pipes remain. 3 manuals, 33 speaking stops, 6 couplers, 8 composition pedals. Action partly pneumatic and partly tracker. Blown by "Duncan" water motor. Organist: F. H. Burstall.

LIVERPOOL.—St Saviour's Church. Built by Lewis. 3 manuals, 36 speaking stops, 9 other stops, 11 composition pedals, 2 tremulants, 2 Swell pedals. Blown by electric motor. Organist: John Herbert England

LIVERPOOL.—St. Silas Church. Built 1845 by Bewsher & Fleetwood. 2 manuals, 14 speaking stops, 2 other stops, 3 composition pedals. Great organ, pure quality of tone. Organist: J. Foxley, 3, London Gardens, Princes Park, Liverpool.

LIVERPOOL.—Sefton Park Presbyterian Church Built 1878 by Hill. Enlarged 1892 by Hope Jones. New action, etc., 1909 by Norman & Beard Opened by W. T. Best. 3 manuals, 30 speaking stops, 12 other stops, 1,528 pipes, 16 composition pedals, pistons etc. Tremulant console below pulpit, in middle of choir. Action, tubular pneumatic. Blown by a Bergtheil & Young electric motor. Organist: Richard Francis Lloyd.

LIVERPOOL —Trinity Presbyterian Church, Bootle Built by Booth & Hepworth. 2 manuals, 21 stops. Organist : James Butler Fortay

LIVERPOOL.—West Derby Parish Church Built 1892 by Gray & Davison. 3 manuals, 40 speaking stops, 9 other stops, 2,437 pipes. Organist : Edward Watson, A R.C.O., 7, Tue Brook Terrace, Liverpool.

LLANDUDNO.—St. George's Hotel. Built by Positive Co. 2 manuals, 7 speaking stops, 6 couplers Tubular pneumatic action throughout.

LLANDUDNO —St. John's Wesleyan Church Built 1900 by Young 2 manuals, 23 speaking stops, 4 couplers, 1,200 pipes, 7 composition pedals, balanced Swell pedal Blown by hydraulic "Ross" engine. Organist. Miss L. Mudd.

LLANDUDNO.—St Paul's Church, Craig-y-Don. Built 1910 by Hill 30 speaking stops, 6 couplers, 6 combination pistons Tubular pneumatic action throughout Opened by the late Dr. A. L. Peace. Organist and Choirmaster : L. H. Summerfield, "Lyncroft," Sylva Gardens, Llandudno.

LLANDUDNO.—Welsh Wesleyan Church Built by Conacher. Gift of R. D. Owen, Esq. 2 manuals and pedal, 17 speaking stops, 3 couplers, 6 composition pedals. Blown by hydraulic engine. Organist : W. A. Ll. Evans.

LLANELLY —Capel Newydd Calvinistic Methodist Chapel. Built by Blackett & Howden 2 manuals and pedal, 22 speaking stops, 8 couplers, 6 composition pedals, Great to Pedal " on and off." Tubular pneumatic action throughout. Blown by hydraulic motor. Organist : Brinley Morgan.

LLANELLY.—Parish Church. Built 1854 and 1906 by Bevington. 2 manuals, 15 speaking stops, 5 couplers, etc.

LLANFAIRFECHAN.—CHRIST CHURCH. Built 1902 by Hill. Opened by present organist. 3 manuals, 37 speaking stops, 10 other stops, 2,096 pipes. Hydraulic blowing. Oak case. Organist : Llewelyn Jones, F.R C.O.

LLANGOLLEN.—PARISH CHURCH. Built by Willis. Restored 1898 by Young. 2 manuals, 17 speaking stops, 3 other stops. Organist : Charles Morton Bailey, MUS. BAC. DUNELM, F.R.C.O.

LONDONDERRY.—ST. COLUMBS CATHEDRAL. Built 1887 by Conacher. Opened by D. C. Jones. 4 manuals, 45 speaking stops, 11 other stops, 2,507 pipes. Blown by electric motor. Organist : Sydney Weale, B. MUS., F.R C.O.

LONG EATON.—TRENT COLLEGE (Nr.). Built 1870 and restored 1909 by Gray & Davison. 3 manuals, 24 speaking stops, 6 other stops, and 1,582 pipes. Blown by hand. Organist : R. M. Cadman, M A , MUS. BAC. OXON , F.R.C.O

LONGWOOD.—WESLEYAN CHURCH. Built by Conacher. 3 manuals and pedal, 32 speaking stops, 8 couplers, 6 composition pedals, 6 pneumatic pistons, pedals and pistons for Great and Swell to Pedal "on and off." Blown by h draulic engine. Tubular pneumatic action throughout. Pitch pine case varnished.

LOUGHBOROUGH.—PARISH CHURCH. Built 1904 by Ingram & Co. 4 manuals, 63 stops. Blown by electric motor and rotary fan. Organist : R. T. Bedford.

LOUTH.—HOLY TRINITY CHURCH. Built 1870 by Foster & Andrews. Opened by present organist. 3 manuals, 24 speaking stops, 6 couplers, 1,540 pipes A very fine spotted metal claironet in choir organ, also splendid open diapason. Organist : H. W. C. Foster.

LOUTH.—ST. JAMES' PARISH CHURCH. Built by Gray & Davison. Rebuilt by Norman & Beard. 3 manuals, 49 stops. Tubular pneumatic action. Oak case. Organist : Owen M. Price, F.R.C.O., L T.C.L.

LOWESTOFT.—ST. MARGARET'S PARISH CHURCH. Rebuilt 1902 by Forster & Andrews. 4 manuals, 31 speaking stops, 5 couplers. Organist : Ernest Banks.

LOWESTOFT.—ST JOHN'S CHURCH. Built 1904, and enlarged 1908 by Norman & Beard. Opened 1904 by Dr. Bates. 3 manuals, 33 speaking stops, 9 couplers, 2 tremulants, 9 composition pedals, 12 pistons. Blown by Kinetic Blower Organist : C. J. R. Coleman, A.R C.O., 8, Cleveland Road, Lowestoft.

LUDLOW.—PARISH CHURCH. Built 1764 by Snetzler. Restored by Walker, Gray & Davison, and Hill (1900) 4 manuals, 47 speaking stops, 12 other stops, 2,844 pipes. Detached console. Tubular pneumatic action throughout. Organist : H. C. L. Stocks, MUS. BAC. OXON., F R.C.O.

LUTON.—KING STREET CONGREGATIONAL CHURCH. Built 1911 by Binns. The gift of Mrs. Hucklesby in memory of her husband, the late Alderman A. J. Hucklesby, J.P. 3 manuals, 42 speaking stops, 15 couplers, 13 pistons, 9 composition pedals, 1 combination, 2,432 pipes Binns' patent tubular pneumatic action throughout, with detached console placed in front of pulpit. The length of tube from keyboard to pipe is over 60 ft. Electric motor and fan. Oak case. Organist : Edgar Knowles, L.R.A.M. (organ).

LUTON.—LUTON HOO MANSION PRIVATE CHAPEL. Built 1906 by Norman & Beard. 4 manuals, 50 stops, 18 pistons, 8 composition pedals, and 2 Swell pedals to Swell and Solo organs. Blown by electric motor and Kinetic blower Organist. Frederick James Gostelow.

LUTON.—LUTON PARISH CHURCH. Built 1889 by Holdich. Rebuilt 1899 and 1909 by Norman & Beard. 3 manuals, 48 stops, 7 composition pedals and Great to pedal " on and off " pedal. Detached console. Tubular pneumatic action Balanced Swell pedals to Swell and Choir organs. Blown by 2 Swanton hydraulic engines. Organist : Frederick James Gostelow.

LUTTERWORTH.—ST. MARY'S PARISH CHURCH. Built 1886 by Gern. Opened by J. Stimpson. 2 manuals, 23 speaking stops, 5 other stops, 1,500 pipes. Pneumatic action. Console facing choir. Organist : G. J. Haswell.

LYTHAM.—LYTHAM PARISH CHURCH. Restored 1903 by Ainscough. 3 manuals, 35 speaking stops, 8 couplers. Tubular pneumatic action. Blown by 2 water engines. Organist : Samuel Hull Broughton.

LYMINGTON.—ALL SAINTS' CHURCH. Built by Norman & Beard, 1909. 2 manuals, 11 speaking stops, 3 other stops, 458 pipes. Electric motor for blowing. Organist : Miss Madge Bruce. Choirmaster : H Wakeford, F.R.C.O., M I S.M.

LYMINGTON.—PARISH CHURCH. Built 1831 by Walker. Rebuilt and enlarged 1911 by Brindley & Foster. 3 manuals, 34 speaking stops, 8 couplers, 10 composition pedals, 16 pistons, 15 transformers, " Brindgradus " pedal and other accessories. Placed in West Gallery. Blown by electric motor. Organist : H. Wakeford, F.R.C O.

LYMM.—PARISH CHURCH OF ST. MARY THE VIRGIN. Built by Forster & Andrews. 3 manuals, 30 speaking stops, 7 other stops. Organist : William Cook, F.R.C O.

MACCLESFIELD.—ST. MICHAEL'S PARISH CHURCH. Built 1885 by Hill. 3 manuals, 28 speaking stops. Blown by Crossley gas engine. Organist : Charles Seal.

MAIDENHEAD —ST. MARY'S CHURCH. Great organ of nine stops, and Swell organ of seven stops, with sub-octave coupler and tremulant. Two 16ft. stops on the pedals, the 16ft. open being added by Jones in 1877. Clarinet replaced the old trumpet in 1887. Originally a chamber organ, and is enclosed in a fine old Spanish mahogany case. Organist and Choirmaster : Charles Silvester Banwell.

MAIDSTONE.—ALL SAINTS' PARISH CHURCH. Built by Lewis. Restored by Adams. Rebuilt 1911 by Rushworth & Dreaper. 3 manuals, 40 speaking stops, 10 couplers, 10 composition pedals, 12 pistons. Tubular pneumatic action throughout. Wind generated by 6 feeders, operated by an electric motor. Organist : F. Wilson Parish.

MALDON —ALL SAINTS WITH ST. PETER'S. Restored 1896 and 1903 by Bishop. 3 manuals, 27 speaking stops, 6 other stops, 1,632 pipes. Organist : Thos. W. Hayes.

MALMESBURY.—ABBEY CHURCH, THE. Built 1660 by Father Smith. 3 manuals, 7 stops on Great organ, 17 speaking stops. Removed from Church of St. Benetfick nr. Royal Exchange to Bath, and to Abbey in 1840.

MANCHESTER.—ALBERT HALL. Built 1910 by Wadsworth. 4 manuals and pedal, Great 12 stops, Swell 12, Choir 9, Solo 4, Pedal 9, 14 couplers, 2 tremulants. Swell, Choir and Solo in separate boxes. Blown by electric motor and Kinetic blower.

MANCHESTER.—BRIDGE WESLEYAN CHURCH, RADCLIFFE. Enlarged 1899 by Cousans. Opened by M. Field, MUS. BAC. 3 manuals, 32 speaking stops, 7 other stops. Tubular pneumatic action. Organist : Edward Barnes, A R.C.O.

MANCHESTER.—CATHEDRAL, THE, AND COLLEGIATE CHURCH OF ST. MARY, ST. GEORGE AND ST. DENYS. Built 1871 by Hill Presented by Sir William Houldsworth, Bart. Rebuilt 1910 by Hill. 5 manuals, 66 speaking stops, 20 other stops. Tubular pneumatic action throughout. There is a second organ in the " Ely Chapel," built by Father Smith in 1680. 1 manual and pedal, 7 sounding stops. Organist : Sydney H. Nicholson.

MANCHESTER.—CHOWBENT UNITARIAN CHURCH, ATHERTON. Built 1901 by Young 3 manuals and pedal, 31 speaking stops, 7 couplers (2 tremulants), about 2,000 pipes, 9 composition pedals.

MANCHESTER.—DIOCESAN CHURCH HOUSE. Built 1911 by Hill. 32 speaking stops, 7 couplers Tubular pneumatic action. Electric blowing

MANCHESTER.—DROYLSDEN PARISH CHURCH Built 1904 Twice enlarged by Young. Opened by present organist 3 manuals, 31 speaking stops, 10 other stops, 1,583 pipes. Pneumatic action to Pedal organ. Cor Anglais—free reed—made by specialist in Paris. The tremulants operated by drawstops and movable key-strips (pneumatic action). Organist W. W. Hornby.

MANCHESTER.—FREE TRADE HALL. Built by Jardine. 3 manuals, 50 speaking stops, 8 other stops. Organist : Charles H Fogg.

MANCHESTER.—HENSHAW'S BLIND ASYLUM. Built 1894 by Wadsworth. 3 manuals, 35 speaking stops, 6 couplers and tremulant. Pneumatic action to Great, Swell and Pedal organs Blown by electric motor. Organist : Isaac Davidson, MUS. BAC. DUNELM., 54, Broad Street, Pendleton, Manchester.

MANCHESTER.—HIGHER BROUGHTON PRESBYTERIAN CHURCH. Built by Young 2 manuals and pedal, 19 speaking stops, 4 couplers, 6 combination pedals, 6 combination pistons, 1 crescendo pedal Tubular pneumatic system. Console detached. Organist : Edgar Halstead, A.R.C.O.

MANCHESTER.—PLYMOUTH GROVE WESLEYAN CHURCH. Built 1895 by Wadsworth. Opened by William Mullineux, F.R.C O 3 manuals, 27 speaking stops, 6 other stops. Pneumatic relief valves applied to lower octaves of Swell and Great organs. Pedal organ tubular pneumatic. Carved oak case with spotted metal front. Organist and Choirmaster : Clifford Davies, M.I.S.M.

MANCHESTER.—ROYAL COLLEGE OF MUSIC. Built 1894 by Wadsworth. 4 manuals, 9 stops on Great organ, Swell 8, Choir 8, Solo 3, Pedal 5, couplers 5, balanced pedal to Swell and Choir. Tremulant by pedal. Blown by electric motor. Professor of the Organ at the College : Dr. J. Kendrick Pyne.

MANCHESTER.—ST. AUGUSTINE'S CHURCH. Rebuilt 1908 (a portion from the old Church) by Richardson. 3 manuals, 26 speaking stops, 5 couplers, 4 composition pedals. Tubular pneumatic action to the heavy stops. Organist : Arthur Edward Sandiford.

MANCHESTER.—ST. BRIDE'S PARISH CHURCH, OLD TRAFFORD. Rebuilt 1907 by Benson. 4 manuals, 64 speaking stops, 11 other stops, 3,728 pipes, 18 pistons. Tubular pneumatic action throughout. Wind supplied by a Kinetic Swanton blower, worked by a 4h.p. electric motor. Formerly in use at St. Peter's, Manchester. Organist : George Pritchard, MUS. BAC. DUNELM.

MANCHESTER.—ST. CHRYSOSTOM CHURCH. Built by Hill. 3 manuals, 24 speaking stops, 7 couplers, 1,585 pipes. 6 combination pistons, 3 combination pedals, 1 double acting pedal. Tubular pneumatic action throughout. Blown by electric motor. Organist : Ellis Standring.

MANCHESTER —ST JAMES CHURCH, HOPE, PENDLETON. Built 1861 by Hill. Opened by Henry Wilson. Restored 1909 by Wadsworth. 3 manuals, 27 speaking stops, 8 other stops, 1,800 pipes. Blown by hand. Organist : Robert Rayner Clark.

MANCHESTER.—ST. MARY'S CHURCH, CRUMPSALL. Built by Conacher. Opened by Dr. J. Kendrick Pyne. Enlarged by Jardine, 1912. 4 manuals, 36 speaking stops, 10 other stops. 2 balanced crescendo pedals to Swell and Choir. Organist : Charles H. Fogg.

MANCHESTER.—ST. MICHAEL'S PARISH CHURCH, FLIXTON. Built 1900 by Young. Opened by David Clegg. 2 manuals, 23 speaking stops, 5 other stops, 1,242 pipes. Blown by hydraulic engine. 7 double-acting composition pedals. Tubular pneumatic action. Oak case " Gothic " tracery. Organist : Thomas M. Ferneley.

MANCHESTER.—ST. PAUL'S CHURCH. Built by Hill. Opened by Dr. Watson. 4 manuals, 34 speaking stops, 7 other stops, 1,800 pipes. All stops go through. Organist : Alfred Smith, F.V.C.M , F.I C.C.M.

MANCHESTER —ST. THOMAS' CHURCH, RADCLIFFE. Built 1904 by Hill. Opened by W. Mullineux, F.R C.O. 3 manuals, 36 speaking stops, 11 other stops, 2,232 pipes. Blown by electric motor. Organist : W. E. Taylor, F.R.C.O.

MANCHESTER.—SOUTH MANCHESTER NEW CHURCH. Built 1904 by Binns. Opened by present organist. 3 manuals, 25 speaking stops, 11 couplers. Builder's tubular pneumatic action throughout. Choir organ enclosed in separate swell box. Blown by Crossley gas engine, working 3 independent feeders in room below organ. Binns' patent interchangeable combination pedals applied to Great, Swell and Pedal organs. Organist : John Holgate, MUS. BAC., F.R.C.O.

MANCHESTER.—TOWN HALL. Built 1877 by M. Aristide Caville-Coll. Paris. 4 manuals, 51 speaking stops, 11 couplers, Choir and Swell, tremulant by pedals. Barker lever throughout. Organist · Dr. J. Kendrick Pyne.

MANCHESTER.—WALKDEN PARISH CHURCH. Built 1904 by Wilkinson. 3 manuals, 29 speaking stops, 7 couplers, 8 combination pedals Organist : B. Higham, A. MUS. T.C.L.

MANCHESTER —WHITWORTH HALL, OWEN'S COLLEGE Built 1902 by Willis. 4 manuals, 12 stops on Great organ, Swell 13, Choir 10, Solo 8, Pedal 10, couplers 10. Swell and Great pistons to composition pedals, 5 pistons to each manual. Tubular pneumatic action throughout. Lever pedals to Swell and Solo organs Blown by 3 electric motors. Organist : Dr. J. Kendrick Pyne.

MANCHESTER.—WITHINGTON CONGREGATIONAL CHURCH. Built 1906 by Binns. Opened by present organist. 3 manuals, 38 speaking stops, 12 other stops, 2,249 pipes Interchangeable combination pedals. Electric blowing. Tubular pneumatic action throughout. Detached console. Five wind reservoirs. Organist : Frank Greenwood.

MANSFIELD.—ST PETER'S PARISH CHURCH. Built 1872 by Brindley & Foster. 3 manuals, 26 speaking stops and couplers. Blown by hydraulic engine Organist and Choirmaster ; George P. Allen, MUS. DOC. DUNELM, F R C.O., I, R.A.M.

MARGATE.—HOLY TRINITY CHURCH. Rebuilt 1904 by Browne 4 manuals, 42 speaking stops, 14 other stops, 2,216 pipes Detached console ; tubular pneumatic action throughout. Wind supplied by electric motor. Stops controlled by 19 pistons, 2 balanced swell pedals Crescendo pedal. Organist : Edward Johnson Bellerby.

MARGATE.—ST. PAUL'S CHURCH Built 1877 by Brindley & Foster. 3 manuals, 27 speaking stops, 7 other stops Great and Swell organ South side of Chancel Choir organ (pneumatic action) north side of Chancel in a swell box Organist : Joseph William Pearson.

MARLBOROUGH —COLLEGE CHAPEL. Built 1877 by Foster & Andrews. Opened by W S. Bambridge. 3 manuals, 35 speaking stops, 6 couplers, 1,936 pipes. Pneumatic action to Great Oak case designed by G F. Bodley. 2 stops prepared for Organist : George Dyson, MUS. BAC. OXON., F.R.C.O., A.R.C.M.

MARLOW —ST JOHN THE BAPTIST CHURCH Built 1864. Restored 1907 by Norman & Beard. 2 manuals, 9 speaking stops, 4 other stops, 454 pipes. Opened by Dr. P. Bath. Organist : William Copas.

MATLOCK.—CONGREGATIONAL CHURCH. Built 1882 by Lloyd. Rebuilt 1907 by Adkins Opened by David Clegg and William Wolstenholme, MUS. BAC. 2 manuals, 25 speaking stops, 5 other stops, and 1,300 pipes. Special features : diapason Phonon (leathered), on Great organ (Hope Jones principle). Organist : Harry Douglas.

MAYNOOTH.—ST. PATRICK'S COLLEGE CHAPEL. Built 1896 by G Stahlhuth, Aix la Chapelle. 2 manuals, 33 speaking stops, 8 couplers, 1,924 pipes. 6 composition pistons, 2 pedals affecting Great, Swell and Pedal. Pedal helps Collective crescendo Pedal. Drawstops in shape of keys. Electro-pneumatic. Organist : Rev. H. Bewerunge.

MERTHYR TYDFIL,—" CARTREFLE." Private Residence of E T Davies, F.R.C.O. Built 1904 by Vowles. Claribel flute added 1910 by Norman & Beard. 3 manuals, 12 speaking stops, 6 other stops. Pitch pine case with decorated pipes and beautiful small Gamba of unique tone. Kinetic Swanton hydraulic blowing. Neatly constructed in a spacious music room.

MERTHYR TYDFIL.—ST. DAVID'S CHURCH. Built 1850 by Gray & Davison. Opened by E. Lawrence. 3 manuals, 34 speaking stops

1,200 pipes. Old two-manual restored 1888 by Vowles, who added the Choir organ. Organist and Choirmaster: H. Percy Birmingham, F.G.L.D.O

MERTHYR TYDVIL.—St. Mary's Catholic Church. Built 1905 by Corps. Opened by A. D. Sibley, O.S.B. 2 manuals, 23 speaking stops, 3 couplers, 6 composition pedals. Instrument built in two parts Separate reservoir to each wind chest. Tubular pneumatic action throughout. Blown by hydraulic power.

MIDDLESBROUGH.—St. Barnabas Parish Church, Linthorpe. Built by Hope Jones. 3 manuals. Electro pneumatic. East and West end organ. Organist: Warner Yeomans, A.R.C.O.

MIDDLESBROUGH.—St. Paul's Parish Church. Built 1873 by Gray & Davison; rebuilt 1911 by Norman & Beard. 3 manuals, 26 speaking stops, 9 other stops, 1,452 pipes. Organist: John Alfred Copeland.

MIDDLESBROUGH.—Town Hall. Built 1898 by Hill. 4 manuals, 51 speaking stops, 12 couplers, 2 tremulants, 8 combination pistons, 4 combination pedals, 3 balanced swell pedals. Tubular pneumatic action throughout. Blown by electric motor. Organist: Felix Corbett.

MIDDLETON —Holy Trinity Church. Opened by Dr. J. K. Pyne. 2 manuals, 19 speaking stops, 4 couplers. Organist: John Marsden, 29, Glebeland Terrace, Cross Street, Middleton, Lancs. Appointed Organist 1878, Choirmaster 1892. Music Teacher.

MINEHEAD.—St Andrew's Church Built 1880 by Walker. 1 manual, 9 speaking stops. Organ situated in organ loft above the choir on north side. Organist: F. Walton Evans.

MINEHEAD.—St Michael's Parish Church. Built 1902 by Norman & Beard Opened by Rev. Dr. Davis. 3 manuals, 28 speaking stops, 6 other stops. Electrical blowing installation. Tubular pneumatic action throughout. Detached console. Organist: F. Walton Evans.

MOFFAT.—United Presbyterian Church. Built 1889 by Bevington, 2 manuals, 20 speaking stops, 10 couplers, etc. Tubular pneumatic action. Console 50ft. from organ. Gas blowing. Organist: George Hermon Allatt, A.R.C.O.

MONMOUTH.—Parish Church. Built 1885 by Nicholson & Lord. 3 manuals, 25 speaking stops and couplers. Tracker action. Organist: Miss Enid Payne, "Trafalgar," Hereford Road, Monmouth.

MONTROSE.—Melville Parish Church. Built 1882 and restored 1906 by Forster & Andrews. 2 manuals, 19 speaking stops, 4 couplers and tremulant, 5 composition pedals. Fine diapason tone throughout. Opened by Dr. A. L. Peace. Organist (blind): Alfred B. Grieve.

MORPETH —St. James's Church. Built 1870 by Harrison. 3 manuals, 44 speaking stops, 10 couplers. Organist and Choirmaster: Mr. Henry William Radford.

MORPETH —St. Mary's Church. Built 1800. Rebuilt 1868 by Nicholson & Newbegin. 2 manuals, 13 speaking stops, 3 couplers. Organist and Choirmaster: Henry William Radford.

NEATH.—GNOLL ROAD CONGREGATIONAL CHURCH. Built by Abbott & Smith. 2 manuals, 19 speaking stops, 7 couplers, 1 tremulant, 6 composition pedals. Blown by electric motor. Detached console. Tubular pneumatic action Organist ; Arthur Ll. Dennis.

NENAGH —ST. MARY'S PARISH CHURCH. Built by Nicholson & Lord. 2 manuals. Organist : W. Herbert Pullan, F.I.G.C.M., L.V.C.M.

NEWARK-ON-TRENT.—CHRIST CHURCH. Built 1880 by Harston. Opened by the late S. Reay, MUS. BAC. 2 manuals, 19 speaking stops, 5 other stops, 1,068 pipes. Previous organ given by the late W. E. Gladstone. Organist : James Harston.

NEWARK-ON-TRENT.—PARISH CHURCH. Built 1804 by England. Rebuilt 1886 by Willis. Rebuilt and enlarged 1910 by Hill. 4 manuals, 51 speaking stops, 9 couplers, and 8 composition pistons. Wind supplied by 2 of Hill's hydraulic engines, acting upon independent feeders in a separate chamber. Organist : William Thompson Wright, A.R.C.O., R.C.M.

NEWBURY.—CONGREGATIONAL CHURCH. Built 1907 by Hunter. Opened by Dr. F. Huntley. 3 manuals, 38 speaking stops, 9 other stops, 2,051 pipes, 19 pneumatic pistons, 11 composition pedals. Tubular pneumatic action throughout. Electric blowing. Choir in separate Swell box. 2 balance Swell pedals. Organist : H. Flint. Deputy Organist : Walter Midwinter.

NEWBURY.—ST. JOHN'S CHURCH. Built 1874 by Bevington. 2 manuals, 13 speaking stops, 10 couplers.

NEWBURY —ST. NICHOLAS CHURCH. Built 1863-67 by Bevington. 3 manuals, 30 speaking stops, 10 couplers.

NEWCASTLE-ON-TYNE.—CATHEDRAL, THE. Built 1882 by Lewis. Re-constructed and enlarged 1911 by Harrison. 4 manuals, 75 speaking stops, 22 couplers, 8 combination pedals, 29 combination pistons, 4 reversible pistons, 1 reversible pedal, 2 reversible foot pistons for tremulants, 3 balanced crescendo pedals. Electro-pneumatic action throughout. Blown by 2 electric motors of 7 and 5 h.p. respectively, and 2 large feeder-bellows with 10 feeders. Organist : J. E. Jeffries, F.R.C.O.

NEWCASTLE-ON-TYNE.—CONGREGATIONAL CHURCH, HEATON Built by Blackett & Howden. 2 manuals and pedal, 17 speaking stops, 7 couplers, 4 composition pedals, balanced swell pedal. Detached console. Tubular pneumatic action throughout. Blown by electric motor.

NEWCASTLE-ON-TYNE.—ELSWICK ROAD WESLEYAN CHURCH. Built 1878 by Lewis. Rebuilt 1906 by Nicholson & Newbegin. Opened by J. M. Preston. 3 manuals, 31 speaking stops, 8 other stops, 1,752 pipes. Detached console centre of front pews. Tubular pneumatic action throughout on 6in. wind. Swell chorus reeds on 5in. wind. 9 interchangeable pneumatic pistons to Great, Swell and Pedal organs. 3 pistons to Choir organ. Blown by electric motor operating 3 throw crank gear. Organist : George Dodds.

NEWCASTLE-ON-TYNE.—ST. GABRIEL'S CHURCH, HEATON. Built 1905 by Abbott & Smith. Opened by N. J. E. Jeffries, F.R.C.O. 3 manuals, 32 speaking stops, 8 couplers, 9 composition pedals. Electric blown. Tubular pneumatic action. Detached console. Handsome oak case.

NEWCASTLE-ON-TYNE.—St. Hilda's Church, Jesmond. Built by Blackett & Howden. 2 manuals, 19 speaking stops, 5 couplers, 6 double-acting composition pedals. Blown by electric motor.

NEWCASTLE-ON-TYNE.—St. Mary's R. C. Cathedral. Built 1869 by Lewis. Opened by Mr. Corelli Beare. 3 manuals, 34 speaking stops, 5 couplers, 2,035 pipes. " A noble sample of high-class work." Organist : Nicholas Hodgson Brown, MUS. BAC. (DUNELM), A.R.C.O.

NEWCASTLE-ON-TYNE.—St. Thomas The Martyr. Built 1901 by Vincent. Opened by present organist. 3 manuals, 34 speaking stops, 2,356 pipes. pneumatic action Blown by electricity. Situated in gallery at west end. Organist : Frederick William Smallwood, MUS. BAC. (DUNELM), F.R.C.O., F.G.O.

NEWCASTLE-ON-TYNE.—Town Hall. Built 1862 by Gray & Davison. Rebuilt and enlarged 1901 by Vincent. Re-opened by Dr. A. L. Peace. 4 manuals, 53 stops. Tubular pneumatic action throughout. Hydraulic blowers.

NEWCASTLE-ON-TYNE.—Westgate Hall. Built 1912 by Vincent. 3 manuals, 40 stops. Pneumatic action. Detached console. Electric blower. Opened by J. H. Preston. Organist : Hardy Spark.

NEWCASTLE-UNDER-LYNE.—St. Giles' Parish Church. Built 1911 by Steele & Keay. Opened by G. R. Sinclair, MUS. D., F.R.C.O., HON. R.A.M 3 manuals and pedal, 53 speaking stops, 10 couplers, 1 combination coupler, 14 double-acting pistons, 5 combination pedals, 2 self-balancing pedals, 1 reversible pedal. Tubular pneumatic action throughout. Blown by " Rotary " fans driven by 3 h.p. electric motor. Oak case. Organist : Geo. W. Clay, 1, Station Street, Longport, Staffs.

NEW MALDEN.—Parish Church. Built by Monk. 3 manuals. Organist and Choirmaster : James Griffin, School of Music, New Malden.

NEWMARKET.—St. Martin's Church, Exning. Built 1908 by Harper. Opened by C. Englehardt, MUS. BAC. 2 manuals, 17 speaking stops, 5 other stops, 852 pipes. Blown by hand. Organist : George A. Sarvent.

NEWMARKET.—St. Mary's Church. Built 1910 by Brindley & Foster. 3 manuals, 32 speaking stops, 12 other stops, 14 pneumatic combination accessories, 11 composition pedals. Blown by electric motor. Organist: J. F. Hindell, A.R.C.O., Connaught House, Newmarket.

NEWPORT, I.W.—Carisbrooke Church. Built 1910 by Bevington. Opened by Dr. Prendergast. 2 manuals, 19 speaking stops, 11 other stops. Blown by hand. Organist : John T. Read.

NEWPORT, I.O.W.—St. John's Church. Built 1890 by Bryceson. Opened by W. Scadding. Rebuilt 1909. Choir added and placed in a 3in. box. Organ now is 3 manuals 32 stops, 1,260 pipes. Fine tone. Organist : Alexander S. L. Scadding.

NEWPORT, I.O.W.—Wesleyan Church. Built by Forster & Andrews. 2 manuals, 20 speaking stops. Blown by hand. Organist : Ernest John Henry Quarrier.

NEWPORT, MON.—Congregational Church, Victoria Road. Built 1886 by Vowles. 3 manuals, 30 speaking stops, 8 other stops, 1,300 pipes. Opened by G. Rogers. Organist : Herbert Frank Nicholls, A.R.C.O.

NEWPORT, MON.—GREAT CENTRAL HALL. Built 1907 by Binns. Opened by present organist. 3 manuals, and pedals, 33 speaking stops, 14 other stops, over 2,000 pipes. Blown by electric motor. Divided organ. Detached console ; well placed in capacious hall. Greatly in demand for choral concerts. Organist : Arthur E. Sims, L.R.A.M.

NEWPORT, MON.—HAVELOCK ST. PRESBYTERIAN CHURCH. Built 1886 by Conacher. Opened by G. Rogers 2 manuals, 11 speaking stops, 3 other stops, 578 pipes. Organist. Miss G. Hall Jones, L.R.A.M., 169, Commercial Street, Newport, Mon.

NEWPORT, MON.—PARISH CHURCH. Built 1878 by Vowles. 3 manuals, 7 stops to Great, Swell 9, Choir 6, Pedal 2, couplers 7. Organist : John Augustus Gaccon, F.R.C O.

NEWPORT (MON.).—VICTORIA WESLEYAN CHURCH, MAINDEE. Built by Blackett & Howden. 3 manuals and pedal, 27 speaking stops, 9 couplers, 1,438 pipes, 6 composition pedals, Great to Pedal " on and off." Tubular pneumatic action throughout Blown by electric motor. Organist : Charles P. Simmonds, Brincliffe, Newport, Mon.

NEW ROMNEY.—ST. NICHOLAS CHURCH. Built 1887 by Speechly. Restored by Kearsley Brown. 3 manuals, 35 speaking stops. Formerly a 2-manual Tracker action, but through the generosity of the late R. R. Daglish was in 1905 rebuilt, a Choir organ added, and tubular pneumatic action installed throughout. Added in 1910, by Mrs. R. R. Daglish at a cost of £350, a blowing chamber with 6 h.p Crossley gas engine and Kinetic blower, in memory of her husband, R. R. Daglish, Mayor of New Romney. Organist : Edward Charles Mitchell, A.L.C M.

NEWRY.—ST MARY'S CATHEDRAL. Built 1910 by Telford & Telford. 3 manuals and pedal, 35 speaking stops, 7 couplers, 8 combination pistons. Hydraulic blowing Situated in West gallery. Tubular pneumatic action throughout. Organist and Choirmaster : L. Seymour, 2, Courtenay Hill, Newry.

NEW TREDEGAR.—PARISH CHURCH. Built 1903 by Sweetland. Opened by H. Evans, F.R.C.O. 2 manuals, 17 speaking stops, 3 other stops, 1,100 pipes Organist. Frank Lewis.

NEWTON ABBOT.—CHURCH OF ST. PAUL. Rebuilt 1889 by Hele. Opened by present organist. 3 manuals, 25 speaking stops, 5 other stops. Stands in Organ Chamber on south side of Chancel, one front as usual. Pneumatic action. Hydraulic blower. Organist : W. J. Bown, A R.C O.

NEWTON STEWART.—ALL SAINTS' CHURCH. Built 1878 by Harston. Opened by Mr Denny. 2 manuals, 15 speaking stops, 2 other stops, 734 pipes. Blown by hand. Organist. L. F. Baguley.

NEWTON STEWART —ST. ANDREW'S CHURCH. Built 1910 by Ebrall. 2 manuals, 10 speaking stops, 4 other stops, couplers, etc., 498 pipes. Blown by hand. Organist : L. F. Baguley.

NEWTOWN, N. WALES —CONGREGATIONAL CHURCH. Built 1881 by Conacher. Opened by Mr E. Minshall. 2 manuals, 14 speaking stops, 4 other stops. All stops run through. Organist : William Pugh Phillips.

NEWTOWN, N. WALES.—ST. MARY'S PARISH CHURCH. Built 1849 by
   Willis. Rebuilt and enlarged 1909 by Bishop. 3 manuals, 28 speaking
   stops, 9 couplers, 7 composition pedals. Organist: A. J Bibb, F.R.C.O.

NORTHAMPTON.—ALL SAINTS' CHURCH. Rebuilt 1912 by Brindley &
   Foster. 4 manuals, 41 speaking stops, 17 other stops, 11 composition
   pedals, 43 pneumatic combination accessories, balanced swell pedals.
   Blown by " Centrifugal " blower. Organist: Brook Sampson, MUS.
   BAC. OXON., F.R.C.O., Beethoven House, Northampton.

NORTHAMPTON.—CATHOLIC CATHEDRAL. Built 1887 by Bevington.
   Opened by the Right Rev. Monseigneur Scott, D.D., V.G. 2 manuals,
   20 speaking stops, 10 other stops. Blown by hand. Organist:
   John Tonks.

NORTHAMPTON.—HARDINGSTONE CHURCH. Built 1894 by Bevington.
   2 manuals, 11 speaking stops, 9 couplers. Pneumatic action throughout. Separate and reversed console. Organist: Henry Clarke, 5,
   St. Michael's Mount, Northampton.

NORTHAMPTON.—MOUNT PLEASANT BAPTIST CHURCH. Built 1909 by
   Bevington. 2 manuals, 20 speaking stops, 13 other stops, 1,120 pipes.
   Blown by electricity. Tubular action throughout. Separate and
   reversed console. Organist: W. Tebbutt.

NORTHAMPTON.—ST. MARY'S CHURCH. Built 1888 by Walker. Opened
   by Dr. H. Keeton. 2 manuals, 10 speaking stops, 5 couplers, 555
   pipes, 4 composition pedals. Excellent quality. Organist: Reginald
   W. Bartle, F.R.C.O.

NORTHAMPTON.—ST. MATTHEW'S CHURCH. Built 1895 by Walker.
   4 manuals, 48 speaking stops, 11 couplers, 14 composition pistons,
   8 composition pedals. Tubular pneumatic action to manuals and
   pedals, 2,925 pipes. Drawstop action, electric pneumatic. Blown by
   2 electric motors. Organist: Charles J. King.

NORTHAMPTON.—ST. MICHAEL'S AND ALL ANGELS'. Built by Bishop.
   2 manuals, 12 speaking stops, 4 couplers. Renovated 1902 by Walker,
   and new tubular pneumatic action applied to Pedal organ. Organist:
   John C. Dunlop, A.R.C.O., A. MUS. T.C.L.

NORTHAMPTON.—ST. PAUL'S CHURCH. Built 1894 by Binns Opened
   by Dr. H. Keeton. 2 manuals, 23 speaking stops prepared for, 3
   couplers. Organ at present in-complete. Tubular pneumatic action.
   Balanced Swell Pedal. Excellent quality, especially diapasons and
   reeds. Console on level with choir stalls. Body over head. Organist:
   Cyril Davis.

NORTH BERWICK.—PARISH CHURCH. Built 1886 by Forster & Andrews.
   2 manuals, 14 speaking stops, 4 couplers. Tracker action throughout.
   Blown by hydraulic motor by Melvin, Glasgow. Situated on north
   side of Chancel.

NORTH BERWICK.—ST. BALDRED'S CHURCH. Built by Forster & Andrews.
   Rebuilt 1906 by Norman & Beard 3 manuals, 29 stops and accessories.
   Pneumatic action throughout. Organist: Ernest W. Hardy, A.R.C.O.

NORTHOP.—PARISH CHURCH. Built by Chas. Whiteley. 2 manuals, 16
   speaking stops, 4 other stops, 5 combination pedals. Tracker action.
   Organist: Charles Lewis Jones, MUS. BAC. DUNELM, L.R.A.M., A.R.C.O.

NORTH SHIELDS.—WESLEYAN MEMORIAL CHURCH. Built 1908 by Nicholson & Newbegin. 3 manuals, 34 speaking stops, 7 couplers. Detached console. Organist . H. Yeaman Dodds.

NORTHWICH.—ST WILFRED'S CHURCH, DAVENHAM. Built 1870 by Wadsworth. 2 manuals, 19 speaking stops, 3 other stops, 1,070 pipes, 6 composition pedals. Situated in a chamber on North side of Chancel. Fine clarinet and straight diapasons. Organist : T. J. Candlin.

NORTHWICH.—WHITLEY PARISH CHURCH. Built 1907 by Rushworth & Dreaper. 2 manuals, 18 speaking stops, 5 other stops, 902 pipes. Tubular pneumatic action to Pedal, front pipes and basses. Radiating and concave pedal board. Angular stop jambs 2 diapasons in. Great, the second being of small scale for choir accompaniment Organist : Rev. Joseph Clare Trampleasure.

NORWICH —CATHEDRAL, THE. Built 1889 by Norman & Beard. 5 manuals, 64 speaking stops, 14 couplers, 4,148 pipes. Tubular pneumatic action applied to whole organ excepting Echo organ, which is controlled by the latest electro-pneumatic connection. Splendid tone of diapasons, and fine Echo organ. Organist : Frank Bates, MUS. DOC. Sub-Organist : R. J Maddern-Williams, A R C O.

NORWICH —ST. PETER MANCROFT. Built 1912 by Hele. 4 manuals, 47 speaking stops, 13 other stops. Hele's patent key stops. 13 pistons. Wind pressure from 2¾"—14". Detached console. Blown by 6 h p. electric motor. Organist . R. J. Maddern-Williams, F.R.C.O.

NOTTINGHAM —ADDISON STREET CONGREGATIONAL CHURCH Built 1885 by Lloyd. 2 manuals, 21 speaking stops, 5 other stops, 1,112 pipes. Organist : John Thorton Masser

NOTTINGHAM.—ALBERT HALL, NOTTINGHAM Built 1910 by Binns. Gift of Sir Jesse Boot 59 speaking stops, 18 couplers, 18 pistons, 10 combination pedals, 16 interchangeable combination pistons. Tremulant to Swell, Choir, and Solo Tubular pneumatic action throughout. Patent electric motor, working 4 discus blowers. Organist : Bernard Johnson, B.A., MUS. BAC. CANTAB., F R C O.

NOTTINGHAM.—ALBION CONGREGATIONAL CHURCH, SNEINTON ROAD, Built 1905 by Lloyd Opened by Sir Walter Parratt, M.V.O. 3 manuals 37 speaking stops, 9 couplers, 10 combination touches. Tubular pneumatic action throughout, excepting pedal couplers Organist : Gilbert Ryde, 6, Victoria Villas, Sneinton Dale, Nottingham.

NOTTINGHAM —ALL SAINTS' CHURCH, ANNESLEY Built 1908 by Rothwell. 3 manuals, 23 speaking stops, 6 other stops Opened by Norman Hibbert, MUS. BAC. Organist : William Henry Renshaw.

NOTTINGHAM —CANAAN PRIMITIVE METHODIST CHURCH, BROAD MARSH. Built 1907 by Lloyd 2 manuals and pedal, 21 speaking stops, 6 couplers, 6 double-acting combination pistons. Tubular pneumatic action throughout. Opened by Norman Hibbert, MUS. BAC., F.R.C.O. Organist : A. Hodgkinson.

NOTTINGHAM —OLD BASFORD PARISH (ST LEODEGARIUS) CHURCH. Built 1902 by Jones 2 manuals, 22 speaking stops, 4 couplers, 1,185 pipes. Pneumatic action to Pedal organ. Tracker to manuals.

NOTTINGHAM.—PRESBYTERIAN CHURCH, MANSFIELD ROAD. Built 1898 by Cuthbert. Opened by Dr. G. Bennett. 3 manuals, 18 speaking stops, 2 other stops, 1,054 pipes. Pneumatic action to manuals. Tracker to pedals. Balancing Swell. Organist: Arthur Charles Walker.

NOTTINGHAM.—ST. JOHN'S PARISH CHURCH, BEESTON. Rebuilt 1909 by Lloyd. Opened by present organist. 3 manuals, 28 speaking stops, 10 couplers and tremulant, 1,689 pipes. Balanced Swell pedal. Compass, 5 octaves (to C). Pipes acted on by stop-keys. Combinations by pistons. Organist: Horace Vernon Kington, F.R.C.O., L.R A M.

NOTTINGHAM —ST MARY'S CHURCH. Built 1873 by Bishop. 3 manuals, 42 stops, and couplers. Organist: Fred Dunnill, F R C O , A R.C.M.

NOTTINGHAM.—ST. MARY'S CHURCH, Arnold. Built 1876 by Brindley & Foster. 2 manuals, 15 speaking stops, 1 other stop, 678 pipes.

NOTTINGHAM.—ST. PETER'S PARISH CHURCH Built 1770 by Green for York Minster, and removed to St. Peters in 1815 Enlarged 1863 and improved 1911 by Lloyd. 3 manuals, 25 speaking stops, 6 other stops, 1,200 pipes Fine case. Removed from Western gallery to the side of Chancel, 1878. Organist. Vincent W. Trivett, Member R.C.O.

NOTTINGHAM —ST SAVIOUR'S CHURCH. Built 1867 by Forster & Andrews. Rebuilt and enlarged 1906 by Lloyd. Opened after restoration by the present organist. 2 manuals, 20 speaking stops, 6 couplers, 1,000 pipes. Four stops on the pedals. Tubular pneumatic action is applied throughout. Solid ivory draw-knobs Organist: Herbert Frederick Smith, A R C O.

NOTTINGHAM.—PRIVATE ORGAN OF J. T MASSER, 32, MAPPERLEY ROAD. Built 1848 by John Nicholson, Bradford. Rebuilt 1908 by Lloyd. 3 manuals, and pedal, 22 speaking stops, 8 couplers, 4 composition pedals, lever pedals to Swell and Choir 1,010 pipes Blown by electric motor and fan.

NOTTINGHAM.—WESLEYAN CHAPEL, LANGLEY MILL Built by Young. 2 manuals, 20 speaking stops, 5 couplers, 3 composition pedals, balanced swell pedal. Organist: J. Arthur Frost.

OBAN.—ST COLUMBA PARISH CHURCH. Built 1899 by Brindley & Foster 2 manuals, 20 stops. Divided console in centre Pneumatic action throughout. Organist: Julian H W. Nesbitt, A. MUS., T C.I.

OKEHAMPTON.—ALL SAINTS PARISH CHURCH. Rebuilt 1902 by Hele. Opened by Rev. Arnold D. Culley. 3 manuals, 24 speaking stops, 5 other pipes, 1,300 pipes Organist Sydenham J Janes Born 1864 at Okehampton. Educated at Torrington. Appointed 1884.

OLDHAM.—ST. MARY'S PARISH CHURCH. Built 1830. Rebuilt 1896 by Elliott & Hill Opened by Mr Knyvett. 3 manuals, 33 speaking stops, 6 couplers, accessories, 1,836 pipes. Organ in west gallery. Re-modelled, made tubular, pneumatic throughout by Hill, 1908 Blown by a " Discus " blower, attached to a 3 h p electric motor. Organist: G Wilmot-Cooper, MUS DOC , Queen's College, Oxford, L R.A.M

OLDHAM.—ST PETER'S CHURCH. Built by Young. 3 manuals, 40 speaking stops, 10 couplers, 9 double-acting pedals, 2,348 pipes. Tubular pneumatic action throughout. Blown by electric motor.

OLDHAM.—St. Thomas' Church. Built 1881 by Hill. Opened by W.T. Best. 4 manuals, 52 speaking stops, 10 other stops, 2,852 pipes. 3 crescendo pedals to Choir, Swell, and Solo, 6 composition pedals. Organist and Choirmaster : W. Norman Mellalieu, A.R.C.O.

OLD MALDEN —St. John The Baptist Church. Built 1905 by Norman & Beard. 2 manuals, 16 speaking stops, and 4 couplers. Pneumatic action to manuals and couplers, tracker to pedals. Organist : John Cawley, A.R.C.O.

OMAGH —Church of the Sacred Heart. Built by Positive Co. 32 speaking stops, 9 couplers.

OSSETT.—Holy Trinity Parish Church. Built 1880 by Abbott & Smith. 3 manuals, 40 speaking stops, 5 couplers, 8 composition pedals, 2 Swell Pedal, Swell and Choir. Tracker and pneumatic action. Two blowers. Organist : B. Whitworth, A.R C.O.

OSSETT.—Wesleyan Church. Built 1884 by Abbott and Smith. 3 manuals, 32 speaking stops, 6 other stops, 1878 pipes. Splendid tone and balance. Diapasons good. Reeds full and mellow. Organist : J. T. Taylor.

OSWESTRY.—Parish Church. Built 1860. Rebuilt and enlarged 1910 by Hill 3 manuals, 36 speaking stops, 8 other stops Organist : Alfred E. Floyd, MUS. BAC. OXON.

OXFORD —Christ Church Cathedral. Rebuilt 1884 and 1910 by Willis. 4 manuals, 40 speaking stops, 10 couplers, 7 composition pedals, 10 pneumatic pistons. Organist : Henry George Ley.

OXFORD.—Church of the Society of St. John the Evangelist. Built 1897 by Beale & Thynne. Opened by Dr. Pearce 2 manuals. 11 speaking stops, 3 other stops. Fine case (see page 54) by G. F. Bodley, A.R.A. Organist : Basil C. Bucknall.

OXFORD —Cowley Church. Built 1858 and restored 1896 by Bevington. 3 manuals, 24 speaking stops, 8 other stops. Blown by hand. Organist : M. E. Creaton, A L.C M.

OXFORD —Exeter College Built 1861 by Hill. 3 manuals, 24 speaking stops, 5 other stops. Organ in West gallery.

OXFORD —Magdalen College Chapel. Built by Gray & Davison, and Binns 4 manuals, 50 stops. Organist : John Varley Roberts, MUS. DOC., F R.C O.

OXFORD —Merton College Chapel. 2 manuals, 14 speaking stops ; 8 great, 4 Swell, 2 Pedal, 3 couplers Composition pedals to Great organ. Hand blown. Organist : Walter K. Stanton.

OXFORD.—St. Barnabas Church. Built by Martin & Coates. 4 manuals, 39 speaking stops, 10 other stops. Blown by Swanton Kinetic blower. Organist and Choirmaster : Herbert C. Warrilow, F.R.C O.

OXFORD —S.S. Philip and James' Church. Built 1860 by Hill. Rebuilt and brought up to date 1904, by Gray & Davison. 3 manuals, 36 speaking stops, 8 couplers, 10 composition pedals Electric blowing. Tubular pneumatic action throughout. Organist : Norman Cocker.

OXFORD.—WADHAM COLLEGE CHAPEL. Built 1886 by Willis. 2 manuals, 18 speaking stops, 5 couplers. Light tracker action with tubular pneumatic to pedals, 5 composition pedals. Radiating concave pedal board. Organist: A. J. Derrick.

PAIGNTON —CHRIST CHURCH. Built 1889 by Hele. Enlarged 1906. Opened by present organist. 3 manuals, 30 speaking stops, 6 couplers, 1,788 pipes. Organist: F. W. Benson, F.R.C.O., L.R.A.M., A.M.T.C.L.

PAIGNTON.—WESLEYAN CHURCH Built 1904 by Forster & Andrews. Opened by Dr. O. A. Mansfield. 2 manuals, 20 speaking stops, 4 other stops, 1,032 pipes. Radiating concave, R.C.O. Pedal board. Tremulant. Organist: Madame Queenie Clark.

PAISLEY.—CANAL STREET UNITED FREE CHURCH. Built 1899 by Bishop. 2 manuals, 14 speaking stops, 5 other stops, 708 pipes. Pneumatic action Detached console. Organist: James Black.

PAISLEY.—HIGH PARISH CHURCH. Built 1899 by Hill. 2 manuals, 24 speaking stops, 5 other stops, 1,366 pipes. Tremulant by pedal. Blown by 2 Melvin engines. Organist: Robert A. Chatterton, L.R.A.M., A.R.C.O.

PAISLEY.—SHERWOOD UNITED FREE CHURCH. Built 1893 by Lewis. Opened by Alfred Hollins, F.R.C.O. 2 manuals, 18 speaking stops, 5 other stops, 964 pipes. Blown by hydraulic engine. 8 Electro pneumatic action; crescendo pedal over whole organ. Balanced Swell pedal. Organist: H. Sandiford Turner.

PEEBLES.—PARISH CHURCH. Built by Gern. 3 manuals, 28 speaking stops, 13 other stops. Pneumatic action throughout. 5 pistons to each manual; 7 composition pedals Organist: Horner Whalley, F.R.C.O.

PENRITH.—ST ANDREW'S PARISH CHURCH. Built 1799 by Green. Rebuilt 1870 by T. H. Harrison, Rochdale; 1887 by Wilkinson: 1906 by Keates. Opened by E. Godfrey Brown. 3 manuals, 37 speaking stops, 6 other stops. Organist: J. Pollard, F.R.C.O.

PERSHORE —ABBEY THE. Built by Nicholson. 3 manuals, 41 speaking stops. Organist: Frank Alfred Charles Mason.

PERTH.—CATHEDRAL, THE. Built 1856 by Robson, Smith, Conacher. Rebuilt 1901 by Miller. Opened by T. H Collinson, MUS. BAC. 4 manuals, 45 speaking stops, 10 other stops, 2,652 pipes, 10 composition pedals. Tubular pneumatic action. Organ in South choir aisle. Console in North choir aisle. Patent stop key action to Console. Organist: Stephen Richardson.

PERTH.—NORTH UNITED FREE CHURCH. Built 1894 by Miller. Opened by Dr. A. L Peace. 2 manuals, 21 speaking stops, 7 other stops, 1,188 pipes, 6 composition pedals Moving console, with Hope Jones electric action. Organist: Edward Nicol.

PERTH.—ST. JOHN'S EPISCOPAL CHURCH. Built 1908 by Binns 3 manuals, 51 stops. Fitted throughout with the builder's patent pneumatic action and patent interchangeable combination stop action. Blown by electric motor. Organist: Harold Helman.

PERTH.—St. John's Parish Church. Rebuilt 1893 by Hope Jones.
New electric action added 1905 by Scovell. 3 manuals, 30 speaking
stops, 11 couplers. Electric action throughout, excepting the Rachet
Swell pedal, which is mechanical. 10 composition pedals. Organist:
Frederick Midgley, F R C.O.

PERTH —St. Paul's Church. Built by Harrison. 2 manuals, 22 speaking
stops, 3 other stops. Blown by water engine. Organist: John Edward
Pirrie.

PERTH.—West U.F. Church. Organ built by J. W. Walker & Sons,
London, in 1896. Opened by W. Stevenson Hoyte. 2 manuals, 20
speaking stops, 4 couplers, 6 composition pedals, one double-acting
pedal, controlling Great to Pedal coupler, stands behind pulpit. Tubular
pneumatic action throughout. Blown by Melvin hydraulic engine.
Organist: R. E. C. Taylor.

PETERBOROUGH.—Cathedral, The. Built 1894 by Hill. 4 manuals,
68 speaking stops, 13 other stops, 4,917 pipes. Organist: Haydon
Keeton, MUS. DOC. OXON., F.R C O.

PETERHEAD —Parish Church. Built 1911 by Brindley & Foster.
2 manuals, 29 speaking stops, 5 other stops, 1,681 pipes, 31 pneumatic
combination accessories, 9 composition pedals, tremulant, balanced
swell pedal Blown by hydraulic engine. Organist. J. M. Collyer,
29, St. Peter's Street, Peterhead.

PLYMOUTH —Christ Church. Built 1857 by Squire. Opened by Mr. W. S.
Yeo. 2 manuals, 24 speaking stops, 4 other stops, 1,300 pipes.
Organist: James Henry Lucas, A.T C L., A.T.S.C., 1st. MUS. BAC. OXON.

PLYMOUTH —Guildhall, The. Built 1882 by Willis. Rebuilt and
enlarged 1907 by Hele, when Echo organ was added in separate Swell
box 4 manuals, 73 speaking stops, 14 couplers Tubular pneumatic
action, 2 tremulants. Blown by 4 hydraulic engines. Borough Organist: Harry Moreton, MUS. BAC., F.R.C.O

PLYMOUTH —Holy Trinity Church. Built 1848 by Dicker 2 manuals,
21 speaking stops, 5 other stops, 1,131 pipes. Organist: William
George Warden.

PLYMOUTH.—St. Andrew's Parish Church. Built 1726 by Parsons,
Brought up to date 1909 by Hele 4 manuals, 54 speaking stops, 11
couplers 3 hydraulic engines Tubular pneumatic action throughout.
Organist Harry Moreton, MUS. BAC. DURHAM, F.R.C O.

PLYMOUTH.—St. Catharine's Church. Restored by Hele 3 manuals,
26 speaking stops, 7 other stops, 1,378 pipes. Gamba Gambette, and
Clarinet (Choir organ) in a separate Swell box. Organist: Manley
Martin, F.R C O.

PLYMOUTH.—St. Jude's Church. Built 1877 by Hele. 2 manuals, 20
speaking stops, 3 other stops, 5 composition pedals. Blown by " Ross "
hydraulic engine. Organist: Thomas W. Luger.

PONTERDAWE.—St Peter's Church Built 1872 and enlarged 1912 by
Vowles. 3 manuals, 29 speaking stops, 6 other stops, 1,692 pipes.
Detached Console Pneumatic action throughout. Has two fronts of
speaking pipes, beautifully decorated. Pitch pine case. Organists:
Joan Williams, A.R.C.M. (English); Daniel Howells (Welsh).

PONTEFRACT.—PARISH CHURCH. Built 1895 by Binns. Opened by A. Hollins. 3 manuals, 36 speaking stops, 9 other stops, 2,100 pipes, 7 composition pedals. Tubular pneumatic action throughout. Organist : Frank A. Chapple, MUS. BAC., F.R.C.O.

PONTYPRIDD.—ST. KATHERINE'S CHURCH. Built 1904 by Hill to specification of present organist. 3 manuals, 32 speaking stops, 6 couplers, 8 combination pistons. Tubular pneumatic action. Hydraulic blowing. Organist and Choirmaster : W. J. Granger, F.R.C.O.

PORT GLASGOW.—PARISH CHURCH. Rebuilt 1897 by Binns. 3 manuals, 26 speaking stops, 9 couplers. Detached console in body of Church. Pneumatic action throughout. Solid oak console and case. Organist : Charles Edmund Midgley.

PORT GLASGOW.—TOWN HALL. Built 1902 by Binns. 3 manuals, 35 speaking stops, 11 couplers, 3 Binns' interchangeable combination pedals to Great and Swell, and interchangeable pistons to Choir. Pneumatic action throughout. Pitch pine case. Organist : Charles Edmund Midgley.

PORTSMOUTH.—CHRIST CHURCH, SOUTHSEA. Built by Hunter. 2 manuals, 22 speaking stops, 4 other stops, 6 composition pedals. Variety of tone. Pedal board straight to concave. Organists : George Ernest Longyear and C. Masher.

PORTSMOUTH.—ST JOHN'S, PORTSEA. Built 1789 by England. Restored 1901 by Dyer. 3 manuals, 29 speaking stops, 6 other stops, 1,470 pipes. Organist : Edward Buckle.

PORTSMOUTH.—ST. JUDE'S CHURCH, SOUTHSEA. Built 1912 by Hill. Tubular pneumatic action. 45 speaking stops, 7 couplers. Organist : — Martin.

PORTSMOUTH.—ST. MARGARET'S CHURCH, SOUTHSEA. Built by Monk. 3 manuals, 28 speaking stops, 5 couplers Built in three arches, elevated twenty feet from floor. Console under organ connected by tubular pneumatic action.

PORTSMOUTH.—ST. MARY'S PARISH CHURCH, PORTSEA. Built 1892 by Walker 3 manuals, 38 speaking stops (Solo organ of 5 stops prepared for), 8 couplers, 1 tremulant, 4 combination pistons, 4 composition pedals. Pneumatic action to drawstops. Blown by 3 h.p. Crossley gas engine. Organist : Hugh A. Burry.

PORTSMOUTH.—ST. MICHAEL'S AND ALL ANGELS. Built 1879 by Walker. 3 manuals, 21 speaking stops, 7 other stops, 1,268 pipes. Organist : Percy Ramsey, L. MUS. T.C.L.

PORTSMOUTH.—ST. SIMON'S CHURCH, SOUTHSEA. Built 1871 by Ivimey. Restored 1901. 2 manuals, 26 speaking stops, 6 other stops, 1,354 pipes. Organist : A. Shaw.

PORTSMOUTH.—TOWN HALL. Built by Gray & Davison. 4 manuals, 52 speaking stops, 12 other stops, 3,259 pipes.

PORTSMOUTH.—WESLEY CHURCH, ARUNDEL STREET. Rebuilt 1890 by Bevington. 3 manuals, 21 speaking stops, 12 couplers.

PORTH.—CONGREGATIONAL CHURCH   Built 1910 by Bevington. 2 manuals, 17 speaking stops, 11 couplers, etc. Tubular pneumatic action throughout. Hydraulic blowing.

POTTERS BAR.—ST. JOHN THE BAPTIST CHURCH. Built by Brindley & Foster. 2 manuals, 13 speaking stops, 3 other stops, 676 pipes.

PRESTON.—CHRIST CHURCH, FULWOOD   Built by Richardson. 3 manuals, 29 speaking stops, 7 other stops, 1,476 pipes, 5 composition pedals. Great to Pedal and Swell to Great by horse-shoe pedals. Blown by hand. Organist : Thomas Hogg, F R C.O , 15, Stanley Place, Preston, Lancs   Appointed 1907.

PRESTON.—PARISH CHURCH. Built 1802 by Davis   Restored 1888 by Hill. 3 manuals, 48 speaking stops, 7 couplers   Blown by 2 hydraulic engines. Organist   James Edward Adkins, MUS. BAC. (DUNELM), F.R C O.

PRESTON.—PUBLIC HALL. Built 1882 by Wilkinson. Improved and enlarged 1912 by Ainscough. 4 manuals, 54 speaking stops, 13 couplers, 12 combination pedals, 23 pneumatic pistons   Organist : James Tomlinson, 8, Starkie Street, Preston.

PRESTON.—ST MARY'S CHURCH, GOOSNARGH   Built 1905 by Ainscough. Opened by J Tomlinson. 2 manuals, 18 speaking stops, 5 other stops, 930 pipes. Blown by a Vacher hydraulic motor. Oak case. Organist : William Ernest Cooke, A.R.C O , A. MUS T C L , A C.P.

PWLLHELI.—HENMONT CALVINISTIC METHODIST CHURCH. Built by Blackett & Howden. 3 manuals and pedal, 25 speaking stops, 9 couplers, 6 composition pedals, Great to Pedal " on and off," balanced swell pedal. Tubular pneumatic action throughout   Blown by hydraulic motor.

READING.—ALL SAINTS' CHURCH. Built by Willis. 3 manuals, 36 speaking stops, 7 other stops   Organist : W. D Boseley, MUS BAC. OXON., A R C.M., F.R C.O

READING.—CHRIST CHURCH. Built by Jones   Restored by Hill. 3 manuals, 26 speaking stops, 6 other stops   Blown by hand. Organist : Arthur Willis Moss, L R A.M , F R C.O.

READING.—GREYFRIARS' CHURCH   Built 1887 by Monk. 3 manuals, 35 speaking stops, 5 couplers

READING.—ST. GILES' PARISH CHURCH   Restored 1867 and 1888 by Walker   3 manuals, 32 speaking stops, 6 other stops, 1,214 pipes, 7 composition pedals. Organist ; P R. Scrivener, L.T C.L , F.R.C.O.

READING.—ST. MARY'S CHURCH, CASTLE STREET. Built by Monk. 3 manuals, 34 speaking stops, 6 couplers.

READING —TOWN HALL. Built by Willis. 4 manuals, 37 speaking stops, 9 other stops. Hydraulic blowing. Organist : W. D. Boseley, MUS. BAC. OXON., A R.C.M , F.R.C.O.

REDDISH.—ST AGNES' CHURCH. Built 1912 by Hill. Tubular pneumatic action. 22 speaking stops, 7 couplers.

REIGATE.—Parish Church. Built 1911 by Norman & Beard. 3 manuals, 44 speaking stops, 13 other stops, 2,477 pipes. Heavy pressure reeds, Tuba, pistons, balanced crescendo Pedals to Swell and Choir. Blown by electric motor. Organist: John W. Gritton, F R C O.

REIGATE.—St. Mark's Church. Built 1899 by Willis. Opened by Mr. H. L. Balfour. 3 manuals, 28 speaking stops, 6 other stops, 1,742 pipes. Good reeds. Organist: Charles Robert Palmer, A.R.C.O.

REPTON.—School Chapel. Rebuilt 1904 by Keates. 3 manuals, 34 speaking stops, 10 couplers, etc. Pneumatic action. Organist. Dr. G. G. Stocks.

REPTON.—Pears' Memorial Hall, Repton School. Rebuilt and modernised 1910 by Keates. 3 manuals, 31 speaking stops, 10 couplers, etc. Swell reeds to Choir switch. Ventil for combinations, " on and off " pedal. Fine oak case Organist: Dr. G. G. Stocks, F R C O.

RETFORD.—St. Saviour's Church. Built 1878 by Bevington. 2 manuals, 17 speaking stops, 9 couplers, etc. Organist: L. F. Sellen, A R C M.

RICHMOND (Surrey).—St. Matthias' Church. Built by Walker. Choir organ added by Gray & Davison. Solo organ by Hill; and balanced pedals, etc. by Lewis. 4 manuals, 53 speaking stops, 10 other stops. Rebuilt 1911, on the " Burns " plan of construction. 22 ranks, 73 draw-notes, 4 swell boxes, electric blowing, 3 manuals, and a pedal of 13 speaking stops, 5 of which are flexible. Organist: Kenneth Glencairn Burns.

RICHMOND (Surrey).—Wesleyan College Chapel. Built by Hill. 3 manuals, 14 speaking stops, 6 other stops, 3 composition pedals.

RICHMOND (Yorks).—St. Mary's Parish Church. Built 1809 by England. Restored 1883 by Abbott & Smith Rebuilt 1912 by Harrison Contains pipework by each of the builders 3 manuals, 43 speaking stops, 10 couplers, 5 combination pedals, 13 combination pistons, 3 reversible pistons, reversible pedal, balanced crescendo pedal. Tubular pneumatic action. Blown by two hydraulic engines and feeders Reeds on Great transferable to Choir. Action and heavy reeds on 10in. wind. Organist: Edward Brown, MUS. BAC., F.R C O.

RIPON.—Cathedral, The. Built 1878 by Lewis. Restored 1902 by Hill. 4 manuals, 52 speaking stops, 11 couplers. Solo organ of 6 stops prepared for. Organ originally built by Father Smith. Rebuilt 1912 by Harrison, when all reeds were re-voiced and mitred, the flue work re-scaled and re-voiced, the Solo organ of 6 stops added, and the Choir organ boxed and placed on North side of the Choir, and blowing apparatus transferred to the crypt. Blown by gas engine. Organist: Charles Harry Moody.

ROCHDALE.—St. James' Church. Built by Bevington. 3 manuals, 22 speaking stops, 7 couplers, 5 combination pedals.

ROCHESTER.—Cathedral, The. Built 1791 by Green. Rebuilt 1905 by Walker. Opened by Sir F. Bridge. 3 manuals, 41 speaking stops, 6 other stops. Organist: Bertram Luard-Selby.

ROSS-ON-WYE.—St. Mary's Parish Church. Built 1884 by Eustace Ingram. 3 manuals, 31 speaking stops, 6 other stops. Organist: H. M. Goodacre, F.R.C.O.

ROTHERHAM.—CHRIST CHURCH, PARKGATE. Built 1887 by Conacher. Opened by Dr. Spark. 2 manuals, 20 speaking stops, 3 other stops, 1,156 pipes. Organist : Henry Thomas Cawthorne, Certificate L.C M.

ROTHERHAM.—PARISH CHURCH, EASTWOOD. Built 1876 by Brindley & Foster. Opened by Dr. E. H. Turpin. 2 manuals, 18 speaking stops, 4 other stops. Organist : H. Crackel, F.R.C.O.

ROTHERHAM.—TRINITY CHURCH, WENTWORTH. Built 1877 by Willis, 2 manuals, 22 speaking stops. Organist : W. J. Dickie, L.R.A.M., Exhibitioner R.C.M.

RUGBY.—ST. MATTHEW'S PARISH CHURCH. Built 1878 by Bryceson. Rebuilt 1905 by Forster & Andrews. 2 manuals, 18 speaking stops, 4 couplers, 1 tremulant, 918 pipes. Organist . Herbert Lane, A.R.C.M., A.R C.O.

RUGBY.—SCHOOL, CHAPEL. Built 1872 by Bryceson. Modernised by Norman & Beard. 4 manuals, 55 speaking stops, 16 couplers, 3,131 pipes. 18 pistons, 4 reversible pistons, 10 composition pedals, 2 reversible pedals, balanced Swell pedal to Choir, tremulants to Swell and Choir organs. Blown by Kinetic blower. Organist : Basil Johnson, B.A. OXON.

RUGBY.—SCHOOL, SPEECH ROOM. Built 1890 by Bryceson. 3 manuals, 40 stops. Organist : Basil Johnson, B.A. OXON.

RUGELEY —ST. ANNE'S SCHOOL. Built by Bishop. 2 manuals, 11 speaking stops, 3 other stops. Organist : Miss Chadwick.

RUNCORN.—HOLY TRINITY CHURCH. Built 1908 by Rushworth & Dreaper 3 manuals, 31 speaking stops, 9 couplers, 9 composition pedals, 8 pistons. Tubular pneumatic action throughout. Organist : A. Savage.

RUSHDEN.—ST. MARY'S PARISH CHURCH. Built 1874 by Trustam. Opened by Mr. Harrington. 2 manuals, 15 speaking stops. Pipes spotted metal. Organist and Choirmaster : Joseph Enos Smith.

RYDE, I.W.—HOLY TRINITY CHURCH. Rebuilt 1898 by Bevington. 3 manuals, 30 speaking stops, 12 couplers Part tubular Electric blowing. Organist : A. Percy James, 7, Trinity Villas, Winton Street, Ryde, I.O.W.

RYDE.—ST. JOHN'S CHURCH. Built 1876 by Bevington. 2 manuals, 17 speaking stops, 4 couplers, tremulant, 5 composition pedals. 2 stops prepared for. Organist : Sidney L. Torr.

RYDE.—PARISH CHURCH OF ALL SAINTS. Built 1872 by Willis. Restored 1911 by Hill. 3 manuals, 40 speaking stops, 12 other stops, 2,386 pipes. Blown by Discus blower and electric motor. Organist : R. Yates Mander, MUS. DOC. OXON., F.R.C.O., L.R.A.M.

RYDE —TOWN HALL. Built by Abbott & Smith. 3 manuals and pedal, 28 speaking stops, 7 couplers, 9 interchangeable combination pistons, 6 composition pedals, 2 balanced crescendo pedals and tremulant. Gift of the townspeople to commemorate Diamond Jubilee of Queen Victoria. Organist : R. Yates Mander, MUS. DOC. OXON., F.R.C.O., L.R.A.M.

RYE.—St. Mary's Parish Church. Built 1902, removed, rebuilt and enlarged 1912 by Norman & Beard. 3 manuals, large scale. Tubular pneumatic action Organist: W. Sprigg Walker.

SAFFRON WALDEN.—Parish Church of St. Mary the Virgin. Restored 1885 by Lewis Restored 1911 by Norman & Beard 3 manuals, 40 speaking stops, 14 other stops, 15 pistons, 9 composition pedals, Choir and Swell each enclosed in Swell-box Organist: Herbert Mahon, mus. bac. (dunelm), a. mus. t.c.l.

ST. ALBANS —Cathedral, The Built 1861 by Hill. Restored and enlarged 1907 by Abbott and Smith Expense entirely borne by Lord Aldenham. 4 manuals, 49 speaking stops, 12 couplers, 7 composition pedals, 13 composition pistons, one Great to pedal, 3 Swell pedals Organist: W. L Luttman, m a., mus. bac. cantab, f.r c.o, a.r.c.m.

ST. ALBANS.—Tabernacle Baptist Church. Rebuilt 1907 by Hewitt. Opened by F. Gostelow. 2 manuals, 22 speaking stops, 4 other stops, 1,144 pipes, 7 composition pedals. Beautiful design and tone Organist: M. L Parker.

ST. ALBANS.—Baptist Church, Dagnall Street. Built 1885 by Bevington. Restored in 1898 by Hill. 2 manuals, 16 speaking, 5 other stops, and 846 pipes Opened by F. Gostelow. Organist: F. J. Hobbs.

ST. ANDREWS.—St. Andrew's Episcopal Church. Built 1870 by Forster & Andrews. Restored 1909-10 by Miller. Opened by Sir H. Oakley, m a., mus doc 3 manuals, 27 speaking stops, 7 couplers, tremulant, 1,872 pipes, 6 composition pedals. Pneumatic action. Hydraulic engine. Fine tone Beautiful carved oak front. Console detached. Organist · Charles Freeman.

ST.-ANNE'S-ON-SEA.—St. Thomas' Church. Built 1905 by Hill. 3 manuals, 26 speaking stops, 9 couplers. Tubular pneumatic action. Electric blowing Organist. H W. Fisher.

ST. ASAPH.—Cathedral, The Restored 1898 by Hill. 4 manuals, 42 speaking stops, 9 couplers, 7 composition pedals. Organist and Master of the Choristers: W. E. Belcher, m a. cantab, f r c.o., a.r c.m.

ST. BEES.—Priory Church Built 1899 by Willis. Opened by T. H. Collinson, mus. bac. 3 manuals, 40 speaking stops (including one or two additions by Harrison), 14 couplers and accessories. Specialties —Number of very fine reeds on 15, 7 and 3½ inches pressure ; Pedal open wood pipes, made by W. Allen for Lincoln Cathedral, 1826 ; patent pneumatic Swell pedals ; interchangeable combinations ; also magnificent oak front by R. Hedley, of Newcastle, added in 1908. Organist: F. J. Livesey, b.a.

ST. BEE'S.—School, The. Built 1907 and enlarged 1911 by Wilkinson. Opened by present organist. 2 manuals, 18 speaking stops, 3 other stops. Organist: James William Aldous, m.a.

ST. DAVIDS.—Cathedral, The Built 1882 by Willis. 3 manuals, 34 speaking stops, 7 couplers Organist: Herbert C. Morris, m.a. cantab., f.r.c.o., a.r.c m, l.r.a m.

ST. HELENS —All Saints' Church. Built 1900 by Brindley & Foster. 2 manuals, 21 speaking stops, 4 other stops.

ST. HELENS.—Holy Cross R.C. Church. Built 1863 by Hedgeland. Blown by electricity. Organist: Joseph Barr.

ST. HELENS.—PARISH CHURCH. Restored by Whiteley. 2 manuals, 31 speaking stops. Has undergone several alterations and additions. The original organ (2 manual and pedals, built by G. M. Holdich in 1848), which had been in use at Westminster Abbey, and afterwards placed in the Old Town Hall, St. Helens, was burnt down many years ago. Rebuilt and enlarged with pneumatic action in 1909 by P. Conacher & Co., of Huddersfield. Containing 3 manuals, 41 speaking stops, and 14 couplers. Organist : E. Heywood, F R C.O.

ST. IVES (HUNTS).—ALL SAINTS' CHURCH. Built 1894 by Gern. Restored 1904 by Notetman. Opened 1894 by T. Noble and 1904 by B. Luard Selby. 3 manuals, 18 speaking stops, 10 other stops, 956 pipes. Ch. organ on East side of Chancel arch. Beautiful case on screen (see page 55). Organist : H. J. Hatton, Broadway, St. Ives, Hunts. Appointed 1902.

ST. LEONARDS-ON-SEA.—ST. MATTHEW'S CHURCH. Built 1890 by Willis. Opened by H. L. Balfour. 3 manuals, 23 speaking stops. Organist : Henry George Baily.

ST. NEOTS.—ST. MARY'S PARISH CHURCH. Built 1856 by Holdich ; opened by Sir F. A. Gore Ouseley. Restored 1900 by Bishop ; opened by Dr. A. H. Mann. 3 manuals, 29 speaking stops, 5 other stops, 1,350 pipes. Organist : Fred E. E. Harvey, M.A. (CANTAB.), L.R A M , A R C.O.

SALCOMBE.—EAST PORTLEMOUTH CHURCH. Built 1905 by Bevington. 2 manuals, 16 speaking stops, 8 couplers.

SALFORD.—TECHNICAL INSTITUTE. Built by Young. Gift of Lees Knowles, Esq., M.P. 3 manuals and pedal, 33 speaking stops, 7 couplers, 1,786 pipes, 8 composition pedals. Blown by two hydraulic engines.

SALTBURN.—PARISH CHURCH. Built 1907 by Harrison. Opened by T. T. Noble. 3 manuals, 31 speaking stops, 8 other stops, tremulant. Detached console. 6 couplers, 8 combination pistons, 4 combination pedals. Harmonic trumpets to play on Great or Choir at will. Organist : William Houston Boynes.

SALISBURY.—CATHEDRAL, THE. Built 1876 by Willis. 4 manuals, 55 speaking stops, 11 couplers. Organist. Charles T. South.

SALISBURY.—WESLEY CHURCH. Built 1912 by Burton. 2 manuals and pedal, 14 speaking stops, 5 couplers, tremulant, 5 composition pedals. Tracker action to manuals and couplers. Tubular pneumatic to Pedal.

SANDRINGHAM.—ST. MARY'S CHURCH. Built 1909 by Walker. Presented by H.M. King Edward VII. 3 manuals, 25 speaking stops, 11 couplers, 1,429 pipes, 7 composition pedals, 3 poppet pedals, balanced crescendo pedal to Swell and Choir organs. Tubular pneumatic action to manuals, pedals and drawstops. Carved oak case. Wind generated by silent Watkins & Watson " Discus " blower. Driven by electric motor. Organist. Frederick A. Keene.

SCARBOROUGH.—CHURCH OF ALL SAINTS, FALSGRAVE. Built 1895 by Corps. Opened by Dr. S. S. Wesley. 4 manuals, 40 speaking stops, 7 couplers, 9 composition pedals, 2 Swell pedals. Splendid tone. Placed on South side of chancel. Organist : Dr. Thomas Ely.

SEAFORD.—PARISH CHURCH. Built 1909 by Morgan & Smith. 2 manuals, 22 speaking stops, 5 couplers. Blown by hydraulic engine. Organist : Herbert J. Boden.

SEDBURGH.—PARISH CHURCH. Built by Norman & Beard. 2 manuals, 19 speaking stops. Organist : A. E. Thorne.

SEDBERGH.—SEDBERGH SCHOOL CHAPEL. Rebuilt 1897 by Norman & Beard. 3 manuals, 30 speaking stops, 7 other stops, 1,582 pipes, 7 composition pedals, 6 thumb pistons Tubular pneumatic. Hydraulic blowing. Organist : A. W. Ogilvy, F R.C.O.

SELBY —ABBEY, THE Built 1909 by Hill. 4 manuals and pedal, 57 speaking stops, 13 couplers, 2 tremulants, 16 pistons, 10 pedals, 3 double acting pistons for couplers. Tubular pneumatic action throughout. Blown by three hydraulic engines. Organist : F W. Sykes, MUS. BAC., F.R.C.O., Abbey House, Selby.

SELBY —WESLEYAN CHURCH. Rebuilt 1904 by Abbott & Smith. 2 manuals, 24 speaking stops, 5 other stops, 1,480 pipes. Fine diapason tone and solid foundation. Organist : Wansbrough Poles, A R.C.O., L R A.M.

SETTLE.—CHURCH OF THE HOLY ASCENSION. Restored 1912 by Binns. 2 manuals (compass CC to C), 22 speaking stops, 8 couplers, 6 composition pedals with interchangeable combinations Pneumatic action throughout Hydraulic engine. Organist and Choirmaster John Goddard Barker, A.R.C.O.

SEVENOAKS —ST. NICHOLAS PARISH CHURCH. Built 1798 by Avery. Restored 1896. 4 manuals, 40 speaking stops, 8 other stops, 2,293 pipes, 6 composition pedals. Blown by Watkins hydraulic engine. Mellow tone of old pipes, together with the beautiful new stops. Organist : W. A. Soyer, F R C O.

SEVENOAKS.—WESLEYAN CHURCH. Built 1884 by Jones. Opened by F. Meen. Restored and moved to new church 1904 by Morton Ellis. 2 manuals, 15 speaking stops, 4 couplers, 910 pipes. Blown by hand. Organist : Sidney Edwards.

SHAW (LANCS.).—HOLY TRINITY CHURCH. Built 1887 by Hill Opened by A. E. Bostock 3 manuals, 27 speaking stops, 8 other stops, 1,580 pipes. Blown by two hand levers. Pneumatic action to Great organ and couplers Organist and Choirmaster : John Jawton.

SHEFFIELD —ECCELSALL CHURCH Rebuilt and enlarged 1909 by Keates. 3 manuals, 31 speaking stops, 10 other stops. Pneumatic action. Electric blower. Detached console.

SHEFFIELD.—HATHERSAGE PARISH CHURCH. Built 1907 by Keates. . 2 manuals, 17 speaking stops, 5 other stops Balanced Swell pedal. College of organists scale. Stops at an angle of 45°. Organist : Frederick Walker Hulme.

SHEFFIELD.—PARISH CHURCH. Built 1888 by Brindley & Foster. Restored 1905. 4 manuals, 56 speaking stops, 12 couplers. Double acting composition pedals, pistons, etc. Organist : Thomas William Hanforth, MUS. BAC. DURHAM , F R C.O.

SHEFFIELD.—PITSMOOR CHURCH. Restored 1894 by Keates. 3 manuals, 26 speaking stops, 7 other stops, 1,624 pipes. Unpolished oak case. Placed in chamber south of Chancel. Pedals and heavy pipes pneumatic. Good full toned diapasons on Great. Organist : W. H. Peasegood.

SHEFFIELD.—St. Augustine's Church. Built 1899 by Keates. 3 manuals, 29 speaking stops, 9 couplers, etc. Handsome oak case. Tubular pneumatic action throughout. Organist : E. B. Glossip.

SHEFFIELD.—St. Luke's Church (Sale Memorial Church, Dyer's Hill). Rebuilt by Keates. 2 manuals, 18 speaking stops, 4 other stops. Organist : Cyril Cantrell.

SHEFFIELD.—St Marie's R C Church. Built by Lewis. 3 manuals, 28 speaking stops and couplers.

SHEFFIELD.—Wesleyan Church, Carver Street. Built 1901 by Forster & Andrews. 3 manuals, 34 speaking stops, 7 other stops, 1,912 pipes. 8 composition pedals. Blown by electric motor. Organist. John Duffell, mus. bac.

SHEFFIELD.—Wesley Church, Fulwood Road. Built 1898 by Brindley & Foster. 3 manuals, 37 speaking stops, 8 other stops Organist Joseph William Ibberson.

SHEPPERTON.—Littleton Church Built by Monk. Additions by Bishop. Opened by J. Griffin. 3 manuals and 35 stops Celestial organ in the tower, 50ft away from main instrument and connected by tubular-pneumatic action, this organ has 8 stops Pedal organ of main instrument contains a fine metal open 16, which forms a portion of the front of the organ. The organ is very orchestral, having 3 different celestes, also vox humana, orchestral oboe and clarinet Organist. Arthur Leslie Griffin.

SHERBORNE —Abbey, The. Built 1851 by Gray & Davison. 3 manuals, 36 speaking stops, 7 other stops. Organist : A. R Mote, b a., mus. bac. oxon. et dunelm.

SHERBORNE.—School Chapel. Built 1898 by Hill 2 manuals, 12 speaking stops, 3 other stops. Tubular pneumatic action. Detached console. Organist : Archibald Frank Tester, f r.c o , l .r.a.m.

SHERBORNE.—School. Big Schoolroom Organ Built 1884 by Gray & Davison 2 manuals, 21 speaking stops, 5 couplers Tubular pneumatic action. Detached console. Organist : Archibald Frank Tester, f.r.c.o., l.r.a.m.

SHIFNAL.—St. Andrew's Parish Church. Built by England. Rebuilt 1893 by Abbott & Smith 3 manuals, 32 speaking stops, 5 couplers, 2,326 pipes. Organist : W Brennard Smith.

SHIPLEY.—Parish Church, Windhill. Built 1830 by Ward Enlarged 1864 by Kirkland & Jardine Rebuilt 1892 by Binns 3 manuals, 50 stops. Organist · James Arthur Firth, 36, Westcliff Road, Shipley.

SHIPLEY.—St. Peter's Church. Built 1912 by Brindley & Foster 3 manuals, 31 speaking stops, 9 other stops, 1,754 pipes, 25 pneumatic combination accessories, 10 composition pedals, tremulant, balanced swell pedal. Blown by electric motor.

SHREWSBURY.—Abbey Church, The. Built 1911 by Hill. 3 manuals, 38 speaking stops. Blown by electric motor. Organist. P. W. Pilcher, m.a. cambridge, a r c.o.

SHREWSBURY.—ST. CHAD'S PARISH CHURCH. Built 1905 by Norman & Beard. 3 manuals, 37 speaking stops, 8 pneumatic pistons, 8 composition pedals, tremulant to Swell. Pneumatic action throughout. Blown by electric motor. Organist: W. R. Ebrall, Ebor House, Shrewsbury.

SHREWSBURY.—ST GILES' CHURCH. Built by Gray & Davison. 3 manuals, 25 speaking stops, 7 other stops.

SHREWSBURY.—ST JULIAN'S CHURCH. Built 1850 by Groves & Mitchell. Restored 1901 by Gray & Davison. 3 manuals, 29 speaking stops, 5 other stops, 1,495 pipes. Blown by hand. Organist: Alfred Thomas

SHREWSBURY.—ST MARY'S CHURCH. Built 1911 by Binns. Opened by present organist. 4 manuals, 56 speaking stops, 20 couplers, 3,120 pipes. Tubular pneumatic action. Interchangeable pistons. Electric motor and feeder. Organist: Arthur Johnson.

SHREWSBURY.—SCHOOL CHAPEL. Built 1890 by Forster & Andrews. 2 manuals, 22 speaking stops, 8 other stops. Tubular pneumatic action to Pedal organ. Tracker action to manuals. Pitch pine case. Hand blown. Organist: Walter Henry Moore, M A., Worcester College, Oxford

SIDMOUTH.—PARISH CHURCH. Built 1881 by Hill. Opened by Dr H. A. Harding. 3 manuals, 28 speaking stops, 10 couplers, 6 combination pedals. Tremulant to Swell. Number of Solo stops of great beauty. Organist J. A. Bellamy, MEMBER I.S.M.

SKELMORLIE.—PARISH CHURCH. Built by Binns. 3 manuals and pedal, 30 speaking stops, 12 other stops, 10 accessories. Pneumatic action. Organist: Arthur S. Mansfield, A R C.M.

SKIPTON.—CHRIST CHURCH. Built 1906 by Harrison. Opened by Dr. Bairstow. 3 manuals, 26 speaking stops, 8 other stops, 1,528 pipes. Electro pneumatic. Console at East end, organ at West end. Organist: James Lambert A. Firth

SMETHWICK.—OLD CHURCH. Built 1904 by Porritt. Opened by C. W· Perkins. 3 manuals, 27 speaking stops, 7 other stops. Choir in separate Swell box. Tubular pneumatic action throughout. Fine Swell. Organist· Frederick T. Cox, 17, Fountain Road, Edgbaston, Birmingham Born 1848. Appointed 1880.

SOUTHAMPTON.—ALL SAINTS' PARISH CHURCH. Built 1867 by Bevington. Opened by Dr S. Wesley. Restored and enlarged 1901. Reopened by Dr G B Arnold. 3 manuals. Tubular pneumatic action. Blown by electricity. Organist and Choirmaster: Lionel A. Ladbrooke, A R C M., I R.A M, " Cairo," Highfield, Southampton.

SOUTHAMPTON.—AVENUE CONGREGATIONAL CHURCH. Built 1902 by Ingram & Co. 4 manuals, 18 speaking stops, 15 other stops, electro-pneumatic action throughout. Detached console in centre of Chancel. Organist J. E. Pearson, MUS. BAC. (DUNELM), A R.C O.

SOUTHAMPTON.—JESUS CHAPEL. Built 1902 by Gray & Davison. Completed 1906 by Burton, chiefly through the generosity of Mr. Andrew Carnegie. Pneumatic action inserted. Choir organ of 7 stops and 4 additional Pedal stops, including an extension of the Tuba. Total speaking stops 33, couplers 12, composition pedals 10. Blown by 2 hydraulic engines (Watkins & Watson). Wind pressures, 3¼, 5 and 7 inches. Designed by the Organist, W. J. Phillips.

SOUTHAMPTON.—Lock's Heath Church Built by Burton. 2 manuals, 18 speaking stops, 5 couplers, 920 pipes. Tubular pneumatic action.

SOUTHAMPTON.—Pear Tree Green Church. Built by Burton. 4 manuals and pedal, 34 speaking stops, 12 couplers, 1,862 pipes, 10 composition pedals

SOUTHAMPTON.—St. Mark's Church. Built 1896 by William Ginns. Opened by Sir George Martin. 2 manuals, 20 speaking stops, 5 other stops Tubular pneumatic action throughout. Console with player facing the Choir Oak case Organist: George Leake, MUS. BAC. (DUNELM), F.R.C.O., A.R.C.M., L.R.A.M.

SOUTHAMPTON.—St. Mary's Church. Built 1879 by Willis Enlarged 1894. 3 manuals, 36 speaking stops, 8 couplers, 7 composition pedals. Organist: R. Sharpe

SOUTHAMPTON —St Michael's Church. Built by Sims. 2 manuals, 20 speaking stops, 5 other stops. Organist: S Franz Somers, Diploma Leipzig, HON. REP. R.A.M.

SOUTHEND-ON-SEA.—Cliff Town Church. Built 1901 by Eustace Ingram. 3 manuals, 31 speaking stops, 9 other stops. Organist: J. R. Griffiths, MUS. BAC. DUNELM.

SOUTHEND —Holy Trinity Church, Southchurch. Built 1860-1911 by Bevington 2 manuals, 17 speaking stops, 9 couplers. Originally built for Swedish Church, St. George's, London, E. Organist: A. T. Cowdrey.

SOUTHEND-ON-SEA —St. Alban's Church, Westcliff. Built 1911 by Hill. 22 speaking stops, 8 couplers Tubular pneumatic action. Electric blowing. Organist W. J. Slape.

SOUTHGATE —Christ Church Built 1870 and enlarged by Walker. Opened by T. Kilner, of Christ Church, Highbury. 2 manuals, 22 speaking stops, 5 other stops, 1,436 pipes. An instrum nt much admired for its beauty of tone. Organist. John Harman Judd.

SOUTH MOLTON.—St. Mary Magdalene. Built 1900 by Vowles. Opened by Dr Wood. 3 manuals, 25 speaking stops, 5 couplers, 1,392 pipes. Tubular pneumatic action to Key, Pedal and Choir drawstops. Oak case. Organist. Michael Watson, M I.S M.

SOUTHPORT.—All Saints' Church. Built by Young 3 manuals and pedal, 40 speaking stops, 10 couplers, 3,560 pipes, 8 composition pedals Divided organ Tubular pneumatic action. Blown by electric motor. Organist: A. C. Waggett, A R.C.O., 23, Mill Lane, Southport.

SOUTHPORT.—Christ Church. Restored 1900 by Lewis. Opened by present organist. 3 manuals, 26 speaking stops, 9 other stops. Tubular pneumatic action throughout. Organist: William Silkstone Dobson, L R A M, L MUS. T.C.L.

SOUTHPORT —High Park Wesleyan Church. Built 1911 by Rushworth & Dreaper 2 manuals, 15 speaking stops, 6 couplers, 5 composition pedals. Tubular pneumatic action. Blown by electric motor. Organist and Choirmaster: Charles Porter.

SOUTHPORT.—St. ANDREW'S CHURCH. Restored 1903 by Gray & Davison. Opened by Dr. A. L. Peace. 3 manuals, 45 speaking stops, 9 other stops, 2,754 pipes. Blown by 2 Watkin's and Watson's hydraulic motors. Organist: Benjamin Lofthouse, MUS. BAC OXON, F.R.C O.

SOUTHPORT.—St. JOHN'S PARISH CHURCH, BIRKDALE. Renovated 1910 by Rushworth & Dreaper. 3 manuals, 24 speaking stops, 6 couplers, 6 composition pedals. Organist: Fred W. Jackson, L.N.C.M.

SOUTHPORT.—St. MARIE'S CATHOLIC CHURCH. Built 1900 by Steele & Keay. 2 manuals and pedal, 22 speaking stops, 4 couplers, 6 double-acting composition pedals, self-balancing crescendo pedal. Tubular pneumatic action to Pedal. Electric blowing. Organist: W. Wilkinson, Mersey Bank, Windsor Road, Southport.

SOUTHPORT —St. PHILIP'S CHURCH. Rebuilt 1910 by Rushworth & Dreaper. Opened by present organist. 3 manuals (4th prepared for), 34 speaking stops, 10 other stops. Tubular pneumatic action throughout. Electric blowing. The organ had originally electric pneumatic action, and was built in 1903 by Hope Jones & Ingram. Several Hope Jones fancy stops incorporated in present scheme. Organist: John Brook.

SOUTH SHIELDS —PARISH CHURCH. Built by Nicholson & Lord. 3 manuals, 30 speaking stops. Organist: Arthur Docksey, MUS. DOC., F.R.C.O.

SOUTH SHIELDS.—St. PAUL'S PRESBYTERIAN CHURCH. Built 1896 by Hope Jones. 2 manuals, 11 speaking stops, 9 other stops, 5 composition pedals. Detached console Electric action Organist William J. Davison.

SOUTH SHIELDS —St. THOMAS' CHURCH. Built 1912 by Vincent 3 manuals, 33 stops. Electric blower. Tubular pneumatic action. Opened by D. Farrer, F.R.C.O. Organist: C Burcham.

SOUTHWELL.—CATHEDRAL, THE Built 1892 by Bishop. Opened by present organist. 4 manuals, 54 speaking stops, 11 other stops, 3,000 pipes, 11 combination pistons. Tremulant. Tubular pneumatic action throughout. Spotted metal pipes Blown by gas engine. Organist: R. W. Liddle, HON. VICE-PRESIDENT G.O.

STAFFORD —St. MARY'S PARISH CHURCH. Built 1907 by Harrison. 4 manuals, 50 speaking stops, 3 couplers. 5 combination pedals, 18 combination pistons, reversible pedal to Great and Pedal, reversible piston Great to Pedal, reversible piston Swell to Great, two balanced crescendo pedals to Swell and Solo organs. Tubular pneumatic action throughout, except the manual to pedal coupling action, which is mechanical. Organist: C. F. Rowland.

STAMFORD.—St. MARTIN'S CHURCH. Built 1890-1911 by Bevington. 2 manuals, 17 speaking stops, 8 couplers.

STAMFORD.—St. MARY'S CHURCH. Built by Wood, Stamford. 2 manuals, 19 speaking stops, 6 other stops, 880 pipes. Organist: J Clare Billing.

STAMFORD —THE HALL, KETTON. Built 1870. Enlarged 1874 by Cavaillé Coll, Paris. 3 manuals, 47 speaking stops, 17 other stops. Identical with organ by same builder in Manchester Town Hall Wind supplied by three pairs of horizontal feeders stored in three large main reservoirs, from thence conveyed to eight smaller reservoirs (at different pressures) disposed inside organ near respective sound boards. Console is reversed, so that organist faces audience. 17 pedals to combination Pneumatic lever action. Organist : J. Clare Billing.

STANMORE.—St JOHN THE EVANGELIST PARISH CHURCH. Built 1863 by Walker. Restored 1906 by Bishop 3 manuals, 27 speaking stops, 6 other stops. Blown by a Swanton hydraulic engine. Choir organ and pedals pneumatic action ; Great and Swell organs, tracker. Organist : Albert Ernest Denman, F.R.C.O., L.R.A.M., A.G.S.M.

STEVENSTON.—EPISCOPAL CHURCH Built 1894 by Bevington 2 manuals, 13 speaking stops, 9 couplers, etc.

STEYNING.—St. ANDREW'S PARISH CHURCH Built by Monk. 3 manuals, 32 speaking stops, 7 other stops Organist : E Burritt Lane, MUS. B., etc., " Hayes," Steyning, Sussex.

STIRLING.—ALLAN PARK UNITED FREE CHURCH. Built 1898 by Foster & Andrews. Opened by Thos. Berry, MUS. BAC. CANTAB. 2 manuals, 21 speaking stops, 5 other stops. The organ and Choir at first situated in organ loft behind pulpit. In 1905 pneumatic system was introduced, and now console and Choir are on a platform in front of pulpit. Organist and Musicmaster : D. Burns-Jamieson, MEMBER OF INCORPORATED SOCIETY OF MUSICIANS.

STOCKPORT.—St. PAUL'S CHURCH, HEATON MOOR. Built by Benson. Opened by C. H. Fogg 3 manuals, 29 speaking stops, 7 other stops, 1,688 pipes. Tubular pneumatic action to Swell and Pedal organs. Blown by electric motor. Organist : F. Handel Woodward, MUS. BAC. (DUNELM).

STOCKPORT.—TRINITY WESLEYAN CHAPEL. Built by Young. 3 manuals and pedal, 31 speaking stops, 7 couplers.

STOKE-ON-TRENT —TOWN HALL. Built 1912 by Binns Opened by Herbert Walton 4 manuals, 64 speaking stops, 24 couplers, 3,185 pipes. Binns' patent tubular pneumatic action and Binns' interchangeable combination pistons Worked by electric motor and fan.

STOURBRIDGE —KINVER PARISH CHURCH Built by Conacher. 3 manuals and pedal, 30 speaking stops, 9 couplers, 6 composition pedals, 6 combination pistons. Tubular pneumatic action throughout. Blown by Crossley gas engine. Oak case.

STOURBRIDGE.—OLD SWINFORD PARISH CHURCH. Built 1901 by Norman & Beard. Opened by present organist.' 3 manuals, 30 speaking stops, 6 other stops, 1,790 pipes Builders' patent. Tubular pneumatic action throughout. Handsome oak case. Good diapasons and reeds. Organist · Hedley Satchell, LEIPSIC CONSERVETORIST.

STROUD —HOLY TRINITY CHURCH. Built by Nicholson. Restored 1910 by Liddiatt & Sons, Leonard Stanley. 3 manuals, 20 speaking stops, 5 other stops. Organist : R. H. Whall, MUS. B. DUNELM, F.R.C.O.

STROUD.—St. LAWRENCE'S PARISH CHURCH. Built 1906 by Norman & Beard Opened by C. W Perkins. 3 manuals, 31 speaking stops, 11 other stops, 1,660 pipes. Tubular pneumatic action throughout. Detached console facing East. Choir organ in Swell box. Balanced Swell pedals. Large Pedal organ with 8 stop keys. Organist and Choirmaster : S. W. Underwood, A.R.C.O.

SUDBURY.—ALL SAINTS' CHURCH. Built by Brindley & Foster. Rebuilt and enlarged 1882 by Bishop. Opened by Sir G. C. Martin. 3 manuals, 29 speaking stops, 9 other stops, 1,584 pipes. Lever pneumatic action to Great organ. Organist : Miss Lilian E. Hicks.

SUDBURY.—ST. PETER'S CHURCH. Built 1911 by Lewis. 3 manuals, 40 speaking stops, 17 other stops. Opened by Dr. A. H. Mann. Organist : E. E. Vinnicombe.

SUDBURY.—TRINITY CONGREGATIONAL CHURCH. Built by Conacher. 2 manuals and pedal, 16 speaking stops, 5 couplers, 6 combination pedals, 6 combination pistons. Tubular pneumatic action throughout. Detached console. Organist : William Trant.

SUNDERLAND.—GRANGE CONGREGATIONAL CHURCH, THE. Built 1899 by Vincent. 4 manuals, 43 stops. Pneumatic action. Electric blower. Organist : H. S. Vincent, 21, Argyle Square, Sunderland.

SUNDERLAND.—NORTH BRIDGE STREET PRESBYTERIAN CHURCH. Built 1893 by Vincent. 3 manuals, 32 stops. Pneumatic action. Electric blower. Organist : A. S. Young.

SUNDERLAND.—ST. GEORGE'S PRESBYTERIAN CHURCH. Built 1900 by Vincent. 3 manuals. Pneumatic action. Organist : Henley Pratt, L.R.A.M., 34, Fawcett Street, Sunderland.

SUNDERLAND.—ST. IGNATIUS THE MARTYR. Built 1893 by Vincent. Opened by T. H. Collison, MUS. BAC. OXON. 3 manuals, 31 speaking stops, 9 couplers, 1,782 pipes. Tubular pneumatic action. Both Swell and Choir organs enclosed. Complete system of control with 13 thumb pistons, 3 central balanced pedals acting respectively on Swell, Choir and Great. Organist : Frederick William Newrick, L.R.A.M., A R.C M.

SUNDERLAND.—ST. PAUL'S CHURCH. Built 1896 by Vincent. 3 manuals, 39 stops. Tubular pneumatic action. Electric blower. Organist : J. L. Smith, A.R.C.O., 7, Tunstall Terrace, Sunderland.

SUNDERLAND.—ST. PETER'S CHURCH, MONKWEARMOUTH. Built 1886 by Willis. Rebuilt and enlarged 1911 by Vincent. 3 manuals, 30 stops. Tubular pneumatic action. Organist : F. R. Jarman, MUS. BAC., F.R.C.O., 32, Ewesley Road, Sunderland.

SUNDERLAND.—TRINITY PRESBYTERIAN CHURCH. Built 1877 by Vincent. 3 manuals, 30 stops. Pneumatic action. Electric blower. Organist : A. Phillips, F.R.C.O.

SUNDERLAND.—UNION CONGREGATIONAL CHURCH. Built 1896 by Vincent. 3 manuals, 28 stops. Pneumatic action (divided). Organist : G. F. Dodds.

SUNDERLAND.—VICTORIA HALL. Built 1906 by Vincent. Opened by Dr. Peace. 4 manuals, 50 speaking stops, 15 couplers, 2,547 pipes. Tubular pneumatic action throughout. Kinetic blower driven by electric motor.

SURBITON.—CHRIST CHURCH. Restored 1905 by Norman & Beard, Opened by Dr. Alcock. 3 manuals, 34 speaking stops, 8 other stops. 1,864 pipes. Tubular pneumatic action throughout. 7 composition pedals. Kinetic blower driven by 3½ h.p. electric motor. Organist : C. I. Clapperton, 24, The Avenue, Surbiton Hill, Surrey.

SURBITON.—St. Mark's Church Built 1896 by Norman & Beard. 3 manuals, 30 speaking stops, 7 couplers, 1,722 pipes. Tubular pneumatic action except to pedal couplers and drawstop. Blown by electric motor Organist: R. Frederic Tyler, F.R.C.O., L. MUS. T.C L.

SUTTON (SURREY).—Christ Church Built by Brindley & Foster. 4 manuals, 43 speaking stops, 10 couplers and tremulant, 5 patent interchangeable pedals, 6 composition pedals, 2 reversing pedals. Blown by electric motor. Tubular pneumatic action throughout. Organist: H. M. Higgs.

SUTTON COLDFIELD.—Parish Church. Built by Hope Jones, Electric Organ Company, and Norman & Beard. 3 manuals, including diaphonic organ in West end of Church, Great, Swell and Choir organ in South-East transept, console in North-East transept. Organist: William Hardley, "Ridgecote," Sutton Coldfield, Warwickshire. Appointed 1891.

SUTTON-IN-ASHFIELD.—Parish Church. Built 1907 by Norman & Beard. Opened by E. Perkins. 2 manuals, 24 speaking stops, 3 other stops. Tubular pneumatic action. Organist: Arthur Howard Bonser, A.R C.O.

SWADLINCOTE.—Wesleyan Church. Built 1905 by Young. Opened by present organist. 3 manuals, 23 speaking stops, 7 other stops, 1,428 pipes. Blown by hand. Organist: Walter Jones, MUS. BAC., F.R.C.O.

SWANAGE.—Parish Church. Built by Vowles. 3 manuals and pedal 29 speaking stops, 7 couplers, 1,760 pipes, tremulant, 6 composition pedals. Double-acting pedal for Great to Pedal. Detached console. Pneumatic action throughout.

SWANSEA.—Christ Church, St. Helens. Built 1875-86 by Bevington 2 manuals, 17 speaking stops, 9 couplers, etc. Organist: C Johnson, F.R.C.O., Bryn-y-mor Road, Swansea

SWANSEA.—Holy Trinity Church. Built 1883 by Conacher. 3 manuals, 28 speaking stops, 7 other stops, 1,702 pipes. Organist: Louis H. Torr, F.R.C O , L R.A.M., L.T C.I.

SWANSEA.—Parish Church. Built 1904 by Norman & Beard. 4 manuals, organ on South side and console on North side of chancel Electric action. Blown by electric motor. Organist: Arthur Hey, MUS. BAC. (DURHAM), F.R.C.O., L.R A.M.

SWANSEA.—Walter Road Congregational Church Built 1873 by Jones. 2 manuals, 20 speaking stops, 3 couplers Tremulant action by pedal. Organist. James F. Fricker, A.R C.O., ETC.

SWANSEA.—St. Gabriel's Church. Organ built 1892 by Conacher. 3 manuals, 29 speaking stops, 6 other stops, 1,772 pipes

SWANSEA.—St. Paul's, Sketty. Built 1909 by Halliday. 2 manuals, 20 speaking stops. Organist: T. O. Jones, "Dalmore," Dillwyn Road, Sketty, Swansea.

TAMWORTH.—Parish Church. Built by Green. Restored 1887 by Bryceson. 3 manuals, 28 speaking stops, 4 couplers, 5 composition pedals. Blown by hydraulic motor. Organist: H. Rose, A R.C.O.

TAUNTON.—St. James's Parish Church. Built 1863 by Hill. Restored by Minns. 3 manuals, 26 speaking stops, 6 other stops prepared. Organist : J. Herbert Chalmers.

TAUNTON.—St. Mary Magdalene Church. Built 1882 by Willis. 3 manuals, 35 speaking stops, 9 other stops Good reeds. Organist : Harold A. Jeboult, F.R.C.O., A.R.C.M., L. MUS. T C.L.

TEDDINGTON.—St. Alban the Martyr. Built 1895 by Lewis. Opened by Alfred Hollins. 3 manuals, 32 speaking stops, 6 couplers, 1,836 pipes. A fine instrument and somewhat unique, inasmuch as there is no Choir organ, the 3rd manual being a Solo organ. Electric action to Solo organ and tracker action to the other 2 manuals, and pneumatic action to pedals and drawstops Solo stops beautifully voiced and very orchestral in tone. The large open diapason is very fine. Organist : William Ratcliffe, F R C O, L MUS. T.C.L.

TENBURY.—St Michael's College Rebuilt and enlarged 1874 by Willis. 4 manuals, 55 speaking stops, 9 other stops, 3,130 pipes Blown by hand Organist : Norman C. Woods, M A., MUS BAC CANTAB.

TETBURY.—St Mary's Parish Church. Built 1863 by Nicholson. Removed to South side of chancel from West gallery, 1901. Rebuilt and enlarged by Binns, 1912 3 manuals and pedals, 41 stops. Tubular pneumatic action. Organist : Frederick Nathaniel Baxter, MUS. BAC. (DUNELM), F.R C.O.

TEWKESBURY.—Abbey Church (St. Mary) Grove Organ. Built 1885 by Michell & Thynne. Built for inventors exhibition, where it obtained silver medal for tone. Presented to Abbey to commemorate Queen Victoria's Jubilee. 4 manuals, 55 stops. Blown by 2 hydraulic engines. Organist : Percy Baker, F.R C O, L MUS. T C.L.

TEWKESBURY.—Abbey Church (St Mary) Milton Organ. Brought in 1737 from Magdalen College, Oxford. Built by John Harris, the grandfather of Renatus Harris. By Cromwell's orders it was removed to Hampton Court, and is said to have been played by Milton, Cromwell's secretary. In 1660 the organ went back to Oxford, and was repaired in 1662, 1690 and 1796. Enlarged by Willis 2 manuals, 26 stops The Grove and Milton organs are sometimes played together. Organist : Percy Baker, F.R.C O., L. MUS. T.C.L.

THORNHILL.—Morton Parish Church. Built 1886 by Harrison. Opened by Law Starkay. 2 manuals, 21 speaking stops, 3 other stops. Blown by hydraulic engine. Organist : Alma Shuttleworth, A. MUS. T.C.L.

TIPTON.—Gospel Oak Wesleyan Church. Built 1908 by Steale & Keay. 2 manuals and pedal, 21 speaking stops, 5 couplers, 6 double-acting composition pedals. Tubular pneumatic action to Pedal. Pitch pine case.

TIVERTON.—Blundell's School Chapel. Restored 1906 by Osmond, Taunton. 3 manuals, 26 speaking stops, 8 other stops, 1,468 pipes. Tubular pneumatic action throughout. All stops run through Open diapason on big scale and separate wind pressure (4½in.) Organist : Francis Herring, M.A.

TIVERTON.—St. Georges' Church. Built 1903 by Hele. Opened by Dr. Wood. 3 manuals, 24 speaking stops, 6 couplers, 6 composition pedals and tremulant. Organist : W. H. Pengelly, The Retreat, Tiverton.

TIVERTON.—St. Peter's Church Built 1696 by Father Smith. Restored 1870 by Willis 3 manuals, 40 speaking stops. Blown by hand. Very fine instrument with a handsome case, supposed by Gibbing. Organist : R. Barcham, F.R.C.O.

TODMORDEN.—Parish Church. Built 1875 by Gray & Davison. Restored 1904 by Jardine. 3 manuals, 30 speaking stops, 6 other stops. Tubular pneumatic action throughout. Organist : William A. Wrigley, MUS. BAC. OXON Appointed 1884.

TONBRIDGE.—Parish Church. Restored by Norman & Beard. Opened by Dr. A. H. Brewer 3 manuals, 34 speaking stops, 7 other stops, 1,906 pipes. Organist . J. W. G. Hathaway, MUS DOC. OXON., F.R.C.O

TONBRIDGE —St John the Baptist Parish Church, Penshurst Rebuilt 1907 by Walker. Opened by Sir Frederick Bridge 2 manuals, 21 speaking stops, 7 other stops, 1,066 pipes, 6 double acting combination pedals. Balanced Swell Detached console on floor of church Tubular pneumatic action throughout. Hydraulic blowing gear. Organist : Reginald E. Groves, A R C.M., A R.C.O , L.R.A.M.

TORQUAY.—Belgrave Church Built 1908 by Osmond 4 manuals, 38 speaking stops, 12 other stops, over 2,000 pipes. Solo, Choir and Pedal are pneumatic ; Great and Swell tracker action. Organist . A W. Fletcher, L T S C.

TORQUAY.—St. Luke's Church Built 1864 and restored 1904 by Walker. 3 manuals, 33 speaking stops. Manuals placed out from the organ and organist faces the choir. Organist . J Heaton-Bailey, A R C.O

TORQUAY.—St Matthias Church Built 1886 by Hill 3 manuals, 30 speaking stops, 7 other stops. Blown by electric motor. Fine quality tone. Organist : Walter L Twinning, F R C.O

TOTTENHAM.—Christ Church, West Green Rebuilt 1891 by Willis. Opened by H. L. Balfour, MUS BAC , F R C O 3 manuals, 32 speaking stops, 7 other stops, 1,830 pipes. All stops run through. 7 composition pedals to Great organ, Great to Pedal " on and off." Tremulant by pedal. Organist : Thomas Alfred Berry.

TOTTENHAM.—Parish Church. Built 1817 by Elliott. Restored 1862 by Willis and 1880 by Hedgland. 3 manuals, 25 speaking stops, 5 other stops, 7 composition pedals. Organist : Harry Fellowes Wilkinson, F.R C.O.

TOTTENHAM.—St. Katharine's College. Built by Willis. 2 manuals. Organist : Edith A. Chubb, MUS. B. DUNELM , A R.C.M.

TOTNES —Parish Church. Built 1861 by Willis Enlarged 1896 by Hele. 3 manuals, 30 speaking stops, 6 couplers, 4 composition pedals Organist : Herbert Worth.

TOWCESTER.—St. Lawrence's Parish Church. Built 1817 and rebuilt 1885. Reopened by Dr. Turpin. 3 manuals, 25 speaking stops, 9 other stops, 1,538 pipes. Enlarged 1906, when tubular pneumatic action was added by Nicholson , then opened by Dr Keeton Handsome carved case Organist : A. Ward, High Street, Towcester

TOWYN —Parish Church Built 1911 by Morgan & Smith. Some of the stops used from original organ by Ingram. 2 manuals, 17 speaking stops, 5 couplers. Detached console. Pneumatic action throughout. Handsome carved oak case. Blown by hydraulic engine. Organist: R. O. Jones, C.P.T.C.L.

TRAMORE.—CATHOLIC CHURCH, THE. Built 1895 by Telford & Telford. 3 manuals and pedal, 28 speaking stops, 7 couplers, etc., 4 composition pedals.

TREHARRIS, GLAM.—BRYNHYFRYD BAPTIST CHURCH. Built 1897 by David & Sons. Opened by J. F Fricker, A R C.O. 2 manuals, 19 speaking stops, 5 other stops, 5 composition pedals, 1,138 pipes. Wind supplied by pair of diagonal feeders worked by a Melvin motor. Organist and Choirmaster: T. D. Edwards, A.R.C.M., F.T S.C , L.R.A.M.

TREETON.—ST. HELEN'S CHURCH. Restored 1900 by Keates. 2 manuals, 12 speaking stops, 5 other stops. Blown by hand. Organist: Herbert Antcliffe

TROWBRIDGE.—ST JAMES' PARISH CHURCH. Restored 1908 by Hele. 3 manuals, 30 speaking stops, 6 other stops, 1,714 pipes. Pneumatic lever to Great and couplers. Tubular pneumatic to pedals. Organist: Cyril T. Weigall, F R.C.O.

TRURO.—CATHEDRAL, THE Built 1887 by Willis. 4 manuals, 55 stops. Pneumatic action, hydraulic engines for blowing. Organist M. J. Monk, MUS DOC. OXON , F.R C O.

TRURO.—ST. JOHN'S CHURCH. Built 1883 by Forster & Andrews 2 manuals, 18 speaking stops, 5 other stops, 932 pipes, 3 composition pedals. Tracker action. Blown by hand.

TUNBRIDGE WELLS.—HOLY TRINITY CHURCH. Built 1883 by Walker. 3 manuals, 38 speaking stops, 1,956 pipes. Electric motor blowing apparatus added in 1905. Organist: Mr. E Harding, 25, Standen Street, Tunbridge Wells

TUNBRIDGE WELLS.—ST MARK'S CHURCH Built 1867 by Walker; enlarged 1884 and 1896, rebuilt 1906 by Walker. 3 manuals, 28 speaking stops, and 5 other stops Very fine diapasons and flutes. Organist · William Wooding Starmer, F R.A M , L MUS T.C.L.

TUNBRIDGE WELLS.—ST. PETER'S CHURCH Built 1876 and enlarged 1889 by Bevington 2 manuals, 14 speaking stops, 4 couplers Organist. Alfred G. B Archer, L.T C L

TUNBRIDGE WELLS.—PEMBURY PARISH CHURCH Built by Hill. 1 manual, 9 speaking stops, 2 other stops. Organist . William M. Brooke.

TUNBRIDGE WELLS.—ST. PETER'S CHURCH, PEMBURY. Built by Hill. 2 manuals, 13 speaking stops, 3 other stops. Organist William M. Brooke.

TUNSTALL.—CONGREGATIONAL CHURCH. Rebuilt 1912 by Steele & Keay. 3 manuals and pedal, 28 speaking stops, 7 couplers, 6 double-acting composition pedals, 1 reversible pedal, 1 self-balancing pedal. Tubular pneumatic action to Pedal The organ is blown by an electrically driven fan of the builders' own design. Oak case Organist: Amos Birchall, Tunnell Terrace, Chatterley, Tunstall, Staffs.

TUNSTALL.—St. Chad's Church. Built 1909 by Steele & Keay. 2 manuals and pedal, 13 stops, 5 couplers, 4 double-acting composition pedals, 1 self-balancing crescendo pedal. Gothic case.

TWICKENHAM.—All Saints' Church. Built by Dyer. 3 manuals, 30 speaking stops, 8 couplers, 8 composition pedals. Balanced Swell pedal. Blown by electricity. Diapason and flute stops excellent. Organist and Choirmaster : Malcolm Donald Ramsay, A.MUS.T.C.L.

TWICKENHAM.—St. Mary's Parish Church. Rebuilt by Ingram & Co. 3 manuals, 24 speaking stops, detached console. Organist : F. Holloway, F.R.C.O., Fortescue House, Twickenham.

TWICKENHAM.—St Stephen's Church. Built 1881 by Willis. 3 manuals, 25 speaking stops, 5 other stops, 1,322 pipes. Tracker action to manuals, pneumatic to pedals, tremulant to Swell. 6 composition pedals. Organist : A. Livingstone Hirst, MUS. BAC. (DUNELM), F R.C.O.

TYNEMOUTH.—St. George's Church, Cullercoats. Built 1884 by Lewis. Opened by Dr. William Rea, F.R.C.O. 2 manuals, 26 speaking stops, 4 other stops. Organist : Frederick Younger Robson, M.I.S.M.

UPPINGHAM.—S.S. Peter and Paul Parish Church. Built by Holdich. Restored and enlarged 1892 and 1912 by Nicholson. Re-opened by Dr W. H. Barrow, F.R C.O. 3 manuals, 30 speaking stops, 5 other stops. Organist : Richard Benjamin Watts, L V C M.

USHAW.—St. Cuthbert's College, 1875 Chapel. Built by Bevington. 3 manuals, 29 speaking stops, 12 couplers. Water blown.

UTTOXETER.—Denstone College Chapel. Rebuilt 1908 by Brindley & Foster. Reopened by present organist. 3 manuals, 32 speaking stops, 7 other stops. Bringradus pedal Pneumatic action throughout. Detached console in West gallery of chapel Organist and Director of the Music : A Rawlinson Wood, MUS. BAC , F.R.C.O., L.T.C.L

UTTOXETER.—Parish Church. Built 1846. Rebuilt 1906 by Hill. Opened by A R. Wood 3 manuals, 30 speaking stops, 6 other stops, 1,916 pipes. Tracker action in South gallery of chancel. Organist : Walter Spinney.

WALSALL.—Salem United Methodist Church, Cheslyn-Hay. Built 1912 by Lloyd. 2 manuals, 22 speaking stops, 7 couplers, 8 combination pistons, " on and off " Great to Pedal. Balanced Swell pedal. Tubular pneumatic action throughout except Pedal couplers. Organist : Arnold S Hawkins, Cheslyn-Hay.

WALSALL.—Town Hall. Built 1908 by Nicholson & Lord. Opened by C W. Perkins. 4 manuals, 51 speaking stops, 12 couplers, 2,882 pipes. 14 pistons, 9 combination pedals, 3 balanced crescendo pedals.

WALTHAM ABBEY CHURCH.—Built 1893 by Walker. 3 manuals, 32 speaking stops, 8 couplers, 6 composition pedals, 1,966 pipes

WANSTEAD —Christ Church. Built by Hill. 3 manuals. Blown by hydraulic power. Organist : Edward L. Holford, F R.C.O.

WANSTEAD.—St. Mary's Parish Church. Built 1847 by Hill. 2 manuals, 15 speaking stops, 3 other stops Tracker action. Situated in the gallery, at the West end of the church. Organist : George Vincent Evans.

WARE.—St. John the Baptist, Great Amwell. Built 1904 by Willis. Opened by F. H Cliffe, M.A., MUS BAC. 2 manuals, 9 speaking stops, 3 other stops, 478 pipes. Stops, pneumatic action ; pedals, concave and radiating, pneumatic action. Organist : Gerald Ambrose Howard, A.R.C.O

WARRINGTON.—Parish Church. Built 1876 Rebuilt 1902 by Young. 40 speaking stops, 10 couplers. Tubular pneumatic action. Blown by electric motor. Organist : Frederick Milman Darby, MUS. BAC. OXON., F.R.C.O.

WATERFORD.—Roman Catholic Cathedral. Built 1861 and restored 1901 by Hill Renovated and rebuilt 1912 by Alexander Chestnutt. 3 manuals, 43 speaking stops, and 6 other stops Tubular pneumatic action. Opened by Rev. Father Herman. Organist : Dr. John Storer.

WATFORD.—Christ Church. Built 1907 by Binns. 2 manuals, 24 speaking stops. Organist : William Charles Kempster, F M.I C L.

WAUNARLYDD.—Sardis Welsh Congregational Church. Built by Blackett & Howden. 2 manuals, 14 speaking stops, 5 couplers, 4 composition pistons. Tubular pneumatic action to Pedal Organ.

WEDNESBURY.—Parish Church. Built 1911 by Brindley & Foster. 3 manuals, 31 speaking stops, 9 other stops, 1,937 pipes, 20 pneumatic combination accessories, 10 composition pedals, tremulant, balanced Swell pedal. Blown by electric motor. Organist : Thomas Troman, A R.C.O.

WEDNESBURY.—Town Hall, Darleston. Built 1903 by Binns Opened by C. W. Perkins 3 manuals, 31 speaking stops, 14 couplers, 2 tremulants, and 1,981 pipes. Interchangeable system, and pneumatic action throughout to stop and key action, both Binns patents. Separate reservoirs to each organ. Blown by electric motor Organist : Thomas Johnson

WEDNESBURY.—Town Hall. Built by Forster & Andrews. 3 manuals, 30 speaking stops, 7 couplers. Blown by hydraulic power. Organist : Thomas Troman, A.R.C.O.

WELLINGBOROUGH.—All Saints' Church. Built 1880 by Hill. 2 manuals, 14 speaking stops, 3 couplers. Organist . Charles John Wood, F.R.C O., MUS. BAC.

WELLINGBOROUGH.—Congregational Church. Built by Hill. Rebuilt 1900 by Binns. 3 manuals, 39 speaking stops, 11 other stops. Tubular pneumatic action throughout. Detached console Kinetic blower. Pedal organ of 10 stops, governed by pneumatic controllers, constructed by F H. Bond in 1910. Organist : Frank Heddon Bond, M A CANTAB., F R C.O.

WELLINGTON (SALOP).—Congregational Church. Built by Conacher. 2 manuals and pedal, 16 speaking stops, 4 couplers, 6 composition pedals, balanced Swell crescendo pedal. Pedal board radiating and concave.

WELLINGTON (SALOP).—Parish Church. Built 1879-1899 by Bevington. 3 manuals, 28 speaking stops, 14 couplers. Part tubular. Hand blown. Organist : M. Allison, MUS. BAC , L R A M , F.R.C O , Waterloo Road, Wellington.

WELLINGTON, SOMERSET.—PARISH CHURCH. Built 1837 by Gray. Rebuilt 1868 by Dicker, and 1903 by Hele. Opened by Dr. D. J. Wood. 3 manuals, 26 speaking stops, 5 other stops. Erected in the South-East corner. Organist : Percy E. Clarke, F.R.C.O.

WELLS.—CATHEDRAL, THE. Rebuilt 1664 by Robert Taunton ; 1786 by Green ; 1857 (and restored 1891) by Willis ; rebuilt and considerably enlarged 1909 by Harrison. 4 manuals, 55 speaking stops, 21 couplers, 2 tremulants, 6 combination pedals, 20 combination pistons, 2 reversible pistons, 2 balanced crescendo pedals. Tubular pneumatic action throughout, except the manual to pedal couplers, which are mechanical. Blown by 3 hydraulic engines Organist : Rev. Thomas Henry Davis, B.A., MUS. DOC., F.R.C.O.

WELLS.—ST. CUTHBERT'S CHURCH. Restored 1906 by Sweetland. 3 manuals, 28 speaking stops, 6 couplers R.C.O. radiating and concave pedals. 6 composition pedals to Swell and to Great.

WEST BROMWICH.—PARISH CHURCH. Built 1898 by Brindley & Foster. Opened by Sir F. Bridge. 3 manuals, 32 speaking stops, 9 other stops, 1,700 pipes. Blown by Melvin hydraulic engine Organist : Alfred J. Smith, F.C.O.

WEST BROMWICH.—ST. PHILIP'S CHURCH. Restored 1906 by Nicholson & Lord. Opened by James Randall Cooke. 3 manuals, 26 speaking stops, 6 other stops, 1,452 pipes. Tracker action to manuals, pneumatic to pedals.

WESTBURY.—PARISH CHURCH. Built 1867 by Bevington. 3 manuals, 19 speaking stops, 7 other stops.

WEST HARTLEPOOL.—HOLY TRINITY CHURCH, SEATON CAREW. Built 1893 by Nicholson. 2 manuals, 16 speaking stops, 4 other stops. Organist : Frederick W. Hard.

WEST HARTLEPOOL.—ST. GEORGE'S CONGREGATIONAL CHURCH. Built 1904 by Binns. Opened by Dr. Peace. 3 manuals, 27 speaking stops, 12 other stops, 1,529 pipes. Choir organ in separate Swell box. Tubular pneumatic action throughout. Triple feeders worked by electric motor. Organist : G. Nutton, West Hartlepool.

WEST HARTLEPOOL.—ST. OSWALD'S CHURCH. Built 1904 by Ingram & Co., and opened by present organist. 4 manuals, 35 speaking stops, 29 couplers, 1,982 pipes Blown by electric motor. Current to organ supplied by transformer. Electro pneumatic action. Organist : Edward Vernon Pickersgill, MUS. BAC. (DUNELM), F.R.C.O.

WESTON-SUPER-MARE.—PARISH CHURCH Built 1883 by Walker. 3 manuals, 24 speaking stops, 5 couplers, 1,330 pipes. Organist : E. G. Bentall, Shelston, Weston-Super-Mare. Appointed 1883.

WEYMOUTH.—ALL SAINTS CHURCH, WYKE REGIS. Built 1884 by Jones. 2 manuals, 15 speaking stops, 4 other stops, 750 pipes, 2 composition pedals.

WHITCHURCH (MIDDLESEX).—ST. LAWRENCE'S CHURCH. Built 1715 by G. Schmidt, a nephew of Father Smith. Restored 1818 by H. Jones; 1867 by W. Hill ; 1877, by Brindley & Foster. 2 manuals, 15 speaking stops, 4 other stops, 796 pipes, 3 composition pedals Played upon by Handel when organist to the Duke of Chandos (1718-1721). Gilt pipes and beautiful oak case of original organ still remains. Organist : W. J. Honey.

WHITCHURCH (SALOP).—PARISH CHURCH. Built by Conacher. 3 manuals and pedal, 34 speaking stops, 6 couplers, 7 composition pedals, pedal for Great to Pedal " on and off." Oak case. Organist and Choirmaster : William Edwin Rogers.

WHITEHAVEN.—ST. JAMES' PARISH CHURCH. Built 1909 by Norman & Beard. 3 manuals, CC to A3 ; 26 speaking stops, 12 other stops. Blowing apparatus, two Watkins and Watson hydraulic engines. Pedal board radiating and concave. Tubular pneumatic action. 10 composition pedals. Two Swell pedals. Organist : George Tootell, F.R.C.O.

WHITEHAVEN.—ST. NICHOLAS' PARISH CHURCH. Built 1904 by Harrison. Opened by Dr. W. G. Alcock, M.V.O. 3 manuals, 47 speaking stops, 13 other stops, 2,782 pipes. Blown by electric motor and two Sturtevant fans. Organist : W. Wilson Foster.

WIGAN.—HOPE CONGREGATIONAL CHURCH. Built 1890 and restored 1910 by Jardine. 2 manuals, 25 speaking stops, 9 other stops, 1,715 pipes. Blown by electric motor applied to ordinary feeders. Organist : Richard A. Moss, A.R.C.O.

WIGAN.—PARISH CHURCH. Built 1714. Restored 1902 by Norman & & Beard. 3 manuals, 40 speaking stops, 7 other stops. Tubular pneumatic action throughout. Blown by Swanton Kinetic electric motor. Organist Edgar C. Robinson, MUS. BAC (OXON), F.R.C.O.

WIGAN.—SCARISBRICK ROAD BAPTIST CHURCH. Built by Conacher. 2 manuals and pedal, 20 speaking stops, 7 couplers, 6 composition pedals. Tubular pneumatic action throughout. Blown by electric motor.

WIGAN.—ST. CATHARINE'S CHURCH. Built 1884 by Young. Opened by A. Alexander. 3 manuals, 27 speaking stops, 7 couplers, 1,514 pipes. 3 composition pedals. Pipes of best spotted metal. Tracker action. Trombone stop added to Pedal organ, 1908. Organist : Simon P. Cooke.

WIGAN.—ST. MICHAEL'S CHURCH. Built 1882 by Wilkinson. 3 manuals, 30 speaking stops, 5 couplers, 8 combination pedals. Organist : W. R Newman.

WIGAN.—ST. PAUL'S CONGREGATIONAL CHURCH. Built by Young. 3 manuals and pedal, 30 speaking stops, 9 couplers, 8 composition pedals.

WIGAN.—ST. THOMAS' CHURCH. Built 1908 by Rushworth & Dreaper. 3 manuals, 31 speaking stops, 10 couplers, 7 composition pedals, 4 pistons. Tubular pneumatic action throughout. Blown by electric motor. Organist : Sam Wood, J.P

WILLESDEN.—CHRIST CHURCH, HARLESDEN. Built 1911 by Rushworth & Dreaper. 2 manuals, 18 speaking stops, 6 couplers, 5 composition pedals. Tubular pneumatic action throughout. Organist : R. G. T. Wilding.

WILLESDEN.—ST. GEORGE'S PRESBYTERIAN CHURCH, BRONDESBURY. Built 1890 and enlarged 1900 by Willis. 3 manuals, 22 speaking stops, 5 other stops, 1,124 pipes. Great organ small though powerful. Organist : James Somerled Macdonald, F.R.C.O.

WILLESDEN.—St. Matthew's Church. Built 1905 by Vincent. Opened by W. G. Hopkins, F R.C.O. 3 manuals, 30 stops. Pneumatic action Organist : T. J. Tarbox.

WILMSLOW.—St. Bartholomew's Parish Church. Rebuilt by 1891 Young. 3 manuals, 26 speaking stops, 8 other stops, 7 composition pedals. Balanced Swell pedal. Tremulant pedal. Organist : Frank Osborn.

WIMBLEDON.—St. Mary the Virgin Parish Church, Merton. Built 1847 by Holdich. 2 manuals, 21 speaking stops, 4 other stops. Excepting Clarionet, all stops run through Organist : E. W Pillinger.

WIMBLEDON —Westfield, Wimbledon Common. Private organ, the property of J. M Boustead, Esq Built by Hunter Contains a number of reed stops by Cavaille Coll, of Paris, and a Cor Anglais of William Hill & Son. Contains four 32ft. stops and one 64ft. acoustic Pipes are in a basement below music room, and action is electric, the ordinary magnets used for electric bells being used, wound to a high resistance, and current supplied by the secondary batteries in the house Electric motors for blowers. The effect sitting at the keys in the music room is that of a cathedral organ. Pipes of pure tin or best spotted metal ; wood stops of pine. There are 5 manuals, 3 pedals, 108 speaking stops, 6 gongs, 78 pistons, 8 composition pedals, 3 touch pedals, 33 kicking pedals, and 2 swell pedals.

WIMBORNE —Canford Magna Parish Church. Built 1882 by Bevington Enlarged by Brindley & Foster. Opened by H Wakeford, F.R C O 2 manuals, 10 speaking stops, 3 other stops, 522 pipes. Pedals latest R C O pattern. Organist , Mr. Ronald Gomer.

WIMBORNE.—Minster, The. Built 1664 by Hayward Rebuilt 1764, 1844, 1865 and 1899. Opened by E. H. Lemaire, 1899. Removed from choir screen to south choir aisle 1856. Hydraulic system added in 1901. 3 manuals, 35 speaking stops, 8 other stops, 2,330 pipes Tubular pneumatic action to manuals, pedals and drawstops Organist : Albert Edward Wilshire, F.R C.O., L.R.A.M.

WINCHESTER —Cathedral, The. 4 manuals, 69 stops Built by Willis, for the Great Exhibition of 1851, and bought by the Dean on the advice of Dr. S. S. Wesley, organist of the Cathedral. Set of diapasons added by Hele, 1905. Organist : William Prendergast, mus. doc oxon.

WINCHESTER —College Chapel. Built 1681 by Renatus Harris ; repaired 1804 by Green ; entirely rebuilt 1875 by Bishop , enlarged later by Hill ; rebuilt 1909 by Norman & Beard. Organist : E. T. Sweeting, mus. doc. oxon , F R C.O.

WINCHESTER —Congregational Church. Built by Burton. 3 manuals, 33 speaking stops, 11 couplers, 1,896 pipes, tremulant, 5 composition pedals. Detached Console. Electro-pneumatic action. Blown by electric motor.

WINCHESTER.—Private Residence of C. Boyd, Esq., Sillwood Weeke, Winchester. Built by Burton. 3 manuals and pedal, 28 speaking stops, 7 couplers, 12 pneumatic pistons, 1,319 pipes. Tubular pneumatic action.

WINCHESTER.—St. Maurice Church. Rebuilt by Burton 3 manuals and pedal, 28 speaking stops, 11 couplers, 1,624 pipes, 8 pneumatic pistons, 6 composition pedals Tubular pneumatic action. Organist : C. Stuart, Colnebrook, Winchester.

WINDERMERE.—St. Mary's Church. Built 1912 by Wilkinson 2 manuals, 26 speaking stops, 5 couplers, 8 combination pedals.

WINDSOR.—Parish Church. Built 1906 by Hunter. 3 manuals, 47 speaking stops, 10 couplers, 21 pistons. Tubular pneumatic throughout. Blown by electric motor. Reeds spotted metal throughout. Organist : Albert Melleo.

WINSFORD.—Primitive Methodist Church, High Street. Built 1912 by Steele & Keay. 2 manuals and pedal, 18 speaking stops, 5 couplers, 5 double-acting composition pedals, self-balancing crescendo pedal. Tubular pneumatic action to Pedal. Pitch pine case.

WINSFORD.—Primitive Methodist Church, Station Road. Built 1907 by Steele & Keay. 2 manuals and pedal, 20 speaking stops, 4 couplers, 6 double-acting composition pedals, self-balancing crescendo pedal. Tubular pneumatic action to Pedal. Pitch pine case

WINSLOW.—Parish Church of St. Lawrence. Built 1911 by Bevington. Opened by H. G. Ley, of Christ Church Cathedral. 3 manuals, 26 speaking stops, 7 other stops, 1,418 pipes. Blown by hand Tubular pneumatic action throughout, except composition pedals and drawstop action. Organist : G. Herbert Thompson, L. MUS. T.C.L.

WISBECH ST. MARY.—Parish Church. Built by Conacher. 2 manuals and pedal, 15 speaking stops, 3 couplers, 6 composition pedals. Oak case. Pedal board radiating and concave. Organist and Choirmaster : J. Sutcliffe Smith, MUS. BAC. DUNELM, A.R.C.O.

WOKING.—Christ Church. Built 1909 by Hunter. 3 manuals, 32 speaking stops, 12 couplers, 18 pistons. Tubular pneumatic throughout. Blown by electric motor. Reeds spotted metal throughout. Organist : W. D. Boesley, MUS. BAC.

WOKINGHAM.—All Saints' Parish Church. Rebuilt 1897 by Walker. Opened by J. D. Chandler, F.R.C.O. 3 manuals, 28 speaking stops, 5 other stops, 1,512 pipes. Bellows placed in roof of chamber. Organist : Sidney A. Mosdell, F.R.C.O.

WOLSTANTON —Wesleyan Church. Built 1898 by Steele & Keay. 3 manuals and pedal, 28 speaking stops, 8 couplers, 6 double-acting composition pedals. Tubular pneumatic action to Pedal and front pipes. Pitch pine case. Organist : G. H. Heath, Belmont, Wolstanton, Stoke-on-Trent.

WOLVERHAMPTON.—St. Mark's Church. Built 1902 by Norman & Beard. 3 manuals, 34 speaking stops, 5 other stops. Blown by hydraulic engines. Organist : Ernest Darby, MUS. BAC. (DUNELM), A R.C.O.

WOMBWELL.—Parish Church. Built 1906 by Brindley & Foster. Opened by P. Jones. 2 manuals, 22 speaking stops, 5 other stops, 1,334 pipes, 8 composition pedals. Tubular pneumatic action throughout. Organist : Arthur Banks Linford.

WOODBRIDGE.—Parish Church. Built by Gray & Davison. Rebuilt 1886 by Monk and 1911 by Bishop. 3 manuals, 40 stops. Tubular pneumatic action. Organist and Choirmaster : Alfred J. Dye, L.MUS. T.C.L., I.S.M., Townley House, Woodbridge.

WOODFORD.—ALL SAINTS' CHURCH, WOODFORD GREEN. Built 1890 by Willis. 3 manuals, 27 speaking stops, 4 other stops Enlarged from older instrument. Swell box for both Swell and Choir. Organist: E. Markham Lee, M A , MUS. DOC. CANTAB., F R.C O

WOODFORD.—HOLY TRINITY CHURCH, HERMON HILL. Built 1889 by Walker. Opened by Dr. W. S. Hoyte. 3 manuals. Enlarged and set up by Monk, from old organ in Woodford Parish Church. Presented by R Roberts, Esq. Organist: —. Wright

WOODFORD —PARISH CHURCH. Built 1850 by Hill. Opened by W. S. Hoyte. Originally a 4-manual chamber organ belonging to Mr. Baxter, of The Minories, E.C. Rebuilt 1912 by Hill 3 manuals, 45 draw knobs. Tubular pneumatic action throughout. Usual pistons and accessories. Hydraulic blowing and console in North transept. Opened by Dr G. F. Huntley. Organist: John W. Cox.

WOODFORD.—ST. MARY'S PARISH CHURCH Built 1850 by Hill. Opened by W. S. Hoyte. Rebuilt 1912 by Hill. 3 manuals, 32 speaking stops, 8 couplers. Tubular pneumatic action throughout. Hydraulic blowing Originally a chamber organ. Given to the church, 1889, by Mr. Baxter Organist: J. C Cox.

WORCESTER.—CATHEDRAL, THE Built 1896 by Hope Jones 4 manuals, 55 speaking stops, 25 other stops. Organ divided into 3 sections, console behind stalls, North aisle of church is connected with various parts of organ by single flexible cable. Wind supplied by Kinetic blower. Organist: Ivor Atkins, HON, R.A M., MUS BAC. OXON , F.R C.O.

WORCESTER.—CLAINES PARISH CHURCH Rebuilt and enlarged 1902 by Nicholson. 3 manuals, 21 speaking stops, 18 other stops, 945 pipes. Tubular pneumatic action throughout. Blown by Crossley oil engine and " Fan." Organist. Arthur H. Whinfield.

WORCESTER.—ST. GEORGE'S CHURCH Built 1898 by Nicholson. 2 manuals, 22 speaking stops, 3 other stops, 1,206 pipes. Tubular pneumatic action Organist: Percy G Tyler.

WORCESTER.—ST. JOHN IN BEDWARDINE, CHURCH. Built 1865. Rebuilt 1900, by Nicholson. 3 manuals, 29 speaking stops, 6 other stops, 1,596 pipes. Blown by hand Choir organ in box. Organist: George Street Chignell.

WORTH (SUSSEX).—PADDOCKHURST, THE RESIDENCE OF LORD COWDREY. Built by Bevington. 3 manuals, 20 speaking stops, 11 couplers Hydraulic blowing.

WORTHING —ST ANDREW'S CHURCH Built 1901 by Hunter. Opened by Monsieur Wigand 3 manuals, 42 speaking stops, 9 other stops Tubular pneumatic action throughout. Separate reservoirs to each manual. All reeds spotted metal. Blown by hydraulic engine. Organist: Horace A Hawkins, F.R.C O.

WORTHING.—HEENE PARISH CHURCH. Built 1881 by Chas Whiteley. Restored 1893 and 1909 by Walker. 3 manuals, 33 speaking stops, 6 other stops, 2,000 pipes Blown by hand 6 composition pedals. Tremulant pedals and 4 stops on Choir organ, enclosed in a Swell box. Organist: Arthur Boyse, F.R.C.O.

WORTHING.—WESLEYAN CHURCH, STEYNE GARDENS. Built 1912 by Brindley & Foster. 2 manuals, 17 speaking stops, 6 composition pedals Balanced Swell pedal Blown by electric " Fan." Organist : Alfred Walter Fisher, L R A M , A R C.O

WREXHAM —PARISH CHURCH Built 1894 by Forster & Andrews. 3 manuals. Choir organ particularly good. Organist : Frank Pullein, A R.C.O.

WREXHAM.—PENYBRYN CONGREGATIONAL CHURCH, SALISBURY PARK. Built 1868 by Bevington. Opened by J. R. Griffiths, MUS. BAC. Restored 1899. 2 manuals, 22 speaking stops, 9 other stops. Organist : H. Ewart Jones.

WREXHAM.—PRIMITIVE METHODIST CHAPEL, POYSER STREET. Built 1912 by Abbott & Smith. Opened by F. Pullein, A.R.C.O. 2 manuals, 15 speaking stops, 8 other stops. Organist : A. E. Mudd

WREXHAM —ST MARK'S CHURCH Built 1874 by Chas. Whiteley. 3 manuals, 28 speaking stops, 7 other stops Organist : J. Jones, A.R.C.O.

YEOVIL.—ST. JOHN THE BAPTIST CHURCH Built 1894 by Norman & Beard. Restored 1904 by Hope Jones. Opened by C H. Lloyd. 3 manuals, 24 speaking stops, 10 other stops, 1,220 pipes Swell and Choir organs in transept at north-east of church. Great divided in West tower. Very fine console at East end. Electro-pneumatic action, and blown by Ross engine. Organist : Frederick George Risdon, F R.C.O , A.R.C.M.

YORK —MINSTER, THE. Built 1829 by Elliott & Hill. Improved 1860 by Hill. Entirely rebuilt 1903 by Walker. 4 manuals, 70 speaking stops, 13 couplers, 2 tremulants, 21 electric pneumatic combination pistons, 14 electric pneumatic combination pedals Blown by 4 hydraulic engines Console on south side. Organist : T. Tertius Noble, F.R.C.O., A R C.M.

YORK.—ALL SAINTS' CHURCH, PAVEMENT. Built 1898 by Hopkins. 3 manuals, 26 speaking stops, 6 couplers. Organist : Arthur Hopkins, 48, Bishopthorpe Road, York. Appointed 1883.

YORK.—BOOTHAM ASYLUM. Built 1910 by Crompton. Opened by T. T. Noble. 2 manuals, 20 speaking stops, 4 other stops. Blown by electric fan. Organist . Bertram G W Dunsford.

YORK —ST. ANDREW'S CHURCH. Restored 1905 by Hopkins. 2 manuals, 16 speaking stops, 5 other stops. Organist : Cecil Daly Atkinson, A. MUS. T.C.I , M R C O.

YORK.—ST PHILLIP AND ST. JAMES'S. Built 1905 by Hopkins. Opened by T. T. Noble. 2 manuals, 30 speaking stops, 6 other stops. Blown by hand. Organist : Bertram G. W. Dunsford.

Organ Builders

WHOSE INSTRUMENTS ARE REPRESENTED IN THIS WORK.

ABBOTT & SMITH, Blackman Lane, Leeds.

AINSCOUGH, H , Derby Road, Preston.

ANDREWS, WILLIAM, City Organ Works, 31, Crampton Street, Bradford.

ARUNDELL, G., & Co., New Cross Organ Works, 49, New Cross Road, London, S.E.

BANFIELD, J. C., & Co., City Organ Works, Branston Street, Birmingham.

BENSON, G., 60, Cornbrook Road, City Road, Manchester.

BEVINGTON & SONS, Manette Street, Charing Cross Road, London, W.

BINNS, J. J., LTD , Bramley Organ Works, Leeds.

BISHOP & SON, 20, Upper Gloucester Place, London, N.W. and Westbourne Mills, Ipswich.

BLACKET & HOWDEN, Grafton Street, Newcastle-on-Tyne.

BRINDLEY & FOSTER, 21, Buckingham Street, Strand, London, W.C. ; Suffolk Road and Fornham Street, Sheffield ; and 147, Bath Street, Glasgow.

BROWNE, F. H. & SONS, 21, Stour Road, Canterbury.

BRYCESON BROS., 155a, Marlborough Road, Upper Holloway, London, N.

BURTON, W. J., St. George's Street, Winchester.

CHESTNUTT, ALEX, Manor Works, Waterford, Ireland.

COMPTON, JOHN H., Organ Builder, Nottingham.

CONACHER, P., & Co., Springwood, Huddersfield ; and 12, Fleet Street, Dublin.

CORPS & SON, 28, Oxford Road, Finsbury Park, London, N.

COUSANS, SONS, & Co., City Organ Works, Lindum Road, Lincoln.

DALLADAY, S. F., Sussex Organ Works, Manor Hall, Hastings.

DRIVER & HAIGH, Snowdon Street, Bradford.

DYER, H., & SON, 64, Burghley Road, Highgate, London, N.

ENGLAND, A., Victoria Road, Westbury Park, Bristol.

FORSTER & ANDREWS, 43a, Dock Street, Hull.

GERN, AUG., Turnham Green Terrace, Chiswick, London, W.

GRAY & DAVISON, 6, Pratt Street, Camden Town, London, N.W. and 128, Holt Road, Liverpool.

HARRISON & HARRISON, The Avenue, Durham ;
    Church House, Westminster, London, S.W.
    and 50, Wellington Street, Glasgow.
HALMSHAW BROS., Palmerston Road, Sparkbrook, Birmingham.
HAMILTON, C. & F., 18, Bread Street, Edinburgh.
HARPER & Co., Organ Builders, Newmarket.
HARSTON & SON, 40, Stosman Street, Newark-on-Trent.
HELE & Co., Earl's Acre, Pennycomequick, Plymouth ; and
    11, Elm Grove, Hammersmith, London, W.
HEWITT, H. W., Myrtle Road, Highfields, Leicester.
HILL, W , & SON, York Road Organ Works, Islington, London, N.
HOLT, JOHN, Pioneer Works, Station Road, Harborne, Birmingham.
HOPKINS, T., & SON, 56, Skeldergate, York
HUNTER, A., & SON, 87, High Street, Clapham, London, S.W.
INGRAM, EUSTACE, 32, The Avenue, Bedford Park, London, W.
INGRAM & Co., St. George's Hall, Hereford.
JARDINE & Co., Elsinore Road, Old Trafford, Manchester.
JOHNSON, G., & Co., 10, Dighton Street, Bristol.
JONES, H., & SONS, 70, Park Walk, Fulham Road, London, S.W.
JONES, T S., & SON, 168, Marlborough Road, Upper Holloway,
    London, N.
KEATES, A., Sheffield Organ Works, Charlotte Road, Sheffield.
KIRKLAND, A., 155a, Marlborough Road, Upper Holloway,
    London, N.
LAYCOCK & BANNISTER, Aire Street, Crosshills, Keighley.
LEWIS & Co., LTD., Ferndale Road, Brixton, London, S.W. ;
    916, Sauchiehall Street, Glasgow ; and
    2, Empress Road, Kensington, Liverpool.
LLOYD, C., & Co., Brighton Street, Nottingham.
MAGAHY, T. W., 23, Lr George's Street, Cork.
MARTIN & COATE, 54, Pembroke Street, Cowley Road, Oxford.
MILLER, J. R., Dundee Organ Manufactory, 11, Caldrum Street,
    Dundee.
MINNS, J. E., 32, North Street, Taunton.
MONK, A., 49, Crayling Road, Glissold Park, London, N.
MORGAN & SMITH, LTD., Organ Works, Milbury Bridge, Hove,
    Brighton.
NICHOLSON & Co., Palace Yard, Worcester.
NICHOLSON & LORD, Vicarage Place, Walsall.
NICHOLSON & NEWBEGIN, Dunn Street, Newcastle-on-Tyne.
NOBLE, W., & SONS, 13, Heathfield Road, Acton, London, W.
NORMAN & BEARD, LTD , 61, Berners Street, London, W. ; and
    Chapelfield Road, St. Stephen's Square,
    Norwich.
NOTERMAN, A., 111, Frithville Gardens, Shepherd's Bush, London, W.
POSITIVE ORGAN Co., LTD , 44, Mornington Crescent, London, N.W.
PHIPPS, G. P., Gloucester Green, Oxford.
PORRITT, J., & SON, 84, London Road, Leicester.

RAYSON, JOHN, & SONS, 15, High Street, Ipswich.
REIGER BROS., 54, Great Marlborough Street, London, W.
RUSHWORTH & DREAPER, LTD., 3, Great George Street, Liverpool.
RUTT, ROBERT SPURDEN, Cedars Lawn, Leyton, London, E.
SPEECHLY, HENRY & SONS, Camden Organ Factory, St. Mark's
      Road, Dalston, London, N.E.
STEELE & KEAY, Market Place, Burslem.
SWEETLAND ORGAN BUILDING CO., LTD., Bath.
TAYLOR, STEPHEN & SON, Purcell House, 34, Nelson Street,
      Leicester.
TELFORD & TELFORD, 109, St. Stephen's Green, Dublin.
VINCENT, H. S., & CO., St. Mark's Organ Works, Sunderland.
VOWLES, W. G., LTD., 3, St. James's Square, Bristol.
WADSWORTH BROS., 35, Oxford Street, Manchester.
WALKER, J. W., & SONS, 27, Francis Street, Tottenham Court
      Road, London, W.C.
WEDLAKE, HENRY, 142, Tollington Park, London, N.
WHITELEY, CHARLES, Crane Lane, Chester.
WILKINSON & SONS, Church Organ Manufactory, Kendal.
WILLIS, H., & SONS, Rotunda Organ Works, High Street, Homerton,
      London, N.E.
WORDSWORTH & CO., Hanover Avenue, Park Lane, Leeds.
YOUNG, A., & SONS, 29, Eldon Street, Upper Brook Street, Man-
      chester.

Some French Historical Organs.

Contributed by Dr. G. Bedart, University of Lille.

Notre Dame de la Dalbade, Toulouse, France.

BUILT by Moitessier, of Montpellier, in 1849, on a tubular system of aspirating wind or attenuated air, patented by the builder in 1840, under the name of " Abrège Pneumatique " (the full description of this patent to be found in " Hinton's Organ Construction," page 110).

This organ opened by Lefebur Wely, of Paris, in 1859, is the first in which tubular system was applied, and lasted with its original aspirating wind tubular system till 1889, having performed a 40 years' career ! It was a masterpiece of joinery , but the pistons, running into cylinders bored in wood pieces, did not remain air-tight with time, and caused numerous ciphering and a great loss of blowing power. When this quite historical organ, the first of all tubular organs, was overhauled and enlarged to 54 speaking stops, by Theodore Puget, of Toulouse, this builder put Barker levers to each manual, and electro pneumatic pedal in 1889 (two swell boxes and pneumatic drawing for stops).

Church of St. Volusien Foix in the Departement of Ariege, South France.

Twenty-eight speaking stops by Firmis, a schoolmaster in Hauterive, near Toulouse ; built in 1868, with tubular pneumatic system (tubes starting from the keyboard) supplying 6 inches wind to the pneumatic levers.

This organ is also an historical one. The swell compartment was on show during the Paris exhibition in 1867, and Mr. Henry Willis was much struck with this system, and turned his energies to developing an improved form of tubular work.

The Foix organ is actually in good action, no structural repair has been done since its erection, but its action is rather slow compared to modern tubular, and it is a great wind-eater.

It must be noticed that M. Peschard, when performing his electro-pneumatic trials, 1864, had also tried to move the valve of pneumatic lever by tubular action with compressed air.

St. Francois Xavier of Paris.

Sixty-six speaking stops, 3 manuals ; built in 1878 by Firmis (the builder of tubular organ in Foix, 1868), associated with Percy. This fine organ has its original system of tubular action ;

Cavaille Coll only introduced a pneumatic lever for controlling the mechanical tracker action, opening the valves, and admitting wind into the tubes.

Originally this organ possessed tubular action to drawing stops, with interchangeable combinations, but actually these combinations do not work very well, and are not very much used.

The voicing is by Ferat, and the organ a very good one, but it is a great wind consumer, and needs five men for blowing.

The Organist is Adolphe Marty, the highly reputed blind professor of organ in National Institution for Young Blind Scholars, of Paris. His name ought to be remembered as the first of Parisian organists to prove that tubular action was quite compatible with an artistic playing of the organ, as well as with the Barker lever system.

When the three-manual organ of the Blind Institution was restored in 1897, Marty obtained, against the dicta of his Parisian colleagues, the adoption of the tubular system, which was added by Puget, of Toulouse, the pioneer of tubular in France.

St. Michel's, Dijon.

This small organ (16 stops) is also a remarkable one. It was built in 1882 by Gheys, on the tubular system, and contains an undivided wind chest. The Austin wind chest device for drawing stops and moving the valves corresponding to each pipe, is only a slight modification of Ghey's system.

This organ had not been repaired in 1911, and was in perfect action. ----

St. Laurent Parish Church, Salon, near Marseilles.

This Church possesses the " Dean " of all electric organs in the world, for not only was it the first built with electro-pneumatic transmission (1866) by Peschard in collaboration with Barker, but actually in 1912—forty-six years after its erection—is in good order, working upon the primitive electro-pneumatic device !

This quite historical organ is a two-manual of 28 speaking stops The electro-magnet governs the small valve of pneumatic lever put outside the chest.

In the cleaning of 1904, M. Franc, the organist, preserved all the electric part *just as it was affixed by Peschard and Barker*, only refitting new copper needles where damaged in the quicksilver contacts. Before this cleaning, the organ had been devoutly kept in good survey by the organist M. Payen ; therefore, we are indebted to these gentlemen for preserving in good order the first electric organ built in the world.

It is an intact proof of the excellence of Peschard-Barker system, although fitted with quicksilver contact, and requiring a heavy consumption of electricity—6-10ths ampere by 8 volts for each key.

PART III.

The Organist's Who's Who.

Brief Biographical Notes of the leading British Organists.

The Organist's Who's Who.

ABBOTT, ARTHUR, 140, Montague Street, Blackburn. Born at Blackburn. Assistant Organist and Choirmaster, St. James', Blackburn, 1900-5 ; and Organist and Choirmaster of same, since 1905.

ABBOTT, WALTER S., 34, Albany Street, Leith, Edinburgh. Born 1867 at Lewisham. Trained under Dr. Bentley, F.R.A.M., Ex-examiner Cambridge University. F.I.G.C.M. Organist St. James', Hatcham, 1896 1902 ; St. Mark's, New Cross, 1902-5 ; Christ Church (Episcopalian), Edinburgh, 1905-11 ; St. Thomas', Edinburgh, since 1911. Formerly Conductor St. James' Orchestral Society ; All Saints' Orchestral Society ; St. James' Choral and St. Mark's Choral. Conductor Leith Choral Society since 1905. Freemason.

ABDEY, ALFRED WILLIAM, 69, Florence Road, Brighton. Born at Brentford, 1876. Educated at Brighton. MUS. BAC. OXON., F.R.C.O. Organist and Choirmaster St. Andrew's, Burgess Hill, Sussex, 1898-1903 ; Chapel Royal, Brighton, 1903-1910 ; St. Augustine's, Brighton, since 1910. Composer of organ and piano pieces.

ADAMS, JOHN HENRY, 8, Castle Road, Bedford. A.R.C.O., L.R.A.M. Organist Freshwater, I.O.W., 1888-90 ; St. Margaret's, Hollinwood, Oldham, 1890-5 ; St. Cuthbert's, Bedford, since 1895.

ADAMS, WILLIAM, Woodcote, Chiswick Lane, London, W. Born at Plymouth in 1875. Educated at Plymouth and Trinity College, London, F.R C.O., A.T C.L. Organist and Choirmaster All Hallows, Bromley, E., 1894-1902 ; St. Saviour's, Shepherds Bush, 1902-5 ; St. Bartholomews, Dalston, London, N.E., 1906-8 ; Chiswick Parish Church, since 1908. Publications : Anthem, " Christ is Risen " (Vincent).

ADCOCK, ARTHUR F., 5, Petworth Street, Battersea, London S.W. Organist St. Mary the Less, Lambeth, 1879-1883 ; St. Mary's Parish Church, Battersea, since 1883.

ADKINS, JAMES EDWARD, 23, Fishergate Hill, Preston, Lancs. Solo Chorister Ely Cathedral. Studied under Dr E. T. Chipp, organist of Ely Cathedral, and at the Royal College of Music, London. MUS. BAC. (DUNELM), F.R C.O. Formerly organist St. Anne's, Wandsworth, London ; All SS., Grovenor Road, London ; St. Stephen's, East Twickenham ; Parish Church, Esher, Surrey. Organist Parish Church, Preston, since 1890.

AKEROYD, ARTHUR T., Elm Bank, The Grove, Ilkley, Yorks. Born 1861 at Bradford. Trained by F. C. Atkinson, ESQ., MUS., BAC., Organist Norwich Cathedral ; Dr. W. Creser (harmony and composition) ; Mr. Henry Blower (singing). A.R.C.M. Organist Oswestry Parish Church, 1879-81 ; Ellesmere Parish Church, 1881-89 ; St. Paul's, Bradford, 1889-99 ; St. Margaret's, Ilkley, since 1899. Singing Master, Girls' Grammar School, Bradford, since 1895 ; Singing Master, Ladies College, Harrogate, since 1908. Hon. Sec. Yorkshire section, Incorporated Society of Musicians. Conductor Ilkley Vocal Society, since 1895 ; Wharfedale Orchestral Society, since 1907. Publications : Minuet and Trio in D ; Wedding Chorus in E flat, for organ ; A Masque of May Morning, fairy cantata for schools ; anthems, part songs, songs, pianoforte pieces.

ALDOUS, JAMES WILLIAM, West Road, Lancaster. Born 1866 at Witham, Essex. Educated privately, and with Dr. G. M. Garrett, Cambridge University organist, M.A., Downing College Cambridge. Organist and Choirmaster Christ Church, Lancaster, 1886-1906; St. Bees', School, Cumberland, since 1907. Director of music, St. Bees' School since 1886. Publications: Pianoforte pieces, part songs, etc. Recreations: Golf and cycling.

ALLATT, GEORGE HERMON, 3, Beach Grove, Moffat. Born 1888 at Heckmondwike. Trained under J. Allatt, F.C.O., J. Bowling, and H. A. Fricker, MUS. B., F.R.C.O. City Organist, Leeds. A.R.C.O. Organist 1905-09 and Organist and Choirmaster 1909-11, Wellhouse Moravian Church, Mirfield. Organist and Choirmaster Well Road U.P. Church, Moffat, since 1911.

ALLEN, GEORGE, P., The Terrace, Mansfield, Notts. MUS. DOC. DUNELM, F.R.C.O., L.R.A.M. (Pianoforte playing). Organist and Choirmaster Parish Church, Netherseale, Ashby-de-la-Zouch, 1896-7, St. Peter's Stapenhill, Burton-on-Trent, 1897-1911; Parish Church (St. Peter's) Mansfield, since 1911. Conductor Burton-on-Trent Orchestral Society, 1903-7; Matlock Choral and Orchestral Society, 1909-1911; Mansfield and District Choral and Orchestral Society, 1912. Publications: Communion Service, Evening Service; organ pieces, etc.

ALLOTT, JOEL. Fern Cottage, Church Street, Heckmondwike. Born 1862 at Liversedge. Trained privately. F. GLD. O. Organist Liversedge Parish Church, 1887-1889; Heckmondwike Parish Church, 1875-1887; and since 1889. Hobby and recreation: Choral work and bowls. Clubs: Conservative and Glee Union.

ANDERSON, JAMES SMITH, 46, Great King Street, Edinburgh, F.R.C.O. (1878). MUS. BAC. OXON (1878). Organist and Choirmaster Wesleyan, 1872-77; Abbey Parish Church, 1877-9; St. Thomas' Episcopal, 1879-81; St. Andrew's, Edinburgh, since 1881. Hobby: Golf.

ANDREWS, GEORGE F., The Cottage, Rectory Avenue, High Wycombe. A.R.C.O. Organist All Saints' Parish Church, High Wycombe, since 1895. Conductor High Wycombe and District Choral Association. Music Master Royal Grammar School.

ANSTEY, SIDNEY HERBERT, 8, Kensington Gardens, Haverfordwest. Born 1891 at Poole. Trained at Royal Normal College, Upper Norwood. A.R C.O. (Winner of Lafontaine prize, 1910). Organist St. Mary's, Haverfordwest, since 1912.

ANTCLIFFE, HERBERT, 102, Gell Street, Sheffield. Born 1875 at Sheffield. Trained privately. Organist St. Helen's, Treeton, Yorks. since 1911. Publications: Lives of " Brahms " and " Schubert " in Bell's Miniature Series; " Living Music " (Joseph Williams, Ltd.); " Advice to the Music Teacher " (Augener, Ltd.). Recreation: Walking.

ARCHER, ALFRED G. B., Alverstoke, The Drive, Prospect Road, Tunbridge Wells. Born 1872 at Tunbridge Wells. L.T.C.L. Teacher of music. Organist Mt. Pleasant Church, Tunbridge Wells, 1890-5; St. Peter's, Pembury nr. Tunbridge Wells, 1895-7; St. Peter's, Tunbridge Wells, since 1887. Recreation: Fishing.

ARGYLE, S., Hursley. Born 1861 at Sheffield. Trained at Culham College, Oxon, and under J. S. Liddle, MUS. BAC., Dr. Turpin, and others. A.R.C.O. Organist Culham College, 1881. Organist and Choirmaster Parish Church, Thelnetham, Suffolk, 1882; Parish Church, Smallthorne, Staffordshire, 1886; Parish Church, Kintbury, Berks, 1894; Parish Church, Hursley, Hants, 1906.

ARNOLD, GEORGE EDWARD, Market Place, Knaresborough. Born 1861 at Burnley, Lancs. Educated under Matthew Arnold, Hadyn Fisher, and J. Allanson Benson. Fellow and Hon. Examiner, Incorporated Sight Singing College, London. Organist Parish Church of St. John, Knaresborough, since 1887. Hobbies: Gardening, photography, and M.R. shooting.

ASPINALL, WILLIAM, Rockleigh, Ashton-in-Makerfield, Lancs. Born at Platt Bridge, Hindley. Educated at Wigan. Chemist and dental surgeon. Deputy Organist, 1887-1902, and Organist since 1902, Congregational Church, Ashton-in-Makerfield. Recreation: Golf.

ATKINS, IVOR, 8, College Yard, Worcester. HON. R.A.M. MUS. BAC., OXON., F.R.C.O. Organist (assistant), Hereford Cathedral 1890-3; Collegiate Church of Ludlow 1893-7; Worcester Cathedral since 1897. Conductor Worcester Festival; Worcestershire Orchestral Society; Worcester Festival Choral Society; Worcestershire Ladies' Choral Society.

ATKINSON, CECIL, DALY, Bishopthorpe, York. Born 1872 at Hull. Educated at Tenbury and Oxford. A. MUS., T.C.L., M.R.C.O. School Master 1891-1901. Conductor Bishopthorpe Choral Society; Darrington Ladies Choir. Musical Director of the Pontefrait, and District Musical Competitions, 1902-7. Curate of Market Weighton 1904-5. Priest-organist and choirmaster St. Andrew's Church, York, since 1905. Domestic chaplain to the Archbishop of York. Hobby and recreation: Music and cycling. Club: Oxford and Cambridge Musical, Leicester Square.

AYRTON, T., 187, Westburn Road, Aberdeen. Formerly organist Trafalgar Street Church, Burnley. Organist East United Free Church, Aberdeen, since 1900. School Teacher. Hobby: Music.

BAGULEY, L. F., A.R.C.O., Fairholm, Station Road, Newton Stewart, N.B. Born at Nottingham, 1880. Educated by Mr. R. W. Liddle, organist of Southwell Minster. Conductor of Newton Stewart Orchestral Society. Sub-organist of Southwell Minster, 1897-1902. All Saints', Newton Stewart, N.B., 1902. Hobby: Photography.

BAILEY, CHARLES MORTON, 2, Arfryn, Llangollen. Educated at Ripon Cathedral MUS. BAC. DUNELM, F.R.C.O. Organist St. Catherine's, Wigan, 1889; St. Mark's, Wrexham, 1890-1906; Llangollen Parish Church, since 1906. Conductor Llangollen Amateur Operatic Society. Publications: Organ pieces, piano pieces, Evening Service, Benedicite, scale and arpeggio manual.

BAILY, HENRY GEORGE, 12, St. Matthews Road, St. Leonards-on-Sea. Born 1851. Educated at Marlborough College. Solicitor. Hon. Local Representative for Hastings and District of the Associated Board of R.A.M., and R.C.M. Organist St. Matthew's, St. Leonards-on-Sea, since 1885.

BAIRD, ANDREW LAUDER, 2, Trinity Place, Leven, Fife, N.B. Born 1867 at Edinburgh. Trained George Herrot's School, Edinburgh. Teacher of music. Organist Greenside Parish Church, Edinburgh, 1887; Inveresk Parish Church, Musselburgh, 1890; St. Paul's Free Church, Edinburgh, 1892; St. Cuthbert's U.F. Church, Edinburgh, 1895; St. James' U.F. Church, Edinburgh, 1901; Sconnie Parish Church, Leven, since 1909. Recreation: Golf.

BAIRSTOW, EDWARD C., 10, De Grey Road, Leeds. Born 1874 at Huddersfield. Trained under Sir F. Bridge. MUS. DOC. DUNELM, F.R.C.O. Organist All Saints', Norfolk Square, W., 1894-99: Wigan Parish Church, 1899-1906; Parish Church, Leeds, since 1906. Publications: Church music, organ music, songs and part songs.

BAKER, ARTHUR HENRY, St. Cecilia., Wellington Road, Camborne. Born and educated at Torquay, F.R.C.O., F.T.C.L., L.R.A.M., A.R.C.M. Teacher of organ, piano, violin, singing. Organist Bovey Tracey Parish Church, 1897-1903; St. Petroc's, Bodmin, 1903-1907; St. Martin's, Camborne, since 1910. Composer of sacred song, " My Father in Heaven."

BAKER, ARTHUR J., 33, Knowle Road, Bristol. Born 1882 at Bristol. Trained privately. Organist and Choirmaster St. George's Church, Brandon Hill, Bristol, 1897-1911; Holy Nativity, Knowle, since 1911. Hobby and recreation: Engineering and cycling. Club: Bristol Savage.

BAKER, ERNEST WILLIAM, F.R.C.O., St. Cecilia, Padstow, Cornwall. Born at Leicester, 1876. Educated at New College School, Oxford, Dresden Conservatoire of Music, and Norwich Cathedral. Organist and Choirmaster Hingham Parish Church, Norfolk, 1895-7; Halton Parish Church, and resident Music Master at The Chilterns, Tring, 1897-1900; Organist and Choirmaster to Evelyn Countess of Craven's Private Chapel, Ashdown Park, Shrivenham, 1900-4; St. Michael's, Bishop's Stortford, 1904-12; Padstow Parish Church since September, 1912. Conductor Bishop's Stortford Musical Union (orchestral and choral). Publiactions: Magnificat and Nunc Dimittis in E; Benedicite in C; chants, hymn tunes, etc.

BAKER, HENRY JOHN, 7, Ferrestone Road, Hornsey. Born 1850 at Bluntisham, Hunts. Educated at Tottenham Grammar School and Cambridge, F.I.S.SC., London, Associate Philharmonic Society, London. Teacher of organ, pianoforte and singing. Organist St. Paul's, New Southgate, 1870-1874; St. Michael's, Bowes Park, 1874-1889; St. Mary's Parish Church, Hornsey, since 1889.

BAKER, PERCY, Hazeldene, Gloucester Road, Tewkesbury, F.R.C.O., L. MUS., T.C.L. Organist, formerly (assistant), Tewkesbury Abbey, St. James', Piccadilly, W. (Organist), St. Thomas', Regent Street, W., St. Thomas', Clapton Common, St. Matthew's, Upper Clapton, London, Tewkesbury Abbey and Walton, Cardiff, since 1910. Conductor of the Tewkesbury Festival. Published compositions, piano pieces and Church msuic. Conductor to the Philharmonic Society. Contributor to " Musical Opinion " and " Musical Standard." Author of Studies in " Musical History," Acoustics, etc.

BAKER, RALPH HINDLE. Born at Woolton Hill, near Liverpool. Past and present appointments: Hon. Organist and Choirmaster of Gateacre Parish Church, near Liverpool; Hon. Conductor of the Wavertree Amateur Musical and Dramatic Society; Founder and Hon. Secretary of the Liverpool Church Choir Association; Member of the Committee of the Liverpool Philharmonic Society; Musical Secretary of the Liverpool Cathedral Foundation Stone Laying Ceremony; Musical Director of the Liverpool Pageant; Hon. Treasurer of Liverpool Cathedral Choir Fund; Warden of Liverpool Cathedral. Compiler of " The Organist and Choirmaster's Diary." Patentee of " The Patent Sheet-Music Repair Slips."

BALFOUR, HENRY LUCAS, Westwinch, Elmwood Road, Croydon. Born 1859 at Battersea. Educated R.A M., and National School of Music. MUS. BAC., F.R.C.O. Organist and Choirmaster, St. Saviour's Croydon, 1885-

1902; Holy Trinity, Sloane Street, S.W., since 1902; Royal Choral Society, Albert Hall, London, since 1895; organ professor, Royal Normal College for the Blind, since 1896; Music Master, Whitgift Schools, 1899; High School for Girls, Croydon, since 1902; Conductor, Croydon Philharmonic Society, 1885-1900; Musical Director of South London Musical Club; Member of Philharmonic Society and The Madrigal Society.

BAMBRIDGE, WILLIAM SAMUEL, The Waimate, Marlborough. Born 1842 at The Waimate, New Zealand. Educated privately. Musically at R.A.M., MUS. BAC. OXON., F.R.A.M, F.R.C.O., J.P.; Alderman and Ex-Mayor of Marlborough. Organist Clewer Church, Windsor, 1853-64; Marlborough College Chapel, 1864-1911. Hobbies and recreations: Freemasonry, cricket, football, and athletics generally.

BANDEY, E., The Myrtles, Goldington, Bedford. Born at Goldington, 1849. Studied music privately under the late Mr. P. H. Diemer, Bedford. Organist and Choirmaster Godmanchester Parish Church, 1874; St. Cuthbert's Church, Bedford, 1875; Moravian Church, St. Peter's, Bedford, since 1895; Pianist of the Bedford Musical Society from 1888 to 1902; Local Representative of the London College of Music. Composer of pianoforte solos, songs, anthems and part songs. Recreation: Cycling.

BANKS, ERNEST, Hazeldene, Corton Road, Lowestoft. M.A. CANTAB. Organist Queen's College, Cambridge, 1887-1902; St. Margaret's Parish Church, Lowestoft, since 1902.

BANWELL, CHARLES SILVESTER, 35, Norfolk Road, Maidenhead. A Tonic Sol fa C., L.V.C.M. First-class Certificated vocalist, Society of Arts, London. Organist and Choirmaster St. Mary's Church, Maidenhead, since 1889.

BAREHAM, RICHARD, 33, St. Andrews Street, Tiverton. Born at Pokesdown in 1874. Educated under H. Moreton. MUS. BAC., F.R.C.O. St. Andrew's Plymouth. Organist Lynton Parish Church, 1894-1897; Tiverton Parish Church, 1897.

BARKER, JOHN GODDARD, Penyghent View, Settle, Yorks. Born at Ashby-de-la-Zouch, Leicestershire, 1860. Educated at the Derby School of Music. Teacher of organ, piano, singing, and harmony; pianoforte tuner, and salesman. Associate Royal College of Organists. Organist and Choirmaster, Matlock Bath, 1884-9; All Saints, Matlock, 1889-92; Ashover, 1892-5; Fulford, York., 1895-6; Giggleswick Parish Church, 1896-03; Church of the Holy Ascension, Settle, since 1903. Publications: Military March (Anglican Organist Book XII.); "Berceuse" "Minuetto," and "Sylvan Scenes," for pianoforte; songs, "A Parting Prayer," in B flat and D, and "Ever with Thee," in F and A flat. Hobbies and recreations: Cycling and reading.

BARNES, ARCHIE FAIRBAIRN, Farnborough School, Hants. Born 1879 at Bristol. Educated at Bristol Grammar School; Royal College, of Music; and Oxford (1898-1902). B.A. Formerly exhibitioner R.C.M., Organ scholar Keble College, Oxford. MUS. BAC., F.R.C.O. Music Master, Farnborough School, Hants, since 1907. Music Master Llandovey College, Wales, 1903. Organist and Choirmaster, Christchurch, Hampstead, 1904. Hobby: Roses.

BARNES, EDWARD, 101, Blackburn Street, Radcliffe, Manchester. Born 1867 at Whitefield. Educated at Radcliffe and Bolton. A.R.C.O. Organist Holy Trinity Church, Bury, 1889-1900; Bridge Wesleyan, Radcliffe, since 1900.

BARROW, WILLIAM HENRY, 4, Saxe Coburg Street, Leicester. Born at Leicester 1857 Privately trained. MUS. DOC., Trinity College, Dublin; MUS. BAC , CANTAB., F.R C O., L R.A.M., etc. Organist and Choirmaster Wigston Parish Church, 1875; St. George's, Leicester, since 1876. Hobbies: Entomology (coleoptera), microscopy, law Club: Leicester and County Liberal.

BARTLE, REGINALD W., 58, Euston Road, Northampton. Born 1874 at Derby. Educated at Northampton. F R C.O Professor of music. Organist St. Lawrence's, Northampton, 1892-1901; St. Mary's, Northampton, since 1901. Hobby: Fishing.

BARTLETT, EDWARD, Maltravers Street, Arundel, Sussex. Fellow Royal College of Organists. Formerly assistant Organist Chichester Cathedral, and Organist of the Sub-deanery Church. Organist Arundel Parish Church, since 1876.

BARTLETT, E. P., 24, Clarendon, Trowbridge. Born at Westbury, Wilts. Organist Westbury Leigh, Wilts, 1907-09; North Bradley, Wilts, 1906-07; Bradford-on-Avon, 1909; Holy Trinity Parish Church, Bradford-on-Avon, since 1912.

BATES, FRANK, Upper Close, Norwich. Born at March, Cambridgeshire. Educated privately. MUS. DOC., Trinity College, Dublin. Formerly Organist St. Baldreds, N. Berwick, N.B.; St John's, Edinburgh. Organist Norwich Cathedral, since 1885 Conductor Norwich Philharmonic Society, 1900; Norwich Choral Society, 1901; Norwich Diocesan Church Choral Society. Recreation: Golf.

BATES, THOMAS, 3, Ford Place, Finnart Street, Greenock. Born 1859 at Durham. Trained under Dr. Ford at Carlisle Cathedral Teacher of Music. Organist and Choirmaster Dunblane Cathedral, 1881; St. John's Episcopal, Greenock, since 1883. Accompanist Greenock Choral Union.

BATES, WILLIAM HENRY, Grove Road, Ash, nr. Aldershot. Born 1854 at Banbury, Oxon. Educated at Banbury. F.G.O. Professional musician. Formerly Assistant Organist at Bloxham, Oxon, Music Master, Banbury Academy Organist and Choirmaster Crookham, nr. Aldershot; Whitwell, I.O.W.; Organist, St. Thomas, Ye Martyr, Oxford, for five years; Organist and Choirmaster, Whitehaven, Holy Trinity Church, for 12 years, and Choirmaster to Deanery of Gosforth. Organist and Choirmaster, St. Saviours, Dartmouth; Fleet, Hants; and Wonersh, Guildford. Organist and Choirmaster St. Peter's Parish Church, Ash, nr. Aldershot, since 1898. Publication: Evening Service in D.

BAXTER, FREDERICK NATHANIEL, Northfield, Tetbury,{Gloucester. Born 1859 at Risely, Beds. Educated privately. MUS. BAC (DUNELM), F.R.C.O. Organist Parish Church, Colerne, Wilts , 1871; St. Mary's Parish Church, Tetbury, since 1880. Conductor Tetbury Philharmonic Society. Publications: " Notes on the Organs of Tetbury Church," " Notes on the Church of St. Mary Magdalene, Tetbury,"; cantatas, " By the Cross " and " The Norman Baron "; part songs, and Church music. Hobby: Photography.

BEARDWELL, DAVID, 38, Patshull Road, London, N.W. Born in London, 1850. Trained as a chorister and as a musician, at Lincoln's Inn Chapel, under the late Mr. Josiah Pittman and Dr. C. Steggall, 1860-67 ; the Royal Academy of Music, 1868-69 ; the Dresdener Conservatorium fur Music, 1870, and privately under the late Mr. T. G. Baines, former Organist of St. Margaret's, Westminster. Frequently he acted as deputy for Mr. Baines at St Margaret's ; the late Mr. John Hullah at the Charterhouse ; Dr. Steggall at Lincoln's Inn, the late Mr. James Higgs at St. Andrew's, Holborn, etc., etc. A.R.A.M., Member of the Incorporated Society of Musicians. Professor of Pianoforte, Harmonium and Accompanying at the Guildhall School of Music, having been on the staff of Professors since its establishment in 1880. Was Organist Congregational Church, Hampstead Road, 1869 ; All Saints' (English) Church, Dresden, 1870. Music Master, Organist and Choirmaster Elstree School, 1871-1912 The present Organist and Choirmaster of St. James', Clerkenwell. Accompanist, Organist and Conductor, Alexandra Palace, 1873-1882 Formerly Conductor St. John's Choral Society, Holloway ; the Athenæum Amateur Orchestral Society ; Assistant Conductor Highbury Philharmonic Society, etc., etc , and Private Accompanist to the late Madame Patey. Composer of church music, etc Initiated into Freemasonry, 1883, in the Guildhall School of Music Lodge, No 2454 (P. Dep. G. O. Eng. ; P.P.G.O., Herts) and holds and has held other very important offices.

BECK, HENRY JAMES, 70, Silchester Road, North Kensington, London, W. Born 1890 At work in father's printing office Organist Holy Trinity Church, N. Kensington, London, W., since 1907. Recreations: Cycling, swimming.

BEDFORD, R T., Loughborough. Formerly Organist St. Andrew's, Lambeth; Church of Good Shepherd, Lee, S.E. Articled pupil and Sub-Organist to Dr A M Richardson, Southwark Cathedral. Organist : Loughborough Parish Church since 1903.

BELCHER, W. E., Bryn Gobaith, St. Asaph, N. Wales. M.A. CANTAB., F.R.C O., A R.C M. Organist and Master of the Choristers, St. Asaph Cathedral. Formerly Organist St. Matthew's, Duddeston, Birmingham ; Parish Church, Kingston-on-Thames ; St. Michael's, Headingley, Leeds ; (Deputy) Leeds Corporation Choral scholar King's College, Cambridge. Music and Mathematical Master Bromsgrove School. Student R C M. London ; Hon. Local Examiner, Royal College of Music ; Hon Local Representative, Royal Academy of Music.

BELL, ANDREW J., 21, Charterhall Road, Edinburgh. Born 1883 in London. Trained under Thomas Richardson. Organist and Choirmaster Gaylockhart Parish Church, Edinburgh, 1904-11 ; W. St. Giles Parish Church, Edinburgh, since 1911.

BELLAIRS, RALPH HAMON, Western Lodge, Cheltenham. Born at Belgaum, India, 1867. Educated Westminster School, Balliol College and R C.M. M A , MUS DOC OXON , F.R.C O , A R C M. Hon. Examiner, R C.M (1904). Organist Bradfield College 1893-6 ; Christ Church, Cheltenham since 1901. Publications : " Daily Studies for Organ," etc.

BELLAMY, J. A., Glenavon, Sidmouth. Born 1866 at New Barnet. Educated at Grantham Member I S.M. Organist Barkston Parish Church, 1885-88 ; St. Mark's, St. Helens, 1888-94 ; Parish Church, Sidmouth since 1894. Hobby : Microscope.

BELLERBY, EDWARD JOHNSON, Ravensworth, Margate. Born 1858 at Pickering, Yorks. Educated at York Minster. MUS. DOC. OXON., L R A.M Formerly Assistant Organist York Minster. Organist: Selby Abbey Church 1879-81; Parish Church, Margate, 1881-4; Holy Trinity, Margate, since 1884. Hobbies : Chamber music, gardening and astronomy.

BENNETT, GEORGE JOHN, North Place, Lincoln. Born 1863 at Andover. Educated at Winchester College Choristers School. MUS. DOC. CANTAB., F.R.A.M., F.R.C.O. Conductor Lincoln Musical Festivals, 1896, 1899, 1902, 1906 and 1910 ; Lincoln Musical Society since 1896 ; Organist Lincoln Cathedral since 1895. Composer of music. Club . German Athenæum, London.

BENNETT, R. STERNDALE, Tudor House, Uppingham. Born 1880 at Southwold, Suffolk. Educated at Derby School and R C M. London, and St. John's College, Cambridge University. B A. CANTAB , A R C M , A.R.C.O., Stuart of Rannock scholar (Cambridge University) in sacred music. Director of Music and Organist, Fettes College, Edinburgh, since 1905. Assistant Master St. Andrew's School, Eastbourne, 1904-5. Hobbies and recreations : Mounted Infantry, Queen's Edin. R.V., football, rifle shooting, etc. Publications : 6 songs from R. L. Stevenson's " A Child's Garden of Verses " (Patterson). Club : Oxford and Cambridge Musical, London.

BENNETT, THOMAS HERBERT, Belmont House, Friar Gate, Derby. Born 1869 at Derby. F.R.C.O., L.R.A.M., M.I.S.M. Professor of Music. Organist St. George's ; St. Luke's (Deputy) ; and St. Thomas', Derby, 1888-96 ; also St. Chad's, 1896-1905 ; and All Saints', Derby, since 1906.

BENSON, F W., Dimora, Headland Park Road, Paignton. Born at Birmingham. Educated at Newcastle-under-Lyme. F.R.C O., L.R.A.M., A.M.T C.L. Professor of Music. Organist St. Oswalds, Small Heath, Birmingham 1895-1904 ; Christ Church, Paignton, since 1904. Publication : " Gondoliera " Pianoforte Solo. Recreation : Walking.

BERRIDGE-HICKS, W. Woodvale, Augusta Road, Moseley. Partner in pianoforte business. Organist St. John de Sepulchre, Norwich, 1888 ; Kingsbury, Warwick, 1890 ; St. Oswald's, Smallheath, 1893 ; St. Aidan's, Smallheath, 1895 ; St. Anne's, Moseley, since 1897. Conductor Moseley Choral Society since 1897. Hobbies and recreations : Dogs, shooting and gardening.

BERRY, THOMAS ALFRED, Knebworth, Station Road, New Barnet. Born at Tottenham. Educated at Tottenham Grammar School. Banker's clerk. Deputy Organist All Saints, Tuffnell Park, 1908 ; Christ Church, Spitalfields, 1909. Organist Christ Church, Tottenham, since December 25th, 1909.

BEWERUNGE, REV H., St. Patrick's College, Maynooth Born 1862 at Letmathe. Educated at Wuerzburg and Ratisbon. Diploma Ratisbon School of Church Music. Organist St. Patrick's College Chapel. Maynooth. Publications : Six five-parts Motets by Palestrina, arranged for five male voices ; the Vatican Edition of Plain Chants ; A Critical Study Die Vatikanischen Choralausgabe Eine Kritische Studie ; Der Vatikanischen Choralausgabe Zweiter Teil.

BIBB, A. J., F.R.C.O. Formerly articled to Mr. H. C. Morris, M.A. CANTAB., F.R.C.O., L R.A.M., A.R.C.M , St. Davids Cathedral. Assistant Organist and Choirmaster, St. Davids Cathedral, for five years. Organist and Choirmaster, St. Mary's Parish Church, Newtown, since 1909.

BIGGS, ALLAN, Waverton, Christchurch Road, Boscombe. L.R.A.M., F.R.C.O., Hon Local Representative R.A.M. Writer of annotated programmes for Symphony Concerts Winter Gardens. Musical critic " Musical News " and " Bournemouth Graphic." Formerly Organist Sheffield, Stamford, Manchester and private organist to the Earl of Scarbrough. Organist Royal Arcade, Boscombe, and St. Katharine's, Southbourne.

BILLING, J. CLARE, Milverton House, Stamford. Educated at Stamford Grammar School. A R.C.O. Organist St. Peter's, Southampton, 1887 ; St. John's College, Lancashire, 1890 ; St. Mary's, Stamford, 1898 ; Ketton Church, 1905 ; The Hall, Ketton, since 1900 ; St. Mary's, Stamford, since 1907.

BIRCHALL, AMOS, Tunnel Terrace, Tunstall, Staffs. Born 1879 at Tunstall. Trained locally. Organist Tunstall Congregational Church, since 1897.

BIRD, E. W , 42, Blackfords, Cannock. Born in 1874 at Chadsmoor. F.I.G.C.M. Organist St. Chad's, 1893. Publications · "A Passing Thought." For Pianoforte, Mors-Rose Waltz, Vesper Hymns, Kyries, etc.

BIRD, HENRY RICHARD, 8, Longridge Road, Earl's Court, London, S.W. Born 1842 at Walthamstow. Articled pupil to the late Mr. James Turle. F.R.C.O., F.T.C.L. Organist St. John's, Walthamstow, 1851 ; St. Mark's, Myddleton Square, 1858 ; Holy Trinity, Sloane Street, 1860 ; St. Gabriel's, Pimlico, 1866 ; St. Mary Abbots, Kensington, since 1872.

BIRMINGHAM, H. PERCY, 6, Lancaster Terrace, Merthyr Tydfil. Born abroad. Educated at Blundell's School, Tiverton ; Exeter, Winchester and Continent Cathedral. F.G.L.D O. Professor of Music. Formerly Organist Alford Parish Church ; St. Andrew's, Pau, France ; St. Andrew's, Willesden, London, N.W. Organist and Choirmaster St. David's, Merthyr Tydfil, since 1899. Hobbies : Architecture and pictures.

BISHOP, EDWARD J., 78, Rochester Street, Chatham, Kent. Born 1861 at Rochester. Organist Ebenezer Congregational Church, Chatham, since 1889.

BISSELL, THOMAS FREDERICK, 24, Whitehall Road, Handsworth, Birmingham. Formerly Conductor Wednesbury Choral Association , Studley Choral Association. Formerly Choirmaster Sutton Coalfield Parish Church. Formerly Organist St. Paul's, Tipton. Organist : Wednesbury Parish Church 1872-1910 ; Wednesbury Town Hall 1872-1910.

BLACK, JAMES, 131, Albert Road, Langside, Glasgow. Born (1885) and trained at Glasgow. T.C.L. Certificate. Organist and Choirmaster South U.F. Church, Barrhead, 1905-06 ; Wellpark U.F. Church, Dennistoun, Glasgow, 1906-08 ; Canal St. U.F. Church, Paisley, 1908. Hobby and recreations : Photography, golf, tennis and cycling.

BLACKBEE, FELIX D,, Junr. (Son of R. Felix Blackbee, late celebrated organist of London), Dental Institute, 212, Holdenhurst Road, Bournemouth. Born 1869. Educated in London. Organist and Choirmaster Christ Church, Boscombe, 1894-7. Organist Catholic Church, Bournemouth, since 1901. Publications : " March Progressive," etc. Hobbies : Photography, inventing. Catholic Institute Dramatic Club.

BLACKMAN, ERNEST A., 24, Picton Road, Waterloo, nr. Liverpool. L.L.C.M. Organist Litherland Parish Church, nr. Liverpool, 1901-5 (partly as assistant and partly as Organist and Choirmaster). Organist and Choirmaster Christ Church, Kensington, Liverpool, 1905-1911 ; St. Matthew's, Bootle, since 1911.

BLAIR, HUGH, Osnaburgh House, Regent's Park, London, N.W. (Trained at Worcester Cathedral, and under Dr. Garrett.) M.A., MUS. DOC., Cambridge. Organist Christ's College, Cambridge, 1884-87 ; (Assistant) Worcester Cathedral, 1887-92 ; Organist Worcester Cathedral, 1892-97 ; Holy Trinity, Marylebone, London, since 1889. Conductor Festivals of three Choirs, Worcester Cathedral, 1892-97 ; London Church Orchestral Society, 1910. Publications : Cantatas, anthems, organ and orchestral music.

BLAKE, ALFRED J., 238, Verdant Lane, Hither Green. Born 1885 at Cardiff. Trained privately. Organist Roath Park Congregational Church, Cardiff, 1898;-1905 ; Catford Wesleyan Church, since 1908.

BLAKEY, T. W., School of Music, New Market Street, Falkirk, N.B. Born at Otley, Yorks. Educated at R.A.M., London. Member of Council, Edinburgh Section, Incorporated Society of Musicians. Music Master and Organist Loretto School and St. Peter's, Musselburgh, 1883 ; Oundle School, Northants, 1888 ; West U.F. Church, Falkirk, since 1891. Conductor Falkirk Operatic Society and Falkirk and District Orchestral Union. Publications : Three sketches and gavottes for piano ; 3 leaflets for violin and piano ; 2 part songs for mixed voices ; scales and arpeggios for piano and violin, etc. Hobby and recreation : Golf. Free Mason.

BOND, FRANK HEDDON, 30, Hatton Avenue, Wellingborough. Born 1875 at Manchester. Educated at Wakefield and Cambridge. M.A. CANTAB., F.R C O. Music Master Truro College, 1898-1900. Organist Wesleyan Church, Exmouth, 1900-2 ; Wesleyan Church, Leamington, 1902-6 ; Congregational Church, Wellingborough, since 1906. Conductor Wellingborough and District Nonconformist Choir Festivals, Wellingborough Glee Club.

BONNEY, REV. EDWIN, St. Cuthberts College, Ushaw. Born 1873 at Blackburn. Trained under Dr. Armes, Durham. Organist and Choirmaster St Cuthbert's College, Ushaw, Durham, since 1899.

BONSER, ARTHUR HOWARD, Forest Lodge, Sutton-in-Ashfield, Nottingham. Educated at Mansfield Grammar School. A.R.C.O. Organist St. Peter's, Mansfield, 1889-1902 ; Parish Church, Sutton-in-Ashfield, since 1906 J.P. Notts County. Ex-Chairman Mansfield Board of Guardians. Conductor Sutton-in-Ashfield Choral Society. Composer of Music. Member Notts County Education Committee.

BOOTH, JOSIAH, 20, Coolhurst Road, Crouch End, London, N. Born 1852 at Coventry. Educated at Oxford and R.A.M. A.R A.M. Organist Wesleyan Church Banbury, 1868-76 ; Park Chapel, Crouch End, London, N., since 1877. Publications : Services, anthems (Novello), one hundred hymn tunes (Simpkin, Marshall), cantatas, part songs (Curwen), songs (Weekes). Hobbies and recreation : Chess, billiards and golf.

BOOTH, THOMAS, Kenmore, Carlton Road, Bolton. MUS. BAC. (DUNELM), A.R C.O. Organist and Choirmaster Bradshaw Parish Church, 1892. Deputy Organist St. John's, Bolton, 1885 ; Worsley Parish Church, 1889. Organist and Choirmaster St. George's Church, Bolton, since 1892. Hon. Sec. Bolton Musical Artistes' Association.

BORLAND, DR. JOHN ERNEST, 81, Bromley Road, Catford, London, S E. Born 1866 in London. Educated R.C.M. and private. MUS. D. OXON., F.R C O. Lecturer and writer on musical subjects. Various organ posts 1881-1898. Organist St. Botolph Without, Bishopsgate, London, E.C., since 1898 ; Director of Music at Bermondsey University Settlement, since 1891 ; Conductor of Choral and Orchestral Societies ; Editor " Musical News," 1895-1902 ; Musical Adviser to Education Department of the London County Council, since 1908. Publications : Magazine articles, lectures, church music. Hobby : Gardening.

BORWELL, MONTAGUE, 124, Walm Lane, Cricklewood London N.W. Born at Eastville, Lincs., 1866. L.R.A.M., A.G.S.M., M.I.S.M. Organist and Choirmaster St. Ethelburga, Bishopsgate, 1887-94 ; St. John's Stamford Hill 1895-1903. Principal baritone Lincolns Inn. Publication : " How to Sing."

BOSELEY, W. D., 200, King's Road, Reading. MUS. BAC. OXON., A.R.C.M., F.R.C.O. Organist Sonning-on-Thames, 1892 ; St. Lawrence, Reading, 1898 ; Holy Trinity, Sunningdale, 1907 ; All Saints', Reading, since 1907 ; Reading Philharmonic Society, since 1898. Music Master St Mary's Convent, South Ascot. Member Staff University College, Reading.

BOSTOCK, ALFRED EDWARD, 297, Bolton Road, Edgworth, Nr. Bolton. Formerly Organist Union Street Wesleyan, Rochdale (nearly 2 years) ; Parish Church, Shaw (3½ years) ; now Organist and Choirmaster St. Anne's Turton, since 1889.

BOWDEN, HAROLD DUNCAN, 47, Arnold Street, Liverpool. Studied under J. Herbert England. MUS. BAC., F.R.C.O., A.R.C.M. Deputy Organist Our Lady of the Annunciation, Wavertree, 1905-6. Organist St. John's, Kirkdale, 1906 ; St. Clare's, Sefton Park, Liverpool, since 1908. Club : Liverpool and District Organists' and Choirmasters' Association.

BOWDEN, W. J., 47, Arnold Street, Liverpool. Born 1857 and educated at Liverpool Institute. Formerly Organist St. Bernard's, Liverpool, for 2 years. Organist St. Patrick's Roman Catholic Church, Liverpool, since 1887. Local correspondent of " Musical Standard " (London), " Musical Courier " (New York). Musical critic " Liverpool Porcupine."

BOWLING, JOHN, Cleckheaton. Born 1880 at Heckmondwike. Educated at Bradford Grammar School. Engineer. Organist Birstall Congregational Church, 1895-6 ; West Lane Wesleyan Church, Gomersal, Leeds, 1896-1908 ; George Street Congregational, Heckmondwike, since 1908. Hobby : Model engineering.

BOWN, W. J., 1, Claremont, Newton Abbott. Born 1847 and educated at Wells. A.R.C.O. Formerly Assistant Organist Wells Cathedral. Organist Church of St. Paul, since 1879. Hobby : Gardening.

BOYNES, WILLIAM HOUSTON, Windsor Road, Saltburn-by-the-Sea. Born 1876 at Durham. Teacher of music. Organist St. Columbus, Darlington, 1897 ; Parish Church, High Coniscliffe, Darlington, 1897-1900 ; Parish Church, Norton, Stockon-on-Tees, 1900-04 ; Parish Church, Saltburn-by-the-Sea, since 1904 ; Sometime Organist and Choirmaster, private chapel of the Marquis of Londonderry, Wynyard Park, Durham. Professor of music at " The Bowers " Ladies' School. Conductor Choral and Orchestral Society.

BOYSE, ARTHUR, Byron Lodge, Byron Road, Worthing. F.R.C.O. Organist Heene Parish Church, Worthing, since 1886.

BRADFORD, FREDERICK GANDY, 12, Dix Field, Exeter. Born at Heavitree, Exeter. A.R.C.O. Assistant to Dr. Wood, Organist Exeter Cathedral. Organist and Choirmaster All Hallows-on-the-Walls, Exeter, 1902-5 ; St. Edmund's, Exeter, 1905-9 ; St. Matthew's Parish Church, Exeter, since 1909.

BRADLEY, CHARLES, 31, East London Street, Edinburgh. Organist St. Michael's, St. Mary's, and St. John's, Wakefield, Yorks, 1871 ; St. Paul's, Middlesborough-on-Tees, 1871-1882 ; St. George's, Edinburgh, 1882-4 ; Abbey Parish Church, Edinburgh, 1886-7 ; South Leith Parish Church, since 1887 ; Edinburgh Choral Union, 1893-1910.

BRADLEY, WILLIAM, 5, Jowitt Lane, Carlton Hill, Leeds. Born at Leeds. Educated privately. MUS. DOC. DUNELM., F.R.C.O. Organist and Choirmaster Temple Newsam, 1893 ; St Matthew's, Leeds 1896 ; Christ Church, Upper Armley, Leeds, since 1902 Publications Evening Service, pianoforte pieces, masonic songs, etc

BRAZIER, FRED P., 14, Capstone Road, Bournemouth. Born 1885 at Bournemouth. Trained under A E Cottam, MUS. BAC., and Dr. Holloway Member Tonic Solfa College, London. Organist Springbourne Wesleyan Church, Bournemouth, 1900-02 ; St Mark's Presbyterian Church, Bournemouth, since 1902.

BRENNAN, CHARLES JOHN, 5, Upper Crescent, Belfast Born 1876 at Gosport, Hants. Educated privately. MUS. BAC. (DUNELM), F.R.C.O., L.R.A.M. (Teacher of Singing). Formerly Organist and Choirmaster All Saints, Clifton, Beds ; Parish Church, Strabane, Co. Tyrone, Elmwood Church, Belfast Organist and Choirmaster Belfast Cathedral since 1904. Organist and accompanist to Belfast Philharmonic Society ; Conductor of Belfast Operatic Society and City Organist, Past Provincial Grand Organist of the Masonic Province of Down. Publication : " Words in Singing " (handbook on Phonetics, for singers).

BRENTNALL, HENRY, 16, Glanmire Road, Cork. Born 1859, at Lenton, Notts Educated at Radford, Notts Council Member I S M. and F G O Professor of Music Precentor, Military Church, Cork, since 1883. Organist St. Paul's, Paul Street, Cork, 1892-1902 ; and Glanmire Parish Church, since 1902. Composer of festival services, hymn tunes, chants, etc.

BREWER, JOHN FRANCIS, 84, Oxford Gardens, London, W. Born 1865 in London. Organist Farm Street R C. Church since 1883.

BREWERTON, R H. Organist Great George Street Congregational Church, Liverpool. Studied under H. E. Petre at the Royal College of Music, Manchester Formerly Organist and Pianist to the most Noble the Marquis of Cholmondeley for nearly two years.

BRIDGE, SIR FREDERICK, The Cloisters, Westminster Abbey, London. Born 1844 at Oldbury, Worcestershire. Trained at the Cathedral School, Rochester. M.V.O. (1902), C V O (1912), M.A., MUS DOC. OXON, F.R.C.O. Chorister Rochester Cathedral, 1850-89 ; Assistant Organist Rochester Cathedral 1865 ; Organist Holy Trinity, Windsor, 1865-69 ; Manchester Cathedral 1869-75 ; Westminster Abbey since 1875. Gresham Professor of Music since 1890 ; Conductor Royal Choral Society since 1896 ; Professor of Music, London University since 1902. Publications : Cantatas, oratorios, theoretical works, church music, etc. Recreations : Fishing and shooting.

BRIDGE, JOSEPH C., Christ Church Vicarage, Chester. M.A., MUS. DOC. OXON. and DUNELM., F.S.A., HON. R.A.M., F.R.C.O. Formerly Chorister and Assistant Rochester Cathedral Assistant Manchester Cathedral, Organ Scholar Exeter College, Oxford. Organist Chester Cathedral since 1877. *Professor of Music University of Durham, since 1908.*

BRIDGER, JOHN HENRY, 39, Morland Avenue, Addiscombe, Croydon. Born 1869 at Farnborough, Hants. Educated at Guildford MUS. BAC. DUNELM, F.R.C.O., A.R.C M., L.T.C.L. Professor of Music. Organist Farnborough Parish Church 1893-1910. Publications: Pianoforte pieces and Church music; also book, " How to Harmonize Melodies." Hobbies : Astronomy and gardening.

BRIDSON, C. W., 37, Sheil Road, Liverpool. Born and educated at Liverpool. F.R.C O. Organist St. Saviour's, Liverpool, 1899. Choirmaster Speke Church, near Liverpool. Organist and Choirmaster St. Nicholas', Liverpool, since 1903.

BRIGHT, PERCY SIBTHORPE, 106, Thornlan, West Norwood. Born 1867 at Southsea. Trained at the Royal College of Music. MUS BAC. LOND. A.R.C.O. Organist Christ Church, Battersea, 1893-96 ; St. Luke's Parish Church, West Norwood, since 1896. Publication : Evening service.

BRINKWORTH, F. W , 31, Albert Mansions, Albert Bridge Road, S.W. Born 1884 at Chippenham. Trained privately. A R.C.O. Organist and Choirmaster St. Mary's Church, Hullarington, 1904-11 ; Church of the Ascension, Blackheath, since 1912. Recreations : Tennis and billiards.

BRITTAIN, JOHN W., Ladywood Road, Egbaston, Birmingham. Born 1880 at Aston, Birmingham. Elementary School Master. Trained in choir at Aston Parish Church and St. John's College, Battersea. Organist Dyson Hall, Aston 1895-99 and 1901-03 ; St. James' Parish Church, 1903-08 ; St. Barnabas Parish Church, Birmingham, since 1908.

BROOK, JOHN, Carlowrie, 115, Duke Street, Southport. Born (1863) at Elland, Yorkshire. Educated at Elland and at Putney, Surrey. Formerly Organist Bethesda Church, Elland ; St. Stephen's Church, Copley ; St. Paul's Church, King Cross, Halifax ; Elland Wesleyan Church ; Hoghton Street Church, Southport. Organist St. Philip's Church, Southport, since 1902. Conductor West Vale Prize Choir. Choirmaster St. Mark's Church, Scarisbrick, Ormskirk, and West Vale Baptist Church. Conductor Blowick Musical Society. Musical critic, " Southport Visiter." Secretary Southport Vocal and Instrumental Competitive Festival Hobbies: Golf and photography.

BROOKE, WILLIAM M., Harriett Villa, Pembury, near Tunbridge Wells, Kent. Born 1861 at Wimbledon. Educated privately and Malvern College. Organist Trinity Presbyterian, Notting Hill, 1890-2 ; St. Andrews Episcopal, Maniton, Colorado, U.S.A., 1892-4 ; St. David's Cathedral, " *pro tem.*" 1896 ; Parish Church and St. Peter's Church, Pembury, since 1899. Composer of music. Hobbies and recreations : Chess, lawn tennis, mountaineering.

BROUGHTON, SAMUEL HULL, 3, West Bank Avenue, Lytham. Born 1864 at Burnley. Educated privately. MUS. BAC. OXON , F.R.C.O Organist St. James', Blackburn, 1890-97 ; Lytham Parish Church, since 1897, Conductor Lytham Amateur Operatic Society, 1903.

BROWN, EDWARD, Bank House, Richmond, Yorks. Trained at Ripon Cathedral and privately. MUS. BAC., F.R.C.O., A.T.C.L. Formerly Assistant Organist Ripon Cathedral and Organist Parish Church, Southbank. Organist Parish Church and Trinity Church, Richmond, since 1908 Music Master Richmond School, since 1908. Publications: Church music, songs, etc. Recreations: Outdoor sports.

BROWN, E. GODFREY, I, Fernbank, Holywood, Belfast. Born 1874 at Barrow-in-Furness. Educated at R.C.M. London. Teacher of piano, violin, organ and singing. Formerly Organist and Choirmaster Parish Church, Grange over Sands, Lancs (12 years) and Parish Church, Penrith (6¼ years). Now Organist and Choirmaster Parish Church, Holywood, Belfast. Conductor Belfast Philharmonic Society; Penrith Biennial Musical Festival; Penrith Amateur Operatic Society. Recreation: Rose growing. Commission in Territorials (King's Own Royal Lanc. Reg.).

BROWN, JAS. ARTHUR, 31, Plough Lane, Sudbury, Suffolk. Born (1845) and educated at Sudbury. Organ tuner. Organist Twinstead Church, 1862-7; All Saints, Sudbury, 1867-1908 (41¼ years).

BROWN, EDMUND JAS., Clyde Cottage, Amesbury. Born at Amesbury. Assistant Organist Amesbury Parish Church, 1875. Organist and Choirmaster Amesbury Parish Church, since 1903. Hobby and Recreation: Photography and Boy Scouts work.

BROWN, NICHOLAS HODGSON, Morton House, Tynemouth. Born and educated at Newcastle-on-Tyne. MUS. BAC DUNELM, A R.C.O. Professor of Music. Organist St. Andrew's (R.C), Newcastle-on-Tyne, 1875; St. Dominic's, 1883; St. Mary's R.C. Cathedral, since 1885. Hobby: Reading.

BROWN, RALPH WORTHINGTON, 10, Peel Street, Westhoughton. Born 1872. Educated at Sunnyside Institute, Bolton. F. GLD O., and A T.C L Organist St. George the Martyr, Bolton, 1895; Lever Bridge Church, Bolton, 1900; Parish Church, Westhoughton, since 1902. Publications: "First Steps," "Local Organs and Organists," "Choirs and Congregations," "Musicans' Corner," a number of hymn tunes, chants, etc.

BROWN, T. BORDONEL, 36, Grove Street, Liverpool Born 1861 at Dublin. Organist R C. Pro. Cathedral, Liverpool, since 1880; Choirmaster since 1911. Professor of singing, Blind Asylum, Liverpool, since 1885. Organist and Musical Director, St. Edward's College, since 1895. Publications: Many Masses and Latin motetts.

BROWN, WILLIAM AELRED, Morton House, Tynemouth. Born at Newcastle, and educated at Westminster Cathedral and Ushaw College, Durham Organist St. Cuthbert's College, Ushaw, 1907; St. Patrick's, Felling, 1909. Hobby: Classical literature.

BRUCE, ROBERT HALLIDAY, Lower Royds, Heckmondwike. Born 1879. Educated at Dewsbury Grammar School Cotton Merchant. Organist George Street Congregational, Heckmondwike, 1889-1907; Organist and Choirmaster, King's Cross Wesleyan Church, Halifax, since 1908.

BRUNDELL, WILLIAM CHARLES FREDERICK, 9, Broom Hill Road, Ipswich. Born 1882 at Christchurch; educated at Ipswich A.R.C.O. Organist St. John's, Needham, 1900-01; St Mary's, Burstall, 1902-03; Playford, 1903-04. Organist All Saints' Parish Church, Ipswich, since 1904. Hobbies and recreations: Photography, physical culture, football, etc.

BUCKLE, EDWARD, Briarville, Stubbington Avenue, Portsmouth. Organist (assistant), All Saints, 1887-9 (assistant), St. Mary's, Kingston, 1889-92 ; St. Luke's, Southsea, 1890-5 ; St. John's Portsea, since 1895.

BUFFEY, THOMAS GOODBURN, 18, Hull Street, Hull. Born 1859 at Hull. MUS. DOC. DUNELM., L.R.A.M. (violin). Organist and Choirmaster St. Mark's, Hull, 1878 ; Choirmaster St. Silas', Hull, 1886. Organist and Choirmaster St. Matthew's, Hull, since 1889. Organist and Choirmaster to Hull Incorporation for the Poor. Publications : Pieces for piano and violin, part songs, scale and arpeggio manuals, for violin.

BULL, GEORGE, 254, Newport Road, Cardiff. Born (1869), and educated at Cardiff. A.R.C.O. Organist Wood St. Congregational Chapel, 1881-6 ; Clifton St. Presbyterian Church, 1887-1901. Organist and Choirmaster Richmond Road Congregational Church, since 1901. Built small organ for private use.

BUNNEY, WALTER JOSEPH, 59 Highfield Street, Leicester. Born 1866 at Leicester. Educated under various professors. F.R.C.O., L.R.A.M. A.R.C.M. Organist and Choirmaster Holy Trinity, Leicester, 1885-1905 ; St. Peter's, Leicester, since 1905. Hon. Conductor Leicester Philharmonic Society, since 1910. Hobby and recreation : Bowls and golf.

BURCHILL, GILBERT, Hampden House, South Road, Kingswood, Bristol. Educated privately. M.I.S M., R.C.O. Professor of music. Organist and Choirmaster St. Barnabas Parish Church, Bristol, since 1896.

BURGESS, FRANCIS, 3, Kelfield Gardens, North Kensington, W. F.S.A. (Scot.), member I.S·M. Organist St. Mary the Virgin, Primrose Hill, 1900 ; St. Mark's, Marylebone Road, London, 1902 ; St. Columb's, North Kensington, London, W., since 1904. Publications : " Textbook of Plainsong," "Handbooks to the Opera " (6 vols.), " A Primer of Gregorian Music." Musical Director of the Gregorian Association, and Director of the Plainsong and Mediæval Music Society's Choir.

BURGESS, M. GORDON, 8, Deerbrook Road, Herne Hill, S.E. Born at Brentwood, Essex. Trained at Guildhall School of Music. B.A. OXFORD, F.R.C.O., A.G.S.M. Organist St. Michael's College, Tenbury, 1908-10 ; Wadham College, Oxford, 1904-07 ; Dulwich College Chapel, since 1910.

BURLEIGH, MISS CELIA, 78, Ditchling Road, Brighton. Trained at Brighton School of Music. MUS. BAC. DUNELM , F.R.C O. Organist Chapel Royal, Brighton, 1892-1903 ; Church of the Sacred Heart, Hove, 1903-09 ; Union Congregational Church, Brighton, since 1909.

BURLEY, A. E., Oak Cottage, Harrow. Born 1874 at Birmingham. Trained under Thos. Facer and W. Jenkins, of Birmingham. Secretary Birmingham Choral Union, 1894-1898. Sub-Organist Soho Hill Congregational Church, 1893-1898. Hon. Organist and Choirmaster Harrow Presbyterian Church, since 1905. Hobbies and recreations : Tennis, cycling and gardening. Member Grove Tennis Club, Harrow.

BURNS, FELIX, Arcade, Scotch Street, Carlisle. Born 1864 at Perth, N.B. Organist Our Lady and St Joseph's Church, Carlisle, for twenty years. Musical Director and Accompanist for Carlisle Corporation. Publications (latest compositions): " My Colleen," " Woodland Echoes," " Old Malabar," " Moorland Flowers," " Kansas Koon," " Shuffling Samuel," " Silver Moonbeams," " Spring Serenade," " Fairy Bells," Choir of Angels," " Woodland Serenade."

BURNS, KENNETH GLENCAIRN, 6, Chisholm Road, Richmond, Surrey. Born 1872 at Knockmaroon, Co. Dublin. Educated at Clifton College. Expert on organ construction. Gave first performance in Richmond (Surrey) of Bach's " Matthew " Passion. Compositions published: song, " Country and King." Organist St. Mary's, Greenwich Park, 1896-8; Christ Church, Beckenham, 1898-1901; Thirsk, 1901-2; Elland, 1902-3; Parkfield School, Hayward's Heath, 1903-6; St. Matthias', Richmond, since 1906. Publications: " Reform of the Church Organ." Hobbies and recreations: Photography, genealogy and heraldry, sailing, punting and fencing. Primrose Club, St. James', S.W.

BURROWS, BENJAMIN, 30, Highfield Street, Leicester. Born 1891 at Leicester. Organist St. Mary's Church, Leicester, since 1910.

BURRY, HUGH A., 5, Cavendish Road, Southsea. Formerly Chorister, St. Paul's Cathedral; Conductor, Oxford House (University Settlement), Bethnal Green; Organist and Choirmaster, St. Augustine and St. Faith, City of London. Now Organist St. Mary's Parish Church, Portsea, and Conductor Portsmouth Philharmonic Society.

BURSTALL, FREDERICK HAMPTON, 20, St. James' Road, Liverpool. Born 1851 at Liverpool. Educated privately. Composer of music. Organist Childwall Parish Church, 1870; Wallasey Parish Church, 1876; The Cathedral, Liverpool, since 1880.

BURTON, HARRY ORAM, 48, Beacon Hill, Lichfield, Staffs. Born 1866 at Kandy, Ceylon. Educated Ashby Grammar School and Lichfield (privately) F.GLD.O., A.R.C.O., Hon. Loc. Examiner, scholarships, R.C.M., London; Probate Court Clerk. Organist Wexford, 1880; St. Chad's, Lichfield, 1885; St. John's, Lichfield, 1892; St. Michael's, Lichfield, since 1894. Hobbies: Painting, etc.

BUTLER, FRANK, 33, Fonthill Road, Hove, Sussex. F.R.C.O. Formerly Organist St Nicholas', Brighton; Chapel Royal, Brighton; Emmanuel Brighton; and St. Luke's, Prestonville, Brighton. Organist All Saints, Hove, since 1894.

BUTT, W. J. D., 30, College Road, Cheshunt, Herts. Born 1866 at Ely. Educated privately, and at Westminster Abbey. L. MUS., T.C.L. Organist Holy Innocents, Hornsey, 1872; All Saints, Brighton, 1886; Grosvenor Church, South Audely, St. W. 1889; St. Mary's Parish Church, Cheshunt, since 1891. Publications: 2 marches for piano, small pieces for beginners; Evening Service in G.; and hymn tunes, etc Hobby and recreations: Fishing and walking. Hon. Conductor of Cheshunt Choral Society.

CADMAN, REGINALD MANDEVILLE, Trent College, Derbyshire, and The Garlands, Scarborough. Born 1878 at Malton, Yorks. Educated at R.A.M. and private. M.A., MUS. BAC. (OXON.), F.R.C.O. Musical Director United Services College, Windsor, 1895-98; Fonthill Preparatory School, East Grinstead, 1904-07. Director of Music, Trent College, since 1908. Publications: Church music. Hobby and recreation: Shooting and lawn tennis. Member of Union of Directors of Music in Secondary Schools.

CAIRD, CHARLES CLAGGETT, Clinton Villa, Brecon Road, Abergavenny. Born at Liverpool, 1832. Educated at Edinburgh. L C.M. Organist St. Barnabas', Bristol, 1848; and subsequently 1858-83 at St. Andrew's,

St James', and St. John's, Bristol, Almondsbury Church ; St. Law-rence's, Appleby ; and St George's, Tredegar ; Llanthewy Parish Church, nr. Abergavenny, since 1883 ; was also private organist to Crawshay Bailey, Esq , of Maindiff Court, Abergavenny.

CAMIDGE, JOHN, Highgate, Beverley, Yorks. Born at York, 1853. Edu-cated Christ Church, Oxford Professor of music. Organist The Minster, Beverley, since 1876. Publications · 2 Evening Services, 1 anthem. Chants in New Catholic Chant Book, and the Collegiate Psalter.

CANDLIN, T. J., Davenham, Northwich Born (1857), and educated at Dawley. Professor of music Organist Lever Bridge, Bolton 1876 ; St. Wilfred's, Northwich, since 1881. Conductor, Davenham Choral Society. Music Master, Wincham College. Publications : songs. Hobbies and recreation . Cricket, billiards and bowls.

CANTRELL, CYRIL, 86, Woodhead Road, Highfield, Sheffield. Born 1891 at Sheffield. Trained under local professors. Organist Birley Carr U.M. Church, 1907-09 ; St. Luke's, Dyer's Hill, Sheffield, since 1909.

CARPENTER, THOMAS, Stanton, 50, Radford Road, Leamington Spa. Born 1884 at Leamington Spa A T C L , Member of I S.M. Formerly Assistant Organist Leamington Parish Church. Organist and Choir-master Moreton Parish Church (Gloucester) Organist and Choir-master Warwick School Chapel since 1909. Hobby and recreation . Shorthand and walking.

CARR, W. R , Lulworth House, Abergavenny. Associate Royal College of Organists Organist St. Mary's Parish Church, Abergavenny. Past positions : Organist St James' Church, Hereford ; Holy Trinity, Hereford ; Assistant and Acting Organist Hereford Cathedral.

CASSELS, ROBERT, Willowdene, Linlithgow Born 1867 at Glasgow Educa-ted at Edinburgh University. Music Master Linlithgow Academy. Conductor Linlithgow A O Society Organist St Michael's Parish Church since 1893.

CAWLEY, JOHN, 51, Kingston Road, New Malden. Born 1880 at Rhyl. Educated at Birkenhead School and Bradfield College, Berks A.R.C O. Organist St Alban's Church, Windlesham, 1906 ; St. Mary Magdalene, Woodstock, 1907 ; to the Duke of Marlborough, at Blenheim Palace, 1907. Articled Assistant Organist St. Albans Cathedral, 1908 ; St. John the Baptist Church, Old Malden, 1909.

CAWTHORN, HENRY THOMAS, 18, Mangham Road, Parkgate. Born at Saltley, Birmingham. Educated at Batley. Certificate L O M. Organist Christ Church, Parkgate, since 1889. Hobbies : Gardening and green-house work and photography.

CEILEY, GEORGE R , Highcroft, Muswell Hill Road, London, N Born and educated at Great Yarmouth. L.R A.M., A R C.O Vocalist and Conductor. Formerly Assistant Organist St. George's, Great Yarmouth. Organist and Choirmaster of Parish Church, Aylsham, Norfolk ; St. John's, Kilburn, N.W. Assistant Organist and Choir-master St. James', Piccadilly. Organist and Choirmaster All Saints', East Finchley, since 1901. Professor of Solo Singing at the Battersea Polytechnic, London, S.W. Publication : Song, " Dream-Singing." Hobbies : Craft and Arch Masonry.

CHALMERS, Herbert J., 6, Carlton Terrace, Taunton. Born at Rock, Worcestershire. Organist Parish Church, Burton, Westmorland, 1885-90 ; Holy Trinity, Henley-on-Thames, 1890-1900 ; St. James' Parish Church, Taunton, since 1900. Operatic and Military Band Conductor. Hobby and recreation : Tennis and golfing.

CHANDLER, James D., Sunbury, Methuen Road, Bournemouth. F.R.C.O. Late articled pupil, Sir George Martin, M.V.O., of St. Paul's Cathedral. Organist and Choirmaster St. John's, Farley Hill, Reading, 1891 ; Parish Church, Wokingham, 1892. Organist and Choirmaster St. Peter's, Bournemouth, since 1905. Conductor Wokingham and Bracknell Choral Societies, 1892.

CHAPPLE, Frank A., The Mount, Pontefract. Born 1881 at Cardiff. Trained at Llandaff Cathedral. MUS. BAC. (DURHAM), F.R.C.O. Professor of music. Organist All Saints', Llandaff, 1899-1902, and Sub-Organist Llandaff Cathedral ; Avenue Church, Southampton, 1902-04 ; Monmouth Parish Church, 1904-08 ; Parish Church, Broadstairs, 1908-09 ; Pontefract Parish Church since 1909, and King's School since 1909. Music master Pontefract High School for Girls since 1911. Conductor Ackworth Choral Society since 1910. Publications : "There's not a Joy," anthems, and hymn tunes.

CHARLTON, James, 66, Fernroyd, The Avenue, Leigh. Born 1846 at Tyldesley. Educated at Leigh and Manchester Grammar Schools. M A. St. John's College, Cambridge. Organist St. Mary's Parish Church, Leigh, since 1869.

CHATFIELD, Alfred, Orsett House, Kidderminster. Born 1874. F.R.C.O., A.R C.M., L.R A.M. St. Paul's Church, Finchley, 1898-1904. Organist Kidderminster Parish Church, since 1904. Recreations : Tennis, golf.

CHATTERTON, Robert A., 1, Townhead Terrace, Paisley. Born 1872 in Cheshire. Educated at Motham Grammar School. L.R A.M., A R.C.O. Organist Hayfield Parish Church, 1887-97 ; Carvu Memorial Church, 1897-1902 ; High Parish Church, Paisley, since 1902.

CHEADLE, J. W., 37, Castle Street, Dumfries. Born at Newton Heath, Manchester. Studied music under Dr. Henry Hiles and J. Kendrick Pyne, Esq (now Doctor) both of Manchester. Organist Brunswick Wesleyan Church, Manchester, 1884 ; Whalley Range Wesleyan Church, Manchester, 1889 ; St. Michael's Parish Church, Dumfries, since 1900.

CHENOWETH, Wilfred John, Penthesiléa, Formby, Liverpool. Born 1879 at Torquay. Educated at Leamington. A R.C.O., M I.S.M Formerly Assistant Organist St. Mark's, Leamington ; Lillington Parish Church. Choir Master St. John's R.C. Kirkdale, Liverpool. Choir Master St. Anne's R.C. Church, Ormskirk. Organist Our Lady of Compassion, since 1902.

CHIGNELL, George Street, Hill View, 1, St. John's Hill, Worcester. Born 1870, at Havant, Hants. Trained at St. Michael's College, Tenbury ; Salisbury Cathedral and Selwyn College, Cambridge. Assistant Organist Salisbury Cathedral, 1886-9. Organist and Choirmaster Dilton Marsh, Westbury, 1887-9. Organ Scholar Selwyn College, Cambridge, 1889-91. Choirmaster Malvern Priory, 1893. Assistant Organist Worcester Cathedral, 1893-96. Organist and Choirmaster St. John in Bedwardine, Worcester, since 1893.

CHIGNELL, PHILIP, Hessle, near Hull. Born 1872 at Leighton Buzzard. Chorister St. George's, Windsor, 1882-7 ; Pupil Norwich Cathedral, 1888-92. F.R.C.O., 1896. Organist Kirkley, Suffolk, 1892-1901 ; All Saints', Hessle, since 1901. Hon. Sec. Hull Philharmonic Society ; Conductor Howden Rural Deanery Choral Association ; Professor Hull and East Riding College of Music. Recreations : Lawn tennis, golf, chess.

CHUBB, EDITH A., 59, St. George Street, Hastings. Born at Wellingborough, Northants. Educated at Hastings. MUS. BAC, DUNELM., A R C.M. Organist St. Anne's School 1907-11 ; Organist and Lecturer in Music St. Katharine's College, Tottenham, N., 1911.

CHURCH, CYRIL GERARD, 10, Wiltie Gardens, Folkestone. Organist 7 months at Helmsley, Yorks, 1891 ; Tenby, South Wales, 1891-5 ; Romford, Essex, 1895-9 ; St. Agnes, Kennington Park, London, 1899-1905 ; and Folkestone Parish Church, since 1905.

CHURCHILL, SAMUEL WILLIAM, Donnington, Foster Hill Road, Bedford, and 60, Berner's Street, London, W. Born at Bedford, 1877. Privately educated. Teacher of singing. A.R.C.M , L.R.A.M., A.R.C.O. Professor, Bedford Ladies Crescent House College. Organist : St. Peter de Merton Parish Church, Bedford, since 1892. Recreation : Motoring and golf.

CHUTER, HERBERT WILLIAM, 8, Henley Villas, Tankerton, Kent. Born (1875) and educated at Andover, Hants A.R.C.M , F.R.C.O. Teacher of organ, piano, theory of music. Organist St. Jude's, Gray's Inn Road, London, W.C , 1891 ; St. Michael's, Sittingbourne, Kent, 1896 ; The Abbey, Sherborne, 1900. Conductor Male Voice Choir since 1906. Hobby and recreation : Lawn tennis and reading aloud.

CLARK, ROBERT E., Rosedene, Falmouth. MUS. BAC. OXON , A.R.C.M. Organist and Music Master Magdalen College School, Brackley, 1892. Organist St. Nicholas' Collegiate Church, Galway, 1894 ; Winkfield Parish Church, Windsor, 1895 ; and Falmouth Parish Church, since 1900.

CLARK, ROBERT RAYNER, 2, Edmund Street, Seedley, Manchester. Born 1861 at Lambeth, London. Educated at Manchester. Formerly Organist St. Bartholomew's, Salford ; Pendleton Congregational ; Irwell Street, Wesleyan, Salford ; St. Saviour's, Cheetham ; St. Clement's, Chorlton-cum-Hardy. Organist St. James', Hope, Manchester, since 1904. Hobbies : Literary work.

CLAYPOLE, ARTHUR GRIFFIN, Kent College, Canterbury. Born at Peterborough, 1882. Educated at Peterborough Cathedral (1899-1903) ; and Royal Conservatorium of Music, Leipzig. MUS. DOC. DUNELM., F.R.C.O., L.T.C.L., Cert. Leipzig Royal Conservatorium (1903), Music Master of Kent College, Canterbury (appointed 1904). Assistant Organist, Peterborough Cathedral, 1902-3. Publications : Anthems— " The Lord is my Shepherd," " I will lift up mine eyes," " Jesu, thou Joy of Loving Hearts." Winner of Coronation Prize Anthem— " Musical Journal." Articles in various musical journals.

CLIFFE, HERBERT WILLIAM, 13, Devonshire Road, Blackpool. Professor of Organ, Pianoforte, Singing, Harmony, Counterpoint, etc. Formerly Organist Rawtenstall Parish Church ; Christ Church, Moss-side, Manchester, etc., etc. Organist Christ Church, Blackpool, since 1907.

COCKER, NORMAN, 33, Beech Croft Road, Oxford. Born 1889 at Somerby Bridge. Educated at Magdalen College School, Oxford. School Organist Magdalen College School, 1904-6 Organ Scholar Merton College, Oxford, 1907-9. Organist and Choirmaster SS. Philip and James' Church, since 1909. Music Master, Magdalen College School, since 1910 Hobbies and recreations : Photography, magic arts and sleight of hand, organ construction.

COCKRELL, EDWARD GORDON, 16, Melling Road, Southport. Born 1858 at Manchester. Educated at King William's College, Isle of Man ; Old Trafford School and Owen's College, Manchester ; and Guildhall School of Music, London Fellow of the Guild of Organists Organist and Choirmaster Harmondsworth Parish Church, Middlesex, 1880 ; St. John's, Bedford Hill, Balham, 1882, St. John's, Cheetham, Manchester, 1885 , St. Elizabeth's, Reddish, 1888 ; Emmanuel Parish Church, Didsbury, 1895 ; Eccles Parish Church, 1896 ; St Benedict's, Ardwick, Manchester, 1898 ; St. Mary Magdalene Parish Church, Ashton-upon-Mersey, 1906-8 , Woolton Parish Church, 1908 , Ainsdale Parish Church, since 1910. Conductor Beethoven Society's Orchestra, since 1888.

COE, GILBERT H., Weston Villa, Albury, nr Guildford. Born at Albury, 1874 Educated at Eastbourne and Basle (Switzerland). Fellow Royal College of Organists. Organist, Catholic Apostolic Church, Albury, since 1891. Conductor, Albury Musical Society, 1899. Hobbies and recreations : Electrical engineering, rifle shooting, and mountaineering

COLCHESTER, ALFRED MARKHAM, 28, Poet's Road, Canonbury, London, N. Born at Enfield. Educated at The Palace School. A R.C.O. Organist St Mark's, Old Street, 1868 , St Andrew by the Wardrobe, 1873 ; St. Augustine's, Highbury, 1878 , Christ Church, New North Road, 1886 , St Paul's, Canonbury 1903 , Alexander Palace, 1900 ; St. Mary's Parish Church, Islington, since 1907. Hobbies : Bees, canaries, fishing.

COLDWELL, DAVID JOHN, Penge, St Thomas' Road, Launceston Born at Walton-on-Thames. Educated at Portsmouth Grammar School F.R.C.O. Formerly Assistant Organist All Saints', Ryde, I W. ; St. Anne's, Soho, W. Organist and Choirmaster St. Mary's, Hadleigh, Suffolk, 1896-1907 ; St. Mary Magdalene, Launceston, since 1907. Publications . Communion and Evening Services

COLEMAN, HENRY, 181, Preston New Road, Blackburn. Born 1888 at Dartmouth Articled pupil of S. H. Nicholson, M A , MUS BAC., of Carlisle and Manchester Cathedrals. Studied piano under Mr. Percy Walker, Professor of Matthay School of Pianoforte. F.R.C.O. Organist and Choirmaster St Stephen's, Carlisle, 1908-09. Sub-Organist Manchester Cathedral, 1910-12 Organist and Choirmaster Blackburn Parish Church, since 1912. Club : Old Rectory, Deansgate, Manchester.

COLLEDGE, A N McLEOD, Rosemount, Douglas Road, Hawick. L L.C M. Organist St. John's Episcopal, Selkirk, 1894-1898 ; Walkerburn Parish Church, 1898-1901 ; Hawick Parish Church since 1901. Music Master to Buccleuch Higher Grade School.

COLLINGS, R PERCY, Cannon House, Chagford. A.R.C O. (July 1911). Born at Chudleigh, Devon, 1884. Studied music under Mr. W J. Bown, A.R C.O , Newton Abbott ; and Mr. Stanley Chipperfield, F.R.C.O., Organist of Richmond (Surrey) Parish Church. Assistant

Organist Richmond (Surrey) Parish Church, 1902-4 ; Organist and Choirmaster St. Barnabas Church, Acton Vale, W., 1903-4 ; Chagford Parish Church, Devon, since 1904. Conductor Chagford Choral Society. Hobbies and recreations : Photography, billiards and cycling. Club : Chudleigh Constitutional.

COLLINSON, THOMAS H., 5, Portgower Place, Edinburgh. MUS. BAC. OXON , F R C.O. Organist St Mary's Cathedral, Edinburgh, since 1878 ; Organist to Edinburgh University.

COMBEN, A. WHITE, 16, Tregarvon Road, Clapham Common, S.W. Born 1876 in London. Organist Claverton Street Wesleyan Church, S W., since 1896

CONWAY, M.P., La Rona, King's Avenue, Eastbourne. Born in London 1885 Educated privately, and at the Royal College of Music. MUS. BAC (OXON), F R C.O , A R C.M. Organist Upperton Congregational Church, Eastbourne, 1900-2 , Assistant Organist St. Saviour's, Eastbourne, 1902-9 ; All Saints', Eastbourne, since 1908 Recreation Boating.

COOKE, JAMES RANDALL, 9, Dudley, Road, West Bromwich. Born (1865), and educated at West Bromwich. Professor of music Conductor of Choral Society and West Bromwich Male Voice Choir Conductor of The Dudley Operatic Society , formerly West Bromwich Operatic Society , Oldbury Operatic Society Organist St Philip's Church, West Bromwich, 1899-1909 , St. Luke's, Dudley, since 1909.

COOKE, SYDNEY HERBERT, Dunevis, Pitlochry, N B. Born and educated at Warwick. Organist St Nicholas Parish Church, Warwick, 1887-1900 ; St Margaret's Episcopal Church, Aberlour, 1900-4 ; Holy Trinity Episcopal Church, 1904-8. Conductor Pitlochry Musical Society and Orchestral Society Published .compositions include songs , Pianoforte pieces, " Cradle Song " for violin and Pianoforte (dedicated to, and played by Miss Marie Hall), anthems, etc.

COOKE, SIMON P., 28, Wallace Lane, Whelley, Wigan. Born 1853 at Downall Green, N Ashton-in-Makerfield. Educated at Seneley Green Grammar School. Clerk and cashier Organist Billinge Parish Church, 1864-9, St. Catherine's, Wigan, 1869 to 1887 ; Bolton, Park Street Church, 1889 to 1894 ; St. Catherine's, Wigan, since 1895.

COOKE, WILLIAM, Brookfield Road, Lymm. Born 1874 at Widnes. Educated at Runcorn. F R C O. Professor of Music. Organist St Paul's, Widnes, 1896-1900 , All Saints, St. Helen's, Lancs., 1900-1908 , Lymm Parish Church, since 1908. Hobby and recreation : Walking and cycling.

COOKE, WILLIAM ERNEST, Schoolhouse, Goosnargh, Preston, Lancs. Born 1870 in London. Educated at Yorks. A.R.C O , A MUS. T.C L., A C P. Head Master, Oliverson's C E. School, Goosnargh Organist St. Mary's Goosnargh, Preston, since 1899 , Staveley, Derbys, 1894-6 ; Hixon, Stafford, 1896-9.

COOPER, MISS ELLEN MARY, 38, Hamilton Road, Highbury, London, N. Born at Highbury. Educated privately. Teacher of the pianoforte and organ. Organist St Jude's, Mildmay Park, 1867-9 ; St Michael's, Queenhithe, 1869-70 , Christ Church, Hampstead, 1870-9 ; Christ Church, Highbury, since 1880.

COOPER, L. C., 4, Pulteney Avenue, Pulteney Road, Bath. Born November 27th, 1887. Educated at London. Formerly Organist Halwill Church, N. Devon, at age of 16, for four years. Organist of St. Matthew's Church, Bath, October 1st, 1909.

COPAS, WILLIAM, Little Marlow, Bucks. Born (1872), and educated at Newbury, Berks. Organist Golden Common, nr. Winchester, 1891-3; Church of the Holy Cross, Newton Ferrers, Plymouth, 1894-1900; St. Lawrence's Church, Whitchurch, 1900-1908. St. John the Baptist Church, Little Marlow, since 1908.

COPE, Miss MARIA J. 1, Lanark Mansions, Maida Vale, W., London, W. Born and educated in London. Teacher of music. Musical trainer, Church Choral Society. Organist King's College, Hospital Chapel since 1892; Holy Trinity, Kingsway, London, since 1865

COPELAND, JOHN ALFRED, 85, Ayresome Street, Middlesborough. A.R.C.O., L.R.A.M., L.T.C.L. Organist St. James' Parish Church, Darlington, 1900-03; St. Paul's Parish Church, Middlesborough, since 1903.

CORBETT, FELIX, Southfield Villas, Middlesborough. Organist Parish Church, Middlesborough since 1882, and Middlesborough Town Hall since 1898. Composer of numerous songs, pianoforte, and organ composition. Organ recitals are given each Saturday from September to June; average attendance 700.

CORBETT, S., Burns Street, Nottingham. Born at Wellington, Salop. Educated privately. MUS. DOC. (CANTAB), F.R.C.O., L T.C L. Professor at Midland Institution for the Blind. Organist Holy Trinity, Bournemouth, 1892-7; St. Andrew's, Nottingham 1905 to 1908; Battlesford Church, since 1908. Publications: Songs, pianoforte and church music.

COTTRILL, WILFRED, E., 17, Summer Street, Glossop. Born 1867. Organist St. Mary's R.C., 1881; Littlemoor Chapel, 1886; Glossop Parish Church since 1887. Musical Director, Theatre Royal, Glossop. Hobbies and recreations: Fishing, shooting and natural history.

COULTER, ALBERT JOHN HUMPHREY, Down Cathedral, Downpatrick, Co. Down, Ireland. Soprano Chorister, and bass soloist, Down Cathedral, 1877-98; Organist Down Cathedral, since 1898. Festival Conductor, and Feis Adjudicator. Publications: Te Deum in B flat, anthem "Lift up your heads," Latin and English hymns, chants, carols, kyries, German and English song, "Es zogen drie Bursche," Rudyard Kipling's "Recessional" etc.

COVENEY, SIDNEY LOUIS. Born (1878), and educated at Dover. F.R.C.O., A. MUS. T.C.L. Teacher of music. Organist Buckland Wesleyan, Dover, 1895-1900; Congregational, Dover, 1900-04; St. John's Wesleyan, Llandudno, 1904-11; Queen's Road Baptist, Coventry, since 1911.

COX, JOHN W., Inglewood, Empress Avenue, Woodford Green. Born at Coggeshall. Formerly Organist and Choirmaster St. Saviour's, Walthamstow. Organist Woodford Parish Church, since 1910.

COX, MISS M. V., Berwyn, Abingdon, Berks. Born at Abingdon. Educated at Abingdon and Reading. Principal of Girls' Private School. Organist Congregational Church, Abingdon, Berks.

COX, VICTOR E., Frankfort House, Clevedon. Born 1887 at Clevedon. Trained under H. E. Marchant. Organist St. Andrew's Parish Church, Clevedon, since 1911. Profession : Master of Art School, Clevedon, specialising in wood and stone carving, sculpture, etc. Hobby : The organ and music generally.

COXALL, PHILIP HERRMANN, 17, Brandreth Road, Upper Tooting, London, S.W. Born 1877 in London. F.R.C.O. Organist St. Philips, Battersea, 1899-1906 ; Holy Trinity, Richmond, Surrey, 1906-7 ; Christ Church, St. Marylebone, N.W. 1907-11 ; St. Saviour's, St. George's Square, Pimlico, since 1911.

CRACKEL, H., Branksome, Fitzwilliam Road, Rotherham, Yorks. Born 1876 at Rotherham. Educated privately. F.R.C.O. Organist St. John's, Masbro', Rotherham, 1889-91 ; Parish Church, Eastwood, Rotherham, since 1901. Contributor of organ compositions to the following :—" The Organ-Loft," " Ecclesiæ Organum," " The Recital Organist " and the " Choir " series of organ compositions, etc., etc.

CRADDOCK, CHARLES S., 9, Anne Street, Clonmel, Ireland. Born at Padstow, 1861. Educated at Torquay. Music Master New College, Margate, 1885. Organist Parish Church, Clonmel, since 1888 ; Garrison Church, Clonmel, since 1897. Conductor Clonmel Choral Society. Composer of : " Song of the Wrens," " Gather ye rosebuds," " Days that are no More," " When he who adores Thee " ; part songs, and " All Thy Works praise Thee " anthem, all of which have obtained prizes at the Irish Musical Festival, Dublin. Club : Donoughmore, Clonmel.

CRAPPS, JOHN, Heatherdene, Henfield, Sussex. Born at Brighton, 1845. Pupil of Chas. Goodban, MUS. BAC. (who was a pupil of Vincent Novello, who took lessons of Joseph Haydn). Organist and Choirmaster St. Andrew's, Hove, 1869-1900 ; All Saints, Brighton, 1900-1906 ; St. Peter's Parish Church, Henfield, since 1906. Musical Director to the Brighton Corporation, 1896-1901. Conductor of numerous Choral Societies.

CRAWFORD, THOMAS J., 2, Elizabeth Street, Eaton Square, London, S.W. MUS. BAC. DUNELM., F.R C.O., M.I.S.M., 1st Prize Leipzig Conservatoire. Organist All Saints', Leipzig, 1894-98 ; Holy Trinity, Eltham, 1898-9 ; St. Paul's, Camden Square, 1899-1902 ; St. Michael's, Chester Square, since 1902. Publications : Pieces for organ, piano ; songs and Communion Service. Hobby : Model engineering.

CREATON, M. E., Hollow Way, Temple Cowley, Oxford. Born at Oxford. A.L.C.M. Organist Cowley Church, Oxford, since 1911.

CRERAR, PETER, 14, Hillend Road, Arbroath. Formerly Organist and Choirmaster St. James' Parish Church, Edinburgh. Organist St. Vigean's Parish Church, Arbroath, since 1896.

CRIMP, HERBERT E., 65, South Street, Leominster. Born 1870. Formerly a member of Savoy Theatre Company ; theatrical conductor on tour ; reader for a music publishing firm, and Organist Holy Trinity Church New Barnet. Composer of music. Organist Priory Church, Leominster, since 1905.

CROAGER, EDWARD GEORGE, Flint Cottage, Amersham Common, Bucks. Born 1861. A.R.A.M. Sub-Organist St. Andrew's, Wells Street, 1877-83 ; Organist and Choirmaster Quebec Chapel, 1884-7 ; St. Mark's,

North Audley Street, 1888-90 ; St. James', West Hampstead, 1891-7 ;
St. Paul's, Avenue Road, London, N.W., since 1898. Publication :
" Our Watchword " (Patriotic Cantata). Hobby : Beekeeping. Club :
R.A.M.

CROMPTON, WILLIAM, 12, Kildare Street, Farnworth. Born at Farnworth
and educated at Worsley. A.R.C.O. Music Teacher. Organist St.
Stephen's, Kearsley, 1885-89 ; St. John the Baptist, Little Hulton,
since 1889. Publications : " Sweet Lily " (Schottische) and " Joyous
Moments " (Gavotte).

CROSSLEY, WALKER, Stanley Bank, New Road, Radcliffe. Born 1883 at
Radcliffe. Educated under Dr. Walter Carroll, at Victoria University
(Queen's College), R.C.M. and Bury Parish Church. MUS. BAC. DUNELM.,
F.R.C.O. Assistant Organist Bury Parish Church, 1905. Organist and
Choirmaster St. Matthew's Parish Church, Little Lever, Bolton, since
1910.

CROSSLEY, WILLIAM T., 197, Undercliffe Street, Bradford, Yorks. Born
(1867) and educated at Bradford. Associate Royal College of Organists.
Deputy Organist St. Paul's, Manningham, Bradford, 1885-7. Organist
Mannville Chapel, 1888-9 ; and Wesley Church, Lowmoor, Bradford,
since 1889. Publications : " Yorkshire Songs," prize anthems and
hymn tunes. Recreations : Reading and walking.

CROUCH, WALTER CHAPMAN, 43, Chesterton Road, Kensington, London,
W. Born 1884 in London. Trained under H W. Weston, Esq.,
MUS BAC., F.R.C.O., A.R.C.M. A. and L.L.C.M Assistant Organist
Brunswick Wesleyan Church, 1902-4 ; Organist Brunswick Wesleyan
Church, 1904-6 ; Victoria Wesleyan Church, 1906-1911 ; Denbigh
Road Wesleyan Church, since 1911. Publications : Vesper Hymn,
" Through the Day Thy Love Hath Spared Us " ; Children's Hymn,
" Onward, Children, Onward."

CROWE, FREDERICK JOSEPH WILLIAM, St. Peter's House, Chichester.
F.R.A.S., F.R. HIST., SOC. Born near Weston-super-Mare. Educated at
Wells Cathedral and Milan. Formerly Assistant Organist Wells
Cathedral ; Organist, Ashburton, and St. Mary Magdalene, Torquay.
Founder and Conductor of vairous Choral Societies in Devon. Past-
Grand Organist of Grand Lodge, Grand Chapter, and Mark Grand
Lodge of England. Organist and Master of the Choristers Chichester
Cathedral, since 1902. Professor of Music Bishop Otter Training
College for Teachers. Hon. Conductor Cathedral Oratorio Society,
Chichester Orchestral Society, Chichester Amateur Operatic Society,
and Bognor Musical Society. Hobbies and recreation : Astronomy,
architecture, Free Masonry.

CROXALL, THOMAS BERTRAM, 14, Regent Street, Church Gresley, Burton-on-
Trent. Born at Church Gresley, 1881. MUS. BAC. DUNELM., 1904 ;
F.R.C.O., 1902 ; L.R.A.M, pianoforte, 1899. Organist Woodville
Wesleyan, 1897-1900 ; Egginton Parish Church, 1900-2 ; Swadlincote
Parish Church, since 1902 ; and Swadlincote Harmonic Society, since
1906

CRUSH, GEORGE T, Lynwood, Hampden Terrace, Eastbourne. Born 1877
at Horsebridge, Sussex. Trained under H Baillie and Smallwood
Metcalf. Organist Central Wesleyan Church, Ea tbourne, since 1893.
Conductor Eastbourne Musical Fraternity.

CRUSHA, EDWIN ARTHUR, 19, Church Street, Lower Edmonton, London, N. Born 1863. Educated at Edmonton Grammar School. F R.C.O., L. MUS. T.C.L. Teacher of Music Organist All Saints' Church, Edmonton, N , since 1889. Singing Master since 1889. Publications : Services and organ pieces.

CULLEY, REV. ARNOLD DUNCAN, The College, Durham. Born at Great Yarmouth, Norfolk. Organ Scholar Emmanuel College, Cambridge. M.A., MUS. BAC. CANTAB., M.A. DUNELM., F.R.C.O., A.R.C.M. Norfolk and Norwich scholar. R.C.M. Trained at R.C.M. Sub-Organist Exeter Cathedral, 1900-1906. Organist and Master of the Choristers Durham Cathedral, since 1907. Minor Canon and Precentor, Durham Cathedral, since 1906. Curate Chapel Royal, Brighton, 1894-1897. Deputy Priest-Vicar, Exeter Cathedral, 1897-1906.

CUNNINGHAM, GEORGE DORRINGTON, 6, Leaside Avenue, Muswell Hill, London, N. Born in London. F R C O , A R.A M Organist Alexandra Palace since 1901 ; St. James', Muswell Hill, since 1901.

CURRAN, JOHN, Ventnor House, Myatt's Park, London, S E Born 1872 in Bombay. Educated at City of London School. F.RC.O. Assistant Organist St. Luke's, Camberwell, 1887 ; St. Peter's, Brockley, 1889. Organist St. Mary's, Byfleet, 1891 ; All Saints', Norfolk Square, 1892 ; Wesleyan Church, Putney, since 1894. Accompanist St. Peter's Choral Society 1892, and Secretary 1900. Local Secretary Trinity College of Music. Professor Solo Singing, South London Institute. Conductor Oratorio Choir, Putney. Publication : Service music. Hobby and recreation : Cycling, drama.

CURRY, THOMAS, 442, High Road, Chiswick. Born 1885 at Pimlico Trained under G. R. Egerton. Organist All Saints', Acton, 1875 ; Holy Trinity, Richmond, 1896 ; St. Andrew by the Wardrobe, City, 1909 ; St. John's, Clapham, since 1910. Publication : Congregational Responses. Recreation : Cycling.

CURTIS, SIDNEY M , Norfolk House, Norfolk Crescent, Bath. Born at Bath, 1869 Professor of the Violin. Organist and Choirmaster Holy Trinity, Bath, since 1885. Publications : Romance for Violin and Piano (Vincent Publishing Company) ; Gipsy Dance for Violin and Piano ; anthem, " The Glory of God " ; text book, " The Ornaments used in Music " (Hutchings & Romer).

CUSTARD, EDWARD REGINALD HERBERT GOSS, " Thornleigh," St. Matthew's Avenue, Surbiton. Born 1877 at St. Leonards-on-Sea. Educated under his father, Walter Goss Custard. Organist St. Mary's, Battle, 1894-1900 ; (Assistant) St. Margaret's, Westminster, 1900-2 ; St. Margaret's, Westminster, since 1902 Publications : Twenty original compositions for organ and numerous arrangements.

CUSTARD, HENRY GOSS, 7, Esmond Gardens, Ealing, London, W. Born 1871 at St. Leonards-on-Sea, MUS. BAC. OXON. Organist Christ Church, Blacklands, Hastings, 1887 ; Holy Trinity, Hastings, 1890 ; St- John's, Deptford, S.E., 1902 ; St. Saviour's, Ealing, London, W., since 1904, also Hon Borough Organist Publication : Communion service. Hobby : Fishing.

DAGLISH, WILLIAM THOMAS, East View, Dipton, R.S.O., Durham. Organist St. John the Evangelist, Dipton, 1887-1905 ; St. Thomas', Collierly, since 1905.

DALE, A. V., 25, Pagitt Street, Chatham, Kent.   Born in 1871 at Rochester. Educated at the London Academy of Music.   F.R.C O. Borstal, Rochester. Publications : Organ Music (Donajowski), Services (Weekes), Anthems (Culley).

DALTON, HORACE MONTAGUE.   Born 1884 at Garforth, near Leeds.   Educated at Hook Memorial Church and private.   A.R.C.O.   Sub-Organist Hook Memorial Church, Leeds, 1898-1902.   Organist and Choirmaster St. Paul's, Shadwell, Leeds, 1902-07 ; St. John's, Collingham, Leeds, 1907-09 ; St. Bartholomew's, Sheffield, 1909-10 ; St. George's, Leeds, since 1910.   Conductor Collingham and Linton Choral Society, Bardsley Choral Society.

DANSIE, REDGEWELL, 28, Gleneagle Road, Streatham, S.W., and Bechstein Studios, 40, Wigmore Street, London.   Born 1883 in London.   Educated privately and R.A.M.   F R C.O., A.MUS.T.C.L., INTER. MUS. BAC. DUNELM.   Silver Medalist and Certificate R.A.M.   Vocalist.   Assistant Organist and Choirmaster St. Matthew's, Denmark Hill, 1900.   Organist and Choirmaster Christ Church, Camberwell, 1902 ; Christ Church, Hendon, 1905 ; Camden Parish Church, 1907 ; St. John's Church, Clapham, since 1911.   Principal of Ffrangcon-Davies School of Singing, London.   Hobby : Literature.

DARBY, ERNEST, Clifton Terrace, Chapel Ash, Wolverhampton.   Born (1873) and educated at Wolverhampton.   MUS. BAC. DUNELM., A R.C.O. Organist Bushby Parish Church, 1896-8 ; St. Mark's, Wolverhampton, since 1899.   Conductor Albrighton Choral Society, 1900 ; Bannock and District Choral Society, 1901 ; Wolverhampton Choral Union, since 1905.

DARBY, FREDERIC MILMAN, 2, Salisbury Street, Warrington.   MUS. BAC. OXON., F R.C.O.   Organist St. John's, Eastbourne, 1892-5 ; Cliffe, Lewes, 1895 ; St. Peter's, Eastbourne, 1896-1909 ; Parish Church, Warrington, since 1900.

DAVIES, CLIFFORD, Ilkeston, Chalford Road, Whalley Range, Manchester. Born 1864 at Manchester.   Educated by C. B. Grundy, Esq.   Member of the Incorporated Society of Musicians.   Professional musician. Organist Oxford Road Wesleyan, Manchester, 1885-90.   Organist and Choirmaster Methodist New Connexion, Boston Street, Manchester, 1891-96 ; Plymouth Grove Wesleyan, Manchester, since 1897.   Hobby Reading.

DAVIES, E. T , Cartrefle, Merthyr Tydfil, S. Wales.   Born 1879 at Dowlais. Educated at Dowlais, and Merthyr Tydfil High School   F.R.C.O. Hon Examiner and Local Representative R.A.M., R.C.M.   Local Secretary Trinity College London.   Member of Council (South Wales Section), Incorporated Society of Musicians.   Organist Pontmorlais Welsh Methodist Church, Merthyr, since 1902.   Toured with Welsh concert party in America, 1899 ; Ben Davies' concert party, 1905 ; Evangeline Florance, 1906.   Conductor Merthyr and District Choral Society, Dowlais Operatic Society.   Music Master County School, Merthyr.   Adjudicator, Conductor, Organist, and teacher of singing, etc.   Composer of anthems, part songs, and pianoforte works.   Recreations : Tennis, golf, and reading.

DAVIES, ROBERT WORDSWORTH, 39, Fern Grove, Sefton Park, Liverpool. Born 1860 at Liverpool.   Educated under Dr. Röhmer.   Organist St. Peter's Parish Church, Rock Ferry, Birkenhead, since 1879.   Publications : Songs, etc.

DAVEY, HERBERT W., 52, Avenue Road, North Finchley, London, N. Born 1885 at Clapton. Trained under Herbert Swain, I.S.M. Organist Hackney Baptist, 1907-8; Dalston Baptist, 1908-9; Enfield Town Baptist, 1909. Hobby and recreations: Photography, cycling and gardening. Recitalist London and provinces.

DAVIES, T., 15, Westbourne Crescent, Cardiff. Born at Brecon 1853. MUS. BAC. (DUNELM), A.R.C.O., A. MUS. T.C.L. Harmony Prizeman, 1882, T.C.L. Choir Trainer to the Arch-Deaconry of Brecon. Organist and Choirmaster St. Edmund's, Crickhowell, up to 1889; and St. Mary The Virgin, Cardiff, since 1889. Hon. Local Examiner, R.C.M.

DAVIS, CYRIL, 19, St. George's Place, Northampton. Born 1889 at Gloucester. Educated at Culham College, Oxon. Assistant Master. Organist of Culham College, and deputy Conductor of the Choral and Orchestral Society, 1907-9. Organist and Choirmaster St. Paul's, Northampton, since 1909. Compositions: " Crossing the Bar " (quartet); anthems—" Abide with Me," " Out of the Deep," " God is a Spirit "; Vesper Hymn, Quintuple Amen, hymns and chants. Hobbies and recreations: Music, tennis, boating, organ tuning. Culham Club.

DAVIS, HENRY JAMES, 6, Alfred Street, Bath. Born (1869), and educated at Bath. L.R.A.M. Organist Bathampton Church, 1882; accompanist, Bath Philharmonic Society, 1884; Assistant Organist, St. Mary's, Bathwick, 1884. Organist and Choirmaster Christ Church, Bath, since 1888. Hon. Conductor, Orpheus Glee Society, since 1900. Has given over 160 monthly organ recitals on Sunday afternoons, from October to May.

DAVIS, REV. THOMAS HENRY, The Liberty, Wells Born 1867 at Birmingham. Educated at King Edward's School, Birmingham. B.A., MUS. DOC., F.R.C.O. Clergyman. Priest-Vicar Wells Cathedral, 1895-99. Organist and Choirmaster Wells Cathedral since 1899. Prebendary of Combe VIII., Wells Cathedral, 1912.

DAVISON, WILLIAM J., 17, Osborne Avenue, South Shields. Born 1882 at Jarrow-on-Tyne. Educated at Higher Grade School, South Shields and Armstrong College, Newcastle. Assistant Schoolmaster. Organist St. Andrew's Congregational, South Shields, 1900-1906; Ocean Road Congregational Church, South Shields, 1906-9. Organist and Choirmaster St. Paul's Presbyterian Church, South Shields, since 1909.

DAWSON, GEORGE CUMMINGS, 64, Bon Accord Street, Aberdeen. Born at Durham. Educated at Durham Cathedral. Head Music Master, Aberdeen High School for Girls. Organist St. Machar's Cathedral, Aberdeen, since 1893. Past positions: Organist St. Andrew's, Aberdeen, and Holburn Parish Church, Aberdeen. Hobby: Cycling.

DAWSON, E. INMAN, 30, Brunswick Street, Westboro', Dewsbury. Born 1875. A.L.C.M. Teacher of music. Organist Dewsbury Moor Parish Church, since 1895.

DAWSON, HERBERT J., 6, Liverpool Road, Ealing, London, W. MUS. BAC. (CANTAB), L R.A.M., F.R.C.O. Formerly Assistant Organist Norwich Cathedral; St. Baldreds, N. Berwick; Eltham Parish Church. Organist Parish Church, Ealing, since 1903.

DEAR, James, R., Kildare, Arundel Road, Eastbourne. Born at Ventnor, I.W. Educated at Westminster Abbey, and privately. MUS. BAC., F.R.C.O. Organist St. Giles Church, South Myms, 1889, St. Lukes, Uxbridge Road, W., 1893; St. James', West Hampstead, 1898; St Saviours, Eastbourne, since 1899. Composer of " Leap of Kurroglou " for baritone solo, chorus and orchestra, " Songs of the Open Air " for baritone solo, chorus and orchestra (produced at Brighton Festival, 1910), church music, part songs, songs, etc. Recreations: Golf and tennis.

DEAVIN, Herbert Charles, 108, London Road, Gloucester. Born 1888 at Bowbridge, Stroud. Trained under C. H. Deavin, sen. A R.C.O. Chorister Gloucester Cathedral, 1898-1903. Deputy Organist St. Michael's, Gloucester, 1903-06. Organist Matson Parish Church, Gloucester, 1906; St. Mark's, Gloucester, since 1906 Assistant Master Archdeacon Street Council School, Gloucester. Publications: Songs, " The Sea Hath its Pearls " and " Two Songs of Farewell "; hymns, " An Auxiliary Hymn Book "; carols, " It Came upon the Midnight Clear " and " In a Lowly Stable." Recreations Rowing, cricket and most outdoor sports. Hobby : Study of English literature. Member of Gloucester Choral Society.

DENHAM, George, L.R.A.M., A.R.C.O. Music Master South Eastern College, Ramsgate, for seven years. Organist and Choirmaster Emmanuel Church, S. Croydon, since 1906.

DENMAN, Albert Ernest, Ivy Cottage, Stanmore, Middlesex Born 1875 at Croydon. Educated at Guildhall School of Music. F R C O , L.R.A.M , A.G S M Organist St. Mark's, Camberwell, 1892-1904 , St. Peter add Vincula, Tower of London, 1894-1896; St. John the Evangelist Parish Church, Stanmore, since 1898.

DENNIS, Arthur Llewelyn, 93, London Road, Neath. Born 1882 at Neath. Trained under L. H. Torr, F.R.C.O., Swansea. Organist Maes-y-rhaf Welsh Congregational Church, Neath, 1896-1903. Choirmaster Wesley Church, Neath, 1907-11. Organist and Choirmaster Gnoll Road Congregational Church, Neath, since 1912.

DERRICK, Alan James, Wadham College, Oxford. Born 1889 at Nottingham. Trained under F. Dunnill. Organist and Choirmaster St Mark's, Nottingham, 1907-09. Acting Organist Boston Parish Church, 1910 ; St Augustine's, Nottingham, 1910 ; St. Ive's Parish Church, Cornwall, 1911. Organist Wadham College, Oxford.

DERRICK-LARGE, W. H , 76, Wellington Park, Belfast. Educated, St. John's College, Hurstpierpoint. Organist Holy Trinity, Melrose, N.B., 1890 ; Belfast Y.M C.A. 1906-09 ; Christ Church, Belfast ; St. Thomas's, Belfast, since 1904. Conductor Belfast City Choral Society. Publications : Settings of kyries, and Benedicite. Hobby : Photography.

DERRY, H. Bromley, St. Mawes, St. Mary's Road, Ealing. Born 1885 at Stratford-on-Avon Educated at King Edward VI. School, Stratford-on-Avon. F.R.C.O. (1907). Professor of Organ, Piano, Singing, 'Cello, Harmony and Counterpoint. Assistant Organist Stratford-on-Avon Collegiate Church of the Holy Trinity, 1903. Organist and Choirmaster St. Mary's, Vauxhall, S.E., 1908 ; All Saints', Ealing, since 1908. Studied under Sir Walter Parratt, Sir F. Bridge, Drs. Alcock, Reed and Hoyte. 1906-10 at R C.M. Council Exhibitioner in Organ Playing, 1909-10.

DIBB, FRANK, 35, Worcester Road, Bootle, near Liverpool. Born 1872 at Liverpool. Educated at Newton School, Rockferry. Studied the pianoforte under Mynheer M. E. P. Zepher, and later under Herr Adolph Kransse, at the German Institute of Music, Liverpool. Studied the organ under Mr. R. Wordsworth Davies, of St. Peter's, Rockferry. F.R C.O. Organist and Choirmaster St. Luke's, Tranmere, 1889 ; Wallasey Parish Church, 1896 ; St. Paul's, Birkenhead, 1899 ; St. Catherine's, Tranmere, 1902 ; Christ Church, Bootle, since 1906.

DICKIE, W. J. I., Kirklands, Rawmarsh, Rotherham. Born 1875 at Wentworth. Educated R.C.M., L.R A.M Exhibitioner R.C.M. Violinist and Choral Conductor. Organist Trinity Church, Wentworth, since 1901. Hobbies : Hunting and shooting.

DIXON-SMITH, J., Daledene, Stanhope Road, Deal. Born 1882 at Norwood. Educated Royal College of Music. F.R.C.O. Musician. Organist Lambeth Palace Chapel, 1906 ; St. Anne's Parish Church, Limehouse, 1906 ; St. George's, Deal, since 1908 Clubs : R. C. M. Union, member I.S.M.

DOBSON, WILLIAM SILKSTONE, 5, Alma Road, Birkdale, Southport. Born 1869 at Manchester. Educated at Southport, Liverpool, and London. L R.A.M., L. MUS. T.C.L. Organ recitalist. Teacher of organ, pianoforte, singing, harmony, etc. Organist Methodist Free Church, Duke Street, Southport, 1886-8 ; Christ Church, Southport, since 1888. Sub-Organist, St. Peter's, Eaton Square, London, S W., since 1907.

DOBINSON, MARK, Tigh Ruadh, Crieff. Born at Bassenthwaite, Cumbs. Educated in music, Carlisle Cathedral. Music Master, Girls' School, Morrison's Academy, Crieff. Formerly Organist St. Mary's, Carlisle ; Parish Church, Inverleithen. Organist Crieff Parish Church, since 1889. Hobby : Gardening.

DOCKSEY, ARTHUR. Educated R.A.M MUS. DOC., F.R.C.O. Formerly Organist St. Aisan's, South Shields. Organist Parish Church, South Shields, since 1903.

DODDS, GEORGE, 4, Warrington Road, Westmorland Road, Newcastle-on-Tyne. Born 1876 at Newcastle. Educated R.C.M. and private. MUS BAC. (DUNELM), L R.A M , A R.C.M. Teacher of singing and voice production. Organist Corbridge Parish Church, 1892-94 ; St. Paul's, Newcastle, 1894-1900 ; Elswick Road, Wesleyan, since 1900. Conductor Newcastle Philharmonic Society, 1901-7, Jarrow Philharmonic Society, Newcastle and District Nonconformist Choir Union, 1912. Clubs : " Pen and Palette," Newcastle, Newcastle Liberal Club.

DODDS, H. YEAMAN, 61, Fern Avenue, Newcastle-on-Tyne. Born 1878 at Newcastle-on-Tyne. Educated R.C.M., London. A.R.C.M , L.R.A.M. Organist Wesleyan Memorial Church, North Shields, since 1899. Hobbies : Fishing and Motoring. Club : " Pen and Palette," Newcastle.

DOORLY, C CARTE, Church House, Beverley, E., Yorks. Organist St. Stephen's, Hull, 1889 ; St. Michael's, Appleby, 1894 ; St. John's Episcopal, Dumfries, 1895 ; Yaxham Church, Norfolk, 1896 ; St. Mary's, Beverley, since 1897.

DOUGLASS, ERNEST, Prideaux, Gosport. A.R C.O. Organist Holy Trinity, Gosport, 1893-9 ; St. Mary's, Alverstoke, Gosport, since 1899. Conductor Gosport and Alverstoke Choral Society.

DOUGLAS, HARRY, The Rowans, Matlock. Born at Matlock. Educated at the Cavendish School, Matlock. Organ diploma, Incorporated Society of Musicians; Member of Royal College of Organists; Member of the Derby and District Organists' Association. Composer of organ pieces (Novello and Co.), hymn tunes, etc. Secretary, Matlock Choral Union, since 1902; Organist, Congregational Church, Matlock, since 1902; Secretary, Matlock Orchestral Society, since 1907. Hobbies and recreations: Rifle shooting, golf, motor cycling and stamp collecting Clubs: English XX., Matlock Conservative Club, The Matlock Club.

DOULTON, HUBERT, The Blue House, Dulwich Common, S E. Born in 1864 at Dulwich. Educated private. M.A. Oxford. Master of music at Dulwich College, September, 1901.

DOWNES, PERCY WALTER, Vine Cottage, Bromley Street, Stepney, London, E. Born 1882 at Poplar. Educated at Poplar. Municipal Officer. Organist St. Dunstan's, Stepney, since 1903. Hobby: Photography.

DUCKET, HENRY ARMSTONE, Bresby, Perivale, West Ealing, London, W. Born 1877 at Birmingham. Educated at private boarding school, Hungerford, Berkshire. Organist Perivale Parish Church, Ealing, London, W., since 1903.

DUFFELL, JOHN, 107, Millhouses Lane, Sheffield. Born 1871 at Tipton, Staffs Educated privately. Professor of Music. Graduated B. MUS. London, 1899. Organist St. John's Wesleyan Church, Sheffield, 1892-1900; Wesleyan Church, Carver Street, since 1903. Conductor Sheffield Choral Society, Sheffield Amateur Instrumental Society, Sheffield Grand Opera Society, Sheffield Teachers' Operatic Society, Worksop Operatic Society. Music Master Eton House High School, Sheffield. Instructor in Music Sheffield University Training College Department. Composer of music. Recreation: Cycling and walking.

DUNLOP, JOHN C., 33, Adnitt Road, Northampton. Born and educated at Westminster. Formerly Organist Seaford Parish Church, Sussex; St. Michael's, Appleby, Westmoreland; St. Luke's, Newcastle-on-Tyne. Organist St. Michael's and All Angels', since 1902. Hobbies: Cycling, reading.

DUNN, MATTHEW, 114, Clonmore Street, Southfields, London, S.W. Born 1872 at Glasgow. Educated privately. A.R.C.M., F I.S.C. (honours), Society of Arts medalist and prizeman. Voice specialist. Sub-Organist St. Luke's, Brondesbury, 1896-98. Organist St. John the Baptist, Putney, S.W., since 1898. Publications: Church music, songs and pianoforte music. Hobby and recreation: Reading and cycling.

DUNSFORD, B G. W., 15, Longfield Terrace, Frome, Somerset. Born at Frome in 1890. Educated as chorister, York Minster. Pupil of T. Tertius Noble, Esq. Organist Garrison Church, York, 1907-1910; St. Philip and St. James', Clifton, Whit Sunday, 1910; Bortham Asylum Chapel, July, 1910.

DYE, ALFRED JOHN, Townley House, Woodbridge, Suffolk. Born at Lowestoft. Trained under well-known London men. L. MUS. T.C.L. Member I.S.M. Organist and Choirmaster St. Martin's, Haverstock Hill, London, 1869; Eaton Episcopal Chapel, Eaton Square, S.W., 1870-73; Christ Church, Crouch End, N., 1873-1907; Parish Church, Woodbridge, since 1907. Publications: Church music, violin solos, piano solos, part songs, military band and full orchestra marches. Hobby: Photography.

DYSON, GEORGE, The College, Marlborough. Trained at R.C.M. and abroad. MUS. BAC OXON., F.R.C.O., A.R.C.M. Formerly Organist Parish Church, Greenwich and Royal Naval College, Osborne. Organist and Director of Music, Marlborough College.

EDWARDS, ARTHUR CHARLES, Tan-y-graig, Trinity Road, Aberystwyth. Born at Peterborough, 1869. Educated at King's School, Peterborough. Trained at Llandaff and Southwark Cathedrals. MUS. BAC. OXON, Fellow Royal College of Organists. Organist St. Neot's, Hunts, 1892 ; Framlingham College, 1894 ; Bridlington Parish Church, 1896 ; St. Andrew's, Croydon, 1902 ; Holy Trinity, Aberystwyth, since 1906. Publications : Anthems, etc. Recreations : Cycling, Climbing, mathematical problems.

EDWARDS, ALBERT H., 20, St. Dunstan's Road, West Kensington, London, W. Born at Chelmsford, 1869. Educated Trinity College, London, and Rochester Cathedral. MUS. D. (Trinity College, Dublin), F.R.C.O. Organist St. George's, Barrow-in-Furness, 1891 ; St. Mary's, Brecon, 1894 ; Christ Church, Doncaster, 1896 St. Mary Magdalene's, Bradford, 1899 ; St. Mary's, West Kensington, 1911. Publications : "200 Melodies for Harmonization," "100 Transposition Tests," "250 Rhymical Figured Basses," choir, organ and pianoforte music, songs, etc.

EDWARDS, BURMAN HERRICK, 27, Clarendon Road, Lewisham, London, S.E. Born at Erdington, Warwickshire. Educated at Cheltenham. A.R.C.O. Assistant Organist Holy Trinity, Cheltenham, 1897-1900. Assistant to Dr. Warwick Jordan, at St. Stephen's, Lewisham, and St. Paul's Cathedral, for the Festivals of the London Gregorian Choral Association, 1900-1909. Organist St. Augustine's, Grove Park, Lee, S E., 1903-1908. Organist and Director of the Choir St. Laurence, Catford, S.E., 1908. Organist and Director of the Choir (Plainsong) at All Saints' Boys' Orphanage, Lewisham, since 1904. Member of the Committee of the London Gregorian Choral Association, 1909. Hobbies and recreation : Railways, photography and cycling. Club : The Railway Club, Victoria Street, Westminster.

EDWARDS, NELSON VICTOR, 99, Keighley Road, Colne. Born at Bath, 1888. Educated privately. F.R.C.O., L. MUS. T.C.L., L.I.S.M. Professor of Music. Assistant Organist St. Mary's Bathwick, Bath, 1905-7. Assistant Music Master Bath College, 1906-7. Assistant Organist Norwich Cathedral, 1907-8 ; Organist and Choirmaster Ellacombe Parish Church, Torquay, 1908-11 ; Parish Church, Colne, since 1911. Hon. Conductor Ellacombe Choral and Orchestral Society, 1908-9. Professor of Music, Colne Technical School, since 1911.

EDWARDS, SIDNEY, 147, High Street, Sevenoaks. Born 1865 at Southwark, S.E. Educated privately under Drs. Marchant and McIntosh. Organist Wesleyan Church, Sevenoaks, since 1882.

EDWARDS, T. D., L.R.A.M., A.R.C.M., F.T.S.C, School of Music, Treharris, Glam. Born at Pittston, Pa , U.S. America. Organist and Choirmaster Brynhyfryd Baptist Church, Treharris (formerly of Salem Baptist Church, Porth). Conductor of the Brynhyfryd Choral Society and the Pontypridd Musical Society. Organist of the Porth Harmonic (Oratorio) Society. Hon. Local Representative of the Royal Academy of Music, London ; Local Representative and Examiner of the Tonic Sol fa College, London; Member of the Free Church Musician's Union and Royal College of Organists ; Organ Recitalist, Eisteddfod Adjudicator, Conductor of Choral Festivals. Composer of popular songs, pianoforte pieces, part songs, anthems, etc.

EGGLETON, WALTER LAWRENCE., 3, Walnut Tree Road, Greenwich, S.E. Born 1885 at Greenwich. Trained privately and at City of London College. Organist and Choirmaster Greenwich Road Congregational Church, 1906-10 ; Bishopsgate (Congregational) Chapel, since 1910. Hobby and recreation : Reading and tennis.

ELLIS, JOHN, Music Studio, 31, Spring Bank, Hull. Born 1865 at Kingston-upon-Hull Formerly Organist Lincoln Street P.M. Chapel, Hull (at the age of 17) and Baptist Church, Beverley Road, Hull. Organist and Choirmaster St. John the Evangelist Church, Hull, since 1907.

ENGLAND, JOHN HERBERT, 2, Edith Road, Seacombe, Cheshire. Trained at Woodhouse Grove College, Apperley Bridge, Yorks. MUS. BAC. DUNELM, F.R C.O., L.R.A M , A.R.C.M. Professional Musician. Organist and Choirmaster St Matthew's, Leeds, 1891-95 ; St Thomas', Leeds, 1896-98 ; All Souls', Halifax, 1898-1904 ; St. Saviour's, Liverpool, since 1904 Hobby . Medical work.

EVANS, F. WALTON, Kirkleigh, Highertown, Minehead. Born 1876 at Bala, North Wales. Educated at Marlborough College, and Keble College, Oxford. Music teacher. Assistant Organist Keble College, Oxford, 1893-96 ; St. Asaph Cathedral, 1897-1901 Organist Ellesmere College, 1896-1902 ; St. Michael's Parish Church, Minehead, since 1902. Hobbies and recreations : Hockey, football, shooting, etc.

EVANS, G STEPHEN, 3, Lisburne Terrace, Aberystwyth. Born at Crickhowell, Breconshire. A.R.C.O. (1901) Organist and Choirmaster Potterne Parish Church, Wilts, 1898 ; Leigh Parish Church, Kent, 1899 ; Berkeley Parish Church, Gloucester, 1901 ; English Congregational Church, Aberystwyth, since 1904. Conductor Berkeley Choral Society, 1901 Contributor to Bristol Chant Service and Anthem Book, Donajowski Castle Series of Organ Books, '' Weekly Mail '' Music Gallery, etc , etc.

EVANS, GEORGE VINCENT, 13, Spratt Hall Road, Wanstead Born 1889 at Enfield, Middlesex. Trained under B. Weller, Esq., MUS BAC , and Dr Davan Wetton, of the Foundling Hospital Chapel. Organist St. Bartholomew's, Islington, N , 1907-08 Organist and Choirmaster St. Stephen's, Poplar, E , 1908-10 ; St. Mary's Parish Church, Wanstead, since 1910.

EVANS, WILLIAM ARTHUR LLEWELYN, Llyo Arthur, Mostyn Avenue, Llandudno. Born 1893 at Llandudno Trained under C T Dee, F R C O., Organist of Holy Trinity Church, Llandudno. Organist Welsh Wesleyan Church, Llandudno, since 1912 Hobby : Photography

EVELEIGH, WILLIAM GEORGE, 5, Fernhurst Avenue, and 54, South Mall, Cork Born 1868, at Meerut, India. Educated at Cambridge University. Trained under Sir J. Benedict, for piano ; C E. Willing, Esq and Dr. J Bridge, for organ. MUS. DOC. OXON , F R C.O., A.R C.M Examiner Royal College of Music, London Formerly Organist Parish Church, Bramley ; Parish Church, Holywell, N. Wales ; Holy Trinity Episcopal, Ayr, N.B Organist Cork Cathedral since 1903. Composer of pieces for violin, piano, organ, church services, songs, etc.

EVERITT, JAMES, Lansdowne House, Alton, Hants Born and educated at Brighton. MUS. BAC. DUNELM (1898), M.I S.M. Professor of Music. Organist Christ Church, Southwark, 1874 ; Cheam, Surrey, 1880 ; St Lawrence's Parish Church, Alton, since 1892. Conductor Alton Choral Society Publications : Evening Service in D, and anthem '' I will greatly rejoice.''

EYRE, ALFRED J., Penybryn,Fox Hill, Norwood, S.E. Born 1853. Educated in London. M.R.A.M, F.R.C.O. Teacher of organ, pianoforte, singing and harmony.Professor of Choral Singing at the Royal Normal College for the Blind, Norwood. Late Organist of Crystal Palace. Organist St. Peter's, Vauxhall, 1868-1880, except for eighteen months at St. Ethelburga, Bishopsgate. Organist and Choirmaster St. John Evangelist, Norwood, since 1880. Publications: Communion and Evening Services in E flat, C and D. Recreation: Reading and walking.

FARNELL, GEORGE HARRY, 4, Abyssinia Street, Belle Vue Road, Leeds. Born and educated at Leeds. A.R.C.O. Deputy-Organist Belle Vue Primitive Methodist Church, Leeds, 1902-05; Salem Central Hall (Congregational), Hunslet Lane, Leeds, since 1905.

FAULKES, WILLIAM, Amhurst, Priory Road, Anfield, Liverpool. Born November 4th, 1863, in Liverpool. Composer, pianist and teacher. Organist St. John the Baptist, Tue Brook, Liverpool, 1882-6; St. Margaret's, Anfield, Liverpool, since 1886. Publications: Numerous organ compositions, pieces for pianoforte, violin, violoncello, etc.

FERNELEY, THOMAS M, 10, Barlow Moor Road, Chorlton-cum-Hardy. Born 1850 at Salford. Trained privately and at Owen's College, Manchester. Organist St. Philip's, Hulme, 1874-76; St John's, Manchester, 1876-78; Parish Church, Chorlton-cum-Hardy, 1878-82; St. Clement's, Chorlton-cum-Hardy, 1882-96; Wesleyan Church, Stretford, 1897-1900; St. Michael's Parish Church, Flixton, since 1901. Hobby: Musical literary work. Musical Director and Conductor Stretford Orchestral Society, 1879-1886; Didsbury Orchestral Society, 1882-1885; Stretford Philharmonic Society, 1883-86; Ferneley's Orchestral Concerts, 1884-86; Promenade Concerts, Manchester, 1886-87; Chorlton-cum-Hardy Choral Society, 1889-1903; Manchester Orchestral Society, 1889-91; Urmston Choral Society, 1890-1905; Manchester S C. Operatic Society, 1900-1907; Chorlton Operatic Society, since 1907.

FERTEL, FREDERICK, Holmcroft, Holwood Road, Bromley, Kent. Born in London. Trained privately. Organist St. Mark's, Bromley, 1886; Parish Church, Bromley, since 1896. Publication: Communion Service in E flat. Hobbies: Photography, gardening and Masonry. Bromley and County Club.

FIELD, J. T., Montana, Blackheath, S E. Born near Manchester. Organist Christ Church, Lee Park, S.E., since 1874. L.T.C.L. Assoc. Phil. Society. (London). Publications: Offertory, Sentences, Service in D, etc. Hobby: Photography.

FIELDING, HENRY, 39, High Street W, Glossop. Born 1863 at Glossop. Trained under W. P. Fairclough, MUS. BAC., F.R.C.O. Organist Wesley Church, Glossop, since 1880 and Choirmaster also, since 1898. Recreation: Golf.

FIELDING, S. H., 31, Bicknell Street, Blackburn. Born 1873 at Blackburn. Educated St. John's, Blackburn. Schoolmaster. Organist and Choirmaster St. Peter's, Accrington, since 1897. Junior Conservative Club.

FIRTH, JAMES LAMBERT A, 44, Keighley Road, Skipton. Born 1880 at Leeds. Teacher of music. Organist St. Stephen's R.C. Skipton 1898-1903; Giggleswick Parish Church, 1903-4; Christ Church Skipton, since 1904. Conductor Skipton Permanent Orchestra. Hobby: Painting. Music Master, Skipton Grammar School.

FISHER, ALFRED WALTER, Hove Academy of music, 93, Church Road, Hove. Born 1874 at Folkestone. Educated at Worthing and Brighton. L.R.A.M., A.R.C.O., Principal Hove Academy of Music. Formerly Organist Worthing Baptist; Holland Road, Hove; and Norton Road, Hove. Organist Steyne Gardens Wesleyan Church, Worthing. Publications: Various articles, lectures, and songs. Hobby: Oil painting.

FITTON, J. W., 65, West End Avenue, Harrogate. Born 1864 at Dewsbury. Educated privately. MUS. BAC. DUNELM., F.R.C.O. Organist Hopton Congregational, Mirfield, 1881. Organist and Choirmaster Congregational, Batley, 1887; Heaton Parish Church, Bradford, 1887; Heaton Parish Church, Bradford, 1894-1906; Trinity Wesleyan Church, Harrogate, since 1909 Teacher of Music Leeds Institute, 1890. Conductor Frizinghall Choral Society, Bradford, 1896, Bradford Old Choral Society, 1902-1906. Principal Leeds School of Music, 1898. Recreation: Reading.

FITZGERALD, JAMES F., 27, Upper Merrion Street, Dublin. B.A. CANTAB. Born 1873. Educated Uppingham, Trinity College Cambridge, and R.C.M. Organist Assistant Christchurch Cathedral, 1901; Molyneux Church, 1902; Joint.and Master of Choristers, Christchurch Cathedral, Dublin, since 1904. Sole Organist since 1906. Choirmaster Portobello Garrison Church, 1909.

FLACK, ARTHUR MORGAN, Glendene, 96, Woodberry Avenue, Winchmore Hill, N. Born 1864 at Holloway. Trained under G. Wetton Spencer, A. MUS. T.C.L., and W. H. Smart, MUS. BAC. DUBLIN. Assistant Organist Old Parish Church, Hornsey, 1881; St. Anne's, Brookfield, Highgate, 1885. Organist and Choirmaster St. Peter's, Hornsey, 1886; Christ Church, West Green, S. Tottenham, 1889; Holy Innocents, Hornsey, since 1909. Publications: Benedicite in D (Novello); five canticle chants (Orpheus Co.). Hobby and recreations: Gardening, walking and reading.

FLETCHER, ALBERT, 48, Frederick Street, Mexboro. Born 1877 at Mexboro. Trained under J. W. Phillips Teacher of Music. Organist St George's Church, Mexboro, 1903-1908. Organist and Choirmaster St. Peter's Church, Conisboro, since 1908. Hobby and recreation: Reading and cycling.

FLETCHER, ALFRED WILLIAM, L.T.S.C., "Tinta-Nyoni," King's Road, Paignton. Born at Derby. Trained under T. T. Trimmel, MUS. BAC. Organist and Choirmaster Victoria Street Congregational Church, Derby, for over twenty years; North Adelaide Baptist Church, South Australia, for eight years; Belgrave Congregational Church, Torquay, since 1912. Publications: Cantata, "The Christmas Star"; part songs, songs, anthems, etc. Hobby: Carpentry.

FLETCHER, FRANK EDWARD, 20, Brockman Road, Folkestone. Born at Oxenhope, Yorks. MUS. BAC. (Trinity College, Tor.), F.R.C.O. Organist Formerly of South Cliff Church, and Queen Street Wesleyan Church, Scarborough. Christ Church, Folkestone, since 1886. Recreation: Tennis, cycling, golf.

FLITCROFT, JOHN THOMAS, 52, St. George's Terrace, Bolton, Lancs. Born at Bolton 1851. Professor of music. MUS. BAC., T.U.T., F.R.C.O., L.R.A.M. gold medallist, F.T.C.L. Academic Life Member of Trinity College of Music, London. Organist Wesley Chapel, Bolton, 1868-80; Organist and Choirmaster St. Paul's, Astley Bridge, Bolton, 1880-95; Bank St. Unitarian, Bolton, since 1895. Hobbies and recreations: Mechanics, joinery, and reading.

FLOYD, ALFRED E., 34, Victoria Street, Oswestry. MUS. BAC. (OXON).
Music Master Oswestry Grammar School. Conductor Choral Society.
Formerly Assistant Organist of Winchester Cathedral. Organist
Oswestry Parish Church since 1904.

FOGG, CHARLES H., Springfield, 470, Moss Lane E., Manchester. Born (1859)
and educated at Manchester. Formerly Organist Cavendish Chapel
for 12 years. Organist St Mary's Church and Free Trade Hall, Manchester, since 1891 ; The Halle' Concerts. Composer of music.

FOORT, REGINALD J., 22, Sutherland Avenue, Maida Vale, London, W.
Born 1893 at Daventry. Trained R C M. F.R.C.O. Organist Rugby
Lower School, 1907-09 ; Newbold Parish Church, 1908-09 , St. Mary's,
Bryanstone Square, W., since 1910. Hobby : Photography.

FORD, ERNEST HARTLEY, 5, Wimborne Gardens, Ealing, London W. Born
1865 in London. Educated at Mill Hill School. Professor of music.
Organist St. James', Ealing, 1895-8 , St. John's, Ealing, since 1898.

FORD, THOMAS JAMES, 74, Goldington Avenue, Bedford Born in London,
1848. Educated Collegiate School, Maida Hill. Local Examiner
for R C M scholarships Organist London Road Congregational,
Chelmsford, 1863-67 ; Bunyan Meeting, Bedford, since 1867

FORDHAM, CHARLES HENRY, 2 and 4, Chaloner Street, Guisboro', Yorks.
Born (1856), and educated at Leeds F.G C.M. L. MUS., V C.M. Clerk.
Organist Beeston Hill Congregational, 1870-2 ; Holbeck, St. Matthew
1873-6 , and St. Nicholas', Guisboro', since 1876.

FORSTER, CLAUDE ALAN, 2, Edward Road, Forres Born 1888 at Norwich.
Educated at Norwich Cathedral, under Dr F Bates, 1905-1910.
Chorister of Norwich Cathedral, 1897-1903 ; Horsford Parish Church,
nr. Norwich, 1905 ; St Clements Church, Norwich, 1906, and Assistant
Organist of Norwich Cathedral. Organist St John's Episcopal Church,
Forres, since April, 1910 Hobby and recreation : golfing and cycling.

FORSYTH, W FORBES, 59, Cecil Street, Hillhead, Glasgow. Born at
Stirling Educated at Glasgow High School L.R.A.M., A.R.C.O.
Organist Hyndland Chruch, Glasgow, since 1907. Accompanist to
Glasgow Choral Union.

FORTAY, JAMES BUTLER, 5, Abercromby Terrace, Oxford Street, Liverpool.
Born 1856 at Liverpool. Musical lecturer Liverpool Corporation 1891-
1910, and elsewhere. Writer for the Press. Organist St. Columba's
Church, Liverpool (when a boy) , St. Ambrose' 1874-9 , Emmanuel,
Liverpool, 1879-91 ; St. Michael's-in-the-Hamlet, Liverpool, 1891-98 ;
Trinity Presbyterian, Bootle, Liverpool, since 1898. Composer of
music. Recreations : Reading, and seaside and country walks.

FORTUNE, ALLAN, Exley Head, Keighley. Born in 1890 at Keighley.
Organist St Peter's Church, Keighley, since 1909.

FOSTER, W. H. C , 39, Ramsgate, Louth, Lincolnshire. Born 1846, and
educated at Louth Music seller Organist Oakamoor Church, 1866-67 ;
Holy Trinity, Louth, since 1867.

FOSTER, W. WILSON, 7, Scotch Street, Whitehaven. Born 1885 near
Rudstone, Yorks. Trained at Bridlington and Peterborough. Organist
Clifton Parish Church, York , St. Nicholas Parish Church, Whitehaven.
Formerly Music Master The College, Scarborough Publication :
Benedicite in F. Recreation : Billiards.

FOWLER, WILLIAM ERNEST, 8, Elmdale Road, Tyndall's Park, Bristol. Born 1871 at Bristol. Educated musically under the organists of Bristol and Gloucester Cathedrals. L.R.A.M., A.R C.M. Professor of pianoforte and organ. Organist Pro. Cathedral, Clifton, 1885-96 ; All Saints, Bristol, since 1896. Founder of the Bristol Eisteddfod in 1903, which has proved one of the most successful competitive musical festivals in the country.

FOWLES, BERNARD, Glenthorn Cottage, Hillingdon, Middlesex. Born 1871 at Portsmouth. Trained at R.C.M. (Witcombe Scholar 1885-7) and privately. L.R.A.M. Teacher of Music. Organist Downe, Kent, 1903-5. Professor Beckenham School of Music, 1893-1908. Organist St. Alkmund's, Derby, 1907-11 ; returned to London, 1912. Principal Midland School of Music, Derby ; Spalding and Skegness Schools of Music. Music Master Orient College and Orient Girls' College, Skegness Clubs : " Nobodies," London ; Spalding Constitutional ; Derwent Rowing, Derby.

FOX, G. HOLLAND, 1, Granville Terrace, Darlington. Born in London. Educated at Cheltenham and Winchester. Formerly Music Master Trent College, Notts, and one of the Glasgow Corporation organists. Organist Holy Trinity, Darlington, since 1901 ; also Choirmaster of St. James' Church, and Etherley Parish Church. Composer of songs, piano pieces, and writer of musical articles, recitalist. Hobby and recreation : Humorous musical sketches.

FRASER, WILLIAM HENRY, Grasmere, Orsett Road, Grays, Essex. Born (1874), and educated at Luton, Beds. F.I.G.C.M., L.L.C.M. Formerly Organist St. Andrew's, Luton ; Parish Church, Northfleet, Kent ; and St. Hilda's, Whitby Organist Grays Parish Church since 1894. Conductor Grays and District Choral Society, 1906. Author and composer of " Fleeting Thoughts " waltz, for piano. Recreation : Cycling.

FREEMAN, ANDREW, 57, Buckleigh Road, Streatham, S.W. B.A. (CANTAB), 1896 ; MUS. B. (CANTAB), 1903 ; F.R.C.O., 1905. Organist and Choirmaster Wesleyan Church, Newbury, 1892-1900 ; Congregational Church, Guildford, 1900-2 (assistant), St. Peter's, Eaton Square, London, 1902-3 ; Congregational Church, Newbury, 1903-09 ; Immanuel Church, Streatham Common, S.W., since 1909. Music Master Newbury Grammar School, 1904-8. Conductor of the South London Orchestral Society, 1910.

FREEMAN, CHARLES, 64, North Street, St. Andrews, N B. Born at Longboro'. Educated at Moreton, Glos. Teacher of music. Organist Todenham, 1870-3 ; Worting, 1873-78 , St. Andrew's Episcopal, St. Andrews since 1878. Hobby and recreation : Cycling and bowling.

FREER, THOMAS, Glasgow. 487, Cathedral Street, Glasgow. Born at Glasgow. Educated at Free Church College. Piano and organ merchant. Organist and Choirmaster Anderston Parish Church, Glasgow, since 1899 ; and to the Corporation of Glasgow. Arlington Club.

FREW, ROBERT FOX, 7, Athole Gardens, Newlands, Glasgow. Born at Glasgow. MUS. DOC. DURHAM., L. MUS. T.C L., A.R.C.O. Organist Belmont Parish Church, 1893-6 ; Largs Parish Church, 1896-8 ; and Govan Parish Church, since 1898.

FRICKER, HERBERT AUSTIN, 17, Cavendish Road, Leeds. Born 1868. Educated Cathedral School, Canterbury. F.R.C.O., MUS. BAC. DUNELM. Organist (Deputy), Canterbury Cathedral, 1884-90 ; Holy Trinity

Church, Folkestone, 1890-98; Town Hall, Leeds, since 1898; St. Michael's All Angels, 1904-8. Chorus Master Leeds Musical Festival, Leeds Philharmonic Society; Bradford Festival Choral Society. Conductor Leeds Saturday Municipal Orchestral Concerts, and Morley Choral Society. Music Master Leeds Grammar School.

FRICKER, James F., Sturndale, St Helen's Road, Swansea Born at Swansea. A.R.C O Local Examiner R C M ; Local Representative R A M., Member Incorporated Society of Musicians. Formerly Organist St. Andrew's, Swansea ; Christ Church, Swansea Organist Walter Road Congregational Church. Composer of organ, pianoforte and vocal music.

FROST, Charles Joseph, 72, Wickham Road, Brockley, S.E. Born 1848 at Westbury on Trym. MUS. DOC., CANTAB , F.R C O. Organist Holy Trinity, Westbury on Trym, 1867-9 , Holy Trinity, Weston-Super-Mare, 1869-73 , Holy Trinity, Lee, S E , 1873-7 ; St Mary, Haggerston, E., 1875-80 , Christ Church, Newgate St , E C , 1880-4 ; St. Peter's, Blockley, since 1883. Publications : Organ music ; 55 hymn tune voluntries, 22 marches, 11 andantes, 36 short and easy voluntaries; 13 original voluntaries ; a collection of 24 pieces, 40 postludes and 20 soft voluntaries, 4 sets of variations, 6 hymn tune voluntaries (2 staves) ; 55 piano pieces ; 28 songs , 2 books and 12 pieces for harmonium , 11 church service settings ; 15 anthems ; 2 cantatas ; 12 part songs, and choruses.

FROST, J. Arthur, The Grove, Aldercar, Langley Mill, Notts. Born at Derby. Organist and Choirmaster Wesleyan Chapel, Langley Mill, Notts, since 1901.

GACCON, John Augustus, Clyro, Caerau Road, Newport, Mon. Formerly Organist St. John the Baptist, Newport, Mon. Organist Parish Church, Newport, Mon., since 1895.

GARRETT, Louis J., Ardeevin, Connaught Avenue, Cork. Chorister at Cork Cathedral under the late Dr Marks Teacher, voice, piano, organ. Formerly Assistant Organist Cork Cathedral. Organist and Choirmaster St Nicholas, Cork, 1896-1902 ; Holy Trinity (Christ Church), Cork, 1902-1908 ; St. Luke's, Cork, since 1908. Music Master, Cork Grammar School, since 1900 Publications · Anthems, services, carol songs, etc

GATER, William H., 19, Victoria Avenue, Donnybrook, Dublin. B.A , MUS. DOC , T.C.D., L. MUS. T.C L. Organist St. Stephen's, Dublin. Formerly at Christchurch, Bray, Co. Wicklow. Professor of Pianoforte, Wesley College, Dublin. Conductor East Meath Church Choral Association.

GATES, Horace W., Carlton House, 101, Ditchling Rise, Brighton Born at Brighton. A.R.C.O. Assistant Organist St. Bartholomew's, Brighton, 1897-1900 ; St. Barnabas Church, Hove, 1900-1909 ; Chapel Royal, Brighton, since February, 1910.

GAUNT, John H , 39, West Bars, Chesterfield. Born (1858) and educated at Chesterfield. Pianoforte dealer, etc., and music teacher. Organist Mount Zion Primitive Methodist, Brampton, 1867-88 ; Chesterfield Congregational since 1888. Composer of several hymn tunes and songs. Hobby : Photography.

GAUNTLETT, CHARLES TREVOR, The Chantry, Berwick-upon-Tweed. Formerly Organist and Choirmaster St. Luke's, Newcastle-on-Tyne; Parish Church, Oswestry. Organist and Choirmaster Parish Church, Berwick, since 1899. Music Master Berwick Grammar School and Conductor Choral Union. Local Secretary Trinity College, London.

GIBBONS, MISS LUCY J , Westonwood, 25, Parham Road, Gosport. A R.C.O. Born at Gosport. Organist Student Royal College of Music, South Kensington, January 1908—July 1909.

GIBSON, FREDERICK, 30, Whitehall Street, Dundee. Born 1878 at Gateshead-on-Tyne. Trained under Dr. W. Kea, Dr Chas Chambers and Dr. Huntley. L.R.A M., L.T.C.L. Organist Leighton Memorial, Heaton, Newcastle, 1898 ; Bainbridge Memorial, Newcastle, 1898-1900 ; Church of St Paul, Whitley Bay, Northumberland, 1900-11 ; Gilfillan Memorial Church, Dundee, since 1911. Publications: Post Benedictions and Evening Service in D. Recreation : Walking.

GILL, FREDERICK J., 12, Gainsborough Road, Bedford Park, London, W. Born (1878) and educated at Birmingham and London Organist and Choirmaster Wesleyan Methodist Church, Ponder's End, London, N., 1901-4 ; Hinde Street Wesleyan Methodist Church, since 1906.

GILL, HERBERT CHARLES TOMS, " Kenmure," Wells Way, Bath. Associate Royal College of Organists ; Member Incorporated Society of Musicians ; Academic Member Trinity College of Music, London. Organist St. James's Church, Bath, since 1900.

GILBERTHORPE, HENRY TYAS, Lismore, Uxbridge Road, Hampton Hill, Middlesex. Born 1877 at Chesterfield Trained under Mr. H N. Biggin, Dr F Bates and Dr. A. E. Tozer. F.R.C.O., L MUS. T.C.L. Organist St. John Baptist, Felixstowe, 1899 ; Hunstanton Parish Church, 1900 ; Lynton Parish Church, 1901 , Dunster Priory Church, 1902 ; Christ Church, Ellacombe, Torquay, 1904 ; Walton-on-Thames Parish Church, 1908. Organist and Choirmaster St James' Church, Hampton Hill, and Conductor of Hampton Hill Choral Society, 1911. Publications : Benedicite in C , and numerous articles in " Musical Opinion." Hobby and recreation : Cycling and walking. Clubs : Walton, Oatlands and Hersham Conservative

GODFREY, ARTHUR E, 64, Clifton Hill, London, N.W. Born 1868 in London. Educated at St. Paul's Cathedral Choir School and Royal Academy of Music Accompanist. Musical editor and adviser Robert Cocks & Co., 1890-8 ; Gould & Co , 1898-1902 Manager Hopwood & Crew, 1902-4. Organist and Choirmaster St. John's, Waffing, 1883-6 ; All Saints', Finchley Road, N.W., 1886-97 ; St Mary the Virgin, Primrsoe Hill, 1897-1900 ; St. Andrew's Presbyterian, Frognal, since 1903. Hobbies and recreations : Golf, bowls, bridge, and billiards.

GODFREY, GAVIN, 32, Polwarth Terrace, Edinburgh Born 1871 at Edinburgh. Trained privately, and at Royal Academy and Trinity College. L R A.M., A R C O Organist Elder Street Church (now St James', McDonald Road), 1882-1886 ; Tron Church, 1886-88 ; Old Greyfriars Church, 1888-93 ; Lauriston Place U.F. Church, 1893-95 ; St Michael's, North Merchiston, since 1895. Conductor Lauriston Musical Association, 1893-95 ; St. Michael's Musical Association, since 1895. Edinburgh Western Choral Society, 1901-09 ; Markinch Choral Society, 1904-09 ; Juniper Green Choral Society (Mid-Lothian), 1905-08. Music Master, Morelands School, Grange, 1890-1900. Director of

.nale choir, All Saint's Church, 1900-01. Organist and accompanist to the Edinburgh Roayl Choral Union since 1910. Teacher to the Edinburgh Royal Choral Union Theory Classes, 1912. Hobby and recreation Gardening and golf Member of Baberton Golf Club.

GODFREY, GOODHART, Ivy Hatch, Horsham, Sussex. Born 1843. Educated at Leeds Grammar School. Organist St. Bartholomew's, Southsea, 1863; Park Chapel, Chelsea, 1867; Christ Church, Ealing, 1871; St. John's, Sevenoaks, 1882; Lucens, Switzerland, 1888; All Saints', Roffey, since 1893.

GOODACRE, H. M., Ashfield Park, Ross, Herefordshire. F.R.C.O. Assistant Organist Peterborough Cathedral. 1900. Organist St. Mary's Parish Church, Ross, since 1902. Conductor Ross Choral Society, 1902. Trained at Peterborough Cathedral.

GOODMAN, EDWARD PERCY, 67, Amesbury Avenue, Streatham Hill, London, S.W Born 1864 at Holloway Educated at Framlingham, Suffolk; London and Paris. Organist Lambeth Presbyterian, Kennington Road, London, S.E., 1901-10. Publications : Hymn tunes in Bible Christian Sunday School Hymnal, Primitive Methodist Sunday School Hymn Book, carols, Communion Service in D flat, etc.

GOODYEAR, ARTHUR C., 25, St. George's Road, Aldershot. Born 1874 at Belbroughton, Worcestershire. Educated at Belbroughton School. Assistant Organist All Saints', Aldershot, 1894-1896. Organist and Choirmaster St. Mark's, Hale, Surrey, 1896-99; St. George's Miltary Church, since 1899. Recreation Gardening.

GOSTELOW, FREDERICK JAMES, 29, Upper George Street, Luton. A.R.A.M., A.R.C.M , F.R.C.O. Formerly Organist at various chapels at Luton. Organist Luton Parish Church, since 1899; Luton Hoo Mansion (private chapel) since 1900.

GOUGH, JOHN B., " Homelea," Windmill Lane, Belper. Born at Belper, 1859. Educated at the Old Lancastrian School, Belper. Late Hon. Conductor ; Belper Amateur Orchestra, and Belper Nonconformist Choral Union Hon. Sec. Belper Orpheus Glee Singers, since 1889. Conductor of singing by the United S.S. Scholars, Diamond Jubilee, 1897 ; also the Coronation, 1902. Organist Belper-Pottery Wesleyan Church, 1874-8 ; Belper Wesleyan Church since 1878. Vice-President Derby and District Organists' Association, 1912. Profession : Cashier.

GRANGER, WILLIAM, Cross Bank House, Kendal. A.R.C.M. (teaching singing), F I.S.C., I.S.M. Solo Chorister and Assistant Organist, Lichfield Cathedral for 12 years. Formerly Organist St. Michael's, Lichfield ; Parish Church, Omagh, Ireland ; All Saints, Southport. Organist Parish Church, Kendal, since 1898.

GRANGER, W. J., Fernleigh, Church Village, Nr. Pontypridd. Born 1868 at Netherton, Nr. Dudley. F.R.C.O. Formerly Assistant Organist Parish Church, Dudley , Parish Church, Scarborough ; and Parish Church, Huntingdon. Organist St. Augustine's, Holly Hall, Dudley, 1883 ; St. Mary's, Brampton, Huntingdon, 1886. Organist and Choirmaster St Saviour's, Dartmouth, 1890 , St. Mark's, Portsmouth, 1891 ; Parish Church, Pontypridd, since 1902. Formerly Professor Southsea School of Music. Publications : Triumphal March for the Organ ; song, " A Letter From Afar." Hobby : Gardening.

GRANT, VERNOR, 22, Kelvin Road, Highbury, London, N. Born 1872 in London. Trained partly at Guildhall School of Music. Assistant Organist Italian Church, Hatton Garden, 1890-94 ; Spa Fields Chapel, 1894-98. Organist and Choirmaster Catholic Church, Homerton, 1898-1903 ; Catholic Church, Stoke Newington, 1903-07 ; St. Joseph Retreat, Highgate, since 1907.

GRAY, ALAN, York House, Chaucer Road, Cambridge. Born at York 1855 Educated at St. Peter's School, York, and Cambridge. L L.M., MUS. DOC. CANTAB., F R.C.O. Organist Wellington College, 1883-92 ; Trinity College, Cambridge, since 1892. Conductor Cambridge University Musical Society.

GRAY, ALBERT J., 109, Great Western Road, Glasgow. Born at Lenzic, 1871. L.T.S C. Organist and Choirmaster Burnbank United Free Church, Glasgow ; Visiting Singing Master Govan Parish School Board , one of the Organists to the Corporation of Glasgow. Formerly Organist of St. Peter's Episcopal Church, Glasgow. Recreations : Golf and fishing Club : I S M.

GREEN, MISS ADA H , Stranhope, New Barnet. Born in London. Trained, at North London Collegiate School and Royal College of Music F R C O. A R C M Publications : Pianoforte music. Hobby and recreations : Theatricals, riding, cycling.

GREEN, CHRISTIE, 7, Barrs Hill Terrace, Radford Road, Coventry MUS. DOC. OXON , F.R.C.O. Organist St. Thomas', Sutton-in-Craven, 1883-91. Assistant Organist Leeds Parish Church, 1891. Organist and Choirmaster Emmanuel Church, Leeds, 1891-1900 , Blackburn Parish Church, 1900-12 ; Holy Trinity Church, Coventry, since 1912.

GREEN, FREDERICK, Congleton, Cheshire. Born at Bollington, Macclesfield 1883 Educated privately A R C.M. (London) 1907 ; L R A M , 1904. Deputy Organist Bollington Parish Church, 1896-1900. Organist, Wesleyan Church, Bollington, 1900-6 ; St. Peter's Parish Church, Congleton, since 1906. Hobbies : Motoring and engineering. Club : Masonic

GREEN, JOSEPH ERNEST, 33, Avignon Road, Brockley, S E Born in London. Trained privately MUS. B., DUNELM., L. MUS T C.I, Gold Medallist, L A.M. Lecturer in Music under L.C C., 1900-7. Organist and Choirmaster Rye Lane Baptist Church, Peckham, S.E , since 1893 Publications " Our Father," anthems, hymn tunes and vespers.

GREEN, J. H., 206, Burnley Road, Accrington Organist Parish Church, Accrington, 1869-78, and 1905-7 : Boxenden Church, 1894-1905

GREENISH, FREDERICK R., 15, Queen's Avenue, Muswell Hill, London. Born at Haverfordwest. Educated at Exeter and Paris MUS DOC. OXON. Organist St. Martin's, Haverfordwest, 1881-7 ; and St Mary's, 1888-1909. Adjudicator at National Eisteddfod of Wales at Carnarvon, 1906 Hobbies, etc : Cycling, golf and philately

GREENWOOD, FRANK, 6, West Street, Rochdale. Born 1877 at Todmorden. Formerly Organist Providence Congregational, Rochdale. MUS BAC. (DUNELM), F.R C.O., A.R C.M. (PIANO). Organist Withington Congregational since 1904.

GREENWOOD, GILBERT H , Longwood, Alsager, Cheshire Born at Dewsbury. Educated at Bristol and London. MUS. BAC. Professor of Music. Formerly Organist St. John's, Dewsbury, and St. Mary's Parish Church, Boston Spa Organist St. Mary Magdalene Parish Church, Alsager, since 1906. Hobby: Gardening.

GREGORY, GEORGE HERBERT, Church Close, Boston, Lincs. MUS. BAC. (OXON), F.R.C.O. Organist and Choirmaster Holy Trinity Episcopal, Melrose, N.B , 1872-4 ; Tamworth Parish Church, 1874-5 ; and Boston Parish Church, Lincs., since 1876.

GREGORY, JAMES LIVELY, York House, Hertford. Born 1860 at Windsor. MUS. BAC. DURHAM, 1892 ; F.R.C.O., 1883 ; L.T.C.L , 1889. Organist Holy Trinity, Melrose, 1875-6 ; Parish Church, Welford, 1877-9 ; Parish Church, Ware, 1880-1901 ; All Saints, Hertford, since 1901. Organist and Music Master Christ's Hospital, Hertford, since 1901. Conductor E. Herts Choral and Orchestral Society, since 1892 ; Hon. Conductor Hertford Festival Choir, 1906 ; Hertford Amateur Operatic Society, since 1903. Music Master Hertford Grammar School. Publications : Organ and pianoforte pieces, songs, part songs, and church music.

GRICE, HERBERT, Fairdays, Barlows Road, Edgbaston Born at Birmingham Educated for organ under R. A E. Payne, Organist at Carr's Lane. Birmingham ; for harmony under Henry Taylor, MUS. BAC. ; for violoncello under A J. Priestley and W. E Whitehouse (London). Present position since 1904.

GRIEVE, ALFRED B., 45, Ferry Street, Montrose. Born 1878 at Liverpool, Trained at Royal Blind School, Edinburgh, and under Henry Marshall. Dundee. Certificate for piano in connection with R C M and R A.M. Organist Butter Burn U F Church, Dundee, 1900-03 ; Abbey Parish Church, Arbroath, 1903-4 ; Melville Parish Church, Montrose, since 1904. Hobby and recreation Esperanto and chess.

GRIFFIN, ARTHUR LESLIE, Epsom Villa, Shepperton-on-Thames Born in 1878 at London Educated at Kingston College, Yeovil. Organist (1893) Charlestown Parish Church, Cornwall, 1895, St. Mewen Church, Cornwall ; Sub-Organist at Alexandra Palace, London. N., 1899-1902 ; Organist at Angelus Hall, 1905-6 ; Organist Littleton Parish Church, since 1896.

GRIFFITH, WILLIAM, 67, Dean Street, Kilmarnock. Born 1867 at Syresham. Educated, Magdalen College School, Brackley. MUS BAC DUNELM., F R.C.O , L. MUS. T.C.L. Chemist, by examination of the Pharmaceutical Society. Formerly Organist St. Paul's, St Mary's, Barrow in Furness ; Church of the Holy Sepulchre, Northampton, 1895-1901. Conductor of the Northampton Amateur Operatic Society, 1897-1901 ; King Street U F. Church, Kilmarnock, 1901-9. Member of the staff of the Athenaeum School of Music, Glasgow, 1902-8 Music Master Kilmarnock Academy, since 1906 Conductor to the Kilmarnock Society of Musicians, 1906. Organist Parish Church of Kilbarchan, Renfrewshire, since 1909.

GRIFFITHS, J. R , 28, Satanita Road, Westcliff-on-Sea. Born 1857 at Buckley, N. Wales. Organist Greville Place Church, St. John's Wood, since 1876 ; Highgate Church, 1877 ; Christ Church, Westminster Bridge Road, London, 1881 ; Cliff Town Church, Southend-on-Sea since 1905 Hobbies : hymn tune studies.

GRIGGS, WILLIAM GEORGE JAMES, A.R.C.O., 18, Lower Brook Street, Ipswich. Born in 1887 at Ipswich, and educated at Great Yarmouth. Teacher of music etc. Deputy Organist, St. Mary's Church, Southtown, 1903-06. Organist S. Helen's Church, Ipswich, since 1907. Deputy Conductor and accompanist to Ipswich Male Voice Choir.

GRITTON, JOHN W., Talfourd Cottage, Reigate. F.R.C.O. Formerly Organist St. Mark's, Reigate; St. Michael's, Betchworth; St. Paul's, Dorking, St. Barnabas, Ranmore. Organist Parish Church, Reigate, since 1887.

GROOCOCK, EDWARD WILLIAM, Lynton House, 81, St. James' Road, Croydon. Born 1872 at Milton-next-Gravesend. Educated at Park House School, Gravesend. Professor of music. F.R.C.O., A.R.C.M., L.R.A.M., A G S M. Late Conductor of Wallington and Warlingham Musical Societies. Organist St. Mark's, S. Norwood, 1891-1900; St. Andrew's, Croydon, 1900-1; and St. Saviour's, Croydon, since 1902 Conductor Croydon Choral Society, since 1901. Composer of an anthem for All Saints Day; Benedicite; setting of the Pater Noster, etc. Recreation: Long country rambles.

GROVES, REGINALD E., Rose Cottage, Penshurst, Kent. Born 1879 at Lewisham. Educated at Tunbridge Wells. A.R.C.M., A.R C.O., L.R.A.M. Musician. Formerly Assistant Organist St. James' Church, Tunbridge Wells. Organist St. John the Baptist Parish Church, Penshurst, since 1899. Conductor Penshurst Choral Society; Penshurst Orchestral Society; Toys Hill Choral Society. Hobbies: Photography, Electricity.

GUEST, LANGFORD, Ambleside, Care Road, Wallington. Born at Streatham. Educated at Croydon. F.R.C.O. Organist (Sub) St. Michael's and All Angels, Beddington, 1904-6; St. Mary the Virgin, Soho, W., since 1908.

GUYER, T. S. 37, Amherst Road, Bexhill. Born at Speen, Newbury, Berks. Educated privately at Speen Hill Academy. F.R.C.O. Teacher of music. Formerly Assistant Organist St. John the Evangelist, Edinburgh. Organist St. Baldred's, North Berwick; Eltham Parish Church; St. Bartholmews, Brighton; St. Mary Magdalen, St. Leonards. Organist and Choirmaster Parish Church, Bexhill, since 1910.

HAAN, GUST, F. S , 4, Montgomery Street, Carlow, Ireland. I.S M. Professor of Gregorian Chant, St. Patrick's College, Carlow; Professor of music, St. Mary's, Knockbeg. Organist Carlow Cathedral.

HAGUE, ALBERT, St. Mark's College, Woodhouse Lane, Leeds. Born 1867 at Rotherham. Trained R C M. F.R.C.O. Organist All Saints', Colchester, 1890-97; St. Mark's, Leeds, 1897-1912; St. Michael's, Headingley, Leeds, since 1912.

HALES, FRANCIS, S., 1, Broadwater Road, Brucegrove, N. Born 1882 in London. Educated at London College. Cert. S.A. Organist St. Peter in Chains, Stroud Green, London, since 1905. Pianist, Stroud Green Choral Society. Hobby: Music.

HALEY, WILLIAM MEACHAM, 160, Millfields Road, Clapton, London, N.E. Born 1885 at London. Educated at East London Technical College, Mile End, E. Studied the organ under R. Bernard Elliott (Organist and Choirmaster St. John of Jerusalem, South Hackney). Organist

St. Alban's, Windlesham (Surrey), 1902-1903. Organist and Choir-master, Ram's Episcopal Chapel, Homerton, N.E., 1904-1908 ; St. Bartholomew's, Dalston, 1908-11 ; St. Mary the Virgin, Soho, 1912 ; Christ Church, S. Hackney, since 1912 Hobbies and recreations : Cycling and photography.

HALLAM, E. PERCY, 115, Northgate Street, Bury St. Edmunds. Born at Nottingham. MUS. BAC , F.R.C O., L. MUS T.C.L Educated privately, and at Manchester Cathedral. Formerly Organist (assistant) St. Thomas', Nottingham ; St. Bartholomew's, Nottingham. Organist New Church of St. Chad, Manchester, 1907-1909 ; St. Mary's Parish Church, Bury St. Edmunds, since 1909 Publications and composi-tions : Magnificat and Nunc Dimittis in A flat, anthems. Music Master Bury St. Edmunds Grammar School. Founder and Con-ductor St. Cecilia Choral Society ; Conductor Amateur Operatic Society. Recreations · Walking and book collecting

HALLER, GEORGE DENNIS, 47, Tunnard Street, Boston, Lincolnshire. Born 1876 at Hornsea. Trained at Royal Normal College and Academy of Music. F.R.C.O., M.I.S.M. Organist and Choirmaster Headingley Wesleyan Church, Leeds, 1901-04 ; Boston Wesleyan Church, since 1904. Publications : An Andante for the Organ, three piano pieces and anthem, " Great is our Lord." Hobby : Esperanto.

HALLS, ALBERT ERNEST, 39, Madras Road, Ilford, Essex. Born 1882 at Chelmsford. Trained at Little Ilford. Clerk. Organist St. James', Little Heath, Ilford, 1899-1901. Deputy Organist Hospital Chapel, Ilford, 1902-4 ; St. Ethelburga, Bishopsgate, E.C. (week-day services), 1898-1902. Hon Organist Ilford Chapter of Guild of Servers since 1904. Assistant Organist St. Michael and All Angels, Little Ilford, since 1904.

HALSTEAD, EDGAR, 18, Kilnhurst, Todmorden. Born 1885 at Todmorden. F.R.C.O. Organist Castle Grove U.M. Church, Todmorden, 1909-12 ; Higher Broughton Presbyterian Church, Manchester, since March 1912.

HAMILTON, RICHARD B., 44, Clare Avenue, Hoole, Chester. Born (1881), and educated at Liverpool. Organist St. Aidan's, Liverpool, 1903-5 ; St. Mary's Parish Church, 1905-10 ; All Saints', Hoole, Chester, since 1910 Recreation : Cycling.

HAMMET, WESLEY, 106, Narbonne Avenue, Clapham Park, London. Born at Taunton, Somerset. Educated R.A M. A.R.C.O. Formerly Organist Temple Chapel, Taunton ; Wesleyan Church, Norbiton ; Chelsea Congregational Church Organist Wesleyan Church, High Street, Clapham, since 1899. Hobby Photography.

HANCOCK, B. J., Rosedene, 4, Parkside, Eltham Park, S.E. MUS. BAC. OXON , F.R.C.O. Organist and Choirmaster St. Thomas', Charlton, 1893-1903 ; Holy Trinity, Eltham, S.E, since 1903 Choirmaster Royal Military Academy Chapel, Woolwich, S.E. Conductor Eltham Choral and Orchestral Society. Publications : Church music, children's cantata, school songs, pianoforte pieces, etc.

HANCOCK, CHARLES, De Montfort Square, Leicester. Born 1852 at Islington. Educated St. George's, Windsor. MUS. BAC. OXON., F.R.C.O. Formerly Organist St. Mary's, Datchet, Windsor ; St. Andrew's, Uxbridge. Organist St. Martin's Church, Leicester, since 1875. Conductor Leicester New Musical Society. Theoretical Examiner, I.S.M. and Local Examiner Royal College Music. Composer of music.

HANFORTH, THOMAS WILLIAM, 24, Northumberland Road, Sheffield. MUS. BAC. DURHAM, F.R.C.O. Trained at York Minster. Organist to the late Archbishop Thomson, 1885-88; St. Martin's-le-Grand, York, 1888-92. Professor of Music York School for the Blind, 1889-92; Organist and Choirmaster Parish Church, Sheffield, since 1892. Bandmaster Fourth W.R.Y. Vol. Artillery, 1900-03. Composer of music.

HANN, SIDNEY, 59, Drewstead Road, Streatham Hill, S.W. Educated at St. James' Chapel Royal and Royal Academy of Music. A R.A.M. Professor of Pianoforte. Organist St. James', Clapham Park, 1886-88; St. Mary's, Islington, 1888-1907; Independent Church, Brixton, since 1907.

HARD, FREDERICK WILLIAM, 65, York Road, West Hartlepool. Born 1886 at West Hartlepool. Trained at Osborne High School and under Organist of Durham Cathedral. Musician. Organist and Choirmaster Holy Trinity, Hartlepool, 1904-1909; Seaton Carew Parish Church, West Hartlepool, since 1909. Pianist to late West Hartlepool Philharmonic Society. Hobby and recreations: Reading and indoor games.

HARDING, HERBERT JEFFERY, Belmont, Oldfield Park, Bath Teacher of piano, organ and singing Conductor St. Paul's Musical Society. Organist St. Paul's, Bath, since 1902.

HARE, HAYDON, 84, St. George's Road, Great Yarmouth. Born 1869 at Stamford, Lincs. Educated at King's School, Peterborough, where he was chorister at the Cathedral. Articled pupil with Dr. Keeton (Organist of Peterborough Cathedral). MUS BAC. DUNELM, F.R.C.O., A.R.C.M. Organist and Choirmaster All Saints' Church, Stamford, 1885; Great Yarmouth Parish Church, since 1895. Choirmaster Bourne Abbey Church, 1893. Conductor Great Yarmouth Musical Society. Chorus Master Norfolk and Norwich Musical Festival. Composer of part songs, etc.

HARRIS, CLEMENT ANTROBUS, Ellangowan, Crieff. Born 1862 at York. A.R.C.O., A. MUS. T.C.L. Music Master Ardvreck School. Organist St. Matthew's, Leyburn, 1884; Thirsk Parish Church, 1885; St. Paul's, Middlesborough, 1887; Ledbury Parish Church, Hereford, 1893; St. Columba's, Crieff, since 1894. Publications: "Notes on the Singing of Hymns," "Scale and Arpeggio Fingering," "How to Write Music," "Curios of Musical History," "A Chronometrical Chart of Musical History," "Snippet-Thoughts of a Country Organist," articles in quarterly reviews and other magazines, etc.

HARRIS, CUTHBERT, 48, Braxted Park, Streatham Common. S.W. Born 1870 in London. Trained privately and London Academy of Music, MUS. D. DUNELM, F.R.C.O. Organist Parish Church, Welwyn, Herts, 1891-93; St. Andrew's, Streatham, 1893-1903; St. Leonard's Parish, Church, Streatham, since 1903. Publications: Anthems, services, songs, part songs, cantatas, organ pieces, piano pieces, books on music. Recreations: Fishing and golf. Club: Norbury Golf.

HARRISON, GEORGE, 38, Connaught Street, Phibsboro, and 4, Upper Sackville Street, Dublin. Born 1878 at Dublin. Trained at the Royal Irish Academy of Music. Organist and Choirmaster St. George's Parish Church, Dublin. Professor Church of Ireland Training College, Mountjoy College, Townsend Street Training College. Conductor of North City Choral Society. Hobby: Engineering.

HARRISON, Julius Alan Greenway, 44, Talbot Road, Highgate, N Born at Stourport Educated at Birmingham School of Music A R C.O. Organist Areley Regis 1901-5 ; St. James' Parish Church, Hartlebury, 1906-9 ; Union Congregational Chapel, Highbury, London, since 1909. Publications : " Cleopatra Cantata," album of songs, part songs for female voices, Harvest Cantata, six pianoforte miniatures, various songs, pianoforte pieces, etc.

HARRISON, Lewis, 28, Windsor Road, Gillingham, Kent. Born 1889 at Rochester. Trained under A. V. Dale, F R.C O., and others. Formerly Organist Union Chapel, Chatham. Organist and Choirmaster St. Andrew's Presbyterian, Chatham, since 1906. Publications Songs. Hobbies : Painting, and novel and poetry writing.

HARSTON, James, Abbeywood, Newark-on-Trent. Born (1857) and educated at Magnus School, Newark. Pianoforte and music dealer. Organist St. Wilfred's Church, S. Muskham, 1870-89 ; Christ Church, Newark-on-Trent, since 1890.

HART, Leonard, 9a, Warwick Avenue, Paddington. Born 1880 at Kilburn. Trained privately and R.A M. F.R.C O., A.R.A.M. Organist St. Stephen's, Westbourne Park, 1897-1911 ; St. Saviour's, Warwick Avenue, since 1911. Recreation : Reading.

HARVEY, Fred E. E., New Street, St Neots, Hunts Born (1877) and educated at Cambridge and R C M M.A. (CANTAB), A R C.O., L R.A.M. Lecturer in Music, Cambridge University Training College for Schoolmasters. Music Master, County School for Boys, Cambridge. Organist St. John the Evangelist, Clapham Rise, S.W., 1901-3 ; St Mary's Parish Church, St. Neots, since 1903

HARWOOD, Basil, Woodhouse, Almondsbury, near Bristol. Born at Woodhouse, Olveston, Glos., 1859. Educated at Charterhouse and Trinity College, Oxford M.A., MUS. DOC OXON Composer of music. Organist Trinity College, Oxford, 1878-1881 ; St. Barnabas, Pimlico, 1883-7 ; Ely Cathedral, 1887-92 ; Christ Church Cathedral, Oxford, 1892-1909.

HATHAWAY, J. W. G , Glenville, Tonbridge Born 1870 Educated at R.C.M. MUS. DOC OXON., F.R.C O. Organist Wincanton Parish Church, 1889 ; Parish Church, Tonbridge, since 1895. Publications : Cantatas, Church services, songs, pianoforte music, etc Club : Primrose.

HAVELOCK, George, 10, Thorne Road, Doncaster Born 1862 at Erith. Trained at Blackheath College. L.R.A.M., L.T.C.L., MUS. D. TORONTO. Organist Malta Cathedral, 1883 ; Dudley Parish Church, 1886 , Duke of Connaught's Church, 1888 ; St. James', Doncaster, and St Michael's, Rossington, since 1908. Publications Two Communion Offices, six organ pieces, songs, etc Essays and short stories.

HAWKER, Henry W., 39, Bath Road, Exeter. Born 1869 at Exeter, and educated at King's Lodge College, Exeter. Pianoforte tuner. Organist Clyst Honiton Parish Church, 1899 ; Friernhay Church, Exeter, 1900 , and Bedford Church, Exeter, since 1905.

HAWKINS, Arnold S , Grasmere, Cheslyn-Hay. Born 1878 at Cheslyn-Hay. Trained under Mr. Amos Keay. Examiner I S.M. Organist United Methodist Church, Cheslyn-Hay, since 1894. Hobby and recreation ; Gardening and shooting.

HAWKINS, HORACE A., Bedfordleigh, Winchester Road, Worthing. F.R.C.O. Organist and Choirmaster St. Andrew's Church, Worthing. Conductor Symphony Orchestra. Music Master at All Souls' Collegiate, London, N.W., and at Wykeham House School, Worthing. Formerly Organist and Choirmaster at St. Paul's Church, Southampton. Sub-Organist at Winchester Cathedral. Singing Master at Handel College, Southampton Choirmaster at Hospital Chapel, Southampton, and Conductor of the St. Paul's Orchestral and Choral Societies. Hobbies : Foreign travel, angling.

HAYES, THOMAS W., Maldon. Born 1877. Directly related to Dr. William Hayes, late Organist Exeter Cathedral. Organist Langford Church, 1897-1909 ; All Saints', Maldon, since 1909.

HAYHURST, JOHN, 20, Montague Street, Blackburn. Born at Blackburn, 1834. Studied music privately. Appointed Organist St. Ann's Catholic Church, Blackburn, 1856, a position he still holds, thus making a record of 56 years' service.

HAYHURST, JOHN W., 19, Newton Street, Clitheroe. Born 1858 at Clitheroe. Organist Moor Lane Chapel, Clitheroe, since 1872. Publications : Popular hymn tunes. Hobby : Literature.

HEAPS, ROBERT, 3, Clydesdale Avenue, Chichester Born at Carlisle. Educated at Preston, Lancs. Lay Vicar Chichester Cathedral. Choirmaster St. George's and St Pancras, Chichester. Organist St. Olave's, Chichester Music Master Chichester Grammar School. Conductor of Felpham and Middleton Choral Society. Formerly Lay Clerk, of Felpham and Middleton Choral Society. Formerly Chorister Carlisle Cathedral ; Bangor, 1896. Lay Vicar of Salisbury, 1899-1902. Recreation : Cycling.

HEATH, ALFRED, Cleveland, Alfred Road, Cromer Born 1882 at Compton, Wolverhampton. Educated at Wolverhampton Grammar School, and Lichfield Cathedral Choir School. Assistant Organist St. Mary's, Stafford, 1900-3 ; Norwich Cathedral, 1903-5. Organist and Recitalist Cromer Parish Church, since 1905. Recreation : Golf, bowls.

HEATON-BAILEY, J., Ryde, Morgan Avenue, Torquay. A.R.C.O. Organist St. John's, Ryde, I.O.W., 1886-90 ; St Luke's, Torquay, since 1890.

HEDGCOCK, WALTER W., 81, Thornton Avenue, Streatham Hill, S.W. Musical Director Crystal Palace, S.E. Born 1864 at Brighton. Deputy Organist St. Michael's, Brighton, 1877 Organist and Choirmaster Patcham, near Brighton, 1878-1881. Organist St Agnes', Kennington, 1881-83. Organist and Choirmaster St. Agnes', Kennington, 1883-99 ; All Saints, Norwood, 1899-1903. Organist Crystal Palace since 1894. Musical Director Crystal Palace, since 1903. Conductor Crystal Palace Orchestral Society, Crystal Palace Choir and Organist Handel Festivals. Professor of Organ at Guildhall School of Music. Publications : A Suite de Ballet, on Overture " Easter " for orchestra ; a song cycle to Captain Basil Hood's lyrics on a " Robin Hood " subject ; many songs, etc.

HEK, FREDERICK WILLIAM, 47, Cromwell Road, Montpelier, Bristol. Born 1870. Educated at Shebbear College, N. Devon. A.R.C.O. Organist St. Michael's, Two Mile Hill, 1892 ; Winscombe Parish Church, 1894 ; Assistant Organist Wells Cathedral, 1896. Organist and Choirmaster Bedminster Parish Church, since 1897. Music Master Hart House School, Burnham. Conductor Bristol Aeolian Male Voice Choir. Recreation : Tennis.

HELMAN, HAROLD, 18, Charlotte Street, Perth. Born at Hull. Educated at Worcester Cathedral and private. Organist at Shustoke Parish Church, St. Nicholas Church, Droitwich; St. John's Episcopal Church, Perth (June, 1911). Publications: Magazine articles, organ music. Recreation: Motor cycling.

HEMSTOCK, A., Mere Street, Diss, Norfolk. Born (1845) and educated at Bingham, near Nottingham. Teacher of Music, tuning, etc. Formerly Organist at Bingham, etc. Organist Choral Society, Corn Hall; and Diss Parish Church, since 1864. Publications: "Practical Guide to Organ Tuning," church and pianoforte music. Recreations: Fishing, billiards.

HEMY, HENRI C., 27, Lovaine Place, Newcastle-on-Tyne. Born 1854 at Newcastle-on-Tyne. Educated privately. MUS. DOC. TRIN. Toronto and Toronto Universities. Formerly Organist St. Dominic and St. Andrew's R.C. Newcastle; St. Benet's, Monkwearmouth; St. Cuthbert's R.C. North Shields. Publications: "Westminster Hymnal," etc. Recreation: Literature. Club: Pen and Palette.

HENDERSON, A. M., 3, St. James Place, Glasgow. Born at Glasgow, 1879. Studied music in Berlin at the Klindworth-Scharwenka Conservatorium, principally under Scharwenka; later under Pugno, in Paris. Diplomé of the Klindworth-Scharwenka Conservatorium, Berlin. L.R.A.M. Organist of Glasgow University since 1906. Author of two volumes of Transcriptions for Piano from the works of Bach (Bayley & Ferguson) and has edited two organ albums for the same firm. Hobbies: Literature and pictures.

HERD, WILLIAM A., 44, Devonshire Road, Aberdeen. Born and educated at Aberdeen. Teacher of pianoforte, organ and singing. Organist Rosemount Parish Church, 1885-1897; Holburn Parish Church, since 1897.

HERRING, FRANCIS, Redlands, Tiverton, Devon. Born 1862 at Deptford. Educated at Cambridge. M.A. Organist Blundell's School Chapel, since 1885. Hobby and recreation: Gardening and bicycling.

HEWITT, JOSEPH HALL, 16, Lord Street, Liverpool. Born 1887 at Liverpool. Educated under F. H. Burstall, Liverpool Cathedral Organist. Organist Parish of Frankby, Cheshire, 1906; Parish Church of St. John the Baptist, Toxteth, 1907; Allerton All Hallows, 1909.

HEY, ARTHUR, 17, Walter Road, Swansea. MUS. BAC. DURHAM., F.R.C.O., L.R.A.M. Organist St. James', Swansea, 1885-1904; Parish Church, Swansea, since 1904.

HEYWOOD, E., 142, North Road, St. Helens, Lancs. Born (1876) and educated at Huddersfield F.R.C.O. Organist Parish Church, Thurstonland, near Huddersfield, 1889-92; Parish Church, Newmill, 1892-6; St. Mark's, St. Helens, 1896-1907; Parish Church, St. Helens, since 1907.

HEYWOOD, JOHN, Hanbury House, 38, Camp Hill, Birmingham. Born and educated at Birmingham. Trained R.A.M. London M.I.S.M. Organist and Choirmaster St. Judes', Birmingham, 1863; St. Mary's, Aston Brook, 1863-5. Assistant Organist Holy Trinity, Bordesley, 1864-6. Organist and Choirmaster St. Margaret's, Ward End, 1865; St. Paul's, Balsall Heath, Birmingham, since 1865. Publications: "Art of Chanting" (Clowes), "Choral Office of Matins and Evensong" (Novello). Hobbies: Acting and reciting.

HIBBERT, NORMAN, Oxford House, Burton Road, Derby. Born 1868 at Staneley, Derbyshire. Trained under H. N. Biggin and Dr. H. Keeton, Peterboro. MUS. B. OXON., F.R.C.O. Organist Finedon, Northants, 1887; Wisbech, Cambs, 1889; Christ Church, West Hartlepool, 1893; All Saints', Derby, 1894; St. Luke's, Derby, 1901; St. Werburgh's, Derby, since 1912. Publications: Bass songs, Fantasia on Hymn Tune. Recreations: Walking, cycling and swimming.

HICKOX, EDWIN J., The Cottage, Bagshot. Born 1869. A.R.C.M., F.R.C.O. Private Organist to Earl of Aberdeen, 1887. Organist Christ Church, Endall Street, 1888; St. Paul's, Paddington, 1890; St. Anne's Parish Church, Bagshot, since 1894. Professor of Pianoforte, Guildhall School of Music, London. Publications: Album of songs (Weekes), part song, " The Last Day of Autumn " (Weekes).

HICKS, MISS LILIAN E., 56, Friars Street, Sudbury. Born at North Shields, Northumberland. Educated at Brussels. Studied under the late Dr. Rea; Mr. C. W. Todd, MUS. BAC. and Mr. T. W. Ritson, MUS. BAC. F.R.C.O. Hon. Deputy Organist for nine years (seven years under Mr. C. W. Todd, MUS. BAC.) of Tynemouth Priory, Northumberland. Organist All Saints' Church, Sudbury, since 25th December, 1910.

HIGGS, FRANKLIN, Bath Villa, 43, Park Road, Gloucester. Born 1837 at Gloucester. Organist and Choirmaster Southgate Congregational, Gloucester, since 1863. Had previously been Organist and chorister with various choirs.

HIGHE, FRANCIS GARDNER, The Grove, Castleacre, Norfolk. Born 1876 at Castleacre. Educated privately. F.I G.C.M., CERT. TRIN. COLL. LOND, Independent gentleman. Organist St. James' Parish Church, Castleacre, since 1893. Publisher of various songs. Hobbies: Acting, play-writing, billiard playing, fishing and shooting.

HILL, MISS, Spring View, Ecchinswell, Newbury. Born at Ecchinswell. Trained under J. Liddle, MUS. BAC., and A. H. Drury, A.R.C.O. Organist St. Lawrences', Ecchinswell, Newbury, since 1878.

HINTON, JOHN WILLIAM, Bridge House, Stoke Prior, Bromsgrove. M.A., MUS. D. TRINITY COLLEGE, DUBLIN. Organist St. Michael's and All Angels', Woolwich, 1891-1909; Church of the Ascension, Blackheath, 1909-12 Author of " Organ Constructions " and " Story of the Electric Organ."

HIRST, A. LIVINGSTONE, Naburn House, East Twickenham. Born 1874 at Batley, MUS. BAC. DUNELM., F.R.C.O. Organist St Stephen's, East Twickenham, since 1894. Publications: " What is Counterpoint," organ recital pieces, " Harmony in Eight Pages," pianoforte works, church music, songs. Hobbies: Photography and bookbinding.

HITCHCOCK, WILLIAM REUBEN, 107, Salcott Road, Clapham Common, London, S.W. Born 1869 in London. A.T.S C. Organist Northcote Road Baptist Church, Wandsworth, since 1892.

HOBY, CHARLES, Royal Marine Barracks, Chatham. Born in London. Educated privately and Royal College of Music. A.R.C.M. (double diploma), L.R.A.M. (conductorship). Associate the Philharmonic Society, London. Formerly Director Natal School of Music. Conductor Durban Orchestra, Municipal Choir, Male Voice Choir. Instructor in Music Natal Education Department, 1891-1906. Band Master Royal Marines (Chatham Division) since 1907. Organist Duke of York's

Royal Military School, 1890-1; Parish Church, Durban (Natal), 1893-1906; St. Luke's, Redcliffe Square, South Kensington, since 1906. Hobby and recreation: Photography and riding.

HODGE, HERBERT, 40, Ashmead Road, St. John's, London, S.E. Born 1869 at New Cross. Trained R.C.M. F.R.C.O., A.R.C.M. Sub-Organist St. Brides', Fleet Street, E.C., at age of 11; St. Anne's, Soho, 1884; St. Mary Abbots, Kensington, 1885; Marylebone Parish Church, 1886. Organist and Choirmaster Hornsey Parish Church, 1888; St. Peter's, Cranley Gardens, S.W., 1893; St. Nicholas Cole Abbey, E.C., since 1905. Assisted Sir George Martin at St. Paul's Cathedral, 1888-93. Professor (and afterwards Director of Music) at the Royal School for the Indigent Blind, St. George's Circus, London, S.E., 1885-1902.

HODGSON, JOHN EDWARD, 2, Ann Street, Hillhead, Glasgow. Born 1873 at Drighlington, Yorks. Educated at Turton Hall College, Gildersome, Leeds. MUS. BAC. DURHAM, F.R.C.O. Organist Gildersome Parish Church, 1887; Congregational, Dewsbury, 1893; Lansdowne Church, Glasgow, since 1905; Organist Choral and Orchestral Union, Glasgow, since 1906.

HOGG, HERBERT, 29, Belvoir Street, Princes Avenue, Hull. Born 1876 at Hull. A.R.C.O. Organist and Choirmaster Congregational, Cottingham, near Hull, 1896-1903; St. Stephen's, Hull, since 1905. Conductor North Clive Choral Society, 1904; Hessle Choral Society, since 1906. Recreation: Cycling.

HOGGETT, THOMAS JAMES, 7, Hillary Place, Leeds. Born 1864 at Darlington. Educated at Durham Cathedral. MUS. BAC DUNELM., F.R.C.O., L.R.A.M., A.R.C.M., L.T.C.L. Organist St. Ninian's, Whitby, 1886-96; All Souls Church, Leeds, 1896-1901. Conductor Whitby Orchestral Society, 1891-96; Bramley Choral Society, 1896-98. Musical Director Rev. the Marquis of Normanby's School, Mulgrave Castle, Whitby, 1892-1904; Girls' High School, Harrogate, 1897-1907. Girls' High School, Ilkley; Girls' High School, Chapel Allerton, Leeds; St. Mary's College, Leeds. Teacher of Harmony, Composition and Art of Teaching, Leeds City School of Music; Lecturer in Music Educational Department Leeds University; Lecturer in Music West Riding Training College for Women, Bingley. Teacher of music. Hobbies: Reading, literature.

HOLFORD, EDWARD L., F.R.C.O., 3, Grove Villas, Nightingale Lane, Wanstead. Formerly Organist St. Peter's, Limehouse; St. Matthias, Plaistow; St. Anne's Parish Church, Limehouse; and St. Stephen's, Bow. Now Organist and Choirmaster, Christ Church, Wanstead.

HOLGATE, JOHN, Rufford, 198, Upper Chorlton Road, Manchester. Born (1871) and educated at Manchester. MUS. BAC. DUNELM., F.R.C.O Organist Cross Street Chapel, Manchester, 1893-7; Lauriston Place U.P. Church, Edinburgh, 1897-1900, South Manchester New Church' since 1900. Composer of music.

HOLLANDS, HIRAM ALFRED, St. Rest, Eversley Road, Silverhill, St. Leonards on Sea. Born 1884 at Hastings. Educated at St. Leonards Senior Honours (piano) L.C.M. Assistant Master Tower Road Council School. Organist Wellington Square Baptist, Hastings, since 1907. Late Conductor Gensing Choral Society. Publications: "La Garde Imperiale Marche Militaire " (piano); " School Chums " Polka March; " Bravo Boys " Quick Step (2 violins or mandolines and piano); " Cantilene " (organ); " The Aerial Post " (piano); " Off to the Seaside " (piano); " Rollicking Pete " (piano); " Valse Caprice " (piano). Hobbies and recreations: Music, cycling, gardening, and drawing.

HOLLINGSHEAD, FREDERICK E, 5, Burlington Street, Bath. F.R.C O., A R.C.M. Formerly Organist Uttoxeter Parish Church and St James', Nottingham. Now Organist and Choirmaster St. Andrew's Church, Walcot, Bath.

HOLLOWAY, FREDERICK WILLIAM, 39, Lanercost Road, Tulse Hill, S W. Born 1873 at St. Ives, Hunts Educated at London F.R.C.O. Teacher of singing, composition, and pianoforte. Organist St. Paul's, Herne Hill, 1894-1909. Appointed All Saints', West Dulwich, 1909 Publications · Organ music, pianoforte and songs, church services, etc. (Novello ; Vincent Music Co ; Arthur Schmidt Co., Boston ; Collard Montrie ; Richards, Stainer & Bell, Bosworth).

HOLLOWAY, REGINALD F. C , National School, Farnborough, Hants. School teacher. Organist College Chapel, Winchester, 1906-8. Assistant Organist Farnborough Parish Church, 1908-10. Organist Farnborough Parish Church, since 1910.

HOLMAN, MELBOURNE, Albion House, Bovey Tracey. Born at Torquay, 1885. Educated at Torbay College. Piano tuner and Teacher of Music. Assistant Organist St John's, Torquay, 1905-6 Organist St. Raphaels, Torquay, 1907-8. Organist and Choirmaster St Thomas A-Becket Parish Church, since September, 1908 Hobbies and recreations : Swimming, cycling and church history. Club · Bovey Tracey Constitutional.

HOLMES, GEORGE AUGUSTUS, Auckland House, Linden Grove, Peckham Rye, London, S E Born 1861 and educated privately. Director of Examinations, London College of Music. Organist St George's, Camberwell, 1880-1903 ; London College of Music since 1903. Has given recitals at International Fisheries Exhibition, 1883 ; Inventions Exhibition, 1885. Publisher of numerous well-known musical works, chiefly of educational nature. Hobby and recreations : Collecting old music, golf, cycling and motoring

HOLTHAM, T. KING, 52, Cherrington Road, Hanwell, London, W. Born 1857 at Gloucester. Educated at Bedford Grammar School. Organist Ely Cathedral, 1872-7 ; St. Margaret's, Lee, Kent, 1879-86 ; All Saints', Acton, since 1886 Conductor of Acton Choral and Orchestral Society. Hobbies : Gardening and engineering.

HONEY, WILLIAM JOHN WHITE, 13, Stormont Road, Lavender Hill, London, S.W. Born 1863 in London. Educated privately Commercial clerk. Organist St. Bartholomew's the Great, West Smithfield, 1880-4 ; St. Mary's, Holmbury, Dorking, 1885-6 ; British Consular Chapel, Pernambuco, 1888-9 ; Church Army End Church, London, 1900-1 ; St. Catherine's, Hatcham, S.E , 1902-8 ; Church of the Ascension, Lavender Hill, S.W , since 1909.

HOPKINS, NOEL T., 48, Bishopthorpe Road, York. Organist Clare College, Cambridge.

HOPKINSON, BERTRAM, Dovecote Cottage, Ashover, Chesterfield. Born (1887), and educated at Ashover. Senior Honours T C L Organ Builder Assistant Organist Wesleyan Chapel, Ashover, 1908-1910. Organist Ashover Parish Church since 1910.

HORNBY, W. W , 340, Woodhouse Grove, Droylsden, Manchester. Born 1867 at Droylsden. Educated privately. M.I.S M. Lecturer on

Singing. Conductor Droylsden and District Philharmonic Society, Droylsden Co-operative Society. Organist Droylsden Parish Church, since 1888. Hobby and recreation: Literature and tennis.

HORSFIELD, GEORGE, 12, Third Avenue, Halifax. Born 1876 at Halifax. Organist St. Mary's, Halifax, 1901-8; All Saints', Salternebble, since 1908. Formerly of St. Thomas', Halifax.

HORSFIELD, WILLIAM, 32, Bull Green, Halifax. Born at Queensbury, 1852. A.R.C.O. Organist St. James', Halifax, since 1879.

HORTON, H. N., 42, Church Street, Barnsley. F.R.C.O., A.R.C.M. Formerly Organist St. John's, Wilton Road, London, S.W., and Organist and Choirmaster Holy Trinity Church, Maidstone. Organist and Choirmaster Parish Church, Barnsley, since May, 1912.

HOWARD, GERALD AMBROSE, Hope Villa, 91, New Road, Ware, Herts. Born 1889 at Ware. Organist Holy Trinity, Wareside, 1905; St. John the Baptist Great Amwell, Ware, since 1905. A.R.C.O., July, 1910.

HOWE, ALBERT PERCY, "Cecilia," 1, Linden Road, Bexhill-on-Sea. Born at Battle, 1885. Teacher of music, singing, pianoforte, organ, and theory. MUS. BAC. (DUNELM), F.R.C.O., L. MUS. T.C.L. Organist St. Andrew's, Bexhill, 1900-4; St. Stephen's, Bexhill, 1904-7; St. Barnabas', Bexhill, since 1907. Conductor Bexhill Musical Society. Recreations: Walking, cycling, swimming, and tennis.

HOWELL, JAMES, A.R.C.O., 272, Upper Parliament Street, Liverpool. Born 1877 at Liverpool. Trained under Mr. Ernest H. Smith, F R.C.O. St. Bede's Church, Liverpool, and Dr. J. C. Bridge, M.A, Chester Cathedral. Organist and Choirmaster St. Mary's (Parish) Church, Birkenhead, 1908-1909; Emmanuel Church, Liverpool, 1909-1912; St. Dunstan's Church, Liverpool, 1912; Bandmaster 3rd West Lancashire Brigade, R.F.A.

HOWELLS, DANIEL, Heatfield Road, Pontardawe, Glam. Born 1893 at Pontardawe. Clerk. Organist St. John's Church, Alltwen, Pontardawe, 1907-8; St. Peter's Church, Pontardawe, since 1908.

HOYLE, WALTER, Haldon, Manor Road, Coventry. Born at Exeter. Music Master King Henry VIII School, and High School for Girls. F.R.C.O. Late Organist St. Petrox, Exeter. Sub-Organist of Exeter Cathedral for 7 years (was selected for this post in open competition, out of 250 applicants). Conductor St. Michael's Festival Society, and Organist St. Michael's, Coventry.

HUGHES, MILLWARD, 9, Park Road, S. Birkenhead. Born Birkenhead, 1862. Professor of music. Organist and Choirmaster St. Anne's Church, Birkenhead, since 1887. Publications: 42 pianoforte works, 15 songs, 4 organ works, 15 hymns, anthems, etc. Recreation: Golf.

HULBERT, ARTHUR W. H. Chislehurst, Sydenham Villas Road, Cheltenham. Born 1861 at Cheltenham. Articled pupil and assistant to J. A. Matthews, Esq., L. MUS, Cheltenham. Deputy Organist Church of the Holy Trinity, 1877-1880. Organist Church of the Holy Trinity, Cheltenham, since 1880. Hobby: Photography.

HULL, A. EAGLEFIELD, 48, New North Road, Huddersfield. MUS. DOC. (OXON), F R C O   Formerly Organist, Market Harborough ; St. Mary's, Plaistow, E. ; Parish Church, Bishop's Stortford. Lecturer on Musical subjects ; organ recitalist, coach for University degrees.   Director of Huddersfield Chamber Music Society.   Organist, Huddersfield Parish Church   Author, " Organ Playing : its Technique and Expression " ; editor, " Modern Organ Composers " (Augener) ; reviser of the whole of the W. T. Bast Edition of Bach's Organ Works ; co-editor with Dr. Carl of New York and M. Bonnet of Paris of the complete Guilmant Organ Works ; author of Handbook to Bach's Organ Works. Principal Huddersfield College of Music.   Writer for " London Musical Record " and " Huddersfield Examiner."

HULL, PERCY CLARKE, Castle Green House, Hereford   Born 1878 at Hereford.   Articled pupil to Dr. Sinclair (Hereford Cathedral).   L R A M., A.R C.O., Hon. Local Examiner, R C.M   Assistant Organist Hereford Cathedral, since 1898.   Choirmaster, St Peter's Church, Hereford Lecturer in Music Hereford Training College and Music Master Cathedral School and Shrewsbury High School   Recreations : Cycling and walking.

HULME, FREDERICK, WALKER 16, Hanover Square, Sheffield.   Born 1865 at Sheffield   Professor of music.   Organist and Choirmaster Hathersage Parish Church, 1900-3 , Conisboro' Parish Church, 1903-8 ; Hathersage Parish Church, since 1908.   Publications : Songs and organ music. Hobby : Gardening.

HUNN, WILLIAM RICHARD, 14, Regent Road, Great Yarmouth.   Born at Great Yarmouth, 1879   A R.C.O. (1902), F.R.C.O., L.R.A.M. (1911), A R.C.M (1912).   Professor of Music.   Assistant Organist Great Yarmouth Parish Church, 1897-1904.   Organist St. Mary's Parish Church, Southtown, Great Yarmouth, since 1899.   Director of Music, Britannia Pier and Pavilion, Great Yarmouth, since 1902.   Conductor of Norfolk Military Band.   Past Provincial Grand Organist of Suffolk ; Organist United Friends Lodge, No. 313 ; St. Andrew's Lodge, No. 1631.   Teacher of singing, organ and pianoforte.   Music Master Yarmouth College. Publications   Anthems—" Blessed are they that dwell in Thy House," " O Send out Thy Light and Thy Truth," " O give thanks unto the Lord," " Thanks be to Thee for now and evermore " , Quartette— " Bow down thine ear," " Save me, O God."

HUNT, EDWIN, Clifton House, Towcester.   Born (1857), and educated at Bristol.   Music Warehouse, piano and organ tuner.   Organist St. Lawrences Parish Church, Towcester, 1876-1900 , Easton Neston Church, Towcester, since 1900.

HUNT, HUBERT, W ,2, Upper Byron Place, Clifton, Bristol. Born at Windsor, 1865.   Educated at St. George's School, Windsor Castle   Violinist. Organist and Choirmaster Clewer Parish Church, 1883-6 ; Christ Church, Clapham, 1886-7 , St. Jude's, South Kensington, 1887-1901 ; Bristol Cathedral, since 1901.   Club : Bristol Musical.

HURST, JAMES, 64b, Patrick Street, Cork.   Born 1857, at Barley, Herts. Educated at Cavendish Grammar School, Suffolk   Agent for " Irish Times."   Organist Cavendish, Suffolk,‖1872-78 ; Long Melford, Suffolk, 1878-9 ; Eastham, Cheshire, 1879-84 ; St Catherine's, Long Melford, 1885-90 ; St. Mary's Shandon, Cork, 1890-8 ; Christchurch, Cork, 1898-1902 , St. Michael's, Blackrock, Co Cork, since 1902   Secretary Sunday's Well Boating and Tenins Club, and Cork Golf Club.

HUXLEY, THOMAS DAVIDSON, 45, Lime Grove, Hoole, Chester Born at Chester, 1876. Educated at Holy Trinity School, Chester. F.R.C.O. Solicitor's cashier Organist Waverton Church, 1895-8 ; Christleton Church, 1900-2 ; St Mary's, Chester, since 1902. Recreations : Reading, cycling, and walking

IBBERSON, JOSEPH WILLIAM, 41, Durham Road, Sheffield. Born at Sheffield. Educated at Sheffield and Paris. Organist Wesley Church, Fulwood Road, Sheffield, since 1888.

ILIFFE, FREDERICK, 13, Warnborough Road, Oxford. Trained at Kibworth Grammar School and private. M.A , MUS. BAC. OXON Organist St. Barnabas', Oxford, 1879-83 ; St. John's College, Oxford, 1883 ; Oxford University, 1900 , St Mary the Virgin, Oxford, since 1900 Conductor Queen's College Musical Society, 1883-1904. Examiner for Musical Degrees, Oxford, 1908 Publications : Oratorio—Visions of St. John the Divine ; Eight-part Motette—Sweet Echo ; Cantatas—Morning, Evening, Power of Song, Via Crucis ; anthems, services and part songs. Recreations : Canoeing, fishing and gardening.

IRELAND, JOHN NICHOLSON, 54, Elm Park Mansions, Chelsea, London, S.W. MUS BAC., F R C O , A.R.C M (Late Composition Scholar, R.C.M., London) Formerly Organist St Mary's, Hornsea Rise , All Saints', Tufnell Park ; St Jude's, Upper Chelsea, 1894-1904 Organist St. Luke's Parish Church since 1904 Sub-Organist Holy Trinity, Sloane Street, since 1898. Choirmaster, St. Jude's, Upper Chelsea, since 1907.

IVIMEY, JOHN W., 1, Arundel Mansions, Fulham, London S W. Educated privately. B MUS. OXON., F R.C O , A.R.C.M. Organist (assistant) and Music Master Wellington College, 1888 , Harrow School, 1890-94 ; Organist St. Paul's, Onslow Square, 1891-1906 ; Dulwich College Chapel, 1906-1910 ; Grand Organist of Grand Lodge of Freemasons, 1910-1911 ; Grand Organist Mark Masons, 1912. Publications : Choral, orchestral, and chamber music, operas, etc Hobby : Writing. Clubs ; Savage and Three Arts.

IVORSEN, MISS GRACE, The Lodge, 81, Drewstead Road, Streatham, London S.W. Educated Royal Academy of Music, London. A R A.M., A.R.C M·, A.G.S M. Gold medal for pianoforte playing. Organist Magdalene Hospital, Streatham, S W. Hobbies and recreations : Reading, cycling, walking, modern languages. Successor to Miss Stainer (sister of Sir John Stainer, MUS. DOC.), for 50 years Organist to the Magdalene Hospital.

JACKSON, FRED W., Hopefield, 154, Liverpool Road, Birkdale, Southport Born and educated at Eccles F N C M Formerly Assistant Organist Christ Church, Patricroft, Manchester Organist St John's Parish Church, Ainsdale, Southport, 1895-1910 ; St John's Parish Church, Birkdale, Southport, since 1910 Publications : '' Crossing the Bar '' (song) ; and male voice part song ; '' Love's Repose '' (waltz)

JAMES, CHARLES KENNETH, Invergordon, Allerton, Liverpool. Born 1875, at Liverpool. Educated at Merchant Taylor's School Insurance manager Organist St. Matthias, Liverpool, 1897 ; All Saints', Stoney-croft, 1898 , St John's, Waterloo, 1902 ; St. Nicholas', Blundellsands, 1903 ; St. Peter's Parish Church, Woolton, since 1908. Musical Director, New Brighton Amateur Operatic Society, and Blundellsands and Formby Operatic Society, since 1905. Hobby ; Water colour drawing

JAMES, HAROLD W. W., 48, Adelaide Road, Brockley, London, S E. Born 1881. Trained under Dr. Madeley-Richardson, M.A., at Southwark Cathedral. Organist Corpus Christi College Mission, 1904-07 ; St. Paul's, Dock Street, E., 1907-08 ; Potter's Bar Parish Church, 1908-09 ; Peckham Parish Church, S.E., since 1909.

JAMIESON, D. BURNS, 87, Port Street, Stirling. N.B. Born 1877. at Linlithgow. Educated at Falkirk and Edinburgh M I.S.M. Teacher of music. Organist East U.F. Church, Linlithgow, 1892-8 ; Allan Park U.F. Church, Stirling, since 1898. Publications : 5 anthems, 3 hymn tunes, 2 vespers, and one song.

JARMAN, ROBERT FRANCIS, 32, Ewesley Road, Sunderland. Born 1874 at Stockton-on-Trees. Trained privately. MUS. BAC. DUNELM, F.R.C O. Organist and Choirmaster St. Stephen's, Ayres Quay, Sunderland, 1890-94 ; St. Peter's, Bishopwearmouth, 1897-1902 , Monkwearmouth Parish Church, since 1902. Music Master Bede Collegiate Boys' School, Sunderland Publications : Songs, anthems, etc. Hobbies : Music and shooting. Member Sunderland Rifle Club.

JARRATT, OWEN SINCLAIR, Bridge House, Honiton. Born 1884 at Goodleigh, N Devon. Trained under Dr Wood at Exeter Cathedral. M.I.S.M Professor of Music. Organist and Choirmaster Parish Church, Clyst St. George, 1902 ; Assistant Organist St. Anne's, Soho, 1904-7. Organist and Choirmaster Parish Church, Honiton, since 1909.

JEBOULT, HAROLD A , 1, Birch Grove, Taunton Born and educated at Taunton. F.R.C O., A R C M , L. MUS., T.C L Organist Holy Trinity, Taunton, 1888-97 , St. Mary Magdalene, Taunton, since 1897. Conductor, Taunton Madrigal Society. Organist Lodge " 261 " Hon. Conductor Taunton Deanery branch of the Bath and Wells Diocesan Choral Association. Local representative and examiner for R A.M., also R.C.M.

JEFFREY, H. C., 22, N Hamilton Street, Kilmarnock. Born at Dreghorn, Ayrshire. Trained at Kersland Barony School. A.R.C O. Teacher of Music. Formerly Organist, Calder U.F. Church, Lochwinnoch, when 16 years old ; U.F. Church, Skelmorlie. Organist and Choirmaster King Street U.F. Church, Kilmarnock, since 1910. Conductor of King Street Musical Association. Hobby and recreation : Photography and golf.

JEFFERIES, JOHN EDWARD, 166, Westmorland Road, Newcastle-on-Tyne. Born at Walsall. Trained at Royal College of Music. F.R C O. Formerly Organist and Choirmaster Walsall Parish Church Organist and Choirmaster The Cathedral, Newcastle-upon-Tyne, since 1905. Publications : Oratorio, " The Annunciation " ; Evening Service in E flat, etc. Member Northern Conservative and Unionist Club, Newcastle-upon-Tyne.

JENNER, JOHN CARTER, 7, De Crespigny Villas, Camberwell, London, S E. A.R C M. Formerly Organist Christ Church, Bexley Heath, and Parish Church, Northfleet. Organist St. Giles', Camberwell, since 1890.

JOB, JONATHAN, 67, Fonnereau Road, Ipswich Born 1875 at Little Aston, Sutton Coldfield. Educated at Lichfield Grammar School F R C O. Articled pupil Lichfield Cathedral. Organist Finedon Parish Church, Northants, 1896-1900 ; St. Margaret's Parish Church, since 1900. Other appointments Conductor Ipswich Amateur Opera Company; Felixstowe Choral Society Recreations : Golf and cricket.

JOHNSON, Arthur, The College, Sutton Road, Shrewsbury. Born at Norwich. Trained at Norwich Cathedral and Leipsic Conservatoire. Diploma Leipsic. Formerly Organist at Elgin and St. Giles, Shrewsbury. Organist St. Mary's, Shrewsbury, since 1910.

JOHNSON, Basil, West Vale, Rugby. Born (1861), and educated at Malvern College, Magdalen College, Oxford, and the Royal College of Music. B.A., Oxon. Formerly Organist St. James, Norlands, Notting Hill; St. Gabriel's, Pimlico. Organist School Chapel, Rugby, since 1886. Director of music in Rugby School. Conductor of the Rugby Philharmonic Society, and the Rugby School Subscription Concerts. Examiner for the Associated Board of the Royal College and Royal Academy of Music.

JOHNSON, Bernard, Clinton Terrace, The Park, Nottingham. B.A., MUS. BAC., CANTAB. F.R C.O. Organist Choir and Music Master, Framlingham College, Suffolk, 1889-91. Organist, Choir and Assistant Master, Leeds Grammar School, 1891-1905 Conductor Leeds Musical Union, 1902-5 Organist Priory Church Bridlington, 1905-10; Albert Hall, Nottingham (city organ), since 1910.

JOHNSON, Thomas, 69, Gillott Road, Birmingham Born at Wednesbury. Educated at Mason College, Birmingham. MUS. BAC. CANTAB. Conductor Darlston Choral Society since 1896. Organist Darlaston Town Hall (see under Wednesbury); All Saints', Darlaston, 1882-9; Christ Church, Summerfield, Birmingham, since 1889.

JONES, Arthur E., Orrisdale, 418, Chorley Old Road, Bolton. Born 1869 at Bolton Trained privately. F.R.C O., L.T.C L. Organist St. Augustine's, Tonge Moor, Bolton, 1883-7; Bridge Street Wesleyan Church, Bolton, 1887-96; Parish Church, Farnworth, since 1896; Bolton Borough Organist, since 1909 Publications: Anthems, organ pieces and pianoforte pieces Recreations. Cycling and walking. Organist Freemason's Lodge, No. 221, St. John, Bolton, since 1906.

JONES, Charles Lewis, The Gables, Northop Educated at Chester Cathedral MUS. BAC. DUNELM , L R.A.M., A.R.C.O. Organist Hereford County College, 1883; Highbury School, St. Leonards-on-Sea, 1884 9; All Saints', Princes Park, Liverpool, 1889-1901; Parish Church, Northop, since 1903. Music Master, St Clare's Convent, Pantasaph, since 1903. Conductor, teacher, orchestral player. Recreation: Cricket.

JONES, Ernest, Holland Villa, Bodafon, Llandudno. Formerly Organist St. Paul's, Craig-y-don; Parish Church (St. Hilary and St. Mary), Llanrhos Musical Director, piano soloist (with orchestra); accompanist viola. Hobby: Gardening.

JONES, H. Ewart, 19, Talbot Road, Wrexham. Born 1882 at Wrexham. Trained under John Morris, I S.M. Organist Penybryn Congregational Church, Salisbury Park, Wrexham, since 1903.

JONES, J., Gerald Street, Wrexham Born 1883 at Wrexham. A.R.C.O. Organist Brymbo Parish Church, Wrexham, 1901-10; St. Mark's, Wrexham, since 1911.

JONES, Llewelyn, Haulfre, Llanfairfechan. Born 1870 at Llandudno. Educated at Great Malvern. Teacher of music, F R.C.O. Organist Beaumaris Parish Church, 1888-9; Sub-Organist Bangor Cathedral, 1889-1902; Christ Church, Llanfairfechan, since 1892.

JONES, R. O., C.P.T C L , 9, High Street, Towyn. Born 1883 at Festiniog, N.W. Educated at Wrexham and Llangollen. Music teacher. Organist Engedl, Festiniog, 1899-1907 ; St. Cadvan's Parish Church, Towyn, since 1907 Bandmaster Towyn Silver Prize Band ; Conductor Towyn Orchestral Society ; Member Royal College of Organists Recreations : Walking, cycling, golfing.

JONES, WALTER, Handel House, Swadlincote, Burton-on-Trent. Born 1860 at Woodville. Trained privately. MUS. B. DUNELM, F.R.C.O., L. MUS. T.C L. Teacher of Music. Organist Holy Trinity, Ashby-de-la-Zouch, 1885-87 ; Parish Church, Swadlincote, 1888-1902 ; Wesleyan Chapel, Swadlincote, since 1905. Conductor Swadlincote Harmonic Society. Member of Derbyshire County Council. Court of Governors of Birmingham University. Hobby : Politics. Recreations . Tennis and bowls.

JONES, WALTER OWEN, Everart House, Kings Lynn Born 1843 at Kings Lynn Educated musically under J. F. Reddie, Organist St Margaret's, Kings Lynn Studied harmony and counterpoint under Dr. E. T. Chipp, Organist of Ely Cathedral. Local Secretary Trinity College London. Formerly Organist All Saints' Church ; St. John's Church, Kings Lynn Organist All Saints', Kings Lynn, since 1880 Examiner Open Scholarships R.C.M Composer of music Hobbies : Boating, swimming and skating.

JONES, W. PERCY, 71, Church Road, Gorleston. Born in 1891 at Fulham. Educated under Dr. Bates, Norwich Cathedral Organist St. Margaret's Church, Reydon, 1906 ; St Andrew's, Hingham, 1909 ; St. Andrew's, Gorleston, since 1911. Assistant Organist St Peter's, Mancroft, Norwich, since 1910.

JUDD, JOHN HARMAN, Lamb's Cottage, Lower Edmonton, N. Born 1847 at Lower Edmonton Educated at Lower Edmonton Registrar of Births and Deaths. Organist St. Michael's, Wood Green, Middlesex, 1861-63 ; St Thomas', Islington, London, 1864 ; Christ Church, Southgate, London, N., since 1864. Hobby : Topographical books and country rambles.

JUPP, CHRISTIE W. S., Fairview Villa, North Berwick. Born 1887 at Edinburgh Educated at Edinburgh Teacher of music. Organist and Choirmaster Livingston Parish Church, 1903-1904 ; St. Margaret's Parish Church, Edinburgh, 1904-1908 ; North Berwick Parish Church, 1908-1911 , Warrender Park U.F. Church, Edinburgh, since 1911. Hobbies . Golf and billiards.

KARN, FREDERICK JAMES, 106, Haverstock Hill, London, N.W. MUS BAC. CANTAB , MUS DOC. TRIN. UNIV. TORONTO Principal of the London College of Music. Organist and Choirmaster Church of the Holy Redeemer, Clerkenwell, E.C , since 1904. Publications : Book on harmony, Educational works on music, Classical works, etc.

KEECH, WILLIAM JOHN, 5, Kingsfield Terrace, Faversham, Kent Trained privately. MUS. BAC. DUNELM, F.R.C.O. Organist and Choirmaster St. Mary's, Bedford, 1894-1903 , Faversham Parish Church, since 1903. Conductor Faversham Philharmonic Society and Sittingbourne and District Musical Society Music and Singing Master Queen Elizabeth Grammar School, and also Wreight's School, Faversham.

KEIGHLEY, THOMAS, 12, Blair Road, Alexandra Park, Manchester. Born at Stalybridge. Educated privately. Trained at Royal Manchester

College of Music. MUS. D. VICT., F.R.C.O., A.R M C M., A R.C.M., L R A.M. Organist Christ Church, Stalybridge, 1887; St John's, Dukinfield, 1887-97, Albion Congregational Church, Ashton-under-Lyne, 1897-1911. Professor of Harmony and Counterpoint, Royal Manchester College of Music, since 1897. Lecturer in theory and singing, Victoria University of Manchester, since 1904. Conductor Stockport Vocal Union. Publications: Part songs, etc. Recreations: Golf and tennis.

KEMPSTER, WILLIAM CHARLES, 29, Victoria Road, Watford. Born 1876 at Watford. Educated privately. P.M.I.C.L. Professor of Music. Formerly Organist at Watford Union Chapel. Organist Christ Church, Watford, since 1905. Conductor Christ Church Orchestral Society. Publications: Morning and evening services. "Marche Religieuse" Recreation: Walking.

KENNETT, GEORGE, "Turville," New Cubbington, Leamington Spa. Born 1856 in London. Educated Westminster Abbey. Organist Parish Church, Folkestone, 1872-75; St. Mark's Parish Church, Leamington Spa, since 1875. Composer of music.

KERR, ALFRED HERBERT, The Glen, Victoria Drive, Eastbourne. Organist and Choirmaster St Mary's Parish Church, Eastbourne, since 1909. Formerly Organist Christ Church, Mayfair, for 9 years; St Mary's, Alverstoke, for 12 years.

KETTON, HAYDN, Thorpe Road, Peterborough Born 1847 at Mosborough. Educated at Windsor MUS DOC Organist Datchet Church, 1866-9, Aldin House (OXON F R.C O.) Slough, 1869-70; The Cathedral, Peterborough, since 1870. Conductor Peterborough Choral Union and Orchestral Society.

KING, ALFRED, 54, Compton Avenue, Brighton. MUS. DOC., OXON., F.R.C O., L.T C L. Organist and Choirmaster St Michael's, Brighton, since 1865. Parish Church, Brighton, 1878 Organist The Dome, Royal Pavilion, Brighton, since 1880 Composer of Oratorio, Epiphany, Mass in B flat, Prize Coronation Glee, Madrigal Society prize, 1909, services, part songs organ music, etc. Hobbies Philosophical studies and Freemasonry.

KING, CHARLES J., Brookdene, Kingsley Park Terrace, Northampton. Born 1859 at Brighton. Trained at St. George's Chapel, Windsor. Teacher of music Organist Farnham Royal 1877; Parish Church Hinckley, 1878, St. Sepulchre's, Northampton, 1890; St. Matthew's, Northampton, since 1895. Publication: Communion Service. Hobby: Reading.

KINGTON, HORACE VERNON, F R C O, L R A M., School of Music, Melrose Avenue, Beeston, Nottingham Born 1880 at Derby. Trained under A Rawlinson Wood, Esq., Mr Norman B Hibbert, and Mr. T. H Bennett Assistant Organist St Luke's, Derby, 1898-1903. Organist St. George's, Derby, 1897; Beeston Parish Church, Notts, since 1903. Recreations: Boating, cycling, motoring, walking, etc.

KIPPS, ARTHUR, 361, New Cross Road, London, S.E. Born 1868 in London. Educated at New Cross. Pianoforte dealer and importer. Organist St. Luke's, Deptford, 1883-8; Holy Trinity, Greenwich, 1888-94; Licensed Victuallers' Asylum Chapel, since 1894. Hobbies: Reading and billiards

KIPPS, WILLIAM JOHN, 93, Lewisham High Road, London, S.E. A.R.A.M., F.R.C.O. Professor and Examiner R A M Professor of Piano at Black-heath Conservatoire of Music. Trained at R A M. Formerly Organist St Saviour's, Denmark Park, S.E ; St Mark's, Lewisham, S.E. Started career as organist at 11 years of age. Organist St. Martin's-in-the-fields, London, since 1899.

KIRBY, CLARENCE HASTINGS, " Truro," Holmdene Avenue, Herne Hill, S E. Born 1869 at West Newington. Educated at Newington Grammar School and Camberwell (Wilson's) Grammar School A R C O. Organist St. Mark's, Walworth, 1886 ; Assistant Organist Newington Parish Church, 1887 ; Organist and Choirmaster All Souls', Grosvenor Park, 1890 ; Organist and Choirmaster Camden Parish Church, Camberwell, since 1912.

KIRBY, W. E, 22, Alexandra Road, Hemel Hempstead. Born 1877 at Fenny Stratford. Trained at T C L and privately. F.R C.O. Organist Fenny Stratford Parish Church, 1898-1907 ; All Saints' and St John's, Bedford, 1910-11 ; Parish Church, Hemel Hempstead, since January, 1912.

KIRBY, WILLIAM RAYMENT, Coolinge, Mount Nod Road, Streatham, S W. Born at Kennington Educated at City of London School MUS BAC DUNELM., F R C O. Organist St Mary's Parish Church, Newington, Surrey, 1882-1892. Organist and Choirmaster St George's Parish Church, Southwark, 1894-1896. Organist St. Mary's Parish Church, Newington, 1897 and Organist and Choirmaster since 1907.

KIRTLAND, J. S. R., Westover, Lytham Road, S. Blackpool Son of James Kirtland, Organ Builder. Born at Manchester, 1852 Educated under the Rev. L. W. Riley, M A., St. Cross, Knutsford. MUS. DOC (Toronto), F R C.O. (England). Organist St. Cuthbert's Parish Church, Lytham, 1870-4 , (Honorary), Holy Trinity, South Shore, Blackpool, 1883-7 ; and Christ Church, Blackpool, 1892-1907.

KITSON, C. H., St Filian's, Kimberley Road, Leicester. Born 1874 at Leyburn. Educated at Cambridge. M.A., MUS. DOC OXON. Assistant Music Master Haileybury College, 1897-98 ; St. Edmund's School, Canterbury, 1898-1901 Organist and Choirmaster St. John the Baptist, Knighton, since 1901. Publications : " The Art of Counter-point," " Studies in Fugues," anthems, organ pieces, etc.

KNOTT, ALBERT EDWARD, Taunton Road, Ashton-under-Lyne A R C O., M.I.S M Professor of Music. Musical Editor " Ashton-under-Lyne Herald " Organist Christ Church, Ashton-under-Lyne, since 1888. Hobbies and recreations . Literature, art and cycling

KNOWLES, CHARLES EDGAR, Kilmorie, Castle Street, Luton. Born 1887 at Luton. L.R A M Trained under Stanley Marchant, MUS. BAC., F R.C.O., A R A M. Organist and Choirmaster King's Street Congrega-tional Church, Luton, since 1904.

LAIDLAW, HUTTON ROGERS, 23, East Hermitage Place, Leith. Born 1884 A L.C.M. Trained under W. B. Ross, MUS B. OXON , F R C.O. Organist Gorebridge East U F Church, 1904-05 , South Queensferry U F Church, 1905 , Dean Street U.F. Church, Edinburgh, 1905-07 ; Guthrie Memorial U F. Church, Cowdenheath, 1907-09 ; Burnt Island Parish Church, since 1909. Recreations : Golf, cycling and walking

LANE, EDGAR ALFRED, Holly Bank, Dorchester. Formerly Sub-Organist Ripon Cathedral; Music Master, Magdalen College School; Organist Brackley Parish Church; Organist St. Peter's Church, Dorchester. Organist and Choirmaster Holy Trinity, Dorchester, since 1909. Principal Dorchester School of Music. Music Master Dorchester Grammar School. Conductor Dorchester Vocal Association and Madrigal Society, and Charminster Choral Society. Local representative Royal Academy of Music.

LANE, E. BURRITT, Hayes, Steyning, Sussex. Born 1849 at Christchurch, Hants. Trained T.C.M. and privately. MUS. B., DUNELM., F.T.C.L., Assoc. Phil. Soc. of London. Gold medallist, Examiner and Member of the Board of T.C.L. Formerly Organist Parish Church, Bromley, Kent; Holy Trinity, Twickenham; King's Weigh-house, London. Organist and Choirmaster Steyning Parish Church, since 1910. Publications. Te Deum and other Church music. Divisional Secretary for the University of Durham in the Union of Graduates in Music. Chairman of the Steyning Branch C.E.M.S.

LANE, FREDERICK, 28, Aygyle Road, Ealing. Born 1872 in London L.N.C.M. Organist and Choirmaster West Ealing Baptist Church, 1893-1906; St. James' Parish Church, Ealing, since 1908. Pianist, accompanist, and Conductor, Frederick Lane's band. Recreations: Boating and fishing. Club: Ealing Conservative.

LANE, HERBERT, 1, Grosvenor Road, Rugby. Born 1874 at Earlstown. Educated at Rugby. A.R.C.M. (pianoforte teaching), A R C O. Organist St. John the Baptist, Hillmorton, 1892-95; St. Thomas', Catthorpe, 1895-1900, St. Matthew's Parish Church, Rugby, since 1900. Conductor St. Matthew's Choral Society, 1901; Rugby Male Voice Choir, 1907. Organist, Rugby Philharmonic Society, 1910. Occupation: Cashier. Hobby: Model steam engines.

LANE THOMAS, 27, St. Alban's Road, Darwen. Organist St. Anne's, Warrington, 1880; St. Barnabas', Pimlico, S.W. (Deputy), 1885-6; St. John's, Pimlico, 1886; Walton Church, Warrington, 1888-98; Littleborough Parish Church, Rochdale, 1900-3; Darwen Parish Church, since 1903.

LANGDALE, BERNARD, 121, Park Grove, Barnsley, Yorks. Born at Bradford, 1876. Educated at Bradford and Leeds. Teacher pianoforte, organ, singing, and theory. L.I S.M., A.R.C.O. Organist St Mary's, Laisterdyke, Bradford, 1892; Parish Church, and Conductor Orchestral Society, Thornton, Bradford, 1900. Organist and Choirmaster St. George's, Barnsley, since 1903. Publications: Wild Anemone," Mazurka de Salon (pianoforte).

LAWSON, JOHN ADELBERG, Beethoven House, East Parade, Harrogate. F.R.C.O., F.T.C.L. Professor of music. Principal Beethoven School of Music (established 1898), Harrogate. Music and Singing Master, Pannal Ash College, Harrogate, since 1898. Organist and Choirmaster St. Paul's Presbyterian, Harrogate, since 1903. Director of Music St. Robert's R.C., Harrogate, 1898-1903; and at Blyth, Northumberland. Publications: Pianoforte compositions, anthems, etc. Hobbies: Cycling and photography.

LAWSON, JAMES BROOM, Bath House, Ardrossan. Organ expert. Organist Wesley Church, Dumfries, 1877; Skelmorlie Parish Church, 1883; Ardrossan New Parish Church, since 1887. Member Incorporated Soicety of Musicians. Pupil of Dr A. L. Peace.

LAWSON, JOHN RICHARD, 108, Grafton Street, Hull. Born 1889 at Hull. F.R.C.O., L.R.A.M. Trained at Royal Normal College and Academy of Music for the Blind. Organist Portobello P.M. Church, since 1911. Recreation : Reading.

LAWSON, J. WILLIAM, 7, Canyngi Square, Clifton, Bristol. Born 1844 at Bristol. Professor of Music. Organist St. Mary Redcliffe, Bristol, 1862-1906 (retired). Hobbies : Photography and gardening.

LAWTON, JOHN, 54, Wellington Street, Oldham. Born 1866 at Oldham. Educated privately (under William Lawton, Esq., and Jas. F. Slater Esq.). MUS. BAC. DUNELM, F.R.C.O. Formerly Organist Regent Street Congregational Church, Oldham ; Hope Congregational, Oldham ; All Saints, Oldham. Organist Holy Trinity Church, Shaw, since 1905. Hobby : Photography. Club : Freemasons Hall (Union Club).

LEAKE, GEORGE, 97, Hill Lane, Southampton. Born 1859 at Derby. Educated at Lichfield Cathedral. MUS. BAC. (DUNELM), F R.C.O , A.R.C.M., L.R.A.M. Lecturer on music, Hartley University College. Examiner to the Associated Board of the R.A.M., and R.C.M. Teacher of singing, pianoforte. Organist Holy Trinity, Halstead, Essex, 1880-99 ; St. Mark's, Southampton, since 1899.

LEE, BENJAMIN SANDBERG, 8, Devonshire Road, Claughton, Birkenhead. Professor of music. Formerly Organist Birkenhead Board of Guardians. Organist and Choirmaster Christ Church, Higher Bebington ; St. Mark's, New Ferry, Cheshire. Organist St. Mark's, Birkenhead since 1897. Publications : Church music, services, anthems, etc.

LEE, E. MARKHAM, Riffel, Woodford Green, N.E. Born at Cambridge. Educated Emmanuel College. M.A., MUS. DOC. CANTAB., F.R.C.O. Organist Emmanuel College, Cambridge, 1894 ; All Saints, Woodford Green, London, N E., since 1896. Professor G.S.M (1905). Examiner I.S.M (1904). Director Woodford Chamber Concerts (1901). Publications : Anthems, services, books on music, etc. Extension Lecturer University of Oxford (1909). Hobby and recreation : Mountaineering. Clubs : Oxford and Cambridge Musical.

LEEDS, FREDERIC, 22, Clarendon Road, Lewisham, S.E. Born 1866 at Lee, S.E. Educated musically at R.C.M. MUS. BAC. CANTAB., F.R.C.O. Specialist in voice production. Organist, St. Mark's Church, Lewisham, 1886 ; Organist and Choirmaster Christ Church, Brondesbury, 1890 ; St. Luke's Parish Church, Charlton, S.E , 1893 ; St. Mary's Parish Church, Lewisham, 1895 ; St. Margaret's Parish Church, Lee, since 1899. Publications : Evening Service for A.T.B. (Novello), sung at Westminster Abbey and Royal Chapel, Windsor ; Evening Service for S.A.T.B. in Bristol Service Book ; " Home and Liberty," part song ; etc.

LEWIS, FRANK, Welwyn House, Duffryn Terrace, New Tredegar, Mon. Born 1868 at Newport, Mon. Educated at Aberdare, South Wales . Organist Parish Church, New Tredegar, Mon., since 1900.

LEY, HENRY GEORGE, Christ Church, Oxford. Born 1887 at Chagford Rectory, Devon. Trained at St. George's Chapel, Windsor, and Uppingham School. Council Exhibitioner, Royal College of Music. A.R.C.M., MUS. BAC. Organist St. Mary's, Farnham Royal, Bucks, 1905-06 ; Organ Scholar Keble College, 1906-09 ; President of Oxford University Musical Club, 1908. Organist Christ Church Cathedral, Oxford, since 1909. Publications : Morning Service in C Minor ;

anthem for S.A.T.B. or A.T.T.B., " God so loved the World " ; part song for S.A.T.B., " How Sweet the Moonlight " ; Evening Service in C Minor, S.A.T.B. or T.T.B.B. ; anthem for T.T.B.B., " The Lord is My Shepherd " ; anthem for S.A.T.B., " Let all the World " ; carol in S.A.T.B., " In the Bleak Mid-winter." Recreations. Motoring, cycling, and golf.

LIDDLE, R. W., Vicar's Court, Southwell, Notts Born (1864), and educated at Durham. Hon. Vice President, G.O. Violinist. Organist St. Baldreds N. Berwick, N.B. 1886-8 ; Southwell Cathedral, since 1888 Conductor Mansfield Harmonic Society, 1898 ; Orchestral Society, 1906 Organist St. Peter's Church, Mansfield 1904. Conductor Newark and District Orchestral Society.

LILWALL, NORMAN ALFRED, 147, Ilford Lane, Ilford, Essex. Born at Tottenham. Professor of music. Organist St. Peter's, Regent Square, London, W.C., 1894-98 , Parish Church, Wembley, 1898-9 ; Christ Church, South Hackney, 1899-1905 ; St. Barnabas, Clapham Common. since 1905. Composer of organ, pianoforte, and Church music. Conductor St. Barnabas' Choral Society.

LINDSAY, THOMAS, 175, High Street, Arbroath. Formerly Organist and Choirmaster Moffat Parish Church, Lochee Parish Church. Organist Erskine U.F. Church, since 1884.

LINEKAR, THOMAS JOSEPH, Bryn Deryn, Queen's Park, Colwyn Bay. Born 1858 at Hoylake. Educated at Hoylake and Liverpool. Organist at Hoylake 1878-81 , Frankby, 1881-2 ; Hoylake 1882-3 ; Llandrillo yn Rhos (Colwyn Bay), 1883-7 ; St. John's Colwyn Bay, since 1887. Composer of " The Blacksmith," " Knights Love Song," " Sigh of the Breeze," " Angel of Dreams," " Entreat me not to leave Thee," " Jesu, Lover of my Soul " (chosen for contralto test, Royal National Eisteddfod, Colwyn Bay, 1910) ; three school songs (Curwen) ; three part, " Song of April " (female voices) ; Berceuse for organ (also arranged for piano) ; Bridal March , Rydal Mount March ; Isora Valses ; Tarantella for piano ; vesper, " God be with you till we meet Again " (also in post card form) ; hymn tunes arranged for organ students, including studies in the alto and tenor clefs, with instructive notes (just published).

LINFORD, ARTHUR BANKS, Carlton Villa, Wombwell, nr. Barnsley. Born and educated at Barnsley. Architect and Surveyor. Organist Wombwell Parish Church, 1886-7 ; Darfield Parish Church, 1887-1905 ; Wombwell Parish Church, since 1905 Composer of music. Hobbies . Painting and photography.

LISHMAN, GEORGE, " Ferney Cottage," Hatfield, Herts. Matriculated Queen's College, Oxford. Member Union of Directors of Music in Secondary Schools. Music Master Dagmar House School, Hatfield, Herts. Organist and Choirmaster Parish Church, Lemsford, and Hatfield House Music Master Hitchin Grammar School, two years ; Thorne Grammar School, two years , Ludlow Commercial School, eight years. Organist Richard's Castle Parish Church, two years ; Ludford Parish Church, two years ; Ludlow Parish Church (assistant), two years ; Local Secretary Trinity College of Music since 1904. Publications : (Vincent & Co) Benedicite, Te Deum, and Benedictus in chant form , vesper hymn, Nine Fold Amen. (Novello & Co) Hymn for beginning and end of term. The " Chester " series of school songs : No. 1, " Our Dear Old England " , No. 2, " Beneath the Flag " , No. 3, " A Song of Britain " ; No. 4, " A Cricket Song." " A Football Song," " Christmas Bells," " Our Heroes "

LITCHFIELD, ASA, 13, Nether Hall Road, Doncaster. Born at Hoyland, nr. Barnsley. Educated at Byegates Academy, West Malton, nr. Rotherham, and trained at the R.A.M. Music Dealer. Organist Hoyland Wesleyan, nr Barnsley, 1886-8 ; and Priory Place Wesleyan, Doncaster, since 1888. Teacher of music.

LIVESEY, F. J., B.A., St. Bees, Cumberland. Educated at Hereford Cathedral School and St. John's College, Cambridge. Deputy Organis-Hereford Cathedral 1883-4. Organist Priory Church, St. Bees, since 1887. Hobby : Photography.

LLOYD, RICHARD FRANCIS, 142, Upper Parliament Street, Liverpool. Born (1871) and educated at Liverpool. MUS. BAC. Surveyor and ganger. Organist Sefton Park Presbyterian Church, Liverpool. Chairman of Liverpool and District Organists' and Choirmasters' Association.

LOARING, JAMES, Brunswick House, Yeovil. Born 1838 at Yeovil. Trained under Sir J. Goss and George Cooper. MUS. BAC. OXON, F.R.C.O., L. MUS. T.C.L. Organist Trinity Church, Yeovil (at age of 12), 1850 ; St. Sepulcure, City of London, 1880 ; St. Leonard's, Shoreditch, 1890 ; St. Peter's, Tiverton, 1894. Recently resigned. Composer of Church music and pianoforte pieces.

LOCKETT, HENRY GERALD, Liszt House, Leyland. Born at Dunoon, Argyleshire, 7th August, 1878. Educated at Edinburgh Collegiate School and Sandringham House School, Southport. Associate of the Royal College of Music (organ playing and choir training). Assistant Organist St. Luke's Church, Leyland, 1898-1902. Organist and Choirmaster Holy Trinity Church, Preston, 1902-3 Conductor Leyland Glee and Madrigal Society, 1903 and 1904. Organist and Choirmaster, St. Andrew's Church, Leyland, since 1903. Hobbies and recreations : Mechanical pursuits, motor-cycling, and yachting.

LOFTHOUSE, BENJAMIN, Ashfield, 23, York Road, Birkdale, Southport. Born 1867 at Tadcaster, Yorks. Trained privately and at York Minster, under Dr. Naylor, MUS. BAC. OXON., F.R.C.O. Organist Tadcaster Parish Church, 1882 ; St. Martin's, Coney Street, York, 1892 ; St. Andrew's, Southport, since 1897.

LOMAN, RUDOLPH, 36, Heath Street, Hampstead, London, N.W. Born in Amsterdam. Trained at Leipsic Conservatoire and Cologne. Organist Austin Friars Dutch Church, London, since 1885. Engaged as Solo Pianist at annual Dutch Musical Festival, 1898. Hobby : Chess.

LONGYEAR, GEORGE ERNEST, St. Margate Road, Southsea. Born 1879 at Portsmouth. Educated at Portsmouth Higher Grade Secondary School. Professor of Music. Formerly Organist St. Patrick's Church, Pennar, Pembrokeshire. Assistant Organist Royal Dockyard (P. DR. Yard). Organist Arundel Street, Wesleyan, Portsmouth ; Christ Church Congregational, Southsea, since 1909.

LOTT, CLARENCE (son of the late Edwin M. Lott, MUS. DOC.), Kildare, Park Farm Road, Kingston-on-Thames. Born (1879) and educated in London Organist St Stephen's, Shepherd's Bush, 1892-93. Deputy Holy Trinity, Hammersmith, 1893-94. Organist and Choirmaster St. Raphael's, Kingston-on-Thames, since 1894. Composer of music. Recitalist, England and the Continent.

LOTT, JOHN B., Lombard Croft, Lichfield. MUS. BAC OXON., F.R.C.O. Formerly Organist St. Dunstan's ; St. Paul's, Canterbury ; Parish Church, Margate. Organist The Cathedral, Lichfield, since 1881.

LOVETT, SYDNEY H., 131, Saltram Crescent, Maida Hill, London, W. Born 1881 in London. Educated R.A.M. and private. F.R.C.O. Organist Christ Church, Brondesbury, N.W., 1897-1903 ; Harrow Weald Parish Church, 1903-1905 ; St. Augustine and St. Faith, since 1905.

LOW, WILLIAM GEORGE, 18, Eatington Road, Whipps Cross, Essex. Born 1880 in London. Educated privately. Organist St. Mary's, Benfleet, 1898 . Christ Church, Spitalfields, 1899-1906 ; Christ Church, Surbiton, 1906-9 ; St. Matthew's, Upper Clapton, since 1910.

LOWE, FRANK, 45, Trinity Road, Handsworth. Born 1888 at Birmingham. Trained under W. W. Randall. Gained two silver medals and a National Prize in Senior Examination of Trinity College, London, 1908. Organist Birchfields Wesleyan Church, Birmingham, since 1905, and Choirmaster also, since 1909. Recreations : Tennis and reading.

LUARD-SELBY, BERTRAM, The Precinct, Rochester. Born 1853. Educated at Tonbridge School and Oxford. Organist St. Barnabas, Marylebone, 1876 ; Salisbury Cathedral, 1881 ; St. Barnabas, Pimlico, 1885 ; Rochester Cathedral, since 1900. Composer of music. Hobbies : Fishing and sketching.

LUCAS, JAMES HENRY, 62, Hill Park Crescent, Plymouth. Born at Plushay, Cornwall. Educated at Borough Road College, Plymouth. A.T.C.L., A. Tonic Sol-fa College. Deputy Organist St. Peter's, Plymouth ; Christ Church, Plymouth, since 1901. School-master. Publications : Hymn tunes and anthem " I will worship." Recreations : Walking, geological science.

LUGAR, THOMAS W , 1, May Terrace, St. Jude's, Plymouth. Born (1867) and educated at Plymouth. Assistant Organist St. John's, Plymouth, 1885-9 , St Matthias, Plymouth, 1889-99. Organist Bickleigh Church, Roborough, 1899-1900 ; St. Jude's, Plymouth, since 1900.

LUMB, HORATIO ALBERT, Triangle, Halifax. Educated at Knaresborough. Trained under Dr. Roberts of Oxford. Formerly Conductor Halifax Orchestral Society, Greetland Choral Society, and Massed Choir Festivals. Judge Choral Contests. Organist and Choirmaster St. Mary's, Sowerby and Christ Church, Sowerby Bridge. Organist All Saints', Salterbibble, Halifax, 1887-1907. Conductor Ripponden Choral Society. President Halifax Dickens' Fellowship ; President Sowerby Bridge Literary and Scientific Society ; Lecturer in Musical Theory and Acoustics to Workers' Educational Union, Halifax ; Vice-President of Halifax Foreign Circle. Hobbies : Scientific and mechanical subjects, modern languages, rifle shooting, etc.

LUMSDEN, ANDREW S., 14, Bruntsfield Avenue, Edinburgh. A. MUS. T.C.L., L.C.M. Teacher of music. Organist Borthwick Parish Church, Midlothian, since 1897.

LUMSDEN, JAMES C., 69, Hanover Street, Edinburgh. Concert Director and Musical Agent. Organist Whitekirk Parish Church, 1898-1903, and Pilrig U.F. Church since 1903.

LUTTMAN, WILLIE LEWIS, Park Street, Frogmore, St. Albans. Born 1874 at High Wycombe. Studied at R.C.M.., 1891-1894, M.A., MUS. BAC. CANTAB., F.R.C O , A R.C.M. Organist Tylers Green Parish Church, Buckinghamshire, 1888-91 ; Hughenden Parish Church, 1894. Organ scholar St. Peter's College, Cambridge, 1894-97 ; Banbury Parish Church, 1898-1907 ; St. Alban's Cathedral, since 1907. Principal of St. Alban's School of Music. Conductor of School of Music Choral and Orchestral Society.

LUTTMAN, WALTER CHARLES, Havenfield, Banbury. F.R.C.O. Formerly Organist Parish Church, Llangollen, St. Paul's, Maidstone, Kent; Banbury Parish Church, since 1906.

MACDONALD, JAMES SOMERLED, 10, The Avenue, Brondesbury, London, N.W. Born 1876 in London. Educated privately and Guildhall School of Music Organist St. George's Presbyterian, Brondesbury, London, N.W., since 1892. Publication : Cantata and carols.

MACDONALD, PHIL., Briavels, Grove Lane, Kingston-on-Thames. Born 1869 at Islington Trained privately Organist St. Paul's, Covent Garden, 1891-1901 ; St. Stephen's, Hounslow, 1901-03 ; St. Matthew's, Surbiton, 1903-05 ; St. Paul's Parish Church, E. Molesey, Surrey, since 1906. Publications : Magnificat and Nunc Dimittis in B flat, Preces and responses and male voice music. Recreation : Cycling.

MACKINTOSH, ALFRED ALEXANDER, Nairn, Compton, Guildford. Born 1860 at Lowestoft. Educated privately. F.R.C.O. Teacher of music Organist St. Peter's, Kirkley, Lowestoft, 1880 ; St Mary's, Kippington, Sevenoaks, 1881 ; All Saints', Huntingdon, 1885 ; Godalming Parish Church, since 1890.

MACPHERSON, G. W. WILSON, 18, Goldsmid Road, Brighton Born at Bath, 1856. Educated at Sidney College, Bath. Articled pupil to Dr. Arnold, Winchester Cathedral. M.I.S.M. Teacher of music. Organist and Choirmaster St. Marychurch, Torquay, 1878 ; Parish Church, Camberwell, 1883 ; Parish Church, Sidmouth, 1889 ; St. Margaret's, Brighton, since 1894. Publications : Chant services. Recreations : Cycling and boating.

MACTAGGART, JOHN, 30, Bellevue Crescent, Ayr, N.B. A.R.C.M., L.R.A.M., Fellow Tonic Sol-fa College ; Certificated Vocalist, Trinity College, London. Formerly Organist and Choirmaster Kelton Parish Church ; St. George's U.F. Church, Castle Douglas ; Darlington Place U.F. Church, Ayr. Formerly Conductor Castle Douglas Choral Society, Ayr Amateur Opera Company, Ayr Philharmonic (Orchestral) Society, Paisley Philharmonic (Orchestral) Society, Conductor Gowan Choral Society, and Western Amateur Orchestra, Glasgow. Organist and Choirmaster St. Leonard's Parish Church, Ayr, since 1911.

MADDERN-WILLIAMS, R. J., 130, Cambridge Street, Norwich. Born 1885 at Pendeen, Cornwall. Educated R.C.M. and Wells Cathedral. F.R.C.O. Organist Wells Parish Church and Assistant Wells Cathedral, 1904-06 , Nave Organist Norwich Cathedral, 1906-08 Sub-Organist Norwich Cathedral. Organist and Choirmaster, St. Peter, Mancroft, Norwich. Music Master Norwich Pageant, 1912. Music Master Boys' High School. Conductor Mancroft Choral Society. Local Secretary T.C.L., representative of the R.A M.

MADDOCKS, JAMES, 19, Jermyn Street, Leicester. Born at Springwood, Chesterton. Trained under Mr. J. Alcock and Mr. W. Barrow. Organist Hovingham, Nr. Malton, 1882-3 ; Chesterton, N. Staffs, 1884 ; St. Michael and All Angels' Church, Leicester, since 1886. Publications: School songs and chant services. Hobbies : Gardening and fishing.

MAHON, HERBERT, The Gables, Saffron Walden. Born 1871 at Leigh-on-Mendip. Educated at Bloxham. MUS. BAC. DUNELM., A. MUS. T.C.L. Formerly Music Master Honiton School. Organist Holy Trinity, Lambeth ; All Hallows, Southwark. Organist Parish Church of St. Mary the Virgin, Saffron Walden, since 1898. Conductor North

Essex Association of Church Choirs, 1899 ; Saffron Walden Musical Society, 1905. Music Master Newport Grammar School, 1911. Recreation : Tennis.

MAISEY, W. H., 32, St. Margaret's Road, Manor Park, Essex. Born 1852 at Oxford. Associated with choir work since 1858. Organist St. John's, Wapping, London, since 1901.

MALONE, ROBERT, 3, Pembroke Road, Carlow, Ireland. Born at Dublin, 1847. Educated at St. Patrick's Cathedral, and Trinity College, Dublin. MUS. DOC , T.C.D. Organist St. Michan's, Dublin, 1866 ; Roscrea, 1868 ; St. Mary's, Carlow, since 1880. Conductor Leighlin Choir Festivals. Lecturer and Writer on Music, and Literature. Provincial Grand Organist S.E. and Midland Counties, Ireland. Composer of evening services, chants, pianoforte music, etc.

MANDER, RICHARD YATES, Claverdon, Argyll Street, Ryde, I.O.W. MUS. DOC. OXON, F.R.C.O., L.R.A.M. Organist St. John's, Leamington, 1879 ; St. Philip's, Birmingham, 1888. Music Master Royal Naval College Osborne, 1904-08 ; Blind College, Worcester, 1892-97. Organist Parish Church, Ryde, I.O.W., 1898 ; Town Hall, Ryde, since 1899.

MANFIELD, ARTHUR S., Maryfield, Skelmorlie. Born at Leeds. Educated at Glasgow Cathedral. A.R.C.M. Organist St. John's Episcopal, Glasgow. Assistant Organist Glasgow Cathedral, 1898-9 ; Canal Street United Free Church, 1899-1908 , Pobbok Street U.F. Church, Glasgow, 1908-1910 ; Parish Church, Skelmorlie, since 1910. Conductor Skel morlie and Wemyss Bay Choral Union. Publication : Anthem, " Oh Every One That Thirsteth " (Vincent).

MANSFIELD, ORLANDO AUGUSTINE, Glenhaven, Avenue Road, Torquay. Born 1863 Horningsham, Wilts. Educated privately. MUS. DOC. University of Toronto, MUS. DOC. University of Toronto F.R.C.O., L. MUS. T.C.M., L.MUS. L.C.M., F.A.G.O. Examiner, recitalist, author, teacher of organ, piano, singing and theory. First President of Free Church Musicians Union. Organist Belgrave Church since 1890, where he has given nearly 50 recitals. Over 500 publications

MANSFIELD, PURCELL JAMES, 24, Lynedock Street, Glasgow. Born 1889 at Torquay. Trained privately. F.R.C.O., A.R.C.M., L. MUS. T.C.L., L.C.M. Gold and bronze medalist. Professor of Music. Organist, Wesleyan Church, Paignton, 1905-08 ; Wesleyan Church, Bideford, 1908-10 ; Park Church, Glasgow, since 1910. Publications : Pianoforte, organ, and vocal compositions. Hobby and recreation : Photography and cycling.

MANN, GEORGE HOWARD, Chief Loman, Prospect Road, Moseley, Birmingham. Born at Moseley, 1868. Formerly Assistant Organist St. Paul's, Balsall Heath, Birmingham ; Moseley Parish Church, 1892 ; and Organist of the same, since 1903. Recreations : Golf, cricket, tennis.

MARCHANT, MISS FANNY ELLEN, Drayton Villa, Clevedon. L.R.A.M. (piano). Teacher of piano, organ, violin, theory. Organist Christ Church, Clevedon, since 1899.

MARCHANT, HENRY ERNEST, Drayton Villa, Queen's Road, Clevedon. Born 1837 at Brabourne, Kent. Educated at Canterbury, and articled to the late Dr. W. H. Longhurst. Teacher of pianoforte, organ, violin, theory. Organist Deal Parish Church, 1864, and Clevedon Parish Church, 1870-1911.

MARKHAM-LEE, W. H., 10, Bellvue Road, Ayr, N.B. Born (1875) and educated at Cambridge. Teacher of organ, pianoforte, theory and singing. M.I.S.M , A.R.C O. Organist Horningsea, 1889-91 ; Stow-cum-Quy, 1892-4 ; St. Columbas Presbyterian, Cambridge, 1894-5 ; All Saints', Wyke Regis, Weymouth, 1896-12 ; Ayr Parish New Church since 1912. Hobbies and recreation : Golfing, gardening, philately, entymology.

MARKS, T. OSBORNE, Armagh, Ireland. Born at Armagh, 1845. Educated at Armagh Cathedral MUS BAC. OXON , MUS DOC. T C.D. Organist St. Patrick's Cathedral, Armagh, since 1872 ; also St. Mark's Parish Church, Armagh. Conductor Armagh Musical Society. Publications : Anthems, services, hymn tunes, etc., chiefly in MSS.

MARSDEN, LOUIS DELABENE, 42, Heath Street, Hampstead, London, N W. Born 1867 at Louth, Lincs Scholarship holder of the Harrow Music School under Mr. John Farmer, 1879. A.R.C.O. (1904). Organist St. Peter's, Arkley, High Barnet, 1886 ; Stoke Poges Parish Church, 1887 ; Poplar Parish Church, 1895 , Chislehurst Parish Church, 1897 ; All Hallows', North St. Pancras, 1898 , St Peter's, Belsize Park, 1903. Publications : Songs and pianoforte pieces

MARSTON, ARTHUR, 14, Morley Road, Bournemouth. Born 1884 at Birmingham. A R C O Organist St. Mark's, Washwood Heath, Birmingham, 1900-5 ; St. Andrew's, Boscombe, Bournemouth, since 1906.

MASON, BERKELEY, 297, Spring Bank, W , Hull. Born 1882 at Bradford. Trained R C M. London F.R.C O., L R A.M Organist and Choirmaster Wycliffe Congregational Church, 1903-12 ; Queen's Hall, Hull, since 1912

MASON, FRANK ALFRED CHARLES, Broad Street, Pershore Born 1878. Educated privately. Assistant Organist Worcester Cathedral, 1893-9 ; St. Asaph Cathedral, 1899-1900 ; Denbigh Parish Church, 1899-1900. Conductor Abbey Choral Society, Pershore. Organist The Abbey, Pershore, since 1900 Hobby and Recreation : Classics and bicycling. Club Pershore Club

MASON, HENRY HAWTHORNE, 20, Castleford Road, Sparkhill, Birmingham. Born 1874 at Birmingham Trained under Dr Herbert Sanders (organ), Mr. Kimberley Smith, and (theory) at Midland Institute, Birmingham Deputy Organist Camp Hill Presbyterian Church, Birmingham, 1890-96 , Sparkhill Wesleyan Church, Birmingham, since 1899 ; Saltley Sisterhood since 1911.

MASSER, JOHN THORTON, 32, Mapperley Road, Nottingham. Born 1855 at Bradford, Yorks. Trained at Bramham College, Tadcaster. Solicitor. Formerly Organist Bramham College ; Hornton Lane Chapel, Bradford ; Addison Street, Nottingham, for 20 years. Publications : Tune book, Psalter, Harvest Cantata, services and anthems, various piano pieces. Recreation : Cycling Club : Cyclists' Touring.

MARTIN, SIR GEORGE CLEMENT, 4, Amen Court, London, E C. Born 1844 at Lambourn, Berks. M.V O., MUS DOC, OXON ET CANTUAR , F.R.C.O , HON. R A.M. Formerly Organist Lambourn Church. Private Organist to Duke of Buccleuch, 1871 ; Master of the Choristers, St. Paul's Cathedral, 1875 ; Sub-Organist St. Paul's Cathedral, 1876. Organist and Director of the Music St. Paul's Cathedral since 1888 Hobby and recreation : Shooting and golf. Club Constitutional.

MARTIN, MANLEY, 5, Napier Terrace, Plymouth. Born (1870), and educated at Plymton Grammar School. F R.C.O. Professor of music. Organist St Jude's, 1885-8 ; St. George's, Stonehouse, 1888-99 ; St. Matthias, 1899-1905 ; St. Catharine's, Plymouth, since 1905. Conductoi Mannamead and Mutley Choral Society, Plymouth Hon. Conductor The Three Towns Choral Union Composer of Music. Hobby and recreations : Cricket, fishing, football.

MATTHEWS, J., St. Stephen's Villa, Rocquettes, Guernsey. Born at Liskeard. Educated at Plymouth and Dresden. R C.M., Dresden-Associate. Organist and pianist. Trinity College London Organist St. James', Swansea, 1883-4 ; St. Austell Parish Church, 1887-9 ; St. Stephen's, St. Peter Port, Guernsey, since 1889. Publications . " Handbook of the Organ " (Augener) ; " Violin Works of Beethoven " (" Strad " Library) ; etc.

MATTHEWS, JOHN A., Wesleyville, St. Luke's Square, Cheltenham. Born and educated at Gloucester. Conductor of Festival Society. F. GLD. O., L. MUS. T.C.L Hon. member R.A. Roma. Formerly Organist St. John's and St. Mark's, Gloucester ; St. Mary's, Lydney ; Parish Church, Cheltenham Deputy and Organist *pro tem*, Gloucester Cathedral, 1857-65 ; St Matthew's, Cheltenham, 1866-1907 ; late Organist and Conductor Gloucester Choral Society. Local Secretary T.C.L. ; local representative R.A.M. (London). Examiner higher examinations T.C.L. Writer on musical topics ; author and composer of part songs, piano music, Church music, elementary works on singing and sight reading.

MAXFIELD, W. HENRY, Ivy Bank, Ashley Road, Altrincham. Born at North Somercotes, Lincs., 1849 Educated at Manchester. Music and singing Master. Lecturer on musical composers MUS BAC. (gold medalist), Trinity University, Toronto. Fellow Royal College of Organists. Organist St. Peter's, Levenshulme, 1866 ; St. Thomas', Norbury, 1872 , St. George's, Altrincham, 1879 , St John the Evangelist, Altrincham, since 1884. Publications : Cantatas, anthems, part songs, organ and pianoforte compositions, editions of popular song books, etc. Recreations : Sketching and walking

McBRATNEY, J. HENRY, 75, Fitzwilliam Street, Belfast, and 14, Park Parade, Lisburn, Ireland. Born 1882 at Belfast, and educated under Belfast professors. Organist Derriaghy Parish Church, 1897 , St. Stephen's Church, Belfast, 1900 , The Cathedral, Lisburn, since 1906.

McKNIGHT MISS EDITH L., Castletown, Isle of Man. Born at Coventry. F.R C.O. Organist Alfreton Parish Church, Derby, 1881-92. Organist, teacher of music, and choir trainer, King William's College, Castletown, I.O M., since 1892. Recreation : Cycling.

McLEAN, J. CHARLES, 3, Queen's Terrace, Aberystwyth. Born Portmadoc, 1875. Educated privately and R.C M. London. Fellow Royal College of Organists. Organist Salem, Portmadoc, 1894. Professional accompanist, Kymric Ladies Choir, and Gwalia Male Voice Choir, London, 1900-1. Organist Welsh C. M. Tabernacle Chapel, Aberystwyth, since 1906, and is also Conductor Choral Society, Portmadoc. Singing Master County School, Portmadoc. Publications : Prize anthem, songs, hymn tunes, and organ compositions. Recreations : Fishing and golf

MEACHAM, C J. B., 9, Calthorpe Road, Edgbaston, Birmingham   Studied music at Ely Cathedral.   MUS BAC , CANTAB   Organist St. Philip's Church, Birmingham, 1871-88 ; St. George's Church, Edgbaston, Birmingham, since 1888.   Composer of services, anthems, etc.

MEACHEN, GEORGE NORMAN, 11, Devonshire Street, W., and 18, Forest Drive West, London, N.E   Born 1876 at Beccles   Educated at Guy's Hospital.   M.D., B.S LONDON, M R.C.P , MUS. T.A.C I,   Physician and Dermatologist.   Formerly Organist (assistant) St. Philip's Church, Buckingham Palace Road, S.W ; Richmond Road Wesleyan Church, Hackney, and St. Bartholomew's Church, Islington, N.   Organist St. Paul's Church, Canonbury, London, N , since 1907.   Publications : " The Place of Music in the Healing Art," " Silent Night " (carol). Hobbies and recreations : Photography, reading, and motoring.

MEAD, HENRY GEORGE, Cranleigh, Salway Hill, Woodford, Essex.   Born 1862 at Mile End.   Trained under S G Benson, Esq , R A.M , at East London Organ School, and H. Lister Esq , MUS. BAC   Fellow of Society of Science and Literature, and F.G O.   Organist St. Mary's, Theydon, 1886-8 , St. Stephen's, Buckhurst Hill, 1888-93 ; All Hallows, London Wall, 1893-1905 , St. Cyprian's, Canning Town, 1905-7 , St James', Kennington, 1907-9 ; St. John's, Kilburn, since 1909.   Publication . Communion in E flat.   Hobby and recreation : Shooting and cycling.

MEALE, JOHN ARTHUR, 42, Milton Park, Highgate, N.   Born 1880 at Slaithwaite   F.R.C O   Organist Marsden Congregational, 1896-9 ; Selby Wesleyan, 1899-1905 ; Queen's Hall, Hull, 1905-12 , Central Hall, Westminster, S.W., since 1912.   Drew up specifications for the City Hall organ, Hull   Draw-stops number about 140.   Includes a whole octave of drums.   Organist to the Nonconformist Choir Union Festival, Crystal Palace.   Publications : About eight anthems, two books, organ pieces, and various others.

MEARING, ARTHUR, Crabswood Cottage, Lyme Road, and Music Stores, South Street, Axminster   A MUS T C.L., A MUS. L.C M., M I S.M. Professor of music.   Musical instrument dealer.   Organist and Choirmaster Parish Church, Axminster, 1906-12

METCALFE, RICHARD D , 24, Manor Road, Stoke Newington, N. Born at Stepney.   Educated privately.   MUS. BAC DUNELM, A R.A M.   Organist Stepney Meeting Congregational, 1881-7, and 1891-8 , Children's Home, Victoria Park, 1887-90 ; St. Michael's and All Angels, Stoke Newington, 1898-1903 ; St Alban's, Wood Street, London, E.C , since 1903.   Publications : anthems, part songs, etc.

METZGER, STANLEY GUSTAVE, F.R C O   Trained by H Coy, MUS. DOC., F.R.C.O.   Assistant Organist Christ Church, Moss Side, Manchester ; St. Thomas' Church, Heaton Chapel.   Organist St George's Church, Altrincham, 1905.   Now Organist Bowden Parish Church.

MIDGLEY, CHARLES EDMUND, Croftholme, Farquhar Road, Port Glasgow Organist at age of 16, Wesleyan Church, Almondbury, Huddersfield, 1876-1880 ; Parish Church, Port Glasgow, since 1880 ; Town Hall, Port Glasgow, since 1902

MIDGLEY, FREDERICK, 18, King Street, Perth   Born at Todmorden, Yorks. F.R.C.O.   Organist St. John's Episcopal Church, Perth, 1891-1902 ; St. John's Parish Church, since 1902.   Conductor St. John's Choral Society.   Hobby : Golf.

MILES, JOHN, Lyndene, Heaton, Bolton   Born at Blackburn, 1841.   Educated at Market Rasen, Lincs., and at Tyldesly, Manchester   Alderman and J.P. for the Borough of Bolton   Mayor in Coronation year and year after.   Chairman of many public and private companies.   Freemason P.P.G.O., P.M., East Lancs., P P.G.S.D.   Organist and Choirmaster St. Mary's, Parish Church, Deane, Bolton, since 1864.   Club: Bolton Conservative

MILLARD, WILLIAM, The Schools, Ascot, Berks.   Schoolmaster   Organist Cranbourne, 1870-4, All Saints', Ascot, Berks, since 1874.   Recreation: Bowls.

MILLER, REV. CYRIL W., St Cuthbert's Clergy House, Philbeach Gardens, S.W.   Born at Moseley, Warwickshire   Educated R C.M.   MUS BAC., DUNELM., F R C O   Organist St. John Baptist's, Kensington, 1892-1900;   St Cuthbert', Kensington, since 1900.

MILLER, KENNETH J., B.A OXON., F R C O, Wadham College, and Close Hall, Wells, Somerset.   Organist St. Matthew's, Wookey, 1905;   Parish Church, Wells, 1906; (Assistant), Wells Cathedral, 1906;   Wadham College Chapel, 1907-1910.   Organist and Music Master St Oswald's College, Ellesmere, Shropshire, 1910.

MILLS, C. NORMAN, 36, Old Queen Street, Westminster.   Born at Westminster   Educated privately.   Musician   Organist and Choirmaster St. Mark's, Walworth   Hobbies and recreations   Musical compositions, boating and cricket.

MILLS, E. E., 22, Ashgrove Street, Ayr   Born at Birmingham.   Trained G.S.M. London and privately   Organist St Cuthbert's, Lockerbie, 1910; Darlington Church, Ayr, since 1911.

MILLS, EDWARD, 32, Sisters Avenue, Clapham Common, London, S.W.   Born in London.   Educated at St. John's College   MUS. BAC. OXON.   Organist St. John's College, Battersea, since 1870

MILLS, E P., Thornhill, Wellfield Road, Cardiff.   Born at Pontypridd, 1865.   Studied music under the late Hugh Brooksbank, Esq.   Organist Llandaff Cathedral.   MUS. BAC. (OXON.), F R C O   Formerly Organist Clifton Street Church, Cardiff, and Wesleyan Church, Pontypridd.   Now Organist (since 1908) Ebenezer (Congregational) Church, Cardiff.   Composer of anthems, songs, organ and pianoforte pieces.   Recreations: Cycling, reading, tennis, bowls, billiards, etc

MILNES, JAMES, 5, Hyde Park Terrace, Leeds   Born at Leeds.   Diploma Leipzig Conservatorium of Music   Formerly Deputy Organist for 5 years, at Leeds Parish Church.   Organiser and Director of the choir, All Hallows' Church, Leeds.

MINSHALL, EBENEZER, Bryntirion, Folkestone   Born 1845 at Oswestry.   Educated privately.   Retired Organist.   Organist City Temple, London, 1876-1893   Late editor of " The Musical Journal "   President of The Nonconformist Choir Union   Author of " Organs, Organists and Choirs," " Fifty years Reminiscences of a Free Church Musician."   Composer of anthems, etc.   Hobby   Photography.

MITCHELL, EDWARD CHARLES, Amhurst, New Romney.   A.I. C M   Formerly Organist (Assistant) Christ Church, Tunbridge Wells; St. Peter's, Southborough; Christ Church, Southborough.   Organist St. Nicholas, New Romney, since 1892.

MONK, M. J., Pendrea, Truro. MUS. DOC OXON , F R C O   Conductor Truro Philharmonic Society, 1890-97. Formerly assistant, York Minster. Organist an1 Choirmaster Truro Cathedral since 1890. Publications : Pianoforte and organ pieces, songs, Church services, anthems, etc.

MONTGOMERY, WILLIAM AUGUSTUS, 16, Gladstone Street, Gainsborough. Born 1872 at Hawick, N.B. Educated at St. Martin's Grammar School, Scarborough. MUS BAC DURHAM, F R.C O., L R A M., L. MUS. T C L   Teacher of piano and singing Formerly Organist St. Modoc's Doune ; St. Andrew's, Pau, France ; Wallace Hall Academy, Closeburn, N.B ; St. Edmund's, Hunstanton ; S. S. Philip and James, Ilfracombe, and Organist Gainsborough Parish Church, since 1906. Publications : Organ, piano, violin and vocal music.

MOODY, CHARLES HARRY, Woodbridge, Ripon   Born 1874 at Stourbridge, Worcestershire Studied harmony and counterpoint under Dr. Haydn Keeton of Peterborough. Articled pupil at Bangor Cathedral. Deputy Organist Wells Cathedral, 1894. Acting Organist and Choirmaster Wells Cathedral, 1895. Organist and Choirmaster, Wigan Parish Church, December 1895-April 1899 ; Holy Trinity, Coventry, 1899. Organist and Master of the Choristers of Ripon Cathedral, in succession to the late Dr E J. Crow, January, 1902 Lecturer in Music Ripon and Wakefield Diocesan Training College since 1902 Conductor Huddersfield Glee and Madrigal Society ; Music Master Ripon School. Publications : " A History of Selby Abbey," church music, songs, etc. Hobbies and recreations : Architecture, golf and tennis.

MOORE, ROBERT HENRY, 9, Devonshire Street, Keighly, Yorks Born 1856 at Harden, near Bingley. Professor of Music. Organist St. John's, Keighly, 1881 ; St. Andrew's, Bradford, 1887 ; St. Michael's, Haworth, since 1890 , to the Musical Union, Keighly, since 1886. Appointed Conductor of the Musical Union, 1910.

MOORE, WALTER HENRY, The Schools, Shrewsbury Born 1874 at Nottingham. Educated at Nottingham and Oxford. Formerly Assistant School Master at West House Preparatory School, Edgbaston. Organist Emmanuel Church, Nottingham, 1887-94 ; Shrewsbury School Chapel since 1905. Assistant Master at Shrewsbury School.

MORETON, HARRY, 82, Durnford Street, E Stonehouse, Plymouth. MUS. BAC. (DURHAM), F.R C.O. Organist Stoke Damerel Parish Church, 1876 ; Sub Organist Winchester Cathedral, 1879 ; Organist St. Michael's, Winchester, 1879 ; St. George's, East Stonehouse, Plymouth, 1882 ; Town Organist East Stonehouse, 1894. Conductor Launceston Choral Society and Plymouth Vocal Society, 1890. Organist St. Andrew's Parish Church, Plymouth, since 1885 ; Guildhall, Plymouth, since 1899. Conductor Plymouth Guildhall Choir Orchestra and Male Voice Choir.

MORGAN, BRINLEY, Windsor House, Llanelly Trained privately. Formerly Organist Elizabeth Street Church, Dowlais. Organist Capel Newydd Calvinistic Methodist Church, Llanelly, since 1910.

MORGAN, R. T , 12, Redcliffe Parade W , Bristol. Organist and Choirmaster Christ Church, Dorchester, 1891 ; St Andrew's, Hingham, Norfolk, and articled pupil to Dr. Bates, Norwich Cathedral, 1893 ; St. Mary the Virgin, Hayes, Kent, 1895 ; St. Mary Redcliffe, Bristol, since 1906.

MORLEY, FELIX W., 2, Harvey Road and Pembroke College, Cambridge. Born at Bassingbourne. Studied music privately. M.A , MUS. B CANTAB. Organ scholar Pembroke College, Cambridge, 1873 Organist and Choirmaster since 1878 Hon Conductor to the Ely Diocesan Council of Church Music 1902-12 Composer of church services, and vocal and instrumental music

MORRIS, GEOFFREY O'CONNOR, 19, Hogarth Road, Earl's Court, London, S.W. Born 1886 at Thun, Switzerland. Educated at Dublin and R.C M. London. Organist and Pianist. Temporary Organist Black Church, Dublin, at 11 years of age. Assistant Organist St. Bartholomew's, Dublin, from 14 to 17 years of age. Formerly Organist and Choirmaster St. Cuthbert's, Carlisle, and Assistant to the Cathedral Organist at St. John's, Wilton Road, London, S W. Organist and Choirmaster St. Paul's, Onslow Square, since 1910. Hobby and recreation : Acting, cricket and tennis.

MORRIS, HAROLD F., 3, Madiera Place, Leith, Edinburgh. Born 1874 at Scarborough. A. MUS. T C L. Professor of Music. Organist St. Cuthbert's, Hawick, 1896-8 ; and North U P. Church, since 1898.

MORRIS, HERBERT C., The Close, St Davids. M A CANTAB , F.R C O , A R C.M. L.R.A M. Assistant Organist Manchester Cathedral, 1895-6 ; St. Andrew's, Bath, 1896. Organist and Master of the Choristers and Lay Vicar Choral, St. Davids Cathedral, since 1896.

MORRISON, T. R. C., Music Repository, Hornsea, East Yorks. Born 1861 at Ripon. Trained at York School for the Blind. Music dealer and bookseller. Organist Congregational Church, Hornsea, 1886-97 ; Primitive Methodist Church, Hornsea, since 1905. Compositions : Six anthems, eight songs, and a march. "The British National," composed for the Jubilee of H.M. Queen Victoria, from whom he received congratulations. The titles of the songs are · " The Angel's Home," " As the Dawn was Waking," " A Lover's Vows," " The Boats are Coming Home," " The Flowers Appear," " Love that Never Dies," " The Pilot Boat," " There never was an Earthly Dream."

MOSDELL, SIDNEY A., St. Brelade, Wokingham. Born 1870 at Reading. Educated privately. F.R C.O Organist St John's, Caversham, Tring, 1888-91 ; Parish Church, Tring, 1891-1906 ; All Saints' Parish Church, Wokingham, since 1906. Conductor Wokingham Choral Society, since 1906. Hobby and recreations : Freemasonry, shooting, cycling.

MOSS, RICHARD A., Tulchan, Dicconson Street, Wigan. Trained under Jas. Dawber, MUS. B , and J. Crow, MUS. D., Ripon Cathedral, A R C.O. Organist Hope Congregational Church, Wigan. Conductor Wigan Amateur Operatic Society ; St. Helens Amateur Operatic Society ; Crossfields Operatic Society, Warrington. Teacher of Class Singing to Wigan Education Authority. Singing Master Girls' High School, Wigan ; Grammar School, Wigan , Grammar School, Ashton-in-Makerfield. Club : Wigan Conservative.

MOSS, ARTHUR WILLIAM, Rowley, King's Road, Reading Born at Gravesend, Kent. L R.A M , F.R.C O Formerly Organist Parish Church, Wokingham. Organist Christ Church, Reading.

MOSS, CHARLES WALTER, 21, Trafalgar Road, Great Yarmouth Born 1860 at Ipswich Educated at Ipswich and London. F.R C O., M.I.S.M. Professor of Music Organist St Peter's, Ipswich, 1881-4 ; and St. Peter's, Great Yarmouth, since 1884. Conductor Great Yarmouth Orchestral Society. Principal Violin Great Yarmouth Musical Society.

MOTE, A. R , Newland, Sherborne, Dorset. Born 1880 at Sydney, N.S.W., Australia. Educated at Sydney University. B.A. Sydney, MUS. BAC. (Queen's College, Oxford), MUS. BAC. (Dunelm). Professor of Music. Hon. Accompanist Sydney Liedertafel, 1900-1904 Organist University of Sydney, 1898-1904. City Organist at Sydney, 1901-1902. Organist and Choirmaster Sherborne Abbey since 1907. Publications : Anthems, hymns, carols, orchestral pieces and organ voluntaries. Hobbies Sketching and photography.

MOUNTAIN, EDMUND. Born at Bradford 1879. Organist and Choirmaster St. Mary's, Halifax. Formerly at St. Thomas' Church, Halifax.

MOUNTFORD, FRANKLYN, Oakleigh, Harborne. A.R.C.M., L.R.A.M. Professor of Solo Singing and Ear Training, Midland Institute School of Music. Organist Harborne Parish Church, Birmingham, since 1903.

MUDD, A E., Regent Street, Wrexham. Born 1868 at Nantwich. Trained under Mr. Alfred Prince and Miss Hughes, A.R.C.O. Organist Primitive Methodist Chapel, Poyser Street, Wrexham, since 1912.

MÜLLER, F., The Chestnuts, Southcote Road, Bournemouth. Born in Saxony. Educated at Leipzig. PH. D. (University of Leipzig). Organist Wesley Church, Holdenhurst Road, Bournemouth, since 1909.

MUNDY, PERCIVAL D., 23, Southbourne Grove, Bournemouth. Born at Bath 1891. Educated privately. Organist Boscombe Congregational Church, since 1912.

NAYLOR, CHARLES LEGH, Harrogate. Born 1869 at Scarborough. Educated at St. Peter's School, York. M A , MUS. BAC. CANTAB. Organist Emmanuel College, Cambridge, 1888. Assistant York Minster, 1891 ; St. Peter's, Harrogate, 1892. Conductor Harrogate Choral Society, 1899 , Kursaal Orchestra, 1902. General Manager Kursaal and Conductor of Orchestra, 1906. Organist Hook Memorial Church, Leeds, 1911. Musical Editor Methodist School Hymnal (published 1911). Son of Dr. J. Naylor, late Organist York Minster ; brother of Dr. E. W. Naylor, M A., composer of the " Angelus." Lecturer in Music, Emmanuel College, Cambridge , brother of H. Darnley Naylor, M.A., Professor of Classics, Adelaide University, Australia.

NEEDHAM, HARRY ALGERNON, The Coppice, Gravelly Hill, Erdington, Birmingham. Born 1876 at Nechells, Birmingham Educated musically under H. E. Platt, Esq , Erdington Parish Church, and under Dr. F. J. Karn, of London. Guild of Organists' Certificate of Practical Musicianship, 1900. FELL. INCORP'D GUILD CH. MUS. (No. 1905). Organist and Choirmaster St. Clement's, Nechells, Birmingham, since 1900 Publications : Anthem, " Remember Now Thy Creator " ; Communion Service in F ; hymn tunes and chants.

NESBITT, JULIAN H. W., Argyll Mansions, Oban. Educated privately. Formerly Organist Swinton Parish Church ; Dalbeattie Parish Church. Organist St Columba Parish Church since 1899.

NETTLETON, ARTHUR, 120, Somerset Road, Huddersfield. Born in Huddersfield. Trained under late Mr. H. Barratt, Dr. Chambers and Mr. A. Pearson, MUS. BAC., of Huddersfield. A.R.C.O , M.I.S.M Organist Primitive Methodist Chapel, Huddersfield, 1887 ; Ramsden Street Congregational Chapel, Huddersfield, 1890. Organist and Choirmaster Bridge End Congregational Church, Brighouse, since 1892. Hobby : Gardening.

NEWLYN, HERBERT N G , 34, Beecroft Road, Crofton Park, S.E. Born 1884 at Sherborne. Trained privately. Organist St. Hilda's Church, Lewisham, since 1907.

NEWRICK, FREDERICK WILLIAM, 6, St. Bede's Terrace, Sunderland Born at Sunderland. Educated at Sunderland and London L R A M , A R C.M. Teacher of pianoforte and singing Organist Sunderland Parish Church, 1882-8 ; St John's, Ashbrooke, 1888-1905 , St. Ignatius the Martyr, Sunderland, since 1905. Hobby : Old violins.

NICHOLLS, HERBERT FRANK, Dennington, Clyffard Crescent, Newport, Mon. Born 1865 at Bristol. Educated at Kingsdown Grammar School. A.R C O. Professor of Music Organist Congregational Church, Victoria Road, Newport, Mon., since 1886 General Secretary and Founder of Free Church Musicians' Union.

NICHOLSON, SYDNEY H , 6, Wilton Polygon, Crumpsall, Manchester. Born 1875 in London. Educated at Rugby School ; New College, Oxford , Royal College of Music ; and Frankfort-on-Main. M.A., MUS. BAC. OXON. Organist Barnet Parish Church, 1897 ; Lower Chapel, Eton College, 1904. Music Master Wellington House School, Westgate-on-Sea, 1905 ; Carlisle Cathedral, 1905-8 ; Manchester Cathedral, since 1908

NICOL, EDWARD, Paradise Place, Perth Born at Glasgow. Educated there, at Perth and abroad Teacher of music. Organist Markinch Parish Church, 1885-7 ; St. John's (Middle) Parish Church, Perth, 1887-94 ; North United Free Church since 1894 Conductor, Central Men's Brotherhood. Hobby and recreations Cycling, tennis.

NOBLE, T. TERTIUS, 1, Minster Court,York. HON F.R.C.O , A R C.M Organist All Saints, Colchester, 1881 ; St John's, Wilton Road, London, S.W., 1889. Assistant Trinity College, Cambridge, 1890 ; Ely Cathedral, 1892 ; York Minster, since 1898 Conductor York Symphony Orchestra and York Musical Society. Hon. member A.D C and C U M C , Cambridge.

NORTH, THOMAS WILLIAM, Wellington Road, Dudley, Worcester. Born 1883. Professor of Music. Organist St. Paul's Walsall, 1899-1905. Accompanist to Birmingham Triennial Musical Festival, 1903, 1906 and 1909. Conductor Dudley Choral Society, 1905. Organist Dudley Parish Church, since 1905 ; Walsall Town Hall, since 1909.

OCKELFORD, CHARLES HENRY. Born in London. Educated by Mr F. Perkins, A R A.M. Organist Bethnal Green Parish Church, since 1894.

OGILVY, ALFRED WALTER, Sedbergh School, Yorkshire. Born 1877 at Windsor F R C O Organist and Senior Music Master, Bilton Grange, Rugby, 1899-1907 ; Sedbergh School since 1908. Publications Part songs. Recreation · Golf.

OLDING, J. HERBERT, 5, Lydon Road, Clapham, London, S W. A.R C O. F GLD. O. Organist St Stephen's, Clapham Park, S W , 1883-91 , St. Saviour's, Brixton Hill, S W. 1891-1909 ; Christ Church Mayfair, W., since 1909. Composer of anthems, services, songs, and organ voluntaries.

OPIE, BENNETT, Crofton House, The Parade, Leamington Spa. Born 1885, at Redruth, Cornwall Educated at Commercial Academy and Grammar School, Redruth. A R.C.O. Professor of Music. Formerly six years Assistant Organist, Redruth Wesleyan Church and 3 years Organist and Choirmaster of Victoria Wesleyan Church, Weston-super-Mare. Organist Dale Street Wesleyan Church, Leamington Spa, since 1910.

ORTON, ALBERT, 27, Church Road East, Walton-on-the-Hill, Liverpool. L.R.A.M., F.R.C.O. Professor of Music. Organist and Choirmaster Holy Trinity, Toxteth Park, Liverpool, 1900-03; Parish Church of St. Peter, Woolton, near Liverpool, 1903-7; St. Mary's Parish Church, Walton-on-the-Hill, Liverpool, since 1907. Chorus Accompanist, Liverpool Philharmonic Society. Conductor Walton Philharmonic Society, and St. Michael's Church Musical Society, Ditton, Liverpool. Recreations: Cycling and walking.

OSBORN, FRANK, Moelfre Chapel Lane, Wilmslow. Born 1882 at Wilmslow. Organist Alderley Parish Church, 1901-6. Assistant Wilmslow Parish Church, 1906-7; St. Bartholomew's Parish Church, Wilmslow, since 1907. Music Master Wilmslow Grammar School.

OSMOND, HAROLD BARTRUM, Sarum, 34, Gladstone Road, Broadstairs. Born at Southampton, 1869. Educated in London. F.R.C.O. Teacher of pianoforte, singing, harmony, etc. Organist St. Peter's, Bethnal Green, E., 1884; St. Barnabas', Homerton, N.E., 1886; and St. Peter's-in-Thanet, Broadstairs, since 1889. Composer of anthems, Communion Services, etc. Hobbies and recreations: Cricket, tennis, cycling, engineering, architecture and astronomy.

OULD, CHARLES HOPKINS, Forfar, N.B. Born in London Trained at Westminster Abbey. Has held positions in London, Glasgow, United States of America Organist Forfar Parish Church. Conductor Philharmonic Choral Society

PACE, THOMAS JOHN, Fordlands, Ford Bridge Road, Ashford, Middlesex. Teacher of piano, organ, and singing. Organist Holy Trinity Church, Stratford, London, 1890-8; St. Matthew's, Ashford, Middlesex, since 1898. Recreation: Cycling.

PACEY, FREDERICK WILLIAM, 57, Manchester Road, Bolton. Born at Oxford, 1846. Educated at Christ Church Cathedral, Oxford. MUS. BAC. OXON. (1873) Teacher of pianoforte, organ, singing and theory Organist St Paul's, Oxford, 1862-7; St. Clement's, Oxford, 1867-72; Holy Trinity, Bolton, since 1873. Publications: Songs, hymn tunes, chants, anthem and offertory sentences. Recreations: Swimming, rowing, tennis, and golf.

PAGE, CHARLES WILLIAM, Rabymere, Yarborough Road, Lincoln. Moxley, Staffordshire. Trained at Wesley College, Sheffield. Formerly Organist All Saints, Darlaston; St. Mary's, Wolverhampton; Parish Church, Penkridge; St. John's, Wolverhampton; Parish Church, Bracebridge; St. Peter in Eastgate, Lincoln. Organist Wesley Chapel, Lincoln, since 1886.

PAGE, ERNEST VICTOR, 21, St. Lawrence Road, North Kensington, London, W. Trained under A. Livingstone Hirst, MUS. BAC., F.R.C.O., of St. Stephen's, S W. Organist Trinity Presbyterian Church, Kensington, London, W.

PAGE, SAMUEL S, Cairnaquheen, Crathie, Balmoral, N.B. Organist and Choirmaster St. Paul's, West Bromwich, 1898-1900; All Saints' Episcopal, Newton Stewart, N.B., 1900-2; Crathie Parish Church, since 1902. Choir Director R.C. Church, Braemar. Organist on Holidays, etc. Conductor Braemar Choral Union ; Braemar United Free Church Festival Choir ; Ballater Amateur String Orchestra. Publication.: Pieces for piano, R C. and Anglican Church Services, etc. Hobbies and recreations . Cycling, fishing and photography.

PALLISER, JAMES E., 81, Derwent Street, Blackhill. Born 1880 at Blackhill. Trained for organ under late J. W. Gradon, Esq. Assistant Organist Wesleyan Church, Blackhill, 1893-97 ; Organist Primitive Methodist Church, Castleside, 1898-1909 ; Wesleyan Church, Consett, since 1909. Officiated as Organist and Accompanist for Consett and District Contest Choir.

PALLOT, MISS ELIZA, 26, Devonshire Place, St. Heliers, Jersey. Born at St. Heliers. Educated locally and in London. L.R.A.M. Teacher of piano, organ, violin, singing and harmony. Pianist to Jersey Choral Society, 1897-8. Organist United Methodist Church, St. Heliers, since 1879. Composer of " Twelve Original Tunes Set to Favourite Hymns " (Novello), two songs not yet published.

PALMER, CHARLES ROBERT, 60, Croydon Road, Reigate. Born 1881 at East London, South Africa. Educated at Reccles College, Truro College. A.R.C.O. Assistant Organist St. Peter, Mancroft, 1900 ; St. Luke's, Norwich, 1901 ; St Mark's, Reigate, since 1903 ; also at St. Margaret's, Chipstead, since 1904. Hobby : Coaching choirboys at cricket and football.

PALMER, CLEMENT CHARLTON, The Precincts, Canterbury. Born 1871 at Barton-under-Needwood, Staffs. Educated at Repton and Bruges. MUS. DOC. OXON., F.R.C.O. Formerly Organist St. Leonard's, Wichnor ; St. Andrew's, Pau, France ; Holy Trinity, Burton on Trent ; Parish Church, Ludlow. Organist and Master of the Choristers, Canterbury Cathedral, since 1908. Hobby : Architecture.

PALMER, G. MOLYNEUX, The Vicarage, S. Woodford, N.E. Born 1882 at Staines. Educated privately and R C.M MUS. BAC. OXON., A.R.C.M. Organist and Choirmaster Holy Trinity, S. Woodford, N.E., 1905-7. Publications : Songs, cantatas, part songs, etc.

PARISH, F. WILSON, Fernbank, London Road, Maidstone. Born 1869 in London. Educated at Westminster Abbey F R C.O. Organist St. Paul's, Maidstone, 1888-1901 ; All Saints' Parish Church, since 1901. Conductor Maidstone Choral Union, since 1903.

PARKER, R. E., 44, Bessborough Road, Birkenhead. Born 1867 at Burslem. Educated Orme's School, Newcastle-under-Lyme. Studied under Dr. W. S. Hoyte, All Saints, Margaret Street, W. F.R.C.O. Organist and Music Master St. Michael's School, Westgate-on-Sea, 1888 ; Denstone College, 1889. Organist and Choirmaster Wilmslow Parish Church, Manchester, 1890 ; St. Saviour's, Birkenhead, since 1906. Recreation Cycling.

PARRY, ALFRED THOMSON, 53, Sackville Street, Everton, Liverpool Born 1891 at Holyhead. Self trained. Deputy Organist St. Peter's, Everton, 1905-1909 ; Emmanuel Church, Everton, 1909-11. Organist Emmanuel Church, Everton, since March 1912. Recreation : Cycling. Pianist Oddfellows Friendship Lodge.

PARSONS, HAROLD, St. John's Lodge, Leicester. Born 1869 at Birmingham. Trained privately. Formerly Organist Congregational Church, Leicester, for 18 years. Organist Victoria Road Baptist Church since 1905. Publications : Songs, including " What does Little Birdie Say ? " anthems, choral ballads, etc. Clubs : Leicester Liberal and The Aldwych, London.

PARSONSON, C. STANLEY, Glenesk, Launceston. Born 1870 at Winterton, Lincs. MUS. BAC. LONDON, L. MUS. T.C.L. Organist Congregational Church, Whitby, 1900-1902 ; Wesleyan Church, Launceston, since 1902. Recreation : Cycling.

PATTERSON, DANIEL, Ballindean, Tollcross, Glasgow. Born (1874) and educated at Campbeltown. A R.C.O., A. MUS. T.C.L. Private teacher of organ, piano and singing. Organist Tollcross U.F. Church, Glasgow, since 1896. Published song " Hushabye."

PATTMAN, G. T., 3, Holyrood Crescent, Glasgow Born in 1875 at Grantham. Educated at Grantham Grammar School. F R C.O Organist and teacher of singing. Organist All Saints', Scarborough, 1896-1900 ; Bridlington Priory Church, 1901-1904 ; St. Mary's Cathedral, Glasgow, 1904. Recreation : Motoring. Clubs : Pallette, Glasgow ; Glasgow Society of Musicians ; Royal Automobile, London.

PEACOCK, FREDERICK CHARLES, Woodville, Cowfold, Sussex. Born 1889, and educated at Cowfold Grammar School. Assistant Schoolmaster. Formerly Organist Bosham, West Grinstead, Twinsham (age 11). Pupil at Chichester Cathedral. Organist St. Peter's, Cowfold, since 1907. Recreations : Gardening, cycling.

PEARSON, ARTHUR, Cliffe Wood Mount, Shipley, Yorks Born 1868 at Farsley. Trained under F. W. Hird, Leeds. Organist Saltaire Wesleyan Church, 1891-95 ; Westgate Baptist Church, Manningham, since 1895. Conductor Saltaire Prize Choir, 1891-95. Publications : Sacred cantatas, operettas, songs, pianoforte and organ pieces, etc. Regular contributor to " Musical Opinion "

PEARSON, ARTHUR, Rozel, Belmont Street, Huddersfield. Born 1864 at Golcar. MUS. BAC. OXON., F.R.C.O. Teacher of music. Organist Golcar Parish Church, 1880-4 ; St. Paul's, Huddersfield, since 1884 ; and Town Hall, since 1891. Conductor Holmfirth Choral Society, since 1906.

PEARSON, JOHN E., 13, Rockstone Place, Southampton. Trained privately. MUS. BAC. DUNELM., A.R.C.O. Organist and Choirmaster Portland Street, Southport, 1898-1910 ; Avenue Congregational Church, Southampton, since 1910. Publications : Songs, part songs, anthems.

PEARSON, JOSEPH WILLIAM, 44, Godwin Road, Cliftonville, Margate. Hon. Local Examiner R.C.M , 1883 ; Hon. Secretary Kent Section, I.S.M. ; Hon. Sec. Cambridge Local Exam. Organist St. Paul's, Margate, since 1877. Professor of Music.

PEASEGOOD, W. H., 89, Burngreave Road, Pitsmoor, Sheffield. Born (1863) and educated at Sheffield. Professor of Organ, Piano, Violin and Harmony. Organist Pitsmoor Church, Sheffield, since 1875. Hobbies : Billiards and photography.

PEIRCE, CECIL A. J., 71, Norroy Road, Putney, London, S.W. Born 1888 in London. A.I.G.C.M. Organist and Choirmaster Emmanuel Church, Camberwell, since 1912.

PEMBERTON, CHARLES JOHN, Chelston, Somali Road, West Hampstead, N.W. Born 1879 in London. Trained under A. E Godfrey, A.R.A.M., and Alfred Redhead. Assistant Organist All Saints', Finchley Road, N.W , 1895-1900 ; St. Mark's, N.W., 1900-02 ; St. Andrew's, N.W., 1902-04. Pupil-assistant of Dr. Davan Walton at Foundling Hospital, 1904-05. Organist and Choirmaster St John's, Hampstead, 1905-07 ; St. Luke's, Hampstead, 1907-12 ; Rosslyn Hill Unitarian Church, Hampstead. since 1912.

PENROSE, DONALD WILLIAM HENRY, Avonmore, Epping, Essex. Born 1863 at Tramore, Co. Waterford, Ireland. Educated King's College School, London ; studied music under the late Alfred Carder, Clapham Parish Church. Organist St. Augustine's, Clapham Rise, 1888-1890 ; St. John Baptist, Parish Church, Epping, 1890-1904 ; St. Jude's, Upper Chelsea, 1904-1906 ; re-appointed Epping Parish Church, 1906. Conductor Epping Choral Society. Publications : Chants, etc. Recreations : Cycling and rowing.

PARKINS, C W , Town Hall, Birmingham. Born at Birmingham. Organist Town Hall and University, Birmingham.

PHILLIPS, FREDERICK JOHN, Court Hill, Lowther Road, Bournemouth. Born 1875. Chief Assistant Overseer. Organist and Choirmaster St. Augustin's, Bournemouth, since 1896.

PHILLIPS, J ARKITE, 5, Canon Street, Aberdare. Born 1876 Organist Trinity Chapel, Aberdare, since 1891. Oboe and cors anglais player, South Wales Concerts, Bath Festival, National Eisteddfodan, and Palace, Douglas.

PHILLIPS, WILLIAM J., 24, Graham Street, Eaton Square, London, S.W. Born 1873 in London. Educated at R.C.M. and privately. MUS. DOC. OXON., F R.C.O., A.R.C.M. Organist SS. Mary and John, Oxford, 1894 6 ; St John's, Hammersmith, W , 1896-1902 ; St. Barnabas' Church, Pimlico, since 1902. Conductor Harlesden Choral and Orchestral Society ; Examiner Incorporated Staff S. Singing College.

PHILLIPS, WILLIAM JOHN, 6, Cranbury Place, Southampton. Born (1866) and educated at Southampton. Formerly Organist St. John's, Hedge End ; St. Edward's, Netley ; St Barnabas', Southampton. Organist Jesus Chapel, Southampton, since 1897

PHILLIPS, WILLIAM PUGH, J.P., Express Office, Newtown Born at Newtown. Music dealer Organist Congregational Church, Newtown, since 1881. Hobbies and recreation : Bowling, rifle shooting, bridge.

PHILPOTT, BASIL H., Chiltren, Denmark Road, Kingston-on-Thames. Born 1858 in London. Educated privately (father a schoolmaster in Surbiton). M.I.S M., etc. Organist in Ordinary to the King. Teacher of music. Organist Surbiton Park Church, 1878-86 ; H M. Chapel Royal, Hampton Court Palace, since 1886. Music Master Kingston Grammar School, Tiffins Endowed School, Kingston. Hon. Local Examiner R.C.M. Scholarships. Hobby : Mechanics.

PHIPPS, ALEXANDER, MUS. BAC., 44, Princes Road, Liverpool , 71, Deansgate, Manchester ; and 149, Oxford Street, London. Born 1867. Educated R.A.M. and privately under Dr. Steggall, Sir George Macfarren, W. Dorrell, Esq., and W. H. Holmes, Esq. Professor of Music, Solo Organist and Pianist. Formerly Organist St. James', Swansea ; St. John's, Bootle ; Roby Church, Liverpool. Conductor Liverpool

Choral and Amateur Operatic Society. Warden National Conservatoire of Music, Ltd., 149, Oxford Street, London. Principal Liverpool College of Music and Liverpool Conservatoire of Music since 1884. Publications: Guides to Theory and Harmony, Treatise on Voice Production and Pianoforte Technique. Composer of " Opera," " Thea," Degree Ex. " The Ascension." Recreation : Chess.

PICKERSGILL, EDWARD VERNON, 224, York Road South, West Hartlepool. Born 1880. Educated at Ripon Choir and Grammar Schools. MUS. BAC. DUNELM., F.R.C.O. Organist St. Oswald's, West Hartlepool, since 1903 ; St. Paul's Middlesbrough, 1899-1903. Conductor Lyric Voice Choir, since 1905 ; West Hartlepool Choral Union. Publications : " Ode to Joy," and male voice cantata " The Norman Baron." Hobby. and recreation : Reading and cycling.

PIERCE, HERBERT W., 8, Queen's Gardens, Ealing, London, W. Born (1878) and educated at City of London School, etc. A.R.C.O. Banker. Organist St. Andrew's, Gravesend 1898 ; Wesleyan Methodist, Ealing, since, 1900 , Ealing Philharmonic Society, since 1901. Publications : Te Deum and Evening Service in D flat, anthems, songs and part songs, etc.

PIGGOTT, HENRY, The Gables, Alton, Hants. Born at Godstone, Surrey, 1838. Educated privately. Teacher of music. MUS. BAC. CANTAB., 1886, L. MUS. T.C.L., 1878. Organist All Saints', Alton, Hants, since erection of church, 1874. Publications : Sacred music, part songs. Recreation : Gardening.

PILCHER, P. W., 74, Abbey Foregate, Shrewsbury. Born 1866 at Boston, Lincs Educated musically at Boston Parish (under G. H. Gregory, MUS. BAC.) and at Westminster Abbey (under Sir F. Bridge). M.A. CAMBRIDGE, A.R.C.O. Organist and Choirmaster St. John's, Hammersmith, 1889-1892 ; The Abbey Church, Shrewsbury, since 1892. Publications : Six pianoforte pieces, three short organ preludes, two part songs.

PILE, SEYMOUR, 49, Addison Road, Brighton. Born 1868 at Dorking, Surrey. Educated at Cambridge. M.A. CANTAB., L.R.A.M., F.R.C.O. Organist Sid Suss College and St. Mary's the Less, Cambridge, 1888 ; St. Mary's, Boltons, South Kensington, 1895 ; Sedbergh School Chapel, 1897 ; St. John's, Truro, 1907 ; St. Patrick's, Hove, since 1911. Hobbies : Mechanical and electrical engineering. Clubs : Junior Conservative, Oxford and Cambridge Musical.

PILLINGER, E. W., 188, Kingston Road, Merton Park, Wimbledon, London, S.W. Born 1844 at Bath. Educated privately. Organist St. Thomas', Bath, 1864-7 ; Seal Parish Church, Sevenoaks, 1867-71 ; Chipping Norton Parish Church, 1871-73 ; St. Mary the Virgin Parish Church, London, since 1874. Head Master Merton Endowed Boys' School for 37 years. Last Chairman of Merton Parish Council and first Chairman Merton District Council. Clubs : W.M. of the Burgoyne Lodge, 902, in Jubilee year, 1887. A founder of Jubilee Masters' Lodge (Hotel Cecil) ; founder of the Merton Lodge, its first W.M. and Preceptor ; also instrumental in the building of Merton Masonic Hall. President of Clubs, and Trustee or Governor of Secondary Schools and other organisations. Vice Chairman of the Wimbledon and District Higher Education Committee.

PIRRIE, JOHN EDWARD, 22, Victoria Street, Perth. Formerly Organist St. Ninian's Cathedral, Perth. Organist St. Paul's, Perth. since 1890. Publisher of church service music and organ and piano pieces.

PITCHER, RICHARD JAMES, 21, Boundary Road, St. John's Wood, London, N.W. Born 1870 at Devonport. Educated at Clifton Grammar School. MUS. BAC. DUNELM, F.R.C.O., A.R.C.M., Double Diploma as a teacher of singing and pianoforte. Organist and Choirmaster St. John's, Lowestoft, 1892-6; Holy Trinity, Scarborough, 1896-1903; St. Swithin's, London, E.C., 1903-6; St. Mary's, Kilburn, since 1906. Conductor Lowestoft Choral Society; Scarborough Choral Society, 1896-1903 Professor of Singing Guildhall School of Music. Hobby: Photography.

PITMAN, WILLIAM EDWARD, St. Dunstan's, Lyminge, Folkestone. Born 1863 at Southsea. Educated at Southsea and Bristol. MUS. BAC. OXON., 1894, F R C.O., 1894 Organist St. Barnabas, Rotherhithe, 1884; St. Saviour's, Pimlico, 1885; Holmbury St. Mary's, Dorking, 1886-88; Buckland, Dover and Speldhurst, Tunbridge Wells, 1889; Farnborough, Kent, 1890; Convalescent Home, Swanley, Kent, 1890-6; Ide Hill, Sevenoaks, 1897; Kenley, Surrey, 1897-9; Preston, Faversham 1899-1900; St. Mary's Parish Church, Lyminge, Folkestone, since 1901. Hobbies and recreations. Campanology (having rung many peals on church bells), gardening and tennis; much interested in cricket, frequently acting as umpire, and an occasional player. Also deeply interested in theological and ecclesiastical study, and anything bearing on antiquarian matters, historical or geographical.

PLANT, ARTHUR BLURTON, St. Paul's Square, Burton-on-Trent. Born Lichfield 1853. Educated at Cathedral School. MUS DOC. OXON., F.R.C O Singing Master Grammar and High Schools Borough Organist. Organist and Choirmaster St. Paul's, and St. Margaret's, Burton-on-Trent, since 1874. Composer of pianoforte, organ and church music.

POLE, ARTHUR THOMAS, Handel House, 294, Narborough Road, Leicester. Born 1855 at Oldbury. Educated at Leicester. F.N.C.M. Music publisher. Formerly Organist St. Stephen's Presbyterian, Leicester. Organist St. Nicholas, Leicester. Hobby: Collecting curios. Club: Unionist.

POLES, WILLIAM LYDDON WANSBROUGH, Wesley Villa, Selby. Born 1892 at Silsden, Yorks. Trained (piano) at Kingswood School, Bath, under Alfred Beer, Esq., L.R A M , A R C.O.; (organ and theoretical work, etc.) H. T. Head, Esq., F.R.C.O., A.R.C.M., Organist St. Andrew's Church, Bath. Organist Kingswood School, Bath, 1907-1911; Wesleyan Church, Selby, since 1911. Hobby and recreation: Fishing, cycling, and tennis.

POLLARD, JAMES, Brigg House, Sunnybank, Penrith. Born 1884 at Burnley. Articled to W. A. C. Cruickshank, MUS. B., at Burnley Parish Church. F.R.C.O Teacher of piano, organ and theory. Sub-Organist Burnley Parish Church, 1902-04 Composer of organ music. Organist Parish Church, Kenilworth, 1904-12; St. Andrew's Parish Church, Penrith, since 1912.

POLLITT, ARTHUR W., 4, Canning Street, Liverpool. Educated R.C M. Manchester. MUS. DOC. DURHAM, F.R.C.O., A.R.C.M., L.R.A.M., A.R.M.C.M. Music Master St. Mary's School for the Blind. Organist St. Mary's Church for the Blind since 1900. Club: University.

POPPLESTONE, S. MAURICE, The Limes, Pulteney Road, Bath. Born in 1885 at Bath. Educated at Bath Abbey. Fellow of the Royal College of Organists. Organist Walcot Wesleyan Church, 1904-1910; Bradford-on-Avon Parish Church, 1910-12; St. Mark's Church, Bath, since June, 1912. Hobbies: Golf, painting (water colour).

POYSER, ARTHUR, Homewood, Woodstock Road, Golders Green. Born 1876 at Bridlington. Trained at Edinburgh University and privately. Organist St. Mary's, Dunblane, Perthshire, 1895-1900 ; All Saints', Bordighera, Italy, 1900-01 ; All Hallows', Barking by the Tower (City of London), since 1901. Publications : Several operettas ; " The Tower of London " ; the C.T.C. Scottish Road Book ; the Scout Song Book. Recreation : Shooting. Clubs : New Oxford and Cambridge, Pall Mall S.W. and Royal Essex Golf.

PRATT, HENRY SEPTIMUS, 1, Hill House Villas, Stone, near Dartford, Kent. Born 1876 at Kirby Hill, Yorkshire. Late pupil of Davan Wetton, MUS. BAC., F.R.C.O. Late Organist of Thatcham Parish Church, near Newbury, Berks, 1893-1896. Organist and Choirmaster of the City of London Mental Hospital Chapel, since 1896 ; also Conductor of the Hospital Orchestra. Hobbies : Cricket, photography, and fishing.

PRENDERGAST, WILLIAM, The Close, Winchester. MUS. DOC. OXON Formerly Music Master Edinburgh Royal Blind Asylum , Fettes College, Edinburgh. Assistant Organist Winchester Cathedral ; St. Baldred's, North Berwick, 1889 , St. Paul's, York Place, 1891 ; Winchester Cathedral, since 1902.

PRICE, JAMES, St Mary, Russell Road, Ipswich. Born 1858 at Deerhurst. Educated at Horncastle, Lincs. Pianist and music teacher. Organist Bourne Abbey Church, 1875 ; Hexham Abbey Church, 1878 ; St. Margaret's, Ipswich, 1882 ; St Lawrence, Ipswich, 1900. Borough Organist Ipswich, since 1908. Publications Twelve hymn tunes, organ overture " B.H B.," technical studies for piano and various pianoforte works.

PRICE, OWEN M., 6, South Street, Louth. F.R.C.O., L.T.C.L. Born (1870) and educated at Bangor. Organist Llandegai Parish Church, Bangor, 1886-93 ; St. Mary's, Bangor, 1893-7 ; St James' Parish Church, since 1897. Conductor Louth Choral Society, 1898. Singing Master King Edward's VI. Grammar Schools, Louth Recreation : Cycling.

PRINGUER, HENRY T., Aldwych, 4, East Bank, Stamford Hill, N Born 1852. MUS. DOC. OXON., F.R.C.O Organist St Mathew's, Redhill, Surrey, 1870-81 ; St Mary's Church, Stoke Newington, since 1881. Director of Choir, Examiner and Member of Corporation Trinity College of Music. Hobby : Foreign stamp collecting.

PRITCHARD, GEORGE, 230, Upper Chorlton Road, Manchester. Born at Burton, near Chester. Educated at Owens College, Manchester and privately MUS BAC. DUNELM. Organist St Philip's Parish Church, until 1906 ; St Bride's Parish Church, since 1906 Choir Master St. Philip's Parish Church, since 1906. Publications : " Course of Preparation in Theory of Music," Te Deum. Recreation : Cycling.

PULLAN, W. HERBERT, Cudville, Nenagh Born 1869. Educated at Leeds and Bradford F.I.G C.M., L V C M Teacher of music Organist St. Oswald's Parish Church, Leeds, 1888 ; St. Stephen's Parish Church, Belfast, 1894 ; Mariners' Church, Kingstown, Dublin, 1898 ; St. Mary's Parish Church, Nenagh, since 1901. Publications . Anthem, "Consider and Hear Me " ; Evening Service (Magnificate and Nunc Dimittis) in D ; Morning and Evening Service in F (chants) ; Te Deum and Kyrie in G ; Sonatina in A'(piano). Hobbies : Sketching and painting.

PULLEIN, FRANK, 18, Wellington Road, Wrexham. A.R.C.O. Formerly solo boy, Lincoln Cathedral, then articled pupil to Mr. J. Young; then Assistant Organist at Lincoln Cathedral. Organist Wrexham Parish Church, since 1895.

PULLEIN, ERNEST, 66, Canwick Road, Lincoln. Born 1880 at Lincoln. Trained at Lincoln Cathedral. Organist St. Andrew's, Lincoln, 1898-1908. Organist and Choirmaster St. Martin's, Lincoln, since 1909. Publications : Several Evening Services, anthems, organ voluntaries, songs. Recreation : Cricket.

PULLEIN, JOHN, 40, Franklin Road, Harrogate. Born 1878 at Lincoln. F.R.C.O. Choir boy Lincoln Cathedral. Organist St.Swithun's,Lincoln, 1896-1903 ; St. Peter's, Harrogate, since 1903. Music Master Modern College, Harrogate, since 1907. Publications : Songs, part songs, organ and church music.

PULLEIN, W. R., The Green, Calne, Wilts. Born 1865 at Lincoln Articled pupil at Lincoln Cathedral. Late Assistant Organist Lincoln Cathedral and Organist St. Andrew's, Lincoln. Organist to the Marquis of Lansdowne and H. G. Harris, Esq. Organist and Choirmaster St. Mary's Parish Church, Calne. Conductor Calne Musical Society ; Chippenham Amateur Orchestra ; and Chippenham Choral Society, Recreation : Golf.

PYM-BROWNING, GEORGE, F.G.C.M. Born 1884. Formerly Organist All Saints', Warwick. Organist St. Michael-in-Lewes, since 1900. Hobby and recreations : Animated photography and all scientific recreations.

QUARRIER, ERNEST JOHN HENRY, 3, Westminster Terrace, Drill Hall Road, Newport, Isle of Wight. Born 1875 at Newport, Isle of Wight. Teacher of the piano, organ, violin, mandoline, banjo, and guitar; piano and organ tuner ; accompanist. Organist Newport Congregational P S.A. since 1899 ; Wesleyan Church, Newport, since 1904. Publications : Pianoforte album ; " Victorine Waltz " (played before late King Edward VII. by Band of H M. Grenadier Guards ; also by Dan Godfrey's Band, Winter Gardens, Bournemouth ; Sousa's Band, World's Fair, St. Louis, U.S.A.; The Kilties , H.M. Scots Guards, Royal Marine Artillery, etc.) ; song, " I have a Garden " ; two sacred songs, " Saviour Divine " (E flat), and " Wonderful Cleansing Scream " (E flat), sung by Madame Jessie Strathearne, A.R.A.M , Queen of Sacred Song. Composer of a number of publications unpublished.

QUIGLEY, EDMUND, 38, Park Road, Felling-on-Tyne. Born 1890 at Felling. Trained under N. H. Brown, MUS. BAC., of Newcastle. Teacher of Music. Deputy Organist St. Patrick's R.C. Church, Falling-on-Tyne, and Organist since 1911. Hobby : Electric experimenting.

RADFORD, HENRY WILLIAM, De Merley Road, Morpeth. F.I.G.C.M. Formerly Assistant Organist Winchester Cathedral. Organist St. Peter's, Ovington ; St. Mary's, Chester ; St. John's, Earlestown, Lancs. ; St. James', Whitehaven ; St. Mary's and St. James', Morpeth, since 1902.

RAMSAY, MALCOLM DONALD, Hensbury, 6, Gloucester Road, Teddington, Born 1886 at Chelmsford, Essex. Trained Trinity College, London, and privately. A. MUS. T.C.L. Pupil of Dr. G. F. Huntley, of St. Peter's, Eaton Square, and R.C.O., and of Mr. Wm. Ratcliffe, F.R.C.O., Teddington. Chorister at St. Luke's, Kew Gardens, 1897, and St.

Alban's Church, Teddington. Acting Organist Parish Church, Billings-hurst, Sussex, 1907. Organist All Saints' Church, Upper Twickenham, since 1909. Assistant Organist St. Alban's Church, Teddington, since 1906. Honorary Organist of Guild of the Servants of the Sanctuary. Makes special study of boys' voices.

RAMSEY, PERCY, 45, Pelham Road, Southsea. Born 1875 in London. Educated privately at Bournemouth. Organist St. Mary's, Boscombe, 1893-7 ; Parish Church, Poole, 1898 ; St. Michael's and All Angels', Portsmouth, since 1898. Hobbies and recreations : Tennis, chess, bridge. Clubs : Royal Portsmouth Corinthian Yacht Club.

RATCLIFFE, WILLIAM, Glen Lyn, Langham Road, Teddington. Born 1877 at Coventry. Educated at Hampton Grammar School. F.R.C.O., L. MUS. T.C.L. Organist St. John's, Hampton Wick, 1894-99. Assistant St. Alban's, Teddington, 1897-99 ; St. Alban the Martyr, Teddington, since 1899. Conductor Teddington Male Voice Choir, 1903-5 ; St. Alban's Orchestra, since 1902 ; Teddington Philharmonic, since 1905 ; one of the three Hon. Conductors Kingston-on-Thames Madrigal Society, since 1905. Hon. Local Examiner R C M Associate Conductor Imperial Choir Publications : Songs, organ and pianoforte music, hymn tunes and church music.

READ, ARTHUR WILLIAM, Derby Street, Burton-on-Trent. Born 1885. F R C.O., A R.C.M. Organist Primitive Methodist Chapel, at age of 14 ; New Street Baptist, 1901 ; Egginton Church, 1905. Assistant to Dr. A B Plant, at St. Paul's and St. Margaret's, 1905 ; St. John's, Horn-inglow, since 1908. Hobby and recreation : Motoring and engineering.

READ, JOHN T., Little Gatcombe, Carisbrooke Road, Newport, I.O.W. Organist Carisbrooke Church since 1868.

REES, GEORGE HENRY, 5, Fairbridge Road, Upper Holloway, London, N. Born 1886 in London. Trained privately. Organist Caledonian Road, Wesleyan Church, London, 1908-10 ; Crown Court National Scottish Church, Covent Garden, London, since 1910. Publications : Setting of Evening Service.

RENSHAW, WILLIAM HENRY, The Grove, Annesley, Notts. Born at Sutton-in-Ashfield, Notts. Educated at Cheltenham College. Head Master Annesley School, Notts. Music Master New College, Margate, 1889 ; Barnsley High School, 1892. Organist All Saints', Annesley, since 1897. Publications : Nearly 70 compositions

RICHARDS, CHARLES EDGCOME, 41, Uxbridge Road, Ealing, W. Born 1880 at Poplar. Educated Caterham Congregational School F R C.O. Assistant Organist St. Michael's, Chester Square, for a short time in 1900. Organist Congregational Church, Acton, since 1901. Hobbies : Carpentry and mechanical works.

RICHARDS, HENRY W., 6, Norfolk Square, London, W. Born 1865. Educated privately. MUS. DOC F.R.C.O., HON. R.A.M. Professor of Organ and Choir Training at R A M. Examiner L.R.A.M. ; R.C.O. ; Associated Board R.A.M. and R.C.M. Deputy Organist All Saints', Notting Hill, 1877-1879 ; Organist and Choirmaster St. John's, Kilburn, 1879-1886 ; Christ Church, Lancaster Gate, since 1886 ; Kilburn Church Choral Association, 1883-5 Director Philharmonic Society. Musical representative on the Teachers' Registration Council. Member of Council of R.C O. and Union of Graduates in Music. Member of the Committee of Management, R.A.M. Publications : Anthems, lectures, organ music. Recreation : Tennis. Club · R.A.M Club

RICHARDSON, STEPHEN, 15, Barossa Place, Perth. Born 1863 at Durham. Educated at Edinburgh Organist St. Mark's Episcopal Church, Portobello, 1880 ; St. John's Episcopal Church, Perth, 1889 ; The Cathedral, Perth, since 1891. Conductor Perth Choral Society ; Forfar Choral Union ; Alyth Choral Society ; St. Andrew's Diocesan Association. Hon. Local Examiner, R.C.M. Hobbies and recreation : Golf, tennis, painting.

RIDEOUT, PERCY R., 69, Chatsworth Road, Brondesbury, London, N.W. Trained R.C.M. and private. MUS. BAC., 1894 ; MUS. DOC., 1896 ; A.R C.M., HON. F G O. Professor L.A.M , G.S.M., and Hampstead Conserv. Organist and Choirmaster St. Paul's, Wokingham, 1896 ; St Philip's, Regent Street, 1899 ; St Paul's, Great Portland Street, 1900 ; St. George's, Bloomsbury, 1904 ; Wimbledon Parish Church, 1910 ; West London Synagogue, 1904

RIDGWAY, CECIL, " Arreton," Hampton. Born 1877 at Doncaster. Organ Scholar at R.C.M Pupil of Sir Walter Parratt. MUS. BAC. LONDON, 1908, F.R.C.O., A.R.C.M. Organist Holy Trinity, Notting Hill, 1890 ; St. Mary the Virgin, Hampton, since 1896. Recreations Astronomy.

RIDING, HENRY, Chigwell School, Essex. Born at Chorley, Lancs., 1862. F.R.C.O. Organist St. Mary's Parish Church, Chigwell ; Chigwell School ; Epping Choral Society. Conductor Loughton Choral and Operatic Society, etc.

RIDLEY, S. CLAUDE, 1, Gladstone Road, Seacombe, Cheshire. Trained at the Royal Institution, Liverpool. Born 1853 at West Derby, near Liverpool Organist St John's, Tue Brook, Liverpool, 1870 , Liverpool Seamen's Orphanage Church, 1878-1891 ; Unitarian Church, Renshaw Street, Liverpool, 1891-94 ; Congregational Church (Dr. Raffles' Chapel), Liverpool, 1894-1906 ; Egremont Parish Church, since 1907. Teacher of Music. Composer of over 300 musical publications. Recreations : Exercise, fresh air, and books.

RIMMER, THOMAS, Mayfield, Rowsley Avenue, Hendon, London, N.W. Born at Scarisbrick. Educated at Southport. Organist St. Mark's, Scarisbrick (at age of nine), 1874 ; St. Mary's, Waterloo, Liverpool, 1885 , All Saints, Southport, 1886 ; Myrtle Street Church, Liverpool, 1895 ; St Mary's Parish Church, Hendon, since 1907. Organ recitalist at St. George's Hall, Liverpool ; Ulster Hall, Belfast ; and many other important centres. Conductor of the Hendon Choral Society. Publications : Organ, piano and violin pieces, songs, etc., etc.

RISDON, FREDERICK GEORGE, St. Francis, Grove Avenue, Yeovil. Born 1875 at Taunton. F.R.C.O., A.R C.M. Organist Pitminster, 1894 ; St. Andrew's, Taunton, 1895 , Chard Parish Church, 1897 ; Yeovil Parish Church, since 1911.

ROBERTS, JOHN HENRY, 149, Grove Street, Liverpool. Born at Bethesda, near Bangor, N. Wales. Educated privately and R.A.M. MUS. BAC. CANTAB., A.R.A.M., F.T.S.C. Principal, Cambrian School of Music. Organist 1874-8, and Organist and Choirmaster 1878-97, Bethesda Congregational Church. Organist Presbyterian Church, Chatham Street, Liverpool, since 1897. Publications : " God is Our Refuge," solo, chorus and orchestra ; anthems, part songs, songs, etc. Musical Editor of Handbook of Praise, The Sunday School Handbook of Praise, Congregational Tune Book, Novello's Anthem Book, Handbook on the Elements of Music, etc. Adjudicator, Conductor.

ROBERTS, JOHN VARLEY, 18, Holywell, Oxford. Born at Stanningley, Leeds. Educated privately. MUS. DOC., F.R.C.O. Organist St. Bartholomew's, Armley, 1862-8 ; Halifax Parish Church, 1868-82 ; St. Giles' Church, Oxford, 1885-93 ; Magdalen College, Oxford, since 1882. Conductor Choral and Philharmonic Society, Oxford, 1885-93 Publications : "Jonah," "Story of the Incarnation," "Advent," and "The Passion ";. Parish Church Chant Book, Supplement to Cheetham's Psalmody " " Practical Method of Training Choristers," about 60 anthems, five morning and evening church services, part songs, organ voluntaries and songs, hymn tunes and chants.

ROBINSON, ARTHUR WILLIAM, 34, Cartwright Gardens, Tavistock Square, W.C. Born Liverpool, 1881. Educated Merchant Taylor's, Crosby ; Liverpool College of Music. Member Royal College of Organists. Associate Trinity College of Music, London. Organist and Choirmaster Trinity Church, Liscard, 1898-1902 ; Hartington Road Church, Liverpool, 1902-4 ; St. Paul's Presbyterian Church, Birkenhead, 1904-9 ; Trinity Presbyterian, Notting Hill, W., 1909-11 ; Holly Park Wesleyan Church, Crouch Hill, since 1911.

ROBINSON, EDGAR C., 7, Park View, Wigan. Born at Gainsborough. Educated at Lincoln Cathedral MUS BAC OXON., F.R.C.O. Assistant Organist Lincoln Cathedral, 1895-1899. Organist and Choirmaster Gainsborough Parish Church, 1899-1906 ; Wigan Parish Church, since 1906. Conductor Wigan and District Philharmonic Society, since 1907 ; Wigan and District Harmonic Male Voice Choir, 1911.

ROBINSON, W. E., 31, Noel Road, Edgbaston, Birmingham. Born 1875 at Birmingham. Trained privately. F R.C.O., L.R.A.M. Deputy Organist Sutton Coldfield Parish Church, 1895. Organist St. Matthew's Parish Church, Birmingham, 1898 ; St. John's Church, Ladywood, Birmingham, since 1907. Hobby and recreation : Gardening and cycling.

ROBSON, FREDERICK YOUNGER, 8, Bloomfield Terrace, Gateshead. Educated at Dr. W. Rea's School, Newcastle-on-Tyne. M.I.S.M. Music Master Tynemouth School. Teacher of music. Organist St. Luke's, Wallsend-on-Tyne, 1893-6. Choirmaster St. James', Gateshead, 1898-1904. Organist St. George's, Cullercoats, since 1896.

ROBSON, JOSEPH HENRY, Crescent House, Hartlepool. Born 1865 at Hartlepool. Educated at Durham Teacher of pianoforte, organ, theory, etc. Organist Presbyterian Church, Hartlepool, 1882 ; St. Mary R.C., 1884-1895 ; Holy Trinity, Seaton Carew, 1895-1909 ; St. Hilda's, Hartlepool, since 1909. Conductor Castle Eden Choral Society, 1904 ; Hartlepool Amateur Operatic Society, since 1904.

ROCHARD, PAUL, St. Mary's House, Mount Road, Hinckley. Born 1883 at Newport, Mon. Educated at Lycee du Havre and Hereford Cathedral. Professor of Music. A.R.C.M. Organist St. Aidan's, South Shields. 1905-6 ; Holy Trinity, South Shields, 1906-7 ; St. Mary the Virgin, Hinckley, since 1907. Conductor South Shields Glee Singers, 1905 6 ; Hinckley Choral Society. Music Master Hinckley Grammar School. Hobby : Musical and engineering literature.

ROE, W. NORMAN, 22, Albert Road, Brighton. Born 1846 at Islington. Trained under J. E. Roe. Organist Holy Trinity, Hove, 1867-71, Christ Church, New Road, Brighton, 1864-67. Organist and Choirmaster St. Mary's Church, Brighton, since 1872. Publications : Hymn tunes, etc.

ROGERS, BRENDAN J., Eblana Hall, Kingstown Studio, 112, Grafton Street, Dublin. Born at Navan, Co. Neath, Ireland. Trained under his father and elder brother. Organist St. Patrick's Cathedral, Primatial Diocese of Armagh, 1866 ; St. Mary's R.C. Cathedral, Dublin, 1882. Official Organist Irish International Exhibition, 1907 ; winner of first prize Orchestra Competition in Feis Coed, 1894. Holder of many Professorships. Composer of a number of works given in Ireland not published. Hobbies and recreations : Literature, gardening, mechanics, cycling, whist, bridge, etc.

ROGERS, DR. ROLAND, Laurel Bank, Upper Bangor, N. Wales. Born 1847 at West Bromwich. Educated musically under Mr. S. Grosvenor. MUS. BAC. (1870), MUS. DOC. (1875). Teacher of music. Formerly Organist St. Peter's Church, West Bromwich ; St. John's, Woverhampton, 1862-66 ; Tettenhall Parish Church, 1866-71 ; Bangor Cathedral 1871-92 ; St. James', Bangor, since 1902 ; and also Bangor Cathedral since 1906. Publications : Part songs ; cantatas, " The Garden," " Out of the Deep," " Prayer and Praise," " Floribel " ; church services, anthems, organ pieces, school songs, etc.

ROOKE, BARTHOLOMEW WARBURTON, Cranleigh, Monkstown, Co. Dublin. Born (1863) and educated at Wicklow. Professor of Music, Royal Irish Academy of Music. MUS. BAC TRIN. COLL. DUBLIN. Organist Parish Church, Monkstown, Co. Dublin, since 1882. Publications : " Elements of Music," and choral compositions. Recreation : Photography.

ROOTHAM, CYRIL BRADLEY, St. John's College, Cambridge. Born at Bristol, 1875 Educated at Bristol Grammar School, Clifton College, St John's College, Cambridge, and Royal College of Music. M.A.; MUS. DOC. CANTAB. Organist Christ Church, Hampstead, 1898 ; St. Asaph Cathedral, 1901 ; and St. John's College Chapel, since 1901. Club : Royal Societies', St. James' Street, S.W.

ROSE, H , 14, Victoria Road, Tamworth A R C O Formerly Organist Holy Trinity Church, Broadstairs ; Parish Church, Tamworth, since 1886.

ROSS, WILLIAM BAIRD, 2, South Inverleith Avenue, Edinburgh. Born at Montrose, 1871. Trained at Montrose Academy and privately. Organist and Choirmaster Farnell Parish Church, 1885 ; Maisondieu, Brechin, 1890 , St. Luke's, Montrose, 1890 , Broughton Place, Edinburgh, since 1895. Choirmaster Dublin Street Baptist Church, Edinburgh, 1895-1903. Conductor Dalkeith Philharmonic Society, since 1905 ; Philharmonic Orchestral Society, Edinburgh, since 1907 ; and Philharmonic Choral Society of Edinburgh, since 1906. Teacher of pianoforte George Watson's Ladies' College, Edinburgh, 1907. Lecturer in music, New College U.F. Church, Edinburgh, 1909. A.R.C.O. (1891), MUS. BAC. OXON (1896), F.R.C.O. (1899), MUS. DOC. OXON , 1904. Publications : " Ode of the Passions," Cantata for Soli, 8 part chorus and orchestra.

ROWDEN, CHARLES FRANK, The Grammar School, Bedale, Yorks. Born at Ongar, Essex 1871. Educated Salisbury Cathedral School ; pupil and Assistant of C. F. South, Esq. (Organist of Salisbury Cathedral) Head Master of Queen Elizabeth's Grammar School, Bedale Past positions : Assistant Master Salisbury Cathedral School ; Music Master and Organist Ovingdean School, Brighton ; Organist, Choirmaster and Music Master Christ's College, Finchley, 1895-1900. Present Organist St. Gregory's Parish Church, Bedale. Conductor Bedale Musical Society, and at Wensleydale Tournament of Song Concerts.

ROWLANDS, MISS OLWEN, Tawelan, Bangor, N. Wales. L.R.A.M., F.R.C.O., Organist Twrgwyn Chapel, Bangor, since 1900.

RUSHWORTH, WALTER MAYNARD, 65, Heathfield Road, Wavertree, Liverpool. Born (1872) and trained at Liverpool College. Formerly Organist Holy Innocents', Liverpool; Sefton Parish Church; All Hallows, Allerton, Liverpool. Organist St. Andrew's Church, West Kirby. Hobby: Painting.

SANDERSON, WILFRID ERNEST, 7, South Parade, Doncaster. Born at Ipswich. MUS. BAC. DUNELM., F.R.C.O., L.R.A.M., Hon. Local Examiner R C.M. Professor of Music. Pupil assistant Westminster Abbey, 1895-1904. Organist and Choirmaster St. Stephen's, Walthamstow, 1896; All Hallows', Southwark, 1898; St. James', West Hampstead, 1899. Organist and Choirmaster St. George's Parish Church, Doncaster, since 1904. Conductor Doncaster Musical Society and Doncaster Operatic Society. Composer of pieces for organ and pianoforte, songs, etc. Recreations: Motoring and tennis.

SANDIFORD, ARTHUR EDWARD, 181, Acomb Street, Rusholme, Manchester. Born 1872 at Manchester. Educated privately. Formerly Organist Holy Name, St. Aloysius, Manchester. Professor of Piano, Singing. Organist St. Augustine's, Manchester, since January, 1909. Hobbies: Rowing and bowling.

SANDWELL, HAYDN HARPER, Bank House, Huddersfield. Born 1891 at Huddersfield. Trained privately. A R C O (1909), F R.C.O. (1909). Formerly Assistant Organist Huddersfield Parish Church. Organist and Choirmaster Lindley Parish Church since December 1911. Won the Obermeir Pianoforte Competition, 1908. Recreations: Tennis and cricket.

SANGER, N. EDWARD, Avoca, Longfield Avenue, Hackbridge, Surrey. Born 1884 at Salisbury. Trained at Salisbury and at Brinton, under Mr. F. Bellini. Deputy Organist Wesley Church, Salisbury, 1900-1902. Organist and Choirmaster Lambeth Presbyterian Church since March, 1910. Hobbies: Photography and microscopy.

SARVENT, GEORGE A, St Philips Road, Newmarket. Born 1843 in London. Organist St. Michael's, Shoreditch, 1863-1893; St. Agnes, Newmarket, 1893-1899; St. Martin's, Exning, Newmarket, since 1899. Publications: Sets of hymns and tunes. Hobby: Photography. Club: Newmarket Conservative.

SATCHELL, HEDLEY, 50, Hagley Road, Stourbridge. Born 1858 at Banbury. Educated under private tuition and Leipsic Conservatorium. Leipsic Conservatorist. Conductor Peoples' Concert Society, Stourbridge 1884-6, Anglo-American Choral Society, Leipsic, 1887-8; Stourbridge Peoples' Concert Society, 1892-8. Longlands Musical Society and Cradley Choral Society during the first year of their existence. Organist Old Swinford Parish Church, Stourbridge, since 1882.

SAYERS, HERBERT, Ivy Dene, Bensham Lane, Croydon. Born 1874 at London. Educated privately by Professor Prout. Professor of Organ, Pianoforte, and Harmony at St Philomenas, Carshalton; Coloma House, Croydon: Sanderstead High School, &c.; Organist to Sir Henry Irving, 1893-1906. Organist St. Mary's, Croydon, since 1901 Member Royal Society of Musicians. Hobbies and recreations: Whist, Chess, and Horology.

SCADDING, ALEXANDER S. L., Buttovan House, Newport, I O.W. Born 1874 at Cowes, I.O.W. Educated at Cowes and Newport, I.O.W. Director of music warehouse. Organist St. John's, Newport, I.O.W. since 1892.

SCADDING, ISABEL MAY CAROLINE, 31, Holyrood Street, Newport, I.O.W. Born and educated at West Cowes. L.L.C.M. Assistant Organist since 1895, St. Thomas', Newport. Organist St. Mildred's, Whippingham, near Cowes, I.W., since 1904. Daughter of William Scadding, late Organist to her Majesty Queen Victoria, at Osborne Private Chapel, and late Organist at St. Thomas' Parish Church, Newport, for 25 years. Profession : Music.

SCORAH, JOHN N., Alford, Chester. Born 1862 at Liverpool. Educated at Royal Normal College, Norwood. Fellow Guild of Organists. Organist St John Baptist Church, Alford, Chester, since 1879.

SCOTT, DAVID, Clarence Villas, Glastonbury. Born at Wirksworth, 1879. Studied music under Dr. Davis and other teachers. A.R.C.O. Conductor of Glastonbury Choral Class. Organist and Choirmaster St. John's Church, Glastonbury, since 1905. Formerly of St. Columbas Church, Birmingham.

SCOTT, WILLIAM HENRY, 47, New Walk, Museum Square, Leicester. Born Long Sutton, Lines., and educated locally. M I.S.M. Sectional Councillor N. Mid. Section. Teacher of singing, pianoforte, organ, etc. Organist St. Mary Magdalene, Fleet, 1875-86 ; St. Saviour's, since 1886. Hon. Organist and Accompanist Leicester New Musical Society and Hon. Treasurer since 1887. Vice-President of the Leicester Association of Organists and Choirmasters. Recreations. Walking, cycling and bowls. St. John's Lodge Freemasons.

SCRIVENER, P. R., 5, Sidmouth Street, Reading. Born 1872 at Lewisham, Kent. Educated at Asansol, India, and Reading, England. L.T C.L., F.R.C.O. Singing Master. Organist St. Paul's, Asansol India, 1885-6 ; St. John's, Caversham, 1891-5. Choirmaster Holy Trinity, Reading, 1896-1902. Organist and Choirmaster St. Giles' Parish Church since 1895. Conductor St. Cecilia, 1905 ; Reading Ladies' Choir, 1907 ; Singing Master Kendrick Girls' School since 1907 ; Organist Reading Philharmonic Society since 1911. Hobby : Collecting engine picture post cards.

SEAL, CHARLES, 5, Jordan Gate, Macclesfield. MUS. BAC. OXON., F.R.C.O. Organist Great Brington Parish Church, Northants, 1868-73 ; St. Michael's Parish Church, Macclesfield, since 1873.

SENIOR, J. E. R., 22, Royal Crescent, Glasgow, W. Born and educated at Batley, Yorks. F.R.C.O., L R.A.M., L.T.C.L. Local Representative Trinity College, London. Formerly pupil of Dr. A. L Peace, Dr. Hans Von Bülow, Signori Manuel and Gustave Garcia. Teacher of organsinging, piano and harmony. Has given recitals at Crystal Palace, Exeter Hall ; Bow and Bromley Institute ; St George's Hall, Liverpool ; St. Andrew's City Hall Art Gallery, Glasgow ; Govan Town Hall, etc. Formerly Organist George Street Chapel, Heckmondwike (when 10 years old) ; Govan Parish Church, which organ was designed by him Hobbies and recreations : Travelling, cycling, and collecting antique furniture. Publications : Organ, vocal and piano music, Art and Pen and Pencil Clubs.

SEYMOUR, CHARLES F., King Edward Road, Axminster. Born 1874 at Boston, Lincs. A.R.C.M. Formerly Organist and Choirmaster St. Thomas', Boston ; Holy Trinity, Las Palmas ; Cholsey Parish Church ;

St. Mary's Parish Church, Huntingdon Organist and Choirmaster St. Mary's, Axminster Formerly Conductor Boston Orchestral Society. Music Master Wallingford Grammar School, Berks

SHANN, C. J. H , 15, Crown Street, Bury St. Edmunds Born at Leeds. Educated at Royal College of Music. Teacher of voice production, etc. Organist Driffield Parish Church, 1892-6 ; St. James', Bury St. Edmund's, since 1896 Composer of music for Bury St. Edmunds Historical Pageant, 1907. Hobby : Philately.

SHARP, LATIMER TERTIUS, Rosebank, Forsyth Street, Greenock Born at Bradford, Yorks. Trained privately. A R.C.O. Formerly Organist Saltaire Congregational, Yorks ; Prospect Wesleyan, Bradford ; Wesgate Hill Wesleyan, Birkenshaw. Organist Mid Parish Church, Greenock, since 1901 Publications : Hymn tunes, sheet music, etc Hon. Director of Music St John's Lodge of Freemasons, No. 175. Conductor Greenbank Male Voice Choir, Greenock. Hobby . Golf.

SHARPE, E., 3, Carlton Road, Southampton. Organist All Saints',Southampton, 1865-1880 ; St Mary's, Southampton, since 1881.

SHARPE, GEORGE FREDERIC, School of Music, Heath Crescent, Halifax. Born 1863 at Halifax Educated at Park House Academy, Halifax. MUS. BAC OXON , L.R.A.M., A R C M. Principal School of Music, Halifax. Organist St. Mary's, Halifax, 1883 Hon Local Examiner R C.M. Composer of songs, etc. Hobbies . Photography and cycling

SHARPE, J. H Fowler, Haydn House, West End, Ilminster. Born 1873, at High Ham, Somerset Trained chiefly under Albert Ham, MUS. DOC. Organist Kingsbury Episcopal Church, 1889-1896 ; South Petherton, 1896-1907 ; Ilminster Parish Church since November 1907. Publications . Magnificat and Nunc Dimittis in D. Hobby and recreation : Photography and cycling.

SHAW, A , The Rosery, Trinity Grove, Bengeo, Hertford Born 1855 at Hertford. Educated at R A M , London Certificated Organist and Teacher of Music M I S M Professor of Music Assistant Organist Christ's Hospital, 1867, at the age of 12 ; Christ Church, Bengeo, at age of 14, Bayford, 1871-6 ; Holy Trinity, Bengeo, Hertford, 1877-1909 ; St. Simon's, Southsea, since 1910 Hobby Gardening

SHAW, WILFRID, 13, Littledale Road, Egremont, Cheshire Born 1883 at Royton. Educated at Oldham, Rochdale, Manchester and Liverpool Professor of Music. Deputy Organist Wesleyan, Royton, 1899 (age 16) ; Zion Chapel, Lees, Oldham, 1904 , Myrtle Street Baptist, Liverpool, since 1907 Accompanist Orchestral Society, 1898 (age 15), then Conductor of same. Musical Director Wallasey Gentlemen's Glee Club, Cheshire Recreation Golf.

SHEAVES, H MOZART, 11, Orchard Road, Stockport Road, Altrincham. Born (1876) and educated at Manchester MUS BAC. (VICT), F R.C O , A R C M., A R M C M. Teacher of Music. Organist St. Saviours', Cheetham, Manchester, 1897-99 ; Christ Church, Timperley, since 1900. Conductor Timperley Vocal Society since 1900 ; Altrincham Choral Society, 1907-9 , Altrincham Hospital Festival Chorus since 1906

SHEPPARD, SIDNEY HERBERT, 218, High Street, Brentford, Middlesex. Born 1891 at Brentford. Trained at Trinity College of Music, London. A R C.O., L.T.C.L. Formerly Organist St. Faith's, Brentford Organist and Choirmaster Christ Church, S. Marylebone, since February 1911. Recreation . Association football.

SHERWOOD, Sydney V., 14, Daysbrook Road, Streatham Hill, London, S.W. Born 1877 at Brixton, S.W. F.R.C.O. Professor of Music. Organist St. Benet and All Saints', Kentish Town, 1896-7, St. James', Camberwell, since 1897. Assistant St. John the Divine, Kennington. Hobby : Mechanics.

SHINN, Frederick G., 4, Sydenham Park, London, S.E. Born in London. Educated R C.M. and privately. MUS DOC. DUNELM., A.R C.M., F.R.C.O., G.S.M. Professor of the Art of Teaching and of Harmony. Organist St. Bartholomew's, Sydenham, London, S.E., since 1893. Publications : " A Method of Teaching Harmony Based on Eartraining," "Elementary Eartraining," " Musical Memory and its Cultivation." Recreations : Chess and cycling.

SHINN, George, 234, Stockwell Road, Brixton, London, S.W. Born 1837 at Clerkenwell, London. MUS. BAC. CANTAB. Teacher of pianoforte and singing Organist St Peter's, Hackney, 1859 ; St. Jude's, Whitechapel, 1863 ; St. Paul's, Cannonbury, 1866 ; Brixton Parish Church, 1872 ; Christ Church, Gipsy Hill, 1887 ; St. Bartholomow's, Grays Inn Road, since 1900. Publications : Oratorios, " The Captives of Babylon " and " Lazarus of Bethany " ; cantata, " The Treasures of the Deep " ; church services, anthems, organ and piano pieces and numerous other works.

SHUTTLEWORTH, Alma, 27, West Morton Street, Thornhill, Dumfriesshire. Born (1880) and educated at Cononley. Organist United Methodist Free Church, 1895 ; Cononley Wesleyan Church, 1897 ; St. Barnabas', Morecambe, 1901 , Morton Parish Church, since 1903 Hobby and recreation : Shooting, cycling and photography.

SILVER, Alfred J., The Limes, Handsworth Wood, Birmingham MUS. DOC DUNELM., F R.C.O. Formerly chorister St. George's Chapel, Windsor Castle, under Sir George Elvey and Sir Walter Parratt. Assistant Organist St. George's to Sir Walter Parratt. Formerly Organist Clewer Parish Church, Windsor ; Ealing Parish Church, W. ; St. David's, Merthyr Tydfil ; and Parish Church, Carmarthen. Organist Handsworth Parish Church, Birmingham, since 1900. Music Master Handsworth Grammar School. Conductor North Birmingham and Handsworth Choral Society. Composer of music for orchestra, piano, organ, 'cello, church and vocal music, etc.

SIMPSON, James, 6, Castle Terrace, Bridgnorth. Organist Rowley Regis Paris Church, 1880 ; St. James' Parish Church, Dudley, 1882, and St. Mary Magdalene, Bridgnorth, since 1885. Music Master Bridgnorth Grammar School. Publications : Francis & Day's High School Edition " Scale Manual," with English and Continental fingering, " The Irregular Scale Practice," etc.

SIMS, Arthur E., 57, Commercial Street, Newport, Mon. L.R.A.M. Studied under Mr. George Riseley, of Bristol. Formerly accompanist to the Newport Choral Society. Organist to Welsh Choir of 5,000 voices, Crystal Palace Festival of Empire, 1911. Conductor Newport Choral Society (membership 250) since 1905. Organist Great Central Hall, Newport. Hobby : Choral and orchestral conducting.

SINCLAIR, George Robertson, The Close, Hereford. MUS. DOC., F.R.C.O., HON. R.A.M., L.R.A.M. Formerly Organist and Choirmaster St. Mary de Crypt, Gloucester. Assistant Gloucester Cathedral. Organist and Choirmaster Truro Cathedral Past Grand Organist to the Grand

Lodge of England, Grand Lodge of Mark Masons and the Supreme Grand Chapter of the Royal Arch, etc. Organist Hereford Cathedral since 1890.

SLATER, D ALBERT, 25, Grimshaw Street, Great Harwood, near Blackburn. Born at Ribchester, 1878. F.R.C.O. Formerly Organist Holy Trinity, Preston; and Holy Trinity, Blackburn Conductor Great Harwood Male Voice Choir. Teacher Great Harwood Technical School. Organist St Peter's, Blackburn, since 1902. Recreation : Golf.

SLOPER, HUGH VERNON, 74, Charminster Road, Bournemouth. Born at Hendon 1884. Educated at Christ's College, Blackheath, London. Organist Charminster Road Congregational, Bournemouth Pianist to " The Strolling Singers " Concert Party. Recreations : Cycling and boating.

SMALE, PERCY W. DE COURCY, 19, Helvellyn Street, Keswick, and The Festival Office, Morecambe. Born 1875 at Bideford, Devon. Trained at Vevey, Switzerland. Organist Instow Parish Church, 1893 , St. Barnabas, Bell Street, London, W., 1894 , Philberds School, Maidenhead, 1896 ; St. Anne's School, Redhill, 1898 , Lancaster Grammar School and Halton Parish Church, 1900 ; Blairlodge, Scotland, 1901 ; Tonbridge Preparatory School and Ide Hill Parish Church, 1904 , St. Laurence, Morecambe, 1906 , St. John's, Keswick, since 1910 Musical Director Morecambe Musical Festival. Conductor Morecambe Madrigal Society , Yealand Choral Society ; Keswick Madrigal Society ; Keswick Choral Society. Music Master Keswick High School Chorus Master of Morecambe and Keswick Festival Choirs. Recreation : Golf Member Primrose Club.

SMALLWOOD, FREDERICK WILLIAM, 33, Lindon Road, Gosforth. Born (1860) and educated at Durham. MUS. BAC DUNELM., A R.C.O., F G O Architect. Formerly Organist New Connexion Chapel, Durham; Norham Parish Church ; Lord Breadalbane's Private Chapel ; St. John's, Alloa ; Town Hall, Alloa ; All Saints', Gosforth ; St Thomas', Newcastle-on-Tyne. Organist St. Thomas' the Martyr since 1900. Composer of music Author of " Combined Piano and Harmony Tutor " Hobbies and recreations Painting, bowling, cycling, psychology, and any intellectual work. Club : Pen and Palette, Newcastleon-Tyne.

SMITH, ALFRED, 141, Rochdale Road, Harpurthey, Manchester. Born (1860) and educated at Manchester. F.V.C.M., F.I.G C.M. Teacher of music and singing. Organist St. George's, Manchester, 1883-9 ; St Thomas',Heaton Chapel, 1889-91 , St Andrew's, Blackley, 1891-1904 ; St. Paul's, Manchester, since 1904. Hobby : Free Masonry. Club : Harpurthey Conservative.

SMITH, ALFRED GUEST, 151, Grove Lane, Handsworth, Birmingham Born 1880 at Himley Educated privately. F.R.C.O , L-R.A.M. Organist and Choirmaster St. James', West Bromwich, 1902-5 ; St. Andrew's Parish Church, Shifnal, 1905-10 ; St.James', Handsworth, Birmingham, since 1910.

SMITH, ARTHUR F., Malvern House, Uttoxeter New Road, Derby. Born and educated at Derby. MUS. BAC. CANTAB , A R.C O Local Representative R.A.M. Hon. Local Examiner R.C.M Instructor in Music Derby Training College. Organist St. Werburgh's, Derby, 1872-1912. Publications : Pianoforte pieces, part-music, cantata, church music, etc.

SMITH, ALFRED J., Rowena, Hallam Street, West Bromwich. F.G.O. Commercial Clerk. Organist St. Michael's and All Angels', Walsall, 1884-6. Assistant St. James', Wednesbury, 1881-4 ; Parish Church, West Bromwich, since 1886.

SMITH, CHARLES EDWIN, 60, Kyverdale Road, Stoke Newington London, N. Born 1856. Tuition from W. West and Sir F. Bridge, MUS. DOC. Organist Downs Baptist Chapel, Clapton, 1879-96 ; Regent's Park Chapel (Baptist), London, N.W., since 1896 Assistant Secretary Baptist Missionary Society. Musical lecturer Publisher of songs, anthems, tunes, etc. ; Editor of the Chinese Pentatonic Tune Book. (300). Served on Committee in the compilation of the Baptist Church Hymnal. Recreation Cycling.

SMITH, ELI, 75, Avenue Parade, Accrington. Born 1880 at Oldham. Trained at Manchester Cathedral Choir School and Royal Manchester College of Music. L.R.A.M., A.R.M.C.M. 1st MUS BAC. OXFORD. Professor of Music. Organist St. Clement's, Salford, 1898-1904 Organist and Choirmaster St. Martin's, York, 1905-07 ; Accrington Parish Church since 1907. Publication " A Lullaby " for Contralto Recreations : Billiards and cricket.

SMITH, ERNEST H., 35, Hartington Road, Liverpool. Born 1862 and educated at Faversham F R C O Formerly Organist Eastling, Westerham. Organist St. Bede's, Liverpool, since 1892. Teacher and composer of music.

SMITH, GEORGE, 17, Saltburn Place, Bradford. Born 1882 at Manchester. Studied piano with Prof. Chas. Henrich of Bradford Trained for organ under Dr A H. Edwards. Organist and Choirmaster St. Mary Magdalene, Bradford, since 1911. One of the leading First Violinists in Bradford Permanent Orchestra and Festival Choral Society. Piano Soloist

SMITH, GEORGE FREDERICK, Seabourne, Bonham Road, Brixton Hill, London, S W. Born 1856 in London Trained Royal Academy of Music and privately. F.R.C.O., M.R.S.M., L. MUS T.C L., A.R A.M. Sub Professor R A M 1877, Professor G.S.M. 1887, Hon. Examiner R.C M. 1887. Organist St. Barnabas, South Lambeth, 1870 ; Mare Street Chapel, Hackney, 1874 ; St. John's, Angell Town, Brixton, 1875 ; St. Magnus, London Bridge, since 1880. Publications : Songs, pianoforte pieces, part songs, organ music, services, hymn tunes. Recreations Out door sports.

SMITH, GEORGE HENRY, 12, Westbourne Avenue, Hull. Born and educated at Hull MUS. DOC. OXON. Is the Principal of the Hull and East Riding College of Music, and Conductor of the Hull Vocal Society, and the South Holderness Choral Society. Organist Christ Church, Hull, 1881-3 ; Sculcoates Parish Church, since 1883. Publications : Morning and evening service, Benediction Service (R.C.), pianoforte pieces, school songs and anthems, and a " History of Hull Organs and Organists " Recreations : Billiards, cycling.

SMITH, HERBERT FREDERICK, 1, Bridgford Road, Nottingham. Born 1872 at Nottingham. Educated at the People's College, Nottingham ; afterwards privately. A.R.C.O. Teacher of music Principal West Bridgford Music School Articled pupil and assistant of Arthur Page, Esq., F.R.C O , late Organist St. Mary's, Nottingham, 1889-94. Organist St Saviour's, Nottingham, since 1895. Hobby and recreation : Cycling and photography.

SMITH, JOSEPH ENOS, 22, Church Street, Rushden, R.S.O , Northamptonshire. Born (1851) and educated at Stanwick. Certificated Higher Examination Trinity College London in Pianoforte and Organ Playing. Music teacher. Organist Souldrop Parish Church, Bedfordshire, 1872-5 ; St. Mary's Parish Church, Rushden, since 1875 (May). Hobby and recreation : Gardening and cycling.

SMITH, J.TURTON, 4, Victoria Road, Bridgnorth. Born 1879 at Sherrington, Bucks. Trained in London and at St. David's Cathedral. F.R.C.O., L.R.A.M. Organist Conway Parish Church, 1900 ; St. Mary's, Pembroke, 1901 ; St. Luke's, Cork, 1905 ; St. Leonard's, Bridgnorth, since 1908. Music Master, Girls' Public High School, Bridgnorth.

SOAR, JOSEPH, Elm Bank, Swires Road, Halifax, and The Hawthorns, Housley Park, Chapeltown, near Sheffield. MUS. BAC. DUNELM.,A.R.C.M.,F.R.C.O. Twice Exhibitioner R.C.M. London. Formerly assistant pupil Temple Church, under Dr. Walford Davies. Conductor Derby Orchestra. Formerly Organist Parish Church, Chapeltown, Sheffield ; St. John's, Clapham, London, S.W. ; All Saints', Norfolk Square, Hyde Park, W. ; Parish Church, Derby ; Parish Church, Barnsley. Organist Parish Church, Halifax, 1912. Music Master Barnsley Grammar School. Conductor Tankersley Choral Society, Barnsley Amateur Operatic Society, and the S. Cecilia Choral Society, Barnsley.

SOMERS, S. FRANZ, 7, Cranbury Terrace, Southampton. Born 1868 in Hampshire. Educated at Warminster, Winchester and Germany. Teacher of music. Organist All Saints' Church, 1899 ; St. Michael's Church, Southampton, since 1902. Hobbies and recreation : Playing the piano, billiards, gardening and football.

SOMERTON, WALTER, Alveston House, Clevedon. Born 1858. Educated at Clevedon. Organist Deputy All Saints, Clevedon, 1873-4 ; St. Andrew's, Backwell, 1875 ; St. John the Evangelist, Clevedon, since 1876. Clubs : Freemasons and Oddfellows.

SOUTH, CHARLES T., The Close, Salisbury. Organist St. Aske's Hospital, Hoxton, 1866 ; S.S. Augustine Faith, London, E.C., 1868 ; Salisbury Cathedral, since 1883.

SOUTHAN, ARTHUR RICHARD, Lyndhurst, Stourport Road, Bewdley. Member of Guild of Organists, Incorporated. Organist St. Anne's, Bewdley, since 1901.

SOWRY, H. MARSHALL, Gien Lyn, Cheltenham. Born 1882 at Leeds. Trained at Yorkshire Training College of Music. L.R.A.M., F.R.C.O. Organist Roundhay Parish Church 1900 ; St. Matthew's, Cheltenham, since 1908. Conductor Bramhope Choral Society, 1907-08. Recreation: Cycling.

SOYER, W. A., 10, Granville Road, Sevenoaks. Born 1866 at Blackheath. Educated at Roan School, Greenwich. F.R.C.O. Associate Pianist Trinity College London. Clerk in G.P.O. Organist Morden College, Blackheath, 1882-1899 ; St. Mary's, Greenwich, 1899-1901 ; Christ Church, Beckenham, 1901-1908 ; St. Nicholas, Sevenoaks, since 1908.

SPACKMAN, LEWIN, Corsham, Wilts Born (1858) and educated at Corsham. Secretary Gas & Water Company. Organist Free Church, Calne, 1880-2 ; Corsham Parish Church, since 1882. Conductor Corsham Choral Society, since 1883. Composer of Magnificat and Nunc Dimittis in D, six Kyries with Glorias and Gratias Tibi. Hobbies : Astronomy and cricket.

SPANSWICK, J. C., Victor House, 201, Junction Road, London, N., and 33, Clipstone Street, London, W. Born 1852 in London Trained under Tamplin, Gounod, Barnby, and Coward. Music expert, Metzlers (London). Deputy Organist Holy Trinity Church, St. Marylebone, W., 1867-70. Organist Middlesex Hospital, London, W. Publication: Spanswick's Directions on Stop Registrations. Hobbies: Tuning and regulating organs.

SPEER, WILLIAM H., Powyscourt, Balcombe, Sussex. Born in London, 1863. Educated Cambridge and R.C.M. M.A., MUS. DOC. CANTAB., F.R.C.O., A.R.C.M. Music composer. Organist Christ Church, High Wycombe, 1902-3; St. Peter's, Bexhill, 1903-1910. Publications: Numerous musical works, vocal and orchestral. Clubs: Oxford and Cambridge Musical.

SPYER, J., Brenham Cottage, Gordon Road, Camberley, Surrey. F.R.C.O. Organist Royal Military College Chapel, Camberley.

STANDRING, ELLIS, 17, Rupert Street, Reddish. Born 1872 at Oldham. Educated privately. A.R.C.O. Organist and Choirmaster Denshaw Parish Church, 1893; Oldham Parish Church, 1896; St. Chrysostom's, Manchester, since 1898. Conductor St. Chrysostom's Choral Society.

STANTON, T. W., Ardbig, Helensburg, Dumbartonshire, N.B. Born at Leeds. Educated at Manchester. Organist St. Michael's and All Angels' Episcopal, Helensburgh, since 1901. Music Master Landfield School. Conductor Helensburgh Choral Union. Hobby and recreation: Golf and gardening.

STANTON, WALTER K., Merton College, Oxford. Born at Dauntsey, Chippenham, Wilts, 1891. Educated at Choristers' School, Salisbury, and Lancing College, Sussex. Organist Merton College Chapel, Oxford, since 1909. Was a solo boy in Salisbury Cathedral Choir, and presided over the organ there at one service whilst a chorister; has since given three organ recitals in the Cathedral.

STARMER, WILLIAM WOODING, 52, Warwick Park, Tunbridge Wells. Born 1866. Educated at Wellingborough Grammar School and Royal Academy of Music. F.R.A.M., L.MUS., T.C.L. Organist to the Marquis of Northampton, at Castle Ashby, 1883; St. Mark's, Tunbridge Wells, since 1888. Composer of church and organ music. Eminent authority and lecturer on bells, carillons and chimes. Writer of articles in Groves' Dictionary, Cyclopædic Dictionary of Music, and many other important works.

STARK, WALTER E., 164, Amesbury Avenue, Streatham Hill, London, S.W. Born 1861 at Reading. Educated at Reading School. Musician; teacher of pianoforte, organ, harmony and singing. Organist and Choirmaster St. Mary the Virgin, Charing Cross Road, W.C., 1876-7; Wellington College, Wokingham, 1877-80; King Edward VI. School, Browngrove, Worcestershire, 1880-2; St. Margaret Pattens, Rood Lane. E.C., 1882-5; St. Auselin's, Streatham, S.W., 1885-90; St. Andrew's, Streatham, S.W., 1890-2; St. Luke's, Bromley, Kent, 1892-1902; Emmanuel Church, West Dulwich, S.E., since 1902. Recreation: Walking.

STATON, J. FREDERIC, Baslow Road, Chesterfield. Born 1884 at Mosbro. Educated Netherthorpe Grammar School. MUS. BAC. F.R.C.O., L.R.A.M. Organist and Choirmaster All Saints', Ashover, 1899-1909; Chesterfield Parish Church, since 1909. Conductor Chesterfield Orchestral Society, Chesterfield and District Musical Union. Recreation: Golf.

STATHER, HERBERT, 39, Newsome Road, Berry Brow, Huddersfield. Born 1872 at Snaith, Yorks. Self taught. Organist Grove Place Church, Huddersfield, 1892-93 ; Lockwood Baptist Church, 1893-1906 ; Queen Street Wesleyan Church, Huddersfield, since 1907. Publications : Two operattas, 60 anthems, part songs, songs, pianoforte music, etc. Hobby : Studying orchestral instruments.

STEANE, BRUCE, Prospect House, Sundridge, Sevenoaks. Born 1866 at Camberwell. Educated at Dulwich College. Composer of Music. Formerly Organist Parish Church, Whitechapel ; St. Mary's, Cuddington ; St. Mary's, Kemsing ; St. Peter's, Seal ; St. Barts' Convalescent Home, Swanley. Organist St. Bartholomew's Hospital, since 1905. Publications : Opus 350, including 60 anthems, six Te Deums, four morning services, 11 evening services; " The Ascension " (sacred oratorio), 93 organ works, eight Fugues, 12 part songs ; madrigal, " On May Morning " ; songs, " I Heard the Voice " " Come unto Me Ye Weary " ; six pianoforte pieces, eight violin and pianoforte pieces, 60 hymn tunes, 60 single and double chants, two comic operas, pianoforte trio ; symphony, " Dreadnought " ; tone poem, " Grimaldi " ; etc., etc. Hobby and recreation : Rifle shooting and cycling.

STEAR, CHARLES W., Highbank, Trelawney Road, Cotham, Bristol. Born at Bristol, 1870. Educated at Bristol Grammar School. Director of Music and Organist at Bristol Grammar School, since 1886 ; Organist and Choirmaster Chipping Sodbury Parish Church, 1889 ; Holy Nativity, Knowle, 1891 ; St. Mary the Virgin, Tyndall's Park, Clifton, since 1911. Conductor of Bristol Musical Society, Clevedon Philharmonic Society, and Society of Bristol Gleemen. Clubs : University and Literary, Bristol Musical, and " Bristol Savages."

STEDMAN, JOHN, 16, Maida Hill West, London, W. Born 1876 at Hillingdon. Trained under E. H. Turpin, MUS. D. of Trinity College, London. Organist Catholic Apostolic Church, Paddington, since 1902. Recreations : Cricket and cycling

STEGGALL, REGINALD, Beaulieu, 102, Sutton Court Road, Chiswick, W. F.R.A.M., A.R.C.O. Professor R.A.M. Examiner, Assoc. Board R.A.M. and R.C.M. Organist St. Anne's, Soho, 1886-7 ; Lincoln's Inn Chapel, London, since 1905.

STEPHENSON, A. P., St. Helen's, Trinity Road, Bridlington. Born at Hull. Trained at King's College School, London. F.R.C.O. Organist St. Andrew's, Hull, 1883-89 ; St. James', Hull, 1889-94 ; Newington Parish Church, Hull, 1895-98 ; St. Thomas', Hull, 1899-1902 ; Priory Church, Bridlington, since 1909.

STEPHENSON, EDWIN. Formerly Organist and Choirmaster Cartmel Priory Church. Choirmaster and Organist Sunningdale Church, near Windsor , St. Michael's, Brighton ; Parish Church, Brighton. Conductor Professional Symphony Orchestra, Brighton, etc. Organist and Master of the Choristers St. Philip's Cathedral, Birmingham, since 1906.

STEPHENSON, J. C., 83, Franklin Road, Harrogate. Born at York. Pupil of T. T. Noble of York Minster. A.R.C.O. Organist and Choirmaster St. Paul's, York, 1895-1903 ; St. Mary's, Harrogate, since 1903. Club : Masonic.

STEVENS, REV. ARTHUR HENRY, Chattisham Vicarage, Ipswich. Born 1857 at Barnes, S.W. Educated at Eton and Oxford. M.A., MUS. BAC. OXON., Organ Scholar, Worcester College, Oxford. Vicar of Chattisham, Ipswich. Formerly Organist Roehampton, S.W.; St. John's, Hammersmith; Musical Director Dover College, 1882-1906. Chairman R.C.M. Board of Examiners, 1885-1906; Examiner Kent County Scholarship R.C.M. Organist Dover College Chapel, 1882-1906. Publications: Anthems, evening and morning service in G, Christmas carols, school songs, prize hymn tune, contributions to " Organists' Quarterly Journal," " Musical Times," and " Musical News." Noticed in " Biography of British Musicians." Hobby : Fishing.]

STEVENS, CHARLES EDWARD RUSSELL, 25, Bath Street, St. Heliers, Jersey Born at St. Heliers. Educated at Victoria College, Jersey ; Lycee de Rennes, France. Leipzig Conservatorium of Music. Professor of Music. Local Secretary Trinity College, London. Formerly Conductor Jersey Choral Society and Cecilian Orchestral Society. Professor of Music, Highlands College and Jersey Modern School. Organist St. Mark's, St Heliers, Jersey, since 1886. Vice-President Jersey Choral Society and of the Jersey Eisteddfod. Hobby : Lecturing on music. Club : Cæsarean.

STEWARDSON, HENRY WILLIAM, 6, Aspley Villas, Adelaide Square, Bedford. F.T.C.L. Teacher of music. Choirmaster St. Leonard's, Old Warden, Beds, 1903-6 ; St. Mary's Church, Haynes, Beds, since 1901. Organist Bedford Modern School since 1881. Publications : Anthems, " Thou Visitest the Earth " (Weekes etc.) (Harvest) ; " Christ is Risen " (Easter) ; Te Deum, Magnificat, Nunc Dimittis, Benedicite. Additional appointments : Local Secretary Trinity College of Music, Local Examiner Royal College of Music. Hobby and recreation : Photography and cycling.

STOCK, ALFRED R., 21, Sutherland Place, Bayswater, London, W. Born in London. Trained under Sydney Scott, MUS. BAC. (OXON), F.R.C.O., Dr. Cuthbert Harris, F.R.C.O. and several others. A.R.C.O. Organ recitalist. Organist Bayswater United Methodist Church, 1905-09. Organist and Choirmaster Chelsea Congregational Church, Markham Square, S.W., since 1909.

STOCKS, HAROLD CARPENTER LUMB, Ebor House, Ludlow. Born 1884 at Essenden, Herts. Trained at Ely Cathedral and private. MUS. BAC. OXON., F.R.C.O. Organist Littleport Parish Church, 1902-06 ; St. Mary's, Ely, 1906-09 ; (Assistant), Ely Cathedral, 1906-09 ; Yeovil Parish Church, 1909-11 ; Ludlow Parish Church since 1911. Publications : Hymn tunes ; song, " Echoes." Recreations : Walking and cycling.

STONES, JEREMIAH, 16, Church Lane, Kirkstall, Leeds. Born 1874 at Leeds. Trained under R. Dunstan, Esq. and Thos. J Hoggett. Schoolmaster under Leeds Education Committee, 1896-1912. Organist Methodist Church, Armley, 1889-91 Organist and Choirmaster Kirkstall Wesleyan Church, 1891-94 ; Wesleyan Church, Westminster, S.W., 1895-96; Brunswick Wesleyan Church, Leeds, since 1896. Conductor Leeds Nonconformist Choir Union ; Wetherby Choral Society ; Leeds Education Committee's Choral and Operatic Society Music Master City of Leeds Training College since 1912. Recreation : Angling. Member of Leeds Municipal Officers' Guild, Leeds Playgores' Society, Leeds Amalgamation of Anglers' Society.

STORER, JOHN, Academy of Music, Waterford. MUS. BAC. OXON., MUS. DOC. T.U.T. Musical Director Opera Comique, Strand, Avenue and Globe Theatres, London, 1891-6 ; Musical critic of the Morning, Court Circular,

St. Paul's, Madame, and Illustrated Sporting News, 1894-1904. Organist St. Michael's, Whitby, 1879-81 ; Parish Church, Scarborough, 1882-5 ; Parish Church, Folkestone, 1885-88 ; Redempotist Church, Clapham, London, 1888-91 ; St. Marie's R.C. Church, Sheffield, 1904-6 ; Roman Catholic Cathedral, Waterford, since 1906. Principal of the Waterford Academy of Music. Composer of Operas " Punchbowl " Novelty Theatre, 1887 ; and " Gretna Green " Comedy Theatre, 1890 ; Oratorio " Deborah and Barak," masses, cantatas, orchestral symphonies, overtures, chamber music, and a great quantity of songs, part songs, anthems.

SUTTON, FRANCIS W., The Homestead, 59, Loughboro' Park, London, S.W. Born at Brixton, S.W., 1886. Trained at Guildhall School of Music. Held Corporation Scholarship for six years. A.R.C.O. Organist Clapham Congregational Church since 1909. Organist and Accompanist St. Saviour's (Denmark Park) Choral Society since 1905.

SUTTON, WILLIAM STANLEY, 41, East Street, Horsham. Born 1891 at Truro. Educated at Truro Cathedral School. F R.C.O., L.R.A.M. Professor of Music. Articled pupil and assistant to Dr. M. J. Monk, F.R.C.O. (Organist of Truro Cathedral) 1907-1911. Organist Truro Philharmonic Society, 1909-11. Organist and Choirmaster St. Mary's Parish Church, Horsham, since 1911. Conductor and Choirmaster Horsham and District Choral Union Festival.

SWAINSON, S. W., 43, Franklin Road, Harrogate. Born at Harrogate, 1886. Privately trained. F.R.C.O. Organist and Director of the Choir, Bilton Parish Church, Harrogate, since 1908. Recreations : Cycling and swimming.

SWEETING, E. T., Culver Lodge, Winchester. Born 1863. Educated at National Training School of Music. Examiner of the Associated Board of the R.A.M. and R.C.M. Member of the Council, R.C.O. MUS. DOC. OXON., F.R.C.O. Organist St. Mary's, W. Kensington, 1875-1882 ; St. John's College, Cambridge, 1897-1901 Music Master Rossall School, 1882-1897 ; Winchester College, since 1901. Recreations : Golf, cycling and shooting.

TARBOX, THOMAS JAMES, 110, Minet Avenue, Harlesden, London, N.W. Born at Great Berkhamsted, Herts. Trained chiefly under Dr. E. M. Lott. Assistant Organist St. Sepulchre, Holborn, 1886-90; Deputy Organist St. Pancras, 1894-97 ; Assistant Organist Christ Church, Somers Town, London, N.W., 1888-97 ; Organist and Choirmaster Christ Church, Chalton Street, Somers Town, London, N W , 1897-1901 ; Organist Willesden, London, since 1901. Publications : In M S. " Une Ballade " for 'cello, with piano accompaniment separate and orchestral accompaniment separate. Recreations : Chess and 'cello.

TAYLER, EDWIN N., Crewkerne. Born 1873 and educated at Exeter. Music Master Grammar and Girls' Schools. Conductor of Choral Society. Formerly Organist Withycombe Parish Church, St. James', Exeter, and Ilminster Parish Church. Organist Crewkerne Parish Church since 1907 ; Lyme Regis Parish Church since 1910 ; Peek Memorial Chapel since 1910. Composer of services, songs, etc.

TAYLOR, CARDINAL, 7, St. Alban's Street, Leicester. Born 1871 and educated at Leicester. MUS. BAC. DUNELM., F.R C.O. Organist Holy Cross, Leicester, 1887-88 ; St. Peter's, Leicester, 1891-3 ; Humberstone, 1893-99 ; St. Mary's, Whittlesea, 1899-1907 ; St. Paul's, Leicester, since 1907.

TAYLOR, HARRY JAMES, 92, Maison Dieu Road, Dover. Born (1866) and trained at Cheltenham. F.R.C.O. Local Secretary Trinity College, London. Local Examiner R.C.M. Organist (Assistant) St. Matthew's, Cheltenham, 1884 ; Cheltenham Musical Festival Society, 1884 ; Cullompton Parish Church, 1886 ; Christ Church, Dover, 1888 ; St. James', Dover, 1905 ; Parish Church, Dover, since 1908 Editor "Dover Musical Record." Conductor Dover Choral Union, and founder Dover Triennial Musical Festival. Publications : Cantatas, operettas, songs, pianoforte and organ pieces ; "Historical Facts", series of "Musical Booklets," "Miniature Music Manuals," etc. Recreation : Cycling.

TAYLOR, HENRY, 11, Reservoir Road, Edgbaston Born at Derby, 1859. MUS BAC CANTAB., F R C O Assistant Organist Ripon Cathedral, 1876-81 ; Organist and Choirmaster Skelton-cum-Newby, 1876-1881 ; St. John's, Ladywood, Birmingham, 1881-1903 ; and Edgbaston Parish Church, since 1903 Recreation Cycling. University Graduate Club.

TAYLOR, JOHN HENRY, 5, Severn Street, Leicester. Born 1862 at Leicester. Educated privately. Organ blowing expert Organist St. Mark's, Leicester, 1881-84 ; St. John the Divine, since 1889. Hon Conductor Leicester Amateur Music and Dramatic Society. Hobby : Amateur operatic work.

TAYLOR, J. T., Laurel Bank, Ossett Born 1863 at Barnsley. Educated at Darton Grammar School. Pianoforte and music dealer at Wakefield. Organist Wesleyan Church, Ossett, since 1880. Conductor Outward Church Glee Society Teacher of piano, organ and singing, etc.

TAYLOR, PERCY C., 1, Walpole Terrace, Brighton. Born at Brighton. A R.C O Formerly Organist West Grinstead Church and Holy Trinity, Brighton Organist Sacred Harmonic Society, Brighton. Music Master Brighton College and Windlesham House. Hobbies and recreations : Photography, carpentry, cycling, and fishing.

TAYLOR, R. E. C , 5, Priory Place, Perth. Born at Dunbarney, Perthshire. Trained at Perth Academy Member of Official Staff of Messrs. J. Dewar & Sons, Ltd., Distillers Organist Dunning Parish Church, Perthshire, 1894 ; St. Stephen's U.F. Church, 1898 Organist and Choirmaster West U.F Church, Perth, since 1910. Hobbies and recreations : Photography, golf, and cycling. Member Unionist Club, Perth.

TAYLOR, WILLIAM, 132, Croft Street, Galashiels, N B. Born 1878 at Chorley, Lancs A R.C.O. Organist St. Peter's, Chorley, 1893-1901 , St. John's, Galashiels, since 1901.

TEBBUTT, W , 135, Colwyn Road, Northampton. Organist and Choirmaster Mount Pleasant Baptist Church, Northampton, since 1909.

TESTER, ARCHIBALD FRANK, Sherborne. Born 1882 at Tunbridge Wells. Educated at R.A M. London. F R.C.O., L.R.A M. School Music Teacher. Organist Mayfield Parish Church, Sussex, 1901-1903 ; Sherborne School Chapel and Big Schoolroom since 1903. Recreations · Tennis, archœology and travelling. Club : R.A.M. London.

THOMAS, ALFRED, 16, Albert Street, Shrewsbury. Born (1865) and educated at Shrewsbury. Organist Berwick Church, Shrewsbury, 1879-1882. Organist and Choirmaster St. Michael's, Shrewsbury, 1882-1894.

Organist and Accompanist Shrewsbury Harmonic Society, 1892-1909. Organist and Choirmaster St. Julian's, Shrewsbury, since 1894. Hobby: Photography.

THOMAS, CHARLES GEORGE, 140, Marylebone Road, London, N.W. Born 1865 in London. Educated in London and at Leipzig Conservatorium. L T.S.C. Diploma Leipzig Cons. Teacher of singing, piano and composition. Organist Royal English Church, Monbijou Palais, Berlin 1898-1903; St. Mark's, Marylebone, 1905-6; St. Cyprian's, Marylebone, since 1907. Conductor London Bach Society, since 1905. Hobby: Plainsong.

THOMAS, CHARLES VICTOR, 99, Evington Road, Leicester. Born 1887 at Pembroke. Educated St. Bedes College, Hornsea, E. Yorks. F.R.C.O., L MUS. T.C.L., A.R.C.O. Organist Hornsea Congregational Church, 1904; Organist and Choirmaster Dale Street Church, Leamington, 1907; Bishop Street Church, Leicester, 1910. Local Secretary Trinity College of Music.

THOMAS, F. LEWIS, 5, College Road, Bromley, Kent. Born 1857 in London. Trained R.A.M. Organist Christ Church, Lancaster Gate, 1879-1880; St. Mary, Bromley, since 1880. Publications: Piano and violin pieces and anthems. Recreations: Bowls, billiards and bridge.

THOMAS, J., 48, Queenswood Road, Moseley, Birmingham. Born at Haymills. Educated at New College School, Oxford. Late Leading Chorister St. Cyprian's, Haymills, and New College, Oxford. Sang as solo treble at Worcester Festival, 1875, in Wesley's Wilderness (Dr. Wesley at organ) Choir made up of the choirs of Worcester, Gloucester and Hereford Cathedrals, and New College, Christ Church, Oxford, and St. George's Chapel, Windsor. Organist and Choirmaster King's Heath Parish Church, Birmingham, since 1884.

THOMPSON, ALBERT, Bonn, 55, Eaton Rise, Ealing, W. Born 1875 at Grange, Lancashire. Educated at Lancaster, Louth and London. F.R.C.O. Formerly Organist Parish Church, Tatham; Parish Church, St. Neots, Hunts. Organist and Choirmaster Christ Church, Ealing, London, W., since 1901. Conductor Ealing Choral Society; Ealing Orchestral Society; Ealing Male Voice Choir; and Brentham Choral Society, etc. Publications: Part songs, pianoforte music. Hobby and recreations: Egyptology, golf, tennis, croquet.

THOMPSON, G. HERBERT, Station Road, Winslow, Bucks. Born 1871 at Ventnor, I.O.W. Trained under Giuseppe D'Anna, of Ventnor, and Charles Banson, of Parish Church, Sevenoaks. L MUS T C.L. Organist Parish Church, Winslow, Bucks, since 1890.

THOMPSON, JAMES BUCKLEY, Handel Terrace, Queen's Square, Mossley Road, Ashton-under-Lyne. Born 1860 at Stalybridge. Educated under the tuition of Irvine Dearnaley (Parish Church, Ashton-under-Lyne); W. Ffoulkes (St. Andrew's, Southport); and Kendrick Pyne (Manchester Cathedral). Gold medalist. Organist and Choirmaster Wesley Church, Aughton Road, Southport, 1878-1880; Wesleyan Church, Stamford Street, Ashton-under-Lyne, since 1880. Recital Organist and open to engagements

THORNE, A. E., Bainbridge Road, Sedbergh, Yorks. Born 1873 at South Hampstead. Educated at Rossall School, and Sidney Sussex College, Cambridge. B.A. CANTAB. Organist and Choirmaster Christ Church, Newgate; and Sub-Organist St. Anne's, Soho, 1899-1903. Organist and Choirmaster St. Baldred's Episcopal, N. Berwick, N.B , 1903-5 ; Christ Church, Herne Bay, 1905-12 ; Parish Church, Sedbergh, since 1912. Hobbies, etc. : Cycling, tennis, chess, bridge.

THORNE, HERBERT EDWARD, Gorton Lodge, Northside, Clapham Common, London, S.W. Teacher of organ, pianoforte and singing. Organist All Souls', London Road, S.W., 1882 ; St. Saviour's, Brixton Hill, S.W., 1885 ; Clapham Parish Church (Holy Trinity) London, S.W., since 1891.

THORNTON, H. W., 42, Church Street, Barnsley. F.R.C.O., A.R.C.M. Formerly Organist St. John's, Wilton Road, London, S.W., and Organist and Choirmaster Holy Trinity Church, Maidstone. Organist and Choirmaster Parish Church, Barnsley, since May 1912.

TIDNAM, J. EDIS, The College, Dover. MUS. BAC. OXON., F.R.C.O. Organist Chard Parish Church ; Wimborne Minster and Grammar School ; Stroud Parish Church. Organist and Music Master College Chapel, and College Refectory, Dover, since 1906. Publications : Part songs, anthems, etc. Hobby and recreation : Architecture and cycling. Member of Dover Club.

TILTMAN, HENRY T., Stoke Albany Lodge, Bedford. F.R.C.O., L.R.A.M. Formerly Organist St. Martin's, Bedford ; Holy Trinity, Guildford ; St. John's, Clapham Rise, S.W. ; and St. Mary's, Bury St. Edmunds. Organist Holy Trinity, Bedford, since 1905. Publications : Songs and Church music.

TIMS, FREDERICK ROWLAND, 38, Park Lane, Croydon. Born 1886 at Birmingham. Educated at Truro Cathedral Grammar School. F.R.C.O. Professor of Music. Late articled pupil and Assistant Organist to Dr. M. J. Monk, Truro Cathedral, 1902-07. Organist St. Mary's Parish Church, Horsham, 1901-1911. Organist and Choirmaster Parsh Church, Croydon, since June 1911. Conductor of all oratorio performances in the church with full orchestra. Publications : Organ voluntaries and songs. Hobbies and recreations : Motor cycling, swimming, roller skating and yachting.

TIPPING, FRANK, 75, Queen Street, Dumfries. Born 1867 in London. Trained under Dr. John Storer and John Hartmann. Teacher of Organ, Piano, etc. Organist to Lord Arundell of Wardour Castle, Wilts, 1890. Organist and Music Master Ratcliffe College, Leicester, 1891. Organist S.S. Mary and Joseph, Poplar, London, 1893 ; Marquis of Bute, 1895-1910 ; Pro. Cathedral, Dumfries, since 1910. Publications : Several songs (published under the nom de plume of Alban Keighley) and pianoforte pieces. Hobby and recreation : Painting, photography, and cycling.

TOBIN, JOHN, 2, Cranes Buildings, 2, Church Street, Liverpool. Born at Liverpool. Educated privately. F.R.C.O., L.R.A.M. Organist Holy Trinity, Walton Breck, Liverpool, 1908 ; All Saints', Birkenhead, 1910 ; St. Bride's, Liverpool, 1912. Recitalist Japan British Exhibition, 1910.

TODD, CHARLES WILLIAM, Atholl Bank, Fort William. Born at Jarrow-on-Tyne, 1874. Educated privately. MUS. BAC. DURHAM, 1905. Organist and Choirmaster Holy Saviour's, Tynemouth, 1901-8 ; St. Andrew's Church, Fort William, since 1909. Conductor Lochaber Choral Society, 1909.

TOMLINSON, JAMES, 8, Starkie Street, Preston. Organist to the Preston Corporation and Christ Church, Preston. Publications · Organ music— " Angelus " ; Postludes—" Sit laus Sonora " and " Sit laus Jocunda."

TOMLINSON, PERCY R., Rossal School, Fleetwood Born at Pontefract, 1884. Educated at Hymer's College, Hull B.A , MUS. BAC. CANTAB. Organ scholar of Selwyn College, Canterbury, 1903-6 ; John Stewart of Rannoch Scholar, 1906. Organist St. Edmund's College, Canterbury, 1906-10 ; Choirmaster and Organist Rossal School, Fleetwood, since 1910.

TOMLYN, ALFRED WM , 57, Falcon Avenue, Edinburgh. Born 1860, at Plaxtole, Kent. Educated at Trinity College, London. MUS BAC. DUNELM, MUS. T C.I. Organist Wallace Green, Berwick-on-Tweed, 1892-8 ; Girvan Parish Church, 1887-1892 , St Modoc's, Doune, and Conductor of Doune Select Choir, 1884-7 ; and Braid Church Edinburgh, since 1898. Composer of Cantata, " The Forerunner," anthems, part songs, etc. Recreation : Cycling.

TONKS, JOHN, Victoria Road, Northampton. Born January 3rd, 1868. Organist Catholic Cathedral, Northampton, since 1907.

TOONE, ALFRED C., 21, St. Dunstan's Road, Baron's Court, London, W. Born 1872 at Warminster. Educated at Bath. Conductor West Kensington Choral Society.

TOOP, AUGUSTUS, Theydon, 247, Fordwych Road, Cricklewood, N W. Born 1869 at Westminster. Educated at Trinity College, London. F R C O. Organist Italian Mission in London, 1883 , All Saints', Norfolk Square, London, 1886 ; St Peter's, Belsize Park, London, 1891 ; St Peter's, Vere Street, W., since 1891. Publications : Church music and songs.

TOOTELL, GEORGE, 1, Scotch Street, Whitehaven, Cumberland Born 1886 at Chorley, Lancs. Trained at Seafield College. F.R C O. Professor of Music. Organist and Choirmaster (Assistant) Lytham Parish Church, 1903 ; Lund Parish Church, 1906 , St John's Parish Church, Keswick, 1907 ; St. James' Parish Church, Whitehaven, since 1910. Music Master Seafield School ; Lytham and Stamford House Collegiate School, 1905-07 ; Warwick House School, Poulton, 1906-07 ; Keswick School, 1907-10 ; Castlegate School, Cockermouth, since 1908 Conductor Lytham Orchestral Society, 1905-07 , Keswick Musical Festival, 1907-09 , Keswick Choral Society, 1907-10 , Keswick Operatic Society and Whitehaven Harmonic Society, 1910 ; Whitehaven Lyric (operatic) Society, 1911 , Cockermouth Choral Society, 1911 Composer of operas, " Crusader," " Lollipop Land," and " A Knight of the Road."

TORR, LOUIS H., 119, Walters Road, Swansea. Born 1884 at Scarborough. Educated at Southampton F.R C.O , L.R A M , L.T.C L Teacher of music. Organ Recitalist Organist St Deny's, Southampton, 1900 ; Emsworth Parish Church, 1903 Assistant Winchester Cathedral, 1902-4 ; Holy Trinity, Swansea, since 1905.

TORR, SIDNEY L , 81, Monkon Street, Ryde, I.O.W. Born 1888 at Scarborough. Trained at Southampton ; articled to Dr. Prendergast at Winchester Cathedral A R C O. Professor of Music. Organist and Choirmaster St. Stephen's, Sparsholt, Winchester, 1907 ; St. John's, Ryde, I O.W , since 1910.

TOWNLEY, HUGH EDWARD CLAUDE, South View, St. Stephen's, Cheltenham. Organist St. Stephen's Church, Cheltenham, since 1896. Recreations: Cricket and golf.

TOWNSEND, HERBERT, 394, New Cross Road, London, S.E. Born in London, 1870. Educated privately. Professor of Music. Organist St. Luke's, Deptford, S.E., 1889-1906; St. Bride's Church, Fleet Street, London, E.C., since 1909. Publications: Communion Service in G (Wheeler & Kellaway); songs, "I Love Thee" (Novello); "Always be a Man" (Francis, Day & Hunter), "" Good Night, Sweet Flowers" and "Voices Beloved" (Cramer); carols, "Seedtime and Harvest" and "Gracious Lord, We give Thee Praise" (Novello); "O.S.P." March (Wheeler & Kellaway); three Vesper hymns (Hart & Company); "Cathedral March" (Hart & Company); "Lord's Prayer" (Novello), etc. Hobby · Photography.

TOZER, FERRIS, 20, Howell Road, Exeter. Born and educated (Cathedral School) in Exeter. MUS. DOC. OXON. Banker. Formerly chorister Exeter Cathedral. Organist St. David's, Exeter, 1876; and St. Michael's, Heavitree, Exeter, since 1882. Composer of "The Way of the Cross," etc Recreation: Bowling.

TRAMPLEASURE, JOSEPH CLARE, Whitley Vicarage, Northwich, Cheshire. Born 1861 at Liverpool. Educated at Trinity College, Dublin; St. Aidan's College, Birkenhead Organist St. Ambrose, Liverpool, 1882-4; St. Luke's, Tranmere, 1884-5; All Saints', Higher Kinnerton, 1894-1901; Whitley Parish Church, since 1906. Vicar of Nether Whitley. Hobby · Organ construction.

TRANT, WILLIAM, Broxholme, Sudbury, Suffolk. Born 1886 at Brixham. Trained under Messrs. Noble and Vinnicombe. Organist Brixham Baptist Church, 1905-07; Sudbury Parish Church, 1910-11; Trinity Congregational Church, Sudbury, since May, 1911.

TREFFRY, W. H., 10, Baldwyn Gardens, Acton, W. Born 1846 in London. Educated at Trinity College, London. Formerly Organist St. John's, Fulham; St. Matthew's, Ealing Organist French Protestant Episcopal Church of the Savoy, since 1885. Hobbies: Croquet, chess and bridge. Composer of "Dreamland" and other pieces.

TRIVETT, VINCENT W , 5, Edward Road, West Bridgford, Nottingham. Born (1882) and educated at Nottingham. Member R.C O. Teacher of pianoforte, organ and harmony First solo-boy St. Mary's Parish Church, Nottingham, 1893-5 Organist Lady Bay Church, West Bridgford, Nottingham, 1901-6; St. Peter's Parish Church, Nottingham, since 1906. Recreations: Hockey, tennis.

TUCK, RICHARD T , 161, Fosse Road, N. Leicester. Born 1893 at Leicester. Trained under Mr Vincent Dearden of Leicester. Organist Leicester Infirmary, 1905; St. Leonard's Church, Leicester, since 1907. Hobby: Painting (water colour). Member of Leicester and District Association of Organists.

TUPPER, HARRY WILLIAM, 57, Blackpool Street, Burton-on-Trent. MUS. BAC. OXON., F.R C O., L. MUS. T.C.L. Organist St. Peter's, Staines, 1889-91; Parish Church, Bishop's Stortford, 1891-8; Parish Church, Burton-on-Trent, since 1898.

TURNER, H., Sandiford, Tynedale, Greenlaw Avenue, Paisley. Born 1869 at Bury, Lancs. Educated at Henshaw's Institution for the Blind, Old Trafford, Manchester ; Royal Normal College and Academy of Music for the Blind, Upper Norwood, London, under the late Dr. E. J. Hopkins, Temple Church. Played by command before H.M. King Edward VII., 1907. Organist and Choirmaster Row Parish Church, Dumbartonshire, 1888-1898 ; Sherwood U F Church, Paisley, since 1898. Publications : Scherzo in F Minor for Organ and Chanson d'amour. Recreations : Swimming and walking.

TURTON, Miss KATHLEEN B., 31, Waverley Road, Reading. L.R.A.M., A.T.C.L. Organist and Choir Trainer Beenham Parish Church, Berkshire, 1901-1904 ; Ruscombe Parish Church, since 1907.

TWINNING, WALTER L., 13, Torwood Terrace, Torquay. Born 1873 at Cheltenham. Trained under H. J. Taylor, F.R.C.O. Dover Borough Organist. F.R.C.O. Organist and Choirmaster Parish Church, Kingsbridge, 1891 ; Parish Church, Bodmin, 1895 ; Parish Church, St. Marychurch, Torquay, 1903 ; St Matthias Church, Torquay, since 1906. Joint Conductor Torquay Musical Association, 1912. Publications : Church music, violin solos, organ solos, etc. Hobby and recreation : Photography and cycling.

TYLER, PERCY G., School House, Holt, near Worcester. Born (1886) and educated at Worcester. Assistant Organist Holt Parish Church, near Worcester, 1898-1904 ; St. Mary's, Abberley, 1904 ; St. Paul's, Worcester, 1904-5 ; St. George's, Worcester, since 1905.

TYLER, R. FREDERIC, Glengariff, Lingfield Avenue, Kingston-on-Thames. Born 1858 at Charlton, Somerset. Educated privately and at Trinity College, London. Teacher of music. F.R.C.O., L. MUS. T.C.L. Organist West Kington, Wilts, 1872 ; St. James', Plumstead, 1876 ; St. John's, Woolwich, 1880 ; St Mark's, Tunbridge Wells, 1882 ; Holy Trinity, Grays Inn Road, W.C., 1884 ; St John's, Lewisham High Road, 1887, St. Mark's, Surbiton, since 1897. Hobby : Amateur photography.

VALE, W. T., Pittville, Duke's Drive, Eastbourne. Born and educated at Cheltenham. A.R.C.O. On musical staff St. Andrew's Preparatory School. Professor of Music. Organist and Choirmaster St Peter's, Bertham, Gloucester, 1889-1896. Music Master Glengorse, Eastbourne, 1897-1906. Organist and Choirmaster St. Paul's, Eastbourne, 1901-1909 ; and of St Christopher's School Chapel since 1909 Composer of songs, organ, piano and violin music. Fond of walking, cricket, and billiards.

VERNHAM, JOHN EDWARD, 5, Warrington Crescent, Maida Hill, W. Born 1854 at Lewes, Sussex. Educated at St. Paul's, Walworth Choir School and privately. Professor of Music, King's College, London. Organist St. Paul's Church, Knightsbridge, since 1879. Publications : Two primers in the Novello series Communion Service, Evening Service, anthems, carols, " Boys' Voices " (Metzler & Co.), etc. Recreation : Country walks.

VERRALL, MISS MARGARET, 16, Portland Road, Hove. Organist Horsted Haynes Parish Church, 1905-1909 ; St. Barnabas', Hove, since 1909. Publications : Several hymn tunes. Recreations : Tennis and swimming.

VINCE, CHARLES HENRY, Oakleigh, Horsham Road, Cranleigh, Surrey. Born (1886) and educated at Guildford. A.T.C.L. Organist St. Luke's, Guildford, 1901-3 ; Ripley Parish Church, 1903-5. Sometime Assistant Holy Trinity, Guildford ; St. Nicholas', Cranleigh, since 1905. Conductor Cranleigh Choral Society, Ewhurst Choral Society ; and Chorus Master Guildford Choral Society. Recreation : Cycling.

VINCENT, GEORGE F., The Park, Bromley Road, Catford, London, S.E. Educated at Leipzig Conservatorium. Organist Sunderland Parish Church, 1872-4 ; Whitburn Parish Church, 1878-82 ; St. Thomas', Sunderland, 1882-1900 ; St. Michael's, Cornhill, E.C., since 1900. For twenty years Practical Examiner I.S.M. Publications : Operettas, cantatas, four choral fantasias, two fanasias and fugues for two pianos, various pianoforte pieces, various organ compositions, church service in E flat, overtures, pieces for violin, etc.

VINE, W. VIVIAN W., F.R.C.O., L.R.A.M. Organist St. Paul's, Herne Hill, London. Assistant Organist St. Peter's, Easton Square. Member of Council South London Musical Festival.

VINNICOMBE, EDWARD ELLIS, 2 Louth Villas, Sudbury, Suffolk. F.R.C.O. Organist Chagford, Devon, 1893-1901 ; St. Peter's, Sudbury, since 1901. Conductor Sudbury Musical Society ; Sudbury Orchestral Society ; Frinton Choral Society. Music Master at the Grammar School and High School, Sudbury.

WAKEFORD, HARRY, Kenneth, Lymington, Hants. Born 1885 at Southampton. Educated at Southampton and Eastleigh. F.R.C.O., M.I.S.M. Assistant Organist St. John's, Wimborne, 1902-6 ; Sir Richard Glyn's, Wimborne, 1902 ; Canford Magna Parish Church, 1904-1909 ; Lymington Parish Church, since 1909. Choirmaster All Saints', Lymington, since 1909. Hobby and recreations : Cycling, boating, photography, and reading.

WALKER, ARTHUR CHARLES, 54, Burns Street, Nottingham. Born and educated at Nottingham. Teacher of singing. Organist Presbyterian Church, Mansfield Road, Nottingham, since 1903. Secretary Nottingham Sacred Harmonic Society. Recreations : Cricket, rowing.

WALKER, LEONARD HOLMES, Brent'Hill, Hanwell, London, W. Born (1855) and educated at Reading. Schoolmaster. Organist Tylehurst, Reading, 1866-75 ; St. Mark's, Chelsea (Assistant) 1874-5 ; St. James', Fulham, 1876-9 ; St. John's, Fitzroy Square, London, W., 1881-90 ; London County Asylum Chapel, Hanwell, since 1898. Recreation : Cycling. Club : National Liberal.

WALKER, ROBERT S., Park Villas, 414, Osmaston Road, Derby. Born at Derby, 1883. Educated at Derby Higher Grade School. Clerk and Organist at Leys Malleable Castings Company, Ltd. Formerly Assistant Organist St. Chad's, Derby, for four years, and a frequent deputy. Organist Boulton Parish Church since 1903.

WALKER, W. SPRIGG, 5, The Grove, Rye. Formerly Organist All Saints', Hovingham, Yorks. Conductor Rye Choral Society. Organist St. Mary's Parish Church, Rye, since 1899.

WALKER, WILLIAM SPENCER, Moorlands, Whalley Road, Accrington, Lancs. Conductor Accrington Choral Society. Organist Union Street Wesleyan Chapel, Accrington, since 1898. Clef Club and Mechanics' Institute.

WALL, HARRY E., 38, Castelnau Gardens, Barnes, S.W. Born at Aspley Guise, Beds. Educated at Bedford and London (Dr. E. H. Turpin). Teacher of music. Organist Woburn Sands Parish Church, Beds, 1884-7; Rodmersham Church, Sittingbourne, 1887-98; East Farleigh Church, Maidstone, 1898-1903, St. Michael's, Burleigh Street, W.C., 1903-5; St. Paul's, Covent Garden, since 1904. Publications: Pieces for piano (Vincent).

WALLACE, A., 259, Railway Street, Cardiff. Born 1873 at Newport, Mon. Organist Cardiff since 1911.

WALTON, HERBERT F. R., 1, Queen's Terrace, W. Glasgow. Educated at R.C.M. A.R.C.M. LONDON. Formerly Private Organist to the Right Hon. the Earl of Aberdeen and St. Mark's Church, Leeds. Organist Glasgow Cathedral since 1897.

WARBURTON, J. S., 48, Holmecliffe Road, Blackpool, N. A. MUS. T C L. Teacher of organ, piano, composition, etc. Accomplished Organ Recitalist. Composer of " Heidelberg " tune to " Onward Christian Soldiers," and other well-known hymn tunes. Winner of " Musical Herald " prize, March, 1900. Organist Adelaide Street Free Church, Blackpool, since 1892.

WARDEN, WILLIAM GEORGE, Alvington Villa, Lairs, Plymouth. Born 1887 at Plymouth. Assistant Organist St. Matthias, Plymouth, 1907-9. Organist Holy Trinity, Plymouth, since 1909.

WARE, HUGH, Grosvenor Avenue, Wallington, Surrey. Born Sandywell Park, near Cheltenham, 1880. Studied harmony, composition, organ, etc , under Dr. A. E. Tozer; singing under Signor Rizzelli, Trinity College, London; pianoforte, at Virgil Piano School, London. F.R C.O., L.T.C.L. Organist St. Paul's, Swindon, 1896-99; St. Mark's, Swindon, 1901; St. Michael's, Croydon, 1902-5; St. Mary's, Parish Church, Beddington, since 1906. Publications: Evening service in E flat, anthems, organ music, etc. Hobbies and recreations: Photography, fishing, shooting, and other outdoor sports.

WARMINGTON, JOHN HERBERT, Mayfield, 5, Downing Grove, Cambridge. Born 1867 at Lewisham, Kent. Educated at School for Blind, Worcester and Peterhouse, Cambridge. M.A. (Mathematical Tripos 2nd class in 1890). Has been totally blind since age of four. Organist Emmanuel Congregational Church, Cambridge, since 1888. Hobbies and recreations: Rowing, swimming, tandem bicycle riding, bridge, and mechanics.

WARNER, CHARLES F., 6, Grange Road, Canonbury, London, N. Born (1873) and educated at Melton Mowbray. A.R.C.O. Organist Melton Mowbray Wesleyan, 1891-3; Wesleyan Church attached to Westminster College, Horseferry Road, S.W., 1894-5; Highbury Wesleyan, Drayton Park, N., 1895-1904; Wesley's Chapel, City Road, E.C., since 1904. Organist and Accompanist Raleigh Memorial (Congregational) Choral Society, Stoke Newington, 1898-1903; Stroud Green Choral Association, since 1905. Recreations: Tennis and cycling.

WARRELL, ARTHUR SYDNEY, 27, Cotham Vale, Bristol. Born at Farmborough, near Bath, 1882. Educated at Farmborough School, and Merchant Venturers' College, Bristol. Organist and Choirmaster St. Matthias', 1900-1; St. Agnes', 1901-5; St. Alban's, 1905; and St. Nicholas', since 1905, all of Bristol. Teacher of Music, University of Bristol Elementary Training Department (Men), 1909.

WARREN, SAMUEL, 41, Murrayfield Gardens, Edinburgh. Born and educated at Windsor. A.R.C.M. Music Master George Watson's Ladies' College, Edinburgh. Organist Elgin Episcopal, 1886-8 ; St. James' Episcopal, Leith, 1888-1900 ; Palmerston Place U F., Edinburgh, since 1900. Hobbies : Gardening and golf.

WARREN, WALTER, 10, Holly Walk, Leamington Spa. Organist and Choir-master St. Peter's Roman Catholic Church, Leamington Spa, since 1887. Hon. Conductor Leamington Orchestral Society.

WARREN, WILLIAM ALFRED, 64, Southgate Road, Kingsland, N. F.I.S.C. Formerly Organist Old Ford Parish Church, London, E. ; St. Peter's, Hoxton Square, N. Organist Shoreditch Borough Parish Church, since 1898 ; Shoreditch Infirmary, since 1906.

WARRILOW, HERBERT C., 10, Staverton Road, Oxford. Born 1873 at Oundle. Educated at Royal Normal College and Academy of Music for the Blind, Upper Norwood. F.R.C.O. Organist Wilmington, Kent, 1895 ; St. Barnabas, Oxford, since 1904. Choirmaster St. Barnabas, Oxford, since 1911.

WARRINER, JOHN, De Crespigny House, Denmark Hill, S.E. MUS. DOC. TRINITY COLLEGE, DUBLIN, F.T.C.L. Professor of Pianoforte, Sight Reading. Lecturer Training Classes for Teachers of Music. T.C.L., 1890. Member of the Faculty of Music, Board of Studies, and recognized teacher University of London, 1903 ; Divisional Secretary Union of Graduates in Music, 1893. Organist St. Matthew's Church, Denmark Hill, S E , since 1887. Publications : Novello's Primer on Transposi-tion, " National Portrait Gallery of British Musicians," handbook on " The Art of Teaching Music," " Comprehensive " Music Copy Books. Clubs : Primrose, Authors.

WATKINS, ENOS JAMES, The Poplars, Capstone Road, Bournemouth. Born at Wolverhampton, 1876 F R.C.O , A.R.C.M. (singing) Organist Tettenhall Wood Congregational, 1893 , Wolverhampton Presbyterian, 1895 , Poole Congregational, 1898 ; and Richmond Hill Congregational, Bournemouth, since 1899. Conductor Bournemouth Congregational Choral Union, since 1900. Publications : Anthems, part songs, etc.

WATKINS, T. HADLEY, 2, Priory Villas, Oxford Road, Bournemouth. Fellow Tonic Sol-fa College. Examiner R.C.M. Born (1862) and educated at Brecon. Formerly Organist Kensing Baptist Church, Brecon. Conductor Brecon Philharmonic Society Organist Lansdowne Baptist Church, Bournemouth, since 1908. Publications : Anthems, part songs, etc., and contributor to " Anglican Organist," etc.

WATSON, MATTHEW, 10, Outwood Road, Burnley. Born at Burnley, 1874. Studied music privately under Dr. Henry Watson (cousin) of Man-chester. Received first appointment—Organist Bethesda Congrega-tional Church—when 15 ; subsequently Organist Enon Baptist and Salem Congregational Churches, Burnley. Organist Brunswick Chapel, Burnley, since 1906. Member of the Mechanics Exchange, Burnley ; and a Life Member of the Trinity College of Music, London.

WATSON, MICHAEL, Lyn Tor, South Molton. Born 1873 at Stevenage. M I.S.M. Music teacher. Organist South Tawton, Devon, 1891-6 ; St. Mary Magdalene, South Molton, since 1896. Music Master at Devon County School, West Buckland, since 1896. Conductor Choral Society. Hobby : Bowling.

WATTS, RICHARD BENJAMIN, London Road, Uppingham. Born (1866) and educated at Leicester. Organist and Bandmaster Culham College, 1888. Assistant Organist St. Paul's, Leicester, 1880-6. Organist St. Peter and Paul Parish Church, Uppingham, since 1890. Conductor Uppingham Orchestral Society. Head Master Uppingham Church of England School. Past Provincial Grand Organist (Masonic) for the province of Leicestershire and Rutland. Publications: "Floreat Culham," waltz for Pianoforte and a manual of sight singing. Hobbies: Music, masonry, and billiards.

WATTS, THOMAS ISAAC, Lindenhurst, Station Road, Epsom, Surrey. Born 1863, at Broseley, Salop. Educated at Denstone and Queens' College, Cambridge. M.A., MUS. BAC. CANTAB Organ scholar Queens' College, Cambridge. F R C O Organist Trinity College, Glenalmond, N.B., 1887-1895; Walsall Parish Church, 1895-1901; Epsom College Chapel, since 1901. Publications: Cantata, "Ages of Almond"; Magnificat and Nunc Dimittis in D. Hobbies and recreations: Photography, fishing and motor-cycling.

WEALE, SYDNEY HARRY FRANZ, The Cathedral, Londonderry. Born 1881. Educated at Ludlow, Salop. MUS. BAC., F R.C.O., L R.A.M, A.R.C.M., etc Organist M.N.C. Church, Mapplewell, 1894; Westgate Church, Barnsley, 1895; Conisbro Parish Church, 1898 Sub-Organist St. David's Cathedral, 1899; Newark-on-Trent Parish Church, 1901; Southwell Cathedral, 1903; St. John's Episcopal Church, 1904; Organist and Choirmaster the Barony Parish Church, Glasgow, 1909; Organist and Master of the Choristers, Londonderry Cathedral, 1911. Hobbies: Fishing, motoring, and yachting.

WEBB, ARTHUR G., 11, Ellerton Road, Wandsworth Common, S W. Born 1882 at Camberwell. Trained privately under Cecil Usher and Dr. C. H. Frost. Assistant Organist South London Tabernacle, 1900-05. Organist and Choirmaster Walworth Road Baptist Church, 1905-11; Trinity Road Baptist Church since 1911.

WEBSTER, HENRY SMITH, 53, Loraine Road, Holloway, London. Born 1857 at Clerkenwell, London Trained St Andrew's, Wells Street, W. and Trinity College, London. A.R C.O. Sub-Organist St. Andrew's, Wells Street, W., 1870-75 Organist and Choirmaster St. Peter's, Regent Square, W.C., 1874-75; St. Paul's, Great Portland Street, W., 1875-85, S.S. Philip and James' Church, Byfleet Lodge, Surrey, 1886; Kingswalden Parish Church, Hitchin, Herts, 1887-90; St Mark's, North Audley Street, W., 1891; South Place Chapel, Finsbury, E.C., since 1893.

WEIGALL, CYRIL T., Linden, Timbrell Street, Trowbridge. Born 1879 at Salisbury. Trained privately. F.R.C.O. Organist St. Paulinus, Crayford, Kent, 1899; St Mary's Parish Church, Twickenham, 1901; Christ Church, Luton, 1907; St. James', Trowbridge, since 1907.

WELLS, H. WHARTON, Allerton, Atney Road, Putney, London, S.W. F R.C.O, L.R.A.M., L MUS. T.C L. Formerly Organist Parish Church, Long Ditton, Surrey; St. Clement's, Fulham; St. Dionis', Fulham; St. Mary the Virgin, Parish Church, since 1889.

WESTERBY, HERBERT, Townsend Villa, Kirkcaldy MUS. BAC. LONDON, 1901, L. MUS. T.C.L., Tallis gold medallist, 1897; F.R C O., 1901. Organist at Gravesend; Stonehaven; St. George's Cathedral, Grahamstown, S A. (Choir Appointment), Kimberley, S.A.; Collegiate Parish Church, Elgin; Middlesboro'; and Kirkcaldy (Abbotshall

Parish Church), 1911. Recitalist and Conductor Musical Association (London), lectures on " Chromaticism in Harmony " and " The Dual Theory in Harmony." Various series of articles in musical journals: " The Mysterious Chord of the Augmented 6th "; " The Musical Treatment of the Psalms "; " The Accompaniment of the Psalms "; " An Organ Tour in Germany "; etc., etc. Author of " Conversations on the Pianoforte Classics " (Reeves) ; " History of Pianoforte Music." Contributor of articles on " The Relation of Organist and Clergy," etc., in this publication.

WESTON, SYDNEY, 26, Equity Road, Leicester. Born (1883) and educated at Leicester. F.I G.C.M., L.V.C.M. Assistant Organist St. James the Greater, Leicester, 1897-1900. Organist St. James' Church, Aylestone Park, Leicester, since 1900. Teacher of pianoforte, organ, and theory. Accompanist to the Highfields Choral Society, Leicester, since 1898.

WHALL, ROUGHTON HENRY, 6, Whitehall, Stroud, Gloucester Educated National Training School of Music. MUS. BAC. DURHAM, F.R.C.O. Organist Great Marlow, 1887-91, Holy Trinity, Llandudno, 1892 ; Parish Church, Chepstow, 1899 ; Holy Trinity, Stroud, since 1905. Publication: " Abide with Me " (anthem).

WHALLEY, HORNER, Bavelaw, Peebles. Born (1879) and educated at Burnley, Lancs. F.R.C.O. Organist Larkhall Parish Church, 1902-7 ; Duneon Parish Church, 1907. Parish Church, Peebles, since 1907. Hobbies : Golf, tennis, walking, reading, etc. Club : Unionist.

WHEELER, H. WALTER, The Rockets, Belvedere Road, Upper Norwood. Born 1870. Trained privately. Organist and Choirmaster St. Andrew's, Earlsfield, 1893-1900 ; St. Annes', Wandsworth, 1900-10 Hon. Organist All Saints', Tooting, Graveney, since September 1911. Captain Boys' Naval Brigade. Recreations : Yachting and cricket.

WHEELER, LEONARD VAUGHAN, Devonshire Street, Cheltenham. Organist St Mary's, Freeland, Oxford, 1888 ; Church of Scotland, Cheltenham, 1880-3 ; Parish Church, Cheltenham, since 1893.

WHINFIELD, ARTHUR H., Severn Grange, Worcester. Formerly Musical Director of the Royal Victorian Institute for the Blind, Melbourne and Organist of Christ Church, Brunswick, Melbourne. Organist Claines Parish Church, Worcester, since 1898. Principal of Nicholson & Co., organ builders, Worcester.

WHITAKER, ARTHUR W., 135, Thornbury Avenue, Bradford. Born 1865 at Bradford. Studied under J. H. Rooks and H. Newbolt. Organist Catholic Apostolic Church, 1882-1890. Organist and Choirmaster St Thomas', Bradford, for two years ; St. Phillip's, Bradford, eight years ; Zion Chapel, Bingley, three-and-a-half years ; Girlington Baptist Church, since 1910. Choirmaster Catholic Apostolic Church Bradford, since 1882. Publications : Eucharist Service and numerous anthems, " Old Scarborough," Dragoon March, etc. Recreation : Billiards.

WHITE, ERNEST G., 5, Marlborough Road, Lee, S.E. Formerly Organist Pembroke College, Cambridge Mission at Walworth and Mottingham Parish Church, Kent. Organist Church of the Ascension, Blackheath, S.E., 1895-1908 ; Holy Trinity Church, Lee, S.E., since 1908. Publications : " Science and Singing," vocal exercises and songs. Hobby : Gardening.

WHITEHEAD, FREDERICK WILSON, 8, Belgrave Terrace, Glasgow. Born at Heckmondwike, Yorks. A.R C.M., A R.C O Principal, Glasgow School of Singing. Formerly Organist St Luke's, SS. Philip and James', and Whitechapel Church, Cleckheaton ; Elgin Parish Church ; High Church, Inverness. Now Organist and Choir Director Dowanhill Church, Glasgow.

WHITEHEAD, WILLIAM, 191, Algernon Road, Lewisham, London, S.E. Formerly Assistant Organist Southwell Cathedral, and Organist and Choirmaster All Saints' and St Andrew's, Newton Stewart, N.B. Organist and Choirmaster St Mary's Parish Church, Lewisham, London, S E., since 1900

WHITESIDE, JOHN, Church View, Kendal Born 1869 at Calgate, near Lancaster. Educated at Royal Normal College, Upper Norwood. MUS BAC. OXON , F.R C.O Organist St James', Tatham, 1888-92 ; Parish Church, Morecambe, 1892-1906 , St. George's, Kendal, since 1906.

WHITAKER-WILSON, CECIL, 40, Carlton Road, Birkenhead. Born 1886 at Edgbaston, Birmingham Articled pupil for five years to Professor J. C. Bridge, of Chester Cathedral Organist S. Basil Deritend, Birmingham, 1899 ; St Peter's, Waverton, Cheshire, 1905-09 ; Prenton Parish Church, Birkenhead, since 1909 Publications Songs, Church cantatas, carols, services, etc. ; also dance music, teaching pieces, etc., under a nom-de-plume Author of articles in " Musical Opinion," " Musical Student," etc

WHITTAKER, WILLIAM GILLIES, 4, Granville Road, Jesmond, Newcastle-on-Tyne. Born 1876 at Newcastle-on-Tyne. Educated at Rutherford College and Armstrong College MUS. BAC. DUNELM, F.R.C.O., L.I S M. Musical Critic " Newcastle Daily Leader," 1903. Organist St George's Presbyterian, Newcastle, 1893-4 ; St Paul's Presbyterian, South Shields, 1896-1909 Conductor Armstrong College Choral Society ; Newcastle and District Musical Society, 1905-8 ; Tynemouth, Whitley and District Choral Union. Instructor in Music, Armstrong College. Singing Master to the Newcastle Education Committee at Rutherford College for Girls, also in the Central High School for Girls. Hobby and recreation : Reading and walking

WHITWORTH, B , The Chestnuts, Horbury. A R C O. Conductor of Ossett Choral Society. Organist and Choir Master Holy Trinity Parish Church, Ossett

WHOMES, EDMUND, 240-2, Broadway, Bexley Heath. Born and educated at Eltham, Kent. Pianoforte manufacturer. Pianist Paris Exhibition, 1867 Organist St Mary, Cray, 1868-71 ; Christ Church, Bexley Heath, 1871-82 ; St. John's, Woolwich, 1882-93 ; Christ Church, Bexley Heath, since 1897. Hobby : Mechanics (especially motor cars).

WILKINSON, HARRY FELLOWES, Fulford House, The Crescent, South Tottenham, N. Born 1876 at Ashton-under-Lyne, Lancs. Educated at Tottenham A.M.I.C E , M R. SAN I., F R C O. Civil Engineer. Parish Church, Tottenham, 1898-1909 ; Organist and Choirmaster Assistant Organist St. Anne's Church, Tottenham, 1890-4. Organist St. Stephen's Chapel, Tottenham, 1898-1901. Sub-Organist Parish Church, Tottenham, 1898-1909 ; Organist and Choirmaster since 1909. Hobby : Music.

WILKINSON, RALPH WESTROP, 117, Salisbury Road, High Barnet, Herts. Born 1858 at York. Pupil of the late Mr. G. Cooper, organist, Chapel Royal, St. James'; Mr. Walter MacFarren at R.A.M., and Mr. W. Shakespeare. Formerly Organist Shenly; St. John the Evangelist, Upper Norwood; St. Mary's, Hadley. Teacher of Music and Singing.

WILKINSON, ROBERT, Christ's Hospital, Horsham. Born 1874. Educated at R.C.M. MUS. BAC. OXON., F.R.C.O. Music Master and Organist Christ's Hospital, Horsham, since 1902.

WILLAN, HEALEY, 5, Sydney Road, Ealing, London. Born 1880 in London. Pupil of late Dr. W. H. Sangster and Dr. W. S. Hoyte. F.R.C.O. Organist St. Saviour's, St. Alban's, Herts, 1896-1899; Christ Church, Wanstead, 1900-1903; St. John Baptist, Kensington, since 1903. Publications: Anthems, services, part songs, organ music and songs. Recreation: Boating.

WILLIAMS, C. F. ABDY, Myrtle Cottage, Milford-on-Sea. Born 1855 at Dawlish. Educated at Sherborne and Trinity Hall, Cambridge. Musical training at Leipsic. M.A. CAMBRIDGE, MUS. BAC. CANTAB. AND OXON. (Retired from active professional work. Engaged in Musical Literary Work). Organist St. Mary's, Auckland, N. Z., 1879; Dover College, 1881; St. Mary's, Boltons, London, S.W., 1885; Bradfield College, 1895. Various publications Clubs: Saville, Royal Cruising, Hellenic, Travellers.

WILLIAMS, WALTER, 15, Knowsley Street, Bury, Lancs. MUS. BAC OXON., F.R.C.O., A.R.C.M. Formerly Organist and Choirmaster Collegiate Church of St. Nicholas, Galway; and Lecturer in Music, Queen's College, Galway. Organist and Choirmaster Bury Parish Church, since 1904. Conductor Bury Orpheus Glee Club; Hebden Bridge Choral and Orchestral Society. Musical Director Amateur Operatic Society, Bury.

WILLSON, FRANCIS GEORGE, 27, Forest Road, Fishponds, Bristol. Born 1892 at Frocester. Trained under E. M. Cuttle, L.R.A.M., of Holy Trinity, Clifton. Organist St. Michael's, Stoke Gifford, near Bristol, 1910-1912; Stapleton Union Chapel, Bristol, since 1912. Hobby: Music. Profession: Science.

WILMOT-COOPER, G., 24, Barker Street, Oldham. Born 1869 at Silkstone, Yorkshire. Educated at the Royal Manchester College of Music, and privately. MUS DOC. Queen's College, Oxford. L.R.A.M. Professor of Music Organist Holy Trinity Church, Oldham, 1898-1900; Oldham Parish Church since 1900.

WILSHIRE, ALBERT EDWARD, The Cottage, Longfleet Road, Poole, Dorset. Born Potterne, Wilts, 1863. Educated Salisbury Cathedral School. F.R.C.O., L.R.A.M. Professor of Music. Assistant Organist Salisbury Cathedral, 1881-4; Parish Church, Ilfracombe, 1887-1902; Wimborne Minster, since 1902. Conductor Poole and Parkstone Philharmonic Society, 1911; Wimborne Choral Society, since 1902. Composer of 46th Psalm and other music. Publications: " The Timbrels Sound " (choral march), part songs.

WILSON, ARCHIBALD WAYET, Ely Cathedral. Born 1869 at Pinchbeck, Lincs. Educated at Rossall School and R.C.M. Organist Ely Cathedral, since since 1901. Publications: Service in E for mixed voices, Evening Service in Eb for men's voices, cantatas, anthems, and part songs. B.A., MUS. DOC. OXON., F R.C O.

WILSON, FREDERICK ERNEST, 14, Shelley Avenue, East Ham, London, E. Born 1880 at Stratford. Trained privately and under S. Wilson, E. Cuthbert Nunn, and W. F. Kingdon. F R.C.O., L.R.A.M. Organist Christ Church, Stratford, 1893 ; Assistant Organist St. James', Forest Gate, 1896 ; St. John's College, Battersea, 1900 ; Organist St. Michael's and All Angels', Little Ilford, 1904. Publication : " Crossing the Bar," part song. Recreation : Tennis.

WILSON, WILLIAM HAMILTON, 12, Pleasance Avenue, Falkirk. Born 1870 at Motherwell. Educated under Dr. D F. Wilson, Ayr ; and Dr. Varley Roberts F.R.C.O. Magdalen College, Oxford. Associate and Member of Tonic Sol fa College and Matriculated Student, Queens' College, Oxford University. Organist and Choirmaster Annbank Church, 1887-9 ; Auchterarder Free Church, 1889 ; St. Nicholas Parish Church, Broxburn, 1890-1 ; Grahamston Parish Church, Falkirk, since 1891. Conductor Linlithgow Presbytery Choir Union, since 1907. Hobby : Motor cycling.

WILTSHIRE, WALTER B C, 25, Ashburnham Mansions, Chelsea, S.W. Born 1882 at Islington. Trained R.C M., London. F.R C.O , A.R.C M. Organist Christ Church, Brighton, 1901-03 , St. Paul's, Clerkenwell, 1908-11 ; St. Paul's, Vicarage Gate, Kensington, since March, 1912.

WINDER, JOHN SMALLWOOD, Kendal. Violin Master Sedbergh School, Yorks. Music Master High School, Kendal Teacher of piano, singing, etc. Conductor Kendal Choral Society. Organist St Thomas', Kendal, since 1883.

WINDUS, WALTER H., 91, Aigburth Road, Liverpool. Born 1874 at Bournemouth. Trained privately. A.R.C.O. Cert. Trin. Coll. London. Organist and Choirmaster St. Andrew's, Liverpool, since 1907. Formerly Organist and Choirmaster Henfield Church, Sussex, and Emmanuel Church, Liverpool. Recreation : Chess.

WINN, CYRIL E., B.A. OXON , The Rectory, Poplar, London, E. Born in London, 1885 Educated at St. Paul's Cathedral Choir School and Highgate School. Formerly Conductor Exeter College Musical Society and Kidlington Choral Society. Organist Exeter College, Oxford, 1904-1908. Organ scholar Cuddesdon Theological College, 1908-9. Assistant Curate All Saints', Poplar, and St. John-at-Hackney, 1911. Publisher of several songs. Recreations : Football, tennis and cricket.

WITHERS, WALTER G., 16, Laurel Road, Fairfield, Liverpool. Born 1884 and educated at Liverpool. F.R.C O. Professional Musician. Organist St Mary's, Edge Hill, 1901-06 ; St. Catherine's, Higher Tranmere, 1906-07 ; St. Luke's Church, Liverpool, since 1907.

WOLSTENHOLME, WILLIAM, 11, Hilgrove Road, Hampstead, London, N.W. Born at Blackburn. Educated at Worcester. MUS. BAC. OXON. Publications . Works for organ, pianoforte, violin, songs, etc.

WOOD, CHARLES JOHN, 25, Ranelagh Road, Wellingborough. Born (1860) and educated at Lichfield. MUS. BAC. OXON., F.R.C O. Organist St. John's, Ballinasloe, 1880 ; St Nicholas, Tooting Graveney, S.W., 1882 ; St. Saviour's, Croydon, 1883 ; St. Mark's, Tunbridge Wells, 1885 ; St. Nicholas, Galway, 1888 ; All Saints', Wellingborough, since 1891. Music Master Wellingborough Pupil Teachers' Centre, 1905-11 ; Music

Master Wellingborough Technical Institute; Conductor Wellingborough Amateur Operatic Society. Hobbies and recreations: Cycling, skating, mountain climbing, wood-sawing, swimming, and dabbling in languages.

WOOD, EDGAR W., Fox Hill Grove, Bath. Born at Bath, 1865. Educated King Edward's School, Bath. Trained by the late James Kendrick Pyne, James and Joseph Hewitt, and singing and choir training under the late Frederick Helmore. Leading boy Bath Abbey Choir, afterwards Organist and Choirmaster Bathford Church, 1882-3; Laura Church, Bath, 1883-8; St. Matthew's, Bath, 1888-1909. Member Local Committee Trinity College, London. Recreation: Fly fishing.

WOOD, FREDERIC HERBERT, 68, East Park Road, Blackburn. Born in India, 1880. MUS. BAC. DUNELM, A.R.C.M. (singing). Organist and Choirmaster St. Paul's, Blackburn, 1902-5; and St. John the Evangelist, Blackburn, since 1905. Conductor Chatburn and Downham Choral Society; also Clitheroe Choral Union; Blackburn Y.M.C.A. Male Choir. Publications: Songs, part songs, etc. Recreation: Literature.

WOOD, MISS M. L., 2, Albert Terrace, Douglas, I O.M. Born and educated in London. A R.C O , L. MUS. TRINITY COLLEGE. Teacher of organ, singing, theory. Teacher of Singing to the Douglas Secondary School Organist Parish of Peel, 1884-95. Conductor Peel Choral Society, 1884-95. Organist Braddan Parish Church since 1905. Composer of songs, carols, etc.

WOOD, SAM, 147, Wigan Lane, Wigan. Born 1872 at Wigan. Trained under the late Thos. Bullock and J. W. Potter. Organist and Choirmaster Abram Parish Church, 1893-1905; St. Thomas' Church, Wigan, since 1905. Justice of the Peace. Hobby: Municipal work. Club: Manchester Athenæum.

WOODHAM, ALFRED GEORGE, 23, St. John's Avenue, Harlesden, London, N.W. A.R.C.O. Teacher of singing, organ, piano and theory. Organist Oaklands Congregational, Uxbridge Road, London, W., since 1905.

WOODS, NORMAN C., St. Michael's College, Tenbury. Born 1882 at Gosport, Hants. Trained at St. Paul's School, London, and Selwyn College, Cambridge. M.A., MUS. BAC. (CANTAB), A.R.C.O., L. MUS. T.C.L. Organist Parish Church, Chiswick, W., 1906-08; Ludlow Parish Church, 1908-11; St. Michael's College, Tenbury, since 1911.

WOODWARD, F. HANDEL, 51, Greek Street, Stockport. Born at Stockport. Educated at Owen's College, Manchester, and private. MUS. BAC. DUNELM. Organist St. Paul's, Heaton Moor, Stockport, since 1897.

WORKMAN, ALBERT E., Ash Lea, School Lane, Bidston. Born (1863) and educated at Liverpool. Member Incorporated Society of Musicians. Conductor Bootle Orchestral Society; Lecturer Liverpool and Bootle Corporation. Composer of music. Hobbies: Driving and walking. Member of Masonic Fraternity.

WORTH, HERBERT, 24, High Street, Totnes. Organist Littlehempston Parish Church, 1873-6; Parish Church, Totnes, since 1878. Conductor Totnes Choral Society, since 1894.

WORTON, SAMUEL E., South End House, Elland, Yorks. Born at Dudley. Educated at Dudley, London and Leeds. Senior Honours, CERT. R.A.M. Teacher of music Organist Wesleyan, Elland, 1878-83 ; Zion Methodist, Lindley, Huddersfield, since 1884 ; Elland Choral Society. Publications : " Pleasant Hours " morceau for piano , " Giralda " waltz , " I will extol Thee," anthem , " Let the Righteous be Glad," also hymn tunes.

WRIGHT, VERNON OSWALD, 30, Crown Mansions, Glasgow, W , and 4, Prince Albert Terrace, Helensburgh, N.B. Born (1879) and educated at York. Assistant Organist Bangor Cathedral, 1895. Organist Parish Church, Row, since 1897. Professor Glasgow College of Music, 1905.' Music Master Hillside Ladies' School, 1902. Elected A.R.C.M., 1904. Music Master Shandon House, 1910. Hobbies : Sailing and walking. Club : Conservative, Glasgow.

WRIGHT, W. R., 4, Prince Albert Terrace, Helensburgh, N.B. Born at Thirsk. Educated at York. MUS BAC. OXON. Music Master Spins' School Professor Glasgow Athenæum School of Music, for 12 years Late Assistant Organist York Minster, and Local Representative R.A.M. Now Organist West U.F. Church, Helensburgh Publications : Scale and arpeggio manual, etc.

WRIGHT, WILLIAM THOMPSON, The Song School, Newark. A.R C.O., R.C.M. Organist Hornsey Parish Church, 1888-9 , St. Leonard's, Newark, 1899-1903 , Parish Church, Newark, since 1903.

WRIGLEY, GEORGE FREDERICK, Grafton Place, Ashton-under-Lyne. M.A., MUS. BAC OXON , A R A M. Formerly Organist Holy Trinity, Roehampton, S.W. ; St. Alban's, Streatham Park, S.W. Organist St. Michael's, Ashton-under-Lyne, since 1895.

WYLIE, HENRY GLYNN, 239, Woodchurch Road, Birkenhead L R A M. (Class A.) Musician. Organist St Paul's Presbyterian Church, Birkenhead, 1899-1900 ; Princes' Gate Baptist, Liverpool, 1900-1907 ; West End Congregational, Southport, 1907-1909 ; St. Paul's Presbyterian, Devonshire Park, Birkenhead, since 1909.

WYMAN, G. HERBERT, 129, Claude Road, Cardiff. F.R.C.O. Organist St. Margaret's Church, Roath, Cardiff, since 1906.

YARROW, REGINALD, 39, Pelham Street, London, S.W. Born 1874 at Richmond. Educated at St. Paul's Cathedral. Voice trainer and accompanist. F.R.C O , A R.C M. Organist St Mary's, Lambeth, 1892 ; All Hallows', Southwark, 1894 , St. Mary's, Aldermanbury, E.C., 1896 , Chiswick Parish Church, 1898 ; St. Jude's, South Kensington, since 1901 Hobby and recreation : Photography and tennis. Member of South Kensington Conservative Club.

Organ and other Musical Institutions, Etc.
London.

BRITISH COLLEGE OF MUSIC, 139, New Bond Street, London, W. Principal, Pearce Small, Esq.

BRITISH MUSICIANS' PENSION SOCIETY, 21, Albert Embankment, London, S.E. Hon. Sec., Mr. L. W. Pinches. Hon. Treasurer, Mr. C. J. Hoggett.

CHOIR BENEVOLENT FUND. Trustees—Dr. Inge, Dean of St ᵀPaul's, Bishop Ryle, Dean of Westminster, and Dr. Eliot, Dean of Windsor. Sec., Mr. W. A. Frost, 16, Amwell Street, London, E.C.

CRYSTAL PALACE SCHOOL OF ART, MUSIC, AND LITERATURE, Norwood, S.E. Lady Principal, Miss E. M. Prosser. Registrar, Miss L. R. Grey.

GRESHAM LECTURES ON MUSIC, GRESHAM COLLEGE, Basinghall Street, London, E.C.

GUILD OF ORGANISTS. Hon. Secretary and Treasurer, Mr. Fred B. Townend 22, Horney Hedge Road, Gunnersbury, London, W.

GUILDHALL, SCHOOL OF MUSIC, Victoria Embankment, London, E.C. Principal, Landon Ronald. Secretary, H. Saxe Wyndham.

HOME MUSIC STUDY UNION, 12, York Buildings, Adelphi, London, W.C. President, W. H. Hadow, M.A., MUS.D. General Secretary, J. E. Lawrence. Organ, "The Music Student."—Editor, Percy A. Scholes, MUS.B.

INCORPORATED GUILD OF CHURCH MUSICIANS, 18, Berners Street, Oxford Street, London, W. Hon. President, The Very Rev. Francis Pigou, D.D., Dean of Bristol. Hon. Treasurer, G. R. Jellicoe, F.I.G.C.M. Hon. Registrar, J. M. Bentley, MUS D CANTAB., HON. F R.A M.

INCORPORATED SOCIETY OF MUSICIANS. Solicitor and Secretary, Mr. Arthur T. Cummings, 19, Berners Street, London, W.

INTERNATIONAL MUSICAL SOCIETY, 54, Great Marlborough Street, London, W. President, Sir Alexander Mackenzie. General Secretary, Dr. Charles MacLean.

LONDON ACADEMY OF MUSIC, 22, Princes Street, Cavendish Square, London, W. Directors, Dr. T. H. Yorke Trotter, M A , MUS.D. OXON., Signor Denza, Mr. Henry Beauchamp, Mr. Carl Weber, Mr. Rene Ortmans, Mr. Horace Kesteven.

LONDON BACH SOCIETY. Founder, Carl Reinecke. Director, C. J. Thomas, 140, Marylebone Road, London, N.W.

LONDON COLLEGE FOR CHORISTERS, 6 and 7, Blomfield Crescent, Hyde Park, London, W. Director, Mr. James Bates. Secretary, E. B. Golding

LONDON COLLEGE OF MUSIC, Great Marlborough Street, London, W. Principal, F. J. Karn, MUS.D., T.C.D., MUS.B. CANTAB. Secretary, T. Weekes Holmes.

LONDON SOCIETY FOR TEACHING THE BLIND, Upper Avenue Road, Swiss Cottage, London, N.W. Treasurer, C. T. D. Crews, Esq. Secretary, Thomas H. Martin, Esq.

METROPOLITAN ACADEMY OF MUSIC, Earlham Hall, Forest Gate, London. Director, Mr. Frank Bonner.

MUSIC PUBLISHERS' AND CONCERT ASSISTANTS' PROVIDENT SOCIETY, Queen's Hall, Langham Place, London, W. President, Alfred Littleton, Esq. Secretary, Walter Cherry, 186, Broadhurst Gardens, West Hampstead, London, N.W.

MUSIC TEACHERS' ASSOCIATION. President, Sir A. C. Mackenzie, MUS.D., LL.D. Joint Hon. Secretaries, Miss Mary Harker and Mr. A. J. Hadrill.

MUSIC TRADES' ASSOCIATION OF GREAT BRITAIN, LTD., 65, Long Acre, London, W. President, Mr. W. Rushworth, Liverpool. Secretary, W. T. Peat, 100, Sheen Road, Richmond, London.

MUSICIANS' COMPANY. Clerk, T. C. Fenwick, Esq , 16, Berners Street, London, W.

MUSICAL ASSOCIATION. President, Dr. W. H. Cummings, F.S A. Secretary, Mr. J. Percy Baker, MUS.B., F.R.A.M., Wilton House, 12, Longley Road, Tooting Graveney, S.W.

NATIONAL CONSERVATOIRE OF MUSIC, LTD., 149, Oxford Street, London, W. Warden, Professor Alexander Phipps, MUS B.

NATIONAL FEDERATION OF PROFESSIONAL MUSICIANS, 39, Gerrard Street, London, W.C. General Secretary, C. J. Hoggett.

ORCHESTRAL ASSOCIATION, 28, Gerrard Street, Soho, London, W. President, Sir A C. Mackenzie, MUS D. Secretary, Mr. F. Orcherton.

ORGANISTS' BENEVOLENT LEAGUE. President, Sir Frederick Bridge, M.V.O., M.A., MUS.D. Treasurer, Dr. A. H. Harding. Secretary, Thomas Shindler, M.A., LL.B.

ORPHAN FUND FOR THE CHILDREN OF MUSICIANS. Hon, Sec., Mr. H. Chadfield, 19, Berners Street, London, W.

PHILHARMONIC SOCIETY, 19, Berners Street, London, W.

PLAIN SONG AND MEDIÆVAL MUSIC SOCIETY. Hon. Sec. and Treasurer, Percy E. Sankey, 44, Russell Square, London, W.C.

" PROFESSIONAL MUSICIANS' " SICK AND PENSION FUND. Sec , Mr. F. Orcherton, c/o. 28, Gerrard Street, London, W.

ROYAL ACADEMY OF MUSIC, York Gate, Marylebone Road, London, N.W.
Principal, Sir A. C. Mackenzie, MUS.D., ST. AND., CANTAB., ET EDIN.,
LL.D., D.C.L., F.R.A.M. Secretary, F. W. Renaut, Esq.

ROYAL COLLEGE OF MUSIC, Prince Consort Road, South Kensington, London,
S.W. President, H.R.H. Prince Christian, K.G. Director, Sir C.
Hubert H. Parry, Bart., C.V.O., D.C.L., M.A., MUS.D. OXON., ET CANTAB.
Hon. Sec., Charles Morley. Registrar, Frank Pownall, M.A.

ROYAL COLLEGE OF ORGANISTS, Kensington Gore, London, S.W. President,
C. H. Lloyd, M.A., MUS.D. Hon. Treasurer, Dr. C. W. Pearce. Hon.
Sec., Dr. H. A. Harding. Registrar, Mr. T. Shindler, M.A., LL.B.

ROYAL MILITARY SCHOOL OF MUSIC, Kneller Hall, Whitton, Hounslow.

ROYAL NAVAL SCHOOL OF MUSIC.

ROYAL NORMAL COLLEGE AND ACADEMY OF MUSIC FOR THE BLIND, Upper
Norwood, London. President, Right Hon. Lord Howard de Walden
and Seaford. Treasurer, The Right Hon. Lord Stalbridge. Principal,
Sir Francis J. Campbell, LL.D. Hon. Lady Superintendent, Lady
Campbell.

ROYAL SOCIETY OF MUSICIANS OF GREAT BRITAIN, 12, Lisle Street, Leicester
Square. Hon. Treasurer, Dr. W. H. Cummings, F.S.A. Sec., Mr.
J. F. C. Bennett, 4, Bishopsgate, Cornhill, London, E.C.

SCHOLA CANTORUM LONDINENSIS. President, M. Vincent d'Indy. Director,
Mr. C. G. Thomas, 140, Marylebone Road, London, N.W.

SOCIETE DES AUTEURS COMPOSITEURS ET EDITEURS DE MUSIQUE, 32,
Shaftesbury Avenue, London, W.

SOCIETY OF BRITISH COMPOSERS, 19, Berners Street, London, W. Hon.
Treasurer, Ch. Rube, Esq. Hon. Sec., William Wallace, Esq.

SOUTH LONDON INSTITUTE OF MUSIC, Camberwell New Road. Principal,
Mr. Leonard C. Venables.

TONIC SOL-FA COLLEGE, 26, Bloomsbury Square, London, W.C. President,
Sir Walter Parratt, M.V.O., M.A., MUS.D. OXON. Sec., W. Harrison,
M.A., MUS.B. OXON.

TRINITY COLLEGE OF MUSIC, MANDEVILLE PLACE, LONDON. Chairman of
Board, Sir Frederick Bridge, C.V.O., M.A., MUS.D. Organ Professors:
R. d'Evry, F.R.C.O.; F. C. M. Ogbourne; and C. W. Pearce, MUS.D.,
F.R.C.O.

UNION GRADUATES IN MUSIC. President, Sir Charles Villiers Stanford.
Hon. Sec., Dr. E. F. Horner.

VICTORIA COLLEGE OF MUSIC, LONDON, 18, Berners Street, London, W.
Secretary, G. R. Stanton, L.R.A.M., A.R.C.M.

Provincial.

BIRMINGHAM AND MIDLAND INSTITUTE SCHOOL OF MUSIC, Paradise Street and Ratcliffe Place, Birmingham. President, The Archbishop of York, D D. Director, Professor Granville Bantock, M.A. Sec., N. M. Francis.

CITY OF LEEDS SCHOOL OF MUSIC. Registrar, Percy A. Scholes, MUS. BAC. OXON , A.R.C.M.

IRISH MUSICAL FUND. President, Arthur Darley, Esq. Sec., P. J. Griffith, Esq., 9, Merrion Row, Dublin-

LIVERPOOL CHURCH CHOIR ASSOCIATION. Hon. Treasurer, Mr. Eustace Carey, 30, James Street, Liverpool. Hon. Sec., Mr. Ralph H. Baker, Colonial House, Water Street, Liverpool.

MUNSTER ASSOCIATION OF PROFESSIONAL MUSICIANS, Clarence Hall, Cork. Chairman, Wilberforce Franklin, Esq. Hon. Treasurer, Herr H Tils, L R.A M., etc. Hon. Sec., Signor F. Grossi, 61, South Mall, Cork.

ROYAL IRISH ACADEMY OF MUSIC, 36, Westland Row, Dublin. Secretary, C. E. Grahame Harvey.

ROYAL MANCHESTER COLLEGE OF MUSIC, Ducie Street, Oxford Road, Manchester. President, Sir W. H. Houldsworth. Principal, Dr. Adolph Brodsky. Registrar, Stanley Withers.

TRINITY COLLEGE, UNIVERSITY OF DUBLIN. Registrar, H. S. Macran, Esq., Trinity College, Dublin.

UNIVERSITY COLLEGE, CORK, NATIONAL UNIVERSITY OF IRELAND.

UNIVERSITY OF CAMBRIDGE. Professor of Music Sir C. Villiers Stanford, M A., MUS.D., CANTAB.

UNIVERSITY OF DURHAM. 'Professor of Music, Joseph C. Bridge, M A., MUS.D. OXON ET DUNELM, F.S.A., F.R.C.O., HON. R.A.M.

UNIVERSITY OF EDINBURGH. Professor of Music, Frederick Niecks, MUS.D.

UNIVERSITY OF OXFORD. Professor of Music, Sir Walter Parratt, M.A , MUS.D.

ORGAN BIBLIOGRAPHY:

A brief list of some of the Principal Works upon the Organ.

By The Editor.

BARROW, REV. J., Scudamore Organs, &c. (*Bell & Daldy*, 1862)

BISHOP, C. K., Notes on Church Organs, &c. (*Rivingtons*).

BUCH, DUDLEY, Influence of the Organ in History (*W. Reeves*, 1882).

CAVAILLE-COLL, A., Del' Orgue et de son Architecture (*Paris: Ducker et Cie*, 1872).

CASSON, H. T., Reform in Organ Building (*W. Reeves*, 1888).

CASSON, T., The Modern Organ (*T. Gee & Son, Denbigh*, 1883).

CLARK, W. H., Outline of Structure of Pipe Organs, &c. (*Indianopolis*, 1877).

DICKSON, W. E., Practical Organ Building (*Lockwood*, 1882).

EDWARDS, C. A., Organs and Organ Building (*Gill*, 1881).

ELLISTON, THOMAS, Organs and Tuning (*Weekes & Co.*, 1898).

FAULKNER, T., Designs for Organs (*London*, 1828).

HAMILTON's Catechism of the Organ (*R. Cock & Co.*, 1865).

HAYNES, L. G., Hints on the Purchase of an Organ (*Novello*, 1878).

HEMSTOCK's On Tuning the Organ (*Weekes & Co.*, 1876).

HILES, J., Catechism of the Organ (*Brewer & Co.*).

HILL, ARTHUR J., Organ Cases, &c., of the Middle Ages (*Bogue*, 1886).

HINTON, J. W., Guide to the Purchase of an Organ (*W. Reeves*, 1882).

HOPKINS & RIMBAULT, The Organ (*Cocks & Co.*, 1877).

LEWIS's Organ Building (*John B. Day*).

LOCHER, KARL, Erhlärung der Orgelregister, &c. (1887).

MAINE, J. T., Organs in India and America (*Madras*).

NICHOLS, W. G., The Cincinnati Organ, &c. (*Clarke & Co., Cincinnati*).

Advertisements.

By Appointment to H.M.
King George V.

NORMAN &
BEARD, Ltd.

Organ Builders

LONDON & NORWICH.

AGENCIES AT

CAPETOWN,
JOHANNESBURG,
WELLINGTON, N.Z.
SYDNEY, &c.

RESIDENT REPRESENTATIVES—

SWANSEA,
BRISTOL,
GLASGOW,
BIRMINGHAM,
NOTTINGHAM,
BELFAST,
LIVERPOOL, &c.

Address—

61, BERNERS ST., W., opposite Hotel York.

Telegrams—"VIBRATING, LONDON."
Telephone—9145 Gerrard.

A. NOTERMAN

Church and Chamber ♪ Organ Builder. ♪

Postal and Telegraphic Address:

IOI, Frithville Gardens, Shepherd's Bush.

Factory:

III, Frithville Gardens, Shepherd's Bush.

SPECIALITIES:—

Electric and Long Distance Pneumatic Organs Built or Re-built to any Specifications.

LONG DISTANCE PNEUMATIC applied to the following Organs, where Testimonials may be obtained:—

Mr. W. M. Peters, 2, Kidderpore Avenue, Hampstead—2 Manual Organ, fitted with Automatic Self-player, Pneumatic.

The Rev. E. W. Tibbits, Elsworth Parish Church, Cambs.,—new 2 Manual Pneumatic.

The Rev. H. W. Bowstead, Parish Church, Basingstoke—Electric Choir Organ—late Bur. Re-placed by Pneumatic Action.

The Rev. J. B. Croft, St. Matthew's, Great Peter Street, Westminster—late Mr. O Gern, rebuilt two Manuals.

The Rev. Webb Spencer, St. John Baptist, Holland Road, Kensington—late Mr. O. Gern, rebuilt and enlarged, 4 Manuals, Pneumatic.

The Rev. Lawson Foster, Queen's Park Congregational Church, Harrow Road—late Mr. O. Gern, rebuilt 3 Manuals, Pneumatic.

The Rev. O. Wilde, St. Ives' Parish Church, Hunts.—Electric late Mr. O. Gern, rebuilt and enlarged, 3 Manuals, Pneumatic.

The Rev. Alexander Andison, Aberdeen Road, South Croydon Congregational Church—late Mr. Monk, rebuilt and enlarged, 3 Manuals, Pneumatic.

The Rev. Silvester Horne, Whitfield's Central Mission, Tottenham Court Road—new Organ, 3 Manuals.

In Course of Re-construction, St. John's, Red Lion Square—Electric Action, Lewes & Co., Ferndale Road, Brixton.

Enlarging and rebuilding on my Long Distance Pneumatic Pneumatic.

In Course of Construction, 2 Manual Organ, Pneumatic, for Lady Henry Somerset, under the supervision of the Rev. J. B. Croft.

ADVERTISEMENTS

Some Organs built by A. NOTERMAN.

As Built for Whitfield Tabernacle.

Keyboard.

Chamber Organ Built at Hampstead.

——— The ———
New Cross Organ Works

Church & Chamber
ORGAN BUILDERS

Two Manual & Pedal
Student Organs from
🎵 £85-0-0. 🎵

Write for particulars of
our New Model Player
Organs from £60-0 0.

Estimates for Organs to any specification.

**We undertake all kinds of Repair Work,
Rebuilds, Renovations and Tuning Contracts.**

🎵 **VOICING A SPECIALITY.** 🎵

G. ARUNDELL & Co.,
49, New Cross Road, S.E.

Factory : ECKINGTON GDNS., MONSON RD., S.E.

ORGAN BUILDERS.

Estab. 1794. :: 3 Prize Medals.

Tele { grams—BEVINGTON, SOHO, LONDON.
      { phone—GERRARD 9848.

Erected over 2,000 Organs
in all parts of the World.

BEVINGTON & SONS,

Latest
Productions
and Specialities,
Light Pressure,
Pneumatic Action,
Collective and Adjustable
Pistons, Sforzande Movement.

✠

MANETTE STREET,
Charing Cross Road,
LONDON, W.

ESTABLISHED 1874.

ALFRED KIRKLAND

AND BRYCESON BROS.,

ORGAN BUILDERS.

155a, MARLBOROUGH ROAD,
UPPER HOLLOWAY, LONDON, N.

Testimonials and References permitted from a large number
————*of Eminent Musicians, Clergymen, etc.*————

Including the following :—

SIR J. FREDERICK BRIDGE,	DR. A. B. PLANT,
SIR GEORGE MARTIN,	DR. C. C. PALMER,
SIR WALTER PARRATT,	C. J. DALE, ESQ.,
DR. CHARLES W. PEARCE,	F. CUNNINGHAM WOODS, ESQ.,
	MUS.BAC.

Branches : WAKEFIELD & BURTON-ON-TRENT.

W. LAMB, : :

1a, Margaret Street,

Regent Street, London, W.

ESTIMATES FOR PAINTING, —
— GILDING, SILVERING OR
ARTISTICALLY DECORATING
PIPES AND CASES.

SPECIAL DESIGNS.

GRIFFEN & STROUD,

Telephone 305. ORGAN BUILDERS.

Church, Chapel, Concert Hall, and Chamber Organs built
to any design, and fitted on the most modern principles.
ORGANS REBUILT, ENLARGED, REVOICED OR REPAIRED.
Tuning by yearly contract or otherwise.

HEDGEMEAD PARK WORKS, BATH.
(Opposite Walcot Parish Church).

H. S. VINCENT & CO.
Organ Builders, SUNDERLAND.

Specialities. Artistic Voicing, Tubular and Electro Pneumatic
Actions, Self-playing Attachments and Colonial work.

Estimates Free for every description of Organ Work.
Tuning by yearly contract or otherwise.

ESTABLISHED 1880. Telegrams:—" Organs," Sunderland.

Milton Keynes UK
Ingram Content Group UK Ltd.
UKHW030937301124
451950UK00007B/104

9 781015 656734